Path of the Patriots

A Tourist Guide to Paris during the French Revolution

Volume Two

Colophon

Copyright © 2012 Jan Kelley & Kemper Conseil *Publishing*

First Edition

Cover design: Junior Design
Layout: Junior Design
Overview/Metro Maps: Google - Map data ©2012 Google
Location Maps: J.J.M. Bakkers
Photography: Martin Piper

All rights reserved.

No part of this publication may be reproduced, stored in a retrieval system, or transmitted in any from or by any means, electronic, mechanical, photocopying, recording or otherwise without the prior permission of the copyright owner and the publisher.

Notice
No responsibility is assumed by the publisher for any injury/or damage to persons or property as a matter of products liability, negligence or otherwise, or from any use or operation of any methods, products, instructions or ideas contained in the material herein.

Kemper Conseil *Publishing* has done its utmost to ensure that copyrights have been secured for the content in this book, including literary texts, translations, illustrations, maps and photographs. However, despite our intensive research, due to the differing legal situations from country to country, mistakes in attributing rights might nevertheless occur. Please inform us if you become aware of any such errors.

Kemper Conseil *Publishing*
Westvlietweg 67F
2495 AA The Hague
The Netherlands
T: 0031 (0)70 386 80 31
F: 0031 (0)70 386 14 98
E: info@kemperconseil.com
W: www.kemperconseil.com

ISBN: 978 90 76542 515
BIC: HBTV2, WTH, WTL
NUR: 680, 500

TABLE OF CONTENTS

Preface 5

Acknowledgements 7

Foreword 11

How to use this Book 12

Summary of the walks 17

The Walks

V	From the Temple of Reason to the Temple Prison	23
VI	Ghosts in the Place du Carrousel	141
VII	The Route of the Condemned I	247
VIII	The Route of the Condemned II	349
IX	Sans-Culottes, the Terror, and a Path of False Hope	459
X	Power and Glory	581

Glossary of French Terms 675

Bibliography 689

*For Maximilien, Georges, Camille,
and all those who lived - and died - in that turbulent time,
and made France what it is today.*

In writing this book, I have come to feel almost as I knew you.

PREFACE

Particular thanks must go to the following authors, whose works were a permanent fixture on my desk during the writing of this book. They have been invaluable references, enabling me to know and better understand the period of the Revolution, and they will remain on my bookshelves like faithful friends:

CLAUDE MANCERON, whose incomparable series, *Les Hommes de la Liberté*, and *La Révolution Française: Dictionnaire Biographique*, which he wrote with **ANNE MANCERON**, have been invaluable in bringing to life the people who made the Revolution.

JACQUES HILLAIRET, whose *Dictionnaire Historique des Rues de Paris* has been a goldmine of fascinating stories about the people behind those lovely Parisian facades.

SIMON SCHAMA, whose wonderful history of the Revolution, 'Citizens', has been a valuable and constant source for learning and understanding what happened during that turbulent time.

JEAN FAVIER, whose colourful *Chronique de la Révolution* helped to visualise what it was like to live through that time.

LOUIS-HENRI FOURNET, whose *Journal de la Révolution* was like having an 18th-century citizen's diary at hand to verify what happened when.

J.M. ROBERTS AND R.C. COBB, whose book, 'French Revolution Documents', has been a valuable source of information and eyewitness accounts.

Reay Tannahill and the Folio Society, whose collection of eyewitness accounts, 'Paris in Revolution', has also been an excellent source of information in general.

Odile Caffin-Carcy and Jacques Villard, whose two excellent books, *Versailles et la Révolution* and *Versailles, Le Château, la Ville, ses Monuments*, have shed enormous light on a part of Versailles's history that is seldom told.

Monique Lebailly, whose edition of Charles-Henri Sanson's *La Révolution Française vue par son Bourreau* gives a fascinating glimpse into the world of the revolutionary executioner, and has been a wonderful source of eyewitness accounts that bring to life the horror of living during the Terror.

Charles Aimé Dauban, whose wonderful book, *Les Prisons de Paris sous La Révolution*, has provided a unique and incomparable window on the daunting world of revolutionary prisons, and an invaluable source of eyewitness accounts.

G. Lenotre, whose *Vieilles Maisons, Vieux Papiers* and other works on revolutionary Paris have brought to life the people who lived through it all.

And finally...a special thank you to **Restif de la Bretonne** and **Sébastien Mercier**, for being there, seeing it - and writing it all down! Restif's *Les Nuits de Paris* and Mercier's *Tableau de Paris* are veritable canvases of life in late 18th-century Paris

---

Note on Translation. A few of my sources for eyewitness accounts are books already written in English, and I would like to thank the excellent translators of these accounts. Apart from these, the translation of all quotations from books and documents in French has been done by the author. Similarly, translation of all poems throughout the book has been done by the author.

ACKNOWLEDGMENTS

I owe an enormous debt of gratitude to the following two men, both sadly no longer with us, whose wonderful writings started me on an unstoppable journey that culminated in this book: Jacques Hillairet, who opened my eyes to the magical history of the streets of Paris, and Claude Manceron, who brought to life the creators of the French Revolution as no-one else could.

My infinite thanks to Dineke, Fons, Marc, Enno and Gene, and all the team at Kemper Conseil, for your hard work, help, guidance, patience and enthusiasm - and for believing so much in this book. Special thanks go to Marc for being so calm and understanding in the face of my endless questions and anxieties.

I would like to say a special thank you to Frédéric Lacaille, Curator at the Château de Versailles, whose support, encouragement and enthusiasm for my book has helped me enormously in the challenging task of preparing a revolutionary tour of Versailles.

Special thanks also to Marie-Odile Gigou, Curator at the Bibliothèque Historique de la Ville de Paris, and Philippe de Carbonnières, Curator, Cabinet des Arts Graphiques, Musée Carnavalet, for all their invaluable help and advice.

My thanks and appreciation also go to the following people, who have all helped and supported me during the preparation of this book:
Jean-Vincent Bacquart, Director of Publications, Château de Versailles; Denis Verdier, Director, Cultural Development,

Château de Versailles; Yves de Saint-Do, former Principal, Lycée Louis-le-Grand; Joel Vallat, Principal, Lycée Louis-le-Grand; Christian David, Maître d'Hôtel, Restaurant Le Grand Véfour; Gilles Breuil, Director, Restaurant Le Procope; Laurence Dalifard, Director of Communication, Restaurant Lapérouse; Professor Patrice Higonnet, Harvard University; Jean-Jacques Faugeron, Curator, Cimetière de Picpus; Guillaume de Chabot, former Curator, Cimetière de Picpus; Viviane Niaux, Centre de Musique Baroque de Versailles; Odile Caffin-Carcy, Cultural Attachée, Versailles Tourist Office; Jamot Collet, former director, Club Colbert; Christian Lescureux, Societé des Amis de Robespierre; Vinh N'Guyen, Cabinet des Arts Graphiques, Musée Carnavalet; Pierre Blottiere, Cabinet des Arts Graphiques, Musée Carnavalet.

Thanks also go to my family, who have helped, supported and stood by me during the writing of this book: My unique and wonderful mother Joan, my first reader and enthusiast, thanks for all your love during those years before this book was ever thought of, during the years I was writing it, and for always believing I could do it; My daughter Alisa, for all the love you always give me, and for your support, reading, editing, help with revolutionary fashion, advice, ideas, encouragement, optimism, fun and laughs - I couldn't have done any of it without you - you are why I do it all; My son-in-law Martin, for your love, support, advice, help with photos, help with technical things I know nothing about, all the laughs, and for cooking and looking after me when I was working night and day; My gorgeous grandchildren, Alex, Keira and Ava, for giving me so much fun and love - and to Alex for all the great music.

Thanks also to the friends and relatives who have helped me in different ways with the challenge of this book - and who have all been so patient about never hearing from me while I was writing it.

Special thanks go to Tim Hailstone, Patrick Kelley, Daphne Davies, Simon Burton, Dianna Rienstra, David Watkiss, Bertrand Guillou, Roger Burton, Margot Ponce, who have all helped by reading and trying out the walks, or advising on the practical aspects of being a writer; to Marc-Etienne Pinauldt, for giving me such a cosy home in Paris; and to Jean Demetrau, for giving me that first volume of *Les Hommes de la Liberté*, which got it all started.

Finally, my heartfelt thanks must go to the numerous Parisians I've met, questioned, talked and joked with during my wanderings around Paris, all of whom have, in their own way, shed light on my task, and helped me to know better their wonderful city.

FOREWORD

This book begins, in a way, in America. In Boston, to be exact, where I first encountered the fascinating tourist attraction known as the Freedom Trail. This route takes the visitor to the city on a tour of the Boston that witnessed the dramatic and revolutionary events of 1775, events which led to the independence of the American colonies from Britain and the establishment of an American Republic.

The American Revolution was to be the inspiration of a young French soldier by the name of Lafayette, who went to America, initially against the wishes of his king, to help the rebel colonists against the British. He returned to France in the 1780s as a hero, filled with liberal ideologies and political ambition. These new ideas took root in an increasingly turbulent political arena, sifting through from the educated bourgeoisie to the ordinary people of Paris, and culminating in the storming of the Bastille on the 14th of July 1789. This event marked the beginning of the French Revolution.

Paris was the nerve centre of the French Revolution, as Boston was of the American Revolution, and as such deserves its own freedom trail, a route that will take you on a journey through time, and show you the places where ideas and hopes were born, grew, came to fruition, and, at times, tragically destroyed themselves. The Freedom Trail made Boston's Revolution come to life for me, and in this book I hope I can make Paris's Revolution come to life for you.

HOW TO USE THIS BOOK

Path of the Patriots comes in two volumes, and has a total of ten walks. The first four walks are in Volume One, which also gives you an introduction to the Revolution through a brief history of what happened, biographies of the people who made it happen, and a description of what the city of Paris looked like during the revolutionary era. In Volume Two there are six more walks that will complete this unique experience of Paris during one of its most dramatic periods of history. Whichever of these two volumes you are reading right now, get ready to step into the Revolution that changed the world.

Welcome to the world of the revolutionaries, a lost world that you are now going to find again. As you wander around using this book, you will not be having the same kind of experience you have with a conventional guidebook. You will find yourself lost in the lives of people who lived more than two centuries ago, lost in the riots that overwhelmed so many Parisian streets, lost in the hopes and fears of those people, and at times lost in the horror that they lived through. What you won't get lost in however are the streets themselves, since each walk gives you detailed and precise instructions about which street to go down, where to turn left or right, and where to stop and have coffee, lunch or dinner. As you read, look for the ➥symbol that you'll find throughout the walks, showing you where the directions are for following the itinerary. For those of you who have read the walk beforehand, these symbols will enable you to skip the text if you wish, and just follow the directions.

As you walk you'll be reading, so be careful not to bump into things. You should be on the lookout for benches where you can sit and read about what you are going to see next, and if you can't find a bench (Paris needs more of them) you might need to settle for a convenient wall. You will also find yourself crossing the road a lot, going from one house to the next, so watch out, because Parisian traffic is very fast, and drivers don't always stop for pedestrians, even when they're on a crossing.

Throughout the book you will notice some things are in italics. These include eyewitness accounts of events, direct quotes of things people said, the former names of streets and buildings, the titles of contemporary publications, and French words other than present-day street and house names. The following key explains the use of italics for the names of streets and buildings:

>Rue du Jeu de Paume - Present-day street name
>*Rue des Mauvaises Paroles* - Former name of present-day street, or one that no longer exists
>Hôtel de la Chancellerie - Present-day name of a building, house, museum, institution, etc
>*Hôtel de Crussol* - Former name of present-day building, house, museum, institution, etc, or one that no longer exists

Please don't be outraged by the use of words like 'lunatic', 'deaf-mute' or children who are 'backward', which nowadays are inacceptable and have fortunately gone out of use. But they, along with any others you find in the book, were the words used at the time, and I have kept them to maintain the general atmosphere of 18th-century attitudes. I would obviously never use them to talk about the present. The French words *Place* and *Square* (pronounced 'skwar') mean different things. A *Place* is what we call a Square in English (i.e. Place de la Concorde), while *Square* (i.e. Square du Temple) means a public garden - which of course is what a lot of English Squares are.

The book contains numerous references to amounts of money, in *livres*, which was the general unit of French currency in the 18th century. It is incredibly difficult to find a consistent view of the present-day value of the *livre* - trying to do this has driven me mad! But by looking at all the different versions I could find, and using the retail price index and the value of gold then and now, I have managed to arrive at what is hopefully a reasonable estimation of what an 18th-century *livre* might be worth nowadays.

So this is what you do when you come across an amount in *livres*: **multiply the number of livres by 11 for U.S. dollars, 8 for euros and 6 for pounds sterling.** Using these numbers, a dowry, for example, of 6 million *livres* (as the Duchesse de Chartres had) would be the modern equivalent of about 66 million dollars, 48 million euros or 36 million pounds. You might find some discrepancies between these calculations and the official daily exchange rates between the three modern currencies - but this method will still give you an adequate idea of how much the *livres* were worth. And one fact will always emerge - those aristocrats were rich!

The new French republic had its own calendar, and throughout the book you will find some dates written in the revolutionary fashion, the most frequently cited one being 9 *Thermidor*, the day when Robespierre was deposed. The very first day of the revolutionary calendar was September 22nd 1792 (*1 Vendémiaire, An I*). This new system was somewhat complicated, since the year began at the autumn equinox in September, and therefore not always on the same day - some years began on September 22nd, some on the 23rd and some on the 24th. The names of the months were based on the flora, farming or weather associated with that time of the year, and had mostly Latin-based names like *Pluviose* (rain). There were only three 'weeks' in each month, known as *décades*, for they each had ten days, also with Latinate names like *primidi* (1st) and *décadi* (10th). It was this aspect of the revolutionary calendar that made it unpopular, for it only gave people three 'Sundays' in a month, and losing one day of rest every month did not please an already overworked population. Here are the names you will come across in the book.

MONTHS

Vendémiaire: September-October, grape harvest
Brumaire: October-November, fog/mist
Frimaire: November-December, frost/sleet
Nivôse: December-January, snow
Pluviose: January-February, rain
Ventose: February-March, wind
Germinal: March-April, seeds/buds
Floréal: April-May, flowers
Prairial: May-June, meadows/pasture
Messidor: June-July, harvest
Thermidor: July-August, heat
Fructidor: August-September, fruit

DAYS OF THE DÉCADE

primidi (1st)
duodi (2nd)
tridi (3rd)
quartidi (4th)
quintidi (5th)
sextidi (6th)
septidi (7th)
octidi (8th)
nonidi (9th)
décadi (10th)

Since I first started writing this book the open-door Paris of the past has been closed up by the introduction of entry-codes, so sometimes it is not possible to go in and look at the courtyard of a house. But fortunately quite a number of these codes are turned off during the day, and if you press the slightly larger unmarked button (usually above the numbered buttons) the door will open - and sometimes it's enough to just push the door open without pressing any buttons. If you are standing in front of a locked door, reading about the building, chances are someone will come out or go in, so you can at least get a glimpse of the interior as they do so - and if you ask politely, many people are nice enough to let you go in and have a look. But if you do, always bear in mind that most of the buildings are at least semi-residential, so you should always be discreet while looking around - so we can keep this book's good reputation!

Many of the walks include visits to major monuments or museums, and you might choose to make those visits separately, rather than while taking the walk. These are long walks, so some people might prefer to split them up over two separate days - depending on how long you can walk for. But however you do them, I hope you have fun.

SUMMARY OF THE WALKS

Walk Five
FROM THE TEMPLE OF REASON TO THE TEMPLE PRISON
Notre Dame – Hôtel de Ville – Danton's first walk in Paris – Temple

Here you will discover the fascinating Enclos du Temple, the 'town within a town' that was a refuge from the law and a tax haven for thousands of people. It is better known, though, as the prison where Louis XVI and Marie-Antoinette lived their last few months of family life. Between the site of this infamous royal prison and the great cathedral of Notre Dame, you will follow the young Danton as he tries to find his way around Paris for the first time. During this walk, which takes you through the Marais, you meet that singular 18th-century character, Caron de Beaumarchais, and see the house where he wrote 'The Marriage of Figaro' and organized aid to the American rebels. You will also re-live the last violent moments of Robespierre's power, and be a witness to one of the darkest events of the Revolution, the murder of Marie-Antoinette's devoted friend, the Princesse de Lamballe.

Walk Six
GHOSTS IN THE PLACE DU CARROUSEL
The Louvre – Place du Carrousel – The Tuileries

This walk takes you back to the golden days of the Tuileries Palace, home to royalty before becoming a royal prison, and then the seat of the all-powerful Committee of Public Safety. During the revolutionary period the area between the Tuileries Palace and the Louvre was a maze of dark, narrow passages, where the houses of common folk stood side by side with bourgeois mansions. It was through this labyrinth of streets that Robespierre's 'fiancée' hurried to her art classes, where great masters were sold at bargain prices, where Napoléon was nearly assassinated, and where Marie-Antoinette wandered, completely lost, right under the nose of her unsuspecting subjects. When the monarchy was finally toppled, these same subjects, now enraged, poured out of their homes to join the crowd that was heading menacingly across the Place du Carrousel towards the Tuileries Palace.

Walk Seven
THE ROUTE OF THE CONDEMNED I
Their last look at the city
Palais de Justice – Sainte-Chapelle – Conciergerie Pont Neuf – rue Saint-Honoré – Place du Palais-Royal

From the Conciergerie prison sad processions of tumbrils set off each afternoon, transporting the daily batches of victims destined for the guillotine in Place de la Concorde, known then as Place de la Révolution. In walks number seven and eight you will follow in their footsteps, from prison cell to scaffold to grave, at the same time getting to know some of the residents of the area and the events that took place there. During walk seven you visit their prison, see where they were judged by the famous Revolutionary Tribunal, and then follow them as they are jolted around in a tumbril during their long and uncomfortable journey to the scaffold. On the way you'll see where Danton met his first wife, visit the pharmacy where a romantic Swedish count bought ink to write letters to the Queen, and witness the funeral cortege of a slightly less romantic but more famous count.

Walk Eight
THE ROUTE OF THE CONDEMNED II
The guillotine - and after
Rue Saint-Honoré – Place Vendôme – Place de la Concorde – Chapelle-Expiatoire – Parc Monceau

Walk eight re-joins the tumbrils as they roll through the Place du Palais-Royal on their long journey to the scaffold, and along the way you'll see a church where General Bonaparte emerged from the unknown to become a glorious hero. You'll visit the magnificent house where Lafayette spent the first years of his marriage, and in Place Vendôme you can see where Danton ran the Justice Ministry, as well as a house that contained a lot of mesmerised Parisians. This walk takes you through Robespierre's neighbourhood to the site of the famous Jacobin Club, where he reigned supreme during the Terror, and if you want to get better acquainted with this redoubtable revolutionary, you can have lunch or dinner in the same place where he ate every evening with his adopted family. After witnessing the last moments of the most famous patriots in the Place de la Révolution, and then following them to their burial place, you will end your walk at a highly subversive dinner party.

Walk Nine
SANS-CULOTTES, THE TERROR, AND A PATH OF FALSE HOPE
Rue Saint-Antoine – Place de Vosges – Bastille – Faubourg Saint-Antoine – Doctor Belhomme's Clinic – Place de la Nation – The Picpus Cemetery

For four centuries the inhabitants of the faubourg Saint-Antoine lived in the shadow of the grim mediaeval fortress known as the Bastille. For them it was an ever-present symbol of royal despotism, so it isn't surprising they chose it as a target on July 14th 1789, a day in French history that has never been forgotten. As you visit the faubourg Saint-Antoine - which unfortunately has been forgotten by many of today's visitors to Paris - you will be walking with the ghosts of hundreds of unsung popular heroes, for this was the cradle of the sans-culotte Revolution. The sans-culottes of Paris played a vital part in pushing the Revolution towards many of its most radical social reforms. But it was a violent process, culminating in a Reign of Terror that saw hundreds of hard-working citizens denounced, often by neighbours or even their own family. People lived in fear of the guillotine, and would do anything - and pay anything - to avoid being sent before the Tribunal, which meant almost certain death. Some did this by becoming 'patients' at Doctor Belhomme's clinic, where money bought safety. But for how long?

Walk Ten
POWER AND GLORY
Faubourg Saint-Germain – Invalides – Ecole-Militaire – Champ-de-Mars

This walk begins in the faubourg Saint-Germain, seat of the rich and powerful for nearly three centuries, and home to the Empress Joséphine when she was still known as Rose. By 1792 most of its residents had emigrated, and the Revolution moved in, taking over great houses like the Hôtel de Salm, occupied by a political club, and the Palais Bourbon, which became the seat of the Directory government. Here were the roots of today's 7th arrondissement, still a bastion of the republican establishment and home to numerous government ministries. The walk ends on the Champ-de-Mars, where you'll relive the best and worst of the revolutionary era. It was the scene of the euphoric Festival of Federation - the Revolution's greatest moment of optimism - and the execution of Paris's first mayor, astronomer Sylvain Bailly, which must rank among the Revolution's more regrettable acts.

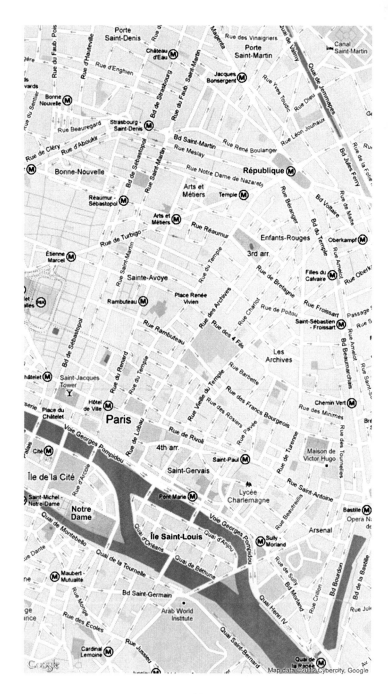

Walk Number Five

From the Temple of Reason to the Temple Prison

Notre Dame - Hôtel-de-Ville - Danton's first walk in Paris - Temple

Here you will discover the fascinating Enclos du Temple, the 'town within a town' that was a refuge from the law and a tax haven for thousands of people. It is better known, though, as the prison where Louis XVI and Marie-Antointette lived their last few months of family life. Between the site of this infamous royal prison and the great cathedral of Notre Dame, you will follow the young Danton as he tries to find his way around Paris for the first time. During this walk, which takes you through the Marais, you meet that singular 18th-century character, Caron de Beaumarchais, and see the house where he wrote 'The Marriage of Figaro' and organized aid to the American rebels. You will also re-live the last violent moments of Robespierre's power, and be a witness to one of the darkest events of the Revolution, the murder of Marie-Antoinette's devoted friend, the Princesse de Lamballe.

From the Temple of Reason to the Temple Prison

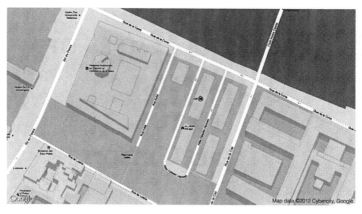

Metro: Cité

Place du Parvis Notre Dame.

➡When you come out of the metro, you see the Préfecture de Police directly in front of you. Veer left diagonally across Place Louis Lépine, turn right on rue de la Cité and then left on to Place du Parvis Notre Dame, where the Hôtel-Dieu hospital is on your left. If you are here on a sunny morning you should bring your sunglasses if you want to look at Notre Dame from here! This vast esplanade is now six times bigger than it was in the Middle Ages, when it stood 2½ metres higher than the ground around it, and was surrounded by a wall. At that time it was the site of the Archbishop of Paris's 'Ladder of Justice', where condemned criminals were brought, barefoot and with a rope around their neck, to make honourable amends for their crime before facing punishment. This was evidently seen as public entertainment for Parisians, for a cartload of rotten eggs and other suitable projectiles was put at their disposal at the foot of the ladder.

To your left, where you now see Hôtel-Dieu, was the *Foundling Hospital*, which received, at any hour of the day or night with no formalities required, about 8,000 babies every year. It was called *Hôpital des Enfants-Trouvés*, created by royal edict in 1670, and it stood on *rue Neuve Notre Dame*, one of the old streets that went across the Parvis. Another foundling hospital for older children was opened at the same time in the Faubourg Saint-Antoine, while the institution here at Notre Dame was only for abandoned newborns. Marie-Antoinette was known to be very fond of children, and on February 10th 1790 she visited this hospital, accompanied by the king and the dauphin, gazing with emotion at the rows and rows of newborn babies who had all been left to their fate in the basket outside the building. It must have been a difficult visit for the queen, for less than a year earlier she had lost her elder son, the first dauphin, and the sight of so many babies must have also brought back poignant memories of her last child, little Sophie, who died in 1787, just eleven months after being born. When a relative had tried to comfort her at the time, she simply replied, '*She would have been my friend.*' Her heart therefore must have been moved, as anyone's would, by the sight of all those tiny potential friends to mothers who would never know them.

On February 10th 1790 Marie-Antoinette visited the Foundling Hospital next to Nôtre-Dame Cathedral, accompanied by the king, the dauphin and Madame Royale. (Courtesy of Musée Carnavalet, Cabinet des Arts Graphiques, Paris)

The Foundling Hospital was demolished in 1877 and the Hôtel-Dieu Hospital built in its place. Up to then the original Hôtel-Dieu had been opposite, on the south side of the Parvis, stretching along the quay from the Pont au Double to the Petit-Pont. Its origins can be traced back to the 9th century, and it owed much of its development to the generous donations of Saint-Louis and his mother, Blanche de Castille. At the time of Saint-Louis the hospital had almost a thousand patients, but by the beginning of the 18th century there were ten times that number, largely due to the unhealthy practice of putting several patients in one bed. These conditions persisted throughout the 18th century, despite the good intentions of the nuns who cared for the patients, and the efforts made by people like Madame Necker to render hospitals more humane. It was not until the 19th century that things began to improve for hospital patients, and by the time the Hôtel-Dieu moved across the Parvis to the new building in 1878, its patients would have had a much better chance of surviving their stay in hospital than their 18th-century ancestors. There is a lovely cloistered garden inside the present building, which you can see if you go in the entrance marked *Urgences*, turn right, go through the glass doors and then turn left into the garden.

Like most hospitals in the past, the Hôtel-Dieu was a pretty unhealthy place, where *'in each bed there was someone ill, someone dying and someone dead.'* Sometimes there could be up to eight patients in a bed, all lying naked next to each other, regardless of their illness, so it isn't surprising that twenty percent of the patients admitted to Hôtel-Dieu left it by way of the morgue. In fact I'm surprised it wasn't more. The building was ravaged by fire in 1737, and again in 1742, this time killing fourteen people, and the hospital faced possible closure. But it succeeded in remaining open, and in 1781 saw several improvements intended to make the hospital less redoubtable. The beds were to be placed in different rooms according to the patients' illnesses, could now contain only one person, and men and women had to be in separate buildings. It didn't seem to change much, though, for in 1789 Louis-Sebastien Mercier described the Hôtel-Dieu in his *Tableau de Paris*. *'It was hoped that the last fire would turn to the advantage of the patients, and that they would build a new, healthier building, but they have left it with almost all the old horrors…it is pestilential, due to its damp and airless atmosphere…they put patients with a dying man on one side and a corpse on the other…there is no-one to console them…the air is full of putrid fumes…the most harmless illness takes on serious complications…and the simplest wound becomes mortal in this hospital.'* (Mercier, 1947)

A ward of the Hôtel-Dieu hospital during the 18th century. (Authors private collection)

Key:
A. *Nun making up the beds of straw with a novice*
B. *Young nuns giving a drink to a patient*
C. *Nuns and a novice carrying a corpse to the mortuary*
D. *Novices cleaning the patients' basins*
E. *Young Novices returning the basins to the patients*
F. *Novice sweeping the ward*

Cathédrale Notre Dame de Paris.

(Open every day 7.45 a.m. - 6h45 p.m.) Directly in front of you is Notre Dame Cathedral, for me the most beautiful building in Paris, and certainly one of the oldest. The first religious monument to occupy this site was one honouring Jupiter, built by the Romans between 14 and 37 A.D. In the 4th century a chapel dedicated to Saint-Etienne was constructed here, followed in the 6th century by another church built on to the west side of the first one. By the 12th century they were both very dilapidated, and since the population of Paris was growing fast, Bishop Maurice de Sully decided to replace them with a cathedral. Mobilizing the entire community, Sully raised enough money from the king, the nobility, the clergy and the general population to realize his dream, and the foundation stone was laid by Pope Alexander III in the spring of 1163. The identity of the architect of this magnificent cathedral remains a mystery, as does his reason for making the north tower wider than the south one - a feature that was later criticized by revolutionary zealots as being an insult to equality. It took approximately 70 years to complete Notre Dame, and Sully died in 1196, having supervised a mere 33 years of construction.

Architecturally the cathedral represents the transition from Roman to Gothic. The great galleried cathedrals like Saint-Denis were on the way out at the time, but with its Gallery of Kings and the colonnades of the Grand Gallery above it, Notre Dame made them a spectacular feature of its façade. At the same time it was the first cathedral to use flying buttresses, and must be one of the finest examples of this Gothic innovation. You will get the best view of them later as we leave the Ile de la Cité. From the 17th century onwards, Notre Dame suffered successive architectural mutilations, including the replacement of its stone funeral slabs by the black and white tiled floor you see today in the interior of the cathedral. Throughout its history this interior has been the scene of grandiose events, beginning with the displaying of the Sacred Crown of Thorns, brought back by Saint-Louis from Constantinople in 1239. The first coronation to be held here was that of the English monarch, Henry VI, who was crowned King of France in 1430 at the age of 9. The second coronation was that of Napoléon I. In 1455 a review was held here of the trial of Joan of Arc, and the cathedral has seen the weddings of two very famous queens - on April 24th 1558 the dauphin François married Mary Stuart, later Queen of Scots, and in 1572 Henri de Navarre married Marguérite de Valois, better known as *La Reine Margot* (Queen Margot).

On the eve of the Revolution, the area around Notre Dame looked very different from what you see now. The Seine to the south was blocked from view by the buildings of the Hôtel-Dieu, which occupied the southern half of the present-day Parvis. The façade of Notre Dame was originally intended to be viewed at close quarters, and many feel that the enlargement of the Parvis has diminished its Gothic impact. The building you see nowadays on the west side of the square facing Notre Dame, occupied by the Prefecture of Police, did not exist. In its place was a maze of little streets linking up with *rue de la Barillerie* and the Palais de Justice - one of the many mediaeval quarters in Paris to be eliminated by Baron Haussmann in the mid-19th century. The beige stones and inscriptions that you see on the ground trace the outline of this vanished neighbourhood, with its main street, *rue Neuve Notre Dame*, and a host of other little streets and buildings, including the church of the Hôtel-Dieu hospital. A huge cloister ran along the north side of the cathedral going right up to rue des Ursins, where the *chanoines* (canons) of Notre Dame lived piously in the service of God. No bridge had yet been built to link the Ile de la Cité with the *Place de Grève* (Place de l'Hôtel-de-Ville), and the Quai aux Fleurs was part of the cloister garden which went down to the river's edge.

During the last years of the *ancien régime* Notre Dame was the object of several attacks on its appearance, beginning in 1750 with one of the cathedral's most tragic losses, the removal of its precious mediaeval stained glass. With the intention of bringing more light into the church, it was replaced by the clear glass bordered with blue and yellow that you will see in a minute when you go into the cathedral. The architect Germain Soufflot can take credit for many admirable works of the pre-revolutionary period, notably the church that would later become the Panthéon, but he should be less proud of his work on the central doorway of Notre Dame, which he mutilated in order to make it wide enough to accommodate the royal canopy on official occasions. One of the first processions to pass through this doorway, with Louis XVI and Marie-Antoinette at the head, was on June 29th 1775, on the occasion of a Te Deum to honour their coronation two weeks earlier. ➡ It's not possible nowadays to follow them in through Soufflot's enormous doorway, so go in through the Porte Sainte-Anne to the right of the central doorway, and look around at the history that has taken place inside this magnificent cathedral.

On February 8th 1779, four years after their coronation Te Deum, Louis and Marie-Antoinette came back to give thanks to the Virgin for the birth of the first royal baby, Madame Royale. On this occasion a hundred couples, all from poor backgrounds, were married in the presence of the king and queen, who offered a dowry to each of the young brides in honour of the royal birth - a gesture that did not impress the population of Paris, who were heartily fed up with the queen's continual extravagance in a period of war and hardship, and showed their contempt by remaining virtually silent as the royal couple entered the cathedral. Three years later on January 21st 1782 a second royal baby was honoured here, but this time the crowd had no complaints, for they were celebrating the birth of a dauphin - the queen had at last given France an heir. The Place du Parvis thronged with people, while the interior of the cathedral was a sea of noble faces, for this was an event no-one would have missed. Among the congregation that day was Madame Adrienne de Lafayette, unaware that her husband had returned home from his glorious victory in America to an empty house.

In 1789 Notre Dame continued to honour the great events of the period, but the nature of those events was altogether different. July 15th saw the cathedral's first revolutionary celebration, when, in the presence of Jean Bailly, the first mayor of Paris, a Te Deum was sung to mark the storming of the Bastille. The abolition of feudal rights on the night of August 4th was also celebrated by a Te Deum, sung the next day by the Archbishop of Paris, Monseigneur de Juigné. On September 27th the archbishop paid further homage to the Revolution by publicly blessing 60 flags of the newly-formed National Guard. But very soon, instead of honouring the Revolution, the cathedral became one of its victims. Church property was nationalized in November 1789, then a year later the Notre Dame chapter was dissolved and the canons expelled from the cathedral, where the following February the nave became a voting office for the election of the city's constitutional bishops and curates. During this time occasional masses were still held, but presided over solely by priests who had sworn the Constitutional Oath, and the fate of the cathedral bells, melted down in June 1791, was an indication of the ravages that lay ahead for Notre Dame.

In August 1792 soldiers from Marseille, who had come to the capital to help overthrow the monarchy, destroyed a statue of Philippe le Bel, and the cathedral's ancient tombs were violated. The two years that followed saw a succession of looting and wanton destruction that robbed the cathedral of many of its sacred relics and precious works of art. The Gothic furniture and fittings disappeared, and most of the statues were destroyed, including the 28 Kings of Juda, which were dragged from their gallery on the main façade and dumped in the middle of the Parvis. Here they were first decapitated and then smashed to pieces. This particular act of vandalism stemmed from ignorance, ordered by the Commune in the mistaken belief that the statues represented the early Capetian kings. The artist David had his own typically grandiose idea about what should be done with the battered remains of the 28 kings, proposing they be used as the base of an enormous statue of Hercules, symbolizing the people of France trampling on the remains of royal oppression - a plan which fortunately never saw the light of day. When Viollet-le-Duc set about restoring the cathedral in 1843 there was not one piece of the broken statues to be found, so they were re-created in the studio of Geoffroi Dechaume and put in the position of the original kings. And to prove that miracles can happen, in 1977 workmen digging at number 20 rue de la Chaussée-d'Antin unearthed 28 stone heads. They were the original heads of the Kings of Juda - a long way from their home - saved nearly 200 years earlier by a royalist sympathizer named Jean-Baptiste Lakanal, who in 1795 had three houses built on rue de la Chaussée-d'Antin (numbers 18-22). Number 20 was the middle house, set back from the street, and led out to a *pathway lined with two rows of poplar trees; the residents of the two neighbouring houses, numbers 18 and 22, were prohibited from throwing anything on to this path or on the trees.* At the end of the path, in the middle of a circular courtyard, was another small building decorated with columns and pillars, and it is possible that this whole interior complex was constructed by Lakanal as a sort of resting place for the heads of the Kings of Juda, which he must have buried beneath it all to protect them from further vandalism. They have now found their final home in the Cluny Museum. A few other statues, notably the Piéta by Nicolas Coustou, were also saved by the intrepid Alexandre Lenoir, who installed them in his *Museum of French Monuments* until they could be safely returned to their present position in the choir behind the high altar.

Temple de la Raison.

On November 7th 1793, with dechristianization at its height, Notre Dame was closed to the Catholic religion and renamed the *Temple of Reason*. A new deity, the *Déesse de la Raison* (Goddess of Reason), was created, and the Commune organized the *Fête de la Raison* to be held on November 10th to inaugurate the new religion. The altar, and anything else in the cathedral that recalled Catholicism, was covered up, and a wooden mountain was constructed in the transept, topped by a Greek temple carrying the inscription 'To Philosophy'. Busts of the great philosophers replaced the saints at the entrance to the temple, which was illuminated by the 'Torch of Liberty', and behind the mountain a burning candle symbolized 'Ardent Truth'.

A huge procession starting out at the Hôtel-de-Ville arrived on the Parvis at about 10 o'clock and filed reverently into the new Temple. Resplendently flanked by two rows of young girls wearing white muslin and crowns of oak-leaves, the Goddess of Reason appeared, seated on an ancient chair and carried along by four citizens dressed like Druids and adorned with oak garlands. According to some the goddess was represented by Mlle Maillard, a singer at the Opera, others say it was a ballet dancer called Mlle Aubry, and a third possibility is an actress called Sophie, wife of the Hébertist Momoro. Whoever she was, she carried out the role to perfection, resembling a Vestal Virgin in her flowing white dress rendered all the more dramatic by a brilliant purple sash and an azure blue mantle that floated around her shoulders. A red Phrygian bonnet, formerly worn by slaves and now the emblem of liberty, served as a crown, and in her hand she carried an ebony pike. Musicians and militia brought up the rear of the procession, coming to a halt at the foot of the mountain, where all those present paid homage to their new goddess.

After receiving the kiss of fraternity from the President of the National Convention, she then took her place next to him, at which point Robespierre got up and left, no doubt furious at the sight of an upstart goddess invading the seat of executive power. But the show went on quite happily without him, as the assembled gathering sang Marie-Joseph Chénier's 'Hymn to Liberty', and the audience's delight reached polytheistic heights when a second goddess representing Liberty was carried in on a verdure throne. The following morning Robespierre took the floor at the Convention and made a scathing attack on the previous day's festivities. Six months later, however, at the pinnacle of his power, a notice over the central door of the cathedral announced, *'The people of France recognize the Supreme Being and the Immortality of the Soul'*. A month after that, Robespierre was to be seen on top of another mountain, this time on the Champ-de-Mars, where, amidst clouds of incense and rose petals, he sang the praises of the Supreme Being and the Goddess of Reason.

At about this time a former count by the name of Claude-Henri de Rouvroi Saint-Simon, known during the Revolution as citizen Simon, came on the scene. Saint-Simon is best known for his writings on philosophy and economics that he began at the beginning of the 19th century and which have since put him amongst the founders of French socialism. Before this, however, he was a rather unprincipled speculator, driven by a desire for wealth, who saw in the Revolution the chance to make a quick fortune. In association with another count, a Prussian diplomat named Sigismond Redern, Saint-Simon acquired all the nationalized property in the department of Orne, and then started buying up state-owned buildings in Paris, including Notre Dame, which he offered to take off the State's hands for 450,000 *francs* payable in *assignats*. Surprisingly his offer was accepted, but before the purchase could be concluded the law put an end to Saint-Simon's career of speculation. He was arrested and imprisoned until after 9 *Thermidor*, sparing Notre Dame from perhaps becoming the 'Temple of Saint-Simonianism', the school of socialism inspired by citizen Simon. The great cathedral thus survived the Terror without being sold, and in the autumn of 1794 the choir was turned into a warehouse for 1,500 barrels of wine - good republican medicine, it seems, for their destination was the nation's military hospitals.

It was not until June 1795 that Abbé Grégoire managed to obtain the keys to Notre Dame and begin the process of returning it to the Catholic faith. In the early hours of the morning of August 15th a purification service took place, and Mass was held that day to celebrate the Assumption. But France was still in a period of transition, and in 1798 the restored Catholic congregation found itself sharing the cathedral with the Theophilanthropists (friends of God and man), a deist cult which became fashionable between 1796 and 1801 and aimed to replace Catholicism. Its ideology was very bound up with the concept of duty - the duty of man towards his fellow men, the duty of children to their parents, and that of parents to their children, as well as the reciprocal duties of married couples. The Theophilanthropists worshipped a god, but one very different from the all-good but all-powerful Christian God, one that forbade all symbolic objects or images in their temples, permitting only baskets of flowers and fruit on the altar. Their inspiration came from Voltaire and Rousseau, as well as certain aspects of the cult of the Supreme Being, and the success of this new religion during this post-revolutionary period was in no small measure due to the support of Louis-Marie de La Révellière-Lépeaux, one of the five chiefs of the new Directory government. His influence permitted the Theophilanthropists to practice their religion in all the major Parisian churches, which were all given new and sometimes prosaic names like 'Agriculture', 'Concord' and 'Social Contract'. The church of Saint-Merri thus became the *Temple of Commerce*, and Notre Dame acquired the rather pragmatic title of *Temple of the City*. This all continued until the end of the century, then on June 23rd 1800 the last constitutional Te Deum to be heard here was sung in honour of France's victory at Marengo. With the first Consulate came religious peace, and an official ceremony restoring the Catholic faith to Notre Dame was held on April 18th 1802. This moving occasion, which was combined with a ceremony of reconciliation between church and government, was presided over by Monseigneur de Belloy, the new archbishop of Paris, who at 92 years old must have been overjoyed to have lived to see this day.

Ten years of alternating vandalism and neglect had left Notre Dame in a dilapidated state, but nothing was done at that time to restore it, apart from the return of certain paintings and three statues saved by Alexandre Lenoir. When Napoléon I was crowned here in 1804 there was an embarrassment of battered statues and holes in the walls ill-befitting an event of such magnitude - it was after all only the second coronation ever to be held in the cathedral, the first one being that of Henry VI of England in 1430. So to preserve the dignity and credibility of the new emperor, the cathedral was hung with tapestries to cover up the devastation. The ceremony was nonetheless a grandiose occasion, and Napoléon evidently liked Notre Dame, for he came back for the baptism of his son on June 9th 1811. At this event, described as the 'apogee of his reign', he lifted his infant son up in triumph before a delirious crowd shouting '*Long live the king of Rome*'. Napoléon's son, who would be known for the rest of his short life by this courtesy title bestowed on him by his father, was proclaimed emperor Napoléon II in June 1815 at the age of 4. His reign only lasted two weeks, and after coming into the world in such a blaze of glory, young Napoléon died of tuberculosis in Vienna at the age of just 21.

It was not until the appearance in 1831 of Victor Hugo's famous novel, 'The Hunchback of Notre Dame', that public attention was focused on the dilapidated state of the cathedral. As a result, extensive restoration work began in 1843, under the direction of the architect, Viollet-le-Duc, who, with a budget of 2½ million *francs*, restored it to its 14th-century glory. During this work, which lasted over twenty years, Notre Dame continued to host historic events, including the marriage of Napoléon III and the Empress Eugénie, and a visit from Queen Victoria in June 1856, before its final re-consecration on May 31st 1864 by the archbishop of Paris, Monseigneur Darboy. Viollet-Le-Duc's restoration returned Notre Dame to its former Gothic beauty, which was enhanced by the addition of a splendid collection of gargoyles that has now become one of the most eye-catching features of the cathedral. Despite the ravages of the centuries some things have survived, such as the stalls of the choir, dating from 1711, the organ case, made in 1731, and the three beautiful circular stained-glass windows, which date from the 12th and 13th centuries and are as old as the cathedral itself.

CLOÎTRE DE NOTRE DAME.

You're now going to have a look at the only part of the old *Cité* that survived Haussmann's modernization. It goes through the former Notre Dame cloister, and will enable you to glimpse back in time at what Danton and his compatriots might have seen while walking around their Paris. ➡ Turn right on leaving the cathedral, then right again into rue du Cloître Notre-Dame, where at number 10 is the Notre Dame Museum (open 2.30-6.00 p.m., tel. 01 43 25 42 92 for more information). Here you can find out more about the history of the Cathedral and the old city from its origins as Lutecia to the present. The 17th-century house at number 14 is now a restaurant called Le Vieux Bistro, but used to be the residence of a canon who was confessor to the famous poisoner, the Marquise de Brinvilliers. Le Vieux Bistro is renowned for its *boeuf bourgignon*, and has a reputation for excellent cuisine and a celebrity clientele.

Numbers 16 and 18 were also canons' houses, where the main gate to the cloister stood. Directly opposite, nestling against the cathedral wall, there used to be a little chapel called *Saint-Jean-le-Rond*, which has left us a story with a very happy ending. One chilly morning in November 1717 a baby boy was abandoned on the steps of this chapel. He was taken in by an orphanage, but immediately put in the care of Madame Rousseau, the wife of a glazier from a neighbouring street. She took him home, christened him Jean le Rond after the chapel where he was found, and brought him up as her own child, although the identity of the baby's real parents was known. The mother was a lapsed nun who was more interested in a life of high-status sex and socializing than in parenting, while his father, an artillery officer, had been away on a mission when his son was abandoned to his fate on the chapel steps. He preferred to remain hidden for reasons of social respectability, but secretly provided enough money for Madame Rousseau to educate young Jean. She sent him to boarding school when he was 12, and five years later he entered Mazarin College, where he was immediately noticed for his brilliance in mathematics, especially geometry. He went on to become a member of the Academy of Science, the Berlin Academy and the Academie-Française, and kept the company of Voltaire and Didérot. It was with Didérot that he co-wrote the monumental 28-volume Encyclopaedia, to which he contributed most of the mathematical and scientific content, and he is better known by the name of Jean d'Alembert, one of France's greatest mathematicians. He was the first to find and solve the wave equation, a solution now known as 'd'Alembert's Solution', and he has been further honoured with a street named after him in the 14th arrondissement.

➥Turn left on rue Massillon, part of the cloister before the Revolution, where at number 4 there used to be a house that was home to the writer Jean-François de La Harpe until his death in 1803. La Harpe was a poet and dramatist who turned his hand to literary criticism on the advice of Voltaire, and he eventually became the greatest literary critic of the 18th century. In 1770 he became chief editor of the newspaper *Le Mercure français,* staying in the post until the early years of the Revolution, which he supported enthusiastically. He was the principal force behind a petition in 1793 demanding payments from the government for academicians, many of whom had been deprived of their income by the closure of the Académie-Française. But like so many others, La Harpe's reputation as a patriot did not spare him from spending several months in prison during the Terror, an experience that changed him radically, for - also like many others - he emerged a committed royalist. When he resumed his classes at the *Lycée* in the autumn of 1794, his lectures were barely disguised tirades against the extremism of Robespierre, and in 1797 he published an essay entitled 'Fanaticism in Revolutionary Language' in which he decries the republican war on morality and common sense.

At number 8 you find the *Hôtel Roger de Gaillon,* which has been occupied since 1455 by the Maîtrise de Notre Dame, a pre-college music school for solo and choral singing. The house was reconstructed in 1740, and during the first part of the Revolution there were fourteen singing masters and a class of twelve children - not a student-teacher ratio you'd find nowadays. When Notre Dame was restored to the faith after the Revolution, the school returned to its former home, and is still here today.

➥At the end of rue Massillon you come out into rue Chanoinesse, which was the main street of the Notre Dame Cloister. There are still many very old houses here, particularly in the part of the street to your left, which has a little of the feeling of a Parisian street Danton might have seen when he first arrived in 1780, except that this particular street, being in the cloister, would have had no taverns (not good for Danton), no workers and no artisans, so it was a lot quieter than the rest of the city. ➡Turning to your right into rue Chanoinesse, the beautiful house with a mansard roof that you see across the road at number 12 dates from the 14th century.

Next door at number 14 was the home of Xavier Bichat, a doctor and anatomist at the Hôtel-Dieu Hospital, whose work with human tissue has made him the father of modern histology and pathology. He was born in Lyon, but fled the revolutionary turmoil there in 1793 when still only 22 and took refuge in Paris, where he was taken in by Pierre-Joseph Desault, a surgeon and anatomist who a few months earlier had been supplying medical care to Louis XVI in the Temple prison. Bichat might well have wondered if he'd chosen the best place of refuge, for in May 1793 Desault was denounced for being offensive to a group of patriots, and spent three days in the Luxembourg prison. At the age of 27 Bichat was appointed physician at Hôtel-Dieu, where he was able to make huge advances in his research into the effects of disease on human organs. He worked constantly, in one six-month period dissecting and examining more than 600 bodies. But this work was not without its dangers. Bichat was constantly breathing in toxic fumes from his experiments on the putrefaction of human skin, which might well have been the cause of a severe bout of coughing up blood that afflicted him for a while. Bichat recovered from this, but it left him in a poor state of health that was worsened by a fall down one of the hospital staircases, provoking a fever from which he never recovered. Bichat once defined life as *'the sum of forces resisting death',* but after two weeks of suffering, his own forces to resist death clearly didn't add up to enough, and he died in this house at the age of 31.

Continue along to number 16, which is also 17th-century, and as well as lodging a notable Egyptian painter called Hamed Abdallah, it is also thought to have been the home of celebrated French dramatist, Jean Racine. Numbers 22 and 24 are both 16th-century former *chanoines'* residences, and hiding underneath the vines and flowers at number 24 you'll find Au Vieux Paris, a restaurant that lives up to its name admirably. The house was built in 1512, and the beautiful cast-iron grille over the ground floor façade was constructed in the 17th century. Just before the Revolution it belonged to a certain Canon Cochu, who was said to have *'more debts than all the canons put together'*, a problem of little consequence for Cochu, who, like many of his colleagues, simply mortgaged the house that had been given to him by the Notre Dame chapter. After the state acquisition of church property the house was occupied by a *hôtelier*, who ran a tavern here during the Revolution, thus launching a new secular life for Cochu's former cloister home. Behind the low stone arch of the main entrance, in the far right-hand corner of the courtyard, some very old steps lead down to an ancient cellar, now owned by the restaurant, where the canons used to store their provisions - and no doubt the wine which put them into such debt!

If you eat at this very romantic restaurant you can go and choose your wine from a 16th-century cellar (not the one in the courtyard, but an equally atmospheric one) and then enjoy the gastronomic delights of cuisine from the Aveyron region, where *patronne* Odette Fau comes from - as does all the meat and produce used in her dishes. The menu includes hot fried *foie gras, boeuf d'Aubrac* with *sauce aux cèpes*, and *fondants au chocolat*. If you feel like a surprise, you can opt for the *Menu Odette* at €90 for two, where Mme Fau will present you with a succession of her specialities. The decor is decidedly revolutionary, with candles, red walls and striped seat covers, and the room upstairs has a wonderful red brocade ceiling in the form of a star. For a private gathering or celebrating a birthday, you can reserve a private room that looks out on to the courtyard - and if you want luxury and atmosphere during your stay in

Paris, ask Mme Fau about the short-term rental apartments in this house. They are wonderful. Telephone 01 40 51 78 52 for more information.

The corner house at number 26, where I was lucky enough to live while working on this book, dates from the revolutionary era and has a courtyard paved with very old tombstones from the various demolished churches in the neighbourhood. This courtyard used to link with that of the house behind, 19 rue des Ursins, and together they formed a little lane giving access to the *Chapelle Saint-Aignan* where legendary lovers Héloïse and Abelard worshipped. ➡As you turn right on to rue de la Colombe you are passing through one of the four former gates of the Notre Dame cloister, the one known as *Porte des Marmousets*. This street has kept much of its 14th-century atmosphere despite having been widened on the left-hand side, and outside number 7 there is a double row of cobblestones on the road marking the position and width of the *Enceinte Lutèce*, the first wall to be built around Paris in 276 A.D.

Behind number 5, in a private courtyard, are the remains of the *Chapelle Saint-Aignan*, founded in 1116 during the reign of Louis le Gros (the Fat). This church was a frequent place of worship for the celebrated lovers, Héloïse and Abélard, as well as Saint-Bernard, who would often come to pray here and bemoan the dissolute life-style of the local students. In 1791 the church was sold at auction and became a barrel warehouse that also served as a front for clandestine religious services. Non-juring priests came here regularly, bringing with them many priests who had taken the Constitutional Oath to save their lives, but continued to practice their religion. They would all gather here, variously disguised as masons, delivery men or water-carriers, to celebrate the Mass in secret. Later the altar was destroyed, and the remains of the 12th-century church were turned into stables, remains that have miraculously survived the ravages of history, and are now all that is left of the 23 little churches and chapels that used to stand in various parts of the old *Cité*. You will probably be as astonished as I was to know that as recently as the 1960s this precious example of Gallo-Roman architecture was being used as a furniture warehouse by an antique dealer! If you are interested in visiting the *Chapelle Saint-Aignan*, which is the oldest Parisian church still standing, you should contact the Association Sauvegarde du Paris Historique, 44-46 rue François Miron, 75004 Paris, tel. 01 48 87 74 31 (you'll be passing by it later in this walk).

On the other side of rue de la Colombe, at number 4, is a wonderful old house that has been a tavern or a restaurant since time immemorial. In the year 2000 it became La Réserve de Quasimodo, a very friendly restaurant - with a wine shop as well if you want to take home a bottle of what you had with dinner. Apart from the excellent food, relaxed atmosphere, a great selection of wine, and evening entertainment, another good reason for eating here is that you will be dining with some very interesting ghosts. The street takes its name from this house, which was known for centuries as *La Maison de la Colombe* (the House of the Dove), thanks to an ancient event that has been charmingly related by a local resident, Mr Jean-Jacques Chaplin. A very long time ago, the house that existed before, on the site of the present restaurant, collapsed when the Seine burst its banks one day without warning, and the inhabitants of the area later discovered a pair of doves imprisoned under the rubble. The male, described romantically by Mr Chaplin as a *'sort of plumed Abelard'*, had succeeded, by some miraculous and totally mysterious means, in finding food for himself and his *Héloïse* throughout their captivity, a marvel that prompted the residents to re-build the house and name it after the magical love-birds. The amorous pair are commemorated by the two doves sculpted over the door, as well as a flying dove on the corner wall.

The House of the Dove merits its reputation as the oldest bar in Paris. The ground and first floors date from the 13th and 14th century, the floors above were added 200 years later, and the wine-merchant's grille that you see over the entrance was made in the 15th century. The lower floor of the restaurant, which is a 13th-century cellar, is quite amazing, and a trip to the toilet there is a unique experience. The original tavern carried the sign *Saint-Nicolas*, much later it was called *Café Desmolières*, and in the 1920s there was an owner who used to serve what he called a *Chupin*. This was white wine in a glass with a broken base - presumably so the drinker could not put it down and thus drank much more quickly - and much more wine. In 1952 it was bought by the American author and illustrator, Ludwig Bemelmans, who is most well-known for his children's books about the Parisian schoolgirl, Madeline. He owned the house for two years, spending much of his time painting frescos on zinc, then sold it to Michel and Beleine Valette, who turned it into the famous *Cabaret and Restaurant de la Colombe*.

There is a very good story associated with this house involving the famous highwayman, Louis Dominique Bourguignon, more commonly known as Cartouche, who terrorized the roads around Paris at the beginning of the 18th century. While looking for victims on the Pont-Neuf one day, he saw a very well-dressed gentleman climb up on the parapet and prepare to throw himself off. Cartouche stopped him and asked him why, and the man explained that he owed so much money to so many people that the only decent thing to do was kill himself. Cartouche promised the man that he would get him out of this difficult situation - all he needed was a list of all the creditors, and how much he owed each one. Cartouche then invited all the creditors to come here to the *Saint-Nicolas* tavern, where he wined and dined them, paid all their debts, not forgetting to get receipts, bade them all goodnight, and left. When all these happy, rather enebriated ex-creditors finally staggered out into the street, they were immediately jumped on by a gang of thieves, who robbed them of all the money they had just put into their pockets. There are no prizes for guessing who the leader was of this band of reprobates. Cartouche made another visit to the *Saint-Nicolas* tavern, this time pursued by the police, but he was able to escape from here by way of an underground passage, part of which still exists.

Later on, during the revolutionary era, the house was a *cabaret* (tavern), and a favourite haunt of the journalist Camille Desmoulins, a well-known customer at many of the city's less salubrious nightspots. Camille was often to be seen here during his 1789 period as a rising star of the revolution, when he was still single, and would spend the evening holding forth on his republican ideas. At that time rue de la Colombe ended at rue des Ursins, and the tavern's address was *21 rue d'Enfer*, the 18th-century name of rue des Ursins. *Enfer* is a corruption of the word *inférieur*, and the street got this name because it was built at a lower level than the other streets within the cloister. You can still see *rue d'Enfer* engraved on the side wall of the House of the Dove.

➡ Turn right into rue des Ursins and follow it along to the steps on the left leading up to the quay. The wonderful house on the corner at numbers 3, 5 and 7, looking like something out of a fairy tale, was originally two different dwellings, one of which was a canon's house, and the other the *Hôtel des Deux Lions*. It is now owned by His Highness Prince Karim Aga Khan, who has apparently tastefully restored it to its former beauty. ➡ As you turn right into rue des Chantres, you are walking through another of the four gates that led into the Notre Dame cloister. Rue des Chantres is a very narrow street with a delightful view at the end of it of a procession of oxidized green saints climbing heavenwards up the spire of Notre Dame. This street owes its names to the *chantres* (cantors), religious singers who had houses here that served as schools for local children - the seeds of the French primary school system were thus planted here.

Along the entire east side of rue des Chantres stood the house where 17-year-old Hélöise lived with her uncle Fulbert, a canon at Notre Dame. In the year 1118 Fulbert had a lodger, Pierre Abélard, a 39-year-old teacher of rhetoric and dialect, who was put in charge of Hélöise's education. Abélard was a musician, a poet, and handsome to boot, so it's not surprising that student and teacher fell passionately in love, and by the end of the year Hélöise was pregnant. Abélard spirited her off to Brittany, where their son, Pierre-Astrolabe, was born. They were married there, in secret, but Hélöise refused to acknowledge the marriage, fearing that Abélard's brilliant career would be ruined by the restraints of a family. So Abélard returned to Paris, where he became an *avant-garde* philosopher, teaching his radical ideas to 3,000 followers among the vineyards of the *Montagne Sainte-Geneviève* (between the Panthéon and the Place Maubert). But old canon Fulbert could not forgive Abelard for taking Helöise away. He took terrible revenge on him by having him castrated, whereupon the tragic lovers both took religious vows and Abélard died in 1142 at the age of 63, having spent his remaining years fleeing from one monastery to another. At his death Hélöise brought his body secretly to the oratory, *Le Paraclet*, founded by Abélard in Nogent-sur-Marne, where she died, also aged 63, in 1164.

➡From rue des Chantres turn left back into rue Chanoinesse, where at number 10 was the second entrance of canon Fulbert's house - the main one being at 9 Quai aux Fleurs, where there is a commemorative plaque. ➡Turn right and you are back in rue du Cloître Notre Dame, which was re-named *rue du Cloître-de-la-Raison* during the Revolution, and here is a good point from which to admire the gargoyles and impressive flying buttresses of Notre Dame. ➡Walk back towards the Parvis, and once you have passed rue Massillon you'll also have a good view of the magnificent north transept, built in 1250. Its arched entrance has two doorways and is known as the *Porte du Cloître*, for these were the doors that for six centuries led from the cathedral into the cloister. Between the two doors you can see the original statue of *Notre Dame de Paris*, which was made in about 1260 by an unknown artist and is the only statue dating from the beginnings of the cathedral.

Quai de l'Archevêché.

➡Turn left into the Parvis and walk along past the façade of Notre Dame for a last look at this magnificent building, then turn left again into the garden that runs along the south side of the cathedral. This area is now known as Square Jean XXIII. In 1161 Maurice de Sully had a large residence built here for the bishops of Paris, who remained until 1622, when Paris became an archdiocese. The archbishops continued to live in the episcopal palace for 75 years, but when Cardinal de Noailles became archbishop he decided to replace it with a more luxurious residence. In 1697 the Archbishops' Palace was built, a magnificent structure that stood alongside the Seine, and, in addition to its fabulous grand staircase designed by Desmaisons, contained one of the biggest halls in Paris. On October 19th 1789 this hall was occupied by the Constituent Assembly for its very first session in Paris after following the royal family from Versailles a fortnight earlier. This was a temporary arrangement, lasting three weeks while the *Salle de Manège* was being re-decorated, but during this short time the Assembly took several measures that set its course for the coming years. In particular, on October 28th it passed the first anti-religious law of the Revolution by voting a ban on the expression of monastic vows, a measure that must have caused a few shockwaves in the Notre Dame cloister next door. Perhaps sitting in a sumptuous palace built for archbishops may have provoked this attack on religion, as well as the one that followed on November 2nd, when they voted in favour of the confiscation of all church property, in order to finance the creation of the notorious *assignats*. It must have been a heated debate, for despite the prevailing resentment toward the wealth of the clergy, more than a third of the deputies voted against the measure.

The limits of revolutionary belief in equality were well demonstrated here on October 22nd, when a delegation of free black landowners from the island of Santa Domingo presented a petition to the Assembly demanding the right to sit as deputies. To justify their demand they explained that they were free, French, and owned property, all of which gave them equal status with white colonials. To further boost their cause they also - somewhat ironically - declared themselves in favour of maintaining slavery in the colonies, well-aware, no doubt, that in opposing it they would be opposing the Declaration of the Rights of Man, which permitted it. But it was the 18th century, and such radical demands made no impression on the white bourgeois deputies, who dismissed their visitors with a smoke-screen of polite ambiguities.

A week later the Assembly dealt a further blow to equality when it passed a controversial law dividing the adult male population into 'active' and 'passive' citizens, a distinction based on income which effectively excluded all but a small minority from eligibility to vote. The same law, known as the 'silver mark decree', placed even heavier income restrictions on membership of an electoral or legislative assembly, thus keeping the running of the country firmly in the hands of the bourgeoisie and the upper-classes. This law was decried by Robespierre, who described it as the 'destruction of equality'. The day before leaving for their new premises in the *Manège*, the Assembly passed a law preventing deputies from being named as government ministers, a measure that effectively blocked communication between the king and the Assembly, and harshly reminded Louis XVI of his diminished role in governing the country. On November 8th the deputies left the Archbishops' Palace, which was used during the rest of the Revolution as a residence by the chief surgeon of the Hôtel-Dieu hospital, while the chapel became an amphitheatre for anatomical dissection. When the palace was demolished in 1837, it was replaced by the garden you see now.

➡Leave the garden at the other end, cross over the road (Quai de l'Archêché) next to the bridge (which should be on your right) and go into the small triangular garden called Square de l'Ile-de-France, where there is a museum to the memory of those deported to concentration camps during World War II. At the end of the 18th century this square was a public garden, but being in the middle of the Notre Dame cloister it was open only to men. By the lovely weeping willow tree at the northern tip of the garden, where the quay meets the Pont Saint-Louis, there used to be a watering place where horses could drink, and where residents of the cloister would fetch their daily water supply. But by the beginning of 1864 the square had become a desolate empty space, and Baron Haussmann decided to move the city morgue here from its old premises on the Quai du Marché-Neuf. The new morgue building had a large hall where bodies were exhibited on marble slabs, and viewed through a window by people looking for missing persons. Clothing was also displayed next to the bodies to help in their identification, and the whole process was made more tolerable after 1881 with the introduction of refrigeration. This macabre establishment continued to function here until 1914.

ILE SAINT-LOUIS.

➡Leave the garden by the exit next to the willow tree, where you see the Ile Saint-Louis to your right. Turn right from the quay on to the Pont Saint-Louis, which links the Ile de la

Cité with the Ile Saint-Louis. The bridges between these two islands have been fraught with disaster, beginning with the first one, a wooden toll bridge completed in 1634. Being very narrow it was limited to pedestrians, and shortly after its completion an argument started between three people over who should be the first to cross. In the ensuing scuffle the balustrade gave way, panic broke out, and many of the people crossing the bridge were trampled on or suffocated. Others, convinced the bridge was going to collapse, jumped into the Seine and drowned. Twenty people died that day and twice that many were seriously injured. At the end of the winter of 1709 the bridge was so badly damaged by cracking ice that it had to be demolished the following year, and was rebuilt in 1717. This bridge, also made of wood, was swept away by the tide at the beginning of the Revolution, and was not replaced until 1795, so crossing from one island to another during this period was impossible. It was replaced twice during the 19th century, and was totally destroyed a second time, also at the beginning of a period of turbulence, in 1939, when a barge carrying an 800-ton water tank ran into it. Later that year it was finished off by a 1,200-ton motor-vessel, which sank the bridge, killing three people instantly. But don't worry, the present bridge is very solid, so you can cross quite safely to the other side, where you will find yourself on the Ile Saint-Louis, one of the quarters of Paris that has hardly changed since the 17th century, having escaped the ravages of Baron Haussmann. It was Henri IV who first planned it as a residential area at the beginning of the 17th century, and many of the beautiful town-houses that you see now were built at that time.

➥Coming off the bridge, bear slightly right into rue Saint-Louis-en-l'Ile, a busy little street that goes right through the middle of the island. You'll probably be tempted to go in to all the wonderful shops on this street, or at least do a bit of window shopping, and you should certainly look into any interesting open doorways. Originally called *rue Palatine*, this street is one of six opened between 1614 and 1646, and it quickly became the principal commercial thoroughfare of the island. At the end of the 18th century many of the boutiques and restaurants you see now were private houses, or served as offices for the lawyers of the Palais de Justice. In 1780 the young Georges-Jacques Danton walked along this street, looking for the offices of Maître Jean-Baptiste François Vinot, an attorney in the Paris Parliament who took on Danton as a legal clerk. He worked and lodged in this street for almost two years, spending most of his free time wooing Gabrielle Charpentier at the Café du Parnasse and taking fencing lessons. Danton also loved swimming, and was one of the first Parisians to use the Seine for this pastime. Wearing a pair of linen long-johns, he would dive in off the quays of the Ile Saint-Louis, to the great amusement of the locals, who would gather on the edge to watch him. He often swam quite long distances, emerging from the water one day not far from the Bastille. As he climbed up on to the riverbank, he remarked to a passer-by, *'That fortress offends me. Will we ever see it knocked down? The day that happens I'll be there - with a pickaxe!'* This was pure bravado, of course, since when the Bastille was attacked Danton stayed well out of it, insisting that he was an orator and had no business on a barricade.

➡ Walk along rue Saint-Louis-en-l'Ile, where at number 54 is the wonderful Hôtel du Jeu de Paume, created out of a 17th-century indoor tennis court. When the owner bought it in the 1980s it was a disused warehouse, but renovation of this former aristocratic playground has produced the most spectacular interior combining 300-year-old beams, stone walls and glass. The majority of the houses from number 50 down to number 22 date from the 17th century, and the beautiful house at number 51, formerly known as the *Hôtel de Chenizot*, was the home of Jean-Jacques Devin de Fontenay, a counsellor in the Parliament. He was 26 years old when in 1788 he married the exquisitely beautiful 14-year-old Thérésia Cabarrus, who would later become famous as Tallien's mistress, and the catalyst for the events of 9 *Thermidor*. In 1789 Thérésia's husband bought himself the title of marquis for a mere 400,000 *livres*, and for a while his young marquess enjoyed a luxurious life in her mansion on the Ile Saint-Louis, surrrounded by a circle of pro-revolutionary friends. But by the age of 18 Thérésia had tired of her arrogant husband whom she'd never loved, and she became the mistress of one of his friends. The marquis responded by having an affair with the chambermaid, at which point the ill-suited couple decided to put an end to their five-year marriage. Thérésia left for Bordeaux, where five months later she captured the heart of the up-and-coming deputy, Tallien. Her disastrous marriage to the marquis had produced a son, named Antoine de Fontenay, who was only 4 when his parents divorced, and who later became a lieutenant-colonel in the Royal Dragoons. He died in this house at the age of 26, and seven years later the property was bought by a wine merchant. In 1840 the government rented it as a residence for the archbishop of Paris, Monseigneur Affre, who was born in 1793 in the middle of the Revolution. In 1848, in the middle of another revolution, when this heroic archbishop tried to mediate between rebels and government soldiers, he was shot and killed as he stood on the barricades with a crucifix held against his chest.

➡ Cross rue des Deux Ponts, and on your right at number 31 is Berthillon, where you might have to queue but you'll get really good ice-cream. At number 19*bis* you find the Eglise Saint-Louis-en-l'Ile, built in 1664. It took 62 years to complete the construction, which was financed largely by a donation of 30,000 *livres* from Jean-Baptiste Lambert, a member of the ubiquitous Lambert-Thorigny family that you will meet very shortly. During the Revolution, after the furniture had been destroyed, the paintings and statues stolen, and the organ pipes used to make bullets, the church became a warehouse for books.

In 1798 it was sold for 60,000 *francs* to a wily entrepreneur called Fontaine, who immediately restored it to the Catholic religion and then re-sold it to the municipality for 150,000 *francs*. The interior of this church is worth a look, and as you enter, look to your right where you'll see a tiny and rather mysterious old staircase. I can't tell you any more about it than that, but it does look intriguing. During the 19th century this church was transformed by one of its curates, Abbé Bossuet, at his own expense, into a gold-mine of art. In the Chapelle de Sainte-Madeleine you'll see a marble bust of Bossuet, and among the statues that he brought here are two that date from the early 17th century. One is of the Holy Virgin (on the right facing the altar) and the other is Sainte-Geneviève (on the left), both of which escaped being vandalised thanks to their being chosen - in a clear lapse of revolutionary rigour - to represent the goddesses of Reason and Liberty. As you reach the altar you will see several beautiful statues, and if you go around to the right behind the altar, the lights cast wonderful shadows of these statues on to the church walls. On October 23rd 1784 a 15-year-old boy was to be seen praying quietly in this church, having just arrived from Brienne on his way to the Military Academy in Paris. His name was Napoléon Bonaparte.

Between numbers 5 and 13 is a large ensemble of houses with a central archway over the entrance to rue de Bretonvilliers. The arched portico is all that is left of the *Hôtel de Bretonvilliers*, built in 1637 by the architect Jean Androuet du Cerceau for Claude le Ragois de Bretonvilliers, who was Secretary to the King's Counsel. The demolition of this mansion, considered for two centuries to be the most beautiful on the island, was the result of Baron Haussman's desire for a clear line of vision between the Panthéon and the Bastille. Number 12 opposite was the home of the engineer and chemist, Philippe Lebon, one of the inventors of the use of gas for lighting and heating. He had been experimenting with this idea since before the Revolution, using his *thermolampe*, a metal box containing logs which, when heated to a high temperature emitted an inflammable gas. One of the major problems was that the gas smelt terrible, and he had to spend many years experimenting before he could present the *thermolampe* to the Institute. Many of his experiments were carried out in this house, and in 1799 he took out a patent on his invention, which caught on much faster in England than it did in France.

Number 6, the *Petit Hôtel de Bretonvilliers*, also owned by the Ragois de Bretonvilliers family, dates from 1639, and at number 4 (number not shown) is the *Petit Hôtel Lambert*, which was reconstructed in 1750. It was one of the many houses owned by the Lambert-Thorigny family, and where Nicolas Lambert lodged his father-in-law. The principal residence of this family was the Hôtel Lambert at number 2, one of the most beautiful 17th-century mansions in the city, designed by architect Louis de Vau and dating from 1642. It belonged to the Lambert family until 1739, by which time they owned fourteen other houses on the Ile Saint-Louis. When the Revolution broke out the house was confiscated by the state from its owner, who had emigrated, but who was able to get it back again when he returned in 1802. The beauty of this residence is somewhat marred by its rather dirty walls and the forbidding bars on the windows, and you should have a look at the strange winged face over the entrance - it rather resembles a flying pig, surrounded by cascades of oak leaves and acorns. In 1975 the Hôtel Lambert was bought by Baron Guy de Rothschild, who kept it until his death in 2007, when his son sold it - in a highly secret transaction - to the Emir of Qatar for 80 million euros.

The house at number 1, a quaint two-storey residence standing alone on the bridge, dates from 1640, and was owned during the latter part of the Revolution by Claude de Beauharnais, the brother of Joséphine's first husband. He held very important offices under the Empire and during the Restoration, but was less responsible in his personal life it seems, for he abandoned his daughter Stéphanie at a very young age, leaving her to be raised by Madame Campan, a former lady-in-waiting to Marie-Antoinette - and to be used later as a pawn in one of Napoléon's diplomatic games. When Prince Charles of Baden lost his fiancée to Joséphine's son Eugène de Beauharnais, Napoléon decided to compensate him by offering him Stéphanie in marriage. In the spring of 1806 when this generous offer was made, the young girl in question was 17, blue-eyed, blonde and ravishing, and shortly after she arrived at the Tuileries Palace to prepare for the great event, Napoléon tried to seduce her himself - without success, though, for she had been warned off by a very jealous Joséphine. Meanwhile, the Prince of Baden had been having second thoughts about the social value of an alliance with a niece of the Empress's first husband, and showed signs of backing out of the arrangement. Napoléon wasted no time in dealing with this problem. He announced his decision to adopt Stéphanie, and was thus able to offer to the Baden family the hand of Princesse Stéphanie-Napoléon, much to the delight of the prince, and the rage of the rest of Napoléon's entourage.

➡ Keep straight ahead at the end of rue Saint-Louis-en-l'Ile and bear left across the Pont de Sully, built in the 1870s. ➡ Look back from the bridge and you will have a panoramic view of the magnificent curved façade of the Hôtel Lambert, with its beautiful balconies bedecked with garlands. ➡ Now continue over the bridge, and in front of you, between the bridge and rue du Petit-Musc, is Square Henri Galli, where you can see the remains of one of the eight towers of the Bastille, the Tower of Liberty, so called because the prisoners in it were free to come out of their cells and walk in the prison courtyard and the governor's garden. It was discovered underneath rue Saint-Antoine in 1899 during excavation work for the construction of the metro, and moved here stone by stone. This relic gives a good idea of just how thick the walls of the sombre fortress were, and makes it easy to imagine why it became a symbol of oppression for the Parisians of the Faubourg Saint-Antoine, who lived constantly in its shadow.

➡ Walk along to the left to number 2*bis* Quai des Celestins (1 and 3 rue du Petit-Musc), where you will see a lovely house that was called *Hôtel Fieubet*, dating from 1681, when it was occupied by the Queen's Chancellor, Gaspard de Fieubet. It was home to a long line of de Fieuberts until 1752, and then continued to have consistently illustrious residents, apart from a short spell in 1816 when a sugar refinery was installed there. The house, which is now a school called Ecole Massillon, was extended in the 19th century and has its main entrance on the quay, while the original red brick wing on the corner, with its magnificent sculpted decoration, has been beautifully restored. Under the windowsills you can see the names and dates of all the de Fieuberts who lived here, and all the others who came after them, right up to 1818, when the *hôtel* was sold to two property speculators who turned it into a residential block. Number 4 was an outbuilding of the *Hôtel Fieubet* belonging to Fieubert's nephew Nicolas de Nicolaï, also sold after the Revolution and turned into apartments. Number 6 dates from the 1650s, and is now a little convenience store - the only one I have ever seen with a 17th-century beamed ceiling.

➡ Continue along the quay until you get to rue Saint-Paul. This part of the quay, between square Henri-Galli and rue Saint-Paul, used to be called the *Port Saint-Paul*, where the city's supply of wine and spices arrived from the provinces. It was one of the departure points for the *galiote* that took people part of the way to Versailles, and it was also the terminus for horse-drawn water-barges that brought passengers by river from provincial towns along the Seine. In 1599 Henri IV's 28-year-old mistress, Gabrielle d'Estrées, arrived here from Fontainebleau on an April afternoon to hear Easter Mass in Paris. She was seven months pregnant with their fourth child, and the king was on the point of rebelling against his ministers and marrying her. But fate intervened cruelly to stop her from becoming queen of France. Gabrielle was seized with stomach pains that same night, after eating a lemon at a dinner party, then she became increasingly ill, gave birth to a still-born son, and died a few days later after atrocious suffering. There are two theories as to what she died of. There was much talk at the time that she was poisoned, for Henri was under pressure not to marry her and was even making negotiations for a possible marriage with Marie de Medici, so there were many who would have liked her out of the way. But the symptoms Gabrielle suffered could also be attributed to eclampsia of pregnancy, which was always fatal in those days. We will never know.

WALKING WITH DANTON.

On October 25th 1784 the young Napoléon Bonaparte arrived for the first time in Paris on the barge from Troyes. He was with four other students from the College of Brienne, accompanied by their principal, Father Berton, all making their way to the Military Academy in Paris. Four years earlier, in 1780, Georges danton had also stepped on to Parisian soil here for the first time when he arrived on the water-barge from his home town of Arcis-sur-l'Aube. He had been advised by an acquaintance in Troyes to head for an inn called *l'Auberge du Cheval Vert* (Green Horse Inn) on rue Geoffroy-l'Asnier, and after asking directions from passers-by, he set off from the port - probably up rue Saint Paul. ➡You are going to follow the route that he might have taken, and wander around some of the other streets Danton might have walked along during those first days in Paris.

The quay at the Port de Saint-Paul was always bustling with activity, and was where both Danton and Napoleon first set foot on Parisian soil after arriving by water-barge from their home towns. (Author's private collection)

➥Turn right on rue Saint-Paul, which has been here under the same name since 1350. I wonder if the residents of the modern apartment building at number 5 on the left know what used to go on here two centuries ago. At that time it was a house belonging to the Marquis de Lignerac, whose dinner-parties with the Marquis de Sade and various actresses of dubious reputation were the talk of the neighbourhood. Number 8 has a wonderful 16th-century tower, and number 9 was where the artist Hubert Robert had his studio before the Revolution. Robert was nearly 60 when he saw the fall of the monarchy that had given him much of his livelihood. After creating his famous masterpiece, the 'Baths of Apollo', at Versailles in 1778, he was designated official designer of the king's gardens, and given lodgings in the Louvre. Gardens were his speciality, in fact, particularly those filled with romantic ivy-covered ruins, which he sketched prolifically in red crayon. So it's altogether appropriate that his house is built right next to the site of the former royal gardens, which you will come to in a moment when you explore the Village Saint-Paul. As his reputation grew, Robert was increasingly sought after by Parisian high society to decorate their town-houses. In his paintings he loved to evoke images of Paris, his native town, and his skill in this regard was celebrated. It was said that he could paint as fast as he could write, so when the Opera caught fire in 1781, he was able to capture the drama as it happened. Despite having spent eleven years in Italy at the beginning of his career, Robert remained a dedicated Parisian and attended all the city's many celebrations and festivals. He was known for his immense charm, his lack of pretension and his brilliant conversation, and seemed in many ways to have a charmed life.

When the Revolution came Robert welcomed it with enthusiasm, continuing to paint romanticized scenes of revolutionary events like the storming of the Bastille, and he was the principal architect of the *Fête de la Fédération* in 1790. But in October 1793 he was arrested and imprisoned in *Sainte-Pélagie*, officially for having forgotten to renew his civic identity card, but the real reason was no doubt his past links with the monarchy. His fellow artist, Jacques-Louis David, who had become a member of the Committee of General Security the previous month, is thought to have been one of the signers of his arrest warrant. But luck continued to follow Robert. The prisoners at *Sainte-Pelagie* had the good fortune, if you can say that, of being only two or three to a cell, and Robert was overjoyed to discover that his cell-mate was his friend, the poet Jean-Antoine Roucher. Prison regulations were quite lenient, so they were able to lead a reasonably agreeable existence, and Robert continued doing pencil drawings of prison life, including one of himself in his cell. The two men were later transferred to the *Saint-Lazare* prison, much less pleasant, where they made the acquaintance of another poet, the young André Chénier. When the fatal roll-call was announced on the evening of July 25th 1794, Roucher and

Chénier heard their names called out. The following morning they were taken away to the Tribunal and guillotined later that day, leaving their friend Robert shocked and alone. But perhaps his life really was charmed, for he was liberated ten days later and went on to become director of the Louvre renovation programme, leaving us some vivid images of this great project in his series of paintings showing the work in progress. He continued to occupy his lodgings at the Louvre until his retirement in 1802, and he died six years later - in the words of a fellow artist, Elisabeth Vigée-Le Brun - *'as happy as he had lived.'* It is often said that Hubert Robert escaped execution because another prisoner with the same name was taken in his place by mistake, but this is probably a myth. Having studied the lists of condemned prisoners during this period, including that of the executioner Sanson, I couldn't find anyone of that name, or even a similar name, who was condemned on the same day as Roucher and Chénier. So I guess Robert's escape from Madame Guillotine was just another of the many lucky breaks that made his life so happy!

Behind Hubert Robert's house, stretching between numbers 7 and 23, is the Village Saint-Paul, a complex of art galleries and antique shops built on the land that was once occupied by the king's gardens. ➡You can wander in and out of this by going through the entrance arcades as you continue your walk along rue Saint-Paul, where you will see several lovely old houses dating back at least to the Revolution, notably at numbers 10, 15, 20, 21, 23, 25, and 26. Since the 7th century there had been a church and a cemetery at numbers 30-32, which was used for the burial of the monks and nuns from certain monasteries in the *Cité*. They were obliged to respect an old Roman law which forbade burials in the city centre, so the bodies were brought by boat across the river and then carried to the cemetery along the grassy path which would become rue Saint-Paul. The original church was demolished and rebuilt by the Normans, who turned the new one into the main parish church, known as *l'Eglise Saint-Paul-des-Champs*. It became a very important Parisian church, for between 1361 and 1559 this was the parish of the kings of France, and during that period all the dauphins and other royal sons were baptised here. When the Revolution broke out it was closed down, sold in 1796, and demolished three years later. One bit of it did remain, however. It had a large clock tower, part of which is still visible, incorporated into the corner house at number 32 (façade on rue Neuve Saint-Pierre).

The adjacent cemetery was also closed at the same time, sold as national property for 70,200 *livres*, and demolished in 1796, which must have been a relief for the local residents, for it gave off a terrible smell. In the last part of the 18th century there were about 600 bodies buried here a year, and the residents of the street used to say that they only had to look at the cemetery to know if it was going to rain, for the increased humidity caused a putrid vapour to rise from the ground. These noxious fumes filtered through the chimneys into the surrounding apartments, changing the colour of the curtains and furnishings and making the residents feel very ill. As soon as the cemetery was closed up, new houses were built on it immediately, before any bones were removed, so under numbers 30 and 32 lie the remains of many well-known people, including the writer François Rabelais, the probable mistress of Richelieu, Marion de Lorme, who poisoned herself in 1650, the architect François Mansart, who popularized the mansard roof, and the celebrated 'Man in the Iron Mask', who was buried here in 1703. There are also the remains of nineteen bodies that were picked up from the streets on the morning of August 11th 1792. These people had been killed during the fighting the previous night when the monarchy was overthrown, and before being buried in the *Saint-Paul* cemetery, they were stripped of every last piece of clothing.

➡ Turn left into Passage Saint-Paul, which apart from the missing central gutter gives you an almost perfect picture of a typical street during the period of the Revolution. It still has the stone blocks by the side of the road (*bornes*) that pedestrians used to run behind for protection - rather vainly I would think - from horses and carriages that often raced through the city's streets at alarming speed. A particular offender in this regard was Louis, 4th Prince de Condé, known as the Grand Condé, who was fond of arriving at top speed outside the pied-à-terre he kept at number 7. This is the lovely little house at the end of the street on the left, right next to the Saint-Paul Church - the prince could have gone straight out of his front door into the church - but I don't think he kept this house for devotional purposes. If you are wondering where he parked his carriage, it could have been in the little lane between the side of his house and the church.

➡ Go back to rue Saint-Paul and turn right, then right again into rue Eginhard, another street to take you back in time. Where the road turns round a corner you can see the remains of an ancient fountain, and a circular window where an old iron transom carved with the initials S.A. recalls the street's former name of *rue Neuve-Sainte-Anastase*. You can see this name carved on the wall of the house opposite number 5. ➡ On leaving rue Eginhard, turn right on rue Charlemagne, which was first opened in the 7th century, and where a great number of the houses date from at least the 18th century. Number 9 is now a public park, where you see part of the city wall known as *Enceinte Philippe Auguste,* and where once stood the home of Jacques-Alexis Thuriot de la Rozière, president of the National Convention during the summer of 1793. He first came to the forefront during the storming of the Bastille, where he was part of the delegation sent in to force Governor de Launay to turn the cannons around and not fire if an attack was made. Despite his relentless persecution of non-juring priests and his strong support for an unconditional death penalty for Louis XVI, Thuriot could never agree with the extremism of Robespierre and Saint-Just, and in November 1793 he was accused of moderation and expelled from the Jacobin Club. After 9 *Thermidor*, he remained faithful to his *montagnard* ideals, and was one of the few die-hard Jacobins to resume meetings at their club. After a further denunciation Thuriot was obliged to flee temporarily, and on his return to politics he was put in charge of interrogating the royalist conspirator, Cadoudal, who persisted in addressing him as 'Mr King-Killer'.

➽ Go to the end of rue Charlemagne, passing number 18 that in 1708 belonged to a judge whose sentences bore a direct relationship to the number of capons and baskets of eggs offered by the accused. Number 18 is on the corner of rue du Prévôt which, from its opening in the 13th century until 1877, was called *rue Percée*, a name that you can see engraved on the wall at either end of the street. If it had had its present name during the revolutionary period, it would certainly have been changed, for it was named in memory of one of its residents, Hugues Aubriot, provost (*prévôt*) of Paris, who ordered the building of the Bastille and laid the foundation stone in April 1370.

➽ Go past rue Prévot up to rue de Fourcy, a 14th-century street also named after a provost in 1684. ➽ Before turning right into this street, cross over and look at the rather neglected Hôtel d'Aumont at 7 rue de Jouy. It was built in 1644 by Michel-Antoine Scarron, a King's Counsellor, whose daughter Catherine lived here with her husband, the Duc d'Aumont. When he died of a fit of apoplexy - an affliction that seemed to run in the d'Aumont family - Catherine soon had plans for a second marriage, but her son Louis had other ideas. Not wanting to see the family fortune in the hands of an outsider, he exercised his filial prerogative and had his mother locked up in a convent. Catherine took her revenge, however, by hiding an enormous part of the said fortune in a place that Louis was never able to find. Women continually seemed to get the better of Louis, including his wife, who, while he was carrying out his duties at Versailles, entertained an impressive series of lovers at the Hôtel d'Aumont. Her following included a marquis, a minister, a Jesuit and an Oratorian, as well as another duke, who on one occasion was obliged to spend the entire day in a wardrobe when Louis came back unexpectedly. The house remained the property of successive dukes of Aumont, several of whom died of apoplexy, until it was sold in the mid-18th century to Pierre Terray, brother of Louis XV's notorious Controller-General, Abbé Terray.

On December 4th 1771 this house was the scene of one of the most brilliant social events of the year, the signing of the marriage contract between Antoine Lavoisier and Marie-Anne Pierrette Paulze, Abbé Terray's great-niece. Lavoisier, who had become a member of the Academy of Sciences at the age of 25, was one of the rising stars of Parisian society, and the house was crowded with courtiers, ministers, scientists, scholars, financiers and General-Farmers. Pierre Terray died in 1780 and the house was inherited by his son, Antoine-Jérôme, intendant of police in the provinces, who was guillotined on April 28th 1794 along with 32 other members of the nobility. Ten days later Lavoisier was also executed with 26 fellow General-Farmers. The house, which had been confiscated by the government, was returned to its owners in 1795.

➡ Now go back and turn left into rue de Fourcy, then left again into rue François-Miron, which was originally the beginning of a Roman road leading from Paris to Sens. On the corner, at number 82, is a beautiful house dating from 1705, and there are four lovely 18th-century façades at numbers 72-78. At number 68 is the beautiful Hôtel de Beauvais, built in

1655 for Pierre Bellier, who started life as a ribbon merchant, and his wife, Cathérine-Henriette, whose sexual talents brought them fame and fortune. Cathérine was a lady-in-waiting and confidante to Anne of Austria, a position that offered her the chance to indulge her taste for romantic adventures. Perhaps this was why the queen later conferred on Cathérine, by then aged 40, the privilege of deflowering the 16-year-old dauphin, future Louis XIV. She evidently did the job well, for the queen was so delighted that she immediately made Pierre Bellier a baron and gave him a job as royal counsellor - even Catherine's father was honoured with the position of Captain of the Hunt. As for Cathérine, not only did she become Baronesse de Beauvais, she also received enough money to have the Hôtel de Beauvais built under the direction of the chief royal architect. On the death of her husband in 1674, Catherine found herself in debt, so she sold the house and paid rent to the new owner, which enabled her to live in it until she died in 1690.

The property had several owners after that, many of whom rented it out, and one of the more illustrious tenants was the Duke of Bavaria's special envoy, Count d'Eyck, who arrived in 1755 and turned it into a very lively gambling house. In 1763 he had visitors, an Austrian family who stayed for five months in rooms on the second floor overlooking the street, while their son did a series of musical concerts at Versailles that charmed Marie-Antoinette and the entire court. This young musical prodigy was still only 7 years old, and already supported his entire family. There are no prizes for guessing that this was Wolfgang Amadeus Mozart, who was thrilled by his success, but nonetheless reported to be crestfallen that Madame de Pompadour had not kissed him when he was presented to the famous courtesan. Count d'Eyck enjoyed himself so much at the Hôtel de Beauvais that in 1769 he bought it, and left it at his death to his three daughters, who rented it in 1785 to a noble called Pierre-Daniel Bourrée, Marquis de Corberon. For having been President of the Paris Parliament - and noble - he was executed in 1794 at the age of 77, along with his son, daughter, son-in-law, and his grandson Armand Bourrée de Corberon, who at just 16 years old was probably the guillotine's youngest victim. The Eyck sisters had sensibly emigrated by then, and their house was confiscated by the government, who turned the ground floor into an office for the administration of provincial coaches. It was sold and re-sold numerous times, and is now the property of the City of Paris, who directed the renovation work that has restored this lovely old house to its former grandeur. While the house was being restored, there were some interesting old shop-fronts on the ground floor, which have all gone now, but you can still see the trace of a painted sign, *Laverie George* (George's Laundry).

Just two houses down from the Hôtel de Beauvais at number 64 was the home of the journalist Jacques-Réné Hébert after his marriage to former nun Françoise Goupil. Soldiers came here twice to arrest Hébert, whose extremist writings often brought him into conflict with the law. Marie-Antoinette was his favourite target, and the first time he was arrested was only a few weeks after he moved in here, for having described her in his newspaper as '*a whore with a crown*'. The Hébert household was a scene of great joy on February 8th 1793 when their daughter, Scipion-Virginie, was born in the huge canopied bed that Françoise had brought with her from the convent. On the wall over the bed was an engraving of Jesus eating supper in Emmaüs, to which Hébert had added the title '*The sans-culotte Jesus dining with two of his disciples in the castle of a ci-devant*'. Hébert was a strangely contradictory character, capable of gazing tenderly into the cradle at his baby daughter, then sitting straight down at his desk and writing '*If justice were to be done, the Austrian tigress should be chopped up like mincemeat*'. In the summer of 1793 the Héberts moved to the *Cour des Miracles* (now rue des Forges in the 2nd arrondissment), an area that throughout the centuries was a veritable den of vice and prostitution. By 1793 it had been smartened up enough for the refined and spiritual Françoise, but still retained enough of its former ambiance to inspire Hébert's crass journalism.

Further down the street at number 50 is a restaurant called Fuxia L'Epicerie, one of a chain of nine throughout the capital opened over the past seven years by Italians Nathalie and Dino. It's a family-run business, offering original recipes made with fresh seasonal produce, a friendly ambiance and reasonable prices. All this has nothing to do with the French Revolution, you might be thinking, and quite rightly, except that this restaurant used to be called *Au Cheval-Vert,* the name of the inn that Danton was directed to. Was this his destination? We don't know, for Danton's *Cheval Vert* was on rue Geoffroy l'Asnier, and there is no record of which number. But this house is on the corner of rue Geoffroy l'Asnier, so who knows - it might have been right here that Georges-Jacques was heading. It has to remain a mystery, but ➡we can imagine, perhaps, that it *was* here - and that gives you a very good excuse to stop and enjoy some traditional Italian fare *chez* Nathalie and Dino, who chose this historic area for its lively atmosphere where 'life doesn't stop at 10 p.m.' Fuxia is open every day from 9 a.m. to 2 a.m., and sounds like just the sort of place for the gregarious Danton.

At this point Danton would have either stopped here if this house was indeed the Cheval Vert of his day, or he would have turned down rue Geoffroy l'Asnier and continued his search. ➡You're not going to follow him for the moment, but are going to continue along rue François-Miron and a few of the other old streets that Danton would have been familiar with - and we'll meet up with him again in a while. At 44-46 there is an interesting 16th-century house that would have seemed very old even to a citizen of revolutionary Paris. It is now the office of Sauvegarde et Mise en Valeur du Paris Historique, where you can get information on historical visits, including the *chapelle Saint-Aignan* where lovers Héloïse and Abelard worshipped. Across the road after crossing rue Cloche-Perce are two wonderful mediaeval houses with open beams and leaded windows. Number 11 is 15th-century, and number 13, with its gabled roof, was built in the 14th century and must be one of the oldest houses in Paris. Look at the ground floor, which is so slanting it seems to lean right over the street. If Danton had stopped to explore the entrances and courtyards of some of the houses on rue François-Miron he would have discovered at number 30 a magnificent Renaissance house. Unfortunately for us it's a private residence, so we're not able to see the fabulous 16th-century house that was the home of Charles IX's mistress, Marie Touchet (anagram of *Je charme tout* in old French - 'I charm all'). The king was devoted to his beautiful and pious Marie, who gave him the only son he would ever have, Charles de Valois, Duc d'Angoulême, and if this child had been legitimate, history would have been very different. A whole succession of celebrated monarchs, including Henri IV, Louis XIV, XV and XVI, would never have reigned, and Georges Danton would most certainly have been walking along this street towards a very different future.

➡ Continue along rue François-Miron, crossing over rue du Pont Louis-Philippe and rue des Barres, and look at the lovely row of houses between numbers 2 and 14 that were all built together during the 1730s. From 138 to 352 A.D. there was a Roman cemetery here that continued as a burying ground after the Romans left. When a wall was built in 1375 to separate the cemetery from rue François-Miron, a host of butchers' shops, fishmongers and greengrocers rapidly sprang up alongside it. These dwellings were rebuilt a century later, and then again under Louis XV, when the large building you see now was constructed by the architect, Gabriel. On its completion in 1737 it accommodated about 60 families, who would no doubt have been much more delighted with their new homes if they'd not been filled with the odour of decomposition that wafted relentlessly through their back windows from the cemetery. Danton may well have suffered a tinge of nostalgia for the sweet air of Arcis-sur-l'Aube as he made his way past the enormous modern apartment block with a lace handkerchief held against his nose! Despite being condemned in 1941, this lovely row of houses was saved from demolition and is now restored to its original appearance. Look at the façade between numbers 10 and 12, where you'll see an old inscription indicating the Place Baudoyer opposite. The balconies of these houses are all decorated with a wrought-iron elm tree, the significance of which you will learn a bit later when you come to Place Saint-Gervais.

One of the first families to take up residence here was that of the composer François Couperin, who had been the organist at the church of Saint-Gervais. In 1734, one year after François' death, the family took an apartment at number 4, which became home for five successive members of this musical family until 1793. Perhaps at this point they were driven from Paris by the Terror, fearing persecution, for it is true that François Couperin had owed his success to a series of aristocratic patrons that culminated in a post as the King's Harpsichordist. Another notable resident was Alexandre Ledru-Rollin, republican and revolutionary of a later vintage, who was born in 1807 at number 10. Violently anti-monarchist, he participated in the revolution of February 1848, from which he emerged as provisional Minister of the Interior. His persistent organizing of insurrections, however, forced him to take refuge in 1849 in England, where he soon became part of a group of European revolutionaries. Ledru-Rollin finally returned to France in 1871, and enjoyed a few months as a deputy in the National Assembly before his death in 1874.

➡Directly opposite this row of houses is the Place Baudoyer, a very ancient square that takes its name from one of the gates in the wall built around Paris during the 11th century. In this square you find the *Mairie*, or town hall, of the 4th *arrondissement*. ➡Go back and turn right off rue François-Miron into rue des Barres, which is one of the oldest streets in this neighbourhood. It already existed in the 12th century, but did not get its present name until the 1600s. Bordering the chevet of the Saint-Gervais Church as it does, the street has retained much of its medieval atmosphere, and its appearance has probably not changed much since Danton walked along it. Look over the entrance to the church and you will see hovering above the street two dramatic gargoyles that I am sure got a second look from Georges-Jacques as he passed by. At number 17 is a house built by Gabriel at the same time as the building you just saw at 2-14 rue François-Miron. Just before the Revolution it was the home of a surgeon at the Hôtel-de-Ville, an unknown man himself, but with a nephew, Eugène Sue, who became famous in 1842-3 with the publication of *Les Mystères de Paris*, the first novel to be published in the form of a serial.

Number 12 looks as if time has stood still since it was built in 1540 as a town-house for the nuns of the Maubuisson abbey. It was later rented to the *Filles de la Croix* (Daughters of the Cross) and became a residential school for young girls, whose families paid 400 *livres* to board their daughters here. Being a religious school, it was closed at the beginning of the Revolution, and at the corner of the house you can still see evidence of the work of revolutionary vandals - the mutilated remains of a *fleur-de-lys*, hated symbol of royalty that was attacked all over France after the fall of Louis XVI. ➡To get a better view of this lovely old house, turn left and look back at it as you walk down rue Grenier-sur-l'Eau, a street dating from the start of the 13th century, maybe earlier. With this view you are very close to seeing Paris through Danton's eyes. ➡Continue on rue Grenier-sur-l'Eau, cross rue du Pont-Louis-Philippe and continue on rue des Justes de France until you get to rue Geoffroy-l'Asnier, which was already in existence at the end of the 13th century, and has had its present name since 1445, when it was the domain of drapers and dyers.

This was the street Danton was heading for in search of his *auberge*, and he may well have stopped to admire the splendid lion's head decorating the entrance of the Hôtel de Châlons-Luxembourg directly opposite at number 26. This house was built in 1600, and one of its earliest owners was Antoine Le Fèvre de La Boderie, whose monogram can still be seen engraved on the window pediments. In 1606 he became ambassador to England, where on one occasion he was given a gift of 150 horses that he brought back to Paris. He didn't have enough room to lodge them in the *hôtel* stables, so he gave them away as presents to his friends, keeping just one horse, the most beautiful one, for himself. He eventually had to give this one away too - to the king, Henri IV, who had remarked rather petulantly, *'Well, am I to be the only one of your friends not to have one of your horses?'* When Danton passed by here in 1780 the Hôtel de Châlons-Luxembourg was owned by Claude Polissart, the king's wine merchant, whose family kept it until 1914. The two houses to the right of it, numbers 20 and 22, both date from the early 18th century, and are worth a look before ➡you turn round and walk back along rue des Justes de France. As you head back towards rue des Barres, it doesn't take much imagination to believe you are back in the Middle Ages.

➡Turn left on rue des Barres, go past Saint-Gervais Church on your right (you'll be visiting it very shortly), and down the hill to the row of houses between numbers 10 and 2, which stand on ground that has witnessed some very bitter justice. It was originally the site of a mediaeval manor, home to a certain Louis de Boisredon, who in 1417 became the lover of

Queen Isabeau of Bavaria. This was not a wise move, for her husband, King Charles VI, was mad, and Louis soon found himself dragged out of his home, sewn into a large sack labelled *'Let the king's justice be done'* and thrown into the Seine. His house was replaced at the beginning of the 17th century by the *Hôtel de Charny*, which was taken over during the Terror by the section committee of the Paris Commune. On the night of 9 *Thermidor* a small group of soldiers was seen coming along rue des Barres carrying a chair, on which was seated a dishevelled young man bound by rope to the back of the chair. He was covered in blood and winced with pain each time his fractured legs were jolted to and fro. It was Augustin Robespierre, younger brother of the Incorruptible, who had just been arrested at the Hôtel-de-Ville. He broke his legs when he threw himself out of the window in an attempt to escape, and the soldiers who gathered him up from the street were not sure what to do with him. Augustin was a likeable personality whose easy-going and sociable nature made him very different from his older brother. But he was devoted to Maximilien, unquestioningly sharing all his opinions, and courageously joined him without a moment's hesitation in his hour of need. *'I am as guilty as he is,'* declared Augustin, *'I share his virtues, and I wish to share his fate.'* The soldiers brought him here to the *Hôtel de Charny* where they were instructed to take him immediately, regardless of what state he was in, to the Committee of Public Safety. So poor Augustin, still tied to his chair, set off again along rue des Barres, for the much longer journey to the Tuileries Palace and the Committee room, where he joined his brother and the rest of their comrades, all of whom were guillotined the following day.

➡ Turn back now and go into the Eglise Saint-Gervais-Saint-Protais by its secondary entrance at 13 rue des Barres. This was the first parish church on the Right Bank, originating in the 6th century as a funeral chapel serving the *cimetière Saint-Gervais* that stood on the north side of the present church. A larger replacement to this chapel was begun in 1213, but work went slowly and it would be more than 200 years before the church was consecrated. Within little over half a century later the second church had become too small for the expanding community, so in 1498 work began on a third one. This was not so much a new church as an enlargement of the old one, incorporating its 13th-century bell-tower, two storeys of which are still there today. Once again work went slowly, taking 163 years this time, so although the new church was built for the most part during the Renaissance, the interior remained in the flamboyant Gothic style of the previous era. But it was 1616 by the time they began work on the façade, which was thus created according to new architectural fashions, and is now the oldest Classical façade in Paris.

Saint-Gervais church used to be the seat of the powerful Brotherhood of Wine Merchants, which might have been how the composer François Couperin met his future wife. He was the church organist here, while the girl in question was Marie-Anne Ansault, daughter of a wealthy vintner whose excellent connections helped the 21-year old François obtain a royal licence to publish his organ music. The post of Saint-Gervais organist was handed down to future Couperins, one of whom, Armand Louis Couperin, was organist during the last years before the Revolution, and in the nave you can still see the organ he played, made in 1758. Armand was killed in a traffic accident in February 1789 while on his way to Saint-Gervais church, so was spared the misfortune of seeing his church attacked and pillaged by revolutionary vandals. Many of the paintings were stolen, and the outside of the building was so badly damaged that the statues of the saints, including Saint-Gervais himself, had to be replaced during the 19th century. During the Directory it was taken over by the new cult of Theophilanthropy, and in 1796 was re-named the *Temple of Youth*. The Revolution was not the only thing to damage this lovely church. In March 1918, on the afternoon of Good Friday, the famous German howitzer known as 'Big Bertha' struck a pillar between the second and third north windows, causing the adjacent arches to collapse on top of the worshipping congregation. The number of dead seems to vary in every account of this incident, ranging from 50 to 200, but it was nonetheless a tragic event.

➡ Leave the church by the main entrance and go down the steps into Place Saint-Gervais, where you will see a lovely elm tree in the middle, surrounded by stone blocks linked with a chain. It was planted in 1912, but was preceded by a much older elm, the famous *Saint-Gervais Elm* that had stood there since the Middle Ages. There has long been a legal association with elm trees, where mediaeval magistrates would sit and dispense judgments, so it is natural that it was next to this tree that local Saint-Gervais residents used to arrange meetings to settle their debts - meetings often not honoured if the debtor didn't have enough money to pay his creditor. From this comes a French expression 'Meet me under the elm', which means making an appointment that you have no intention of honouring. There is also a pejorative term that stems from this legal association with the elm tree - *avocat dessous l'orme* (lawyer beneath the elm), meaning a mediocre or parochial lawyer. The *Saint-Gervais Elm* has been immortalized by the numerous artists who used to come and paint here, and is also echoed in the balconies you saw at numbers 2-24 rue François-Miron, all decorated with a wrought-iron elm tree.

Place de l'Hôtel-de-Ville.

➡ Leave Place Saint-Gervais by turning left on rue Lobau, which was built on the maze of little streets that used to be part of Danton's old neighbourhood before the back of the Hôtel-de-Ville was extended in 1838. At about the point where you leave Place Saint-Gervais, where you now see the rear façade of the Hôtel-de-Ville (see plan), there used to be a church called *Saint-Jean-en-Grève*, where in 1787 the birth was registered of a baby who may have had a famous revolutionary father. We'll come back to this mysterious infant later on.

Danton's Neighbourhood.

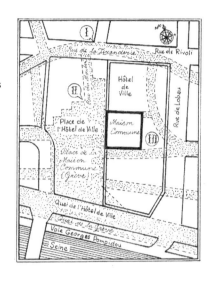

▬▬▬ Modern streets

▬ ▬ ▬ 18th century streets

I   Site of 22 rue de la Tixanderie, where Danton lived

II Site of the gallows, and the lanterne used for lunching

III Site of the church of Saint-Jean-Gréve, where the mystery baby, Jean-Louis, was registered

➡Turn right on Quai de l'Hôtel-de-Ville, known before 1868 as *Quai de la Grève*, ➡and then right again into Place de l'Hôtel-de-Ville, which up until 1830 was called *Place de Grève*. ➡At this point you might want to take a break in one of the cafés and read about what happened in this busy square. There used to be a port here serving the whole of Paris with wine, grain, hay, wheat, wood, coal and salt, all of which was loaded on and off the cargo vessels from several landing docks. These docks, as well as a row of watermills, were built on the sand right at the water's edge, for there was no built-up quay here until later in the 19th century. Over history the *Place de Grève* was well-known as a place of public executions, where all manner of horrible ordeals were inflicted. The gallows, the standard means of capital punishment for ordinary people, stood at the corner of *rue du Mouton*, roughly in the middle of the north side of the present-day square (see plan). As well as hangings, there were decapitations by axe or sword, a noble death reserved for gentlemen, while heretics and witches were burned at the stake, and you could also have your bones broken on the wheel. Crimes against the king were punished with quartering by four horses, and amongst those unfortunate enough to experience this decidedly unpleasant death were Francois Ravaillac, executed in 1610 for killing Henri IV, and an ill-intentioned domestic servant named Robert François Damiens, who in 1757 took it upon himself to remind Louis XV of his duties as a sovereign. Unfortunately he did it by attacking Louis with a rather inoffensive pen-knife, and he soon found himself attached to four horses in the *Place de Grève*.

Another famous victim of this square was the outlaw Louis-Dominique Cartouche, whom you met earlier when he was paying back someone else's creditors at the *Maison de la Colombe*. Based in a notorious slum known as *Cour des Miracles* (later home to Hébert, *Le Père Duchesne*), Cartouche led a gang of over a hundred thieves and murderers, both male and female. This group of brigands, who terrorized Paris on a daily basis at the beginning of the 18th century, is seen as one of the earliest examples of organized crime in France. Like any good 'Godfather', Cartouche didn't flinch from murdering anyone who challenged his leadership, which might well have led to his being denounced in January 1721 by one of his own gang members. He was arrested, condemned to death the following November, and brought to the *Place de Grève* for execution. He was 28 years old, and died by being broken on the wheel, the usual mode of execution for robbers and highwaymen.

Whenever an execution was to take place, the square would begin filling up with people from the first light of day. By the time the appointed hour approached the rooftops would be covered with spectators, and local residents sometimes rented places at their windows for a small profit. It was in the *Place de Grève* that the first execution by guillotine took place, on April 25th 1792, when a highwayman named Nicolas Jacques Pelletier, condemned for robbery with violence, was decapitated by the new machine. People crowded into the square from the break of dawn, standing there all day until the evening came so as to assure themselves a good place. By the time the prisoner was brought out night had fallen, and Sanson had to light the scaffold with candles so he could see what he was doing. But it was all over so quickly. *'Bring back the gallows!'* was the response of some members of the public, who reacted to this new-style execution with great disappointment, finding it too rapid to be of interest.

Although the *Place de Grève* continued to be the place of execution for common law criminals right up to the end of the Terror, it was never used as a theatre of revolutionary justice. There was one notable exception to this, however, when Antoine Fouquier-Tinville and fifteen of his colleagues were guillotined here on May 7th 1795. The square was crowded with people who, having previously harangued Fouquier's victims, had now come to insult Fouquier himself. *'In two minutes you'll be out of the debate!'* someone shouted, while another voice hurled *'Go and join your victims, villain!'* Perhaps the most unpleasant moment for Fouquier was when scores of distraught people began to cry *'Give me back my brother! Give me back my father, my mother, my husband, my sister'*, and worst of all, *'Give me back my children!'* Fouquier remained pale and impassive in the face of all this, but his tired, bloodshot eyes glinted with rage, for he truly believed he was a scapegoat, and that he was guilty only of following the orders of the Committee. Fouquier was the last to be executed, and waited patiently, despite the continuing insults, until at last it was his turn, at which point he shook the executioner's hand and approached the guillotine without a moment's hesitation.

The *Place de Grève* was not only the scene of official judicial killings. On the same corner as the gallows was a street light - generally referred to as *la lanterne* - that on several occasions was used for lynching when the mob took the law into their own hands. One such occasion was July 22nd 1789, in the wake of the storming of the Bastille, when the Intendant of Paris, Berthier de Sauvigny, and his father-in-law, Joseph-François Foulon, were both murdered here. Foulon, a financier, was very unpopular with Parisians, who hated him for his wealth, his ambition to become Necker's successor, and also apparently for the good luck and happiness that had followed him all his life. They were about to change that. They'd heard rumours about Foulon expressing his indifference to the hunger of the people by proposing that they should eat grass - a statement probably as apocryphal as Marie-Antoinette's suggestion that they eat cake. But in those days such a rumour could be as mortal as the plague, and 74-year-old Foulon was seized by a group of villagers in Viry where he had taken refuge. They covered him with hay and stuck thistles to his shirt, then tied him to the back of a cart and made him do the journey to Paris on foot - a long and hard journey during which they quenched his thirst by giving him vinegar and wiped the sweat off his face with stinging nettles. He was brought to the Hôtel-de-Ville, where he sat for six hours, waiting to be put in prison, when suddenly the mob who had brought him from Viry demanded to see their victim again. An eye-witness relates the rest. *'One of their number, a stocky little man, pushed the guards to one side, grabbed Foulon and threw him into the middle of the waiting crowd: he was dragged along, covered in blows, to the fatal lantern…'* One of the crowd then proceeded to lift the poor man on to the lantern, as several others pulled on the rope to hoist him up. By this time Foulon was almost dead, and when the rope snapped *'they separated his head from his trunk, which they dragged in the gutters, while his head was mounted on a pike and carried to the Palais-Royal.'*

While this was going on Berthier was arriving in Paris, accompanied by a heavy escort of bodyguards, when he came face to face with a sea of people waving a pike high in the air. To his horror, on the end of it he recognized his father-in-law's head, dripping with blood, and a handful of straw stuffed savagely into his mouth. Realizing instantly that a similar fate was in store for him, he made a brief attempt to defend himself before giving himself up to the mob, who brought him to the Hôtel-de-Ville. Restif de la Bretonne describes the scene.

'They interrogated him. He replied that he was guilty of nothing, that he had carried out orders...After seven minutes he came out of the Hôtel-de-Ville. In the middle of the steps, hearing cries of rage, he said to a grenadier in the guard: "They frighten me, my friend; don't abandon me!" The grenadier promised him. Was this out of mockery? A group of more than thirty people came up the steps and seized the guard who was leading the prisoner out, dragged him away and beat him. A little urchin of fifteen years old was sitting at the top of the lantern, waiting, shaking the rope... Arriving at the fatal lantern, Berthier, who saw that death was inevitable, shouted "Traitors!" He tried to defend himself, he fought with his executioners. They put the noose round his neck. They lifted him up. He tried to support the weight of his own body with his hand. A soldier went to cut his hand off, but cut the rope...the victim fell and landed on the head of one of the hangmen, whose face was badly torn...They heaved him up again, but the rope broke a second time, so they fell upon him at the foot of the lantern, disembowelled him and cut off his head.' (Restif de la Bretonne, 1986)

General Lafayette was at the Hôtel-de-Ville that day, with Sylvain Bailly, who had just become the first mayor of Paris, but neither of them had dared to intervene to stop this terrible massacre, which the press reported in all its gory detail, including a macabre post-script to the event. Having disembowelled Berthier, the crowd carried his entrails into the Hôtel-de-Ville and ceremoniously presented them to a stunned Lafayette. The general brushed aside this provocative delegation with a few abrupt and defensive words, but walked away heavy with the realization that high-minded ideologies of freedom were no longer enough to stem the tide of popular violence.

But the *Place de Grève* also had more peaceful moments. Three days after the storming of the Bastille, Louis XVI came to Paris, in response to demands by the people to honour the victory of July 14th. He arrived at 6 o'clock in the evening, in a closed carriage, having previously made secret arrangements for his military protection if the worst happened. The square was swarming with people as he got out of his carriage in front of the Hôtel-de-Ville, and Mayor Bailly offered him a tricolour cockade, the new badge of liberty, which Louis attached to his hat with theatrical panache that barely concealed perhaps a small hint of mockery. But perhaps not, for Louis never really knew how to behave in such circumstances, and some say that underneath his self-conscious exterior he was rather moved by the occasion. Whatever he felt, the king's action provoked cries of joy from the assembled spectators, who rushed to the entrance of the Hôtel-de-Ville to greet him. Louis then received a most unexpected honour. Many supporters of the Revolution were masons, and if a fellow mason visited their lodge dressed in noble attire, the members of that lodge would always stand along his path as he entered and join their swords above his head. This was known as the 'vault of steel', a great honour, which was accorded Louis XVI that day when he entered the Hôtel-de-Ville under a triumphal arch of interlocked sabres. The honour was accompanied by a dedication declaring *'You owe your crown to birth, you owe it now only to your virtues.'* As the king walked beneath the steel panoply, people cried with emotion and held out their hands to Louis, who remained silent and embarrassed by this sudden surge of affection and respect.

Three days after the storming of the Bastille Louis XVI visited the Hôtel-de-Ville, and received this masonic honour of the 'vault of steel' as he entered the building. (Author's private collection)

Even Restif de la Bretonne was carried away by borderline royalist sentiments, for his diary that day is bursting at the seams with blessings - he blessed Louis XVI, who was *'more immortal than ten kings together',* he blessed Lafayette, *'hero of two worlds',* for his honesty and dignified command of the nation, and he blessed Mayor Bailly, for bringing humanity, science, morality and wisdom into the city government. But popular affection for the royal family hung on a fine thread, and it was not long before a huge delegation of Parisian women, furious and desperate for bread, assembled in the *Place de Grève.* Undeterred by the rain, they set off for the long walk to Versailles, with the object of bringing back *'the baker, the baker's wife and the little baker's boy'.*

Hôtel-de-Ville.

Place de l'Hôtel-de Ville has been the centre of city government since 1246, when Saint-Louis created the first municipal authority. It had at its head the Provost of Merchants, with the seal of the water merchants as the official seal of Paris, and the last provost, Jacques de Flesselles, would become yet another victim of the Revolution. Accused of complicity with royalty, on July 14th 1789 he was shot through the head by a jeweller named Morin as he was about to leave the square to go to the Palais-Royal for questioning. His head was then cut off and paraded around on a pike along with that of Bastille governor, de Launay.

The heads of Bastille Governor de Launay and Provost Jacques de Flesselles are paraded on pikes in front of the Hôtel-de-Ville. (Author's private collection)

The first municipal building, known as the *Maison aux Piliers* on account of its columned arcades, was built in 1357 in approximately the same place as the present Hôtel-de-Ville. It was replaced between 1553 and 1628 by the Hôtel-de-Ville that Bailly and Lafayette knew, a lovely Renaissance structure that was unfortunately burned down by the Commune in 1871. The building you see now was put up in its place, and is identical in every way to the preceding one, giving you a pretty accurate picture of the revolutionary Hôtel-de-Ville. The only difference is that it was smaller, for the two side wings were added when it was rebuilt during the latter part of the 19th century.

The Hôtel-de-Ville remained the seat of city government up to the Revolution, and the day before the storming of the Bastille the electors of Paris met here for the first time, in the *Salle Saint-Jean*. The vote they took that day resulted in the king's hand being forced on three issues: he would have to move all royal and foreign troops further away from the city, give freedom of action to the Estates-General, and permit the formation of a National Guard. This vote marked the beginning of the Paris Commune, the revolutionary government of the capital that after the fall of the monarchy would become the motor of the *sans-culottes* movement. On the night when Louis XVI was overthrown, the *Place de Grève* was a hive of endless activity, as the Paris sections assembled successive battalions of troops in preparation for the siege of the Tuileries Palace. The commander of the National Guard, Antoine Jean Galiot Mandat, who was a marquis and suspected of royalist sympathies, was shot dead on the steps of the Hôtel-de-Ville (by then renamed *Maison Commune*), and replaced by Antoine Joseph Santerre, the brewer from the Faubourg Saint-Antoine. Inside the building an Insurrectionary Commune formed by political extremists the previous day took over the functions of the Commune. From then on, this illegal body, led by Robespierre, Collot d'Herbois, Billaud-Varenne, Fabre d'Eglantine, Hébert, Chaumette and Marie-Joseph Chénier, would play a determining role in revolutionary government, until its power was usurped by the Committee of Public Safety. It was this Insurrectionary Commune that was responsible for the immediate imprisonment of the royal family in the Temple Prison, and it played an active part in the September Massacres, the downfall of the Girondins and the installation of the Terror.

9 Thermidor - the Fall of Robespierre.

It was also at the *Maison Commune* that the Terror finally came to an end on 9 *Thermidor* Year II (27th July 1794), when, after a tumultuous session at the National Convention,

Maximilien Robespierre and five of his colleagues were put under arrest. As soon as the Commune was alerted, they called a meeting and at 6 o'clock that evening declared their intention to support their arrested compatriots and call for insurrection. At 9 o'clock the alarm bell rang, calling citizens to the *Maison Commune*, where a decision was taken to liberate the prisoners. What they didn't know was that at that very moment Robespierre and his friends were already free, for the prison officials had refused to take them in. But in spite of the Commune's offer of support, Robespierre, would not agree to join them. Incorruptible to a fault, he persisted in respecting the Convention's decision, and continued to consider himself under arrest until the Convention declared him and his friends outside the law. At that point he decided to take refuge at the *Maison Commune*. But the Commune was a shadow of its former self since the Robespierrrists, ironically, had eliminated its most powerful leaders who might have been able to save him. As it was, their insurrectionary movement never really got off the ground, and when Hanriot tried to arouse support in the popular sections of Paris, he was confronted with bolted doors and shuttered windows. People were frightened, and weary of terror and bloodshed, and by the time Barras sent the Convention's troops to the *Maison Commune*, Paris was no longer willing to fight for Robespierre.

Inside the building Robespierre and his friends had locked themselves in the assembly room, known as the *Salle de l'Egalité*, with about 40 members of the Commune. Seated at an enormous table, Couthon and Robespierre were discussing the content of a proclamation they were intending to make. *'In whose name do we put it?'* Robespierre asked earnestly, concerned even at this point to remain within the limits of legality. At about 1 o'clock in the morning they were just putting the final touches to their proclamation, when two columns of soldiers marched into the *Place de Grève*. The troops made their way in heavy rain over the cobblestones of the deserted square, coming to a halt at the entrance of the *Maison Commune*. A small group of *gendarmes* approached the steps of the building, led by Charles-André Merda, a 19-year-old from Gascony who had deserted that day from the Commune *gendarmerie* and who held in his hand a decree from the National Convention. He also had the Robespierrists' password, furnished by another defector, and with this he succeeded in entering the building. His instructions were to get into the room where Robespierre and his friends had taken refuge and wait, all of which he managed to do without difficulty, for on hearing the password the guards at the door of the *Salle de l'Egalité* let him in without any questions.

Walking into that room, Merda had before him a tableau of one of history's most dramatic moments. *'I saw about fifty men in a state of great agitation...In the centre of them, I recognized Robespierre the elder. He was seated in an armchair, his left elbow on his knees and his head leaning on his left hand.'* This was a characteristic position that Robespierre would adopt when reflecting on what to do. At that moment, though, it probably indicated desperation, for as the door opened he was putting his signature to the completed declaration while still in a position of reflection. He only had time to write the initial 'R' before Merda appeared in the doorway, and then it was just a matter of seconds before the room was full of soldiers. Shots were fired, and Merda, still following instructions, took his pistol and pointed it at Robespierre's heart, but in the confusion he aimed badly and hit him in the jaw. The jury remains out as to whether this is really how Robespierre's jaw was shattered, or whether Robespierre shot himself in the jaw in a botched suicide attempt. However it happened, pandemonium broke out, as Philippe Le Bas shot himself in the head and Georges Couthon fractured his skull trying to escape in his wheelchair, which tumbled to the bottom of the stairs with the paralysed deputy still in it. Maximilien's younger brother, Augustin Robespierre, also tried to save himself by climbing out of the window on to a ledge. He stood there for a few seconds staring at the square swarming with soldiers, before jumping on to the cobblestones below, where he was picked up, bloody and injured, by waiting *gendarmes*. In the midst of all this turmoil, Robespierre's devoted follower, Antoine Saint-Just, stood silent and motionless, waiting to be taken away. With the rain still pouring down, the last of the revolutionary chiefs were brought out of the *Maison Commune*, four of them on stretchers, one of them already a corpse, while those who could walk were escorted out by guards, their faces sombre and defeated.

Danton's Bachelor Pad.

When you leave Place de l'Hôtel-de-Ville in a little while, you will go out of it by the north side into rue de Rivoli. If you had been leaving the square in Danton's day, you would be walking past the fatal lantern along *rue du Mouton* (roughly between the two rows of street lamps facing the Body Shop), and into *rue de la Tixanderie*, a narrow, curved street which corresponded to this part of rue de Rivoli along the north edge of the Place de l'Hôtel-de-Ville. You can't take this route easily now, because the fountains are in the way, but if you had been walking in this direction then you might well have seen Danton looking down from his window on to *rue du Mouton*. For it was here, at 22 *rue de la Tixanderie* (approximately where you now see the Body Shop at 68 rue de Rivoli) that Danton took an apartment in 1784. He had just returned from completing his legal studies in Rheims, and he lived here until just before his first marriage in 1787. His apartment, which faced on to *rue du Mouton*, was a stone's throw from the Hôtel-de-Ville, and from his windows Danton had an excellent view of its beautiful Renaissance façade. A less edifying sight, which he could also see very clearly, was the notorious lantern at the end of *rue du Mouton*, and it's probable that being so near to the *Place de Grève* Danton was occasionally an involuntary witness to the work of the executioner Sanson. As he made his way daily across the busy square, could he have possibly imagined that one day he would have so much political influence at the Hôtel-de-Ville - or so close a professional acquaintance with Monsieur Sanson?

Danton had not chosen to live in this particular house by accident. On the same floor as his apartment lived a young woman called Françoise-Julie Duhauttoir, whom he had met in Troyes when he was working as a legal clerk for her uncle. Françoise lived rather well thanks to an inheritance, and divided her time between Troyes, where she took care of the management of her estate, and a *pied-à-terre* in Paris that offered her the anonymity to lead a discreetly liberated existence. This corresponded admirably with Danton's insatiable need for female conquests, and soon after his arrival in Paris in 1780, while he was lodging with Maître Vinot, he began a liaison with Françoise. On February 23rd 1783 she gave birth to a baby boy, whom she named Jean-Louis, and the following month she took the child to the nearby church of *Saint-Jean-en-Grève*, which stood on the site of the rear façade of the Hôtel-de-Ville in rue Lobau. Here Françoise registered the birth, naming herself as the mother, and citing the father as 'unknown'. History has left us no official proof that little Jean-Louis was Danton's child, but what followed, as you will see, certainly gives rise to suspicion.

While living in *rue de la Tixanderie*, Danton had regular evening visits from a group of his old school companions who had also settled in the capital. These were lively events, where they would drink and talk the night away, discussing law, philosophy and politics, and reminiscing about old times. The only woman who ever attended these *soirées* was Françoise, and at one of them Danton unwittingly introduced her to her future husband, Maître Huet de Paisy, a King's Counsellor. It was love at first sight for both of them. In the meantime Danton had fixed *his* sights on Gabrielle Charpentier, and began all the necessary manoeuvres to win her hand, so in 1787 he left *rue de la Tixanderie* and moved to *rue des Mauvaise-Paroles*, near his future father-in-law's café. Françoise and her lover continued to live here, not just in her apartment but also in Danton's now empty one, and it was at this time that Huet de Paisy decided to offer his post as King's Counsellor to Danton - for the not inconsiderable sum of 68,000 *livres*. What's more, 58,000 of it had to be paid immediately, and Danton was hard put to find such a large amount from his meagre resources which at the time amounted to 5,000 *livres*. What was he to do?

For reasons unknown, Françoise came to the rescue and handed over 36,000 *livres* to her old friend Georges, who in turn handed it to Huet de Paisy, who subsequently married Françoise, thus enabling her to get all her money back. It's all the more surprising when we learn that Huet de Paisy had bought the office for only 30,000 *livres*, most of which had never been paid, and Danton agreed to pay off the remainder of the debt. So Huet de Paisy made an enormous profit out of his deal with Danton, and when he married Françoise, he legally recognized her son as his own, all of which could lead to the conclusion that this was part of an agreement between all three of them to avoid Danton being compromised in the eyes of his future father-in-law. If this is the case, Danton paid dearly for his indiscretion, but obviously felt that Gabrielle was worth all the expense. In reality, Mr Charpentier and his daughter were probably both aware of the situation, for Gabrielle's brother, Antoine, worked in the office of the notary who handled the transaction, and was later responsible for ensuring that Danton kept up the payments he had promised to make. But the deal brought him the marriage he wanted, as well as the coveted office, where he unabashedly affixed his name as *Maître d'Anton*, an aristocratic pretence that he continued to use until 1791!

➥Leave the Place de l'Hôtel-de-Ville by its north side, to the left of the fountains, then cross rue de Rivoli, go up rue du Renard and turn left into rue de la Verrerie, a name deriving from a glass factory that was installed here in 1185. Painted and enamelled window glass was produced by a community of artisans who lived in the street, a community that died out during the 18th century when transparent window glass became the fashion. Linking up with rue Saint-Honoré, this street was for centuries part of the city's main east-west artery, and therefore one of the most important streets in Paris. During the reign of Louis XIV it was widened quite considerably, so when the king went to his palace at Vincennes the long procession of carriages could make its way along the street more easily. This end of rue de la Verrerie has retained much of its former atmosphere, thanks to the old stone walls of Saint-Merri Church that run along its north side, and neighbouring streets like rue Saint-Bon, which give you a glimpse of what revolutionary Paris may have looked like. Saint-Merri suffered the same fate as most Parisian churches, being closed in 1793 and turned into a saltpetre factory, then four years later becoming the *Temple of Commerce* for the Theophilanthropists.

At number 83 is a house whose beauty has unfortunately been marred by the construction of a supermarket, but this building actually dates from the 16th century, when it was known as the *Ville de Reims*. In 1690 it became a lodging house called *A l'Image Notre-Dame*, offering accommodation to travellers arriving from Troyes and the Champagne area. Two such voyagers were a certain Comte and Comtesse de la Motte, who arrived here from Saverne in 1781 and rented two furnished rooms that they occupied for a year. During that time the countess would leave every morning for Versailles, where she claimed to have regular audiences with Marie-Antoinette. In fact she spend the day closeted in a dreary little furnished room near the palace, but her supposedly close relationship with the queen enabled her to entangle an unwitting cardinal named Louis de Rohan in a near-perfect confidence trick that would become known as the famous Affair of the Queen's Necklace. The story of this celebrated swindle, which is considered by some to be the real starting point of the Revolution, is told in walk number one on Versailles.

➥Turn right on rue des Juges-Consuls, left on rue Cloître-Saint-Merri, and immediately right on rue Brisemiche. Here you see the Saint-Merri church to your left, and the Centre Pompidou to your right. During the 18th century there was a growing community of Ashkenazi Jews in this part of Paris, and from 1770 they had their synagogue in rue Brisemiche. In 1789 they opened a second one in rue Renard, but both were closed down by the revolutionary government during the Terror. This street is now part of a new square, where you see a pool containing some fascinating imaginary machines, sculptures and colourful creatures, adding a humorous touch to the slightly serious façade of the IRCAM building (a centre for research into modern classical music). This little area between Place de l'Hôtel-de-Ville and rue Saint-Merri was for a long time a notorious district for prostitution, a tradition still carried on in nearby rue Saint-Denis. In his *Tableau de Paris*, written just before the Revolution, Louis Sebastien Mercier described the district around rue Brisemiche as teeming with *'disorderly armies of streetwalkers, who display themselves brazenly in the doors and windows, and flaunt their lascivious charms on the public walkways. They are hired, like public carriages, at so much an hour.'*

➥At the end of rue Brisemiche turn right into rue Saint-Merri, cross rue Renard and continue into the other side of rue Saint-Merri. This part of the street is full of interesting old houses, like number 9 built in 1630, and you should go and look at the inner courtyard of number 12, the former *Hôtel Le Rebours*, which goes back even further to the 16th century. You can still see the old name of the street, *rue Neuve-Saint-Mederic*, engraved on the façade of number 12 (at the corner of rue Pierre-Aulart), with the word *saint* gouged out by revolutionary vandals. This old name appears again on the side wall of number 10, in the cul-de-sac de Boeuf, also with the partially scratched out *St* remaining as a legacy of the Revolution. ➥You should look down rue Pierre-Aulart for a moment, for it is a classic mediaeval street, complete with central gutter. ➥Now cross rue du Temple and continue into rue Sainte-Croix-de-la-Bretonnerie, opened in 1230, where at number 47 (and 24 rue du Temple) you can see a wonderful square turret dating from 1610. This house was once the home of several generations of distinguished surgeons, beginning in 1635 with Turpin, who attended Louis XIII's brother, Gaston d'Orléans.

➥Continue a little further down this road to number 44, which was at the centre of a notorious scandal. During the last part of the 18th century this was the home of a man named Kornmann, a fat banker from Alsace, whose accusations against the writer, Caron de Beaumarchais, made him briefly notorious during the spring of 1787. Kornmann was very taken by the magnetic theories of Dr. Mesmer, who he was convinced had cured his son of a fatal illness, and in 1782 he became a member of 'The Society of Universal Harmony', an association that supported Mesmer in his triumphal return to Paris at the end of that year. A sick child was not the only problem that Kornmann took to the famous doctor. He also confided in him about his matrimonial problems, problems that in 1787 were a major topic of conversation among Parisian society and became known as the Kornmann affair. It all began in 1781, when Beaumarchais was sought out by some of his friends to defend the honour of Madame Kornmann, who had been publicly accused of adultery by her husband, and imprisoned. She had indeed had a liaison, with a young man called Daudet de Jossan, but letters shown to Beaumarchais seemed to prove that Daudet had been secretly encouraged in this affair by Kornmann himself. To make matters worse, Kornmann's wife was pregnant, and likely to give birth in prison if nothing were done to help her.

Madame Kornmann's plight moved Beaumarchais, who confessed to an irresistible weakness for any woman in distress. *'A woman cannot weep without my feeling a pang of anguish. They are, alas, so ill-treated by the law and by men!'* So he paid a visit to the Lieutenant-General of Police, Jean-Charles-Pierre Lenoir, who issued a warrant authorizing Madame Kornmann to leave prison and be put in the care of a midwife. It was with great elation that Beaumarchais went to deliver the news personally to the prisoner, whom he had never met until that moment. When he saw her, his heart took flight into sentimental folly. *'Just imagine,'* he recalls *'a young woman, prisoner since the month of December, and with no other clothing but a wretched summer bed-jacket, pale, worried, pregnant and beautiful! Ah! Pregnant above all, and on the point of giving birth!'* The nature of their subsequent relationship is rather mysterious, but for the next six years Madame Kornmann kept frequent company with Beaumarchais, whom she now called *'my dear papa'*, while he in turn helped her in a long, drawn-out struggle to get back her possessions from her husband.

At the beginning of 1787 the thwarted Kornmann decided to take his revenge. In February Paris was inundated with thousands of copies of a pamphlet written on behalf of Kornmann, exposing his wife as an adulteress, and accusing three people of seduction and defamation of character. The first was, of course, the lover, Daudet de Jossan. However, the second was the unsuspecting Beaumarchais, and the third, even more surprisingly, was the police chief Lenoir! All three of them had probably partaken of the charms of Madame Kornmann, whose reputation was hardly spotless, but Beaumarchais was horrified to be publicly exposed in such a sordid scandal. The pamphlet dragged his character through the mud relentlessly, describing him as loathsome, ambitious, vain, and without any feelings of pity or justice. In addition, *tu* was used throughout the entire document, an insult that some members of the *haute bourgeoisie* would have considered more offensive than the words themselves. Beaumarchais took legal action against Kornmann, but it was not until April 1789, when Parisians were totally preoccupied with the imminent opening of the Estates-General, that he was able to win his case.

➝At number 35 turn right into Square Sainte-Croix-de-la-Bretonnerie, where since the 13th century there had been a convent called *Les Frères de la Sainte-Croix*. As you walk around Paris you are so often walking on the site of former convents, abbeys or monasteries that came to an end, sometimes violently, when the Revolution broke out. The monks here at Sainte-Croix belonged to an order founded in 1211, and spent their time meditating on the Passion and the Cross of Jesus. They were all thrown out when their convent was closed in 1790, and three years later it was sold off as national property. I don't know what happened to the monks, but in 1790 the the odds were certainly stacked against their survival. ➝Turn left out of the square and you will be passing through the convent's former entrance, which opened out on to rue des Archives, opposite another convent, the *Carmes-Billettes*, at number 24. Behind the entrance doors of this old house is the original cloister of the *Carmes-Billettes Convent*, which dates back to 1427. It is only open to the public when exhibitions are held here, so if you can go in you should not miss seeing the magnificent vaulted arcades of this mediaeval cloister, the only one now left in Paris. Next door to the cloister, at number 22, is the church, built in 1756 to replace the original convent chapel that was falling down. It was bought by the government in 1808, when it became a Lutheran church and now houses the Lutheran Cultural Centre. It is here that you find the origins of the *Carmes-*

Billettes Convent, in a dramatic event that popular legend tells us took place in 1290, when number 22 was the house of a Jew named Jonathas. He had lent some money to an old woman, who claimed that in order to get back the clothes she'd left as collateral, Jonathas asked her to bring him the host she received at communion. She did as he asked and gave him the host, which Jonathas proceeded to stab with a small knife, causing blood to spurt out of it. He then threw the sacred bread into boiling water that immediately turned blood-red, at which point the old woman took fright and alerted the entire neighbourhood. As a consequence Jonathas was arrested, tried and burned alive, and the authorities confiscated his house, which then became a magnet for hordes of pilgrims. Four years later a local middle-class citizen was given permission to build a shrine on the site of the house that had become known rather irreverently by the locals as the place where God had been boiled. It was called *Chapel of the Miracle*, and five years later monks known as *Billettes* moved into it, replaced more than three centuries later by the Carmelites. The convent's end was rather less sensational than its beginning. Closed by the government in 1790 and sold three years later, the church was used as a salt warehouse, and the magnificent cloister became a carpentry workshop.

➡ On leaving the cloister turn right up rue des Archives, go back to rue Sainte-Croix-de-la-Bretonnerie and turn right. Number 20 was built in 1696 and was the home of Guy Jean-Baptiste Target, one of the most celebrated lawyers of the old regime who became famous for his courageous defence of Cardinal de Rohan in the Affair of the Queen's Necklace. He was also known in Parisian circles for his tactlessness, on one occasion scandalising the guests at a high-society dinner party by picking up the host's snuffbox and helping himself - a familiarity unheard of in even the most liberal of *salons*. When the Revolution broke out Target cleverly made the transition from defending aristocratic clients to defending the new regime. He was elected deputy to the Third Estate, and it was Target who wrote the famous oath taken in the Tennis Court at Versailles. He later became president of the Constituent Assembly, where he played such a major role in the writing of the Constitution that the royalists referred to it as *La Targette* (meaning the bolt on a door). He organized the Festival of Federation in 1790, and when Louis XVI asked him to defend him at his trial, he wisely refused this rather risky honour on grounds of failing health. In 1794 Target became secretary of his local revolutionary committee, thus surviving the Terror to become a high-court judge during the Directory, and one of the formulators of the Napoleonic Code that forms the basis of modern French law. According to what I have read, Target's house was demolished in 1929, and the grand entrance arch is all that is left of it. However, the last time I was there renovation work was going on, and the house I could see set back in the courtyard was definitely not built since 1929. So until I can find out more, I am reserving judgement on the fate of the house where Guy Target died in 1807 at the age of 74.

Number 18 next door, and 19 opposite, both date from the 18th century, as well as number 16, which was the home of astronomer Joseph Jérôme Le François de Lalande, who in 1760 became a professor at the Collège de France when only 28 years old. He remained in the post until a few months before his death in 1807, thus teaching practically all the French astronomers of the second half of the 18th century. He wrote his famous 'Treaty on Astronomy' in 1764, and four years later became Director of the Paris Observatory, remaining there until his death. It was here that he spent most of the Revolution, studying the stars with his nephew Michel de Lalande, work that resulted in a catalogue of 50,000 stars, entitled 'French Celestial History'. With the mathematician Romme, Lalande created the revolutionary calendar, which started on September

22nd 1792 (*1 Vendémiaire, An I*). The months were divided up into three 10-day 'weeks', and the days were all given Latinate names like *primidi, duodi, tridi*, etc. - the 10th day, *decadi*, was a day of rest. This aspect of the new calendar was not popular, for it gave only three 'Sundays' a month to an already overworked population. Lalande sympathized with this, suggesting, without success, that the fifth day, *quintidi*, should also be a day of rest, although Lalande himself never seemed to stop working. He revised and improved the planetary tables made by Halley, he calculated the distance between the Earth and the Sun, and three years before his death he published his 'Astronomical Bibliography', an impressive chronicle of the science of the era. He was also famous for his curious habit of eating caterpillars.

➡ Continue to the end of the street and turn left on rue Vieille-du-Temple, an ancient street that already existed under the same name in 1270. Before rue de Rivoli was opened this street extended down to the Place Baudoyer, which was the location of the first headquarters of the Knights Templar, a military religious order established in 1119 to protect pilgrims going to the Holy Land. The name of the street originates from its proximity to this site. At number 47 you will see one of the most beautiful houses in the Marais - and one of the most neglected. It is known as the Hôtel des Ambassadeurs de Hollande, a name of mysterious origins, since Holland has never had an embassy here. One explanation is that after the Edict of Nantes churches belonging to Protestant embassies were no longer able to hold services, and the Embassy of Holland, situated in the Faubourg Saint-Honoré at the time, rented part of this house and set up a branch of their church there. It was in this chapel that Germaine Necker, daughter of Louis XVI's Finance Minister and better known by her married name of Madame de Staël, was baptised in 1766. The Hôtel des Ambassadeurs de Hollande is a very old house, built originally in 1395, confiscated in 1420 by the English, who then abandoned it to its fate. It eventually collapsed and different parts of it were reconstructed by successive occupants, before being sold in 1638 to Denis Amelot, a financial advisor to the king. His son Jacques Amelot, who inherited the house in 1655, commissioned the architect Pierre Cottard to construct the building you see today. However, its splendour was somewhat mutilated over the years by various owners, in particular Louis Le Tellier, a royal architect whose professional integrity must be questioned, for he made all sorts of lamentable changes, such as moving staircases and lowering ceilings, and generally destroying the character of the house.

In 1776 Tellier rented the entire residence for 6,600 *livres* a year to Caron de Beaumarchais, who had not yet even heard of Madame Kornmann, and was happily writing successful plays - it was in this house that he wrote *Le Mariage de Figaro, Chérubin* and *Tarare*. Beaumarchais, who began as the son of a clockmaker, had made his dramatically impressive ascent into the upper echelons of Paris society by writing for members of the Court, teaching the harp to Louis XV's daughters, and making prestigious business connections. By 1770 he was a widower for the second time - both his wives had been rich widows - and in November of that year the parents of his first wife (from whom he had appropriated the name Beaumarchais) brought a law suit against him. Their action was possibly prompted by rumours that Beaumarchais had poisoned the first Madame Beaumarchais - and maybe even the second one as well. Although there were many who refused to believe such gossip, the affair left him disgraced and financially ruined, but Beaumarchais was not one to give up, and he re-gained his social popularity by another lawsuit. This time he took the action himself, against a parliamentary counsellor called Goezman, whose wife he claimed owed him money, and his victory was in no small measure due to a series of eloquently venomous pamphlets that he published against Goezman.

By the time he moved into this house he was once again welcome in all the best *salons* in the capital, and was also busy indulging his political interests, one of which was the American revolt against the British. Shortly after moving in, he founded a company called *Rodriguez, Hortalez et Cie* that operated from the house and was generously subsidized by the French and Spanish governments. The company's objective was to aid the American rebels in their struggle against George III by furnishing them with boats, arms and munitions, and within the space of four months Beaumarchais chartered about a dozen 500-ton vessels to set sail for America. Always busy, Beaumarchais had already written *Le Mariage de Figaro* by the end of 1778, but the censors banned it from being performed until 1784, when it was presented by the Comédie-Française. It was an overwhelming success with the public, but its implicit attack on French society brought the disapproval of the king's brother, the Comte de Provence, resulting in Beaumarchais spending five unpleasant days in the *Saint-Lazare* prison. In 1786 he married his mistress, Marie-Thérèse de Willermawlaz, who had been living with him for some time in the luxurious upper floors of the Hôtel des Ambassadeurs de Hollande and with whom he had a 9-year-old daughter, Eugenie. It was during 1787, the last year that he lived here, that the Kornmann affair exploded, and at the end of that year he commissioned the building of another beautiful home in the Faubourg Saint-Antoine, which he moved into two years later.

During the Revolution this house suffered more devastation. It still belonged to Le Tellier's family, who rented it out as a public dance hall, so many of the wall paintings and gilded panels were covered with whitewash. From the beginning of the 19th century the house was used for numerous commercial activities, divided up and mutilated in various ways, until it was barely recognizable. However, in 1924 a new owner undertook radical restoration of this historic *hôtel*, so we are now able to see, as much as is possible, the beauty of the original house designed by Cottard in 1660. It certainly does need a clean, though, but in the meantime you might be tempted by Olivier & Co, a lovely shop on the ground floor, specializing in olive oil.

Take a quick look over the road at number 44 opposite, which is from the 17th century, and number 45 from the 18th, with a very nice oval window and carving over the door. ➥Now go back down rue Vieille-du-Temple, and and turn left into rue des Rosiers, a beautiful name that already existed in the 13th century and originated from the rose bushes in the neighbouring gardens. With rue des Ecouffes and rue Ferdinand-Duval, this street has for a long time been the centre of a community of Ashkenazi Jews, most of whom came originally from Poland and Hungary. It's a goldmine of old houses, some dating from the 17th century (numbers 23, 33, 35 in particular), and there is a tempting selection of Jewish delicatessens and restaurants, the most famous of which has now sadly closed. This was Jo Goldenberg's, at number 7, where you could get a hot pastrami sandwich that would remind any Bostonian of the much lamented Elsie's in Harvard Square!

➥At Jo Goldenberg's turn right into rue Ferdinand-Duval and walk to number 11, once the home of Jean-Pierre Acarie, whose wife, Barbe Jeanne Avrillot, now known as Marie de l'Incarnation, brought the first reformed Carmelite nuns to France in 1604. Their descendants were the sixteen ill-fated Carmelites of Compiègne, whose execution in Paris on July 17th 1794 was one of the most moving spectacles of the Terror. Rue Ferdinand-Duval was also where royalist deputy, François-Antoine Boissy d'Anglas, lived in 1804 when he was a favourite of Napoléon and President of the *Tribunat*. After training as a lawyer he began his political career in the service of the illustrious Monsieur, Comte de Provence, brother of Louis XVI. In spite of this rather royal start, he was elected to the Third Estate, but embraced the Revolution with a certain reserve, always sitting with the moderates on the benches of the Plain, and voting for leniency during the king's judgement. His discretion, however - and a pamphlet that he wrote during the Terror paying some rather unsubtle compliments to Robespierre - enabled him to escape the guillotine, and after 9 *Thermidor* he resumed his correspondence with the Comte de Provence, defended the families of *émigrés* and spoke in favour of religious freedom. In 1795 Boissy d'Anglas was made responsible for food supplies to the capital, but was so disorganized and unsuccessful at the job that he was nick-named *Boissy-Famine* by hunger-stricken Parisians. The food shortages culminated in May 1795 in a revolt known as the *journées de prairial*, when an angry mob invaded the Convention and presented Boissy d'Anglas with the head of one of his colleagues on the end of a pike. His remarkable *sang-froid* in the face of this horror was much appreciated by his terrified colleagues, who did not cease to sing the praises of Boissy d'Anglas for a long time after.

➡ Turn left on rue du Roi-de-Sicile, then left on rue Pavée, where Louis XVI's defence lawyer, François Tronchet, lived at number 12 from 1784 until his death in 1806. It was from this house - another one in need of some love and cleaning fluid - that Tronchet set out in 1792 in the chill of a December morning and headed for the National Convention, where the king was to be tried for crimes against the nation. It would be his job, with his colleagues Malesherbes and de Sèze, to defend Louis's cause and try to save his life. As a deputy Tronchet had always been a moderate, fighting to maintain the royal veto when the Constitution was being drafted, so it's not surprising that he accepted gracefully when Louis XVI picked him out for this dubious honour He did, however, feel just a little inconvenienced, for he was already 67 and had just started what he *had* hoped would be a pleasant retirement surrounded by friends. In the circumstances, he was obliged to hide himself from the public eye until the Terror was over, lest some overzealous patriot reminded the Tribunal of his role at the king's trial. After this Tronchet resumed his pleasant but active retirement, working on the civil code for Napoléon, and becoming President of the Senate in 1802. He died in this house at the age of 80.

Tronchet had scarcely been living here a year when he acquired some unexpected new neighbours, for in April 1785 numbers 14 to 22, which extended across the end of rue Rosier, were transformed into a prison called *La Petite-Force*. It was an extension of *La Grande-Force*, a prison that was already quite familiar to Tronchet for its side walls ran along the end of his back garden. With this new addition he now found himself surrounded by convicted prisoners - a somewhat discouraging situation for a defence lawyer. The entrance was approximately where you now find number 22, and with its double row of barred windows and heavy studded wooden door, it must have given the street a rather grim aspect. *La Petite-Force*, which was reserved for women prisoners, occupied an outbuilding of the Hôtel de Lamoignon at number 24. ➡Before turning right into rue Malher, cross over and take a look at this magnificent house, which is one of the oldest *hôtels* in Paris. It was built in 1584, and before becoming Hôtel de Lamoignon was known as the *Hôtel d'Angoulême*, belonging to Charles de Valois, Duc d'Angoulême, illegitimate son of Charles IX and Marie-Touchet. It was the birthplace of another of Louis XVI's defence lawyers, Chrétien-Guillaume de Lamoignon de Malesherbes, whose grandfather had bought the house in 1688. Born in 1721, Malesherbes grew up with a vast knowledge and deep respect for the philosophers of his time, who were therefore overjoyed when he accepted a post as minister to Louis XVI, for it gave an optimistic boost to their hopes that the new monarch would bring peace and happiness to the nation. But Malesherbes did not stay long at Versailles, preferring to devote his energies to defending oppressed minorities like Protestants and Jews, as well as working for better conditions for prisoners. When Louis XVI found himself facing charges of treason in 1792, he did not have to ask Malesherbes for help. On learning of Target's refusal to take on the role of royal defender, Malesherbes stepped up voluntarily, despite his 71 years, and offered to do the job.

It was with the same philosophical indifference to danger that he faced the terrible fate that the Terror dealt him and his family two years later. He knew he was doomed. He had shared in the creation of the old regime and had enjoyed its sweetness, he had served the king - and he had been happy, which is perhaps what infuriated his persecutors most, and the reason why they unleashed such a relentless campaign against not only Malesherbes, but his entire family. The official reason given for bringing them to trial was contact with *émigrés*, for Malesherbes' younger daughter had left for Switzerland, and he had corresponded with her, even visited her. On April 22nd 1794, he was guillotined along with his older daughter, his grand-daughter and her husband.

The Hôtel de Lamoignon was the scene of Malesherbes' childhood. He became the owner on the death of his father in 1772, by which time the house had been rented out for many years. The original tenant was a book-collector called Antoine Moriau, who left his collection to the city of Paris, who in turn rented the house from the Malesherbes family in order to keep the collection in place. In 1763 this impressive library was opened to the public, but ten years later the entire collection was moved to another location. The following year Malesherbes sold his newly inherited property, and after a succession of owners, it fell prey to the desecration of post-revolutionary irreverence, accommodating a range of activities that included a stocking factory and a boys' institution. For many years of his life Malesherbes was *Directeur de la Librairie*, a post not dissimilar to that of a literary censor, so it is altogether fitting that his former residence has remained in the realm of books, now housing the wonderful Historical Library of the City of Paris. If you want to find out anything about the history of this beautiful city, this is the place to go. (Open 1 p.m. - 6 p.m. every day, 9.30 a.m. - 6 p.m. on Saturdays, closed on Sundays. Tel. 01 44 59 29 40).

PRISON DE LA FORCE.

➡ You should now go back and veer left into rue Malher. When the two prisons of *La Force* were demolished in 1845, rue Malher was built in their place, so as you walk down this street you will be walking right through the middle of them. At this point you are walking through *La Petite-Force*, but at the junction with rue des Rosiers was the wall separating *La Petite-Force* from *La Grande-Force,* which occupied a former noble residence called *Hôtel de la Force*. This was built in the 16th century by Cardinal Meudon, then was bought and sold numerous times before becoming the property of the Duc de La Force, who acquired it through his wife's dowry in 1698. The duke was a *bon-vivant* who would be horrified to see his name forever associated with one of the most unpleasant prisons of the Revolution. Luckily for him, he remained blissfully ignorant of the fate of his little palace of pleasure, where he livened up Parisian society during the reign of Louis XIV with some of the most memorable parties of the era. In 1754 the house was bought by the Comte d'Argenson, Minister of War, and used for various governmental purposes before being transformed into a prison in 1780. *La Grande-Force* was used mostly as a debtors' prison until 1792, when it was merged with *La Petite-Force* and the entire institution became known as the *Prison de la Force.*

During the Revolution, despite being one prison, La Force was made up of two distinctly separate buildings, and imprisoned couples would often find themselves separated from each other in opposite sides of the prison. The only means of communication for these unfortunate people was a sewer that ran under the thick dividing wall, so as you cross rue des Rosiers, spare a thought for Madame Magdelaine Kolly, widow of a Farmer-General who had been executed as a conspirator on May 3rd 1793. She was 35 years old, and was incarcerated on one side of the prison with her 3-year-old son known as Lolo, while her older son, Foucaud, was imprisoned on the other. Magdelaine had been condemned to death as a counter-revolutionary on the same day as her husband, but being pregnant secured her a suspension of the sentence until the child was born. She was thus languishing here in prison for the remaining months of her pregnancy, knowing that as soon as she gave birth she would be taken to the guillotine. A survivor on the men's side remembered her older son Foucaud, who cut a pathetic figure as he went each morning to the sewer to talk to his mother.

'This pious child, who, scarcely adolescent, already knew all the misery of life, knelt before the vile sewer, and with his mouth pressed against the hole, exchanged all the feelings that were in his heart with those of his mother.' During one of these tragic conversations, he spoke to his little brother, who told him, *'Mummy didn't cry as much last night, rested a bit, and she tells you hello; it's Lolo who loves you, who's telling you this.'* On *15 Brumaire l'An II* (November 5th 1793) the suspension of Magdelaine's sentence was lifted, and she was guillotined that same day. Just before her execution it was by means of the sewer that this poor woman was able to pass a bunch of her hair to young Foucaud, at the same time urging him to ensure, if it were possible, that her body be buried with her husband and a family friend who had been guillotined with him. There is no mention of the baby she presumably had just given birth to, or the other two children who were left alone and orphaned in this terrible prison.

As you make your way along rue Malher you are walking where these tragic scenes took place, through the cells of these unhappy people, treading on the putrid straw where they languished within four black walls covered with messages of desperation and boredom. One small barred window permitted a little light during the day, one chair had to be shared by eight prisoners, and a single bucket, emptied once a day, served as a toilet. The prison guards had two enormous dogs, and at the end of each day, as the prisoners returned to their cells, these two intimidating creatures would run up and down the corridors pushing those who were going too slowly.

Living in these grim conditions were numerous former nobles, like the Marechal de Mouchy, a relative of Madame Lafayette, or the Duc de Villeroy, accompanied by his entire domestic staff who were all guillotined with him. There was even an illegitimate son of Louis XV, Jean-Marie Langlois de Villepaille, who was said to be the image of his father, and who ended up on the scaffold. Many prisoners, like Francoeur, former director of the Opera, had no idea why they were there, while others, like Adam Lux, were in no doubt at all. Lux, a deputy from Mayence, was infatuated with Charlotte Corday for her heroic act of killing Marat, and had been imprudent enough to write a poem about her in which he compared her with Brutus. Lux chatted endlessly with his fellow prisoners about the dangers of passion and defective judgement, but faced his death stoically, declaring that *'at 28 years old I am ending a miserable life.'* He spent his last night writing, ate his breakfast heartily, gave his coat to another prisoner and left for the Tribunal at 9 o'clock. By 3 o'clock he was dead. Another prisoner, the handsome Achille de Châtelet, who had lost a leg fighting for his country, preferred to poison himself in the infirmary than suffer an inglorious execution. The imprisonment of 25-year-old Stanislas de Sombreuil, son of the former governor at Les Invalides, was sweetened by regular visits from one of his many mistresses. When he fell ill with a dangerously high fever, this devoted young woman courageously donned her lover's clothes so as not to be recognized by the guards, and stayed at *La Force* for three days and three nights to take care of him. Stanislas got over his illness, only to be guillotined with his 74-year-old father on June 17th 1794.

Some of the more famous people to be imprisoned in *La Force* were Sylvain Bailly, the first mayor of Paris, writer Choderlos de Laclos, author of *Liaisons Dangereuses*, and thirteen Girondin deputies, including Vergniaud and Valazé. In July 1794 the dark walls of *La Force* were lightened by the presence of Thérésia Cabarrus, Tallien's beautiful mistress, who was enraged by the conditions of her short stay here. For 25 days she languished in total darkness, without being able to wash or change her clothes, in a cell that was infested with vermin. A less well-known prisoner, but one who made an impression on prisoners and guards alike, was a fearless Bostonian who alone dared to challenge one of the redoubtable guard dogs. When the agitated animal jumped up at him and seized him by the throat, the American prisoner pushed his finger deftly into the dog's mouth, grabbed hold of its lower jaw in one hand and the upper jaw in the other, and was about to tear the animal's head apart when its owner begged him for mercy. The fate of this Bostonian colossus is not known, but after such a performance the guards no doubt treated him with rather more respect than was usual.

MASSACRE OF THE PRINCESSE DE LAMBALLE.

Of all the massacres to take place in Paris's prisons during the four terrible days between September 2nd and 5th 1792, the most appalling must be the murder of Marie-Thérèse, Princesse de Lamballe, Marie-Antoinette's closest friend. Born in Turin in 1749, she was married at 17 to the Prince de Bourbon-Penthièvre de Lamballe, a debauched noble who died of syphilis a year later. She never married again, preferring to offer her loyalties to the monarchy, and after the departure of Madame Polignac, her rival for Marie-Antoinette's affections, Marie-Thérèse was given the position of mistress of the queen's household. She was not a great beauty, except for her luxuriant head of long blonde hair, which everyone noticed, but she was loved for her sweetness and her capacity for devotion. Despite her soft and pious nature, however, the Princesse de Lamballe was a constant object of popular malicious gossip, referred to as a lesbian whore whose affection for the queen was perverted and unnatural. When Louis and Marie-Antoinette made their attempted escape to Varennes in 1791, Marie-Thérèse left for England, but on hearing of the failure of the plan, she returned immediately to Paris to serve the queen. She was imprisoned with the royal family in the Temple for one week until August 19th, when she was transferred to *La Force*, where she found herself in the company of Madame de Tourzel, the royal children's governess, and three of the queen's chambermaids.

Just prior to the massacres, which neither the Commune nor the Assembly made any attempt to prevent, a last-minute effort was nonetheless made to liberate certain prisoners. Thus Madame de Tourzel and her daughter were taken out of *La Force*, along with the chambermaids and a few other prisoners, but only just in time, for the killing was already in progress as they were leaving. The fact that the Princesse de Lamballe was left there to her fate was no accident, for she was still hated for her supposed influence on Marie-Antoinette, although in reality she had never involved herself in political intrigues. She had no idea why her companions had been set free, or what was going to happen, but as she sat alone in her gloomy cell she could sense the agitated fear that pervaded the prison, and she drew her shawl around her shoulders with a feeling of foreboding.

➥To see where these terrible massacres took place, continue down rue Malher and turn right into rue du Roi-de-Sicile, which by 1792 had been re-named *rue des Droits de l'Homme*. At number 2 you will see a plaque commemorating the site of the prison entrance, which opened out on to a narrow street called *rue des Ballets*, now absorbed by the end part of rue Malher (see plan).

La Force Prison.

Exterior walls of La Force Prison

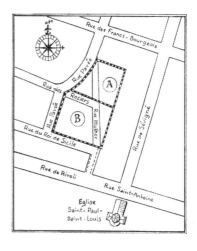

Shows position of former
Rue des Ballets

A   La Petite-Force

B   La Grande-Force

➥Go and stand where rue du Roi-de-Sicile meets rue Malher and look around you, look into the past of this corner where so many people met a frightening and violent death. At half past 2 in the afternoon of September 2nd 1792 an improvised tribunal was set up inside the prison, in the clerk's office. Look over at number 2, and try to picture the prison entrance, where several stone steps led down to the street. If you look hard enough you will see, leaning against the wall on either side of the prison door, about half a dozen hired cut-throats, armed with logs, sabres and axes. They are waiting for the first prisoner to emerge from the 'tribunal', and they will use their weapons to assail their victims as they walk out of the prison. At the sight of the first prisoner appearing in the doorway, they raise their sabres and axes and bring them down on the unfortunate victim.

In the course of that afternoon, one prisoner after another suffered the same fate, trying in vain to fend off the blows, which often resulted in their arms being cut off before they finally died. The bodies were then thrown down the steps and dragged along *rue des Ballets* to the central gutter of rue Saint-Antoine, where they were stripped of their clothing, jewellery and any other possessions worth taking. The accumulated loot from this grisly operation was piled up outside a house in *rue des Ballets*, while the despoiled victims were thrown on to an ever-increasing heap of mutilated bodies outside the prison. The killers received 24 *livres* for this bloodthirsty work, a payment arranged by Jacques Billaud-Varenne, assistant-prosecutor in the Commune, who considered the massacres as a necessary 'national revenge'. One victim, warned of what was in store for him, was clever enough to escape death by leaping so quickly through the door that the blows of his assassins missed him by inches. Before they could catch him he had merged without trace into the crowd of curious onlookers, who did nothing to prevent his escape. Restif de la Bretonne, despite his squeamishness about blood and violence, seemed to be doing the rounds of all the prisons during those terrible days, and saw another prisoner try to escape in the same manner.

> *'I arrived in rue Saint-Antoine, at the end of rue des Ballets at the very moment when a poor unfortunate, who had seen how they had killed the man before him, instead of stopping, took to his heels and ran through the doorway. A man who was not one of the killers, but one of those thoughtless machines that we see so often nowadays, stopped him with his pike. The poor victim was caught by his pursuers and massacred. The man with the pike told us coldly: "How was I to know they wanted to kill him?"* (Restif de la Bretonne, 1986)

Sickened by the sight, Restif was about to leave when he spied two women leaving the prison under escort. One was

Mademoiselle de Tourzel, the 16-year-old daughter of the queen's former governess, and the other was Madame Saint-Brice, a royal chambermaid, who was trying to console her weeping companion. While they were being taken to a nearby church, two more women emerged and were ushered into a waiting carriage. Restif remained, in spite of himself, and was thus witness to the atrocious murder of the Princesse de Lamballe, who had by now been brought out of her cell to be questioned by the so-called tribunal. The judges sat at a long table, while around the sides of the room several assassins, most of whom were drunk, lounged on the benches hurling insults at the trembling princess. She almost fainted several times during her interrogation, during which she was asked to swear that she loved liberty and equality, and that she hated the entire royal family. She agreed readily to the first part of this oath, but refused the second, on the grounds that it was not in her heart, at which point the president of the tribunal (who some say was Hébert) gave the command, *'Let Madame be liberated'*. This along with *'To the Abbey!'* was a code signalling a death sentence, but which duped prisoners into thinking they had been acquitted or were merely to be sent to another prison.

The queen's devoted friend, the Princesse de Lamballe, suffered terrible popular vengeance during the prison massacres, when she was felled by sabres, then beheaded and indecently mutilated. (Courtesy of Musée Carnavalet, Cabinet des Arts Graphiques, Paris)

Restif was waiting in the crowd outside the prison entrance, when he saw the princess appear in the doorway, *'pale as her white linen dress'*, escorted by one of the killers, a giant of a man named Pierre-Nicolas Renier who was known to his friends as 'Big Nicolas'. As she emerged, the sight of a blood-soaked mountain of naked bodies made the princess turn her head away in horror. A man named Charlat, a wig-maker by trade, then began the attack by lifting Marie-Thérèse's bonnet off her head with the point of his sabre, making a small gash across her cheek. She was immediately assailed from all sides, until her body was riddled with blows. When she fell to the ground, she was stripped of all her clothes, thrown on her back on top of the pile of corpses, and left to suffer the lewd mockery of the more insensible members of the crowd.

After two hours her lifeless body was dragged over to the corner of rue du Roi-de-Sicile and *rue des Ballets*, where there was a *borne*, one of the stone blocks that were found in all the narrow streets of 18th-century Paris. This was used as an execution block, on which the princess's head was cut off with a knife by another assassin called Grison, while Charlat, who had begun the massacre, ended it by ripping open her stomach and chest, cutting out her heart and sticking it on the end of his sabre as a trophy. At this point a blood-thirsty hysteria broke out among the other 'workers', who proceeded to amuse themselves by cutting off her breasts, and then inflicting further indecent mutilations on the mangled body of the unfortunate princess. Afterwards a procession formed, headed by Grison displaying the princess's head, her long blonde hair dripping with blood, and Charlat carrying her heart on the end of his sabre. Behind them came her headless body, dragged by the legs, with entrails hanging from its stomach - a grotesquely nauseating spectacle that caused Restif de la Bretonne to faint on the spot. The procession moved slowly into rue Saint-Antoine, turned left and made its way towards Place de la Bastille, where the princess's body was then paraded around the Faubourg Saint-Antoine before being abandoned outside the *Hospice des Enfant-Trouvés* (Foundling Hospital). The remainder of the procession turned left up Boulevard Beaumarchais, carrying the princess's head towards the Temple prison, where the queen was still unaware of the fate of her devoted friend. You will meet up with this gruesome procession again in a little while.

➥Go back now to rue Malher, turn right then immediately left into rue Saint-Antoine, and take a look at the church opposite at number 99, the Eglise Saint-Paul-Saint-Louis, built between 1627 and 1641. This church may have been where Madame de Tourzel's daughter was taken when she was brought out of prison just before the massacres started at *La Force*. If she was, however, she may well have been an unwilling witness to the murder of five priests that took place there on that same day. Before the Revolution there was a shrine in this church containing the hearts of two great French kings, Louis XIII and Louis XIV. When the church was confiscated by the State, these two sacred relics were sold to a painter named Saint-Martin, who mixed the pulverized flesh with oil to make paint of a brown colour known as *mummie*. This paint was much sought after by artists of the time, for no other could give such a beautiful glazed effect, and Saint-Martin no doubt commercialized on the popularity of his product. Louis XIV's heart was the fatter of the two, and Saint-Martin only used a part of it, so when the monarchy was restored, he very reverently returned to the church Louis XIII's unused heart, and what was left of that of the Sun-King. Surprisingly, instead of being outraged at this ignoble use of his ancestors' organs, Louis XVIII compensated Saint-Martin with a gift of a golden snuff-box.

➥Go left on rue Saint-Antoine then immediately left again on rue de Sévigné, which began as a covered walkway around the outside of the city wall. It became a proper street in

1544 with the name *rue Culture-Sainte-Catherine*, changed during the Revolution to *rue Culture*, and in 1867 it got its present name, originating from the Marquise de Sévigné who lived here during the 17th century. The chemist, doctor and politician François-Vincent Raspail, who was born during the Terror, had a clinic at number 5, where a plaque commemorates his work. Raspail was a staunch republican and was active in the later revolution of 1830. In 1834 he founded a newspaper called *Le Républicain*, and was one of the first to proclaim the Republic of 1848. After running as a socialist candidate for President, he was condemned to prison by more moderate republicans, then exiled until 1863. On his return Raspail became a deputy, remaining in the Assembly until his death in 1878, and nine years later one of the capital's boulevards was given his name.

The old house at numbers 7 and 9 was built in 1699 for Poulletier, the Intendant of Finances, then confiscated during the Revolution and used as a government funeral parlour. Number 11 is the site of a house belonging to the Lamoignon family. When it was demolished, the land was bought in 1790 by that most colourful local resident, Caron de Beaumarchais, who had a theatre built on it, supposedly with stones from the Bastille. The *Théâtre du Marais* - one of the numerous theatres to spring up in Paris during the early years of the Revolution - was inaugurated on August 31st 1791 with a performance of *La Métromanie* by Alexis Piron. On June 26th of the following year Beaumarchais presented *La Mère Coupable*, the last of his Figaro trilogy, which was such a spectacular flop the actors could hardly make themselves heard amidst the hooting and whistling from the stalls. The play's failure was partly due to a smear campaign waged against it by actors from the *Théâtre de la Nation*, who had been taken out of the production by the author. Not long after this Beaumarchais was arrested and imprisoned for arms trafficking and the theatre was temporarily shut down. It was finally closed by Napoléon in 1807, then demolished and replaced by another building housing municipal baths, but the façade of Beaumarchais' theatre, with its decorative pillars and wrought iron, is still there. In the courtyard of this house there is a remnant of the outside wall of *La Force* prison, which several prisoners tried to break through during the September massacres. A few months later a group of prisoners had the idea of escaping over the same wall with the aid of several large wooden beams that had been left lying around in the prison yard. They were so pleased with their ingenious idea that they talked about it just a little too loudly within earshot of the guards, who had the beams removed before the plan could be carried out.

Musée Carnavalet.

At number 23 rue de Sévigné is one of the oldest mansions in Paris, the Hôtel Carnavalet, built in 1545, one year earlier than the Renaissance Louvre. In 1572 it was bought by Madame de Kernevenoy, widow of a Breton nobleman, and it is from a corrupted form of her name that we get the name 'Carnavalet'. In 1677 the Marquise de Sevigné rented it and stayed for nineteen agreeable years, finding it possessed of *'fine air, a beautiful courtyard, a beautiful garden and a beautiful neighbourhood'*. The house also had the good fortune not to be confiscated by the revolutionary government, remaining private property until 1866, when its owner Verdot, a teacher at the Lycée Charlemagne, who had used it as a boarding facility for foreign pupils, sold it to the city of Paris. In June 1898 it was inaugurated as a museum of the history of Paris, the basis of which was Alfred de Liesville's private collection from the revolutionary era. The museum was enlarged in 1914, and again in 1989 with the annexation of the Hôtel Le Peletier de Saint-Fargeau at number 29, which was built at the end of the 17th century and now houses the section on the period from the Revolution to the present day.

Number 29 was the birthplace of the wealthy Louis-Michel Lepeletier de Saint-Fargeau, who began as a deputy for the nobility but was later elected to the Convention and voted for the death of the king. He paid for this with his life that same evening in a café at the Palais-Royal. At the outbreak of the Revolution he was still living with his brother Félix here in the Hôtel Saint-Fargeau, which was inherited by Louis-Michel's daughter when he was assassinated. During the 19th century it became the home of the Historical Library of the City of Paris, which remained here until 1968, when plans first began for the annexation of the Hôtel Saint-Fargeau to the Musée Carnavalet. In its thirteen rooms you can see the development of the Revolution in chronological order, from the Estates-General to the beginning of the Empire. Among its collection is the original furniture from the royal couple's prison at the Temple, including their laundry register and a prison key (room 106). In this room you can also see Jacques Necker's plans for the demolition of the Bastille, made before the Revolution, showing his idea for a grand plaza where one of the eight towers was to be kept as a romantic ruin, with a central pyramid made of iron window bars, chains, locks and bolts from the demolished prison. In room 102 is a model of the Bastille, carved out of a stone from the ancient fortress - one of these was sent to each of the newly-formed departments at the time the prison was torn down. You can also see miniature guillotines, which were often sold in the vicinity of the scaffold prior to executions, and one of the museum's treasures is the wheelchair used by the paralysed deputy, Georges Couthon. He attended the National Convention in it, raced around the Committee rooms in it, and was sitting in it when he toppled down the stairs trying to escape on the night of 9 *Thermidor*. In the main courtyard of the museum is a bronze statue of Louis XIV by Coysevox that fortunately survived the Revolution, despite official plans for its demise. It was going to be sent to the national foundry and melted to manufacture arms, but the illustrious Sun King was saved - ironically - by an act of Parisian jingoism by the city Commune, who refused to give it up, claiming it belonged to Paris and not to the nation.

➡ At the end of rue de Sévigné turn left on to rue Parc-Royal, a 16th-century street that in 1907 lost the houses on its south side through the enlargement of the Historical Library in the Hôtel Saint-Fargeau. There are, however, several old houses still remaining on the other side of the street. Number 4 was built in 1620, and number 6 five years later, while number 8 is even older, dating from 1618 or earlier, and counted the Marquise de Sévigné among its residents for a short time. Numbers 10, 12 and 16 are all from the start of the 17th century, and at the end of the 19th century number 12 was used as a lodging-house for poor but honest Christian girls. ➡ Turn left briefly into the street opposite number 12 - rue Payenne - where on your left you will see two squares, Square Léopold-Achille and Square Georges-Cain. At the far end of Square Georges-Cain is the beautiful rear façade of the Hôtel Saint-Fargeau, and between the two squares, at number 14, is its Orangery. It is not hard to imagine the idyllic childhood that Louis-Michel and Félix Lepeletier must have spent here. One of the most interesting relics in Square Georges-Cain is part of the original façade of the Central Pavilion of the Tuileries Palace, consisting of a decorative pediment, a clock, two fluted pillars and an ornate shield with angels and a lion's head.

➡ Go back up rue Payenne, passing number 11 dating from 1572, and the *Hôtel de Châtillon* at number 13, built in 1671 and home to the Duc de Châtillon until six years before the Revolution, when it was bought by the wife of a Public Prosecutor. ➡ Turn left on rue du Parc-Royal and walk up to number 21 (on the corner with number 16 rue Elzévir). This old house once belonged to a cousin of Jean-Baptiste Colbert, Louis XIV's minister. During the Revolution it was home to some friends of Caron de Beaumarchais, who took refuge here on the night of August 11th 1792 when his own house was being visited by the authorities. These *visites domiciliaires* took place all over the capital during the weeks preceding the September massacres, with the object of arresting 'enemies of the people' and putting them in prison to be killed. Beaumarchais was wanted in connection with the purchase of 60,000 guns for which he had supposedly received 800,000 *francs* from the government - an accusation that was probably untrue, but was used by Beaumarchais' enemies to stir up public feeling against him. And these were dangerous times, when popular hatred could have lethal consequences. Beaumarchais later wrote a letter to his daughter telling her about his terrible night in his friends' house at 16 rue Elzévir (then known as *rue des Trois-Pavillons*, which is still engraved on the wall).

'I left without a light for rue des Trois-Pavillons, checking from time to time that no-one was following me...once the door to the street was firmly locked and barred, and one of my friend's servants locked in the house with me, I fell asleep. At midnight, the valet came into my room in his nightshirt, terrified. "Sir," he said, "get up: the entire populace has come to find you; they're knocking down the door. Someone at your house has betrayed you; the house is going to be looted."' Beaumarchais decided to give himself up in order to save his friend's property, but then changed his mind. *'I opened a window that looked out on rue du Parc-Royal...I saw that the street was full of people: I was seized with an insane desire to jump out of the window, but lost my nerve at the last minute. I went down trembling into the kitchen, where, looking through the window, I saw the front door opening and blue suits and pikes coming into the courtyard!'* The terrified Beaumarchais desperately tried to find a hiding-place. *'Near the kitchen there was a sort of office with a huge cupboard where they kept the china. As a last refuge, your poor father, my child, stood in the cupboard behind the door, leaning on a walking-stick...I could see*

candles going up, going down, above my head...I had two pistols in my pocket; I debated with myself at length whether I should use them. I decided that if I did, I would be chopped to pieces immediately, advance my death by one hour and lose my last chance to get help.' (Dauban, 1977)

Beaumarchais spent four hours in this miserable predicament, until he was finally rescued by a friend who was in the National Guard and who by pure coincidence had been sent to the house on another matter. The exhausted but relieved Beaumarchais managed to get a good night's sleep, but his relief was temporary, for a few days later he found himself in the *Abbaye* prison. He was finally liberated, after an intervention on his behalf by Manuel, the Commune prosecutor - and in the nick of time, for it was just four days before the prison massacres.

➡Cross over Place de Thorigny and go into rue de la Perle, where number 16 used to be the home of Jean Lambert Tallien. The number 16 is not marked, but if you walk a little way along the right-hand side of the street you'll see a small red-brick building marked *Crêche Collective*. This is where Tallien's house stood. I wonder if the children and the teachers here realise that they spend their days in a rather historic spot, where one of the most pivotal events in French history was planned. Much criticized, even by his contemporaries, for his complicity in the prison massacres, Tallien wrote in his own defence that *'in times of revolution and agitation, we must draw a veil and leave to history the task of appreciating and honouring the epoch of the Revolution, which has been much more useful than we think.'* Tallien's house had an indoor tennis-court, and was known by its sign *l'Autruche*, meaning ostrich, the irony of which may not have gone unnoticed by Tallien's mistress, Thérésia Cabarrus, who wrote to him from her prison on 8 *Thermidor* accusing him of closing his eyes to her plight - *'I die from belonging to a coward.'* But when her next letter arrived informing Tallien that she was to be judged by the Tribunal the next day, he brought his friends Barras and Fouché here to his house, where they prepared the overthrow of Robespierre. The plan was carried out the following day, and shortly afterwards Thérésia married Tallien, a marriage that brought him the contempt of many colleagues, and one that some say Thérésia entered into out of gratitude.

In spite of all this Tallien was for a while one of the most influential deputies in the Convention, but his power was much reduced from the Directory onwards. In 1804 Napoléon named him Consul in Alicante, but ill health prevented him from keeping this post more than a few months. He was obliged to return to Paris, where he received a small pension that was maintained by Louis XVIII in gratitude for his role in the overthrow of Robespierre. Tallien was later condemned to exile as a regicide, but reprieved on account of his illness, a leprous form of elephantiasis that left him so bloated he was unable to be transported. He died in misery in 1820, abandoned by both friends and family.

➡ Go back to Place de Thorigny and turn left on rue de Thorigny, where at number 5 is the Picasso Museum. It occupies the Hôtel de Juigny, a beautiful house built in 1659 for the ostentatiously *nouveau-riche* Aubert de Fontenay, who had risen from being a footman by way of various speculative actions. One of these was the purchase of the *ferme de la gabelle* (the notorious feudal salt tax), which is the origin of the nickname Hôtel Salé that is still attached to this house ('Salty Mansion' - I like to call it 'Salty Towers'). In 1768 it became the home of the bishop of Châlons, Mgr Leclerc de Juigny de Neufchelles, who in 1781 was made archbishop of Paris, the last before the Revolution. Mgr de Juigny clearly loved a churchly ambiance, for he had all the corridors and staircases of his house hung with purple velvet, and in keeping with the righteousness of his office, the nude figures in the paintings were all given clothes. During the terrible winter that preceded the storming of the Bastille, Mgr de Juigny distinguished himself by his enormous generosity to the near-starving Parisians, but his benevolence did not extend outside the Catholic fold. When a new law was passed giving certain limited civil rights to Protestants, he was among the first to protest, making an official complaint directly to the king himself. His public image further deteriorated at the opening of the Estates-General when he declared himself unequivocally opposed to the merging of the three Orders. Seeing he was in a minority, he decided not to stay around for the undesirable social changes he saw looming on the horizon, preferring to vacate his seat as a deputy and emigrate. In the street outside his house, where you are now standing, a crowd of local residents watched Mgr de Juigny climb hastily into his carriage, which was loaded down with his possessions, and as it rolled away they pelted it with stones. One of them hit the coachman, who leaned down and shouted to his master, *'Monseigneur, if it goes on like this there'll soon be two seats vacant!'*

Opposite the archbishop, at number 6, lived a lawyer named Thiroux de Crosne, who was born in Normandy in 1736, and at the outbreak of the Revolution was the city's Lieutenant-General of Police. Earlier in his career he had worked with Voltaire in the vindication and rehabilitation of a Calvinist called Jean Calas who in 1763 was falsely convicted of murdering his son, and executed on the wheel. Thiroux de Crosne became Police Lieutenant in 1785, taking over from Lenoir, who was later compromised in the Kornmann affair, at which point Thiroux de Crosne may well have found himself in the delicate position of having to question his own predecessor. Another major investigation he conducted was the Affair of the Queen's Diamond Necklace, and he was also responsible for having the municipal cemeteries moved outside the city limits and their remaining bones taken to the Catacombs. In 1786 he signed a warrant for the arrest of Antoine Saint-Just, accused of running away from his home in Blérancourt with his mother's money and jewellery. Thiroux de Crosne must have had a kind-hearted streak in his nature, for he persisted in leniency towards the 19-year-old runaway, despite pressure from his mother's noble defender, Joseph d'Evry, who was determined to see the young tearaway behind bars. He was nonetheless obliged to mete out some kind of punishment to Saint-Just, but made sure it was no harsher than a stay in a supervised *pension* next to the Picpus Convent. Thiroux de Crosne does not present the redoubtable figure one might expect from an 18th-century police chief, and perhaps he was trying to live up to the rather lofty job description drawn up by Colbert when the post was created in 1677.

'Our Police Lieutenant should be a man of the robe and the sword, and if the scholarly ermine of the doctor must float on his shoulders, it is also essential that his foot resound with the sturdy spur of the knight, that he be as imperturbable as the magistrate and as intrepid as the soldier, that he not pale before flood nor plague, before the rumour of the populace nor the threat of the courtier.' In the end Thiroux de Crosne was unable to satisfy this last requirement, for after the violent events of July 1789, he decided to emigrate. In reality he had never been threatened by the populace or any of the new revolutionary 'courtiers', and perhaps it was remembering this that induced Thiroux de Crosne to return to France during the Terror, a foolish move that resulted in his arrest and execution in 1794.

➡ From rue de Thorigny turn left into rue Coutures-Saint-Gervais, a name that refers to the *coutures* (old French for *cultures* meaning farmlands) of a medieval fief belonging to the nuns of *Saint-Gervais*. The road was built on this land in 1620, and you can still see the emblem of this fiefdom, made up of the letters FCSG arranged in the form of a cross, engraved on the corner wall of Mgr de Juigné's *hôtel* (corner of rue de Thorigny and rue Coutures-Saint-Gervais). They are about two metres up, underneath the modern name plaque. The entire side façade of the Hôtel de Juigné runs along the south side of this street, where its gardens, with their entrance at number 1, extended to the end of the block. During archbishop de Juigné's time the north side of the street was mostly inhabited by magistrates.

➥At the end of the street you should turn left on rue Vieille-du-Temple and walk down one block, go across rue de la Perle, continue a few more metres and you will see to your right, at number 87, the Hôtel de Rohan. This now houses the National Archives, but in the 18th century it was the residence of Prince Louis de Rohan-Guémenée, the famous fall-guy in the Affair of the Queen's Necklace. This sumptuous mansion, which was known at that time by its official name, *Hôtel de Strasbourg*, was built in 1705 by Arnaud-Gaston de Rohan, son of the Prince de Soubise and first of four de Rohans to own this hôtel. All four became cardinals and archbishops of Strasbourg, an office they all held with the utmost discretion and dignity - until Prince Louis, the last of their number, came along. He was described in the memoirs of an Alsation baroness called d'Oberkirch as *'a handsome prelate, hardly devout, deeply devoted to women, full of wit and kindness, but with a weakness and a gullibility, for which he would pay dearly.'* Between his Paris home and his château in Saverne, Prince Louis, who became Cardinal de Rohan in 1778, led a truly luxurious life - he had no fewer that 14 butlers and 25 valets, and was famous for his generosity, hospitality and wonderful *soirées*. When in 1761 he was admitted to the Academie-Française, he became part of the small group of members who did not possess the literary background usually required to enter this hallowed institution. The Duc de Nivernois, director of the academy, recognized this in his welcome speech, but assured Prince Louis that *'your name seemed to be needed on our list. In inscribing it there, we do not expect you to be constantly present at our assemblies. We know what great works, what important functions fill your life...you are destined for celebrity; it will follow you everywhere.'* The Duc de Nivernois didn't know how right he was - except for the word 'celebrity', which should have been 'notoriety'.

When the Affair of the Necklace began, the bogus countess, Jeanne de La Motte-Valois, was a frequent visitor here at number 87. Whenever she wished to inform Cardinal de Rohan of the latest development in her 'negotiations' with the queen, she would be seen arriving at rue Vieille-du-Temple decked out in ostentatious finery. Each time there was a crisis to be related, a new piece of trickery to be acted out, another lie to be told, she would come running to the *Hôtel de Strasbourg* and talk in urgent confidence with the unwitting Cardinal. When the whole affair was blown open, and Cardinal de Rohan had to answer to the king and queen for his behaviour, he was arrested and brought to this *hôtel* to pass one last night before going to prison. The next morning the Marquis de Launay, governor of the Bastille, arrived at the *Hôtel de Strasbourg*, and left a short while later with the Cardinal. Accompanying them on their walk to the Bastille were his secretary and two of his servants, who were required to serve the needs of the Cardinal during his stay in the rather pleasant suite of cells that he occupied in the ancient fortress.

➡Now turn round and go back along rue Vieille-du-Temple as far as number 106, which was built in 1621 and bought in 1776 by Antoine Jean-François Megret de Serilly, an aristocratic Farmer-General who successfully combined his role as Treasurer-General with that of capitalist entrepreneur. His involvement in the massive metallurgy empire founded by the de Wendel family at the beginning of the 18th century brought Mégret de Serilly considerable wealth. But he lacked the foresight of Ignace de Wendel, director of the enterprise, who took the prudent step of leaving the country when he saw the Revolution becoming increasingly punitive. Mégret de Serilly and his wife, Anne Marie Louise, remained in Paris and were both arrested and tried along with 23 other prisoners, all charged with being 'co-conspirators' of the king's sister Madame Elisabeth. They were both condemned to death on May 10th 1794, and Mégret de Serilly went to the guillotine that same day along with Madame Elisabeth and her other 'accomplices'. But 31-year-old Anne Marie Louise declared herself pregnant, her sentence was accorded the usual suspension and she was put in the care of the diocese. This saved her life, for a couple of months later Robespierre was deposed and she was liberated. The triangular pediment over the entrance of de Sérilly's house is decorated with sculpted lions and a family coat of arms from the previous owners, and the interior courtyard has a beautiful red brick facade that is visible from 13 rue de Thorigny. After the Revolution the luxurious furnishings and fittings of Madame Mégret de Serilly's boudoir found their way to London's Victoria and Albert Museum.

The house at number 117 became a theatre during the Revolution, when the new liberty of artistic expression gave rise to a deluge of small playhouses reminiscent of the present-day London fringe. After the abolition of the monopoly held by the three national theatres, the year 1791 alone saw the opening of 21 'boulevard' theatres, where thousands of new plays were cheered or jeered according to the whims of Parisian audiences. Many of them satirized the *ancien régime*, or even denounced it, and the new theatres gave the chance for numerous hopeful unknown men - and women - to have their work presented. The revolutionary feminist Olympe de Gouges saw several of her plays produced, notably *L'Esclavage des Nègres,* which delighted the abolitionists in the audience but brought shouts of abuse from the rest. Even the deputies tried their luck, Collot d'Herbois with his nationalistic piece, *La Famille Patriote*, and Fabre d'Eglantine with several plays, some successful, but at least one of which was booed off the stage without mercy. There is no record of what was presented in the little theatre at number 117, which was built entirely out of wood and had several boxes and balconies.

There were several very popular plays at this time about the tragic injustice of Jean Calas's execution, a *cause-célèbre* in French legal history. Jean Calas was a 64-year-old Huguenot cloth merchant in Toulouse, whose eldest son committed suicide in October 1761. Mass hysteria broke out when someone suggested Jean had murdered his son because he wanted to become a Catholic - which he didn't - he hated the Catholic religion as much as his father did, and resented the limitations placed on his career by the anti-Protestant times he lived in. Unfortunately the magistrates found the accusation entirely credible, and poor Jean Calas was arrested with his entire family. They were all tortured, including his wife, and Jean was condemned to death. On March 9th 1762 he died a terrible death lasting two hours, when his bones were broken with an iron bar as he lay stretched on a cart-wheel. Jean protested his innocence to the end, but it was Voltaire, through his heroic and tenacious intervention, who succeeded in clearing the name of this unfortunate man, whose death became a motive force in the drive for religious toleration.

➡Turn right on rue du Poitou, cross rue de Turenne and continue along rue du Pont-aux-Choux, a name that dates from 1610. The *pont* (bridge) used to pass over a sewer that is now covered by rue de Turenne, and the *choux* (cabbage) were grown on the land around it. This street was the birthplace in 1693 of the much romanticized Parisian bandit, Louis-Dominique Cartouche, whom you saw pay for his crimes on the fatal wheel in the *Place de Grève*. ➡At the end of this street you will be at the corner of Boulevard Beaumarchais, which takes its name from the celebrated author's magnificent residence that stood at the Bastille end of this street. At the time it was called *Boulevard Saint-Antoine*, for it ended at the city gate bearing that name. When the macabre procession set off from *La Force* prison carrying the Princesse de Lamballe's head on a pike, they came up this boulevard from the Place de la Bastille, and stopped outside number 113, a house dating from 1773 that you will find on the corner of rue du Pont-aux-Choux. Here they took their gory trophy off the end of the pike and proceeded to wash it in a large bucket of water that had been put outside the house for horses to drink from. After this operation was completed and the princess's head back on the pike, they set off once more for the Temple prison, turning into rue Pont-aux-Choux, then right on *rue Louis* (rue de Turenne), and left on rue de Bretagne, where ➡you will join up with them after taking a short cut through a former convent.

The Princesse de Lamballe's head was paraded in the streets, washed in a bucket and then carried on a pike to the Temple prison, where it was brandished at the window of Marie-Antoinette's prison. (Author's private collection)

➡ To do this, turn left on Boulevard Beaumarchais and immediately left again on rue Froissart. This street was built in 1804 on the site of the *Couvent des Filles-de-Calvaire*, which opened in 1635 for an order of sisters dedicated to the Virgin mourning her crucified son. Just before the Revolution it was taking in boarders for a rent of 600 *livres* - 400 extra for those who came with a chambermaid! Rue Froissart goes right through the middle of this convent, so as you walk along the very last section of the street where it meets rue de Turenne you might be treading the boards with thespian ghosts, for during the Revolution the convent chapel became a theatre. It was called *Théâtre du Boudoir des Muses*, one of the most popular playhouses in Paris, talked about constantly in the newspapers and magazines of the period, and remaining open until 1807, a time when many of the capital's small theatres were closed down.

➡ Cross rue de Turenne and go straight into rue de Bretagne, where you re-join the bloodthirsty procession heading for the Temple. ➡ You are going to walk with them now, as they advance towards the Temple prison with the head of the Princesse de Lamballe held aloft on the end of a pike. As you go you will pass number 41, where you find Paris's oldest covered market, Marché des Enfants-Rouges, originally created in 1615. Its name (Market of Red Children) comes from an orphanage that stood near here during the 16th and 17th century, where the children were all dressed in red. The principal building of this historic market fortunately escaped demolition and has been restored by the City of Paris, which should give a boost to the ambiance of rue de Bretagne.

In 1750 the land this market stands on was acquired by Royal Astronomer, Jacques Cassini, who came from a family of great astronomers. It was his grandson, Jacques-Dominique, Comte de Cassini who, as Director of the Paris Observatory, completed in 1793 the famous 180-page topographical map of

France that had been started by his father, César-François Cassini, the previous Director. Jacques-Dominique was avidly against the Revolution from the start, and when it was proposed in the Convention that the four astronomers at the Observatory be accorded equal status, he protested loudly. A few days later he was arrested and imprisoned, where he found himself in the company of royal governess Madame de Tourzel, her teenage daughter Pauline, and Beaumarchais's third wife. Cassini was lucky, for he was saved by 9 *Thermidor* and lived to the age of 97.

Jacques Cassini kept the market until 1772, when it was bought by a mason and philanthropist, Jean-Claude Geoffroy d'Assy, who extended and renovated it, put in some street lighting, and had a water fountain built for use by the market vendors, even helping them to clear up at the end of a day's trading. But no amount of philanthropic action could obscure Jean-Claude's background as a noble and a financier. He was arrested during the Terror and imprisoned in the Luxembourg, where he was tried on July 9th 1794 as an 'accomplice' in the Luxembourg prison conspiracy. The accusation was completely fabricated, but Jean-Claude was guillotined later on that same day. His heirs took over the administration of the market, which was eventually given to the City of Paris in 1912, and is now is a listed monument.

PRISON DU TEMPLE.
➥Continue along until just beyond rue des Archives, where at number 55 rue de Bretagne there used to be a military post that provided the guards for the Temple prison between 1792 and 1795, when the royal family was there. ➥At this point, where rue de Bretagne intersects with rue des Archives and rue Eugene Spuller, turn right into rue Eugene Spuller. You are now standing on the south-west boundary of the former *Enclos du Temple*, the 'town within a town' where in 1240 the Knights Templar established their domain. They were succeeded

by the Knights of Malta, whose Grand Prior continued to live here until the Revolution. The last person to hold this office was Louis XVI's nephew, the Duc d'Angoulême, whose marriage in 1799 to Louis' daughter, Madame Royale, brought little happiness to either of them. But I wonder, as perhaps you will when you've finished reading the sad saga of the Temple prison, if there was anything that could have ever evoked any real happiness in the heart of this unfortunate royal daughter.

By the 18th century there was a diverse assortment of residents in the Temple enclosure, including wealthy nobles who came here to enjoy the peaceful environment, free-lance artists, and debtors escaping the arm of justice. Just before the Revolution there were about 4,000 people in this little enclave - all living tax-free. The enclosure was surrounded by a wall 8 meters high with round defence towers at regular intervals, and it covered an area approximately between the present-day rues de Bretagne, Picardie, Béranger and Temple (see map).

Plan showing position of Enclos du Temple over present day streets.

➡ Walk up rue Eugene Spuller and stop just before you get to the intersection with rue Perrée. This part of rue Eugene Spuller is where the famous mediaeval tower stood, where Louis XVI and his family were imprisoned. As well as this dungeon, the enclosure also contained the palace of the Grand Prior, extensive convent buildings, a Rotunda, a church, a cemetery, a hospital and a jail. Far from being miles from anywhere or anything, which is the image that some descriptions give of the royal family's final residence, they were living in a very lively neighbourhood where everyday life closely resembled that of a country village. ➡Cross over rue Eugene Spuller at this point, just before the intersection with rue Perrée, and as you cross the road you will be walking right through the legendary prison where the French royals spent their last months of family life. Three of them left for execution, one left to be murdered in another prison, and the youngest one died here of illness and neglect. Only one of them lived to tell the tale - although not surprisingly, she always refused to tell it.

➡You should now walk back along rue Eugene Spuller and turn right into the Square du Temple. When the royal family first arrived at the Temple on August 13th 1792 they were sumptuously received in the palace of the Grand Prior, which stood on the site of this square. Look around and imagine the scene, which seemed more like a national festival than a coup d'état. The residents of the surrounding area were overjoyed, the palace and the gardens were lit up for the occasion, and a luxurious dinner was laid on in the great hall where princes had formerly dined - and where Mozart had played the harpsichord. While the king and queen ate, they were watched by a crowd of local residents - shopkeepers, carpenters, wine-merchants - who had pushed their way into the hall out of curiosity. It was the strangest group of 'courtiers' that Louis had ever eaten dinner with, but he accepted their presence with such grace that they returned the compliment by addressing his as *Monsieur* - a welcome change from *Citizen Capet*. But when dinner was over the royal group were shocked to find themselves conducted to one of the towers (*la Petite-Tour*) of the dungeon, supposedly because nothing else had been prepared yet, but from that moment on they would never again be treated as guests. They became prisoners.

The royal family's first two weeks of incarceration in the formidable tower were deceptively pleasant, for they they were well-fed, in comfortable quarters, and had friends with them in the person of the Princesse de Lamballe, Madame de Tourzel and her daughter. Then in the evening of August 19th came the second shock, when their friends were taken away and imprisoned in *La Force*. This left a family group of five - King Louis, Marie-Antoinette, their daughter Madame Royale, aged 14, the dauphin Louis-Charles aged 7, and Louis's sister, Madame Elisabeth aged 28. They were under the supervision of Antoine Joseph Santerre, Captain of the National Guard, who permitted them to walk in the gardens every day, where the dauphin could play ball and the king would sit on a large stone and read.

During their imprisonment the royal family would walk every day in the gardens of the Temple. Here you see the king's valet, Cléry, playing ball with the dauphin. (Courtesy of Musée Carnavalet, Cabinet des Arts Graphiques, Paris)

It was during one of these daily walks that they heard the news of the prison massacres being shouted outside the wall by a newspaper-seller. The following day the procession you followed on your way here arrived at the Temple and brandished the Princesse de Lamballe's head in front of one of their prison windows. This horrible pantomime was intended for Marie-Antoinette, but fortunately the prison guards showed a little compassion and closed the curtains. The king tried to talk to the crowd, while his valet, Cléry, ensured that the queen was kept away from the terrible sight of her friend's severed head.

After this incident security was increasingly tightened around the captive royals. A high wall was built around the dungeon, separating it from the rest of the enclosure, and the prisoners were transferred to the *Grande-Tour*, where Louis and the dauphin were put on the second floor with their valet, while Marie-Antoinette, Madame Royale and Madame Elisabeth were on the third floor with their servants, a couple named Tison who in reality were spies planted there to observe 'the Austrian woman'. For the next three months life became a daily routine of family meals, sewing, reading aloud, and education for the children, provided by their parents and their aunt. Louis had never before had so much time to devote to his young son, and he spent hours patiently teaching him to read and write French and Latin, and telling him the history of his country. He also introduced him to geography, which was a particular passion of the king and which permitted father and son to escape for a while from the horror of their real lives into the exotic world of the great explorers.

Then on December 11th 1792 Louis was taken to the National Convention, where his trial began for crimes against the people. While the hearings were going on he was not permitted to see his family, and finally, on Sunday January 20th, the Minister of Justice, Dominique Garat, had the terrible task of reading out to the king the sentence of death that had been imposed on him. Louis listened to this as he had listened to his accusers during the trial, with courage, and silent acceptance of his fate. Later that night his valet, Jean-Baptiste Cléry, put out the king's supper, of which Louis ate very little, but asked Cléry to wake him at 5 a.m., and then lay down and slept until the following morning. In stark contrast to the king's apparent calmness, poor Cléry found it impossible to sleep. Consumed by dark thoughts and terrible anxiety, he spent the night sitting in a chair near the king's bed, and by the time the clock struck 5 Cléry was tearful with grief. Louis's fortitude in such circumstances was astonishing, for he gently comforted his valet, telling him he should not be sad for him, but should feel joy, for his ordeal was now at an end. Once breakfast was over, Cléry no doubt had little time to ponder on his own grief, for he was too busy preparing the king for his final departure, as well as delivering various packages containing hair and other mementoes of Louis's family. When the king finally left for the scaffold, he went in the company of his confessor, Abbé Edgworth de Firmont, requesting that Cléry remain at the Temple to look after his son, and to minister to his wife and sister. Unlike most of Louis's requests during his last days of life, this one was granted. Cléry stayed behind at the Temple, desolate and heartbroken for the man he described as 'the best of Kings', and tried to do his best for the family that he left behind. Cléry was the son of a former gardener at the Trianon, and had been long associated with Louis XVI, having been valet to both dauphins, and Louis's valet for the last five months leading up to his execution. Cléry was devoted to the royal family, as was his wife, who rented an apartment near the Temple tower, where she composed and played music whenever the queen walked in the gardens - until the police put a stop to it. Cléry's devotion to the king earned him two periods of imprisonment after Louis's execution, and he only escaped the guillotine himself thanks to the fall of Robespierre. In 1795 he left France and went to Austria to serve

Madame Royale, Louis XVI's daughter, and although he returned more than once to France, he was living in his property in Austria when he died of apoplexy in 1808. The simple inscription on his gravestone could not sum up better this loyal and devoted royal servant. *'Here lies the faithful Cléry.'*

For the six weeks of Louis's trial Marie-Antoinette did not see her husband. Her only sources of news were the scribbled notes that Louis was sometimes able to pass up from his window to hers, and the cries of a newspaper-seller in rue de Bretagne (*rue de la Corderie*) who had been paid by a friend to shout as close to her prison as possible any important developments. It was in this way that she learned on January 20th 1793 that Louis would die the following day. That evening his family were all brought down to his room, where for over two hours the most heartbreaking scene of farewell unfolded before the eyes of their impassive guards. Louis promised his wife he would see her one last time in the morning, but he did not do this, wishing to spare her additional pain. Marie-Antoinette spent the entire night lying fully clothed on her bed, trembling from the cold, and weeping for the husband whom she had grown to love more during their imprisonment than she ever had during 22 years of marriage. At 10.30 the next morning when the cannons announced the death of the king, the royal prisoners were seated around a copious - and rather early - dinner of chicken, lark and rabbit, which none of them could eat. At the sound of the cannon-fire, Marie-Antoinette threw herself down on her bed, shaking with grief, while the little dauphin burst into tears, only half understanding the reality of the situation. Suddenly the queen got up and, taking remarkable control of herself, knelt respectfully before her son and saluted him as the new king of France.

From then on it was to be shock after shock for the traumatized queen. She refused to go out into the garden, unable to bear passing by the door of her husband's room, preferring to sit for hours on end, dressed in widow's weeds, silently knitting by the window of her room. She got thinner and thinner, and her blonde hair began to turn grey and brittle. During this period the queen's most predatory enemy was Hébert, who hated her with a passion, and persisted in publishing violent tirades against her in his newspaper, *Le Père Duchesne*. He often visited the Temple in an attempt to gather evidence against her, a campaign that culminated in the despicable and groundless accusations of incest that he made at her trial. On one of his visits to the Temple, noticing that the queen had put a cushion on the dauphin's chair during mealtimes, Hébert goaded her with a remark typical of *Père Duchesne*. *'What? A cushion for prisoners who ought to be on straw.'*

Hébert was among those responsible for the queen's next shock - the worst one of all for her - when on July 3rd her son was taken away from her and put in the care of the shoemaker Antoine Simon. For two days she could hear him crying continuously in the room below, but in the end the child adapted to his new 'parents', who contrary to legend were not quite the monsters that some suggest. Madame Simon cared for him like any good mother of the era - beginning with an enema in case he had worms. He was excellently fed, had regular baths and each morning she would lay out clean clothes on his bed. Simon found a silver birdcage decorated with crystal and golden garlands that had once belonged to the Prince de Conti and which became a much-loved toy for the young Charles. But to Simon's horror the clockwork birds inside the cage sang a royalist march, so he sent the whole thing to a *sans-culotte* clockmaker, who soon had the birds singing *Ça Ira!* Simon was ferocious in his patriotism, seeing the Revolution as a means to make slaves of the former masters, and he attacked with enthusiasm the task of turning this little king into a little citizen. He taught him to sing patriotic songs, and Charles's increasing facility for revolutionary slang caused Marie-Antoinette to wince in horror as she listened at her window. She could hear him constantly, but never again would she see her little *chou d'amour*, the pet name she had always given him, for at the beginning of August she left the Temple and was transferred to the Conciergerie. The night before her execution on October 16th 1793 she wrote Madame Elisabeth a poignant farewell letter that was never delivered. It nonetheless still exists and can be seen in the Carnavalet Museum.

After the queen's death conditions worsened for the remaining three members of the royal family at the Temple. Madame Elisabeth stayed there until the evening of May 9th 1794, when she was taken away to appear before the Tribunal, and guillotined the following day. Hébert had relentlessly persecuted her too, but did not live long enough to see his mission accomplished, for he was guillotined himself six weeks earlier. Once Madame Elisabeth had gone, the only royal prisoners remaining here were the two children, now completely bereft of any family support - and of each other, for they still occupied different floors of the tower. Madame Royale, known thereafter as the 'Orphan of the Temple', did not leave her sombre prison until 1795, when she was exchanged against four French prisoners and went to join her relatives in exile. She later married and went to England, but she was deeply and permanently scarred by her long ordeal, and to the end of her life would not tolerate any discussion of the Revolution in her presence.

The mystery still remains, however, of the fate of Louis-Charles, the little dauphin, Marie-Antoinette's *chou d'amour*, whose supposed remains lie in the Faubourg Saint-Antoine. On January 19th 1794, when Louis-Charles was still only 8 years old, Simon and his wife moved out of the Temple, and the whole day was spent taking boxes, clothes and linen out from the tower where they had been living. But in fact they didn't leave. They were kept there secretly in a room next to the dauphin's, where they surveyed him and passed his food through a little barred window. There he languished for several months, sick and filthy, covered in vermin, without speaking and hardly moving, totally alone in a room that had neither heat nor light. In addition, he was thought to have been suffering from tuberculosis of the bone, the same disease that had killed the first dauphin in 1789. Louis-Charles's pitiful plight continued until the fall of Robespierre, whom Simon followed to the scaffold, and a little while after this the dauphin was moved to another room. From then on his regime became a bit less severe, but by then it was too late, for he was suffering from rickets and scrofula and had become mentally disturbed. After another ten months of pain and distress he finally died on June 8th 1795 at the official age of 10 years and 2 months. Some locks of reddish hair taken from his head at the autopsy were later shown to the Duc de Grammont, who had known the dauphin personally, and he dismissed them scornfully as false, maintaining that Louis-Charles's hair was golden blonde.

Half a century later, when the bones of this pathetic child were exhumed, they were found to be those of a boy aged between 15 and 18. It is clear that something mysterious happened to Louis XVII, but no one theory can be proved. Maybe he died naturally - his health had never been good - or perhaps by neglect or even by design, but whichever was the case, it was useful for the revolutionary government to maintain the appearance of his existence, for without him the royalist threat from Louis XVI's brother, the Comte de Provence, would have been much more serious. So if he really died around the beginning of January - which is thought to be the case - he was buried in secret next to the dungeon wall, where a skeleton was indeed later discovered. They then took a stray waif from the street and put him in the place of the dauphin, and some theories even claim there were several replacements, which offers an explanation for the enormous number of young men - 43 to be exact - who subsequently claimed to be the dauphin.

With so many sad memories of royal martyrdom, it is not surprising that Napoléon feared the Temple would become a shrine to the monarchy, and in 1808 he ordered its demolition. All that remains now of the ancient community is a fragment of the door to the Rotunda, which you can see in the Marché du Temple (at 8 rue Perrée). ➡Turn left out of the Square du Temple, continue up rue Eugène Spuller, walking once more through the haunted space where the royal prison stood, cross rue Perrée, and when you have passed the market, turn left and take rue Dupetit-Thouars to the corner of rue Gabriel-Vicaire. Here you can see a plan, carved on stone, showing the layout of the Temple enclosure at the time of the royal family's imprisonment. ➡Continue down rue Gabriel-Vicaire, back into the Square du Temple, site of the Palace of the Grand Prior, and have a last look at where the royal prisoners had their first luxurious dinner on arriving. Perhaps this was the last moment of hope they ever had. ➡You should come out of the square on to rue du Temple, turn right and stop at number 158. This is the site of the entrance to the Temple. It was the only one, and it had a drawbridge flanked by two huge round defence towers, making the enclosure a very secure prison. It was here that the royal family entered the Temple in August 1792, and by the same entrance that one by one they left it to be murdered, executed, or exiled - with the exception of the little dauphin, who would never see outside its walls again.

Louis XVI and his family at the Temple prison. (Authors private collection)

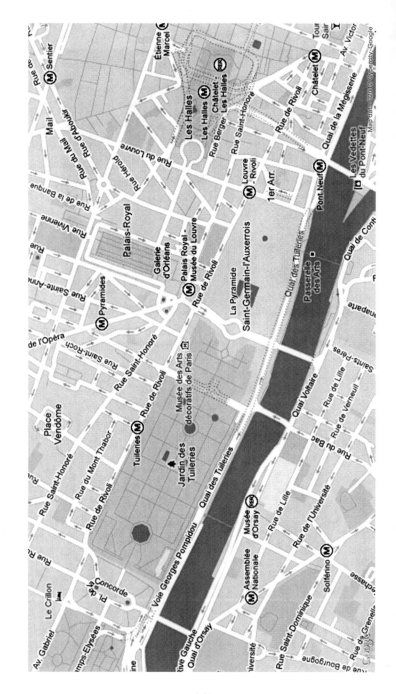

Walk Number Six

GHOSTS IN THE PLACE DU CARROUSEL

The Louvre - The Pyramid - Place du Carrousel - The Tuileries

This walk takes you back to the golden days of the Tuileries Palace, home to royalty before becoming a royal prison, and then seat of the all-powerful Committee of Public Safety. During the revolutionary period the area between the Tuileries Palace and the Louvre was a maze of dark, narrow passages, where the houses of common folk stood side by side with bourgeois mansions. It was through this labyrinth of streets that Robespierre's 'fiancée' hurried to her art classes, where great masters were sold at bargain prices, where Napoléon was nearly assassinated, and where Marie-Antoinette wandered, completely lost, right under the nose of her unsuspecting subjects. When the monarchy was finally toppled, these same subjects, now enraged, poured out of their homes to join the crowd that was heading menacingly across the Place du Carrousel towards the Tuileries Palace.

Ghosts in the Place du Carrousel

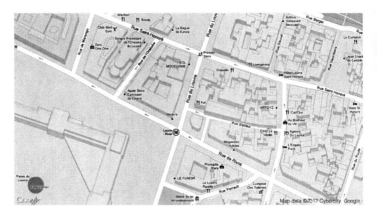

Metro: Louvre-Rivoli

➡ When you come out of the metro you will be on the corner of rue de Rivoli and rue Amiral de Coligny. Walk towards the Seine along rue Amiral de Coligny, where on the left side of the street is the Place du Louvre, and to your right the splendid colonnaded façade of the historic museum. The first building you see on your left as you walk down towards the river is the Town Hall of the 1st *arrondissement*, built in 1859 and the penultimate work of architect Jacques Ignace Hittorf - his last one was the Gare du Nord. Wanting to avoid provocation, Hittorf avoided using the Empire style and created a mixture of Gothic and Renaissance that was intended to be in harmony with the colonnades opposite and the neighbouring church of Saint-Germain-l'Auxerrois. But when the Town Hall was finished he realized there was an unattractive space between the two buildings, so he built a square bell-tower next to it that is graciously linked by an arcade to the church on the other side. Hittorf decorated the tower with a barometer, a thermometer, and a rather pretty clock painted in dark blue and featuring the twelve signs of the zodiac. The tower also contains 38 bells that chime regularly, although since 1960 their peals have been assisted by electric controls. Victor Hugo was not impressed with this trio of buildings, which he said resembled a large oil-and-vinegar cruet set, the bell-tower being the central support and the Town Hall and the church the two flasks.

Hugo's comparison was a bit unfair, particularly regarding the Eglise Saint-Germain-l'Auxerrois, which is a beautiful Gothic achievement by any standards, with its lovely arches adorned with sculpted figures of the saints, and the rather formidable gargoyles hovering dramatically over the entrance. Immediately to the right of the main doorway, which dates from the 13th century, you can see a more light-hearted sculpture showing three figures. The middle one is that First Lady of Paris, Sainte-Geneviève, being tormented by a demon who seems intent on blowing out her candle.

There has been a church here since the 7th century, and the proximity of the Louvre made this parish successively that of kings and artists. The church you see now is the third one, begun in the 13th century, augmented or modified for another four centuries, and finally restored to its present state in 1855. Restoration was badly needed, what's more, for the church had suffered not only the ravages of the Revolution, but also the architectural mutilations of the early 18th century, a period particularly disastrous for Gothic architecture. At this time the central entrance was widened to accommodate official processions, the stained glass was replaced by clear windows to let in more light, the columns in the choir were all altered, and the decorative rood screen disappeared from the entrance to the chancel. Then came the Revolution, when the church was closed and used as a fodder warehouse and a printing works, before being transformed by the Theophilanthropists into the *Temple of Gratitude.* By that time the church had little to be grateful for. Many of its tombs were desecrated, and much more damage would have been done if Alexander Lenoir had not fearlessly stepped in yet again and carried off much of the church's treasure to his *Museum of French Monuments.* Most of what he took eventually went to the Louvre or other Parisian churches, but was never returned to its original home.

The interior of Saint-Germain-l'Auxerrois, with its numerous wall paintings and splendid 17th-century organ case, is worth a visit, and is particularly beautiful when viewed from the central doorway. Here you can best appreciate the lovely Gothic simplicity of the nave, even more enhanced by the radiant blue and magenta stained glass windows that smoulder behind the altar. Some of the stained glass in the transept has survived from the 15th century, and the magnificent pulpit was designed by Lebrun in 1684. Opposite the pulpit there is a beautifully carved churchwarden's pew, made in the same year, where the royal family sat when they attended the church. On June 14th 1787 a still unknown Georges-Jacques Danton stood at the altar of Saint-Germain-l'Auxerrois and watched his blushing bride, Gabrielle Charpentier, as she came up the aisle towards him. She walked on the arm of her father, a café owner and tax inspector, and the church was filled with a huge gathering of lawyers, bankers, financiers, notaries and king's counsellors It was a supremely happy day in 27-year-old Danton's life, a life that would only last for another seven years.

During the 19th century the church of Saint-Germain-l'Auxerrois came very close to being destroyed on two occasions, first of all by Napoléon, who preceded Haussman in the desire for grandiose boulevards to the glory of the nation. With visionary foresight, he planned to build an avenue in the same spirit as the magnificent perspective we have today between the Arch in the Place du Carrousel, the Arc de Triomphe and the

Arche de la Défense, all three of which are perfectly aligned. Napoléon's triumphal route was to begin at the Colonnade of the Louvre and end in the Place de la Nation, so an observer at the palace entrance would have been able to see the famous Elephant in the Place de la Bastille! Luckily Napoléon never got round to carrying out this plan, for it is unthinkable how many other monuments, buildings and picturesque corners of Paris would have been destroyed in the process. There would be no little maze of streets behind the Quai de la Mégisserie, we may well have lost the Tour Saint-Jacques, and many of the old streets on either side of both rue Saint-Antoine and rue Faubourg Saint-Antoine would have been demolished to make the projected avenue wide enough for the imperial ego. The plan was replaced later by a less grandiose one extending rue de Rivoli into the Marais, a project which nonetheless entailed a fair amount of destruction.

Palais du Louvre.

The Colonnade du Louvre.

➨When you come out of the church, stay on this side of the road for a moment and take a look at the Colonnade du Louvre opposite. This imposing structure was designed by the architect, Claude Perrault, who was also a doctor and physicist, and whose younger brother, Charles Perrault, wrote the celebrated Mother Goose fairy tales in 1697. To the modern observer, the perspective of the Louvre has been opened up by the demolition of the Tuileries Palace, the construction of the glass pyramid, and the vast restoration programme that has taken place in recent years. All these things have contributed to making this side of the Louvre seem like the back of the building, but in fact when the colonnade was originally built in 1678, it was the principal entrance to the palace. Although stylistically it bears no relation to the Renaissance lines of the Louvre,

Perrault's Colonnade, with its sweeping row of double Corinthian columns, was completely novel at the time, and launched an architectural style that quickly became fashionable. Thomas Jefferson was a great fan of this façade, classing it among *'the celebrated fronts of modern buildings'*, and took engravings of it back to Washington, where he proposed it as a model to the architects of the new American capital.

The entrance to the Louvre in 1789, going through the Colonnade into the Cour Carrée. Artists were already exhibiting their work in the street outside, a Parisian tradition that still continues to this day. (Author's private collection)

THE QUAI DU LOUVRE.

➥Cross over the road and walk to the left, continuing down towards the Seine. As you walk, turn round for a moment and look up at the top of the church - and you will see an angel waving at you. Turn right on the Quai du Louvre, which originated before the 13th century as a tow-path, and by the time the Revolution began had not been re-surfaced for 70 years. It was paved with large cobblestones and was much lower than it is nowadays, so boats could be loaded and unloaded directly at the water's edge. If you look over the wall to your right you can see how much lower the original level of the quay was. A pedestrian like you in 1789 had to wind his way around customs houses and storage huts, and through a chaotic assembly of officials, guards, dock-workers, street vendors, onlookers, horses and carts, barrels, and other containers waiting to be put on to a boat or taken into town for delivery. The air was filled with the agreeable smells of food being sold or brought by friends and relatives to the men working on the quayside, as well as the less agreeable smells that were a permanent feature of 18th-century urban life.

One pedestrian who often walked here was Nicolas Restif de la Bretonne, the night owl, who arrived on the Quai du Louvre early in the morning of August 11th 1792, having - for once - spent the night at home in bed. He had been woken by the sound of gunfire, and immediately rushed out into the street, where he learned from the gathering crowds that the monarchy had been vanquished during the night and the royal family were in hiding in the National Assembly. Undeterred, despite his horror of violence, Restif started walking towards the Tuileries, deciding to take the Left Bank route, crossing by the Pont Royal which led directly to the Tuileries Palace. '*Arriving at the end of the Pont Royal I saw the gunfire…I saw the Swiss Guards with their throats cut…the National Guard united…I went forward; I saw the dead piled up…I continued on to the quai du Louvre. I saw firing from the windows of the galleries. I pressed myself flat against the wall and a woman, who did not take this precaution, was killed just a few steps away from where I was standing. I saw a butcher's boy fall into the Passage Saint-Germainl'Auxerrois, just 200 paces from the Colonnade du Louvre where the shots had come from.*' (Restif de la Bretonne, 1986)

The Mediaeval Louvre.

➡ Turn right - avoiding the gunshots - through the first archway (opposite the Pont des Arts) that leads into the courtyard of the Louvre known as the Cour Carrée (square courtyard). This was known during the Revolution as the *Grande Cour du Louvre*, and like all public places in the capital where people gathered, there were always government spies hanging around looking for suspicious people. Their investigations sometimes led them to be pleasantly surprised. At the beginning of the Terror one of these official snoopers named Panetier discovered here *'several young people aged from 18 to 20, very good-looking men, who had taken to begging for charity; they have neither hat, hose nor shoes, their hair hangs untidily over their shoulders. Between 8 and 9 o'clock in the evening, I gave alms to several of them so as to get them to talk. The only reason they gave me for doing what they do was poverty. I got the impression that they were very proper young people.'* (Caron, 1910-1978)

The Louvre is one of the most famous landmarks in Paris, and is now the biggest single edifice in the city. But its beginnings were much more modest. ➡ If you stand in the centre of the south west quarter of the Cour Carrée, you will be right in the middle of the original Louvre, known as the mediaeval Louvre, which began as a fort on this spot in the 12th century. When Philippe Auguste built a wall around the city in 1190, on the other side of it at its western extremity was a deserted stretch of land called *Louvre*. One suggested origin of this name relates to the kennels in which the Romans kept their wolf-hounds (*lupara* in Latin), but it is more likely to have come from the old Saxon word *leovar* meaning 'fortified habitation'. Still haunted by stories of the Norman invasions of three centuries earlier, Philippe Auguste set about the creation of a fortress in this stretch of land. The castle that he built against the exterior of the new city wall was a solid quadrangular fortification, with towers at the gate and on each corner. In the middle was a large round donjon tower or keep, surrounded by a circular moat, giving additional security if the outer buildings were invaded. Right now you are standing in the middle of this donjon, which had no prisons, as its name suggests, but contained several bedrooms linked by a spiral staircase.

This great stone building, known as *La Grosse Tour*, was the ancient symbol of French feudalism, and the kernel from which evolved the biggest royal palace in the world. When you visit the museum, you can see the remains of this historic tower, its moat and surrounding walls, in the Mediaeval Louvre exhibition. During Philippe-Auguste's reign the quadrangle of the Louvre had living space only in the south and west wings. The west wall was therefore made particularly thick and protective - they were still scared of invasions from Scandinavian pirates - and its foundations still remain underneath this wing of the palace. When you go into the *Salle Saint-Louis* you can see two pillars and part of the vaulting of one of the original rooms of Philippe-Auguste's palace. Above this, in the *Salle des Cariatides*, the form of the chevet of the original chapel is still visible in the west wall.

It was Charles V (1364-1380) who completed the construction of the quadrangle of the old Louvre, turning it into the fairy-tale castle so beautifully pictured in the mediaeval 'Book of Days', *Les Très Riches Heures du Duc de Berry*. Here, in this one little corner of today's Cour Carrée, the kings and queens resided in luxury with a panoramic view of the Seine, receiving the princes of all nations and entertaining them to sumptuous feasts and celebrations. Their numerous courtiers were lodged in apartments that had painted glass windows illustrating the family coat-of-arms of each occupant. But for Charles V, the creator of this dream residence, it was just a second home, for he lived most of the time in the *Hôtel Saint-Pol* in the Marais. The Louvre was a place where he could retreat from the pressures of Court life to relax and enjoy the solitary delights of his library, which contained nearly a thousand volumes on religion, philosophy, science, medicine, astrology, astronomy, travel, history and poetry. The Bibliothèque Nationale still has the catalogue of this impressive collection that Charles V compiled himself in 1373. Later, during the English occupation, the Duke of Bedford bought most of the books for a pittance and carried them off to England, leaving only about 50 volumes to gather dust on the denuded shelves of the royal library.

The Renaissance Louvre.

François I was the first French king to commit himself to living permanently in the city. This was done as a token of gratitude to his Parisian subjects, who had paid most of the ransom that released him from an unpleasant year of captivity in Italy. So he took up residence in the Louvre, where the air was almost unbreathable due to the putrid water that filled the moat and lapped around the palace walls. Perhaps this is why at first François had the idea of demolishing the entire thing and building a new palace. Fortunately he was persuaded to modernize instead, although he did get rid of the ancient donjon. He then started adding to the existing buildings, and in 1546 called on the services of the architect, Pierre Lescot, who launched three centuries of construction and renovation that culminated in the Louvre we know today.

Lescot re-built the west wing and extended it to the south west, thus introducing the Renaissance style into Paris for the first time. The Tuileries Palace was begun in 1563 by Catherine de Medici, and when Henri IV came to the throne in 1589 he completed the construction of the *Grande Galerie* along the water's edge, with its Pavillon de Flore linking it to the Tuileries. His successor, Louis XIII, built the Pavillon Sully in the centre of the west wing of the Cour Carrée, through which you can now see the glass pyramid, and then extended the wing northwards almost doubling its length. This work, which was completed in 1640, was part of a larger project to quadruple the size of the palace, an idea that had already been envisaged by Henri IV. But when Louis XIII died three years later before being able to complete the plan, his widow, Anne of Austria, left with their 5-year-old son, Louis XIV, and her suspiciously close companion, Cardinal Mazarin, and took up residence in the Palais-Royal. For the next nine years the empty Louvre was a deserted building-site.

The 'Sun-King' in Paris.

When we think of Louis XIV, for most of us it is in the splendour of Versailles that we see him, far from the capital where his people loved him at a distance, and where the Revolution was not yet even a spectre on the horizon. But in fact he lived in the Palais du Louvre for quarter of a century before finally abandoning it for the relative calm and excessive luxury of Versailles. He was only 14 when his mother, no longer threatened by *Fronde* rebels, came back to Paris and chose to settle in the Louvre, where she felt more protected from the sort of invasion she had suffered at the Palais-Royal. When he came of age, Louis resumed his father's plan to quadruple the size of the palace, demolishing what remained of the north and east walls of the mediaeval Louvre, and most of the grand mansions around them. In the space that this created, he extended the south wing, and then closed off the newly-formed quadrangle with two new wings to the north and east, thus forming the Cour Carrée that you see now. From that moment, the palace's new entrance was in the centre of the east wing, and Claude Perrault was called in to add the Colonnade. A decade later in 1678, Louis XIV abandoned his Parisian palace and took up permanent residence at Versailles, leaving a roofless Colonnade that had to wait more than a century to be completed. Voltaire wrote a poem in 1749 to the derelict monument, imploring it to '*be worthy of Louis, your lord and support, break out of this shame, which the universe abhors, and, as Louis shows his glory, let us see yours.*'

THE 18ᵀᴴ CENTURY LOUVRE.

The noble but abandoned palace did eventually break out of its shameful state, although not perhaps in the way Voltaire had in mind. After Louis XIV's departure, the Louvre was gradually occupied by a varied assortment of schemers and dreamers, some from the ranks of the privileged, but with a more non-conformist attitude, preferring the palace's new, rather bohemian 'Court' to the one at Versailles. Some were part of the administrative staff of the various academies and societies that also occupied the Louvre, not only setting up their offices and meeting-rooms there but also installing their personnel in the former royal apartments. One of these was the Academie-Française, founded in 1634 by Cardinal Richelieu. It met in the Louvre from 1643 right up to the outbreak of the Revolution, and it was during this time that Louis XIV, six years before leaving for Versailles, settled definitively the all-important question of armchairs at Academy meetings. Tradition had always held that only the director had the luxury of an armchair, but one day an ancient and gout-ridden cardinal was ceremoniously borne into the meeting-room - in an armchair! Pandemonium broke out at this flagrant defiance of convention, but Louis, who was present in his role of patron of the Academy, quickly restored calm to the occasion by ordering armchairs to be brought in for everyone. Since then, and to this day, the number of armchairs at Academy meetings meticulously corresponds to the number of members present.

Many of the new residents of the Louvre were artists, and in 1736 a son was born in the *Grande Galerie* to one of these painters, who had a very comfortable apartment there. The father's name was Jacques Bailly, inspector of the royal collection, who, in spite of being official painter to the king, showed more aptitude for producing catalogues than for creating works of art. Much to his disappointment, his son, Jean-Sylvain, showed even less talent with a paintbrush, preferring to find fame on the vast canvas of revolutionary politics. Before this, however, he became one of the most brilliant and respected astronomers of his time, was elected to the Academy of Science at the age of 30 and later admitted to the Académie-Française. With his impeccably powdered wig and his calm and gracious manner, Jean-Sylvain Bailly made his presence known from the very start of the Revolution when he sat as a deputy with the Third Estate. He took a leading role in all the events at Versailles during the Estates-General, and it was Bailly who presided over the famous Tennis Court Oath. He became the first mayor of Paris two days after the storming of the Bastille, and for a while was one of the city's heroes, but his enthusiasm for the Revolution waned in the face of mounting popular action. His responsibility for the massacre on the Champ-de-Mars in July 1791 destroyed what remained of his popularity, and the following November his post as mayor was taken over by Pétion. After two years spent out of the public eye, he returned to Paris and was immediately arrested and condemned to death by the Tribunal. His execution on the Champ-de-Mars on November 11th 1793 remains a shameful example of the gratuitous cruelty engendered by the Reign of Terror.

SQUATTERS IN THE LOUVRE.

Certain of the Louvre's new inhabitants at this time were less desirable than others. As a royal domain, it could be legitimately used as a refuge by debtors or those pursued for other misdemeanours, and their presence attracted others who sought to live off them. Ovens were installed by caterers for the provision of food, and the courtyards were piled up with wine barrels. Entertainment came along in all forms, notably that of courtesans, many of whom set themselves up in various rooms in the palace in order to ply their trade. The buildings themselves suffered badly from this invasion, for the new residents did not hesitate to alter their accommodation to suit their tastes or needs. Partition walls were thrown up, unstable mezzanines created, and the walls were riddled with holes of varying sizes to hold anything from a picture-hook to a stove-pipe. And as if the Louvre were not big enough for them, they put up a dozen little houses in and around the Cour Carrée, and even built sheds against the façade of Perrault's Colonnade. This desecration ran its course for nearly 80 years, until de Marigny, Louis XV's superintendent of royal buildings, put a stop to it and threw out all the unwanted residents along with their jerry-built constructions.

ARTISTS IN THE LOUVRE.

Once Louis had got rid of the squatters, some modification and restoration was carried out by the architects Gabriel and Soufflot, including the re-opening of an entrance that had been closed off since the days of François I. The royal authorities lived to regret this, for it facilitated the return of uninvited guests, this time in the form of an invasion of artists, who swept in as if they owned the place, setting up studios, apartments, classes and exhibitions. This was not the first time in history that there had been artists in the Louvre. A century and a half earlier Henri IV, in his goodness, had allotted the three lower floors of his new 'gallery along the water' to a few artists of his choice, so that they could develop their own talents and teach others. But this had been the king's idea, whereas now it seemed the destiny of the royal estate had been taken out of royal hands by a band of creative squatters, which, in addition to artists, included architects, sculptors, silversmiths, carpet-weavers, cabinet-makers and writers. It was of course history in the making, for it would be this community that produced the new ethos of the Louvre, and the backdrop against which a national museum would be created by the Convention in 1793.

➥ Leave the Cour Carrée by taking the archway underneath the Pavillon Sully in the centre of the west wing. As you gradually make your way across this massive space and head towards the Tuileries Gardens, you can use the plan to help you see which pavilion is which and where you should be walking.

Plan of the Louvre showing the pavilions.

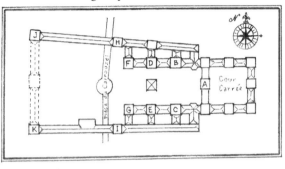

| | | Position of connecting wings of Tuileries Palace | | Pyramid |

A Sully, B Colbert, C Daru, D Richelieu, E Denon, F Turgot, G Mollien, H Rohan, I Lesdiguières, J Marsan, K Flore

Standing on the steps on the other side of the Pavillon Sully, you will have in front of you the controversial glass pyramid built in 1989 by Ieoh Ming Pei, who has created a unique Paris landmark that people seem to either love or hate. More about that later. Right now you should find somewhere to sit and read about how this palace became the most famous art museum in the world. The massive courtyard before you where Pei built his pyramid is called the Cour Napoléon, where on your left are the three pavilions named Daru, Denon and Mollien, and three more to the right named Colbert, Richelieu and Turgot, all added by Napoléon III in the 19th century. Behind them, stretching all the way to the Pavillon de Flore and the Tuileries Gardens, is the *Grande Galerie*, Henri IV's wing by the water, where the tradition of artists in the Louvre began, and it was also here that most of the 18th-century painters lodged. When the young Manon Phlipon (future Madame Roland) came here in 1777 to visit her friend, the artist Jean-Baptiste Greuze, she found herself in an endless corridor with no less than 26 doors each opening on to a studio, each one an expression of the particular creative path of its occupant.

For many of them, probably well-acquainted with the cliché of the starving artist, this was truly paradise, for not only did they have a home and a studio, but they also enjoyed the inspirational company of the capital's artistic elite. At number 2 was Jean-Honoré Fragonard, *le bon Frago* to his friends. *Frago* was famous for his amorous escapades with every model who ever came to pose in his studio, which was seductively equipped with a romantic swing *à la pastorale.* At number 10 lived Hubert Robert, a veritable charmer, whose wife, although equally refined and worldly as her husband, was not too proud to take on the job of cleaning the corridor and keeping the lamps burning. Robert's studio was filled with his canvasses depicting mythical ruins, a style that served him well later on when he immortalized various urban renewal projects in Paris and painted his celebrated view of the ruins of the Bastille. Madame Roland's friend Greuze lived at number 7 with his reputedly awful wife, Gabrielle, whose powdered face and ghoulish blood-red lips terrified everyone, including her long-suffering husband. Poor Greuze had to work most days to the riotous sound of Gabrielle entertaining her friends in the room above.

By the 1780s the tradition of using the Louvre as a lodging-place for artists had become an accepted and desirable aspect of the capital's cultural life, and the former royal palace was now home to numerous painters and sculptors who had been offered the privilege of an apartment and a studio for life. Although this was considered an honour, and may have seemed like heaven for many artists, their accommodation was not always the most luxurious. It was usually in rooms that were dotted around in any available corner of the palace, and one visitor reports having to brave interminable stairs and traverse what seemed like miles of dark corridors in order to get to his friend's studio, which closely resembled a bird's nest tucked under the eaves. The better quarters were reserved for more prestigious occupants such as the academies and associations that had their headquarters there. The Louvre was the seat of two important academies founded by Louis XIV, one of which was the *Academie d'Architecture*. Classes were offered here twice a week by its members, who had a large selection of model buildings at their disposal as teaching aids. In 1789 this academy had as its permanent secretary the author Michel-Jean Sedaine, who owed this honourable appointment, with its free apartment in the palace, to the simple fact of being a mason.

The other academy housed by the Louvre was the *Academie Royale de Peinture et de Sculpture*, which played an all-important role in the evolution of the museum. It had existed since 1648, and counted among its members Marie-Louise Vigée-Lebrun, official painter to Marie-Antoinette, whose portrait she painted more than twenty times. The Academy occupied six enormous rooms that were used for both meetings and classes. The walls were hung with paintings by the French masters, and during any given class the students would all be required to copy the same one, while giving it their individual interpretation. Four grand prizes were distributed each year to the best students, who would then go and study in Rome for three years at the expense of the king. It was thus that in 1775 the young Jacques-Louis David set off for the Italian capital, bringing back with him the love of ancient art that formed the basis of his later revolutionary allegories. Occasionally an outsider triumphed, as in 1752, when the 20-year-old Fragonard walked off with the first prize for a painting called *Jéroboam sacrifiant aux idoles*. Fragonard had presented himself as a candidate after studying with the great master of 18th-century Rococo, François

Boucher, but he felt nonetheless a few apprehensions about not being an Academy student, and confided his fears to his teacher. Boucher had no such anxiety about the situation, however, and even less modesty about his own reputation. '*That won't matter,*' he replied, '*you're my pupil.*' And, of course, he was right.

Every two years, between August 23rd and September 25th, there was an exhibition of the work of Academy members in the *Grand Salon* of the Cour Carrée. Sebastien Mercier often attended these shows, which for six weeks brought masses of people streaming into the Louvre. Mercier was not very impressed with the style of the *Ecole du Louvre*, whose distinguishing feature in his view was the persistent portrayal of powdered wigs and luminous red cheeks. He abhorred the endless busts of men without names, '*these doleful marquesses, anonymous countesses, and useless presidents*' that lined the long galleries. But during the 1780s the increasing dominance at these exhibitions of themes relating to ancient Greece and mythology, and the relative absence of religious paintings, was an indication of the turbulent times that lay ahead. This new focus on things ethical, pastoral and patriotic pleased Mercier, who was supremely grateful for no longer being subjected to '*the faces of executioners and the patient saints that they torture at their leisure.*' Thomas Jefferson attended the Salon of 1787, where the best thing in his view was 'The Death of Socrates' by David, who was Jefferson's undisputed favourite among the artists of the time. He also admired 'five pieces of antiquities' painted by Hubert Robert for the royal palace at Fontainebleau, and several portraits by Madame Vigée-Lebrun, including her celebrated picture of Marie-Antoinette with her children. But Jefferson also remarked that the exhibition contained an '*abundance of things in the style of mediocrity.*'

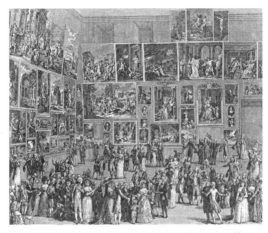

The Salon of 1787 at the Louvre, attended by Thomas Jefferson, whose favourite painting was David's 'Death of Socrates'. You can see it in the bottom row, third painting from the right, almost in the centre of the picture, with a group of four people standing in front of it. You can also see Elisabeth Vigée-Lebrun's portrait of Marie-Antoinette and her children, on the right directly above what seems like an empty picture frame. (Author's private collection)

The most famous revolutionary artist to live in the Louvre during the 1780s was Jacques-Louis David, and it was during these years that David's previously turbulent life took on a degree of calm and stability. He moved into the Louvre and opened his studio to pupils in 1782, the same year that he married 17-year-old Marguérite-Charlotte Pécoul, whose father, a Parisian entrepreneur, provided all the furnishings for David's studio. 1783 and 1784 saw the birth of two sons, who provided Madame David with the attention that she seldom got from her husband, who preferred the matchless company of canvas, brush and palette. His studio was reputed to be faultlessly clean and tidy, and he usually worked wearing a black velvet outfit carefully protected by white over-sleeves. David had been launched into the forefront of the capital's artistic world by the Salon of 1781, where his mother had been quietly in evidence, sitting, proud and smiling, at the foot of her son's pictures. In French painting a new style was in the making, a return to historical sources, and it was David who would turn the page between the

18th and 19th centuries. After his success at the 1785 Salon with *Le Serment des Horaces*, he was hailed as the master of historical painting and sparked off a vogue amongst chic Parisians of dressing *à l'antique*. David was never very pro-royalist, and many art historians have seen the Roman theme of this painting, replete with symbols of the *res publica*, as an artistic herald of the Revolution. He nonetheless enjoyed enormous popularity during these last years of the *ancien régime*, which assured him a constant stream of pupils who came regularly to his studio to study under the fashionable new master.

The Louvre and the Revolution.

In October 1789 the king and the National Assembly moved to the capital and the royal family was installed in the Tuileries Palace. The *Grande Galerie* of the Louvre was linked directly to the Tuileries by the Pavillon de Flore, which was the main entrance used by Louis XVI and his family into their apartments. With the focus of official activity shifted from Versailles to the Tuileries, Paris soon turned its eyes, unavoidably, towards the other palace next to the king's new home. What it saw was a once beautiful building, now dilapidated and dirty, its gracious walls and courtyards cluttered with all manner of shabby huts and stalls. The artists and academies had been joined by an assortment of less cultivated squatters who piled up garbage against the walls and turned the roofs into precarious hanging gardens that were slowly but surely rotting the walls. In short, it was a disgrace - a disgrace that was viewed daily not just by Parisians but also by the numerous foreign visitors who came for a glimpse of the renowned palace. The only possible advantage for the Louvre of all this neglect and abuse is that by the time the Revolution broke out it had ceased to be seen as a symbol of the old regime, which is probably why it was never attacked by enraged crowds or desecrated by anti-royalist vandals.

The idea of a museum in the Louvre was not new. Its origins can be found in the precious collection of paintings and statues that François I accumulated when he lived here. Louis XIV was also a collector, and had an exhibition room in the Louvre for the royal pictures. These numbered more than 2,400 by the time of his death, at which point they were taken from the Louvre and distributed amongst the other royal palaces. During the 18th century various royal ministers envisaged a museum in the *Grande Galerie*, where there were still over 1,000 pictures arranged haphazardly on the walls, but the problem of adequate lighting in a non-electric age always put these projects back into the drawer. It would be the Revolution that transformed the Louvre into a museum.

The first official action took place on May 26th 1791, when a report by the deputy Bertrand Barère was debated in the National Assembly. It resulted in a decree ordering the Louvre and the Tuileries to be united as one '*national palace intended for the habitation of the king and the gathering together of all the monuments of science and the arts.*' This decree was never carried out, however, and after the imprisonment of the royal family in the Temple there was no further need for a royal residence. So a new decree was voted designating the Louvre as the national museum of the arts. This was September 19th 1792, and on July 27th of the following year another decree from the National Convention gave it the name *Musée de la République*, later to become *Musée Centrale des Arts*. It brought together under the same roof the paintings and sculptures collected by François I, the treasures that had belonged to Cardinal Mazarin, objects saved from destruction by Alexandre Lenoir, as well as works from the Tuileries and other royal houses. The same decree appointed Jacques-Louis David as the first president of a commission in charge of managing the new museum.

The official opening took place on August 10th 1793, although it was a modest affair, and of symbolic importance only, for the salons, chaotic and badly-lit as they were, had actually been open to the public since 1791. Works by living artists were exhibited in the *Salon Carrée*, and the royal collections were hung along the *Grande Galerie*, where the walls were still in very bad condition and the lighting did not do justice to the works of the great masters. To promote the cultural life of the new republic, the museum authorities designated certain works as being 'acquired by the nation'. The fact that this honour was given to two portraits by Ducreux of Maximilien Robespierre and Georges Couthon, the two most feared members of the Committee of Public Safety, rather gives the lie to the inspiring preface in the catalogue, which proudly claimed that *'Artists are essentially free: the distinguishing feature of genius is independence.'* Hubert Robert would certainly not have agreed. Having embraced the Revolution with open arms, and immortalized with his paintbrush its first symbolic act, the storming of the Bastille, in October 1793 he found himself in prison. Officially this was for failing to renew his identity card, but everyone knew that his real crime had been designing the royal gardens at Versailles before the Revolution.

When Hubert Robert was released the following August, his fellow artist, David, whose signature had been on Robert's arrest warrant, was spending his second day in prison. During the Revolution David had become the official 'painter of the National Convention', and enjoyed a respected - even heroic - reputation, capturing many of the great moments of the era - the Tennis Court Oath, the deaths of Marat and other revolutionary martyrs, and the last moments of Marie-Antoinette and Danton making their way to the guillotine in a tumbril. His devotion to the Revolution was total, but by allying himself with Robespierre - and then renouncing him after 9 *Thermidor* - he ended up behind bars. Dubbed 'tyrant of the

Arts', he was tried a year later for signing unjust arrest warrants and sending to the scaffold artists whose talent and fame might have eclipsed his own. In the end his judges were swayed away from all this calumny by the relative importance of his role in organizing numerous festivals and painting masterpieces to the glory of the Revolution. The grateful David resumed his work, and when Napoléon came to power, the former 'painter of the National Convention' became the official 'painter of the Emperor'.

In April 1796 the *Grande-Galerie* closed and Hubert Robert was appointed director of an ambitious restoration programme that he recorded in a series of paintings showing the work in progress. His first act as new director was to have the walls painted apple green and olive green, with sky-blue ceilings and stone-coloured cornices, and he then set about designing a system of overhead lighting that he considered essential for the new gallery. Robert and his works committee were responsible for solving a daunting variety of problems, ranging from the best method of hanging and classifying the pictures, to the appointment of guardians and the hours of opening. Whatever they did, it seems, was never good enough for the Minister of the Interior, who ceaselessly criticized them for failing to give the museum '*a character of order, dignity and public utility*'. Nonetheless, Robert remained committed to improving the Louvre, closing the other salons one by one in order to repair more than a century of deterioration, abuse and neglect.

Robert retired in 1802 and it was with much nostalgia and regret that he had to leave the lodgings where he had lived and worked for twenty happy years. He did live to see the fruits of all his labours, though, when the museum re-opened the following year under the name *Musée Napoléon*. Its collection had been substantially enriched during the revolutionary period by the expropriated property of emigrated or guillotined nobility, as well as some controversial works of art pillaged by the French armies in Italy. More treasures poured in later with each victory won by the Empire, and additional wings were built under both Napoléon I (the long north gallery), and Napoléon III, who united the Louvre with the Tuileries. He did this by adding two wings on either side of the Cour Napoléon, where his wonderfully sumptuous apartments can now be seen by visitors. The Ministry of Finance occupied them until the 1980's, when President Mitterrand inaugurated his *Grand Louvre* project which has turned the entire palace into a magnificent museum.

THE COUR NAPOLÉON.

➥You should still be standing (or hopefully sitting) on the steps at the entrance to the Cour Napoléon, which extends to where the two Napoleonic wings end, just beyond the pyramid. During the revolutionary period, the entire area from these steps right up to the triumphal arch of the Carrousel was a maze of dark, narrow passages, where the houses of common folk stood side by side with bourgeois mansions. It was in this labyrinth of streets that Marie-Antoinette wandered, completely lost, right under the nose of her unsuspecting subjects, while she desperately tried to find the carriage that was to take her and her family to safety across the Belgian border. When the monarchy was finally toppled, these same subjects, now enraged, poured out of their homes to join the crowds that were heading menacingly across the Place du Carrousel towards the Tuileries Palace. None of the Louvre buildings to your right existed at that time, and the little streets extended north right up to rue Saint-Honoré and the Place du Palais-Royal. The Napoleonic wing to your left did not exist either, so you would have only seen the *Grande-Galerie*, stretching along the bank of the Seine.

The steps you are standing on are on the site of the former *Place du Vieux-Louvre*, which was a small square, surrounded by houses, between the palace entrance and a street called *rue Fromenteau*. This street ran north-south across the Cour Napoléon, extending to the north right up to rue Saint-Honoré. ➡ If you stand between the present-day Daru and Colbert pavilions, you will be standing in the middle of *rue Fromenteau*, which would have been very risky in 1789, for it was a very busy little street. It was always crammed with traffic, for it linked with the quay by way of a covered passage through the *Grande-Galerie,* and was the usual route for carriages coming from the left-bank to the Opera on rue Saint-Honoré. Some of the traffic on *rue Fromenteau* would have been vehicles coming out of the aristocratic mansions that stood at the south end of the street, nearest the Seine. Many of these had been built during the Renaissance, and there was one, dating from 1309, that would have merited a second look even in the 18th century.

If you'd been walking along *rue Fromenteau* during the Terror, you may well have spotted Eléonore Duplay, daughter of Robespierre's host, hurrying along towards the *Grande-Galerie*. Once a week she would leave her house on rue Saint-Honoré, taking the Terrasse des Feuillants along the north edge of the Tuileries Gardens - which were almost deserted during this dark period of terror - turning right into Place du Carrousel and through the numerous little passages that took her into *rue Fromentau*. From here she entered the long corridor of the *Grande-Galerie* leading to the ground-floor studio of David's self-styled rival, Jean-Baptiste Regnault, one of the resident artists who continued to give painting lessons in the Louvre throughout the Revolution. Here the love-sick Eléonore vainly tried to pour out her unrequited passion for Robespierre on to canvas, while her fellow pupils, a rather privileged group of young ladies, looked on with feelings ranging from dread to contempt. For it was the time of the Terror, and now that Eléonore lived under the same roof as the most feared man in France, she could no longer be like other girls. One of the pupils in Regnault's class, Mademoiselle Hémery, wrote a diary in which she described Eléonore as someone who *'thought she was liked, but in fact she was feared...if ever she turned up unexpectedly, a profound silence fell upon the most lively discussions. Eléonore sat, with furrowed brow, in front of her easel, and worked without speaking; but it would not be long before everyone gathered round her and showered her with questions about her health. I felt inwardly indignant at this flattery which Eléonore appeared to despise, when only an instant before I had heard them talk about her with disdain, criticizing her simple clothes which contrasted with our antique finery.'* (Lenotre, 1906)

Mlle Hémery's diary is a fascinating window on the atmosphere that prevailed during the Terror, and also offers an interesting insight into Eléonore Duplay's character. One day one of the girls, named Vallière, arrived at the studio red-eyed and distraught, announcing with great drama that she was *'going to die. Terrified, I questioned her, and she told me, weeping, that the revolutionary committee of her section had sent to her parents an order obliging her to be in a procession, designating her to represent the goddess at the Festival of Youth. If her family did not obey this order, they would be declared suspect and imprisoned. Vallière's despair was shared by all of us - her parents had said they would rather see her dead than as a goddess...Vallière was convinced she was going to die...thousands of the most extravagant ideas were put forward to ward off this terrible consequence.'* (Lenotre, 1906)

Their conversation was interrupted by the arrival of Eléonore, who knew exactly how to deal with revolutionary committees. *'"I'm astonished" she said "that they didn't think of it before, she's so beautiful. There is only one way to avoid this ridiculous order. Vallière, tell your mother to act enchanted by the committee's choice, to go and ask the president what sort of costume you should put on. Make the costume, show it to all the neighbours, feign joy and make your parents' employees sing the Marseillaise. Then, on the morning of decadi, take three grains of emetic; when*

they come to get you, it'll be easy for you to prove that you are ill. And don't worry, I promise you no-one will ask you anything further." Everything went according to Eléonore's plan. Our dear friend stayed in bed for two or three days...the revolutionary committee was completely taken in by the ruse, and an honest girl was not exposed to the immodest eyes of immoral republican mythologists.'
(Lenotre, 1906)

➡Continue across the Cour Napoléon, veering to the left, and stop by the Denon pavilion, which is at the mid-point of the pyramid. (You can see the names of these pavilions over their arched doorways, but some are a bit faint, so you will have to look hard.) The plan of the area during the Revolution will help you to see where you would have been walking at that time.

Plan of the Louvre and the Tuileries Palace during the Revolution.

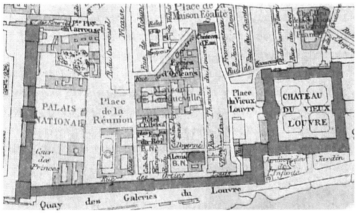

The Louvre and the Tuileries Palace in 1793, showing the maze of little streets between the two palaces, and the revolutionary names given to streets and buildings. The Tuileries Palace is now the Palais National, Place du Carrousel is Place de la Réunion, and the Place du Palais-Royal has become Place de la Maison Egalité. The initials B.N. indicate buildings that have become Biens Nationals (National Property). (Courtesy of Bibliothèque Historique de la Ville de Paris)

As you walk across to the Denon pavilion you are walking right through the grand houses that separated *rue Fromenteau* from another street, *rue Saint-Thomas du Louvre*, which also ran north-south between the present-day Denon and Richelieu pavilions. On its west side, occupying therefore the western half of the pyramid, was a magnificent Renaissance mansion called *Hôtel de Longueville*, which once belonged to Louis XIV and Louis XV. Could this be the *Grand Hôtel du Roi*, said to have been in the Place du Carrousel between the Palais-Royal and the Quai du Louvre, where John Adams lived with his wife Abigail and son John Quincy Adams when he was the American Commissioner in Paris in 1784-5? His own description of it certainly makes this seem likely. *'The Grand Hôtel du Roi, Place du Carrousel, where I had apartments, was situated at the confluence of so many streets, that it was a kind of thoroughfare.'* And if this was indeed the site of the *Grand Hôtel du Roi*, that means two American presidents have lived within this glass wonderland that stands on what is now one of the most visited spots in the capital. It was a spot that was little appreciated by John Adams, however, who recalled with horror his days in *'the putrid streets of Paris'*, living in what sounded like the lodgings from hell. *'A constant stream of carriages was rolling by it over the pavements for one-and-twenty hours out of the twenty-four. From two o'clock to five in the morning there was something like stillness and silence, but all the other one-and-twenty hours was a constant roar, like incessant rolls of thunder.'* We think of traffic noise as a modern phenomenon, but *Rue Saint-Thomas du Louvre* could obviously compete with any present-day city street.

Next door, on the north side of the *Hôtel de Longueville* (between the pyramid and the Richelieu pavilion) was another grand house reputed to be the birthplace of the art of conversation. It belonged to the Marquis de Rambouillet, whose wife, Cathérine de Vivonne, held a *Salon* under the name *Arthénice* (an anagram of Cathérine) in her celebrated blue chamber where the cream of the 17th-century literati gathered regularly to purify the French language and invent courtesy. This house was later sold to the Duc d'Orléans, future Philippe-Egalité - not exactly the doyen of good manners - who used it to stable his horses. In 1785 another part of the house was turned into a dance-hall called *Le Vauxhall d'Hiver*, which remained open during the Revolution under the name *Le Bal du Panthéon*. If you stand by the entrance to the grand pyramid and look at the inside, to your left you will see stairs going down to the museum. Just over two centuries ago you would have seen people dancing here at the *Bal du Panthéon*. If you look to the right there is an escalator, where perhaps you might have seen John and Abigail Adams having a quiet dinner in the *Grand Hôtel du Roi*. Well, probably not so quiet.

Rue Saint-Thomas du Louvre extended north all the way to the Place du Palais-Royal where you found the famous *Café de la Régence*, and at its south end it met *rue des Orties*, which ran alongside the north facade of the *Grande-Galerie* of the Louvre. This was an extremely old street, an ancient tow path that had been there long before the *Grande-Galerie* was constructed, and had buildings only on its north side. These included a church, a college, and a large mansion called the *Hôtel de Matignon*, part of which was destroyed by Henri IV when he built his 'gallery along the water'. Behind this house, parallel with *rue des Orties*, was another small street called *rue du Doyenné* which stood where you now see the wing that links the Denon and Mollien pavilions (look at the plan to see this more clearly). Balzac's description of *rue du Doyenné* in 1838 suggests that by then the Carrousel quarter had lost some of the lively and heterogeneous charm that it had in previous centuries. *'A sombre and deserted block where the inhabitants were probably ghosts, for you hardly ever see anyone...these houses are enveloped in an eternal shadow by the high galleries of the Louvre, which is blackened on this side by the north wind. The darkness, the silence, the icy air...all contribute to making these houses like crypts, tombs for the living.'* Twelve years later the street seemed to have recovered some of its vivacity, for it was the site of a second-hand art market, and if you are an art-lover, you will be amazed to know that here you could find, in good condition and at bargain prices, canvasses by the likes of Boucher and Fragonard being sold on stalls in the open air! Having been supplanted by the Neoclassicism of Jacques Louis David and the artistic fashions that came after him, the works of these great 18th-century masters had gone out of favour and lost much of their original value.

PLACE DU CARROUSEL.

PYRAMIDS.

The main entrance of the *Hôtel de Longueville* opened out on to *rue Saint-Thomas du Louvre*, and its courtyard and gardens stretched westwards up to the *Place du Carrousel* (level with the Lesdiguières pavilion, which you see just after the Mollien pavilion, but set back closer to the Seine, for it was part of the 'Galerie on the Water'). Directly opposite Lesdiguières is the Rohan pavilion, and between these two pavilions was another street, *rue Saint-Nicaise*, running north-south along the eastern side of the *Place du Carrousel*. (This is all much clearer when you look at the plan!) ➡From the Denon pavilion, walk diagonally across to the Turgot pavilion passing in front of the grand pyramid built by the Chinese American architect Ieoh Ming Pei. You have probably decided by now whether you number amongst those who love or those who hate this controversial pyramid, but if you belong to the latter group, you might feel just a little better to know that there is a historical precedent, for this is not the first pyramid to be built here. In fact Parisian city planners seem to have had 'pyramania' for some time now, for Pei's creations have brought to eight the total number of triangular monuments that have graced the capital's horizon. Pei is the fourth designer to build one (he built five, in fact, counting the four small ones), and you have just walked across the site of the pyramid that preceded Pei's, constructed in 1888 in honour of the politician Léon Gambetta. Standing where the elegant garden of the *Hôtel de Longueville* used to be, this gigantic structure was by all accounts a lamentably unaesthetic achievement - and they had plans to put up other even uglier ones in the new Carrousel gardens, plans that were fortunately never carried out. If you are of a certain age, you may have seen the Gambetta pyramid, for it stayed here until 1954. The first time a pyramid was built in the Place du Carrousel, however, was a century earlier than the Gambetta disaster, but it stood in a different place, which you will come to in a little while.

A Near Assassination.

➡From the Turgot pavilion walk to the main road that traverses the Place du Carrousel - the roundabout will be on your left - and you will be standing in the middle of the former *rue Saint-Nicaise*, where on the west side was a building used during the Revolution by the Paris *Opéra* as a school of dance, and for the fabrication of stage sets, and opposite, on the east side, was the house where Arthénice held her courteous conversations. This house was later called *Hôtel de Crussol-Uzès*, and housed the Duc d'Orléans' stables right up to the Revolution. Also on *rue Saint-Nicaise*, but on the other side of the roundabout from where you are standing, was the *Hôtel d'Elbeuf*, home of the deputy Jean-Jacques Cambacérès when he became Second Consul in 1800. Cambacérès was gay, and quite openly so for the time, and would always go for an after-dinner promenade with his friends in the Tuileries Gardens, often watched with great interest by groups of less liberal-minded walkers.

Where you are standing right now, on the north part of the former *rue Saint-Nicaise*, would have been a dangerous place to stand on Christmas Eve 1800. You might have had only a few moments to live. At 8 o'clock that evening the First Consul, Napoléon Bonaparte, came out of his new home in the Tuileries Palace to go to the Opera. Just as his carriage turned left out of the *Place du Carrousel* into *rue Saint-Nicaise*, two royalist conspirators detonated several barrels of gunpowder mixed with scrap iron. The deadly ammunition had been hidden in a cartload of straw that stood unnoticed by the wall of the *Hôtel de Longueville* garden - dangerously near to where you are standing. The explosion shook the entire neighbourhood, damaging many of the surrounding houses, killing several innocent people, but missing its primary target, who arrived at the performance late but unharmed. Napoléon's incredible sang-froid was recounted by his private secretary, who describes how on entering the Opera, Napoléon *'seated himself, according to custom, in front of the box. The eyes of all present were fixed upon him, and he appeared perfectly calm and self-possessed. Lauriston, as soon as he saw me, came to my box, and told me that the First Consul, on his way to the opera, had narrowly escaped being assassinated in rue St. Nicaise by the explosion of a barrel of gunpowder, the blast of which had shattered the windows of his carriage. "Within ten seconds after our escape,"* added Lauriston, *"the coachman having turned the corner of rue St Honoré, stopped to take the First Consul's orders; and he coolly said, "To the opera."'* (Bourrienne, 1829)

A ROYAL DEPARTURE.

➥Cross the road and go through the last archway to your right, then turn left, walk along rue de Rivoli and stop at rue de l'Echelle. On the site of this junction, where you now see the endless traffic of rue de Rivoli, there used to be a little square called *Petite Place du Carrousel*. It connected to the Place du Carrousel by a small street, *rue du Carrousel*, which ran parallel with *rue Saint-Nicaise*. On the evening of June 20th 1791 a coach stood here for two hours, while its occupants became more and more agitated and frightened. Inside the coach were the two royal children, Madame Royale and the dauphin, Prince Louis-Charles, with their governess Madame de Tourzel, and in the driver's seat sat the romantic figure of Count Axel de Fersen, Marie-Antoinette's devoted admirer, who had arranged a daring but badly organized escape that night for the royal family. After taking the carriage out of the Tuileries Palace and driving by way of the quay, the *Place Louis XV* (Concorde), rue Saint-Honoré and rue de l'Echelle, Fersen ended up here in the *Petite Place du Carrousel*. He had arranged to meet up here with Louis XVI and Marie-Antoinette, who were to come to the assigned meeting-place separately on foot. Madame Royale, who was 12 years old at the time, later told the story of this unnerving experience.

Count Axel de Fersen and the royal party waited anxiously for more than two hours before Marie-Antoinette managed to find her way to where the carriage was parked. This attempted escape would eventually end with the arrest of the king in Varennes. (Author's private collection)

'We entered the coach, Madame de Tourzel, my brother and I. Monsieur de Fersen was the coachman. Not to attract suspicion we took several turns round the city. Finally we returned to the Petit-Carrousel...My brother had settled down on the floor of the coach under Madame de Tourzel's skirts. We saw Monsieur de La Fayette pass - he had been to see the king ceremonially to bed - and we remained there waiting for a long hour, without knowing what was happening. Never has time appeared to pass more slowly. Madame de Tourzel was travelling under the name of the Baroness de Korff. My mother was the governess of her children, and called her-

self Madame Rochet; my father was the valet-de-chambre, Durand; my aunt, a companion, Rosalie; my brother and myself the two daughters of Madame de Korff, with the names of Amélie and Aglaé. At last, after an hour, I saw a woman walking round the coach. I was afraid we had been discovered; but I was reassured when the coachman opened the carriage door and it was my aunt. She had escaped alone with one of her attendants. Entering the coach, she trod on my brother who was on the floor, but he was brave enough not to cry out. She assured us that all was quiet and that my father and mother would be coming soon.' (Tannahill, 1966)

The king arrived shortly afterwards, but they had to wait another hour for the arrival of Marie-Antoinette and her bodyguard, neither of whom was familiar with the winding streets of the Carrousel area, and had got completely lost. Once the queen was safely inside, everyone breathed a sigh of relief, Fersen took the reins and pointed the carriage in the direction of the Saint-Martin gate. The royal family's attempt to escape is famous mostly for its failure, and in August of the following year, when the monarchy was finally overthrown, it was in this little square that federal and local troops assembled in preparation for their attack on the Tuileries. On the other side of the wall that separated the *Petite Place du Carrousel* from the palace's *Cour des Suisses,* they could see the royal troops preparing their defence.

A VIEW ON THE PAST.

➡ You should now return directly to the Carrousel garden by going through the entrance of the Musée des Arts Decoratifs. As you go through this museum and back into the gardens, you will be walking through the former *Hôtel de Brionne*, which stood here, next to the *Cour du Manège*, one of the Tuileries Palace courtyards. At number 97 of this courtyard lived the deputy, Georges Couthon, member of the Committee of Public Safety, who by 1792 had been obliged to move from his home in rue Saint-Honoré due to the worsening of his physical condition. Couthon was now in a wheelchair, so needed to be as close as possible to the Committee room, which he could only access by being carried up and down the palace stairs. Right next to Couthon's lodgings was the *Hôtel de Brionne*, where in 1793-4 you found the Committee of General Security busy hunting down suspects and organizing the political policing of the city. Originally created to protect the nation against its internal enemies, this committee became a powerful instrument of the Terror, responsible for hundreds of arrests that usually led to the Tribunal and the guillotine.

➡Coming out of the museum, turn left and walk back towards the Place du Carrousel. As you walk, at first you'll still be inside the Committee of General Security, so be careful not to be arrested, and after that you'll be crossing the former *rue du Carrousel*, a little street that linked the *Petite Place du Carrousel* with the Place du Carrousel. This street would be the other possible site of the *Grand Hôtel du Roi* where John Adams lived, if it was not the *Hôtel de Longueville* that you saw by the pyramid. We can't be certain, since both Place du Carrousel and *rue du Carrousel* have been given as addresses for this house, but I am more inclined to think it was in the Place du Carrousel, since that was a 'confluence of streets', as Adams described it. But listen carefully as you walk - if you hear an American presidential voice complaining about traffic noise, then you will have solved the mystery.

➡Opposite the roundabout, along the northwest side of the square, you will find some stone benches, where you can sit and cast your eyes around today's Place du Carrousel, and if you look hard enough, beyond the streams of traffic and the tourists wandering peacefully between the museum and the gardens, you will see the way the square looked on the pages of history. This vast esplanade has long been a focal point between the Louvre and the Tuileries gardens, and its exact position in the 18th century corresponded to the space between the Arc de Triomphe du Carrousel (to your right) and the large roundabout where bushes surround the top of the inverted pyramid (Pei's slightly smaller glass marvel, which you can see when you go down into the underground shopping arcades).

The first construction to be seen on the site of the Place du Carrousel was a rampart and moat belonging to the *enceinte*, or city wall, built by Charles V in the 14th century. This was the city limit, and beyond the wall was a large expanse of fields containing rich clay used by Parisians to manufacture tiles (*tuiles* in French, from which comes the name *Tuileries*). The rampart stood approximately where you now see the centre of the roundabout, and it was still there at the beginning of the 17th century, when a garden stretched westwards from the moat right up to the Tuileries Palace. This was called *Le Jardin des Tuileries* and was created by Catherine de Medici at the same time as the Tuileries Palace. From 1638, when the rampart was demolished and the moat filled in, the Tuileries Palace was occupied by La Grande Mademoiselle, the daughter of the Duc d'Orléans, and for fourteen years the garden was known as *La Parterre de Mademoiselle*.

THE REAL CARROUSEL.

In June 1662 Louis XIV was still living at the Louvre when he decided to organize a grand festival in honour of the birth of his first child. The highlight of this grandiose affair was a horse-racing tournament - *un carrousel* - and it is from this event that the name of the square originates. The tournament lasted two days and took place on the site of *Mademoiselle*'s garden, which Louis had demolished for the occasion and turned into a vast arena. The space was filled by a square amphitheatre in front of the Tuileries Palace, with a huge semi-circular grandstand holding 15,000 people. The races were in the style of the

Turks, Persians, Indians and Americans, while the Roman quadrille was led by Louis himself, who pranced about in a toga under the admiring eyes of his new mistress, Louise de la Vallière.

THE TRIUMPHAL ARCH.

Later on the arena was separated from the Place du Carrousel by a high wall, and then divided up into three courtyards, the largest being the central *Cour Royale* which formed the principal entrance to the Tuileries Palace. In the centre of the wall was the main doorway, the *Porte Royale*, which was situated where you now see the Arc de Triomphe du Carrousel constructed by Napoléon I in 1808. This archway - an imitation of the Septimius Severus arch in Rome - tends to look a bit lost amid the huge expanse of the present-day Place du Carrousel, but when it was first built it was flanked by decorative wrought-iron railings and formed the grand entrance to the Tuileries Palace. In 1815 the present statue, representing the restoration of the monarchy, was added, replacing the original one that had been put there in 1809. That one had consisted of four horses, pillaged by Bonaparte from the Temple of the Sun in Corinth, pulling a chariot containing a statue of the Emperor himself. This figure was added without Napoléon's knowledge or approval, and when he saw it he reacted in a manner quite uncharacteristic of the man whose name is usually synonymous with megalomania. He fell into a rage and ordered it to be removed from the chariot immediately, shouting at the rather astonished architects, *'It's not up to me to make statues of myself! Let the Victories remain - and the chariot - but leave it empty!'*

A REPUBLICAN FESTIVAL.

During the Revolution the Place du Carrousel continued to bustle with traffic, commerce and pedestrians, especially after May 1793 when the National Convention made its headquarters in the abandoned Tuileries palace. At the beginning of that year the Place du Carrousel was the scene of a zealously republican festival intended to 'purify' the neighbourhood, which was now deemed 'contaminated' by the gambling, prostitution and other vices that flourished in the adjacent Palais-Royal. To this end a 'tree of brotherhood' was planted in the morning in the presence of a delegation of deputies and an immense crowd of patriotic citizens, who all solemnly swore to lay down their lives if necessary for the maintenance of liberty and equality. Then came the festivities, which began with the revolutionary song and dance ritual, the *Carmagnole*, led by the mayor, followed by non-stop dancing that was still going on at 8 o'clock in the evening when the square was suddenly invaded by soldiers. They'd been sent by the Commune with orders to cordon off the area and inspect everyone's identity card. Throughout the entire night people were searched and interrogated, and anyone failing to produce their *carte de citoyen* was arrested on the spot. Terror had not yet been officially made 'the order of the day', but the good republican citizens who ended their festive evening in prison, as well as those who were lucky enough to return to their own homes, must have wondered that night what was becoming of their dreams of liberty.

Conflict and Revolt.

Liberty became an increasingly scarce commodity in Paris as the months went by, and during the later part of the Revolution the Place du Carrousel was frequently the scene of turmoil and revolt. Infuriated mobs passed through it on several occasions prior to invading the Tuileries palace, beginning in June 1792 when the monarchy was humiliated, with a more dramatic repeat-performance the following August when the monarchy was overthrown. In the summer of 1794, when it was the turn of Robespierre to be deposed, the deputy Paul Barras was appointed commander-general of the National Guard, and the first thing he did was to order half the troops of every Paris section to assemble here with a cannon. It was an impressive sight as the 48 section commanders, all patriotic working men, marched into the square followed by their neighbourhood battalion proudly decked out in local colours. It was an army of several thousand that Barras led out of the square that night, on the stroke of midnight, in the pouring rain, towards Robespierre's refuge in the Hôtel-de-Ville.

The Place du Carrousel saw more unrest the following year during the 'Prairial days', when the women of Paris, still hungry for bread despite six years of revolutionary reforms, rose up against the Convention on May 20th. They came in their thousands, from all the city's faubourgs, picking up along the way - sometimes by force - anyone who was standing in a bread queue. They were also joined by hundreds of men as they traversed the capital from all directions, shouting threats and beating drums. It was 2 p.m. by the time they arrived in the Place du Carrousel, they had been marching for nearly two hours, they were tired, they were hungry, and they were ready for revolt. Attached to their red bonnets were tricolour cockades bearing the slogan 'Bread or Death'. Swarming by force through the main gate, across the *Cour Royale*, they then broke into the palace where the National Convention was in session. You will see what happened later when you come to the site of the Tuileries palace, where this dramatic event took place.

On either side of the *Cour Royale* were two smaller courtyards. The one on the north side, which would have been directly behind you (if you are still sitting on the bench in the northwest part of the Place du Carrousel), was the *Cour des Suisses*, often referred to as the *Cour des Ecuries* since it was separated from the *Cour Royale* by the king's stables. On the south side of the *Cour Royale* was the *Cour des Princes*, which you are going to head for now by walking over to the Arc de Triomphe. Stop before going through the arch, and look around. This was where the main entrance to the palace stood, and on the other side of it was the *Cour Royale*, the Tuileries palace's main courtyard that two centuries ago was a theatre of popular action, bloodshed and horror. It was through here that an infuriated crowd surged on June 20th 1792 led by Santerre, the Marquis de Saint-Hurugue and the flamboyant Théroigne de Mericourt, three very different revolutionary leaders but all with the same objective that day, to intimidate and humiliate the king. Before forcing open the main gate into the courtyard, Santerre turned towards the thousands of people who had gathered here from all the faubourgs of the city, and shouted rabble-raising slogans inciting them to invade the royal residence. Once inside the *Cour Royale* the crowd rushed towards the entrance, hacked down the door with an axe and entered the palace.

Less than two months later the crowds returned to the Tuileries, this time with the more serious intention of forcing the king to leave his palace. It was August 10th, and the French monarchy had only a few hours of existence left. Inside the palace the king and queen were wavering between staying and defending their cause, or heeding the advice of those who knew better and taking refuge in the National Assembly. While this agonizing decision was being made, the Place du Carrousel was filling up with large numbers of soldiers, some of whom had succeeded in entering the *Cour Royale* thanks to the complicity of the *gendarmes*, who displayed their hats on the end of their bayonets in a flippant gesture of indifference. Cannons were dragged into the square and placed in front of the main gates and the *Suisses* (the royal troops) retreated into the palace, where the insurgents had succeeded in getting as far as the grand staircase.

All of a sudden there was a thunderous burst of gunfire as cannonballs rained down on the *Cour Royale* from every doorway and window of the palace, killing ten people immediately and wounding numerous others. Many of those in the courtyard beat a hasty retreat back into the Place du Carrousel as 200 *Suisses* charged out of the palace and attacked them. But then suddenly the square was swarming with people. Troops had arrived from the Faubourg Saint-Antoine, thousands of them, side by side with a multitude of armed citizens. Fighting broke out in earnest as cannons roared, the air filled with smoke and the insurgents battled with bayonets and sabres until they were at the palace door, where a valiant group of *Suisses* fired non-stop to the last round of ammunition, in a vain attempt to stop the invasion. For most of them this was their last heroic act in defence of the monarchy, and their fallen bodies joined the piles of corpses, both rebel and royalist, that were strewn all over the courtyard. Once the entrance was taken, the now frenzied crowd rushed into the palace.

More Royal Departures.

You'll find out what happened during these two frightening invasions of the Tuileries when you come to the site of the palace itself. ➥But now you're going to brave the smoke and carnage of August 10th 1792 by walking through the Arc de Triomphe. Once on the other side you are standing in the *Cour Royale*, where on this fateful day you would have been confronted by a veritable war zone, with bodies piled up all around you. Frenzied rebels armed with axes and sabres might be running straight for you, so before it all gets too close for comfort, ➥let's continue on to the *Cour des Princes*, which must be haunted by many royal ghosts, for the palace apartments looked out directly on to it. ➥To get to this courtyard, walk southwards and stand, with your back to the Arc de Triomphe, at the entrance to the little square shrub garden. The wall separating the three Tuileries courtyards from the Place du Carrousel ran north-south at about this point, and going off to your right was the wall separating the *Cour Royale* from the *Cour des Princes*. ➥Turn right into the path that goes around the garden (the second one just before the steps) and you will be walking along that wall, and when you turn left as you continue round the path you will be in the *Cour des Princes*, which is rich in memories of the three years that Louis XVI and his family spent in residence at the Tuileries. On April 18th 1791 you would have seen a carriage standing here. Inside sat the royal family, waiting for authorization to leave for Saint-Cloud, where Louis hoped to celebrate the Easter Mass with a non-juring priest. A number of passers-by noticed Lafayette in the group of people gathered around the carriage, and stopped by the courtyard entrance to see what was going on. The public was still angered by the recent emigration of Louis's two aunts, and some suspected Lafayette of wishing to help the royal family escape. Restif de la Bretonne was among the onlookers.

> *'Lafayette's policy had been to let everyone approach...at that time I still had confidence in Lafayette, believing him to be a partisan of the Revolution...he and the mayor exhorted the people to let the monarch leave, but it fell on deaf ears. A man shouted "Come on, let's unharness the carriage!" Lafayette gave commands; people were threatening him. He was furious, as much as a blond man can be; but you could see that he was champing at the bit. "Ha! You let the aunts leave," cried one man, "but you won't let the king leave!" Lafayette went to talk to the coachman. It was then that the cries and curses against the fugitive aunts doubled. Louis was obliged to descend from the carriage and return to his apartments. It was then that Louis made this admirable statement: "If it must cost even one drop of blood, I will not leave." However, he had much harsher words for Lafayette, for, having agreed to a Constitution that gave liberty to all, he was shocked to be deprived of his own. He lashed out with bitter irony at the agitated General: "It's up to you, Sir, to see what should be done to make your Constitution work."'* (Restif de la Bretonne, 1986)

This letter to a newspaper in March of the same year shows that Louis was not alone in being deprived of his liberty, and gives a hint of the dictatorship to come. *'Dear Sirs, I am outraged by a recent experience that inspires hatred of the odious despotism that is infiltrating the nation. For the past month, being in Paris on business, I have been staying in a hotel, where I was most astonished to be woken up at 3 o'clock in the morning by a policeman demanding my name, my civil status, my place of origin, and finally my marriage certificate. I would like to point out that I was sleeping with my wife, whom he threatened to take to the police station if I could not prove immediately that we were legally married. I can assure you I have never witnessed such atrocious tyranny and insolence. If we are obliged to exhibit a passport when we go for a walk, and our marriage certificate when we go to bed with our wives, then I must start to consider living in another country.'* (Rossel, 1982)

It was here in the *Cour des Princes* that the royal couple's desperate flight to Varennes began on the evening of June 21st 1791. At 10.30 p.m. the carriage arrived in the *Cour Royale*, driven by Axel de Fersen, who slipped discreetly into the *Cour des Princes* and went over to four doors that led into a deserted apartment formerly occupied by the emigrated Duc de Villequier, first gentleman of the royal bedchamber. Here he waited, camouflaged in a great-coat and a coachman's hat, ignored by the palace guards who were used to the comings and goings associated with the king's going-to-bed ceremony, which took place at this hour every night and peopled the courtyard with various members of the royal entourage. Fersen was further protected by a row of coaches lined up along the palace façade, masking the furtive scene that took place as he opened one of the doors and brought out the royal children and their governess, led them through into the *Cour Royale* and bundled them into the coach parked in the middle of the courtyard. They were escorted right up to the coach by Marie-Antoinette herself, which was decidedly risky, but perhaps her courage had been boosted by the exhilarating prospect of escape from the nightmare that her life had become - it certainly boosted her audacity, for as she walked back into the palace she could not resist the pleasure of lashing out with her *badine* (switch) at one of the wheels of Lafayette's carriage. Lafayette, who was in the palace at that very moment seeing the king to bed, had never been a favourite of Marie-Antoinette, who thought he was too ambitious and not to be trusted. The public, however, thought he was her favourite, and some rumours even suggested they were lovers.

It was about 11 o'clock when the queen returned across the *Cour des Princes* and went back into the palace to prepare for her own departure. The first to leave was Louis's sister Madame Elisabeth, who crossed both courtyards without any problem in the company of her equerry, her face unrecognisable under the veil of a large hat. Then out came King Louis, who also had no difficulty leaving the palace with his bodyguard, de Malden. Louis even played his role with a degree of panache. Stepping out into the *Cour des Princes* in a brown frock-coat, closely cropped wig and round hat, he walked nonchalantly, cane in hand, into the *Cour Royale*, where he stopped to re-buckle one of his shoes before going out into the Place du Carrousel. It's a miracle he wasn't suspected, for despite 'disguising' himself as a valet, Louis hardly looked any different from usual.

Soon it was the turn of the queen. She left the palace in the company of her personal guard, managing to cross both courtyards without any hitch, and then passed quickly through the main gateway. If you look over to the Arc de Triomphe du Carrousel, where the gateway stood, you might catch sight of this unfortunate queen, in her grey silk dress, black coat and huge veiled hat, hurrying anxiously through the wooden doors into the anonymity of the Place du Carrousel. As they reached the other side of the square they suddenly heard a loud clatter behind them, and a carriage, lit with torches and escorted by guards, rolled past them. The terrified queen, recognizing the carriage, jumped into a doorway so as not to be recognized by its occupant, Lafayette, who had finished his royal bedtime duties and was on his way home.

The incident threw the queen into a panic, and with one wrong turning she and her companion got hopelessly lost in the confusion of dark and unfamiliar streets that lay directly at her own doorstep. Desperate not to attract attention, they wandered for nearly two hours past churches, shops, warehouses, noble mansions, and the sort of dwellings that Marie-Antoinette, in better days, might have considered suitable for her animals. They roamed through streets she had never seen before - *Orties, Fromentau, Doyenné* - names that were foreign to her cloistered experience - then they were in *rue du Carrousel*, and suddenly there was the carriage, and her beloved Fersen in the driver's seat, waiting to carry his queen to safety.

THE GUILLOTINE.
➡ Walk into the centre of the shrub garden, where you now see a lovely statue by Maillol called 'Night', marking approximately the site of the main entrance to the *Cour des Princes*. This was a simple square doorway in the wall leading from the courtyard out into the street, which was quite wide at this point.
➡ To get into this street, leave the middle of the shrub garden by taking the path to the east, and stop at the point where it joins the path leading to the circular lawn. You are now standing on the spot where, on August 21st 1792, the guillotine ended the life of Louis David Collenot d'Angremont, the administrative secretary of the National Guard, accused of royalist conspiracy. This was the first day that the guillotine appeared in front of the entrance to the *Cour des Princes*, and it remained here for nine months, being moved only on two occasions to the Place de la Concorde, once to decapitate the royal diamond thieves and later for the execution of Louis XVI.

For Collenot d'Angremont's execution, which was carried out in the evening by torchlight, a sizeable crowd of spectators began pushing its way from the Place du Carrousel, renamed *Place de la Réunion*, down the street towards the scaffold. It was an anxious day for the executioner Charles-Henri Sanson, for he had been arrested himself six days earlier, brought out of his prison to carry out d'Angremont's sentence, and returned immediately afterwards. Following the overthrow of the monarchy eleven days earlier, Sanson had been incarcerated by the new authorities for having been an employee of the former despot, and now faced the possibility of becoming a victim of his own machine. Four days later, on August 25th, he was brought out again, this time to execute a royalist journalist named Barnabé Farmian de Rozoy, condemned for publishing monarchist ideas in his newspaper *Gazette de Paris*. At the time of the escape to Varennes, De Rozoy, who was the first journalist to be guillotined by the new regime, had fearlessly offered his own life in exchange for the king's liberty. He died bravely, walking with dignity past the flickering torches that illuminated the guillotine, declaring '*A royalist like me does well to die on Saint-Louis's Day.*'

Sanson came out of prison on several occasions during the month of August for various executions, including one that was the most tragic of his career. It was only two days after de Rozoy's execution, and the story was recounted by an Englishman, John Moore, who was among the spectators that day. '*On the 27th of August three men had their heads cut off for printing false assignats. After the execution it is the custom to hold up the head of the victim and show it to the public. While carrying out this tradition, the executioner's son went too near the edge of the scaffold and fell. He died instantly before his father's eyes.*' The victim, Charles-Henri Sanson's younger son, Gabriel, died from a fractured skull in front of a stunned crowd, who had the unique experience of seeing the imperturbable Sanson standing on the scaffold with tears streaming down his face. He never really got over this terrible event, which produced in Sanson, who had royalist leanings to begin with, a loathing for the revolutionary justice that had taken his son from him at just 23 years old. Later when the Terror obliged him to execute at such an alarming rate, it is said that he took more pleasure in cutting off revolutionary heads than those of the nobility. After the death of Gabriel Sanson, a barrier was put up around the edge of the scaffold.

After the dramatic accident when Sanson's younger son Gabriel slipped and fell to his death, a barrier was put up around the scaffold. Gabriel was just 23, and Sanson never got over the tragedy. (Author's private collection)

On September 25th a venerable and eccentric old man of 72 by the name of Jacques Cazotte, appreciated throughout his life for the charm of his conversation, was brought to this spot to be guillotined. He was one of the first victims of the Tribunal's new chief, Fouquier-Tinville. In his younger days, as Controller of the island of Martinique, Cazotte fought bravely to defend his country when the fort of Saint-Pierre was attacked by the English. But literature was his real passion, and when he returned to France he lived on an inheritance and devoted his life to writing, publishing in 1772 his major work, a fantasy called *Le Diable Amoureux* (The Amorous Devil). His translations of the Arabic fables 'A Thousand and One Nights' are less memorable. After joining a sect known as the *Martinistes* in 1775, his ideas and writings became increasingly strange, and it is said that by the time the Revolution began Cazotte was marginally mad. He was, however, in no confusion about his political loyalties, remaining a staunch royalist who considered the Revolution to be the work of the devil. He embarked on a prolific correspondence with the Court, in which he poured out his hatred for the new regime and offered numerous ideas for the escape of the royal family. These letters were eventually intercepted, leading to the arrest and imprisonment of both Cazotte and his daughter Elisabeth, who saved them both from the September massacres by her desperate pleas for mercy. Having thus escaped popular justice, Cazotte was soon re-arrested and brought here to the *Place de la Réunion*, where he became a victim of official justice, declaring to the crowd, *'I die as I have lived, faithful to my God and my king.'*

ANOTHER PYRAMID.

At the beginning of May 1793 the guillotine was removed from here and taken to the Place de la Concorde. The fact that the National Convention had just moved into new headquarters in the Tuileries Palace probably had something to do with this decision, for few deputies would have appreciated having the sinister death machine permanently on their doorstep. Just over a month later Marat was assassinated and a monument to his memory was built here on the same spot where the guillotine had carried out the revolutionary justice so dear to Marat's heart. This monument took the form of a wooden pyramid surmounted by an inscription reading *'To the spirit of Marat, 13 July Year I. From the depths of his black tomb he makes traitors tremble. A treacherous hand has taken him from the love of the people.'* In front of it stood the famous bath in which Marat had been sitting when the treacherous hand struck him down, and his desk, on which was placed a bust of the dead hero and a selection of some of his most bloodthirsty writings. This pyramid was dismantled after 9 *Thermidor*, and although it was the first one to be built in the Place du Carrousel, it was not the first one to be seen in Paris. There had been one before it, which you'll come to soon.

The Tuileries Palace.

The End of the Tuileries.

➥You should now leave the shrub garden, walk back to the Arc de Triomphe and turn left along the central pathway leading toward the Tuileries gardens. You are now following in the footsteps of all the soldiers, *sans-culottes* and angry women who ran across the *Cour Royale* to invade the Tuileries Palace, which would have been directly in front of you. There is no palace to invade any more, for it was demolished in 1884, after having been seriously burned by the Paris Commune on May 23rd 1871. This occasion was the very last time that violent rebels took this path through the palace courtyard, a path where nowadays leisurely processions of visitors walk side by side with a veritable multitude of revolutionary ghosts.

On that last day of action in the *Cour Royale* in 1871, the intruders were less numerous, and much quieter than their revolutionary predecessors. Just before 9 p.m. they brought into the courtyard five wagons containing gunpowder, liquid tar, turpentine and petrol. Then on the orders of the three principal organizers, Jules Bergeret, Victor Bénot and Etienne Boudin, they scattered the chemicals all over the palace and ignited them. Within minutes the building was a smoke-filled inferno, and in the early hours of the morning Bénot and Boudin led another group who set fire to the Palais-Royal and the Louvre library. It took two days for the Tuileries fire to be completely extinguished, by which time the palace looked like a huge expanse of blackened wall. Bénot and Boudin were arrested and later shot for their role in the siege, but Bergeret managed to escape, first to the isle of Jersey, and then to New York, where he remained until his death in 1905.

THE BEGINNING OF THE TUILERIES.

So where exactly was this palace, whose name is associated in most people's minds with nothing more than a beautiful public garden? ➡Walk along the central pathway and stop directly between the Marsan and Flore pavilions. The palace spanned the long space between these two pavilions - if you're facing the Tuileries Gardens the Marsan pavilion is to your right and the Flore to your left, and you are standing on the site of the domed Central Pavilion with its two connecting wings on either side. ➡Try and find a wall, or somewhere to sit (this terrace needs some benches!) so you can read about the history of the vanished Tuileries Palace, which some say had a curse on it from the start.

In 1564 Catherine de Medici decided to have a new residence that would be independent of the Louvre, and she asked the architect Philibert Delorme to build it for her. But eight years later an ominous horoscope from her astrologer, Cosimo Ruggieri, led Catherine to abandon her plans to live in the new palace that Delorme and his successor, Jean Bullant had created for her. She chose instead to reside in another house built by Bullant, leaving the Tuileries empty and abandoned until 1595, when Henri IV united it with the Louvre by constructing his *Grande Galerie*. After Henri's death the palace was abandoned yet again for half a century, and it was under Louis XIV that it was finally completed. The finished product suffered somewhat from a lack of architectural unity, and was not admired by everyone - an English observer on the eve of the Revolution described it as *'the vilest possible jumble of antique and Gothic, perfectly, utterly bad.'*

The first person to live in the Tuileries Palace was the Duchesse de Montpensier, the *Grande Mademoiselle* who created the original garden in the Place du Carrousel. She was the richest heiress in Europe, so naturally expected to marry a king. But when all her attempts at a good match failed, she threw herself into *Fronde* politics instead, taking up the cause of the Prince de Condé, who repaid her by throwing her out of the Tuileries Palace. She would not be the first person to be forced to leave this palace in a hurry. After the Duchesse de Montpensier came Louis XIV, who spent only three years here before leaving it to another 50 years of emptiness. Louis XV took up residence here at the age of 5, and later the Spanish Infanta, Louis's 4-year-old fiancée, also arrived and was safely cloistered in the *Petite-Galerie* of the Louvre. The riding school (*Manège*) that was built for her on the north side of the Tuileries gardens would later become the seat of revolutionary government.

After six years Louis XV also left the Tuileries abandoned, this time for 67 years, during which time the palace suffered the same fate as the Louvre, being invaded by an assortment of people ranging from aristocrats to artisans. They inflicted the same abuse on the buildings as the residents of the Louvre, even going as far as building new staircases, and laundry was hung out to dry from all its magnificent windows. There were some people who spent a huge chunk of their life there, like the Comtesse de Marsan, who has left her name to the pavilion which she occupied for so many years. While living there she was given a post as royal governess, counting among her young charges the future Louis XVI, whose arrival here in October 1789 escorted by a crowd of Parisian women probably occasioned the countess's hasty departure. Territorial wars were common. Numerous plans still exist from this period showing how certain occupants were continually trying to steal a few precious metres from each other, often provoking ferocious arguments, and disturbing more peaceable residents like the abbot who resided without complaint between two cupboards.

The palace had a theatre, occupied by the Paris Opera in 1763 when their premises on rue Saint-Honoré burned down. They left after seven years and were replaced by the Comédie-Française, who stayed for another twelve while waiting for the completion of their new theatre at Odéon. This was all brought to an end, however, on October 6th 1789, when the women of Paris brought '*the baker, the baker's wife and the little baker's boy*' back from Versailles and installed them in the Tuileries Palace. Every last one of the palace's occupants had been cleared out by 10 o'clock that night, when the royal family arrived at their new home with an entourage of courtiers, staff and servants that totalled 677 people.

The Central Pavilion - Before 1789.
Le Concert Spirituel. If you were standing directly between the Marsan and Flore pavilions you would be in the middle of the Central Pavilion of the Tuileries. There were no squatters in this section of the palace, and from 1725 regular concerts were organized by a composer and musician from the royal chapel named Anne Danican - who was a man, despite the name, which is probably why he went by his surname Philidor (he was older brother to the famous chess player, François-André Danican Philidor). Authorization to hold the concerts was given to Philidor on the condition that they contained no profane music and took place only on Sundays and during religious festivals, so as not to compete with the Opera. Hence the name *Le Concert Spirituel* given to this regular event that was the first private enterprise in the sphere of musical performance in France.

Although Philidor was musically gifted, his objectives in this project were purely commercial, seeing himself as an artistic director, working in conjunction with a sponsoring partner who took care of the business side. But it was aid from the State, in the form of grants and rent waivers, that enabled these concerts to survive financially until the beginning of the Revolution, and even this failed to stave off the numerous law suits that regularly besieged the company. Artistically, however, it was a great success. In addition to boosting Parisian influence on the international music scene, it gave regular work to composers, musicians and performers, who enjoyed a certain cachet in belonging to this new cultural fringe. The concerts attracted many of the great names in European music, such as Haydn, whose symphonies held a monopoly on the first part of the programme. Corelli played here, as well as Mozart, who even composed a new work in honour of the occasion, and Marie-Antoinette often numbered amongst the rich and famous in the audience.

THE NORTH WING OF THE TUILERIES PALACE.
THE SALLE DES MACHINES. ➻Right now you are sitting or standing somewhere at the end of the central path where it intersects with a wide esplanade, the Terrasse des Tuileries. Turn right on this (when facing the Tuileries Gardens) and walk towards the pavilion where the Comtesse de Marsan camped out for so many years. As you walk look to your right, for you are passing by what used to be the north wing of the palace, and it is difficult these days to imagine the grandeur and turbulence that once characterized this empty space, now filled by a beautiful lawn. Most of the north wing was occupied by the *Salle des Machines*, a theatre that got its name from the stage sets and machinery constructed there in the early 18th century and which took up about two-thirds of the wing (the section closest to the Marsan pavilion). The actual auditorium was in the smaller section nearest the Central Pavilion.

➻I'm afraid there are no benches here either, but you can sit on the wall again, and if you look hard enough you'll be able to see what happened more than two centuries ago on this peaceful stretch of grass where the palace once stood. If the weather is good you can sit on the grass and be part of it. You'll see the grand ball held in honour of the arrival of the Spanish Infanta, Louis XV's fiancée, when dazzling crystal chandeliers turned the hall into a wonderland of reflected light. There, in the middle of the hall, sitting alone on his throne, is the very young King Louis, bedecked in precious stones. You can see him rise to greet the 3-year-old princess, bowing gallantly to the tiny figure standing alone and bewildered in the midst of all this splendour. And then, if you keep looking, you'll see Louis offer his hand to a certain Mademoiselle du Charolais for the opening dance, provoking shock-waves of jealousy throughout the hall. Louis was still only 11, but already an object of matrimonial ambition for the young girls at Court. The tiny Infanta, clearly too young to produce an heir, was eventually shipped back to Spain, and Louis married a Polish princess.

A few years later the architect and theatrical scene painter, Jean-Nicolas Servandoni, organized a series of spectacular mime shows and dioramas in the *Salle des Machines*. The first one gave a three-dimensional view of the interior of Saint Peter's Cathedral in Rome, while others offered the audience various glimpses into ancient history and mythology. But the shows were always criticized for lack of movement, so Servandoni tried bringing horses and calves on to the stage to liven up the proceedings. This didn't work either, and merely served to infuriate the safety inspectors.

In 1784 the *Concerts Spirituels* were transferred here from the Central Pavilion. But by this time so many profane works had edged their way into the programme that, according to the ever-cynical Sebastien Mercier, the only thing that distinguished them from the Opera was the costumes. During his five-year stay in Paris the American Minister, Thomas

Jefferson, was an habitué of the *Concerts Spirituels*, which always began at 6.30 p.m. with a couple of Haydn symphonies followed by a varied assortment of shorter pieces. But in October 1789 the royal family moved into the Tuileries Palace, bringing to an end 64 years of *Concerts Spirituels*, the last one of which took place in November of that year.

When the Opera burned down the entire company moved temporarily into the *Salle des Machines*, which was greatly enlarged by putting a new amphitheatre in the space that up to then had been occupied by the machinery (closest to the Marsan pavilion). In 1770 the Opera left and the Comédie-Française took their place. If you are still looking through the empty space into the past, you will see the first ever performances of Caron de Beaumarchais's 'Barber of Seville', which took place here on February 23rd 1775 amidst a public hue and cry over some of its more controversial passages - most of which had been taken out by the royal censors. Fast forward three years, and in one of the elegantly curved boxes you will see the puckish figure of Voltaire, bowing to his fellow spectators as a young lady places a crown of laurels on his head. This gallant ceremony was arranged by the actors of the Comédie-Française to honour the literary giant whose plays formed such an important part of their repertoire. Frantic applause followed, continuing for twenty minutes, and at the end of the evening's performance a bust of Voltaire was brought on to the stage as an actress recited a few more lines in homage to the great writer, whose elfin face was all smiles.

Marie-Antoinette was a frequent visitor to the Comédie-Française, and was in fact the cause of their departure, which was ordered by Louis XVI in 1782. He did this under intense pressure from the queen, who wanted more theatrical diversions in Paris to get her away from the constraints of Court life at Versailles. So the *Salle des Machines* was quickly taken over by an Italian Comic-Opera troupe sponsored by Monsieur, Comte de Provence, but in reality it was Marie-Antoinette's hairdresser, Léonard-Alexis Autié, who received the official funding and authorization to manage the new theatre. At the time Léonard was more well-known as the creator of the queen's spectacular *coiffures* than as an impresario. He specialized in *poufs*, wire and wool frames raised to ridiculous heights, solidified with pomade, and then decorated like a theatre stage with an assortment of topical scenes created with objects, ribbons, fruit, flowers or feathers. Léonard stopped at nothing to reproduce on Marie-Antoinette's head the latest topic of chit-chat in Parisian society, from military victories to innoculation against smallpox.

Perhaps it was this experience of miniature set design that gave Léonard a taste for theatre management. But it was his professional association with the queen, and the royal protection that came with it, that enabled him to have use of the *Salle des Machines* - although he had to pay compensation to the Royal Academy, who were not happy about the competition from this new playhouse, known as *Théâtre de Monsieur*. Monsieur's troupe introduced a new level of frivolity into the theatrical life of the *Salle des Machines*, which for a while became a playground for Marie-Antoinette and her flighty friends. But in October 1789 the royal family were brought from Versailles to live in Paris, and the revolutionary government had other plans for the *Salle des Machines*. Soon the storm-clouds broke over the Tuileries Palace. The curtain fell, the actors disappeared, and the Revolution created a new stage, that of the scaffold, where the king, the queen and the hairdresser would this time all figure among the cast.

LE PALAIS-NATIONAL.
THE NATIONAL CONVENTION. Three days after Louis XVI was overthrown it was proposed that the new National Convention

should move from its rather dilapidated headquarters in the *Manège* and take up residence in the abandoned palace. By the time Louis was executed five months later, the Tuileries Palace had become the *Palais-National*, the Central Pavilion the *Pavillon de l'Unité*, and the Comtesse de Marson's old home was now the *Pavillon de la Liberté*. The *Salle des Machines* was chosen as the Convention's new home, with work already under way to decorate and adapt the former theatre to the needs of a political assembly that was every bit as theatrical as the previous occupants. They had to be, for the acoustics were appalling in their new premises, where, declared Danton, '*one needs the lungs of Stentor to be heard!*' Danton was pretty stentorian himself, but even he had difficulty at times, particularly towards the end of a session, when lack of oxygen in the unventilated hall left most of the Assembly faint and feeble - or asleep. Two months after their first session on May 10th 1793, following complaints from a number of wilting deputies, they tried to improve the air by placing a large urn of water and willow leaves at each corner of the hall. The continual evaporation, in addition to spraying the courtyard with water four times a day would - they hoped - refresh the hall and render the deputies more dynamic. In January 1795 work began on improving the acoustics - carried out at night so as not to interrupt the work of the government - and at the end of that year eight brick ventilators were built in the room below the *Salle des Machines*. The Convention didn't reap much benefit from all this, however, for it was dissolved in October of the same year and replaced by the Directory government.

The National Convention was a busy place. Deputies came and went at all hours, and the normal working day was long and tiring, consisting of eight hours in the Assembly every day, including Sundays, and 'exceptional' sessions in the evening. The exception quickly became the rule in the case of evening sessions, and if you add committee work, meetings, and replying to up to 30 letters a day, you soon had a very exhausted government. '*Never*', declared Desmoulins, '*has any people condemned its legislators to make laws like a blind horse turning a millstone night and day.*' Deputies would often be seen sleeping on camp-beds in some small committee room, like Billaud-Varenne, whose house in rue Saint-André-des-Arts was too far after a long night of debate, and Saint-Just had a magnificent bed installed that was the envy of his colleagues.

Saint-Just, who did everything with style, was always impeccably dressed and well-known for his rather flamboyant earrings. Other deputies - notably the Girondins - kept up a more sober appearance, while a few, like Robespierre, remained faithful to the be-wigged, powdered look of the old regime. Many flaunted the fashionably 'liberated' look of the new age by wearing their shirt open in a provocative style known as *à la Danton* - showing your chest, it seemed, had become a patriotic act. Certain were unique, like Marat, who predictably turned up with long, dirty nails, a filthy open shirt that exposed his diseased skin, leather trousers and the eternal vinegar-soaked handkerchief around his head. As the Terror mounted it became more and more fashionable to look like a *sans-culotte*, so deputies would be seen going about the business of state in the most ridiculous outfits. One of the most popular was the *Carmagnole*, made from the rough striped material used to cover mattresses, and during the winter many deputies would clatter along the corridors of power in clogs. As for red bonnets, it came to a point where there seemed to be more of them in the Tuileries Palace than there were in the Faubourg Saint-Antoine. Even the palace itself had one, an enormous one, sitting in patriotic splendour on top of the dome of the Central Pavilion.

During the time the National Convention met here, the *Salle des Machines* was the scene of dramas more intense and occasionally more horrific than anything that the Opera or the Comédie-Française could have hoped to stage. For over two years its walls, decorated with red bonnets and pikes, sacred symbols of republicanism, resounded to the fiery speeches of Danton and the virtuous logic of Robespierre. Numerous historic laws were passed here, including one on February 4th 1794 that was a pioneer in the fight for racial equality, for it gave liberty and citizenship to all slaves in the French colonies. It was here that the ominous words, '*Terror is the order of the day*', sliced the air like the knife of the guillotine, when on September 5th 1793 an angry crowd invaded the Convention, forcing through this fateful decree that signalled the start of the final and most frightening period of the Revolution. It was during this time that the uncompromising views of the powerful young 'angel of death', Saint-Just, regularly froze the assembled deputies, as he urged them to *'punish not only the traitors, but even those who are indifferent,'* and reminded them that *'what constitutes a republic is the total destruction of everything that is opposed to it.'*

All these lofty speeches and dramatic confrontations took place before the eyes of over a thousand spectators who filed into the public galleries each day, armed with canes and sticks. Anyone could come in, so long as they wore a tri-colour cockade. Some were *tricoteuses* - those same furies who sat by the guillotine cheering and counting the heads as they fell - often paid to come and create 'atmosphere' at the Assembly. In the public gallery the citizens of Paris sat and watched, as the Revolution gradually destroyed itself through factional warfare. From the benches of the immense green-draped amphitheatre successive groups of deputies shouted accusations at their enemies, only to tremble for their own lives later on.

THE END OF THE GIRONDINS. The first of these dramatic watersheds in revolutionary politics was the triumph of the Mountain over the Girondins, 29 of whom, including their leader Brissot, were finally put under arrest on June 2nd 1793, less than a month after the Assembly's first session here. It started on May 31st, when François Hanriot mobilized several columns of armed *sans-culottes*, who descended on the National Convention and demanded that the Girondin deputies be outlawed. There was a repeat performance on June 2nd, when Hanriot brought 80,000 men and 163 cannons to the entrance of the *Palais-National* and once more demanded that the Girondin traitors be handed over. A dramatic scene followed. Some of the deputies who had come out to negotiate with Hanriot tried to calm the agitated crowd. *'What do the people demand?'* asked Hérault de Sechelles with his habitual gentility, *'for the Convention is concerned solely with them and with their happiness.'* Hanriot was not impressed. *'The people have certainly not risen up just to listen to flowery language! They want the traitors arrested,'* he replied, and announced that no deputy would be allowed to leave until the people got what they wanted. *'Seize that rebel!'* shouted Hérault, to which Hanriot riposted, *'Cannons at the ready! To arms, citizens!'* The astonished and terrified deputies looked on in horror, as Marat suddenly left his colleagues and ran over to embrace Hanriot, proclaiming him the saviour of the day. Accompanied by Marat and about a hundred *sans-culottes*, Hanriot entered the Convention to shouts of *'Vive la Montagne!'* and *'Purge the Convention!'* The deputies, lost for words, returned to their seats, and within a few hours the 29 Girondins were all under arrest.

One of the principal Girondins to be outlawed was Jean-Marie Roland, whose wife Manon came to the *Palais-National* twice on the first day of the insurrection in an attempt to save her husband. The first time she found the entrance full of cannons and armed men, but when she returned a few hours later, the stormy session was over, and she tried to find out what had happened from a couple of *sans-culottes* whom she saw leaning against a cannon in front of the palace doorway. *'Oh it was marvellous,'* they exclaimed, *'they all embraced and sang the*

Marseillaise!' When she learned that the Girondins had been put under arrest, she posed so many provocative questions that the two men suddenly interrupted her. *'Who are you, anyway?'* they asked, so aggressively, that Manon beat a hasty retreat. Later on that night she too was arrested .

THE END OF THE HEBERTISTS. After the Girondins it was the turn of the Hébertists and their leader, Jacques-René Hébert, the journalist who wrote under the name of *Le Père Duchesne*. They were denounced in the Convention on March 12th 1794 by Saint-Just, whose position as Robespierre's henchman was making his speeches more and more dreaded, for they generally resulted in arrests. Although Danton supported the persecution of the Hébertists, he walked out of the Convention that day with an uneasy mind, for Saint-Just's denunciation had also hinted ominously at a conspiracy by the *Indulgents*, a faction that included Danton and Desmoulins. Danton soon regained his nerve, and rose to the rostrum a few days later with his usual bravado, imploring everyone not to be frightened by the recent events, which were merely the excesses of a new era of freedom. Desmoulins also openly condoned the execution of Hébert, whom he had slandered without mercy in his newspaper, *Le Vieux Cordelier*. But their enemies operated fast, and this time there was no dramatic denunciation. The warrant for the arrest of the Dantonists was drafted and signed behind the closed doors of the Committee of Public Safety, and carried out that same night without warning.

THE END OF THE DANTONISTS. When the Dantonists were arrested it shocked many deputies, including the butcher, Louis Legendre, who provoked a dramatic moment in the Convention the following day with a courageous plea for his long-time friend Danton. *'Citizens, four members of this Assembly were arrested last night. I know that Danton is one of them, I don't know the names of the others; their names do not matter - if they are guilty...I declare Danton to be as pure as I am. I do not address any particular member of the committees...but I have the right to suspect that personal hate and individual passion are robbing Liberty of the men who have rendered her the most worthwhile service. It falls to me to say this of the man who, in 1792, raised the whole of France by his energetic measures...the enemy was at the gates of Paris: Danton came along, and his ideas saved the nation. He has been in chains since last night; without doubt they fear that his replies would destroy the accusations brought against him. I demand, therefore, that before you hear any report, the prisoners be brought here and given a hearing.'* (Christophe, 1964)

Legendre trembled with emotion as he regained his seat, but the tentative applause that broke out around the amphitheatre came to a sudden halt as Robespierre rose to his feet and turned his frosty eyes on Legendre. *'I ask it of you,'* he said, *'whether the interests of a few ambitious hypocrites should prevail over the interests of the French people?'* Then he addressed the whole Assembly. *'These deputies, whose names Legendre apparently does not know, are well-known to the entire Convention. He spoke of Danton, because he doubtless believes that this name is endowed with privilege. We want no more privileges! We will see today if the Convention knows how to crush a so-called idol, corrupt for so long, or if, in being crushed, it destroys the Convention and the French people.'* (Christophe, 1964). The applause was intense and fearful, and Legendre sat white-faced and motionless as the Incorruptible turned his eyes on him once more. *'They want you to believe that the people are perishing as victims of the Committees! This is a challenge to national justice! I say that whoever trembles at this moment is guilty!'*

THE END OF THE ROBESPIERRISTS. Robespierre was decidedly at the zenith of his power, feared by everyone, and hypnotized by the revolutionary virtues that for him had become a drug. Such a precarious situation could not last for long, and the next time

Legendre challenged Robespierre in the Convention, he was no longer alone. On July 26th 1794 (8 *Thermidor*) Robespierre appeared at the rostrum and made his famous last speech, in which he praised the French Revolution for being the first one to be based on justice and human rights, and then proceeded to hurl a stream of sinister and dangerous threats against the tyrants who were destroying the Revolution. The mistake he made was not naming those tyrants, and there was not a deputy in the house who didn't feel threatened. The next morning - 9 *Thermidor* - when the session began at the customary hour of 10 o'clock, the benches were already crammed with deputies. Within minutes there was chaos as Billaud-Varenne shouted a violent denunciation of Robespierre, who rose to his feet as cries of *'Down with the tyrant!'* rang from every corner of the room. Try as he might, Robespierre could not make himself heard, for every time he began, he was shouted down with accusations of tyranny and despotism. Once more he tried, and his voice failed him in mid-sentence. *'Look, Danton's blood is choking him!'* came a voice from the benches of the Mountain, and when Robespierre's arrest was finally voted, cries of *'Vive La République!'* resounded throughout the hall. But Robespierre was determined to have the last word. *'The Republic!'* he shouted back with contempt, *'The Republic is lost, for the brigands have triumphed!'* With that Robespierre and his colleagues were marched out of the Assembly under armed guard.

THE END OF THE SANS-CULOTTES. After that dramatic session all symbols of the crushed dictatorship were removed from the Convention hall. David's paintings of the deaths of Marat and Le Peletier came down, along with the numerous busts of revolutionary martyrs. But it was a fragile peace that reigned in the post-*Thermidor* Convention, and the *Salle des Machines* was yet to see its most horrific political drama. It came the following May, during the *journées de prairial*, when the man responsible for the city's food supplies, François Boissy d'Anglas, also happened to be president of the Convention. His inefficiency in feeding the capital had earned him the nickname *Boissy-Famine*, and led to the invasion of the Tuileries by that angry crowd of women, with their slogans of '*Bread or Death*', that you saw earlier in the Place du Carrousel. As they were breaking into the palace they came face to face with a deputy named Jean-Bertrand Féraud, who seemed to be trying to stop them. Amidst all the noise the crowd mistook his name for Fréron, another deputy who was hated by Parisians for his violent anti-Jacobinism, so when Féraud tried to defend Boissy d'Anglas they killed him with several shots of a pistol. His head was then cut off, put on the end of a long pike, and taken into the Convention. There it was brandished under the nose of the white-faced Boissy d'Anglas, who rose to his feet with imperturbable calm, removed his hat and respectfully greeted his murdered colleague. With the help of neighbourhood troops, the hall was cleared and those responsible for Féraud's murder were arrested.

When news of these arrests reached the faubourgs, however, the crowds gathered again and returned the next day to the Place du Carrousel for further confrontation. This time the Convention was defended by more than 40,000 soldiers, but they did nothing to drive back the insurgents, resulting in several petitions being heard and numerous promises being made about bread supplies. The people went home reassured, a grave mistake that left them unprepared when government troops invaded the Faubourg Saint-Antoine during the two days that followed. At the end of the siege the once vociferous women of the faubourg watched in resigned silence as 10,000 *sans-culottes* were arrested and taken away.

The Central Pavilion - After 1789.
A Near Escape. It is hard to believe that so much history has been made here on this tranquil lawn, that so many tragic finales have taken place where visitors now amble, happily admiring

the gardens. Things were not any better in the south wing, either, as you will soon see. ➡ Walk back along the Terrasse des Tuileries to the end of the central pathway between the Marsan and Flore pavilions. Here you will once again be in the interior of the Central Pavilion, where you might cross paths with Lafayette fighting off several hundred armed gentlemen on the grand staircase. Brandishing swords and pistols, this noble army managed to get as far as the royal apartments and were about to spirit the king away when Lafayette came along and saved the day. It was a bad day for the former hero of the New World, for he'd begun it by taking all his troops to Vincennes to put down a *sans-culotte* revolt, he was then refused re-entry into the city, and arrived only in the nick of time to foil the royalists here on the grand staircase. When it was all over, Lafayette was, as usual, criticized by both sides. The patriots accused him of inventing the riot at Vincennes and purposely leaving the palace unguarded, while the queen was furious at him for interfering with the attempted escape.

COMMERCE AND CONSPIRACY. During the Revolution the Central Pavilion was re-named *Pavillon de l'Unité*, and, being the main entrance, was always alive with people on their way to the Convention, going to meetings, or coming from committees. Commerce was rife in this busy vestibule, where a citizeness named Lesclapart was always to be seen at the foot of the main staircase selling newspapers, government reports, brochures, committee decrees and lists of suspects. There were stands selling refreshments, and some enterprising patriots had even set up shops here, like citizeness Banguillon, who sold haberdashery, and citizeness Poiré, the wife of a palace doorman, who ran a very popular tobacco shop. Mingling with them all were the inevitable government spies, keeping their eyes on any huddled groups of deputies or any suspicious whispering.

Even before Terror became the order of the day, intrigue and plotting were all around. In May 1793 three figures conversed in lowered tones by the staircase, three deputies named Amar, Lecointre and Bayle. They were talking about Robespierre. '*If there were fifty men like me in the Convention, the tyrant would be no more,*' said Lecointre, and immediately took from his pocket a bill of indictment against Robespierre. His two companions then cited numerous facts proving that Robespierre intended to impose a dictatorship by the scaffold. '*I'll take the stand and denounce the tyrant!*' Lecointre declared in a whisper, his voice full of hate, but Bayle put a hand on Lecointre's arm and tried to calm his agitation. '*This is not the moment.*' he said quietly, and with a lot of good sense, for if Lecointre had done what he proposed that day, he would without doubt have been hastily guillotined. As it was, he left immediately on a mission to Rouen, waited until 9 *Thermidor* made it safe to accuse his enemy, and then survived another eleven years after that.

THE SOUTH WING OF THE TUILERIES PALACE.

➡Once you have passed by the Central Pavilion you are walking alongside the south wing of the palace. Continue southwards along the Terrasse des Tuileries and stop when you get to the hedge that screens off the underpass below. You are almost at the Flore pavilion, re-named *Egalité* during the Revolution, and ➡here you should sit on the wall again and look over at the lawn where the south wing of the palace stood. This was where the royal family's apartments were when they lived here in semi-captivity, and where later on the Committee of Public Safety held its meetings.

THE ROYAL FAMILY AT THE TUILERIES PALACE.

The day after attacking Versailles and forcing the king and queen back to the capital accompanied by the severed heads of their slaughtered bodyguards, the people of Paris permitted themselves a few moments of sentimentality. They massed in the Tuileries gardens around the palace entrance, '*crying like children*' and kissing each other, then demanded the royal family to appear at the window. Marie-Antoinette smiled regally at the crowd, assuring ambassador Mercy-Argenteau that all Paris - from the soldiers of the militia to the fishwives of *Les Halles* - was extending its hand to her, and she would do likewise. Louis XVI also tried to be noble about the whole thing, but he couldn't help wondering how he would survive without his hunting reserves, and was probably already planning where in the new palace he could set up a workshop and continue his experiments as an amateur locksmith. The little dauphin, Louis-Charles, didn't understand anything of what was happening, and when he heard the cries of the people outside, he asked anxiously, '*Mummy, is today going to be like yesterday?*'

The new royal accommodation was initially very basic. The Tuileries had been abandoned to the ravages of squatters for so long that it was in no fit state for royalty when the architect turned palace inspector, Richard Mique, was asked to prepare for the arrival of the king and queen. This awesome task threw the poor man into a panic, particularly as he only had one afternoon in which to do it. He hadn't a minute to lose. The squatters were thrown out amidst much weeping and shouting, recriminations and even threats, all of which were silenced by promises of compensation. These were not empty promises, either. One lucky lady, Madame de la Mark, received 120,000 *livres*, and she was not the only one to receive compensation for being put out on the streets. Mique then set about providing the bare essentials for washing, eating and sleeping during the first few days, but I think the royal family's first night in their new home might well have been a pretty sleepless one. They spent it on camp beds in freezing, damp-ridden rooms empty of even a chair, where the woodwork had rotted from neglect and the windows were all broken. If they did sleep, their dreams must have been very bleak.

Eventually, after the arrival of some slightly more regal furniture and fittings, Louis and his family were able to establish some semblance of a royal lifestyle, but it hardly equalled the splendour that they had enjoyed at Versailles. The number of courtiers was drastically reduced to a few of the most faithful, any thought of festivals, parties or balls was forgotten, and The Capet Family, as they were now known, had to content themselves with an occasional carriage ride, a trip to the theatre, or walking in the public gardens.

THE KING'S DINNER. The new residents of the Tuileries led a very visible life, for their windows were constantly observed by crowds of curious citizens who were ever-present on the garden terraces. On one occasion a few of them even managed to climb in the window and invade the bedroom of Louis's sister, Madame Elisabeth, who was well-known for her extreme modesty. She rushed out of the room in horror and went straight to Louis's apartment, where she begged her brother to give her more secure accommodation. This was quickly arranged, but there was no way she could avoid the uncomfortable experience they all had to tolerate every day in the late afternoon, when the citizens of Paris came to watch their chief executive eat his dinner. Henry Desbassayns, a French colonist from the *Ile Bourbon* (now La Réunion) was living in Paris at the time and recorded in his diary how he witnessed the last vestiges of the Bourbon dynasty being presented as public entertainment.

'I went to the Tuileries Palace to see the King and Queen dine. There was quite a crowd there. I saw Monsieur for the first time since my arrival in France. The wife of the baker whom the people lynched last year, and whose baby was held by the Queen at its baptism, was there, with her little child, who was kissed by the Queen, who was applauded. I was really close to Their Majesties

when they passed by on their way to Mass. There was the King, the Queen, the Dauphin, Madame, the Queen's daughter, Monsieur and Madame, and Madame Elisabeth, and all the ladies in waiting. After the Mass, the King, and all those that I named went by again on their way to dinner. The King and Queen were alone at the table. The others have a separate table in their apartments. After the King's dinner, I wanted to go and see that of Madame Elisabeth, but she was leaving the table when we arrived.' (Desbassayns, 1985)

PREPARING FOR ESCAPE. The bread on the royal dinner-table that day was probably the Viennese style that eventually became immensely popular amongst Parisians. For this they have to thank Marie-Antoinette, and her German baker, who had come from Versailles along with the other staff considered indispensable by the queen - the royal glazier, the royal hairdresser, royal chefs, royal doctors, surgeons and apothecaries, all lodged either in the palace or in the surrounding houses. Louis's needs were somewhat simpler than his wife's, and once he had set up his locksmith's workshop in a little room on the ground floor, he tried to adapt to his new life in Paris. But as the political climate became less and less favourable to the monarchy, he felt more and more like a prisoner, and increasingly open to the idea of escaping. The moment came in June 1791, when the queen's favourite, Count Axel de Fersen, proposed and arranged the famous and badly executed escape plan which culminated tragically in the arrest of the royal family at Varennes. For some time before their departure the royal apartments bristled with covert planning and hushed conversations, which the king and queen's daughter, 12-year-old Madame Royale, never forgot.

'Throughout the day of 20th June 1791, my father and mother appeared to me to be very restless and preoccupied, for no reason I was aware of. After dinner, they sent us away, my brother and me, and shut themselves up alone with my aunt. I have since

discovered that it was then that they told her of their projected flight. At 5 o'clock my mother went out for a walk with my brother and me. During the walk, she took me aside, told me that I must not worry myself about what I would see, that we would not be separated for long, and that we would be together again very soon. My wits were dull, and I understood nothing of all this. She kissed me and told me that, if the attendants asked me why I was not myself, I must say that she had scolded me but that I had made it up with her again. We returned at 7 o'clock; I went back to my apartments very drearily, understanding nothing at all of what my mother had said to me.' (Tannahill, 1966)

But by the following evening Madame Royale was no longer in any doubt about what was going on. *'My brother had been awakened by my mother, and Madame de Tourzel led him to my mother's rooms downstairs. I went down with them. There we found one of the bodyguards, called Monsieur de Malden, who was there to see us safely away. My mother came in to us several times. They dressed my brother as a little girl; he looked charming. Since he was very sleepy, he did not know what was going on. I asked him what he thought was going to happen, and he told me he thought we were about to act a play, because we were in disguise.'* (Tannahill, 1966)

Once the royal children had been escorted out of the palace into the waiting carriage, the king and queen returned to their apartments, where the bedchamber courtiers had taken up their posts in preparation for the royal bedtime. While this ancient ceremony was going on, the king's brother, Monsieur, and his wife, were leaving the palace and heading for Brussels. Marie-Antoinette attended to her night-time toilet, and Louis, the ceremony over, climbed into bed, watching as his valet, Lemoine, closed the curtains around him. During the few short minutes when Lemoine went into the antechamber to change into his night-shirt, Louis slipped quietly through the curtains, closed them again, and left the room. Lemoine came back into the king's bedroom, lay down next to the bed and settled down for the night, unaware that the man he was supposed to be protecting was no longer behind the curtains, but was hurrying in his night-gown down the library staircase.

Once he had changed into his costume and arranged his wig and hat, Louis joined his wife and sister in the empty ground-floor apartment where an hour earlier he had said goodbye to his children. One by one they crept out into the courtyard and began the dangerous walk through the unfamiliar capital. Louis would have been happy never to see the Tuileries palace again, or at least not in those circumstances, but alas he was to be bitterly disappointed, and on June 25th he and his family were once more brought back to Paris by force. But by the time he got there Louis was resigned. Having failed to escape physically from his intolerable situation, he seemed to have escaped mentally into a world of his own, and he walked back into the Tuileries Palace as if in a trance.

Louis Drinks with the People. Within a year war had been declared, people felt frightened of possible invasion, and Louis once more became the target of popular action, this time organized by the Girondins, whom the king had just dismissed from the government. It came at a time when Louis was beginning to be severely affected by all that was befalling him and his family. Madame Campan tells in her memoirs how *'at this time the king fell into a depression that affected him emotionally and physically. For ten days at a time he would not utter a word, even to his close family.'* The queen did her utmost to jolt him out of this state of mind, sometimes with rebukes, sometimes with tenderness, eventually reminding him that he owed it to his family to get himself together. She even went so far as to say that *'if they must perish, it should be with honour, not by waiting for the people to come and snuff out each and every one of them on the floor of their apartment.'* And not long after that the people did come. It was June 20th, and the crowd that you saw earlier in the Place du Carrousel, with feminist actress Théroigne de Méricourt carrying the banner, had first been to the National Assembly on the pretext of celebrating the third anniversary of the Tennis Court Oath. After planting a Tree of Liberty, they broke down the doors of the palace with an axe and ran into the royal apartments, clamouring for the return of the Girondins' 'patriotic Ministry' and immediate action against the threat of invasion.

Louis met the crowd with remarkable calm, and after some discussion of the royal veto, he agreed to put on a red republican bonnet and drink to the health of the nation from the flask of wine that was offered to him by his uninvited guests. Then he sat in the bay of a window and watched passively as the crowd filed past him, insulting him, threatening him, laughing at him in derision, while banners saying '*Down with Veto and his wife*' were waved at him. As the fishwives from Les Halles filed past the royal group hurling insults, the queen is reputed to have asked one of them, *'What have I done to you?',* to which the woman replied, *'Nothing to me, but you harmed the nation.' 'You are mistaken,'* answered the queen, *'I am French, and have no other fatherland; I wish to live and die in France. I was happy when the people loved me.'* At that the fishwife in question is said to have broken down in tears. The dauphin Louis-Charles, also wearing a red bonnet, stood on a table and stared at this ghoulish procession, which seemed a bit like a pantomime to the 7-year-old child. But one thing he didn't like was the expressions on the faces of these unknown people, and who, he wondered, was the miniature woman hanging from the tiny gallows that they brandished in his face? The crowd left at about 10 o'clock in the evening, having spent three hours with the king, during which time the deputies in the Assembly did nothing to intervene. Napoléon Bonaparte, 22 years old and as yet unknown, had been among the crowd that day, and remarked that if he were in Louis's position he would never allow such a thing to happen.

THE IRON WARDROBE. What did Louis XVI do during these years in the Tuileries palace? He made the best he could of his limited freedom and the permanent threat of popular invasion, and tried to present himself as 'cooperative' with the revolutionary leaders. But after his overthrow and removal to the Temple prison, a startling discovery was made in one of the rooms that he had occupied at the Tuileries. It was the notorious *armoire de fer*, or iron wardrobe, revealed by a locksmith named François Gamain, who had built it with the help of the king himself. It was concealed in an alcove behind a revolving wood panel, and Louis had fitted the thick iron door with one of his own very efficient locks. Gamain contacted Roland, who was Minister of the Interior, and poured out the terrible remorse he felt for his complicity with the king in constructing this hiding-place. He took Roland in secret one night to the empty royal apartment, and proceeded to open it in front of the astounded minister, who wasted no time in revealing to the Convention the contents of the wardrobe. In it were stashed piles of papers and letters exposing the double-dealing that Louis had been indulging in since the beginning of the Revolution, and also contained incriminating evidence against Mirabeau, who was dead by then, and could thus escape the consequences of this discovery. But not the king, whose trial for treason against the nation could now no longer be put off in the face of such flagrant evidence.

Louis was taken off and guillotined, but the iron wardrobe remained in his apartment, which a few months later was occupied by the Committee of Public Safety. A committee administrator named Philippe Morice worked right next to it. *'Our office was in the Tuileries, in the apartments that Louis XVI had occupied. The table on which I worked was pushed against this cupboard in which had been found the papers that served partly as the basis of his judgement It was in this cupboard that I used to put my hat and my gloves.'*

THE LAST ROYAL DEPARTURE. In the end no amount of subversive correspondence with foreign monarchies could save Louis and Marie-Antoinette By the beginning of August 1792 their days at the Tuileries were coming to an end, and they would soon know real imprisonment, in a real prison. The final moment came on the 10th, but it took a great deal of persuasion to make the royal couple realize just how much danger they were in. When the Marquis de Clermont came to warn them, the queen replied, *'Can you really believe that they are coming to attack the palace? What madness! That is impossible.'* But the Princesse de Lamballe was seized with terror, shouting *'We won't escape, we'll all be massacred! They are determined to kill us!'* An eye-witness described the panic.

> *'Louis had said his prayers, had confessed to the abbé Hébert, and waited in resignation. The queen, her children, the Princess Elisabeth, ran from apartment to apartment, first to where the king was shut in with the priest, then to the council chamber where the ministers were assembled, receiving advice and discussing with Rœderer how to save the royal family. At 8 o'clock a municipal officer came into the council chamber, where he found the king with his family and the ministers. Joly, the keeper of the seals, shouted to him: "Well, what do they want?" "Dethronement," replied the officer. Joly replied: "Then let the Assembly pronounce it!" "But what will become of the king?" said the queen to the officer. He bowed low, without uttering a single word of reply.'* (Lenotre, 1906)

Just after 8 a.m. when the Procureur-Général, Pierre Louis Roederer, presented the situation to the king, he didn't mince his words. *'Sire, Your Majesty does not have five minutes to lose. There is no safety for him except in the National Assembly.'* No-one could offer them any protection now. As they stood, desperate, in the council room, they could hear above the voices of their advisors violent shouts of rage from the crowd that was getting nearer and nearer to the palace. Heeding the advice of Roederer and the ministers, Louis took his son's hand and ordered his family to *'Start walking!'* As she left, Marie-Antoinette looked back for a brief moment. *'I'll come back and join you,'* she said in a proud attempt to show confidence to those whom she was obliged to abandon.

The royal family left not a moment too soon, for within minutes a huge crowd of people had forced the main gates and surged into the *Cour Royale*. From the palace windows the Swiss guards fired cannons into the crowd, killing them in large numbers, and then came down into the courtyard and charged at them. This attack unleashed the fury of the populace, who, accompanied by the *Marseillais* and other *fédérés*, tried to force the *Suisses* to retreat. At that moment, a contingent from the Faubourg Saint-Antoine arrived, a veritable sea of national guards and *sans-culottes* armed to the teeth with pikes, axes and sabres. A bloody battle ensued, and the insurgents finally got into the palace, where they proceeded to horribly massacre not only the remaining *Suisses* but also several luckless members of the domestic staff. They decapitated them, castrated them, threw them out of windows and impaled them on pikes. Their rage knew no limits. On that terrible night of August 10th 1793 a total of 1,300 people died, 900 royalists and 400 insurgents.

THE COMMITTEE OF PUBLIC SAFETY. Louis and Marie-Antoinette would never spend another night at the Tuileries Palace, and after they moved out the Revolution moved in. There were committees of varying size and importance in rooms all over the Tuileries at that time, but none was more powerful or feared than the Committee of Public Safety. The formation of this notorious institution resulted from General Dumouriez's defection to the enemy in April 1793, and at first its role was to oversee the war effort. But as time went on the Convention gave it more and more power, until it became, at the height of the Terror, the embodiment of revolutionary intimidation.

The committee took over the former royal apartments on the ground floor and first floor of the south wing, so from where you are sitting you can look through the palace windows on to a chilling bit of Parisian history. When the committee was first created, its twelve members, eight of whom were lawyers, met every morning in Marie-Antoinette's bedroom, situated on the ground floor. Later on, as the committee's importance increased, they moved their meetings upstairs to the chamber where Louis XVI had slept. All these rooms looked out on to the gardens, and to get to their meetings the committee members used the queen's staircase that stood against what is now the north wall of the Flore pavilion. Look over at that wall and see if you can see the staircase, and the committee members hurrying up it, eager to get started on their patriotic work. Most of them were there from 8 o'clock in the morning, reading correspondence and preparing for the daily session, which took place amidst the luxurious furniture and magnificent tapestries formerly enjoyed by royalty.

It's 11 o'clock in the morning. Look carefully and you will see the committee members, seated around a long table. Robespierre is there, the committee's de-facto chief, with his steel-rimmed oval spectacles sitting on top of his freshly powdered wig. Next to him are his two closest colleagues, Georges Couthon in his famous wheelchair, and Saint-Just in his not quite so famous earrings. Also at the table are the committee's two most radical members, Billaud-Varenne and Collot d'Herbois, who would both play a major role in deposing Robespierre. The green baize surface of the table is covered with piles of paper - reports, letters, decrees and perhaps a few arrest warrants waiting to be signed. Several reports are read out to the members, followed by lengthy and often stormy discussions, after which decisions are made and sheaves of papers with instructions written all over them are handed to waiting secretaries. Throughout the session documents are passed round the table for signature - documents that as time went on contained more and more bills of indictment, search orders and arrest warrants, which most of the members signed without reading.

It was here that Couthon proposed the infamous Law of 22 Prairial, which took away all hope of defence from victims of the Tribunal and permitted only one penalty - death. Late in the evening of March 30th 1794, as the arrest warrant of the Dantonists was signed and passed on to the secretaries for immediate execution, one of the committee members, Robert Lindet, slipped out of the palace and headed for Danton's apartment to warn him. Lindet was risking his own life by doing this, for he had been one of two committee members who refused to put their signature to the warrant. But Lindet's warning did not prevent the arrest, and while the Dantonists were being judged, Saint-Just presented to the committee his report on a prison conspiracy which resulted in the arrest and execution of Desmoulins' young wife Lucile.

In theory meetings of the committee were public, but fewer and fewer people ventured across its threshold to listen, for Robespierre had let it be known that anyone doing so would be viewed as an enemy spy. The isolation that this imposed on the committee resulted in an intolerably tense atmosphere. Inflamed outbursts of temper were followed by long heavy silences, they contradicted, they threatened, and the spectre of the guillotine was never far from their thoughts. On one occasion Collot d'Herbois and Robespierre came to blows. A group of deputies were huddled around the door in the adjoining anti-chamber, eavesdropping on this spectacular row, when suddenly the door flew open and Robespierre came striding out, his head still turned towards Collot, and shouting at the top of his voice. Collot ran up to him and grabbed him by his jacket, pulled him back into the committee room and began shouting even more loudly. *'Robespierre is despicable, a hypocrite! We love all our colleagues; the patriots are dear to our hearts; it is that man there who wants to murder them all!'* Collot was on the point of beating up Robespierre when Paul Barras happened to pass by and succeeded in separating the two furious deputies.

The committee members continued their deliberations most days until 5 or 6 o'clock in the evening, had dinner, attended the evening session of the Convention, and then returned to the Committee Room at 11 p.m., often going on until 2 or 3 in the morning. These inhuman hours reduced most of the members to a state of exhaustion. *'We no longer sleep at the Committee,'* wrote Couthon to a friend in April 1794, *'and we will stay awake until the Republic is purged of its traitors...I am so overwhelmed with fatigue that I hardly have the strength to write you these few lines; love of my country, however, takes the place of good health, in these great and perilous times.'* For Couthon this exacting schedule was made worse by his paralysis, which kept him in a wheelchair, and meant he had to be carried up and down the palace staircase on a colleague's back. Robespierre too began to fall victim to fatigue in the last months, when increasing bouts of coughing up blood added to his exhaustion. *'I no longer have the necessary vigour,'* he announced to the Jacobin Club, *'to combat the intrigues of the aristocracy. Worn out by four years of tedious and fruitless work, I feel that my physical and moral faculties are not at all equal to a great revolution, and I declare my intention to resign.'*

If Robespierre had carried out his intention, and left the all-powerful Jacobin Club to more moderate leadership, the Revolution may have ended differently, and Robespierre might even have survived it. But he didn't resign. He continued on the path of self-destruction, assuming more and more power and falling more and more under the influence of Saint-Just and Couthon. They were the only deputies allowed to enter Robespierre's little private office next to the Committee Room, which all the others nicknamed 'The Sanhedrin' after another all-powerful seat of justice in ancient Palestine. It was here, in the last month of his life, that Robespierre regularly signed decrees without the knowledge or consent of the rest of the committee, where he received a deluge of denunciations from all over the country, and began compiling lists of 'suspects' and 'traitors'. Many of his fellow committee members began to fear - some with good reason - that their own names would soon appear on Robespierre's lists.

On 5 *Thermidor* (July 23rd 1794) the committee members met together for the last time. Despite the beautiful summer weather, the open windows and the scent of flowers that wafted into the room from the Tuileries gardens, a collective melancholy hung over the heads of the assembled deputies. One feigned optimism, another made a mechanical attempt at conciliation, others shuffled their papers. '*We are your friends,*' said Billaud-Varenne in a hypocritical gesture of reassurance to Robespierre, who seemed fragile and unnerved. Even Saint-Just tried to bring them together. But they all knew that there was no more work for them to do together, for when two forces threaten each other, one must destroy the other.

The next time Robespierre saw the Committee room was four days later. He arrived there on a stretcher, barely alive, his fractured jaw wrapped in a blood-soaked handkerchief. Behind him came Saint-Just, still impeccably dressed, despite the battle he had just lost, his enormous cravat still in place, still tied in a fashionable bow, and on his face the same sober expression that had always accompanied his patriotic speeches. Robespierre's wounded colleagues were placed on the floor at the foot of the queen's staircase, while their fallen leader was carried on his stretcher up to the committee room in the company of Saint-Just and Dumas, who sat in a window alcove and stared out into the gardens below. Robespierre could not stand up, so for want of a bed they put him on the committee table - where he had done so much work, written so many decrees, signed so many death warrants. The table still exists today and can be seen in the Musée des Archives. On that historic day Robespierre was wearing his favourite cornflower blue tailcoat and yellow nankin breeches, and but for the lack of a cravat and the blood-stains on his now open shirt, he could have been dressed for a festival.

For about an hour everyone thought he was going to die, as he lay inertly on the table, his head resting on a wooden box. Then suddenly he opened his eyes and signalled for a cloth to absorb the blood that was filling his mouth. Someone handed him a white animal-skin gun bag on which was written *'To the Great Monarch - Lecourt, supplier to the king and his troops, rue Saint-Honoré'* - probably an intentional insult, for everyone in the room was hurling abusive remarks at their former chief. When the gun-bag could hold no more of the blood that continued to flow from Robespierre's mouth, one man took pity on him and brought over some sheets of paper to help clean the wound. It was not long before a warrant arrived ordering the prisoners to be taken to the Conciergerie. Robespierre's jaw was bandaged by a doctor, then he was seated on a chair and carried out of the palace to begin the painful journey across the city. As the procession of prisoners filed out of the committee room towards the stairs, Saint-Just contemplated a copy of the Declaration of the Rights of Man hanging on the wall, and declared *'At least I achieved that!'*

Robespierre lies wounded and helpless on the Committee room table where he had presided with so much power. Saint-Just and Dumas, also under arrest, stand by a window, observing impassively the downfall of their leader. (Courtesy of Musée Carnavalet, Cabinet des Arts Graphiques, Paris)

The Tuileries Gardens.

➥You are now going to leave the turbulent past of the Tuileries Palace, whose restless ghosts will continue to walk out eternity on the pleasant lawns that have taken its place. ➥Go back to the central pathway along the Terrasse des Tuileries, which first became an esplanade in 1664 when the gardens were renovated for Louis XIV. Up to then the palace had been separated from the garden by a high wall, on the other side of which was *rue des Tuileries*, an extremely squalid public thoroughfare leading down to the Seine. Even then people were rather astonished by this arrangement, which inspired one poet to wonder if it was now the fashion *'to have your house in town, and your garden in the suburbs.'* Louis XIV didn't think it was, so in 1664 he had both the wall and the street demolished and the esplanade built over them.

➥Leave the Terrasse des Tuileries, turning left on the central pathway, down the steps and into the gardens. This was where Louis XVI and his little party of fugitives made their hasty exit from the palace on the morning of August 10th 1792, and ➥you are going to follow them as they head for the National Assembly, which at that time held its meetings on the north side of the gardens in the palace riding-school (*Manège*). ➥Go straight ahead along the central pathway, between the two small ponds, and stop at the large round pond, where for more than a century now children have amused themselves chasing sail boats around with a wooden stick. This pleasantly old-fashioned activity seems to relax everyone around the pond, children and adults alike, so it's is a good place to ➥find a chair, rest your feet and read about these classically French gardens that are so steeped in history. If you sit on the far (west) edge of the pond, looking across the pond towards the Louvre, you will have a good perspective on some of the revolutionary events that took place in this part of the garden.

THE ROYAL GARDEN.

When Catherine de Medici began the Tuileries Palace in 1564 she decided to create a garden at the same time. For this she commissioned the architect Pierre Le Nôtre, who designed an Italian-style garden with a network of pathways that divided the area up into rectangular plantations, each containing a variety of trees and bushes. The garden had a few novelties, including a labyrinth of cypress trees, a grotto made of shells, and a menagerie. Henri IV added an orangery, and a long row of mulberry trees and bramble bushes along the north side. When the garden was a hundred years old the original architect's grandson, André Le Nôtre, was given the job of creating a new garden worthy of the palace's most recent resident, Louis XIV. At the end of seven years Le Nôtre had made a perfect French garden, complete with terraces, esplanades, and lawns. He opened the central walkway along the entire length of the garden, and built the large round pond where you are now sitting, the two smaller ones beside it, and the octagonal pond at the other end of the garden. It was at this time that the two long terraces were built along the north and south sides of the gardens - the Terrasse des Feuillants and the Terrasse du Bord de l'Eau. Because of the downward slope towards the Seine on this part of the right bank, Le Nôtre had to build these two terraces of different heights. Finally, at the far end - next to the present-day Place de la Concorde - he constructed two end terraces each with a large curved ramp leading down into the gardens. When the new gardens were completed in 1673, at the request of Charles Perrault, the author of 'Mother Goose', they were opened to the public. How he had such influence I don't know, but it is said that he found the inspiration for his famous nursery rhymes right here in the Tuileries gardens. Anyone could come in, except soldiers, footmen, or people dressed in rags, and Louis XIV's back garden soon became one of the most popular 'promenades' in Paris.

During the course of the 18th century two great novelties were introduced. One was rented chairs, which enabled visitors to rest for a while as you are doing, and you could pay in advance for the entire summer - Thomas Jefferson's accounts show a payment of 3*fr*12 for a seasonal subscription. The other innovation came in 1780, when, much to the delight of people with children, public toilets were added to the garden's facilities. During the 1780s the Tuileries had a much more respectable reputation than the gardens of the Palais-Royal, and those who came here to walk behaved so well that a group of visiting Italians could not believe their eyes. *'Ah! These good people of Paris! They don't steal anything, they don't break anything; it's amazing!'* The exception to this was Saint-Louis's Day, when there was an open-air musical concert, and the gardens were turned into a funfair. As people danced and drank the hours away in an assortment of improvised cafés, behaviour became decidedly less exemplary towards the late afternoon.

THE TUILERIES GARDENS AFTER 1789.

During the early years of the Revolution the Tuileries remained a favourite 'promenade' for Parisians, who would often come in the hope of seeing the king and queen out for a walk. Marie-Antoinette used to encourage her children to mingle with the public, even talk to them, and every time the little dauphin approached someone, he would run back to his mother asking, '*Did I do it well?*' Henry Desbassayns, the French colonist from La Réunion, was a frequent visitor to the Tuileries, coming here regularly to sit and relax. He was particularly fond of sitting where you are now and looking at the Tuileries Palace in the evening, when the windows were illuminated by the candles and chandeliers of the royal apartments. On one occasion he got some unexpected entertainment. '*We sat under the trees, facing the palace. From there we could see all the palace lights. As we were getting up to leave, we saw a ball of light fly past us, coming from the Seine and heading for the Palais-Royal...it wasn't very high, perhaps three times the height of the Tuileries palace. I think they call this sort of will-o'-the-wisp a meteor. It's not surprising, after the heat that we've had for the last five or six days.*' (Desbassayns, 1985)

After the king tried to escape, security was tightened around the Tuileries, and many citizens were anxious to present a patriotic appearance. Henry Desbassayns came here for his habitual evening walk, only to find the entrance barred. '*I stayed a long time at the gate, examining the faces of those who were allowed in and those who weren't. The latter were not pleased. I had my crucifix under my jacket, which I had buttoned up....I always take care to cross over my jacket and button it, so that my crucifix is underneath...this also makes you less noticed. Otherwise people study you, and nowadays they would say - There goes an aristocrat!*' (Desbassayns, 1985). When Desbassayns came back a fortnight later the gardens were re-opened, but he needed a ticket to get in. Two weeks after that he found them closed again, on the orders of Lafayette, who was responsible for guarding the king. Desbassayns regretted this continual closure of the Tuileries gardens, which he said *'created a void for the idle-rich of Paris.'* The day after Louis XVI sanctioned the Constitution on September 14th 1791, the gardens were once more opened to the public, and a delighted Desbassayns resumed his evening walks. He was there three days later when the king and queen appeared at one of the windows of the palace. Gone it seemed were the bad feelings over Louis's attempted escape. His support of the new Constitution had regained their hearts, and many people in the garden that evening applauded the royal couple and shouted *'Long Live the King and Queen!'*

A fortnight later another Parisian visited the Tuileries gardens, but this was Restif de la Bretonne, so he didn't come when everyone else did, but climbed over the wall after the gates were closed. He soon discovered that he was not alone. *'I chose a place by the terrace along the river, where there was no sentinel, and I got in without obstacle. I saw some people, I slid down and hid under the trees without being noticed.'* Sitting on the chairs underneath the trees was a group of people talking in lowered voices about politics. Restif hid behind a large tree and listened. *'But Monsieur le duc, said one woman bitterly, What is to become of us? Another younger woman added, We have to risk everything, sacrifice everything, to regain our rights. -Prudence! Prudence! said the second man, His Majesty has already regained a great deal; our turn will come.'*

But then Restif had an unwelcome interruption. *'At that moment a fat man got up to come and urinate right near my tree. Fortunately for me a woman told him, You're going too far. He turned round and replied to her, Do you want me to do it right under your nose?'* Restif judged it too dangerous to remain so near to this group of subversive aristocrats, so he slipped silently away to a quieter part of the garden. *'There I saw a tall, young and beautiful woman, walking tenderly arm in arm with a man. -I should be there, she said; they're talking about things of great importance, but you make me forget the entire universe...and yet, what a moment for making love! Perhaps on the eve of a departure...of a bloody war? -If you leave, replied the man, I will follow you to the end of the earth; but without you, never!'* (Restif de la Bretonne, 1986). Restif concluded that it was clearly women who made men emigrate, and with that he left the gardens by sliding down a pole that he found on the terrace.

The First Pyramid.

Less than a year later Louis XVI had to escape from his palace and hide in the Assembly, while the people of Paris took up arms against the monarchy. After the king was deposed, and he and his family imprisoned in the Temple, a solemn festival was held in the Tuileries gardens to honour the victims of the glorious 10th of August. It took place right here in front of you on August 27th 1792, when thousands of soldiers filed one by one past an enormous pyramid that had been built over the large pond. It was a dramatic occasion. During the ceremony a thin black veil was drawn over the pyramid as the soldiers knelt in homage before a huge gathering of widows and orphans dressed in white robes and black belts. A sarcophagus moved slowly through the garden, pulled along by oxen, as mournful music and incense filled the hot summer air. The garden had never looked more patriotic as it did that day, when it was filled with sombre citizens in tricolour cockades, and all the statues wore revolutionary red bonnets.

The National Garden.

Louis XVI would not live to see it, but on April 24th 1793 the Tuileries Gardens were nationalized, and a special guard created to protect the monuments - they had already passed a law two weeks earlier giving two years' imprisonment to anyone caught vandalizing the garden's statues. The new guards were also charged with surveying the promenaders, who were not allowed to take a walk in the *Jardin National* unless they displayed a tricolour cockade. The National Convention was now responsible for the maintenance of the gardens, where much repair work was needed, the result of various *journées révolutionnaires* that had left the pathways and flower-beds ravaged, the ponds damaged and the public benches destroyed. They set about this task with great enthusiasm. All the dead trees were pulled out and an interesting variety of new ones planted, including some dwarf alpine ebony trees, and the flower-beds were adorned with a delightful array of rose-trees, acacia and yellow jasmine. This visual feast raised the hackles of more radical patriots who, at a time when the whole country was suffering from food shortages, took a dim view of this extravagant luxury that seemed primarily for the benefit of the deputies.

The following September the Convention was invaded by a hungry populace demanding bread, leading to a demand that the garden be put to better use. *'The eyes of republicans will rest with more pleasure on this former domain of the Crown, when it produces the basic essentials.'* Five months later the Committee of Public Safety ordered the gardens of Catherine de Medici and Louis XIV to be planted with potatoes, which were later harvested in great quantity and distributed free to the city's poor. Potatoes had become a popular addition to the French diet during the *ancien régime*, when a soldier called Parmentier, who had eaten them while a prisoner in Germany, introduced them to Louis XVI and Marie-Antoinette. By the time of the Revolution they had become popular throughout the whole country, and it was the scarcity of bread that probably prompted the Committee to order the planting of potatoes in the Tuileries. In the spring of 1794 a massive beautification programme for the capital was launched. This naturally contained extensive projects for the improvement of the National Garden, which was celebrating its first anniversary of public ownership on the day that the programme was officially decreed. At the head of the works committee was David, who was enthusiastically organizing a deluge of bronze monuments in honour of Liberty when 9 *Thermidor* came along and put a stop to it all. David was arrested and put in prison, and very little of the proposed makeover was ever achieved.

Festival of the Supreme Being.

Just six weeks before he was guillotined Robespierre reached the pinnacle of his aspirations when the entire population of Paris turned out to honour the new revolutionary deity known as the 'Supreme Being'. It was David who staged this elaborate spectacle, where from 5 o'clock in the morning people began decorating their houses and milling around to the incessant beating of drums. It wasn't long before the National Garden was flooded with people. Women held bouquets of roses, young girls carried baskets of wild flowers and wheat, while fathers and sons marched together amidst an array of flags and banners, a sabre or pike in one hand, a branch of oak leaves in the other. The east part of the garden, where you are sitting, was decorated with busts, garlands and urns, and tricolour flags hung everywhere.

Try to imagine the extravagant scene that was directly in front of you. Against the façade of the Tuileries' Central Pavilion rose a semi-circular amphitheatre with a large platform at the top, where rows of chairs awaited the arrival of the deputies. At the front was a larger chair, raised up on a small dais that was covered with a tricolour carpet. This was reserved for Robespierre. The entire construction was adorned with greenery, flowers, patriotic ribbons and white marble vases, while over the large round pond rose the figure of Atheism, depicted as a monster and surrounded by the smaller but equally fiendish figures of Ambition, Egotism, Discord and False Simplicity. All five models were decorated with the symbols of royalty and coated with sulphur, nitrate and gunpowder. Eight bulls with gilded horns moved slowly around the garden, pulling a red-draped float containing a huge statue of Liberty. Numbered posts marked the spot where each battalion of local troops was to take up its position, and as they filed into the garden it was soon impossible to see the ground, there were so many people. As music filled the air, deputies began appearing on the top of the amphitheatre, dressed in new costumes, while white-clad opera singers, crowned with roses, filed on to the two staircases that descended from the platform to the gardens below At the foot of the amphitheatre a military band stood at the ready.

Robespierre was inside the palace, in the former apartment of the ill-fated Princesse de Lamballe, waiting for the moment when he would appear on the balcony and take his place on the large raised chair that suspiciously resembled a throne. The significance of this was not lost on many of the deputies, one of whom described the event as the catalyst in Robespierre's downfall six weeks later. *'As President of the Convention, Robespierre led the procession...People noticed that there was a considerable gap between his colleagues and himself. Some ascribe this to simple deference, others think that Robespierre was using it to underline his sovereignty. I am inclined to think that it was due to detestation of Robespierre. It seems certain that his downfall was agreed in that triumphal procession.'* Another deputy described how *'intoxicated he seemed; but while the rapturous crowds shouted "Long live Robespierre!" - shouts that are a death warrant in a republic - his colleagues, alarmed by his presumptuous claims, provoked him with sarcastic comments.'* A sans-culotte in the crowd put it more plainly. *'Look at the b——— it's not enough to be master, he wants to be God as well.'* (Cobb, 1988)

When Robespierre finally emerged in his blue tailcoat and wide tricolour sash, he looked across the gardens at the sea

The Festival of the Supreme Being began in the Tuileries Gardens, where a large semi-circular amphitheatre was built on to the facade of the Tuileries Palace. To the sound of a military band, the deputies filed down the steps into the Gardens. (Author's private collection)

of joyful faces below, and his usual austerity and reserve were transformed into euphoria. *'Oh Nature!'* he exclaimed, *'how sublime and delightful is your power! How tyrants must pale at the thought of this festival!'* After delivering a long speech in praise of the Supreme Being, he went down into the gardens, to the sound of choral music, and walked over to the pond. The crowd fell silent as Robespierre seized a flaming torch and set fire to Atheism and her four colleagues, whose burnt ashes floated into the pond, revealing in their place a rather scorched statue of Wisdom. *'Thus into nothingness goes this monster that the spirit of kings has vomited on to France.'* declaimed Robespierre. *'Let all the crimes and misfortunes of the world disappear with it.'* With these apocalyptic words he brought to an end the first part of the festival.

A roll of drums signalled the moment to leave the Tuileries and head for the Champ-de-Mars, where the major part of the ceremony was to take place. Follow the crowd along the central pathway until you arrive at the intersection with the path known as *Allée de Diane* - this name is not marked, but it is where the trees begin. The procession continued down the centre of the garden towards the exit, but ➡you are going to rejoin Louis XVI and his family as they take flight from the palace and head for the Assembly.

THE MANÈGE.
➡To follow in Louis's footsteps, turn obliquely right through the trees and head for the thirteen steps that lead up to the Terrasse des Feuillants. You do this by going around the little pond by the cafe, then veering left through the trees past a huge bronze statue, created in 1992 by Eric Dietman, called *L'ami de personne* (nobody's friend), a name Louis XVI would certainly have identified with as he hurried across the gardens. ➡From here you can see the thirteen steps through the trees, the very same ones that the royal family took on the morning of August 10th. As the king hurried up these steps his way was barred for about fifteen minutes by people shouting '*We want no more tyrants. Death! Death!*' One particularly aggressive soldier named Rocher threatened the king with a dagger, and then grabbed the dauphin from the arms of the queen and carried him off towards the Assembly.

➡When you get to the top of the steps, continue following the royal group as they crossed the terrace and turned immediately right into the National Assembly. You can't follow them all the way, though, because the entrance they used was right in the middle of rue de Rivoli (where it meets rue Castiglione). At that time the Assembly met in the *Manège*, the former royal riding school that had been built in 1720 for the 10-year-old Louis XV and his intended bride, the Spanish Infanta. The *Manège* was a long rectangular building of almost exactly the same width as rue de Rivoli that replaced it. It was 80 metres long and stood along rue de Rivoli taking up about half the block between rue Castiglione and rue d'Alger. Beyond it was a long open lane used for exercising the horses, known as the *carrière de l'escuyerie*, which continued all the way up to rue Saint-Roch. After the Assembly moved into the *Manège* on November 9th 1789 this lane became the principal entrance, linked to rue Saint-Honoré by rue Saint-Roch, which at that time was a cul-de-sac and called *rue du Dauphin*. Later in the Revolution it would become *rue de la Convention*. ➡If you leave the gardens for a minute and turn right along rue de Rivoli, you will be walking inside the *Manège*, probably the very part of it that the royal family hurried into on the morning of August 10th.

The *Manège,* or royal riding school, stood right in the middle of present-day rue de Rivoli. On November 9th 1789 it became the seat of the National Assembly, where three years later the French Republic was founded, and four months after that the king was condemned to death. (Author's private collection)

➡Stop opposite number 230 rue de Rivoli. Here you will find a plaque commemorating the *Manège*, where the Constituent Assembly, the Legislative Assembly and the National Convention all met in their turn to govern the country. It is amazing to think that on September 21st 1792 the French Republic was founded right here in the middle of rue de Rivoli.

➡At this point you should find a café to sit down, have a drink, and read about what happened two centuries ago in the middle of this busy street that became so fashionable for English visitors. If you are a lover of hot chocolate, ➡the best place to do this is at Angélina, the beautiful tearoom just opposite at number 226 rue de Rivoli, where you will have a unique chocolate experience!

Despite renovations ordered by Dr. Guillotin, the *Manège* was not an ideal place for the undisciplined mayhem of revolutionary politics. If it was not bad acoustics, it was the shouting from the public galleries that caused the deputies' voices to frequently be lost, for this was a new era of political involvement, when everyone wanted to have their say. Now that Parisians had the government right on their doorstep, the *Manège* soon became the most popular show in town. People would wait for hours to get in, despite the discomfort of the narrow benches, the lack of ventilation, the freezing chill of winter or the suffocating heat of summer. The deputies chose their position according to their politics, to the right or left of the president's table. This became very complicated when the president, for reasons of acoustics, decided to swap places with the speaker's rostrum opposite, thereby turning the Left into the Right and vice-versa. A most lyrical solution was found to this problem. The Left sat on the highest benches and became La Montagne (the Mountain), the Right sat lower down and were called either La Plaine (the Plain) or Le Marais meaning swamp or marsh. The Montagnards were quick to amuse themselves with this, frequently referring to their right-wing adversaries as *'the toads of the swamp.'*

The atmosphere at the *Manège* was often chaotic, and one description of a typical session here makes you wonder how any laws were ever passed. *'The speakers go one after the other to the rostrum, but you can hardly hear them, for the hall is so long and the public so noisy. In the middle circulate four attendants, in frizzy wigs, black outfits, and gilded swords by their side. They shout incessantly: "Silence! Sit down!" The deputies come and go, tapping their boots with their cane, coughing, spitting, talking loudly and shouting questions at a distance. The president rings his enormous bell, shouts himself hoarse...the attendants clap their hands in vain and exhaust themselves shouting "Sshh!" The deputies take as much notice as undisciplined schoolboys who know very well that the old schoolmaster will not hit them...then the ministers are to be seen coming into the hall; the keeper of the seals holds in his hand an envelope sealed with a large imprint of red wax: it's a letter from the king. Even though most of the deputies on the Left affect the greatest indifference, this short ceremony is not without a certain solemnity. The president rises and reads it to the Assembly. Such is the etiquette followed for the reception of communications from the Court.'* (Lenotre, 1906). At that time, of course, despite his diminished power, the king was still head of state. This was soon to change.

Some of the most dramatic moments associated with the downfall of Louis XVI took place right here in the middle of the traffic on rue de Rivoli. When he and his family finally arrived at the entrance to the Assembly, after their anxious dash through the gardens, there was a crowd milling around the door that for an instant made them fear for their lives. But they were allowed through, and received inside the door by one of the deputies, who took them into the Assembly. Louis strode firmly over to the president and said, *'I am come, gentlemen, to avoid a serious attack, believing that I cannot be in greater security than in your midst.'* Vergniaud, who was presiding, replied, *'You may rely, Sire, on the firmness of the assembly; its members have sworn to die in order to maintain the rights of the constituted authorities.'* But it was forbidden for the Assembly to deliberate in the king's presence, so the royal group were put in the reporters' gallery, a 3 square metre box directly behind the president's desk. As soon as they were installed, one of their servants broke part of the barrier separating the gallery from the Assembly, enabling Louis to watch his own downfall as it unfurled in cinemascope before his eyes. The royal governess, Madame de Tourzel, was also in the gallery that day and described the drama that followed, as a frightened Assembly wavered between defending the king and defending themselves.

Louis XVI watches his own overthrow from the Press Box of the National Assembly, the only place left in Paris where he and his family are safe. (Courtesy of Musée Carnavalet, Cabinet des Arts Graphiques, Paris)

'Roederer appeared at the bar... "We have this moment heard that the palace has been broken into." The assembly passed a decree placing persons and property under the safeguard of the people, and sent a deputation of twenty-five members to convey this declaration. Scarcely had it set out than the noise of cannon and musketry was heard...the assembly was half-dead with fear...some petitioners arrived..."We have set fire to the Tuileries", they said "and we will not put it out until the people have obtained justice to their satisfaction. We...demand the removal from office of the head of the government..." The president replied: "The assembly is watching over the safety of the empire; assure the people that it is about to consider the important measures its safety demands." "Dare you swear," they said to the deputies, "that you will save the empire?" "Yes," replied the deputies, rising to their feet, "we swear it." The concert of all those seditious voices, joined with the noise of cannon and musketry, made us all fearful. Each discharge of cannon made us tremble; the king and queen were in extreme distress...' (de Tourzel, 1988)

The royal party spent nearly fourteen hours in the sweltering heat of the reporters' gallery, and during this time the only sustenance the king took was one peach and a glass of water. Throughout the day the Assembly's desperate deliberations, the cannon fire at the Tuileries, the continuous stream of insults from the public gallery, and the shouts of the crowd as it invaded the Assembly all seemed to merge together, ringing in their ears like a surrealistic symphony. It heralded the beginning of a nightmare for the royal family, only one of whom would come out of it alive. By evening the Assembly had been invaded and the frightened deputies had agreed to the deposition of the king, who was taken with his family to the adjacent Feuillants Club for the night. They came back to the *Manège* in the morning for another day in the reporters' gallery, with a repeat performance again on the 12th, but on the 13th they were taken to the Temple prison.

Louis would not see the *Manège* again until four months later, when he was brought on December 11th to hear the 57 charges made against him. Without the benefit of notes or other preparation, the king made an eloquent response that lasted five hours and left many deputies in a state of palpable amazement and, in some cases, of secret admiration. On January 16th and 17th Louis came back to the *Manège* for his trial. He had not shaved for three days, and the deputies who were to judge him were struck by the pale face and sombre expression of the man who had once addressed them here as their master. Many were surprised by his composure, his *sang-froid,* as he sat on a wooden chair and faced his judges. The writer Sébastien Mercier was there in his role as a deputy, and described the final 72-hour session when Louis was condemned to death by a single vote.

'You picture to yourself, no doubt, an atmosphere of thoughtfulness, silence, a sort of religious awe. No such thing. The far end of the room was transformed into a grandstand, where ladies

The king faces his accusers in the National Convention. Robespierre sits in a green jacket on the front bench, observing closely the fallen monarch, and Danton is third along on the third bench. (Courtesy of Musée Carnavalet, Cabinet des Arts Graphiques, Paris)

in the most charmingly loose attire ate ices and oranges and drank liqueurs... The public galleries during the days preceding this famous judgement were never less than crammed with foreigners, and people of every class; they drank wine and brandy as if they were in a tavern. The betting was open in every neighbouring café...Each deputy went in turn to the rostrum and everyone kept saying: "Is it nearly my turn?" They brought in I know not which sick or convalescent deputy; he came muffled up in his nightcap and dressing-gown. The assembly laughed. Across the rostrum passed faces made more sombre by the pale gleam of the lights; in slow and sepulchral tones they uttered the one word "death". Picture all those countenances succeeding one another; all those voices; those different intonations; Orléans hooting, hissing, when he pronounced sentence of death on his kinsman; others calculating whether they would have time to dine before giving their verdict, while women pricked cards with pins to compare the totals; deputies who fell asleep had to be wakened up to vote.' (Mercier, 1947)

The Terrasse des Feuillants.

Let's leave poor Louis to his judges now, and ➡ go back into the Tuileries Gardens. On re-entering them you should turn immediately right along the Terrasse des Feuillants, which takes its name from the former Feuillant Convent that stood between here and rue Saint-Honoré. Since the construction of rue de Rivoli this terrace is narrower than it was when the deputies used to stroll down here to take the air between debates. From the moment the Assembly occupied the *Manège*, the Terrasse des Feuillants became a political information point, where diverse groups of people jostled each other, harangued each other, sometimes fought each other. There was a café on the terrace, where at the end of a debate deputies would gather to discuss the decisions that had been taken, and the Terrasse des Feuillants soon came to be seen as an integral part of the seat of government. It was known as the *Zone de la Nation* or *Zone de la Liberté*, and was separated by a huge tricolour ribbon from the rest of the garden. The garden itself was full of Swiss Guards defending the palace, and therefore referred to as the *Zone de la Contre-Révolution* or *Zone de Coblenz*, in reference to the popularity of that German city at the time as a meeting-up point for *émigrés*.

La Barrière de Faveur.

After the insurrection of June 20th 1792 the Tuileries gardens were closed and the entire area put under police surveillance. After a few days, however, the public were allowed to walk on the Terrasse des Feuillants, but could not go down into the garden, and Restif de la Bretonne described what happened. *'People did not go down, and it was the public themselves who created and guarded their own barrier.'* This *barrière de faveur* - meaning that people were simply asked politely not to go beyond it - was an unusually civilized phenomenon in an era marked by harsh decrees, strict security, arrests, searches and popular violence. Restif tells how *'an old man, intentionally or by mistake, went down. It was gently pointed out to him that he was emigrating and that he was going to Coblenz. He came back up. A lady of fashion, suspected of doing it on purpose, also went down; she was booed. She wanted to come back, but they wouldn't let her. She had to go and beg the Suisses to let her out on the other side. And that's not all. Soon the barrier was covered with little bits of paper containing the most violent and sarcastic comments against the king, the veto and the Court. I examined all this, and thought to myself - a violent crisis is brewing!'* (Restif de la Bretonne, 1986)

Théroigne's Punishment.

It was on the Terrasse des Feuillants that the feminist actress, Théroigne de Méricourt, suffered a humiliation from which she never recovered. Having made a name for herself in her scarlet riding habit and her sword - which she was not afraid to use - her continued involvement in the republican cause often brought her to the *Zone de la Nation*, where she delighted in haranguing the crowd. In the spring of 1793 she unwisely allied herself with Brissot and the Girondins, who were dangerously close to being expelled from the government and arrested, and two weeks before this happened Théroigne came to the *Manège* and tried to get into the Convention. For the previous few days the doors of power had been policed by a gang of rather formidable Jacobin women who on other occasions would be seen knitting at the foot of the guillotine. They stopped everyone who approached the entrance, scrupulously examining their entry card, and refusing to let in anyone not wearing a tricolour cockade.

When Théroigne arrived with a card she'd obtained through her Girondin connections, they refused to let her past, and regaled her with shouts of '*Here comes Brissot's friend!*' Théroigne regarded these women with contempt, and didn't mince her words in telling them so, before flouncing haughtily away from the door. This so angered some of them that they followed Théroigne down to the Terrasse des Feuillants, where they descended on her with shrieks of laughter, held her down, lifted up her skirts and whipped her. A group of onlookers gathered around, delighted by this unexpected entertainment, and shouted in encouragement, while Théroigne screamed in pain and humiliation - both made worse, no doubt, by the fact that 18th-century women didn't wear underwear. It seems that salvation appeared in the sordidly unkempt figure of Marat, who was not usually known for gestures of gallantry. He happened to be passing by, and - so the story goes - stepped in courageously to rescue Théroigne from this horrible experience. But if Marat saved that day for her, nothing could save her from the mental illness that followed. Some say it was because of her public humiliation, others say it was caused by syphilis, but it resulted in Théroigne spending the rest of her life locked up in an asylum, where she died in 1817 at the age of 55.

➡Continue walking westwards along the Terrasse des Feuillants, where people still like to view the gardens from above as Sebastien Mercier did over two centuries ago. *'When feathers float on the heads of our beauties, it is a very pleasant sight to contemplate from the height of the terrace all these moving, undulating plumes shimmering among a sea of strolling Parisians.'* Walking here in Mercier's time, you were surrounded by greenery on all sides, for there was no rue de Rivoli then. Instead you had the rather more peaceful view of the flower gardens and orchards of the houses and convents that bordered rue Saint-Honoré. ➡Keep walking until you see the back of the Jeu de Paume museum at the top of some steps to the left. This was built in 1853 at the same time as the Orangerie museum on the other side of the gardens. These names are not very logical, for where you now have the last section of the Terrasse des Feuillants and the Jeu de Paume, at the end of the 18th century you had - the *Orangerie*!

➥You will be walking through the former *Orangerie* as you continue straight on to the very end of the Terrasse des Feuillants. Here you should go southwards past the front of the Jeu de Paume, continuing in the same direction once you have passed it until you get to the ramp that leads down to the gardens. As you descend the ramp, keep to the right side of it and stop to look down on the space between the octagonal pond and the garden entrance. On July 12 1789 this was a scene of bloody violence, when Sebastien Mercier's '*sea of strolling Parisians*' fell under the sabres of the Prince de Lambesc and his soldiers. Lambesc, an Austrian officer and relative of Marie-Antoinette, was charged with dispersing the crowds that had gathered in Paris following the dismissal of Necker. Paris was just two days away from a revolution, and that day the American minister, Thomas Jefferson, was passing through the *Place Louis XV* (Concorde) in his carriage. As he went by the Tuileries gardens he noticed a battalion of Lambesc's cavalry lined up by the entrance. Next to them stood a decidedly hostile crowd, their hands already on a pile of stones that had been put there for the construction of the *Pont Louis XVI* (Pont de la Concorde). For a brief moment the future American president came within inches of being the first victim of the French Revolution. *'I passed through the lane they had formed, without interruption. But the moment after I had passed, the people attacked the cavalry...and the showers of stones obliged the horses to retire.'*

July 12th 1789 was a Sunday, and Thomas Jefferson was crossing the square at that time of day when hundreds of families were leaving the Tuileries to go home. The sight of the soldiers massed at the entrance made many of them hostile, and fearing a riot, Lambesc was ordered to force the crowds back into the gardens. The scene is described, rather lyrically, by Restif de la Bretonne. *'Tempted by a beautiful sky, the hardworking city-dweller, taking advantage of a day of rest, went to breathe the pure air of the gardens that Le Nôtre designed, the*

Tuileries. To relieve his pretty companion, the good-hearted Parisian carries his child...arriving on the grass by the shady pond, the husband and his companion sit down to rest, while the child that he carries runs towards other children who are playing: he frolics and makes his mother smile. On the terrace by the river, however, a few thoughtless people are provoking soldiers, assembled for no good reason. A stone, it is said, flew against Lambesc's helmet. The indignant commander trembles. He allows himself to be carried away by foolish advice; he enters on horseback into the king's garden...sacred haven reserved for games, laughter, love, and where Mars should only be seen as a statue...he advances, sabre in hand...piercing cries break out...everyone jumps up. They grab their children. Everyone takes flight.' (Restif de la Bretonne, 1986). This attack resulted in several deaths and a large number of wounded, and Lambesc had to answer for his actions in court, but he was acquitted on the grounds that he was only doing his duty.

Thomas Jefferson usually witnessed more agreeable sights in the Tuileries gardens. One pleasant Sunday in September 1784 he bought a ticket for 6 *livres* and witnessed the ascent of a hot-air balloon by the three Robert brothers. It seemed as if the entire population of Paris had turned out to see this spectacular feat, which ended successfully somewhere in the province of Artois, thus creating a record at the time for the longest flight in history. Parisians were kept in suspense for four days, however, since news of the landing did not reach the capital until the following Thursday. During his stay in Paris Jefferson was among those who came regularly to walk in the Tuileries, and his favourite place was the terrace which ran along the Seine on the south side of the gardens (Terrasse du Bord de l'Eau). From a precarious position on the wall of this terrace he used to admire at length - and at a distance - one of his favourite Parisian mansions that stood on the other side of the river. '*I was violently smitten,*' wrote Jefferson '*with the Hôtel de Salm, and used to go to the Tuileries almost daily to look at it. The woman*

Necker's dismissal generated protest in the capital, and the Prince de Lambesc was charged with dispersing the crowds. He and his soldiers charged into the Tuileries Gardens via the swivel bridge, killing several innocent civilians. (Author's private collection)

who rented chairs - inattentive to my passions - never had the complaisance to place a chair there, so that sitting on the parapet, and twisting my neck around to see the object of my admiration, I generally left it with a stiff neck.'

The Pont Tournant.

➡When you get to the bottom of the ramp, turn sharp right towards the exit. In the 17th century Louis XIII built a new city wall, and part of the moat surrounding it still existed at the western extremity of the Tuileries gardens when the Revolution broke out. What's more it was still filled with water, and made an effective barrier between the gardens and the *Place Louis XV* on the other side. In 1716 a bridge was built over it to allow access to the gardens from the square, but this was not an ordinary bridge. It was invented by an Augustinian friar named Nicolas Bourgeois, and operated rather like a lock gate. In an era when public riots were more and more frequent, this swivel bridge - known as the *Pont Tournant* - was well suited to keeping people out of the gardens as well as letting them in. When the Prince de Lambesc made his charge into the gardens, he fairly quickly saw the error of his decision, and tried to retreat back into the square. One valiant but misguided old man stood in his path and tried to stop him, shouting '*Draw back the swivel bridge!*' Within seconds he found himself on the end of Lambesc's sabre, as the prince ordered his troops back over the bridge.

➡ I'm going to leave you now to explore for yourself the delights of the Tuileries Gardens. In recent years they have been beautifully restored to their former glory, so you can now experience a classic French garden of the kind that André Le Nôtre created in the 17th century. But before you do, ➡ take a brief look outside at the Place de la Concorde, and bid a final farewell to Louis XVI and Marie-Antoinette, who were both guillotined here. From the height of the scaffold, they could see, across the trees of the gardens, the Tuileries palace, where they had lived out their last three years of semi-freedom. The king's final moments were spent in an earnest attempt to address the crowd around him. The queen, by contrast, remained silent, her thoughts elsewhere. The British were able to read about it later in the Annual Register. '*She seldom cast her eyes upon the populace...her spirits appeared to be calm...she ascended the scaffold with much haste and seeming impatience, and then turned her eyes with apparent emotion towards the garden of the Tuileries, one of the scenes of her former greatness.*'

WALK NUMBER SIX

Louis XVI is threatened while fleeing up the steps from the Tuileries Gardens.
(Authors private collection)

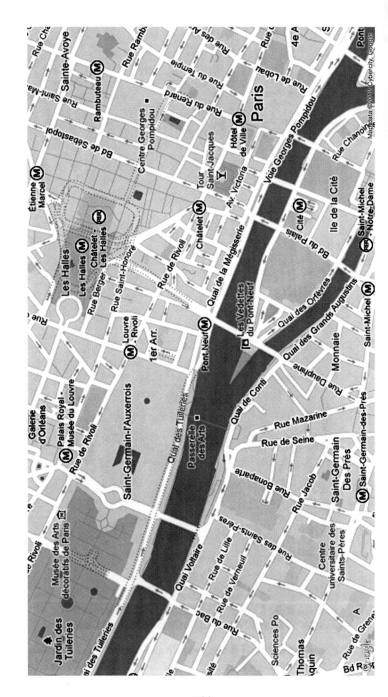

Walk Number Seven

THE ROUTE OF THE CONDEMNED
I. THEIR LAST LOOK AT THE CITY

Palais de Justice - Sainte-Chapelle - Conciergerie - Pont Neuf - rue Saint-Honoré - Place du Palais-Royal

From the Conciergerie prison sad processions of tumbrils set off each afternoon, transporting the daily batches of victims destined for the guillotine in Place de la Concorde, known then as *Place de la Révolution*. In walks number seven and eight you will follow in their footsteps, from prison cell to scaffold to grave, at the same time getting to know some of the residents of the area and the events that took place there. During walk seven you visit their prison, see where they were judged by the famous Revolutionary Tribunal, and then follow them as they are jolted around in a tumbril during their long and uncomfortable journey to the scaffold. On the way you'll see where Danton met his first wife, visit the pharmacy where a romantic Swedish count bought ink to write letters to the Queen, and witness the funeral cortege of a slightly less romantic but more famous count.

The Route of ohe Condemned
I. Their Last Look at the City

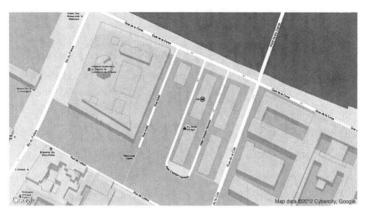

Metro: Cité

Rue de la Cité.

➥When you leave the metro you will find yourself in Place Louis-Lépine. Walk over to the Préfecture de Police, turn left along rue de Lutèce, and you will come to rue de la Cité, which runs along the east side of the square. This street was the result of the joining up in 1834 of two streets that both dated back many centuries. The part to the right, which runs between rue de Lutèce and Quai du Marché Neuf and borders on the Parvis Notre Dame, used to be called *rue de la Juiverie*. Its name comes from the Jewish tradesmen who settled here in the 5th century, establishing themselves as part of the busy commercial centre around the *Eglise Saint-Etienne*, predecessor of Notre Dame. The name of the street then was *Via Judearia*, and it must have been a very exotic kind of market place, for many of the vendors were Syrians selling aromatic oils and spices, jewels and oriental fragrances to the last few generations of Romans who lived here on the *Ile de Lutèce*.

The other part of rue de la Cité to the left, which runs alongside the Hôtel-Dieu hospital and ends at the Pont Notre Dame, used to be called *rue de la Lanterne*. During the Revolution there was a stationery shop in this street owned by a man named Renault, who had a daughter, Cécile Renault, considered to be one of the prettiest girls in the neighbourhood. She was 15 when the Revolution began, and for the next five years she regularly listened in on the endless conversations between her father and his customers, conversations that were invariably about politics, and in particular about a certain Maximilien Robespierre. It was 1794, and Cécile's mind was uneasy, perhaps traumatized by the horror of the daily cortège of tumbrils that left the Conciergerie within sight of where she lived. She was certainly not convinced of the 'incorruptibility' of this new leader, and perhaps had a slight nostalgia for the king that she remembered from her childhood. So she decided to pay Robespierre a visit. When you come to his house during Walk Eight, you'll learn more about what happened when Cécile knocked on his door.

BOULEVARD DU PALAIS.

➡ Turn around now and go back along rue de Lutèce, up to where it meets Boulevard du Palais, and stand on the corner outside the brasserie, *Les Deux Palais* (or go in it if it's time to have coffee or eat - the food here is very good, especially the *crème brulée*.) Rue de Lutèce was formerly *rue de la Vieille-Draperie*, a name originating with the drapers who set up business here in 1183 to replace the Jewish merchants run out of the city by Philippe-Auguste. In 1787 a semi-circular space was created here forming a public square in front of the entrance to the Palais de Justice. This space was called *Place du Palais*, and during the Terror it would fill up daily with people wanting to get a good view of the latest victims leaving the Conciergerie in a tumbril. The north end of Boulevard du Palais (looking right as you come up from rue de Lutèce) was called *rue Saint-*

Barthélemy, where in the 18th century you would have found the *Eglise Saint-Barthélemy*. It stood where you now find the Tribunal de Commerce, and dated back to the 5th century, but in 1772 the king ordered it to be entirely re-constructed. By the time this work was finished the Revolution was brewing, so the new church was very soon closed and sold. It was in this church that the young Manon Phlipon married Jean-Marie Roland, a marriage that turned her into the inspiration of the Girondin faction and one of the victims of the Terror. The church later became *Théâtre de la Cité*, where in 1795 a biting satirical play called 'Inside the revolutionary committees' stirred up the anti-Jacobin fever that was gripping the capital. The church was also used as a masonic lodge, then later the scene of a grand feast attended by Napoléon and Joséphine, and according to my waiter at *Les Deux Palais*, it also used to be a *palais de danse*.

The south end of Boulevard du Palais, to your left, was called *rue de la Barillerie*, where you will see the enormous building housing the Préfecture de Police, constructed in 1865. It was built on the site of two churches (*Les Barnabites* and *Saint-Germain-le-Vieux*) and a market called *Marché Neuf*, which stood on the present-day Quai du Marché Neuf. During the Revolution the two churches were turned into factories for producing soles for shoes, and the massive police building also covers the site of a house occupied by Simone Evrard after the death of her companion, Marat, in 1793. Her address was 33 *rue de la Barillerie*, a house she shared with Albertine Marat, sister of her murdered lover. They were both left in dire financial straits by Marat's death, and at first had to live in wretched lodgings in rue Saint-Jacques. Simone managed to retain an income of 560 *livres* a year from her former possessions, but the two women lived out the rest of their lives in relative misery, and they both died here, Simone from a fall at the age of 60, and Albertine in 1841, aged 83.

Directly in front of you as you emerge from rue de Lutèce is the Palais de Justice, with its famous prison, the Conciergerie, to the right, and Sainte-Chapelle to the left. This impressive complex of buildings stands on the site of the first royal palace built in France, that of the Capetian kings. It began in the 4th century as a fortified residence occupied by Roman magistrates, which was replaced by a king's palace in the 11th century. Philippe-Auguste, who was born there in 1165 and also married there at the age of 15, had a wall constructed between the palace and the Seine, leaving a small space between the wall and the river where several private houses were built. He was not very happy there, however, since despite the protection of the new wall, his palace was plagued by floods and permeated by the intolerable odour of fetid mud that was continually thrown up by the carts in *rue Saint-Barthélémy* (Boulevard du Palais).

In the early 13th century Louis IX, who is known as Saint Louis, enlarged the royal residence with the construction of a church in the palace enclosure. This was the Sainte-Chapelle, which he then linked to the palace via an arcade called *Galerie des Merciers*, as well as extending the north west limits of the palace with the construction of the Tour Bonbec. This is the smallest and the oldest of the four towers on the Quai de l'Horloge, and the only one to be built with turrets. Originally called *Tournelle de la Réformation*, its present name comes from the 15th century, when an interrogation room was set up on the ground floor. *Bec* was a slang word for mouth, and since interrogation in those days was frequently accompanied by torture, prisoners who suffered this would usually give in and talk *(avoir 'bon bec' pour parler)*. During the Terror the two floors of this tower, as well as part of the building that linked it to the Tour d'Argent, became the apartment occupied by Public Prosecutor, Antoine Fouquier-Tinville with his wife and their young twins.

Louis IX's grandson, Philippe-le-Bel, became king in 1285, but he soon found the palace too small to accommodate his growing administrative, financial and judicial staff, and began to make a few changes. He started by getting rid of the wall between the palace and the Seine, and then extending his property almost to the river bank. To do this he had to demolish the houses between the wall and the river, but it wasn't long before new stalls and booths sprang up on the bank against the wall of the new extension, which included two more towers, the Tour d'Argent and the Tour de César. In the new buildings along the side of the river, between the Tour de César and *rue Saint-Barthélemy*, Philippe installed all the communal quarters of the palace, which became a hive of domestic industry comprising such indispensable people as cup-bearers, plumbers, fruiterers, butchers and bakers. Provisions arrived by way of the river and were stored on the ground floor. The Salle des Gardes (Guards' Room) was built at this time, and above it was the *Grande Chambre* of the Parliament, where the king administered justice from his throne known as the 'Bed of Justice.' It was also under Philip le Bel that the two great halls of the Conciergerie were constructed - the Salle des Gens d'Armes (the Room of Armed People, from which we get the word *gendarme*) on the lower floor, and the *Grande Salle* or *Salle Haute* on the upper floor. The palace had two entrances at this time, one that corresponded with the present main entrance to the Cour de Mai, where there was a deep ditch and a drawbridge linking the palace with the street. The other entrance was approximately where the you now find the entrance to the courtyard of the Sainte-Chapelle.

The next king to make additions to the palace was Jean le Bon, who reigned between 1350 and 1364. He completed the north façade along the river with construction of the kitchens in 1353, and the square tower known as the Tour de l'Horloge (Clock Tower) which you can see on the corner of Boulevard du

Palais and Quai de l'Horloge. But the palace was by now living its last days as a seat of kings. On a cold February morning in 1357, Jean le Bon's son, the dauphin, later to become Charles V, witnessed here the brutal murder of the Marshalls of Champagne and Normandy, whose bloodstained bodies were dragged to a stone slab and left exposed to all who passed by. A few months later, the traumatized dauphin left the palace, first for the *Hôtel Saint-Pol*, then for the Louvre, and in 1431 the Capetian palace was permanently abandoned by the kings of France and handed over to the Parliament. The only original parts that still remain are the Salle des Gardes, the Salle des Gens d'Armes, the kitchens and the four towers by the river.

➡ To get into the Palais de Justice and the Sainte-Chapelle these days you have to go through a security check, which usually requires waiting in a rather long line. You'll find the entrance to this across the road and a little down to the left on rue de la Cité. There are two lines, with a barrier between them that seems to serve no purpose, since they both open out to the same place at the end, so ➡ my advice is to join the shorter one. Once you get through, you will come out into the Cour de Sainte-Chapelle, where you should go left to the ticket office. If you want to see the Sainte-Chapelle as well as the Conciergerie, it's best to buy a dual ticket (€11.50) for both of them. The Palais de Justice is free.

The Sainte-Chapelle.

(Tel: 01 53 40 60 93/97). ➡ From just next to the ticket office you go straight into the lower chapel of this 13th-century marvel, where you are met by a blaze of golden arches and painted pillars that immediately evoke the age of knights and crusaders. It was just before setting off on a crusade, in fact, that Louis IX (Saint Louis) had this beautiful chapel built within the walls of his palace. It stands on the site of the *Chapelle Saint-Nicolas-du-Palais*, where Saint Louis had enshrined the sacred

Crown of Thorns that he brought back from Constantinople in 1239. This extremely pious king, dressed in a plain white tunic, had walked barefoot when he brought the Crown into the city, accompanied by his knights bearing the gold and silver caskets that held the sacred relic. Work on the Sainte-Chapelle began in 1243 and it was consecrated in 1248, when the Crown of Thorns was installed in a shrine in the upper chapel. This chapel was reserved for the king and his family and entourage, while the lower chapel was for the palace guards and domestic staff.

The upper room of the Sainte-Chapelle is famous for its magnificent full-length stained glass windows, which give an intensely magical atmosphere to the chapel and achieve perfectly their objective of transporting you to heaven. They were first put there in 1248, but fire and the ravages of the Revolution took their toll on these magnificent works of devotional art, requiring them to be restored during the 19th century. Of the 1,134 scenes depicted, 720 of them contain the original glass, but the restoration has been done with such mastery that it is difficult to distinguish the restored panels from the originals.

In the middle of the apse of the upper chapel are two spiral staircases, which you can see through gilded open panels. On special feast days Saint Louis would go up the staircase on the left, bring out the Crown of Thorns and present it to the privileged group assembled in the upper chapel. The holy object would then be displayed to the public through a glass panel overlooking the courtyard, where people knelt in reverence and prayed. When the Revolution brought dechristianization in 1793, the monumental shrine that held the Crown of Thorns was taken to the Mint and melted, while the Crown itself was sent to the Bureau of Antiques at the Bibliothèque Nationale. It has since been restored to a more sanctified resting place in Notre Dame Cathedral.

The Revolution transformed the Sainte-Chapelle into a flour store before being taken over by a political club during the Directory, and under the Consulate it was a depot for legal and financial archives. However disrespectful it might seem to house financial records in such a sacred place, it was an enormous stroke of luck, for by the time the archives were being installed, this beautiful church already bore a sign over its doors saying, *'National Property - To Be Sold.'* But fortunately all things relating to money and law seem to be held in reverence by any government, and the church was never sold, thus escaping the inevitable demolition that was the fate of most churches auctioned off by the State. When you visit the Sainte-Chapelle, and you stand in awe at its gilded interior and the breathtaking stained glass windows of the upper chapel, you will realize how grateful we should be to those dusty old archives that saved it for us!

Palais de Justice.

➡Coming out of the Sainte-Chapelle, you go through the gate, turn left back into the Cour de Sainte-Chapelle, then turn left again and walk through the arches into the Cour de Mai. This has always been the principal courtyard since the establishment of the original palace, and gets its name from the May trees that were planted here every Spring by law students. Following a huge fire in January 1776, the façade you now see was built between 1783 and 1786, by three architects named Desmaisons, Couture and Antoine. At the same time a master locksmith called Bigonnet made the splendid 40-metre long wrought iron railings to your right, with three gates all decorated in gold, separating the Cour de Mai from the street. The grand stone stairway that leads to the principal entrance was also built at this time, between two small arches. Under the arch to the right is a cafeteria for the Palace staff, who, as they sit happily eating their lunch, hopefully spare an occasional thought for the unfortunate people who passed through their restaurant 200 years ago. For until 1825 this was the only way in to the Conciergerie prison, and it was through this entrance that prisoners condemned by the revolutionary Tribunal were led out of their prison, through the tiny lower courtyard, up the steps and into the Cour de Mai. Here they would be met by the tumbrils that were lined up in the courtyard waiting to take them to the guillotine.

Marie-Antoinette began her final journey by walking up these steps from the small courtyard into the Cour de Mai. The same steps were taken by Danton, Robespierre, Desmoulins, Saint-Just, Bailly, Hébert, Madame Roland, the Girondins and countless other victims of the Revolution. (Courtesy of Musée Carnavalet, Cabinet des Arts Graphiques, Paris)

These few steps leading up into the Cour de Mai have been trodden by all those famous patriots condemned to death by the Revolution they so believed in - Danton, Robespierre, Desmoulins, Saint-Just, Bailly, Hébert, Madame Roland, and the Girondins, one of whom, Valazé, was already dead and had to be carried up the steps. Marie-Antoinette also came up them, in a state of shock, for she had expected a carriage, not a common tumbril, to be waiting for her. For hours before the arrival of the condemned prisoners people would crowd on to the main steps of the Palais de Justice to get a better view of the victims as they embarked on their last voyage. The rooms now occupied by the staff restaurant were the offices of the *greffier*, or clerk of the court, who was responsible for keeping a register of incoming and outgoing prisoners, and it was here that personal belongings were deposited on entering the prison. During the Revolution very few prisoners ever saw those belongings again.

➡ Walk across the Cour de Mai and stop a moment at the foot of the wide steps known as the Grand Escalier and spare a thought for the unfortunate 'countess', Jeanne de La Motte-Valois, that legendary confidence trickster in the Affair of the Queen's Diamond Necklace. After her near-perfect scheme failed, she was condemned here in the Palais de Justice to be publicly whipped and to have a letter 'V' (for *voleuse*/thief) branded on her shoulders with a hot iron. After that her possessions were to be confiscated and she would be imprisoned for life. The execution of this terrible judgement took place right here at the foot of these steps in the Cour de Mai on the morning of June 20th 1786. It was carried out before a crowd of nearly a thousand people, all pressed against the palace railings in an attempt to get a glimpse of the notorious prisoner as she was dragged out into the courtyard. A contemporary account describes what a truly blood-curdling spectacle it turned out to be.

'Up until that day she was unaware of her sentence; in order to make her kneel for the reading out of the judgement, her legs had to be bent by force. She abandoned herself to such a rage on hearing the pronouncement, she let out screams so terrible that they could be heard throughout the entire palace and in the surrounding streets; she shrieked at the clerk of the court and the executioners: "So what have they done to that rogue of a Cardinal, if they treat me like this? Me, of Valois blood!" Five executioners held her down in order to slip the rope around her neck. She rolled about on the ground in the Cour de Mai; she flailed her limbs,

screamed like a fury and uncovered her entire body, which is superb, which has the most beautiful shape according to the reports of those who were present at this execution. The executioners were obliged to tear her bodice and her shift in order to uncover her shoulders, but she struggled so furiously that the red-hot iron slipped on her back, and, sliding under her armpit, burned her beautiful breast. She bit the arm of one of the executioners; a piece of his clothing and his flesh remained in her mouth. She then became extremely faint.' (Manceron, 1972-87)

When Jeanne de la Motte's diamond necklace confidence trick failed, she was sentenced to be publicly branded with a V for *voleuse* (thief). Here you see Sanson approaching her with a hot iron, while several of his assistants hold down the struggling Jeanne. (Author's private collection)

If you're not feeling too faint yourself after such a story, ➡walk up the steps into the Palais, where you will find yourself in the Galerie Marchande (Merchants' Corridor), built by Desmaisons in 1780 on the site of Louis IX's *Galerie des Merciers*. Louis never felt secure in his palace, and lived in constant fear of being murdered, so he built this connecting corridor to enable him to pass directly from his personal apartments to the upper level of the Sainte-Chapelle. This effectively gave him an entirely private floor, thus minimizing the risk of intruders, but the corridor was later filled up with boutiques and bookshops, the last of which remained until 1840.

➡ Turn right on entering the Palais and go to the end of the Galerie Marchande, where you turn left on to the Galerie des Prisonniers, also the work of Desmaisons (the names of these *galeries* are marked on the walls). As you go along this long, rather sombre corridor with its stately colonnades, you are walking with the ghosts of hundreds of doomed prisoners who were conducted through here to the Tribunal. Once on this path, there was very little hope of surviving the next 24 hours, for in the majority of cases the only way out of the Tribunal was in a tumbril. Most of the prisoners taken along this corridor were women, who were brought from their side of the prison by way of a spiral staircase that came up from the Chapel below and emerged at the far end of the Galerie des Prisonniers. It was called the Chapel Staircase, and at the time was barred and bolted at several points to avoid any possibility of escape. Bringing the women up to the Tribunal this way avoided taking them through the quarters reserved for male prisoners, who went to their trial via the Tour Bonbec. Among the more celebrated prisoners conducted to their doom by the Chapel Staircase and the Galerie des Prisonniers were the Girondins and their leader Jacques Pierre Brissot. Marie-Antoinette also came to her trial up the Chapel Staircase, but then went to the Tribunal chamber by way of the *Galerie des Peintres*, now called the Galerie Saint-Louis, an alternative route taken by many prisoners.

➡ Walk along the Galerie des Prisonniers to where it ends, at *escalier* R on the left and the entrance to the Cour de Cassation on the right. If you then turn around and go back to where it meets the Galerie Marchande, you will follow in the footsteps of the Girondin deputies as they walked to the Tribunal, turning left into the Salle des Pas-Perdus. This means 'concourse', but translates literally as 'hall of lost footsteps', where the sounds of walking were inaudible in so vast a space. The Salle des Pas-Perdus was the site of the original *Salle Haute*, built at the end of the 13th century by Philip le Bel, and which bore very little resemblance in either decor or atmosphere to the vast openness of the present-day hall. Go in past the *Acceuil* to the left, look around you and try to picture the original *Salle-Haute*, which must have looked like something out of a fairy tale. It was destroyed by fire in 1618, which is a great loss, for it was a truly magnificent hall, supported by a central row of eight pillars bearing the sculpted figures of 58 kings of France, all painted in gold and azure. The floor was tiled in black and white like a chessboard, and a huge marble dining table constructed in nine interlocking sections served both as a banqueting table and a theatrical stage for entertaining the king. This amazing hall was rendered even more exotic by the crocodile and snake skins that hung from the ceiling, no doubt brought back by crusading knights from their adventures in far-off lands. After the fire the *Salle Haute* was re-constructed in 1622 by Salomon de Brosse, architect of the Luxembourg Palace, but was again destroyed by fire at the hands of the Commune in 1871. It was rebuilt in its original style the following year, when it got its present name of Salle des Pas-Perdus.

THE REVOLUTIONARY TRIBUNAL.

➡As you enter the Salle des Pas-Perdus, look over to your left in the far corner of the hall and you will see a doorway marked Première Chambre du Tribunal Civil. Behind those doors is one of the most historic sites associated with the Revolution, for this was the seat of the *Tribunal Révolutionnaire de Paris*, established here on March 10th 1793 - and contrary to what you might expect, ➡you can go in and look at it. All hearings are open to the public, so even if you see people in there, you can go in quietly, sit down and listen to the proceedings - but I would advise you to ➡first sit on one of the many benches in this hall and read about the Tribunal before going in, for it's not a good idea to rustle pages if there is a hearing going on. When you enter the chamber you will be going through the same doorway that hundreds of prisoners passed through, often in large groups, all accused of the same crime. They were taken to the prisoners' benches, but you should ➡find a place in the public seating area, then look into the centre of the chamber and try to picture what you would have seen there during the Revolution. That is where, on October 16th 1793, Marie-Antoinette sat on a stool facing her accusers, where at 4 o'clock in the morning she heard her death sentence pronounced, then was taken out by her guards and returned to her cell to prepare for the end. Perhaps you can see the much-feared Public Prosecutor Fouquier-Tinville, dispensing justice in his ostrich-plumed hat, or Danton roaring his defence from the prisoners' benches, and the increasingly large 'batches' of mostly innocent people all condemned together as the Terror gathered pace. It is awe-inspiring to be in the very place where these thing happened.

This historic room dates from Philip le Bel's reign, then called the Great Parliament Chamber where the king administered the law from his 'bed of justice.' It was bigger than the room you see nowadays, and had a beautiful coffered oak ceiling painted by Fra Giovanni Giocondo, which unfortunately did not survive the occupation of the hall by the Tribunal. The revolutionary judges were as pitiless with their new premises as they were with their prisoners, for they proceeded to deface all remnants of the previous epoch by destroying not only Giocondo's ceiling, but also a beautiful gilded sculpture of the Lion of Justice, a bust of Louis XV, and all the wall hangings decorated with the *fleur-de-lys*. The room was re-named the Hall of Liberty, and its walls decorated with revolutionary murals, the Constitution and the Declaration of the Rights of Man.

These were dark days for the Palais de Justice, when the very word 'justice' gradually came to mean no more than an interrogation consisting of one question, summary judgement and immediate execution. When the revolutionary Tribunal was originally established, the Minister of Justice at the time was Danton, who considered it essential to have such a court, which would be *'terrible, so as to prevent the people from being terrible.'* He was referring to the massacres that had been carried out by Parisians the previous September, and which he himself had done nothing to prevent. His rationale in creating the Tribunal was that it would eliminate the need for any similar outbreaks of popular justice.

The name that stands out in the history of the Tribunal is, of course, Antoine Fouquier-Tinville, Public Prosecutor, who by the summer of 1794 was condemning to death 200 people a week, and who later, in his own defence, declared that he had been nothing more than *'the axe of the Convention.'* He owed his job to his cousin, Camille Desmoulins, who must have bitterly regretted this act of generosity when Fouquier-Tinville's judgement sent him to the guillotine in April 1794. Fouquier was, in fact, a thorough-going bureaucrat, who followed to the letter the orders of the Committee of General Security. It was this committee that decided who would or would not be arrested, and after that their fate was held in the hands not just of the Tribunal, but also the executioner. For every day, in the early morning, Sanson would go to Fouquier-Tinville's office, where together they would agree on the number of condemnations for that day.

Fouquier was so conscientious about his job that he decided to move out of his home in the nearby Place Dauphine, and install his family in the Tour Bonbec of the Conciergerie. His apartment there was spacious, consisting of an antechamber, lit solely by the light that came from the corridor through a small barred window, a bedroom and a living-room with a view of the Seine. Upstairs was the kitchen and dining-room, and above that, in the mansard roof, were three more small bedrooms. From here Fouquier was able to exercise complete control of his domain, and according to the historian Lenotre, was in his element. *'Fouquier was totally at home at the Tribunal; starting at dawn, he roamed the corridors, he went to the clerk's office, to the public prosecutor's office, to his own office, where the doors were always open, and he surveyed the arrival of employees.'* He also went quite often to the *buvette*, a sort of cafeteria on the first floor of the Tour César, next to the Tribunal chamber, where the judges and jury could refresh themselves during hearings with large quantities of wine. Fouquier's main weakness was wine, and one of his employees later described how, after drinking in the evening, he would *'come and make a terrible din in the offices, breaking up boxes, and insulting the employees.'* But, despite Fouquier's reputation as the monster of revolutionary justice, this particular employee did not condemn him so harshly, adding, *'I have never seen him either cruel or fierce,'* and Fouquier-Tinville insisted to the end of his trial that he merely had orders, and obeyed them.

The Tribunal judged some of the most celebrated figures of the Revolution, including Marie-Antoinette, whose trial lasted two days, ending at 4 o'clock in the morning of October 16th 1793. White-faced and weakened by continual haemorrhages, and scarcely able to see the courtroom on account of short-sightedness, she sat impassively through most of the proceedings, until Hébert took the witness stand and accused her of incest with her young son. Many of the spectators were as shocked as the queen herself at this totally fabricated piece of evidence, and, pressed by the President of the Tribunal for a response, she stood up and looked desperately around the courtroom. *'If I have not replied, it is because Nature refuses to reply to such an accusation made to a mother. I appeal to all mothers here.'* It was the only moment during the trial when she received genuine sympathy from the public, for she had otherwise come to be seen as the personification of all the evils of the old regime, and this prejudice was evident during her trial. At one point one of the officials observed that she was thirsty, and brought her a glass of water. After her condemnation, he was arrested, along with her three defence lawyers, one of whom, Malesherbes, was later executed.

'I appeal to all mothers here'. On trial for her life, Marie-Antoinette made this anguished plea when Hébert accused her of incest with her young son, an entirely fabricated piece of evidence that evoked the only sympathy the queen received during that terrible night. (Author's private collection)

The judgement of the 21 Girondins was held here in October 1793, a trial that also had a dramatic moment when one of the prisoners, Charles Valazé, took a dagger from inside a rolled up paper that he had been holding during the trial, and stabbed himself through the heart. A fellow prisoner, not realizing what Valazé had done and seeing him falter, asked him if he was frightened. *'No,'* replied Valazé, *'I'm dying!'* Another celebrated revolutionary to be tried here for crimes against the Republic was the Duc d'Orléans, Philippe Egalité, whose name Fouquier-Tinville noted in his register of condemnations as *Légalité*, perhaps by mistake, but perhaps out of mockery.

The show-piece of the revolutionary Tribunal, however, was the trial of Georges Danton, who entered the courtroom *'like the bull who surges furiously into the bullring, his horns lowered.'* He thundered his own defence so eloquently that Fouquier-Tinville feared the trial would turn public opinion against the all-powerful Committee of Public Safety. The trial of the Dantonists was, in fact, a veritable piece of theatre, with several of the accused contributing to the entertainment and evoking hoots of laughter and applause from the public gallery. When Camille Desmoulins was asked his age, he replied, *'Thirty-three, the age of the sans-culotte Jesus when he died.'* But it was Danton who stole the show with his loud outbursts of insolent humour and long speeches that the judges tried in vain to suppress. When asked his address, he replied, *'My address? Soon my home will be in the void, and my name in the Panthéon of history!'* He interrupted the proceedings continually from the first official reading of the charges, bringing the court into such an uproar that Herman, the President of the Tribunal, was obliged to rapidly suspend the first session.

The next day, when one of the accused complained that he had not had an initial interrogation, Herman replied contemptuously that this was just a useless formality. Danton did not miss the opportunity. *'We are all here as a "formality"!'* he shouted sarcastically, to roars of laughter from his fellow prisoners. *'I'm the one who created this Tribunal,'* he added with satisfaction, *'I know better than anyone how it should be conducted!'* He lived up to his reputation for coarseness and audacity to the end, answering accusations of conspiracy by suggesting that he would never have had time. *'Me a conspirator? I spend every night in bed with my wife!'* To charges of bribery and corruption he boasted, *'Danton bought? A man of my calibre has no price!'* He ranted on for hours, to the despair and apprehension of those presiding over the trial, for he was clearly getting too much sympathy from the public. His voice could be heard outside in the

Salle des Pas-Perdus and the Galerie Marchande, where crowds of people listened intently to every word and passed it down to those outside on the steps of the Palais, and from there to the whole of Paris. It could also be heard in some of the cells of the Conciergerie, where prisoners waited in anticipation and in the vain hope that Danton would save the day and liberate them from their prisons. Eventually his voice began to fail, he could hardly speak, and Herman seized the opportunity to adjourn the session.

By the time the court next met, the National Convention had issued a decree authorizing Herman to expel from the court any prisoner who obstructed the trial. Without letting the prisoners speak, Herman addressed the jury, who affirmed that they had enough evidence to reach a verdict, and Herman declared the debate closed. *'Closed!'* shouted Danton, *'It hasn't begun yet! You haven't heard our witnesses!'* Then Desmoulins demanded to be heard, and an uproar broke out on the prisoners' benches. But Herman clasped his decree firmly in both hands and, with immense satisfaction, ordered out all the prisoners, who left the courtroom waving clenched fists, spitting vengeance at the judges and shouting abuse. Desmoulins refused to get up from his seat, and had to be forcibly moved by three security guards who carried him out, his arms waving. As he left, Danton hurled his last, not altogether modest words to the Tribunal. *'My name is engraved on every revolutionary institution! The Committees, the Tribunal, the Army, I'm the one who made all that!'* The prisoners never came back into the courtroom, and they were hastily judged and condemned to death in their absence.

The period of the Great Terror began on June 10th 1794, with the passing of the infamous Law of 22 *Prairial* that deprived those accused by the Tribunal of any hope of being able to defend themselves. It radically reformed the judicial procedure applicable to 'suspects' by reducing it to a bare minimum, stating that *'all slowness is a crime, all formality is an indulgence and a public danger; the time it takes to punish enemies of the Nation should only be the time it takes to recognize them.'* Speed had became a necessity in April of that year, following an order that all suspects be brought to Paris for trial. This effectively made Fouquier-Tinville the most powerful public prosecutor in France, and the sheer numbers of prisoners coming to the capital put an impossible strain on an already overworked judicial machine. The Law of 22 *Prairial* would turn it into a judicial pantomime. Under this law the Tribunal could dispense with witnesses if it felt satisfied with the proof furnished, defence lawyers were abolished, and there could be only two possible outcomes, acquittal or death.

The Law of 22 *Prairial* led to the terrifying daily 'batches' of victims, where sometimes as many as 50 people would all be condemned together for the same crime and taken immediately for execution. After having their hair cut and their hands tied, they would be brutally herded into the tumbrils that rolled ceaselessly through the city, towards the guillotine that had been set up in the *Place du Trône-Renversé* (now Place de la Nation). Instead of a seat of justice, the Tribunal became a chamber of terror, where people were despatched to their death sometimes for the simple fact of being related to an *émigré*, for having read a letter from an *émigré*, or simply uttering a sigh of despair against the Revolution. Denouncements became the order of the day, sometimes even within the same family, and people lived in fear of their lives. The number of prisoners' benches increased daily, eventually taking up an entire side of the Tribunal, and those who found themselves on them had little hope of living more than a few more hours, unless they were fortunate enough to be an expectant mother. Many female prisoners managed to gain an extra day by claiming they were pregnant, but as soon as the subsequent examination proved otherwise, they were sent off with the next day's group of condemned prisoners. If a woman was genuinely pregnant, she was given a stay of execution until her baby was born. This was a dubious blessing, however, for these poor women were kept under surveillance in a hospice, where they suffered a pregnancy fraught with anguish and impending horror. At the moment of birth, the executioners would arrive, often immediately, and the new mother would be torn away from her infant and taken to the scaffold. But some women were saved by pregnancy, for 9 *Thermidor* arrived before their babies did. One such woman was Madame Louise-Sylvine de Blamont, whose noble husband Jacques was a former bodyguard. Louise-Sylvine was condemned to death for conspiracy shortly before the fall of Robespierre, but her sentence was suspended until the birth of her baby. She gave birth two weeks after 9 *Thermidor*, was freed by the Committee of General Security, and left Paris for Bellac in central France. There she was reunited with Jacques, also liberated from a provincial prison, and they remained there for the rest of their lives, eternally grateful, I should think, for the child who in a slight reversal of roles had given life to his mother. Louise-Sylvine's husband became mayor of Bellac, and died in 1830, while she lived another 34 years, dying at the age of 91 in 1864, by which time she might well have been the last person still living to have appeared before the revolutionary Tribunal.

Some of the officials who worked for Fouquier-Tinville were not all as cold-blooded as those who have given the Tribunal its sanguinary reputation, and there were some who cracked under the strain of such terrible work. One of the prison warders, a man named Blanchard, burst into tears one day, weeping that he had had enough and that he was going to resign, for the work was making him ill. Some feared for their own lives, and accounts from the Palais de Justice at the time describe one such employee who rushed into the clerks' office traumatized and terrified. *'It's finished!'* he cried, *'No-one is judged any more; we'll all end up at the guillotine, we're all lost!'* His fear was not entirely unfounded, for on 1 *Thermidor*, Fouquier sent one of his clerks, a hard-working family man named Adrien Legris, to his death on some very spurious charges relating to the quality of his work, with the object of making him a salutary example to other employees.

The defence lawyers also lived under threat, until their work was virtually abolished by the Law of 22 *Prairial*. They were all required to have an official 'civic certificate' in order to enter the Tribunal, and anyone who was refused such a certificate was declared suspect. There was a notice posted on the door of the Tribunal chamber, forbidding entry to any defence lawyer who was not in possession of this vital paper. Many lawyers, like Maitre Lavaux, a Public Defender, lived in a permanent state of fear because of this requirement, for certificates were not issued automatically, they had to be requested, and many lawyers dared not ask for one for fear of being refused. Every time Maître Lavaux went past the guards who stood at the entrance to the Tribunal, he trembled with fear in case they asked him for his certificate. Terror was certainly the order of the day. Maître Lavaux described in his memoirs what it was like to work in such an atmosphere.

'I was always having to reassure or console prisoners; I spent my life in the Conciergerie; I saw the condemned prisoners saying their sad goodbyes to their wives, children, relations, friends...' When he tried to gain time for prisoners with some form of appeal he met with a strange reaction. *'My clients would write to the Public Prosecutor, accusing me of negligence, and asking for a prompt decision...right to the last they believed in the justice of the Tribunal, and in the power of their own innocence, persuaded that those whom they saw disappear every day were convicted of a genuine conspiracy. Some merely preferred death to a long imprisonment.'* Fouquier-Tinville would show these letters

to Lavaux, and say, *'Look, read that; why do you persist in trying to paralyze the Tribunal, when your clients can't wait to get themselves guillotined?'* (Lenotre, 1933)

Some people indeed sought to be executed, having lost all desire to remain alive after the condemnation of a loved one. When the royalist publisher, Gattey, was condemned to death, his sister was in the public gallery, where she shouted very loudly *'Long Live the King!'* Everyone tried to silence her, and to save her by moving aside so she could escape. But she remained in her place and continued to shout the same words even more resolutely over and over again. She was arrested, of course, and Maître Lavaux was charged with defending her. *'I did not have much hope,'* he wrote later, *'but I went ahead on the basis of the axiom 'volenti mori non creditur.' Mlle Gattey wanted no part in my efforts, and by irritating her judges with her sarcasm, she got what she wanted.'*

Maître Lavaux's efforts, however admirable, were largely useless in the face of the corruption and gratuitous cruelty of many of the judges and jurors. One particularly odious member of the jury was Joachim Vilate, who adopted the fashionably Roman name of *Sempronius Gracchus* and had ostentatiously taken up residence in the Tuileries Palace in the former apartment of the Princesse de Lamballe. Lenotre describes him vividly but with little sympathy. *'This elegant hedonist, very much in favour...roamed the corridors of the Tribunal, a toothpick in his mouth, without deigning to take part in the deliberations: one day, when the hearing was prolonged, he declared, "The prisoners are now convicted on two charges; here it is, 4 o'clock, and I haven't dined yet: they are conspiring against my stomach."'* Another juror, Châtelet, on receiving the list of prisoners to be judged that day, would scribble the letter F next to the names, indicating *foutu*, slang meaning 'done for'. He would then spend the rest of the hearing drawing caricatures of the prisoners on his desk blotter.

René Dumas, who replaced Herman as President of the Tribunal after the trial of Danton, inspired so much fear that the Tribunal became known as the *Tribunal Dumas*. He would always have two pistols in front of him on his desk, for he too was frightened, and often drunk. *'What is your name?'* was the only question he would ask the people who appeared before him, most of whom he reduced to submissive silence within a few seconds.

The travesties of justice that took place at the Tribunal were flagrant, and tragically numerous. *'You have a brother who is an aristocrat,'* the judge accused one prisoner, who replied, *'I don't have any brothers.'* *'Well,'* retorted the furious judge, *'if it isn't your brother, it's obviously your father!'* On one occasion, Fouquier-Tinville asked one of the bailiffs to bring a certain Duchesse de Biron to the Tribunal. On returning from the prison, the bailiff told him that there were two duchesses of that name. *'Good,'* replied Fouquier, *'they can both come up together.'* The two ladies were both executed the next day.

On another occasion a boy of 17 named Jean-Baptiste Marie-Bertrand Saint-Pern was summoned to the Tribunal in error, for his name wasn't on the official list in front of the judges that day. But he was judged all the same, along with his mother, his sister and brother-in-law. During the hearing he held firmly on to the hand of one of his guards, wishing to show him that he was not frightened. But it was the guard who eventually had to let go of the young prisoner's hand, for he was so moved by the tragedy that he was trembling himself. They were all condemned to death, but Jean-Baptiste's sister, Amélie Saint-Pern, miraculously escaped execution by being in an advanced state of pregnancy. She had the courage to come back the following year to the scene of her ordeal, to testify against Fouquier-Tinville during his trial, when she revealed that her young brother had been judged as his own father, who was unable to be found. The fact that his father was 51 and the boy was a teenager was not deemed sufficient proof of his identity to the judges, who were more interested in quotas than in justice. Amélie's appearance at Fouquier's trial was like that of a phantom, for her escape from death had never been noted, and when you go to the Picpus Cemetery, you will still see her name listed among those guillotined on 1 *Thermidor*.

Another even younger victim, inaptly named Fortuné-Charles de Maillé, was condemned to death with his father at the age of 16. His mother should also have been with them, but when her name was called in the women's prison, the bailiffs mistakenly brought another prisoner called Madame Mayet. Even though the mistake was recognized, the unfortunate lady was judged and executed that day. Madame de Maillé also survived to testify at Fouquier-Tinville's trial, where she gave her account of how she escaped the guillotine. *'I was taken to the Saint-Lazare prison; my son aged sixteen, who had not been arrested, wanted to come with me; on 6 Thermidor he was taken to the Tribunal; I learned that I would not go that day, that a lady named Mayet had been taken in my place, and that she was told, after her judgement, "It's not you we intended to condemn, but at least it's done; today is as good as tomorrow!" When my turn came, on entering the Tribunal and seeing those benches where my son had perished, I fainted: the public were outraged, seeing the terrible state I was in, and managed to get me out of the room.'* One of the judges accused with Fouquier interrupted her, declaring that he had been presiding that day, and that it was he, not the public, who had got her out. But Madame de Maillé was firm. *'It is the people that I must thank for not being judged that day.'* She was then asked if she had proof that her son had indeed been only 16 at the time of his condemnation. *'Here is his birth certificate: he was born in 1777, the 25th of August...his only crime was to have thrown a rotten herring at the nose of grocer who had served it to him...and he was condemned to death.'* (Lenotre, 1933). This 'crime' must have been cooked up by the boy's accusers after his arrival in prison, for he hadn't ever been arrested, but chose to go into captivity with his parents.

On rare occasions the Tribunal could be swayed by the unexpected. In March 1794 a 17-year-old boy called Alphonse-Louis-Dieudonné Martainville, a pupil at the *Collège de l'Égalité* (Louis-le-Grand), appeared at the Tribunal charged with being involved in the publication of unpatriotic tracts. Perhaps his youth was an advantage, but he was acquitted after entertaining the judges with his humour and remarkable sang-froid in the face of possible death. When the President of the Tribunal addressed him as 'de Martainville', the young man stood up, laughed, and then declared to the rather amazed President, *'Citizen President, I am not called de Martainville, but Martainville...Don't forget that you're here to shorten me, not to lengthen me...'* A rare burst of laughter broke out amongst the judges and jury, provoking Fouquier-Tinville into impulsively declaring, *'Well, let's release him then.'* And so they did, and the fortunate young Alphonse walked out of the Tribunal a free man.

The young were not the only hapless victims of this judicial farce. The Maréchale de Noailles was almost 80 when she was condemned to death along with her daughter-in-law, Vicomtesse Anne-Dominique de Noailles. Both were deaf, and in addition the old Maréchale was nearly blind. In order to ask them their names, they had be be brought down right next to the President's desk so they could hear the question, and the Maréchale was so infirm that she had to be supported by guards as she descended the steps of the prisoners' benches. This was the only part of their interrogation that the two women were aware of - they were not even able to hear their own sentence of death - and during the trial someone protested at the charges brought against the Maréchale, citing her age and the fact that she was deaf and blind. Fouquier's reply, difficult to translate, is notorious in the history of the Tribunal. *'In that case she is found guilty of conspiring blindly and 'deafly' against the Republic.'* The Maréchale de Noailles was guillotined later that same day along with her daughter-in-law and her grand-daughter.

Another prisoner, 70-year-old Pierre Puy de Vérine, was also deaf and totally blind since a fall at the age of 3, and the judges found it almost impossible to make him understand what was going on. When they thought he was sufficiently informed, they sent him to the guillotine. Some prisoners were heroic, like Jean-Simon Loizerolles, imprisoned in Saint-Lazare with his wife and his son François-Simon. On 7 *Thermidor* François heard his name called for the Tribunal, and rushed to his father's cell to say goodbye to him. But when he got there he found the old man being dragged out of his bed by two guards, and realized that it was his father who had been called, not him. On his arrival at the Conciergerie, however, Jean-Simon heard the official charge against him, and was surprised to hear it read out in François' name. He didn't say a word, and appeared before the judges as if he was his son. The fact that François was 22 years old, while he was 61 and white haired, seemed to have gone unnoticed, and he was thus able to save his son from the guillotine. Jean-Simon was condemned to death with a 'batch' of 35 prisoners from Saint-Lazare, which also included the poet André Chénier.

Revolutionary justice did not shrink from condemning men of either letters or science, having already guillotined the astronomer Jean Sylvain Bailly in November 1793. In March 1794 the mathematician Marie Jean Antoine de Condorcet was about to be condemned when he decided to take his own life with poison rather than be murdered by the Revolution. On May 8th of the same year the Tribunal made one of its most notorious condemnations, that of the chemist Antoine Laurent Lavoisier, who was guillotined along with 27 other Farmers-

General accused of aiding the enemies of France. In terms of his contribution to the evolution of chemistry as a science, Lavoisier has been compared to Galileo and Newton, a distinction that was of no interest however to Jean-Baptiste Coffinhal, the judge presiding over the Tribunal that day. When Lavoisier asked for a stay of execution in order to complete an experiment, Coffinhal's famous reply showed to what extent revolutionary justice had lost touch with the essence of revolutionary ideals. *'The Revolution has no need of scholars or chemists. The course of justice cannot be delayed.'*

Of the 2,750 people that Fouquier-Tinville's Tribunal condemned to death, a large percentage were judged during the six weeks between 22 *Prairial* and Robespierre's fall from power on 9 *Thermidor*, a day that saw one of the Tribunal's most dramatic moments. On that morning, Dumas, who remained loyal to Robespierre to the end, was presiding over the trial of 24 prisoners. Suddenly several agents from the Committee of Public Safety burst into the room and arrested Dumas, who followed them, pale and frightened, out of the Tribunal. Without further ado, Maire, one of the judges, took Dumas's place and proceeded to condemn to death 23 of the 24 bewildered and stupefied people standing in the dock. After leaving the courtroom, Fouquier-Tinville encountered Sanson, who warned him that there was trouble brewing in the city, and suggested that it might be better to wait until the next day to execute the prisoners who had just been condemned. Fouquier's reply is characteristic. *'Carry on as usual; justice must take its course.'* A few days later Fouquier-Tinville was arrested, and imprisoned with several of his colleagues, but the Tribunal remained active until May 1795, and one of its last acts was to take revenge on its former chief. Fouquier-Tinville was guillotined on May 7th 1795 after a lengthy trial in which he was accused of having sent thousands of people to their deaths under the pretext of conspiracy. When he finally experienced the same ordeal to which he had condemned so many others, he remained cynically calm to the end, waiting patiently while his fifteen colleagues were executed, and shaking the executioner's hand before putting his head through the fatal window. When you leave this historic chamber, as you walk through the door you will not be alone. You will be walking with the ghosts of all those unfortunate people whom Fouquier-Tinville sent to their death, who, after hearing their sentence, all left by this very same doorway. Maybe Fouquier himself is right behind you.

THE CONCIERGERIE.

➥Go back through the Cour de Mai and out on to the Boulevard du Palais, turn left and start walking towards the Seine. This is the route taken by the tumbrils on leaving the Palais de Justice, but ➥first you're going to visit the Conciergerie, where the prisoners spent their last days. The entrance is just a few steps along on the left, opposite the Tribunal de Commerce. The previous entrance around the corner on the quay was a much more atmospheric one, where visitors were confronted by an old wooden door with a small barred window that immediately gave you the feeling you were not entering as a tourist, but as a prisoner! You then had to pass by blackened stone walls and go through a very uninviting iron grille to get in. One of the guards told me there is talk of possibly restoring this entrance - let's hope he's right! The Conciergerie takes its name from the *concierge* of the old Capetian palace, who was an extremely important person, having charge of law and order within the palace and its dependencies. To carry out this post with maximum efficiency, the concierge was allotted a prison area that at first simply consisted of the palace dungeon. As new buildings were added the prison acquired cells and administrative rooms, and by the 18th century it took up almost the entire lower level of the palace.

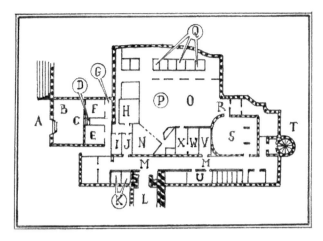

Plan of the Conciergerie during the Revolution.

A Cour de Mai, where tumbrils waited for condemned prisoners
B Small courtyard
C Prison entrance
D Guichet (see glossary for translation)
E Room used by Monsieur Richard, the Concierge
F Clerk's office
G Salle de Toilette (Grooming Room) where prisoners had their hair cut prior to execution
H Marie-Antionette's first cell
I Cell where condemned women prisoners were kept while waiting to have their hair cut
J Room where administrative staff (guichettiers) slept
K Cells where condemned women prisoners spent the night before execution
L Rue de Paris
M Main prison corridor, known as Couloir des Prisonniers
N Le côté des douze
O Women's courtyard
P Stone table, also used as a seat
Q Cells 'à la pistole'
R Small courtyard where the September massacres took place
S Girondin Chapel
T Staircase leading from the Girondins' cell to the Revolutionary Tribunal
U Possible location of the Infirmary
V Cell where Robespierre was kept just before his execution
W Second cell where Marie-Antionette was imprisonment
X Cell used as a Guard Room during Marie-Antionette's imprisonment

The first thing you see when you enter is the enormous Salle des Gens d'armes, a survivor from the old palace of Philip le Bel, and one of the largest and most impressive mediaeval halls in Europe. It has beautiful fluted vaulting on its ceiling, and is divided up by three magnificent rows of pillars, only some of which are decorated, since one half of the hall was built eleven years before the other. The pillars in the central row are much wider and stronger than those on either side, for they support the Salle des Pas Perdus above. You will notice that the floor level of this hall is remarkably lower than that of the street outside, which shows how much the level of the Ile de la Cité has changed since the 13th century. ➡As you come in, go to the first corner on your right and you will see the remains of a mediaeval staircase, obviously as old as the palace itself.

You should forget the movies about the Revolution that show this enormous hall full of prisoners languishing on straw waiting to be guillotined, for the Salle des Gens d'Armes was never used as a prison, even during the Terror. Those prisoners languished in other parts of the Conciergerie that you will see very soon. This hall was about food, serving as a refectory for the king's entire staff, and heated by four huge chimneys that you can still see along each side of the hall. On the right hand side, next to the entrance to the kitchens, is a spiral staircase that goes off from the hall, linking it with the Salle des Pas Perdus above. Unfortunately these wonderful kitchens are closed for renovation work, so you will have to content yourself with the description which is displayed next to the entrance. They are known as the Cuisines Saint-Louis, but in fact were built under the reign of Jean le Bon in 1353, and originally had an upper floor of exactly the same dimensions, also fully equipped with a number of chimneys, each reserved for different kinds of cooking. One was for soup, another for roasting and another for boiling, and every day in these two magnificent kitchens enough food was prepared to feed the 2,000 palace employees who ate here in the refectory. The Cuisines Saint-Louis were not used for very long, for towards the end of the 14th century the palace catering service was moved to another building nearby. On the wall at the end of the hall on the left hand side you can see a fragment of the 14th-century marble table that was used in the *Salle Haute* for banquets and tribunals, and occasionally as a stage.

➥Leave the Salle des Gens d'Armes at the other end, taking the steps on the right by the last chimney, and turn immediately right into the Salle des Gardes, built under Philip le Bel in about 1302 for the soldiers and servants of the king. Directly above it was the *Grande Chambre*, occupied by the king's 'bed of justice' and later the Revolutionary Tribunal, which you've just visited in the Palais de Justice. Look over to the right and you'll see the steps where the former visitors' entrance was, with an old door that looks worthy of a prison. That's because between 1825 and 1914 this *was* the main entrance to the Conciergerie and the one used by incoming prisoners - and outgoing ones (there were many more of those by then than there were during the Revolution). To the right, between the door and the railing, was the office of the prison clerk, where in the 19th century prisoners condemned to the guillotine had their hair cut prior to execution, a procedure rather sadistically called *La Toilette des Condamnés*, a name created during the Revolution.

The wall to your left as you enter the Salle des Gardes (the west wall) is built with several openings, and behind them was the *Grand-Préau* (courtyard) that was transformed during the Revolution into the prison's male quarters. It is still possible to distinguish the old entrance to the men's prison, with its original inscription - *Enceinte Cellulaire* - written over the doorway. The Salle des Gardes was always used as an extension of the men's prison, and was partitioned off into cells that were regularly flooded by the Seine when it rose to the level of the towers. Look around this room and try to picture it during the Terror, when the number of prisoners coming to the Conciergerie was so enormous that the Salle des Gardes was divided by a makeshift ceiling into two storeys, both of which were transformed into *quartiers des pailleux* (straw people's quarters) where floor space covered with damp, fetid straw was allotted to those prisoners unable to afford a cell with a bed (*à la pistole*). Yes, these unfortunate people actually had to pay for the hospitality offered by the Conciergerie! Here is a description of the accommodation at the Conciergerie written in the *Almanach des Prisons* in 1794. It begins by describing one of the cells known as *la Souricière*, a name that conjures up images of large numbers of mice.

'A citizen named Beauregard, an honest and amiable man, was put into this cell on his arrival; the rats ate several different parts of his trousers, without respect for his behind, and he was obliged to cover his face all night with his hand, in order to save his nose, ears, etc. There was hardly any light in these cells; the straw which constituted the prisoners' bedding, quickly made putrid by the lack of air and the stench of the buckets where the prisoners relieved themselves, exhaled such an odour that even the air in the clerks' office was poisoned the moment the door was opened... The prisoners are either à la pistole, à la paille, or in the cells. These latter prisoners have a different regime. The cells are opened only in order to give food, make visits and empty the buckets. The straw quarters only differ from the cells in that their miserable occupants are made to go out between 8 and 9 o'clock in the morning. They are brought back about one hour before sunset. During the day, the doors of their cells are locked, and they are obliged to mope around in the courtyard, or, if it's raining, to crowd into the arcades that surround it, where they must suffer the odour of urine, etc. Otherwise, they have the same inconveniences in their hideous abodes: no air at all, rotten straw, up to fifty people piled up in the same hole, their noses

in their excrement, communicating illnesses...Go and visit these cells, and tell me whether death is not preferable to such an existence...The government should do something to render them healthier, and not forget that innocence is forced to inhabit them. We need a regime that does not degrade those who are obliged to suffer it.' (Dauban, 1977)

The Almanac also describes the quarters known as *à la pistole*, where the prisoners paid rent for the beds they occupied. Prisons, it seems, were quite a lucrative business during the Revolution. *'There are as many beds in each room as it will contain. At first you pay 27 livres for a bed during the first month, and 22 livres a month thereafter. The same bed often brought several rents in one month; during the last days of Robespierre's tyranny, when the tribunal sent victims to their death in cartloads, forty or fifty beds would be occupied every day by a different person, who paid 15 livres for one night; this generated an income of 18 to 22 thousand livres a month.'* (Dauban, 1977)

Many of the cells at the Conciergerie had names, like *Belair*, *le Paradis*, or *la Morgue*, and one of the worst was that named *Bonbec*. It was practically devoid of fresh air, and prisoners slept in beds shaped like coffins, arranged in a circle, with their feet pointing towards the middle. The cells were filled with a variety of nobles, priests, soldiers and ordinary people, and there were large numbers of Parisians, who tended to form little cliques. But there were also increasingly large groups of prisoners from the provinces, who, exhausted by their long journeys, were described by Lenotre as having *'the look of a group of shipwrecked people. A group of peasants from Mont-Blanc after walking for twenty-two days, hardly stayed any time in their cell; Fouquier sent them to the scaffold; twenty poor women from Poitou were sleeping on the stone floor next to their meagre belongings. Their appearance, which showed no awareness of the fate that threatened them, resembled that of cows herded together in the market. When they were called to leave for their execution, the guard had to take away a baby from one woman, who was feeding it, and the mother let out a piercing cry which horrified the whole prison.'* (Lenotre, 1933)

The most highly charged moment of the day at the Conciergerie was when condemned prisoners came down from the Tribunal and crossed the men's prison on their way to the clerk's office, where the executioners were waiting for them. They arrived down the double staircase that you see at the far end of the room, where at that time there was a grille that separated the Salles des Gardes from the staircase. The moment the guards appeared at the grille the prisoners would all congregate in order to see which of their compatriots were to die. It was a sad procession that passed before them, for by the time they were called for their interrogation, most prisoners were in a sorry state. Forget portrayals in movies of imprisoned aristocrats sporting velvet coats and frilled cravats. These were people weakened and debilitated by their terrible living conditions, with matted hair, long beards and filthy clothes that were covered with pieces of straw. As they came past, some walked silently, their eyes lowered in despair, while others tried to laugh, passing their hand across their neck in a theatrical display of bravado. Then there were the goodbyes, the shaking of hands, the kisses and embraces, and many prisoners took this opportunity to hand over possessions to their companions, or to ask for a last favour such as payment of a debt or delivery of a personal memento to a loved one. As they left, their fellow prisoners would try to boost them with shouts of *'Courage!'* and exhorted them not to lose their nerve.

These daily departures left the prisoners shaken and restless, but after a while they reverted to their usual routine. They walked, talked, prayed, and even sang. The prisoners sang a lot at the Conciergerie, to keep up their morale, and to give the image of being unbeaten. When people first arrived they were often surprised to encounter so much jollity, and found the laughing and singing much more unnerving than crying and despair. However, the one thing that stopped the singing was the voice of Fouquier's bailiffs that could be heard every evening, shouting *'Evening Paper!'* In reality they were announcing the distribution of bills of indictment to those who were to appear before the Tribunal the following morning. This fatal piece of paper would be handed over along with sarcastic remarks like *'Here, take this, it's your death certificate.'* Those unfortunate enough to receive one would frantically scan it to see what crime they were accused of, often finding a charge so vague or ridiculous that they felt reassured, believing no jury would ever find them guilty. These poor people would soon be disillusioned.

Once the papers were handed out, night fell, and the prisoners were locked up in their cells. Then the singing would begin again, for it was the tradition that any prisoner who was going to leave for the Tribunal the following morning would be entertained by his cell-mates. They would often sing songs composed by the condemned prisoners themselves, in which they put down their last thoughts about their life, and their opinion of those who had condemned them. As you leave the Salle des Gardes, look down at the old flagstones, and imagine them covered in filthy straw, with people sitting or lying there, wondering if they would be the next to be handed a 'death certificate'.

➡Leaving the Salle des Gardes, you find yourself back in the passage known during the Revolution as rue de Paris. Behind the right hand wall of this corridor was the men's prison, stretching all the way down behind the Guard Room, standing on the site of the *Grand-Préau* (Great Courtyard) constructed during the reign of Philip le Bel, when it was the king's garden. Access to the men's prison was towards the far end of the corridor (next to the Guard Room), through a doorway that also opened on to a staircase leading to the Tribunal. Rue de Paris used to be a very murky place, even for tourists, but since renovation work over the past decade, this once dreaded corridor has become a very pleasant gift/book shop and exhibition area. The renovation has rendered the whole of the Conciergerie much more beautiful, but in doing so has deprived visitors of the delightfully ghoulish experience of really feeling what it must have been like two centuries ago. No-where was this experience more chilling than here in rue de Paris, which really was the hidden inferno of the Conciergerie, and up until a decade ago still left you with a feeling of gloom and doom. Divided up on either side into tiny cells, it left a very narrow passage in the middle that was entirely devoid of air or light, and completely infested with rats. Its name came from the executioner, Sanson, who was generally known as *Monsieur de Paris*, and the 250 *pailleux* who had the misfortune to find themselves crammed together on the putrid straw of this grim passageway would always find their names at the top of his list of victims. For the *pailleux* were the lowest rank of prisoners, stripped of all financial resources, and obliged to spend their last moments in the filth and hopelessness of this infernal corridor. As you stand amongst the gifts and books displayed nowadays in rue de Paris, look around you and try to imagine 250 people living here, lying in their own excrement on decomposing straw, with no light and no air to breathe, waiting to be taken away and beheaded. It is not difficult to believe that this was the place most dreaded by anyone who found themselves a prisoner at the Conciergerie.

➡ You leave rue de Paris through another iron grille which takes you into the Central Corridor or Prisoners' Gallery. This was the principal thoroughfare of the prison. In this corridor you can see three tableaux representing different rooms in the Conciergerie as they were during the Revolution. The two on your left as you enter have been reconstructed in two rooms that at the time were small cells known as 'black cells' since they were completely unlit. This was because they were directly opposite the sleeping quarters of the night clerks, which would have blocked any light from the courtyard beyond. In the first of these two former cells you see a tableau of the Concierge's office. The concierge was the equivalent of a prison governor, responsible for health and security, as well as for the bringing in of provisions. Food came from outside, and the concierge had the complicated job of distributing it to the 800 people within the prison walls. It was a dangerous position. In May 1794 the concierge of another Paris prison was condemned to death for misuse of public funds and bad treatment of prisoners. During the Revolution this post was held here by Citizen Richard, who became an extremely powerful figure at the Conciergerie. Friends and relatives of prisoners did everything to get on the right side of Richard, greeting him with respect and asking after his health. He used to sit in an armchair in his office issuing orders, resolving disputes and listening to prisoners' demands. When he was in a good mood he would smile, but in a bad mood he was extremely morose and unapproachable - *'he was Jupiter, who made Olympia tremble with one look.'* His wife, Citizeness Richard, was of a more benevolent nature, and generally more popular with the prisoners.

But like all prison concierges, their position had its dangers. During the last weeks of Marie-Antoinette's stay here, Richard and his wife were imprisoned themselves for several hours, on suspicion of complicity in a plot to rescue the queen, and after being subjected to a harsh interrogation, were temporarily dismissed. When they later returned to their post, the dangers were still there. One day in 1796, Madame Richard was taking some broth to a despairing prisoner who had just been condemned to twenty years imprisonment. At the very moment that she presented him with the steaming bowl, he plunged a knife into her heart. Within a few minutes she was dead.

In the tableau next to the Concierge's office you see a reconstruction of the *Salle de la Toilette* (Grooming Room), where the ritual of the *Toilette des Condamnés* took place. Condemned prisoners first had their hands tied behind their back and were divested of all their remaining possessions. They were then sat on a stool while the executioner's assistants cut their hair, often purposely nicking their skin or pressing the scissors against their neck to give them a little foretaste of the cold blade of the guillotine. After this unpleasant experience, they were further traumatized by having the neck of their shirt or dress ripped away in preparation for their execution, and finally they were taken out to the Cour de Mai, where the tumbrils were waiting to take them to the guillotine. The actual *Salle de la Toilette* was not where you now see the tableau, but was situated behind the walled-up grille directly to your right at the end of the corridor. This grille was called the *guichet de greffe*, and in the 17th and 18th century was the only entrance to the Conciergerie. Prisoners entering the prison for the first time by way of the Cour de Mai came through the vestibule, which is now the staff restaurant, and then had the grim experience of having to cross the *Salle de la Toilette* before passing through the *guichet* into the central corridor.

On your right as you enter the central corridor is the third tableau, showing the office of the *Greffier*, where all prisoners came on their arrival at the prison. The *greffier* (clerk) was in charge of the prison register *(registre d'écrou)*, in which was logged all prisoners' movements, plus details of the reason for their imprisonment and their condemnation. 130 of these registers still exist, covering the period from 1564 to 1795, but two of the most precious ones unfortunately disappeared during the Commune uprising of 1871.

➡Next to the tableau of the *Greffier*, on the left, is a television room showing films about the Conciergerie and the

Revolution, and from this, to the left, you enter another room containing a reconstruction of Marie-Antoinette's cell as it was during her final imprisonment. This tableau is situated in the room that is adjacent to her actual cell, and at the time was occupied by the gendarmes who guarded the queen. The door linking the two rooms (which was where you see the bed in this reconstruction) has been filled in to give the impression of an enclosed cell. The guards are playing cards, and you can see replicas of the bed, chair, screen and even the peeling wallpaper that characterized Marie-Antoinette's cell. The dark fear and hopelessness that permeates this unhappy scene echoes the general atmosphere of this forbidding prison. To the left as you enter this room is a small display of some interesting relics from the life of the doomed queen. You will soon be seeing the actual room where she was imprisoned.

➡ Now leave the central corridor by the stairs on the left (opposite the Grooming Room tableau), where at the top, to your left, is a room where you'll see listed on the walls the names of the 2,780 people guillotined in Paris during the Revolution. You can also watch here an excellent television film called 'The Conciergerie and the Revolution', with sub-titles in English, giving a very good overview of the whole period and some interesting details about daily life at the prison. To your right after leaving this room is a reconstruction of the different kinds of cells, showing the *chambres à la Pistole*, where those with some means could have the relative luxury of sleeping on a bed and thus avoid the odours and cramped conditions of the cells of the *Pailleux*, where the prisoners had to sleep on straw. I should also tell you, when you read the descriptions next to these tableaux, not to be misled by the use of the word *promiscuité*, which in French can also mean 'lack of privacy.' It is this meaning they are using here - although I'm sure both meanings of the word might well have applied! The third tableau shows a typical cell of the *prisonniers de marque*, who were either rich or famous enough to have a room on their own, enabling them to read or work, although prisoners in these private rooms never stayed there very long, for they were usually executed immediately. The drawings of Hubert Robert and Mariaval in the Carnavalet Museum show very vividly what these cells were like, but it is unlikely there were any at the Conciergerie during the Revolution. Some important prisoners, however, were kept apart from the rest, as in the case of Marie-Antoinette, and Charlotte Corday also found herself in a cell without any other prisoners while she awaited the arrival of the executioner. Sanson was fascinated with this apparently fearless young woman, describing vividly the scene before him as he entered with the bailiffs.

'I saw two people in the condemned cell, a policeman and a citizen who was doing a portrait of the prisoner. She was sitting on a chair, writing against the back of a book. She ignored the bailiffs, but signalled to me to wait... Then she brought her chair to the middle of the room, and sitting down, she took off her bonnet, let down her chestnut hair which was very long and very beautiful, and signalled to me to cut it off. Since Monsieur de la Barre, I had not met with so much courage in the face of death. There were six or seven of us whose job required a minimum of emotionalism, but she seemed less moved than all of us, and even her lips had not lost their colour. I gave her the red robe, which she put on and arranged herself.' (Sanson, 1988). After her hands were bound and she was led out into the Cour de Mai, Charlotte climbed into the tumbril with Sanson and his assistants, refusing the seat offered to her, preferring to stand against the side of the cart.

➥After the tableau of the *Prisonniers de Marque* go left into a series of display rooms containing documents, prints and drawings, with explanatory texts evoking daily life at the Conciergerie. During the Revolution all prisoners scheduled to appear the following day before the Tribunal would be brought to these rooms. There were no social or political distinctions;

they all came here, whether they were celebrated revolutionary leaders, aristocrats, priests, artisans or unknown peasants. Almost 2,800 men and women of all ages spent their last hours on earth here. In the first room is an impressive collection of old prison keys and locks dating from the 18th century, including the original key to the grille between rue de Paris and the cells of the *pailleux* (third key from the left on the top row). In the second room to your right is the original document ordering the transfer of the Girondins from the Conciergerie to the Tribunal. It is dated 1793, and you can see the names of the Girondin deputies written very clearly. You will also see the note that Robespierre and Saint-Just wrote to Couthon on the evening of 9 *Thermidor*, telling him to join them at the Hôtel-de-Ville.

On the wall in the third room is the knife from the guillotine that was used to execute 19th-century murderer, Pierre-François Lacenaire. The first exhibit on the left is a document in Robespierre's handwriting, and the second is a document signed by Herman when he was President of the Tribunal. In it he is requesting the Committee of Public Safety to dispense with the interrogation of prisoners on arrival at the Conciergerie, which he considered to be *'a formality that sheds no light, and takes up considerable time.'* In the middle is a document signed by Fouquier-Tinville, ordering the transfer of 77 prisoners from the Conciergerie to the *Du Plessis* prison (nowadays Lycée Louis-le-Grand). In this room you also see information on some of the people condemned by the Revolution, and one section of the fourth room is all about Robespierre, where you can see two interesting busts made of him during his lifetime in 1791 and 1792. They are the work of Claude André Deseine, who modelled Mirabeau and Marat, and is also said to have been the deaf-mute artist who made a wax effigy of Gabrielle Danton when she was taken out of her coffin by her distraught husband. His likenesses of Robespierre give him a much softer expression than the cold inscrutability that generally permeates paintings of the Incorruptible.

➡As you go down the stairs from this room, you'll see a large wooden ladder that came from the house of the Duplay family, where Robespierre lived. It was probably made by Duplay's carpenters, and legend has it that this ladder served as an access to Robespierre's apartment. Next to it is an ancient door from one of the cells in the Conciergerie, and ➡the stairs lead you into the prison chapel, built in 1779 following a fire that destroyed the original one. At the far end underneath the gallery, a door on the right which is now walled up used to lead to the Chapel Staircase, by which certain prisoners, including the Girondins and Marie-Antoinette, were taken to the Tribunal. This chapel is known as the Chapelle des Girondins, since it is probably the place where the Girondins spent their last night before being guillotined on October 31st 1793. Brissot, Vergniaud and Gensonné were among the 21 condemned deputies who, after sharing a fraternal banquet, spent the rest of the night here laughing and singing patriotic hymns. One of

The twenty-one Girondins sang the Marseillaise as they walked to execution from their prison in the Conciergerie chapel, except for Valazé, who had committed suicide during their trial, but whose corpse was decapitated anyway. (Author's private collection)

their number, Dufriche-Valazé, lay dead on a stretcher, having fatally stabbed himself in front of the entire Tribunal when he heard his death sentence read out. That night stood out in the memory of another prisoner, Baron Riouffe, who wrote that *'this was the first time so many extraordinary men have been slaughtered en masse. Youth, beauty, genius, virtue, talent, all that is interesting in man, was swallowed up in one fell swoop.'* The Girondins went to their death the following day singing the *Marseillaise* - except Valazé, whose corpse was nonetheless guillotined.

There are paintings in the chapel by de la Roche and Boilly depicting the last hours of the Girondins, and opposite these is the well-known painting by Charles-Louis Muller showing the roll-call of the last victims of the Terror. During the three days before the fall of Robespierre, there were 133 executions, 21 women and 112 men. Among these unlucky victims was the 31-year-old poet André Chénier (number 10 in the picture), who was brought to the Conciergerie on 6 *Thermidor*, and spent only one night here, before being tried and guillotined the next day. Before this he had spent nearly five months in the Saint-Lazare prison, where he met and fell in love with Aimée de Coigny, whom he immortalized in his 'Ode to a young Captive'. In the painting of the last victims, you can see Aimée (number 7), who had the good fortune to survive the Terror.

Directly to the left on entering the Girondin Chapel is the Chapelle de Marie-Antoinette. You can't actually go into it, but you can view it through a wide opening in the wall. This chapel was created in 1816 according to the wishes of the queen's brother-in-law, Louis XVIII, and occupies the actual cell where Marie-Antoinette spent the last month of her life. She was moved here on September 14th 1793, after a rescue attempt had been made and the security of her original cell was put into question. Concierge Richard and his wife, who came under suspicion at this time, were dismissed and put in prison themselves, and a new concierge named Bault was brought from *La Force* prison to take over. It is hard to imagine the impact of these new quarters on a queen who had inhabited some of the most sumptuous palaces of Europe. Recall the reconstruction you just saw of her cell, and the conditions she was put into, and you will have no doubt that they were the worst she had ever known. The window to the right, looking out onto the Cour des Femmes, was much smaller than the one you see now, and had horizontal bars from top to bottom. What's more it was almost entirely masked by a sheet of metal, leaving just a small rectangle of light at the top that was covered by a heavy iron grille. There was another smaller window to the left, which looked out on the central corridor, but this one was blocked out entirely. On the left-hand side of the wall directly opposite you was a door which was permanently open, leading into the room occupied by the queen's guards (the room that now contains the reconstruction of the queen's cell). She was surveyed night and day, and certain guards had such contempt for Marie-Antoinette that their surveillance reached provocative proportions in an attempt to humiliate her. She was sometimes able to use a small screen to preserve her modesty, but for the most part her every move was scrupulously observed - or perhaps I should say unscrupulously. Some guards, however, were occasionally more humane, and left her in peace while they played cards, and this time the roles were often reversed, and the queen would stand at the open door and watch *them*. In her happier days at Versailles she had spent so many hours playing cards that she had become a veritable expert, and could seldom resist the temptation to give advice to her guards about how to make their next move.

The sparsely furnished cell contained a trestle bed that was situated under the small blocked-out window to the left, and had two mattresses, a cover and a pillow. The furniture consisted of a table with a wash-basin, a box to hold underwear, two prison chairs and a commode that was emptied each morning by a prisoner. This was one of the dampest cells in the prison, with no air or heating, and the walls were covered with peeling wallpaper, some of which was held in place by nails. However, when the queen arrived, the relatively sympathetic Bault covered the wall with a hanging curtain that was old but not as depressing as the squalid wallpaper. The only other humane touch, which showed a little sympathy for the increasingly severe haemorrhages that Marie-Antoinette was suffering from, was the provision of a small bidet. There was no wardrobe, so the queen had to hang her clothes over a wicker chair at night when she went to bed.

The number of clothes Marie-Antoinette brought with her to the Conciergerie was relatively small for the daughter of an empress, but probably seemed a lot to the young servant, Rosalie Lamorlière, who attended the queen. Rosalie had been placed there clandestinely by royalist friends of her family, although Rosalie herself was probably quite innocent of this fact.

The position of doors, windows and furniture are not accurate, but this print evokes dramatically the despair, the stark loneliness and lack of privacy experienced by Marie-Antoinette during her final days. (Author's private collection)

She showed an immediate affection for Marie-Antoinette, and served her gently and sympathetically to the end. She tried to improve her conditions within the limits of her position, by bringing an upholstered stool from her own room, and replacing the rough bed sheets with some more delicate linen. At 6 o'clock every morning, when the queen awoke, Rosalie would come to the cell with a bowl of hot chocolate or coffee with milk and some rye bread, while her main meal at midday consisted of soup or gruel, duck or veal with vegetables and a dessert. She always drank mineral water, and in the evening ate the leftovers of her lunch. When she first arrived at the Conciergerie the queen had been allowed to keep only one precious possession, her watch, that she had brought with her from Vienna 23 years earlier. She kept track of time from that watch, which she hung up on a nail in the wall on the day she arrived - although according to Rosalie's memoirs, it was taken away from her after only four days. Time passed slowly for Marie-Antoinette, for she had nothing with which to write, sew or embroider, and was only permitted a few books that the concierge considered suitable. She thus spent her daylight hours reading 'The Revolutions of England'.

On October 14th 1793 Marie-Antoinette was sent to the Tribunal. After her judgement and condemnation, she returned to this cell at 4.30 in the morning, exhausted by the prolonged humiliation of the trial, the cold, and the haemorrhages that were getting worse and worse. Here, distraught and heartbroken, she spent her last hours before being executed. Rosalie came to her and persuaded her to take some broth, but she could hardly swallow it, and tears flowed incessantly from her reddened eyes. Sitting at the table by the light of two candles, she wrote on a blank page in her prayer book. *'This 16th October at half past four in the morning: My God, have pity on me! My eyes have no more tears to cry for you, my poor children; adieu, adieu! Marie-Antoinette.'* Then she lay down on the bed and tried to warm herself with the cover, hoping to escape into sleep.

When Rosalie returned at daybreak and found Marie-Antoinette already up and preparing to dress, she stood in front of the bed to hide the queen from view while changing her underwear, but the guard immediately walked across the room and stood by the end of the bed looking at her. She vainly requested that he turn the other way, *'in the name of decency'*, but he insisted that he had orders to watch whatever she did. With a sigh of resignation the queen finished putting on the white linen dress that she always wore in the morning, rolled up her blood-stained undergarments and hastily pushed them into a little space between the wall and the peeling wallpaper. She then knelt and prayed until the executioner, Henri Sanson, son of the man who had executed Louis XVI, entered her cell and proceeded with the task of first cutting her hair and then tying her hands behind her back. She resisted without success this last act, protesting that the king had not been subjected to such an indignity.

It was nearly 11 o'clock when Marie-Antoinette left her cell for the last time, followed by the executioner, who held in his hand the ends of the rope that bound her arms. She left not from this side, but by the door on the other side, going through the guards' room, turning right into the long corridor that led through the Salle de Toilette into the clerk's office. But before leaving the Conciergerie, a worse humiliation was yet to come for Marie-Antoinette. When they reached the clerk's office, she saw through the doorway, beyond the iron grille of the little courtyard, the tumbril waiting in the Cour de Mai to take her to her execution. She reeled in shock. She had expected to be transported in a closed carriage, as the king had been, and the sight of a common cart of the kind used to transport garbage filled her with horror, but not just for the humiliation it represented. She was frightened of being torn to pieces by the crowd.

Her strength suddenly left her, and she was seized with a visceral fear. She asked for her hands to be untied, and in the far corner of the stone floor of the *greffe,* she crouched down and relieved herself in full view of the assembled guards and assistants. Then with as much dignity as she could muster, she rose and offered her hands to be re-tied, before continuing out into the Cour de Mai.

When the queen's cell was reconstructed as a chapel in 1816, a commemorative altar was built carrying an inscription taken from Marie-Antoinette's last letter to her sister-in-law. *'Let my son never forget his father's last words, which I purposefully repeat to him now, that is to never seek to avenge our deaths. I forgive all my enemies for the harm they have done me.'* She could not know that the son she refers to, the little dauphin Louis-Charles, would not live long enough to avenge their deaths, but would die alone and neglected in the Temple prison less than two years later. After the reconstruction of Marie-Antoinette's cell, very little of its original aspect was left for posterity. The

Marie-Antoinette's cell at the Conciergerie was transformed into a commemorative chapel in 1816 at the request of her brother-in-law, Louis XVIII. In the inscription on the altar the queen forgives all her enemies.
(Author's private collection)

window to the right was enlarged and re-glazed with blue and yellow stained glass, the door to the guards' room was closed off, and the smaller window to the left was replaced by a door. The opening you are looking through now was also made at this time, to link the small chapel with the larger prison chapel, the walls were re-plastered, and the old joists and beams of the original ceiling replaced by a vaulted ceiling. The only original feature of the cell that remains is the floor, which is made of bricks placed edgewise in a herringbone pattern. When Marie-Antoinette was here, these bricks were unpolished, and used to leave permanent stains of red dust on her shoes and the bottom of her skirt.

If you look down you will see that the floor where you are standing is exactly the same brick herringbone pattern, for this area was also once another cell that housed a very famous prisoner. At that time there was no opening in the wall separating the queen's cell from where you are standing, and directly behind you was another wall, closing off this second cell from the prison chapel. The small wall immediately to your left did not exist either, and the whole area thus formed another slightly narrower rectangular cell adjacent to that of Marie-Antoinette. So who occupied this room? In July 1794 there was a bed here, containing the dishevelled figure of Maximilien Robespierre, who was brought here on the morning of 10 *Thermidor* to await trial. His face had been hit by a bullet the previous night, and his shattered jaw-bone was being held in place by a blood-stained bandage, but despite the terrible agony that must have marked his last hours, Robespierre remained calm and stoic. When executioner Sanson came in to see him, he was lying on his bed - a bed that, according to some, Danton had slept on a few months earlier. *'He did not complain or moan - he spoke only two or three times, but because of his injury his speech was almost unintelligible. He demanded a surgeon, so he was taken to the Hôtel-Dieu hospital and bandaged a second time. On his return to*

the Conciergerie, he tried to sleep, but the pain prevented him from doing so. He sat up and asked the warden to bring him something to write with; this was refused. Robespierre made an impulsive and threatening gesture of anger, but almost immediately regained his former composure, closed his eyes and retreated into his thoughts.'
(Sanson, 1988)

At midday he was taken to the Tribunal for trial, but having been declared outside the law, it was not really a trial but merely a formal identification. *'Are you Maximilien Robespierre, aged 35, born in Arras and former deputy of the National Convention?'* asked the President of the Tribunal. Robespierre replied in the only way he could, by nodding his head, and he was immediately condemned to death. He came back here after his condemnation, and lay down on the bed exhausted. At 2 o'clock, Sanson and his assistants returned to find him lying with his eyes fixed on the window opposite the bed, his face bathed in a pale ray of sunlight. He didn't move or turn his head when he heard them enter. Sanson tried to lift him up, and Robespierre's eyes momentarily asked *'Why?'*, but he quickly understood and sat up. Supporting his head on his hand, he turned the back of his neck toward Sanson, indicating that he wished to remain on his bed. But Sanson explained that it was impossible to cut his hair without removing the bandage that was holding his jaw in place. So his assistants lifted him up and put him on a chair, and while Sanson cut Robespierre's hair, one of the assistants held the loose ends of the bandage against his temples so his jaw would not fall down. At 6 o'clock that evening he was taken to the *Place de la Révolution* and guillotined with the rest of his entourage.

Robespierre's cell had a door to the left at the far end that was said to lead directly to the Infirmary, so my speculation is that the Infirmary was probably situated directly opposite on the other side of the central corridor, next to the men's cells. It could also have been in this end part of the central corridor, which some accounts say was used as an infirmary - or maybe both these places were used, which is possible since they are adjacent. I can only speculate, since the exact location of the Infirmary is not cited with authority anywhere. But wherever it was, being in a cell close to it was considered a great disadvantage, due to the proximity of numerous dangerous infections, and the Infirmary itself seemed to be dreaded more than the illnesses it claimed to treat. The 1795 *Almanach des Prisons* describes the patients *'piled in twos on miserable pallets...the doctors hardly deigned to examine them...they had one or two tisanes which they administered, with unpardonable negligence, for every illness.'* A prisoner named Beugnot, whose memories of this Infirmary are quite blood-curdling, describes how *'they never thought to change the straw of the pallets, or to wash the covers, so the unfortunate people placed on them would be envelopped in sulphurous fumes...this putrefaction would germinate on the flagstones and you could not pass through the infirmary without your shoes being soiled.'* The medical care offered by the Infirmary was virtually non-existent, consisting, it seems, of the ritualistic prescribing of a *tisane* for every illness, whatever it was. On one occasion an infamous doctor named Thierry went up to a patient and began to take his pulse. *'Ah! he said, he's better than yesterday. —Yes, Citizen Doctor, replied the nurse, he's much better; but it isn't the same person; yesterday's patient died, and this one has taken his place. —Ah! that's different; so let's prepare the tisane, then.'* (Dauban, 1977). Thierry, who owed his position to a letter of recommendation from Robespierre, was described by prisoners as a barbaric and unsociable man who was never known to utter a single kind word or show the slightest compassion for human suffering.

➡From the Girondin Chapel go out into the Cour des Femmes, which was originally a garden belonging to the *Logis du Roi* when the Conciergerie was still a royal palace. Once you are out in the courtyard look back at the little area that you stepped into as you first came out of the door, which was the scene of slaughter in September 1792 when massacres took place in all the prisons in Paris. At the end of the diagonal wall were large iron double doors that separated this little area from the courtyard and opened on the other side on to an enormous cell, where 258 prisoners were murdered on September 2nd 1792. The first killing took place at 8 o'clock in the evening, and the massacre continued throughout the night until about 5 the following morning. Restif de la Bretonne walked around Paris in horror during these terrible days, and describes walking in front of the Conciergerie, where he sees *'a killer who I'm told is a sailor from Marseille. His wrist is swollen from use.'*

It is hard to conceive of this place as a tranquil royal garden, when you look around and see yourself surrounded by barred windows, a reminder that the Conciergerie remained a prison until the beginning of the First World War. During the Revolution this was the exercise yard for female prisoners, as well as a place where they were able to wash, and along the long south side, directly opposite you as you come out, is a covered arcade where prisoners would huddle if it was raining. A row of cells for the *pailleux* situated in the basement underneath this arcade had small high windows that afforded at least a little light, while the windows above belonged to the relatively more comfortable *chambres à la pistole*. On the outside walls of the arcade is a line indicating the level of a flood that occurred on January 28th 1910.

➡Continue round to the east side of the courtyard, and you will see another smaller arcade with more barred windows beneath it. It has sometimes been suggested that Marie-Antoinette occupied one of these cells when she first arrived at the Conciergerie, the one behind the window furthest to your left, next to the iron railing. The reason given for her not remaining here is the drama generated by an alleged escape plot, provoking the authorities to put her in a more secure cell away from the prison entrance. But if we believe Rosalie Lamorlière's memoirs, this was never the case, and the queen went directly to the cell you have just seen. Nonetheless, the plot was real, and did put an end to the relatively relaxed regime enjoyed by the queen during the early part of her imprisonment. At this time she was permitted visitors and given slightly more humane treatment by Madame Richard, who would try to bring her occasional small pleasures such as chicken or peaches. She even brought bouquets of flowers from time to time to brighten up the cell and improve the putrid odour that permeated it.

But all this came to an abrupt end in August 1793, when the queen received a visit from a provincial noble known as the Chevalier de Rougeville. By the time she was transferred to the Conciergerie, Marie-Antoinette looked considerably different from the svelte beauty of earlier days. She had gained weight, her hair was prematurely grey, and she was plagued by painful convulsions that left their mark in her facial expression. Despite all this, however, she still continued to inspire knights like de Rougeville to acts of old-fashioned devotion to their queen. On August 28th, with the help of the prison administrator, he succeeded in getting into Marie-Antoinette's cell, where he conspicuously allowed the carnation he wore in his lapel to drop to the floor behind the stove. The flower contained a rolled-up piece of paper bearing a message of hope and a promise of money. This was the beginning of an attempt to rescue the queen that would come to be known as the 'Carnation Conspiracy', although it is very unclear whether the plan ever got off the ground. Some accounts say that the queen got as far as leaving her cell, passing through several security grilles and reaching the Cour de Mai and the street outside before being stopped. We don't really know, but what is certain is that the plan resulted in the dismissal and imprisonment of the concierge Richard and his wife on suspicion of complicity, and the instigation of a much harsher regime for the queen.

As for the gallant knight de Rougeville, he was arrested as he was leaving the Conciergerie, but after being locked up for only a few hours, he had the incredible good fortune to be confused for someone else and released. He acted quickly and left Paris, where the following day the authorities realized what they'd done and offered a large reward for his re-capture. De Rougeville succeeded in reaching Belgium, and it was only after the fall of Robespierre that he could return to Paris, where he began to boastfully present himself as Marie-Antoinette's last passion. By then, however, he had acquired a fatal taste for conspiracy, and after a string of intrigues he was finally shot on the Champ-de-Mars in 1814 for having 'reprehensible relations' with the Tsar. De Rougeville's accomplice in the Carnation Conspiracy, Jean-Baptiste Michonis, who did not manage to escape, was arrested and guillotined in June 1794 at the height of the Terror.

You cannot see it, but immediately behind this supposed first prison cell of Marie-Antoinette was a small corridor, completely enclosed by iron bars, known as the *parloir*. During the time when communication was still allowed, this was where male and female prisoners could meet. The 1795 *Almanach des Prisons* described it as a place where *'husbands become lovers again, lovers show twice as much tenderness...the most loving kisses are ceaselessly accepted and returned without resistance or scruples; thanks to a little darkness and voluminous clothing, love has seen the crowning of its most tender desires.'* These highly charged exchanges were periodically interrupted by the passage through the *parloir* of condemned prisoners coming down from the Tribunal, a harsh reminder of the reality to come.

Immediately to the left is an iron railing separating the

Women's Courtyard from a small triangular courtyard that was known, for no clear reason, as the côté des Douze (the side of the Twelve) - maybe twelve was the maximum number of people it could hold. It was used by male prisoners to take the air, but it also enabled them to have some contact with the women here in the Cour des Femmes. This little railing must have witnessed many animated conversations, tearful leave takings, and probably quite a few desperate last-minute flirtations before certain death. If you look at the right-hand wall of this little courtyard, behind it were the staff sleeping quarters, and also a cell where condemned women prisoners waited to have their hair cut before execution. The bell above the Côté des Douze dates from the revolutionary period, and was used for keeping to the timetable of daily prison routine. On the wall directly opposite the railing is the original stone fountain where an unlimited quantity of running water, probably the sole luxury in the Conciergerie, enabled the otherwise unfortunate women prisoners to wash themselves and their clothes.

The other interesting relic in the Women's Courtyard is the circular stone table in the centre, used also as a seat, where many a despairing prisoner must have sat and cried. The most famous to have done this were Lucile Desmoulins and Françoise Hébert, two revolutionary widows whose husbands had never been in political accord with each other during their lives. After their husbands were executed, Lucile and Françoise found themselves thrown together by fate in the Conciergerie, where political differences were suddenly less important than the immediate need for comfort. It was on this stone seat that the two women sat, while Lucile, the stronger of the two, put her arm round the shoulders of the weeping Françoise and did everything she could to soothe the distraught widow of her husband's bitterest enemy. Before you leave the courtyard, go and sit for a moment with these two totally innocent but doomed women, and you will feel an unnerving sense of gratitude for your freedom.

Of all the places associated with the Revolution, the Conciergerie is probably the most compelling witness to the terrible perversion of revolutionary ideals that took place during the Terror. I will leave it to a prisoner, writing about the six months he spent here, to finish your tour for you. *'Here finishes my work. Sensitive hearts, do not draw near the Conciergerie. Oh Montesquieu! You would not have guillotined them. A few months of detention would have rendered their serenity; they could have become good husbands and wives, and the Nation would have counted them among its children. Oh Voltaire, oh Rousseau, my divine masters! You would not have guillotined them; you would have made them say a catechism of reason, and they would have become good citizens.'* (Dauban, 1977)

Tour de l'Horloge.

➡ When you leave the Conciergerie turn left along Boulevard du Palais and walk up to the corner, where you will be standing next to the Tour de l'Horloge (Clock Tower) constructed by Jean le Bon in the 14th century. On its façade on the Boulevard du Palais is a magnificent clock, built in 1370. It was the first public clock in Paris, and is beautifully decorated with *bas-reliefs* representing Justice and Law, superimposed on the royal mantle of France. The clock was badly damaged during the Revolution, but its reconstruction in 1849 restored it to its original appearance. On the top floor of the tower there still exists a vaulted room known as the 'Oratory of the White Queen', used in the 14th century as a retreat by Charles V, who would regularly climb up to his little hideaway and stand at the window surveying his domain. There used to be a bell at the top of the tower known as the *tocsin du Palais*, which would chime for three days and three nights on the occasion of the birth or death of a king or his first-born son. Its chimes also heralded the terrible massacre of Saint Bartholomew's Day, when thousands of Protestants were murdered throughout France, and it was for this reason that the Paris Commune had the bell melted down in 1792. At the time when Napoléon Bonaparte proclaimed himself Emperor in May 1804 the ground floor and first floor of this tower were occupied by an optician named Chevalier, who attracted crowds of curious visitors by the enormous thermometer that he installed at the entrance.

Quai de l'Horloge.
At this point the tumbrils crossed over the Pont au Change, but before following them ➡we are first going to turn left and take a detour along the Quai de l'Horloge, which was the alternative route sometimes used by the tumbrils on their way to the guillotine. ➡Keep walking along the Quai de l'Horloge all the way down to number 37. In this lovely house lived the young Manon Phlipon, who, under her married name of Madame Roland, was later to become the inspiration of the Girondin party. Born in Paris in 1754, she was the daughter of an engraver, and her family moved to this house when Manon was not yet 2 years old. They lived on the second floor, in a light, spacious five-room apartment with a view over the Seine. The entrance was on the other side in the Place Dauphine. Manon described herself as *'the daughter of an artist, born in obscurity, but to honest parents, I spent my youth surrounded by the arts, nourished by the charms of scholarship.'* The Phlipons are a sobering reminder of the terrible reality of infant mortality at this time, for they had seven children, all of whom died at birth or in infancy, except Manon. She lived here in the family home until the age of 24, and in her Memoirs written at the Conciergerie, she looks back wistfully on *'the peaceful shelter of the paternal roof'* where she spent a childhood amidst *'flowers and books.'*

The happy atmosphere of the house was shattered in 1775, when Manon's mother died of a mysterious brain fever that the doctors could do nothing to cure. Shortly before dying, however, she gave some last motherly advice to her 21-year-old daughter. *'A good and worthy man has offered you his hand; you are now over twenty; you will no longer have as many suitors as you have had during the past five years; do not refuse a husband who, it is true, does not have the refinement that you value so highly, but who nonetheless cherishes you, and with whom you will be happy.'* She was referring to Jean-Marie Roland, an inspector-general of manufacturing in Lyon, who had been showing a certain interest in this rather studious young girl.

In 1778 the house needed substantial reconstruction work, so Manon and her father moved to new lodgings further down the Quai de l'Horloge. ➡ To get there you should turn left on to the Pont Neuf, walk around the house and turn left again into the Place Dauphine. In October 1787 this lovely triangular square was the scene of a huge demonstration against Louis XVI's exiled Minister Charles Alexandre de Calonne, triggered by a document published earlier that year showing how Calonne had squandered the king's income. The resulting public anger was so high against the now absent Minister that crowds of people surged into the Place Dauphine on October 1st, built a huge bonfire from debris they found on the quay, and threw Calonne's effigy into the flames. To complete the protest they wrote out all their complaints against Calonne, which ended with the statement, *'The said Mr Calonne has been proven guilty of all these crimes and had admitted them by fleeing. He has been denounced in the Parliament and judged by the Nation; this condemnation was executed in the Place Dauphine the 1st October 1787, at 10 o'clock in the evening in the presence of 4,000 citizens, regiments of French and Swiss Guards, and the Paris Guard.'*

➡ Walk right through the Place Dauphine and turn left into rue de Harlay, which is the street where the revolutionary feminist Olympe de Gouges was living at the time of her arrest in July 1793. After a life of radical activity championing and challenging the principles of the Revolution, drawing up a Declaration of the Rights of Women and founding female revolutionary clubs, Olympe was accused of producing writings that went against the desires of the people and encouraged the reestablishment of a monarchical system of government. Her last work, which provoked her arrest, was called 'The Three Urns, or the Salvation of the Fatherland, by an aerian traveller', and proposed a referendum on the kind of government France should have, a republic, a federal government or a constitutional monarchy. After three months in prison trying to defend herself, she was finally condemned to death by the Tribunal, but claimed to be pregnant, telling the court that her blood would never be shed and she would give birth to a citizen or citizeness for the republic. Unfortunately for Olympe this claim was proven to be false later that same day, and she was guillotined the following day at 4 o'clock in the afternoon. Although Olympe de Gouges is chiefly remembered for her feminist stance, it was not this that went against her at her trial so much as her overt criticism of the deputies in the Convention, whom she considered overambitious. It was for this that she was condemned to death.

➡ Walk to the end of rue de Harlay, where you will be back on the Quai de l'Horloge. It was in a house on this corner that the young Manon Phlipon lived with her father for two years, until 1780, when she finally took her mother's deathbed advice and married Monsieur Roland. The marriage took place at the *Eglise de Saint-Barthélemy* (now Tribunal du Commerce, opposite the Palais de Justice), and a reception was held afterwards here at the family home. Her new husband was 20 years older than her, and their relationship was based more on friendship and intellectual companionship than on passionate love. This seemed to suit the serious-minded Manon, who described in her Memoirs her view of Jean-Marie before they were married. *'In M. Roland, I found a friend; his seriousness, his manners, his habits, all consecrated to work, lead me to consider him, so to speak, as without sex, or like a philosopher who exists only by virtue of Reason. A kind of confidence developed…I knew him for nearly five years before he declared any feelings of tenderness towards me.'* After her marriage she continued to esteem her husband, but she was an ambitious woman, and longed in fact to be his equal. *'I did not cease for one single instant to see my husband as one of the most admirable men that existed, and to whom I was honoured to belong; but I often sensed that there was a lack of parity between us.'*

In the 1780s the Rolands lived in the Beaujolais region, where Manon received in her *salon* many friends who would become embroiled in the dramatic events brewing on the political horizon. At the outbreak of the Revolution Roland was sent to Paris to advise the Constituent Assembly on the state of industry in the south, and it is at this time that he made the acquaintance of the Girondin deputies Brissot, Pétion and Buzot. When Manon followed her husband to Paris in 1791, she also met them, and was seduced by their refinement of thought and their elegant rhetoric, which stood out in marked contrast to the overbearing coarseness of Danton and Hébert, both of whom she detested. She immediately made herself noticed by opening her famous *salon* in their apartment in rue Guénégard, where the Girondin deputies met and formulated their policies and strategies. Madame Roland exercised enormous influence on them, with her charm and her intelligence, pushing her husband more and more on to the political scene. The dinners that she gave twice a week for her husband's friends and colleagues brought her heavy criticism from the press, who accused her of offering luxurious banquets while the people of Paris starved.

Despite the media attacks on his wife, Roland became Minister of the Interior when the Girondins took power in the summer of 1792, and fell from power with them the following year. Throughout all the ups and downs of Roland's political career, Manon was by all appearances a dedicated supporter and loyal wife. But she was a dark horse. The day her husband resigned from his post, Manon told him she was in love with another man, namely François Buzot, a leading Girondin deputy, who for some time, it seems, had been providing her with the romantic interest that was lacking in her life with Roland. At the height of this personal crisis, Roland was forced to flee for his life, and Manon was arrested on June 2nd 1793. She was taken first to the *Abbaye* prison, then liberated, arrested again and imprisoned in *Sainte-Pélagie*. Eventually she was taken to the Conciergerie, where she was condemned by the Tribunal and guillotined on November 8th 1793. When he heard of his wife's execution, Roland committed suicide.

While in prison, shortly before her death, Manon wrote a touching letter to her young daughter, Eudora, that captures the mixture of high ideals and deep but controlled emotion that characterized Manon Roland. *'I do not know, my little friend, if I will have the chance to see you or write to you again. Remember your mother. These few words hold all the best things I can say to you. You have seen me happy, by virtue of doing my duty and being useful to those who suffer. That is the only way to be. A strict and busy life is the best safeguard against all dangers; and necessity, as much as wisdom, impose on you the obligation to work seriously. Be worthy of your parents; they leave you a great example, and if you can take advantage of that, you will not have a useless existence. Adieu, dear child, whom I have fed with my milk, and whom I have wished to imbue with all my emotions! The day will come when you will be able to understand how much effort I am making at this instant not to weaken at the thought of your sweet face. I hold you against my breast. Adieu, my Eudora!'* (Roland de le Platière, 1847)

Perhaps you are wondering what became of this sweet-faced young girl, orphaned in such a brutal manner at the age of 12. She did rather well, in fact, thanks to her mother's numerous friends. After Manon was imprisoned, Roland fled Paris, and hid for a while in a house in Montmorency belonging to a friend named Louis Auguste Guillaume Bosc d'Antin, a loyal ally of the Girondin faction and a deeply humanitarian man who spent much of his time sheltering the widows and children of his executed Girondin friends. He thus took Eudora into his care, until he was obliged to leave Paris, and then she went to live with Antoine Creuzé-Latouche, an economist and deputy in the Convention. Although he was not a Girondin, Creuzé-Latouche was a very close friend of Eudora's parents, and when the Rolands saw the danger they were in, it was him, not Bosc d'Antin, whom they asked to take in Eudora and be her tutor. But Bosc d'Antin had been on very affectionate terms with Manon, and it was he who managed to smuggle her Memoirs out of prison. He had perhaps been in love with her, and after Manon's execution Bosc d'Antin seemed to transfer all that sentiment to Eudora. By the time she was a teenager he had not only fallen in love with his young charge, he also harboured thoughts of marrying her. But his feelings were clearly unrequited - Eudora without doubt had no desire to repeat her mother's mistake of marrying a much older man - and Bosc d'Antin, ever the gentleman, took off for America, leaving the 15-year-old Eudora free to marry 19-year-old Pierre-Léon Champagneux, the son of another family friend. Bosc d'Antin came back into Eudora's life in 1800, on the death of Creuzé-Latouche, when he became her tutor and property manager. Eudora and Pierre-Léon had two daughters, Zélia and Malvina, and seemed to have had long and happy lives, marred only by the early death of Malvina at the age of 34. Eudora died in Paris in 1858, aged 77, and Pierre-Léon lived on another six years, until he was 87.

Pont au Change.
➡From rue de Harlay turn right on to the quay and

keep walking back past the Conciergerie to the corner by the clock tower. You are now going to start the route of the condemned, joining the tumbrils as they roll past here and cross over the Pont au Change. From this bridge you can appreciate at a distance the lovely arches of the Pont Neuf to the west, and then, ➥as you cross the bridge, look back at the Conciergerie for a very good view of the ancient stone walls and mediaeval towers of the old prison. This was the view that condemned prisoners had of their last home as the tumbrils carried them across the bridge and along Quai de la Mégisserie opposite. Their journey was long. It took at least an hour and a half to reach Place de la Concorde, and the prisoners, who were usually standing with their hands tied behind their backs, were often unable to keep their balance when the cart tossed and jolted them to and fro as it rattled over the cobblestones. The journey was made even more unbearable by the crowds of onlookers who lined the bridge and all the streets along the route, pitilessly hurling insults at the prisoners, taunting them with sarcasm and sadistic jokes. It is ironic that this bridge, which has seen pass so many victims of the fight against royalty and privilege, originally served to honour the passage of kings.

The Pont au Change dates back to the beginning of the 11th century, getting its present name from the money-changers who traded there after 1305. At that time the bridge was part of the route taken by the monarch when he came into the city to go to Notre Dame. He was always accompanied by a long train of nobles and courtiers, as well as about 2,000 birds that would be released from their cages at the moment the royal procession arrived on the bridge. This delightful show was laid on by local bird sellers in exchange for royal permission to ply their trade on the bridge. An even more spectacular royal entry took place on August 22nd 1389, when the young Queen Isabeau of Bavaria arrived at the bridge after her coronation in Saint-Denis. Just as the procession began to cross, an Italian tightrope walker appeared on a metal wire that was suspended between the top of Notre Dame and the roof of one of the houses lining the bridge. After his dramatic descent, he stepped on to the roof, and as the young queen passed underneath him, he gallantly held a crown over her head. He then further astonished and delighted everyone present by stepping back on to the wire and walking back to the top of the cathedral holding two lighted candles, giving the impression of a departed soul being guided heavenwards by two stars.

During the Revolution the daily processions across the Pont au Change were not so happy or spectacular. A convoy of tumbrils, each containing sometimes up to twenty prisoners, passed each day between the stone houses that lined the bridge. The carts were invariably blood-stained, for after the executions they would be used to transport the bodies to their communal graves. People crowded at all the windows and stood up on the roofs, while in front of the houses was a dense line of spectators, some holding up children to give them a better view, some shouting insults, some throwing things. Some just looked on in silence.

Place du Châtelet.

As the procession approached the other side of the bridge, the sinister outline of yet another ancient prison loomed up ahead in what is now Place du Châtelet. Le Grand Châtelet, for centuries the seat of the provosts of Paris, was originally built as a defence tower in 870 A.D. by King Charles the Bald. This wooden construction was replaced 300 years later during the reign of Louis the Fat by a larger stone building, which, being like a little castle, was given the name Châtelet (*petit château*). It was known as the *Grand Châtelet* because its purpose was to defend the *Grand Pont* (Pont au Change), while another defence tower on the Left Bank by the entrance to the Petit Pont was known as the *Petit Châtelet*. The *Grand Châtelet* prison stood slightly to the left side of the present-day Place du Châtelet, approximately where you now see the Théâtre du Châtelet and a brasserie called Au Vieux Châtelet, and its main entrance faced rue Saint-Denis. This entrance façade had a sundial, a mansard roof and two small towers on either side, while on ground level an arch went through the entire width of the building, from rue Saint-Denis to the quay.

The west side of the building was the administrative wing, housing the law courts and rooms reserved for 'pre-trial interrogation', a euphemism for various forms of torture such as forced ingestion of huge quantities of water, garotting, and stretching on the rack. Naturally most prisoners confessed to their crimes and were then tried, convicted and sentenced to one of the many atrocious punishments that existed right up to the 18th century. Those convicted of murder and grand larceny were hung or broken on the wheel, petty thieves were sent to the galleys, witches, poisoners and heretics were burned alive,

The main entrance to the Grand Châtelet prison on rue Saint-Denis, showing the sundial, the two towers on either side of the entrance, and the wide archway going through the entire width of the building. On this side of the building was the Morgue, and also the room where prisoners were tortured.
(Author's private collection)

swindlers, procurers and those receiving stolen goods were put on the pillory and then exiled, domestic servants guilty of theft or embezzlement had their ears cut off, bigamists had their hair, beard and eyebrows shaved off, and those guilty of regicide were 'quartered', an agonizing procedure where the prisoner's limbs were attached to four horses that galloped off in four different directions. Occasionally, back in the good old mediaeval days, forgers would be thrown alive into a barrel of boiling water. As if this were not enough, condemned prisoners were also subjected, prior to their execution, to a 'post-trial interrogation', where they were encouraged under more torture to give the names of their accomplices.

On the same side of the building, furthest from the square, was the *Morgue*, where they brought the bodies of those who had drowned or been killed in the street. Paris, like all cities, was not a very safe place, and during the 17th century an average of fifteen street murder victims were brought every night to the *Châtelet Morgue*, which was still in use right up to the demolition of the building in 1802. On the east side of the building, right on the square, was the prison, where a thick stone wall and another huge tower enclosed a large square stone dungeon. The *Grand Châtelet* prison was among the worst you could find in Paris, for the building had hardly any windows, so the cells were completely dark and with only just enough air to avoid suffocation. Some had the relative luxury of a bed, but for the most part the prisoners found themselves in huge rooms with up to 100 people sleeping on straw, and some of the cells on the lower level were built in ditches. One of these was in the shape of an inverted funnel, and the prisoners destined for this particularly uncomfortable cell had to be lowered into it by means of a rope and a pulley. Once in there, it was impossible for them to lean against the wall, because it was sloping inwards, and they couldn't sit or lie down, for the floor was swimming with water.

By the time the Revolution broke out, although the role of provost was still accorded VIP status, it carried hardly any political or administrative power. In 1790 the provosts were abolished by the revolutionary government, and the *Châtelet* served as offices for bailiffs and notaries, while still retaining its prison. But because the *Châtelet* prison was uniquely for common-law criminals, it did not house any famous revolutionaries or priests, and for this reason it is surprising that it nonetheless fell prey to the hired killers who during the September Massacres of 1792 murdered about 216 of its 269 inmates. The prisoners themselves were also surprised, for, not being political prisoners, they had rather hoped that the chaos and confusion would provide the opportunity for them to escape. Many of them in fact were all prepared for departure when the execution squad arrived at 11 o'clock in the evening, thirsty for blood after a day's killing at the other prisons of the capital. Only about 50 prisoners managed to escape death, some of them by persuading the killers that they had only ever stolen from aristocrats. After the slaughter, the bodies were piled up at the entrance to the Pont au Change - about where you are standing right now - before being transported to Montrouge for burial.

As you come off the bridge and approach today's Place du Châtelet, with its animated cafés and theatres, it is hard to believe that this was once considered the most horrible neighbourhood in Paris, due to the cries of animals being slaughtered, the raucous shouting of fishwives, the screams of prisoners being tortured, the lingering odour of coagulated blood and waste left by animal skinners, and of course the terrible smell of the *Morgue*. Between 1802 and 1810 the *Grand Châtelet* was demolished, and replaced by a fountain called *La Victoire*, which has since been renovated and moved to the centre of the present-day square.

Quai de la Mégisserie.

➥When the tumbrils reached the end of the Pont au Change, they turned left on to Quai de la Mégisserie and followed it all the way to the Pont Neuf. You should follow them along this quay, which got its name in the 13th century from the tanners (*mégissiers*) who worked here at that time. It was widened in the mid-18th century, when it was known as *Quai de la Ferraille* after the scrap-iron merchants who had set up business. It quickly became one of the liveliest waterfronts in Paris, where the songs of birds being sold in the market mingled with the cries of street vendors, and the appetizing smells of food being sold from open-air stalls wafted along the whole length of the quay.

At number 2, where you see the *Sortie de Secours* (emergency exit) of the Théâtre du Châtelet, was the house where the painter Jacques-Louis David was born on August 30th 1748. His father, an iron merchant who worked on the quay, encouraged his son in his passion for drawing, and enrolled him in the Academy of painting. David's studies brought him the *Prix de Rome* in 1775, and the young artist left to spend five years in the Italian capital, where he developed a love of ancient art. On his return to Paris his studio became a focal point for other aspiring young artists, to whom David often gave free lessons if they had no money. His reputation grew to such a point that by the eve of the Revolution he was being invited regularly to the Duc d'Orléans' salon, and was selling his paintings for huge sums of money. David became an immediate advocate of the Revolution, immortalizing many events of the era with his paintbrush, the most famous being his idealistic representation of the 'Tennis Court Oath.' His genius for quick sketches has left us with exceptionally evocative images of two of the most famous victims of the period, Danton and Marie-Antoinette, on their way to their execution. In order to capture these key revolutionary moments, David would install himself wherever he could get the best view, sometimes perched precariously on a windowsill, or more comfortably at a table on the terrace of a café.

David's devotion to the Revolution led to his election to the National Convention, where he voted for the death of the king. He also voted against Marat being brought before the Tribunal, and painted 'Marat Expiring' in homage to the murdered patriot. He was a member of the Committee of General Security, and the Committee for Public Instruction, where he was responsible for fine arts education. But as a supporter of Robespierre, David's own life eventually fell into danger, and on 8 *Thermidor* he was warned by a colleague not to come to the Convention. Heeding this wise advice, he remained absent until 13 *Thermidor*, when he spoke out against Robespierre in an attempt to disassociate himself from the fallen leader. It was to no avail, however, and he was arrested shortly afterwards and taken to the Luxembourg Prison, where he made use of his time in captivity by painting a self-portrait and his only landscape, 'View from the Luxembourg.' After five months of detention he was released, and went on to become the official artist of the Empire, commemorating Napoléon and Joséphine with a painting of their coronation celebrations. By that time David had become a famous and respected figure, whose studio was frequently visited by Napoléon himself, but when the monarchy was restored, not wishing to pay allegiance to Louis XVIII, David exiled himself to Brussels, where he died in 1825.

PONT NEUF.

➥Continue along Quai de la Mégisserie, looking across the Seine as you go at the wonderful mediaeval towers of the Conciergerie and the Sainte-Chapelle spire - the final view the prisoners had of their last home as they jolted along the quay in a tumbril. Further down you get a lovely view of Manon Roland's first home at the end of the Ile de la Cité. If you can resist the delights of the animal and flower market and the *bouquinistes*, ➡you will soon arrive at the Samaritaine department store (this will be closed for a very long time for decoration work) and the Pont Neuf, a beautiful bridge that was begun in 1578, but remained unfinished until the reign of Henri IV. When construction work was resumed in 1603, Henri visited the site and astounded onlookers by crossing the Seine on a temporary roadway made of loose planks.

On the Pont Neuf you could have your shoes blacked, your teeth pulled, your dog's hair sheared, and buy anything from perfume and paper to flowers and food, while listening to the latest revolutionary songs from travelling balladmongers. (Author's private collection)

This feat had been unsuccessfully attempted by several other people, some of whom had drowned in the process, prompting the king to announce immodestly that *'not one among them was a King as I am.'* After its opening in 1607 the Pont Neuf became an instant hit with Parisians, who delighted in taking walks across the first bridge in Paris to be built with a raised pavement to protect pedestrians from traffic. In addition, there were no houses on either side, so for the first time Parisians could see the river they were crossing, and enjoy a panoramic view of the Louvre.

The Pont Neuf was a veritable market place, always full of a colourful assortment of itinerant merchants - shoeblacks, flower-sellers, dog shearers, cat doctors and tooth-pullers. You could even buy perfume and stationery, as well as fried potatoes to sustain you while haggling over the prices. Another regular attraction on the Pont Neuf were the numerous singers and ballad-mongers who entertained pedestrians, and from time to time fomented revolt with their political ditties. Here you would have seen Ladré, the greatest popular song-writer of the revolutionary period, whose composition *Ah! Ca ira!* became a patriotic anthem. The phrase *Ca ira* means 'Everything will be alright', and was apparently used regularly by Benjamin Franklin when asked about the progress of the American Revolution, and the expression caught the fancy of General Lafayette, who subsequently suggested it to Ladré as a good chorus for a popular song. Ladré was a staunch republican, writing almost exclusively for the *sans-culottes*, and he plied his trade here throughout the entire Revolution. Another regular on the Pont Neuf was a blind balladeer named Duverny, who specialized in peace songs, and whose lyrics could well have been written by a 1960s protest singer. In a song composed for the armies of France and Austria, he begged *'Kings, consuls, emperors'* to end the war and *'console the Earth'*, and looked forward to the time when *'Germans and French, when Europe as a family, at last celebrates peace.'* It does sound rather like a joint effort by Bob Dylan, Joan Baez and John Lennon, doesn't it.

The other distinguishing feature of the Pont Neuf was the *Samaritaine Pump*, which has given its name to the famous department store, Samaritaine, that now dominates the Place de l'Ecole. It stood against the west side of the Pont Neuf, directly opposite the Samaritaine building, which at the time was a row of little cafés. As the tumbrils approached the Pont Neuf their occupants would have seen on the skyline the decorative clock tower of the building that housed this marvel of

Renaissance technology. The *Samaritaine Pump* was another of Henri IV's projects, aimed at improving the water supply to the Tuileries and the Louvre. It was constructed in 1608, against the wishes of the provost of merchants, who claimed it would interfere with the flow of the Seine. Henri IV was not concerned with this, arguing that the bridge had been built with his money and not that of the merchants, and when the pump was completed, he installed the architect, Lintlaër, in the new building as 'governor.'

The Pont Neuf and the Samaritaine Pump in 1789. Built in 1608 to improve the water supply to the Louvre and Tuileries, by the time of the Revolution the Samaritaine Pump had become an object of ridicule, described by one observer as a *'horrid little square building'*. (Author's private collection)

It was a rather precarious construction, and had to be re-built in 1714, but by the time of the Revolution the *Samaritaine Pump* seemed to have become an object of ridicule for more discerning Parisians. The writer Sébastien Mercier, who was born in 1740 in a house that stood in the Place de l'Ecole, described it in his *Tableau de Paris* as *'a horrid little square building'* that ruined an otherwise superb view. He mocked its *famous governor who has among his immense duties the maintenance of the clock which doesn't go. The sundial, seen and consulted by so many passers-by, goes for whole months without marking the hours. The bells are as defective as the clock. When will they get rid of this tasteless building, whose only purpose is to draw water from wells that are dried out for three-quarters of the year?'* (Mercier, 1947). Mercier died in 1814, but not too late to see his wish fulfilled, for the *Samaritaine Pump* was demolished in 1813 and the imperfect bells installed in the belfry of the Saint-Eustache church at Les Halles.

Up until the Revolution the Pont Neuf was crowned by a magnificent bronze statue of Henri IV on horseback. It was made in Italy and set off for France in 1613 in a boat that sank off the coast of Sardinia. A year later the statue was fished out of the sea and brought in triumph to Paris, where it was mounted on a marble pedestal on the Pont Neuf. This was the first equestrian statue to be put up not just in the French capital but in the whole of France, and it had a turbulent career. In 1788 it was adorned with flowers and white ribbons, in 1789 with a tricolour cockade, and in 1790 a military enrolment office was set up in front of it. Two years later it was toppled and broken into hundreds of pieces that were either melted down or thrown into the river. The artist David came up with the idea of replacing it with an enormous statue called 'The Revolutionary Spirit.' On the forehead of this huge figure would be written 'Light', on the chest 'Nature and Truth', on the arms 'Strength' and on the hands 'Work.' The National Convention voted in favour of this grandiose project, but it was dropped after the fall of Robespierre, and in 1818 Louis XVIII ordered the building of the statue you see now, which depicts the entry of Henri IV into Paris. The Pont Neuf, or 'New Bridge', has been restored many times, but the basic construction is the same as that built in 1607, and despite its name, it is the oldest bridge in Paris.

PLACE DE L'ECOLE.
➡If you are standing on the side of the quay by the

bridge, cross over the road to the main building of the Samaritaine store, which stands on the Quai du Louvre between rue de la Monnaie and rue de l'Arbre-Sec. This part of the quay, to the west of the bridge, is called Place de l'Ecole, and in the 18th century the quay was known as *Quai de l'Ecole*, a very lively place with several popular cafés. Construction of the Samaritaine store caused the demolition of a whole row of little cafés that were amongst the most popular in the city. The first in the row was the *Café Manoury*, named after its owner from 1766, where literary figures would meet to discuss ideas, or just read the newspaper. There were also regular customers who came to play draughts, including the 'night owl', Restif de La Bretonne, who described the clientele just before the Revolution as *'four different kinds...draughts players, chess players, chance visitors and café-crawlers.'* Draughts was definitely the game of choice at the *Café Manoury*, where according to Restif, any chess players you saw were *'those not welcome at the Café de la Régence'*. Manoury was a specialist in draughts, and even wrote a book about it, in which he patriotically claims that Polish draughts were in fact invented in France, in a game involving a French officer. Another favourite café here during the Revolution was run by - La Mère Rogomme, who launched a potent brand of *eau de vie* that still bears her name - and to have a *voix de Rogomme* still means having a rasping voice, or one roughened by drinking too much hard alcohol. Mère Rogomme sold her café in 1798 to the innovative Mère Moreaux, who made it famous by being not only the first café to have elegantly-dressed young waiters, but also the first to have a bar where the customers could stand up, while drinking her celebrated plum *eau-de-vie* at two *sous* a glass. Mère Moreaux died in 1852, but her café continued into the 20th century.

From the windows of all these cafés there was a view of the Seine, the Pont Neuf, the *Samaritaine Pump*, and a fountain, adorned with a huge ornamental urn, that stood in the middle of the square outside (corresponding to the middle of the present road, by the traffic lights at the bridge). Local residents would collect water from this fountain, which was a popular meeting point for exchanging the latest gossip. In addition to the cafés there was also a grocery shop in the row called *Au Soleil d'Or*, and one other café, where a young lawyer called Georges-Jacques Danton first found true love. Its official name, inscribed in gold on the door, was *Le Parnasse*, but it was always referred to as *Café de l'Ecole* by the clerks and lawyers who frequented it. Its proximity to the Palais de Justice drew them to the café, but they also loved the quiet and courteous atmosphere encouraged by the proprietor, François-Jérôme Charpentier. He was no ordinary café-owner, for he was also an inspector of taxes, and he understood and spoke the language of the legal profession. His charming Italian wife, Angélique, was a focal point for the clientele, many of whom followed the tradition of the day by paying court to her with discreet gallantry. Danton was no exception, and he had the added advantage of speaking fluent Italian, which, combined with his talent for light-hearted banter, enabled him to easily ingratiate himself with the owner and his wife.

Within a few weeks of his first visit to the café in 1784, Danton was on excellent terms with the Charpentiers, and quickly established himself as a raconteur. Each evening he would come directly from the Palais de Justice to take his modest evening meal of bread and butter and a bowl of coffee with milk. As soon as he began telling stories of his youth in Arcis-sur-Aube, or reciting passages from the classics with outrageously exaggerated gestures, the guests would get up from the marble tables where they were sitting and gather round Danton, fascinated by the seductive ugliness of this theatrical colossus. When, three years later, he asked the Charpentiers for the hand of their daughter, Antoinette Gabrielle, he encountered no resistance, for they could see quite clearly that their daughter had fallen under the spell of her unlikely suitor. The wedding took place in June 1787 at the church of Saint-Germain l'Auxerrois in the nearby Place du Louvre, where Danton was resplendent in black silk breeches and a blue and white striped waistcoat, while Gabrielle blushed beneath yards of virginal white tulle. The reception was held here at the *Café du Parnasse*, where about 100 people crowded together and ate, drank and danced into the early hours, and being the month of June you might well have seen people dancing out here in the street as well.

The future seemed rosy for the newly-weds, although financially it was much rosier for Gabrielle than for Georges-Jacques. By the contract signed the night before, the groom brought to the marriage his position of lawyer, valued at 78,000 *livres*, as well as land and property in his native Arcis-sur-Aube worth at least 12,000 *livres*. For her part, Gabrielle brought a dowry of 20,000 *livres*, but the wily Monsieur Charpentier, determined to take care of his daughter's future, stipulated that Danton had to pay her a 'dower' of 800 *livres* a year, and ensured that the contract placed no responsibility on Gabrielle for her husband's debts. Despite his reputation for amassing money through bribery and corruption, Danton showed a worthy lack of materialism in his choice of bride, for the union certainly did not line his pockets. But he was in love, and seven years later, standing in the fatal tumbril as it rolled through Place de l'Ecole and around the corner into rue de la Monnaie, his bravado momentarily weakened at the sight of the *Café du Parnasse*, and he was heard to whisper '*Gabrielle*' as he took a final look at the scene of his greatest happiness.

RUE DE LA MONNAIE.
➥Keep following Danton's tumbril into rue de la Monnaie, which has been here since the beginning of the 12th century, and owes its name to La Monnaie de Paris (the Mint).

Before it was demolished in 1776 the Mint stood on the right side of the street just before you get to rue de Rivoli - about where the shop Zara is now. Up to the Revolution money in France was very similar to the old English currency of pounds, shillings and pence. One *livre* (pound) was worth 20 *sols*, and one *sol* was worth 12 *deniers*, with 240 *deniers* making one *livre*. On April 7th 1795 a law was passed creating a new unit of currency called the *franc,* which replaced the *livre*. This was divided up, according to the new decimal system, into ten *décimes*, each of which was divided into ten *centimes*, and the gold coin known as a *louis d'or*, bearing an effigy of the king, was of course taken out of circulation. At the time when the tumbrils passed along this street, the Mint had already been demolished and rue Boucher built in its place (you can't see this street as it ends behind the buildings).

When this part of rue de Rivoli was opened in the 1850's, it was on the site of a street going off to the right called *rue de Béthisy*. The last house on this little street, forming a corner with rue de la Monnaie, was the home of author and publisher Alphonse Louis Dieudonné Martainville during the last few years of his life. Martainville was the plucky young man you met earlier when he stood before the President of the Tribunal and joked about being shortened rather than lengthened. Despite his protest then about being given an aristocratic *de* in his name, Martainville was a staunch royalist and remained so all his life. After 9 *Thermidor* he became part of the 'Gilded Youth' who roamed Paris in outlandish clothing, fighting anyone who dared to show any sympathy for the fallen Jacobins. By the time Napoléon became Emperor young Alphonse had grown up considerably and turned his talents to journalism and play-writing, but always with an ultra-royalist agenda underpinning his works. When the monarchy was restored under Louis XVIII he continued his royalist writings, and in 1819 started his own newspaper, *Le Drapeau Blanc*, in which he criticized Louis XVIII for being too liberal. Martainville died in 1830 when he was only 54, but seemed to have been saving up for his old age, for when his house was demolished twenty years later, the delighted owner discovered a concealed cupboard containing 20,000 gold *livres* dating from the reign of Louis XVI. He used this unexpected windfall for the construction of a new house on rue de Rivoli.

➡ The tumbrils continued straight on across the intersection with *rue de Béthisy* and *rue des Fossés-Saint-Germain* (now rue de Rivoli), and into rue du Roule, opened in 1691. In 1789, as the Revolution was beginning, Restif de la Bretonne found himself here on the night after the Prince de Lambesc's attack on the Tuileries, a night when anyone in the street could be killed, and anyone could be a hero. Fortunately Restif wasn't killed, and he did his best to be a hero, in an escapade that is typical of the kind of thing he continually got up to during his night-prowling.

> *'I arrived in rue du Roule...a crowd of people were forcing the door of a gunsmith. A troupe of Guards were advancing, drums beating, flags flying. The troupe dragged the crowd along with them. A young man had stopped there, holding his charming young wife by the hand. He was seized by the marchers and forced to leave her. The young woman tried to hold on to him, screaming. She was pushed back by a lout who punched her with his fist and shouted at her in the most vulgar language. She fainted. I caught her in my arms, and that moment made up for all the other troubles of the evening...I brought her to consciousness with the aid of her flask. "Rest assured," I told her, "your husband will take the first opportunity to escape and return. Don't worry about him...I will take you back home...you can say that I am your father...I have a daughter of your age." "Ha! You're a father!..I trust you, sir!...Take me to my own father!" He was a silk merchant near Les Halles. As we were walking we met someone running as nimbly as a deer, pur-*

sued by two louts armed with long spikes from a roasting spit. "It's my husband!" cried the young woman. I did not reply, but I set about to save her. "Over here! Over here! Quick!" I cried as loudly as possible. The two ruffians stopped and came over to us. That was just what I wanted. I persuaded them to help me take my daughter home. They made a makeshift stretcher out of the spikes and their own jackets, put the girl on it and carried her. The young husband, had seen all this. No longer pursued and his fear gone, he followed us at a distance and returned to his father-in-law's house. As soon as she caught sight of him the young woman came back to life. I left them to return home. Some brigands held me up at the entrance to the Notre Dame bridge. I succeeded in disarming them with my good nature, and went home, where I had to calm my anxious family. That is the picture I can give you of the first night of the Revolution: I only tell what I have seen.'* (Restif de la Bretonne, 1986)

Rue Saint-Honoré.

➡At the end of rue du Roule the procession arrived at rue Saint-Honoré one of the most important thoroughfares in Paris during the revolutionary period. This famous old street, one of the longest in Paris, was a veritable eye-witness to the Revolution. It contained a cross-section of Parisian society, and almost all the turbulent events of the period were acted out here in one way or another, from the euphoria of its beginning to the dark fear and then relief that came at its end.

July 1789: *A hundred members of the Assembly walked the entire length of rue Saint-Honoré, escorted by the citizens' militia and the Swiss Guards. Lafayette and Bailly were to be seen amongst them, as well as Camille Desmoulins, the hero of the previous day, his head held high with pride as he marched along carrying a naked sabre. Flowers rained down on the procession from every window, balcony and roof - a veritable shower of cornflowers, poppies and wild marguerites that transformed rue Saint-Honoré into one big tricolour ribbon.'* (Hénard, 1908-09)

- Celebration of the storming of the Bastille July 1794:
Early in the morning all Paris seemed to arrive in rue Saint-Honoré - reactionary Paris mingled with revolutionary Paris - in the tumult of confusion could be seen people of the most diverse opinions, many of whom had for months been obliged to live out a strange and underground existence, retreating into cellars and secret chambers. The good news had brought them out of their hideouts.' (Hénard, 1908-09)
- Execution of Robespierre

Rue Saint-Honoré is most famous, of course, for being the principal part of the route taken by condemned prisoners, but there was much more to it than that, as you will see when you follow the tumbrils along this dangerously narrow street. Parisian traffic moves fast, so take care when crossing back and forth to look at the buildings. From rue du Roule ➡the procession of tumbrils always turned left on to rue Saint-Honoré, but you should first turn right and and have a brief look at the other side, where you can see, between numbers 33 and 45, a row of 17th-century houses that has unfortunately been a bit defiled by modern commerce. Looking particularly abandoned is number 33, which in 1673 was known by the name *A Jésus Christ* and is now the first house on the street since the demolition of numbers 1-31 during the 1860s. Six years later 33 was acquired by a draper, who also bought number 35, known at the time as *l'Ecrevisse* (Crayfish) then by a succession of names, ending with *Le Renard d'Or* (Golden Fox) in 1766 when the stone figure of a fox was carved over the entrance next to the first floor windows - it's still there. Number 43 had the sign *Au Cygne Couronné* (the Crowned Swan), and its beautifully decorated emblem still exists today, depicting a graceful swan with a red beak.

Stop now and look at the book and record shop called *Parallèles* at number 47. Although there is no commemorative plaque to tell you (and there should be), this dirty, dilapidated but potentially beautiful 18th-century house, which used to carry the sign *La Croix de Fer*, and whose façade is decorated with ornamental masks and ironwork, belonged just before the Revolution to Antoine Lavoisier, the founder of modern chemistry who first identified oxygen and introduced the metric system. Lavoisier was a Farmer-General, and it was while living in this house in 1787 that he became involved in the construction of the wall around Paris to prevent goods being brought into the capital without paying duty. This would prove to be a fatal step for Lavoisier. It was the Farmers-General who received all the revenue from these duties, and for this reason they were hated almost as much as the notorious wall they had built. When the National Convention ordered the arrest of all former Farmers-General in November 1793, despite his reputation as a man of science, Lavoisier was not spared. The Tribunal was indifferent to the fact that, as a deputy in the National Assembly, he had supported all the revolutionary reforms, including the abolition of feudal obligations and the introduction of an old-age pension scheme for the poor. He was condemned along with his colleagues on May 8th 1794 and executed the same afternoon. On the first floor of Lavoisier's old house is a restaurant called Chez Max, reputed to serve dishes from the Landes region.

Number 77 on the corner of rue du Roule hasn't kept much of its old character, but it used to be known as the *Grand Hôtel des Tuileries*, and is where the gallant Chevalier de Rougeville lived in 1792. This was the year before his unsuccessful Carnation Conspiracy of August 1793, which aimed to rescue Marie-Antoinette from her prison at the Conciergerie. It was also at the *Grand Hôtel des Tuileries* that the young Thérèse Louise Thorin stayed after leaving her husband in Blérancourt to follow her young lover, Antoine Saint-Just, to Paris. She and Antoine had been childhood sweethearts, but Thérèse's father had forbidden any talk of marriage, and eventually found another husband for his daughter. This did not stop the love affair from continuing in secret, however, until Saint-Just, weary of his claustrophobic provincial life, ran away early one morning and went to Paris to seek his political fortune. Thérèse could not stand being away from him, and on July 25th 1793 - her seventh wedding anniversary - she fled Blérancourt and went to the capital in search of her true love. But she was to be bitterly disappointed, for Saint-Just had by then found *his* true love, the Revolution, and he sent her away. Heartbroken and humiliated, Thérèse went back to Blérancourt, where her husband refused to forgive her and began divorce proceedings. It was the last she ever saw of Saint-Just, who was guillotined a year later, and Thérèse died poor and alone in Blérancourt in January 1806 .

Number 77 was also the home of Claude Basire, a Montagnard deputy from Dijon. He was the son of a wealthy cloth merchant, and was known from the start for his radical political ideas, as well as for his impressive collection of minerals and rare stones. When he was elected to the Legislative Assembly he immediately allied himself with the extreme left, along with his friend Chabot (see 82 rue Saint-Honoré). Basire was an intense and ardent personality, with a strong streak of violence in his nature that no doubt contributed to his active support of the September massacres. He advocated the death penalty for anyone proposing the restoration of the monarchy, and voted in favour of the law abolishing ecclesiastical costume. He also had a reputation for maintaining certain dissolute relationships, including one with a Dutch baroness who was suspected of spying for the House of Orange. When Chabot turned to denouncing his friends in order to save himself, Basire made the mistake of going with him to the Committee of General Security - perhaps to make sure Chabot didn't denounce *him*! Very shortly afterwards, on November 17th 1793, he found himself in the Luxembourg Prison, and a few months later came past his own house in a tumbril, in the company of the Dantonists. Chabot, who was in the same tumbril, recognized the innocence of his friend, exclaiming *'But you, Basire, what have you done?'* The Directory government it seems also acknowledged Basire's innocence, for they granted a lifetime pension to his otherwise penniless widow. A week before his imprisonment, Basire made his final imprint on the revolutionary period by championing a law, passed on November 12th 1793, abolishing the word *vous* from the French language. This word was considered to symbolize the servitude of the old regime, and all citizens were henceforth obliged to address each other with the more democratic *tu*.

➧You are now standing on the intersection of rue du Roule and rue Saint-Honoré. To your right, on the west corner of rue des Provaires - the street where Cyrano de Bergerac was born in 1619 - you will see number 54 rue Saint-Honoré, constructed in 1700 for a merchant named Boucher. At the time of the Revolution it carried the sign *La Règle d'Or* (the Golden Rule), and on April 2nd 1791 the beautiful balcony that you see was crammed with people, waiting for a view of the funeral cortege of the Comte de Mirabeau, who had died the previous day. It is not difficult to imagine the scene. From the break of day this little intersection had gradually filled up with spectators, with every window and ledge, right up to the rooftops, covered with people eager to get a glimpse of the great man's coffin. After long hours of waiting, the procession finally arrived, preceded by a strange and surprising musical accompaniment of 'tom-tom' drums and trombones. This combination of instruments had never been used before in such a situation, and as the cortege turned the corner, the primitive drumming and the dismal wail of the trombones drifted up to the balcony and tore at the hearts of the awe-struck onlookers as they mourned their departed hero.

Lafayette, splendidly dressed as General of the Citizens' Militia and holding an unsheathed sabre in his hand, was at the head of the procession, followed by a long line of deputies and friends of the deceased. Some were not friends, as in the case of Charles de Lameth, who had been Mirabeau's deadliest enemy, and was even suspected of having poisoned him. Behind the deputies came the Jacobins, who were all dressed in black, with their heads bowed in an air of defeat, and were noticeable for their somewhat ostentatious mourning. Many of them let out little cries of grief and continually wiped their eyes, a performance which, whether sincere or not, was thoroughly appreciated by the crowd. Then came the clergy, followed by the coffin, carried on the shoulders of sixteen citizen-soldiers from the battalion that Mirabeau had commanded. The rear of the procession was made up of members of all the minor political clubs and societies, followed by an endless stream of ordinary citizens whose profound and sincere grief bore witness to the dead orator's enormous popularity with the people of Paris. Amongst them was a young man who, three days earlier, had offered to give his blood to the dying Mirabeau, and the sight of this generous hero provoked floods of tears from many of the women who were watching from the windows and the rooftops. Later in the Revolution the balcony at number 54 was used regularly for observation, for it was a very good place to watch the tumbrils as they came up rue du Roule and slowed down to turn the corner into rue Saint-Honoré.

➥Continue to follow the tumbrils now, westwards along rue Saint-Honoré, and you will immediately see a small row of lovely old houses at numbers 56, 58 and 60, decorated with sculpted masks and beautiful wrought-iron balconies. The house at number 93 has carried the name *Au Bourdon d'Or* since 1637, and until recently has always had a medical association - in 1647 a midwife lived there, followed by an apothecary, and later a barber who specialized in medical bleeding. The house has a beautiful gilded balcony, and on the wall on either side of the first floor window is an exquisite sign which was painted in 1825, when the house was reconstructed in the style of the Directory period by Clérambourg, the resident apothecary at that time. Number 82 is also very old and was the home of François Chabot, the friend of Claude Bazire whom you just met back on the corner. Chabot, a Capuchin monk-turned-deputy who is credited with inventing the term *sans-culotte*, was by all accounts a rather unadmirable character whose suitability to religious orders was highly questionable. Perhaps he was inspired to become a monk during his childhood, which was spent in a religious setting on account of his father's job as cook in a monastery. Chabot entered a Capuchin friary in Rodez in the Aveyron region, but his taste for women, his greed and debauchery soon put him out of favour with his superiors. He also began reading the contemporary philosophers and the Encyclopaedists, as well as various controversial and permissive books whose existence had been revealed to him by his parishioners during confession, but when his reading material began to sift its way into his preaching, it was not long before he was thrown out of the Capuchin order.

Chabot then threw himself into a political career and got elected as a deputy in the Legislative Assembly, where he launched an attack on the royal family and called for the overthrow of Louis XVI. On September 2nd 1792 he was part of a government deputation at the *Prison de l'Abbaye*, where he managed to save the life of one priest, but otherwise did nothing to prevent the massacres that were taking place. After this he was re-elected as a deputy in the National Convention, where he affected the dress and manner of a true *sans-culotte*, and voted for the death of the king. But his scandalous life-style brought increasing criticism as his views became more and more anarchic. *'What is my law, you ask me?'* he said in a speech to the Jacobins. *'My reply is: the natural law, that which says: Poor, go into the homes of the rich; girls, go with the boys; You should all follow your instincts.'*

The year 1793 brought Chabot even more dangerous criticism through his friendship with the Frey brothers, two Austrian bankers who in reality were spies being paid for bribing revolutionaries to renounce their ideas. Chabot married their sister, Léopoldine, three weeks after meeting her, for a dowry of 200,000 *livres*, and from the autumn of that year he came under more and more suspicion for his known speculation in various shady affairs, notably that of the liquidation of the East India Company. Sensing danger, he tried to divert attention away from himself by making a venomous attack on the Girondins and denouncing them with a pack of lies at their trial in October. Denouncing people had always been a favourite activity of Chabot's, but this time the tables were turned against him, and he suddenly found himself the target of multiple accusations.

Then came the most dangerous denunciation of all. Robespierre took the rostrum at the Jacobin Club and made a glacial attack on Chabot for his alliance with the Austrian factions and his involvement in the East India Company affair. Chabot made a desperate bid to clear himself by denouncing his colleagues to Robespierre, claiming that in spite of having received money to falsify documents, he had done this in his capacity of good citizen, infiltrating the plot in order to expose it. He tried to show his sincerity by offering the money to the Committee along with the identity of the conspirators, in exchange for immunity from prosecution. But Robespierre, well aware of Chabot's insatiable love of money, didn't believe him for a minute, and went along with his story only long enough to secure the arrest and imprisonment of all those involved, including Chabot himself. His final days were not distinguished by courage or dignity. When he learned that he was to be judged with the Dantonists, he tried to escape the guillotine by swallowing a horribly corrosive poison that his wife had smuggled into the Luxembourg prison. But the attempt was a failure, for he had not finished taking it before the agonizing effects took hold of him, and his desperate screams for help could be heard throughout the entire prison. The antidote brought by the prison doctor calmed his atrocious convulsions, but left Chabot languishing in severe pain for three days before going to the scaffold.

➡Continue to the junction with rue de l'Arbre Sec (Dry Tree). This street possibly got its name from the gallows which always stood in the middle of the square, known as the *Place de la Croix-du-Trahoir*, in reference to the enormous stone cross which stood next to the gallows to facilitate the last prayers of the condemned. This cross remained here until 1776, and as well as its religious role during executions, the wide steps at its base also served rather less piously as stalls for local butchers and greengrocers on market days. Legend has it that Cyrano de Bergerac and Molière, who was born in 1622 at 94 rue Saint-Honoré, used to play together around the gallows. This was hardly a suitable playground for small children, however, for in addition to hanging, decapitation and breaking on the wheel, various forms of mutilation were also practised here, under the orders of the Bishops of Paris, notably the amputation of the ears of dishonest servants. In these cases, the executioner always cut off the left ear, believing there was a vein on this side that linked with the reproductive organs, thus rendering the offender unable to pass on his undesirable genetic heritage to future generations.

In January 1790, during the Festival of the Constitution, Parisians transformed the former site of the gallows into a joyous altar to the Revolution. On the spot where the sinister wooden gibbet had stood, a platform was erected and decorated with tricolour pennants and garlands of oak and laurel leaves. People flocked enthusiastically to this colourful altar to swear their obedience to the new Constitution. Parents brought their children, schoolteachers brought their pupils, the old and sick were supported by the young and healthy, all raising their hands in ardent displays of loyalty to the new era. But there would still be dark days for the *Place de la Croix-du-Trahoir*. During the winter of 1793-4, when fear hung like a menacing cloud over Paris, bitter cold and food shortages heightened the anguished misery of its citizens. Speculators exploited their desperate plight, resulting in an unprecedented level of looting, theft and violence. For a while a dark, almost mediaeval atmosphere fell upon the city, where famine and plague encouraged wolves to come into the *Place de la Croix-du-Trahoir*, attack children and eat the corpses that were put out in the square.

At number 111 rue Saint-Honoré, on the corner of rue de l'Arbre Sec, you will see a lovely old fountain decorated with garlands rather like a Christmas tree. There had been a fountain in the middle of the *Place de la Croix-du-Trahoir* since 1529, and the original one formed the pedestal for the stone cross. In the 17th century it was moved to the place where you see the present-day fountain, which was constructed in 1775 during the first year of the reign of Louis XVI. This fountain has a Latin inscription in honour of the new king, and is the work of the architect Soufflot and the sculptor Boizot. Opposite the fountain is 94 rue Saint-Honoré, where Molière was born.

Just a few houses along at number 115 you will see a pharmacy that has been here since 1715, and you can still see an inscription on the façade dating from that time, when the owner was Bernard Derosne. To the right above the entrance it says *Manufacturer of extracts evaporated by steam and by vacuum*, and there used to be another one saying *Chemical and pharmaceutical products by Bernard Derosne and Ossian Henry*, but I think that one has disappeared into the mists of time. At the end of the 18th century the newly fashionable mineral water from

Passy was sold at this pharmacy at 7 *sous* a bottle, and it is also generally believed that the Swedish count, Hans Axel von Fersen, bought the ink here that he used for writing his letters to Marie-Antoinette. Whether he was the queen's lover or not remains an unsolved mystery, for in their famous correspondence neither of them ever departed from the formal conventions or forms of address, but his letters are clear evidence of his total devotion and loyalty to both Marie-Antoinette and Louis XVI. Fersen risked his life when he organized the escape to Varennes, an operation in which he took an active part, and he also lent over a million *livres* to the king. Fersen was of the old order, and perhaps a strong element of his feelings for Marie-Antoinette was the chivalrous love that a mediaeval knight would have had for his queen. His letters certainly do not reveal anything more than this, but his relationship with the French queen remains one of history's romantic enigmas. As you walk into the pharmacy, you pass by a magnificent clock on one side and a beautiful mirror on the other, both encased in gilded wood panelling beneath a romantic painted ceiling. Unfortunately commerce comes before romance these days, and the current management has put a soft drink cabinet in front of the mirror. However, if you use your imagination, you might spot the handsome and elegant figure of Fersen, slipping discreetly through the door and out into the street, the bottle of amorous ink carefully concealed beneath the folds of his velvet cloak.

At numbers 121, 123 and 125 there used to be a large house known as the *Hôtel d'Aligre*, where in 1770 Philipp Wilhelm Mathe Kreutz arrived from Switzerland and set up a wax modelling studio. He would later be known as Dr Curtius, who opened the famous wax exhibition in the arcades of the Palais-Royal where Marie Tussaud started her career. In 1769 Mathurin Roze de Chantoiseau opened a restaurant in the *Hôtel d'Aligre*. He had started it three years earlier, in fact, in *rue des Poulies* (now rue du Louvre), very near another restaurant founded by Monsieur Boulanger, whom Roze tried to upstage by claiming that his own establishment was the first restaurant in Paris. But this honour belongs to Boulanger, whose restaurant had opened one year earlier in 1765. Roze's restaurant in the *Hôtel d'Aligre* was nonetheless very successful, for he believed fervently in publicity, and brought out a newspaper in which he advertised his 'house of health', boasting shamelessly about his prowess as a *restaurateur* and the capons that he sold at 3½ *livres* each. He was also an agent for the newly fashionable *eau de Cologne*, and used his restaurant as a depot for this and the various other products he marketed. Roze was a singular character, an idealist, who continued to keep up with the times, so in 1789 he went to Versailles to present Louis XVI with a plan of fiscal reform aimed at reducing the national debt. The plan was by all accounts not a very good one, and Louis was not overly fond of reform, so instead of becoming a financial hero, Roze enjoyed a short stay in prison. The English historian, Rebecca Spang, in her wonderful book about the history of restaurants, gives Roze a rather good epitaph when she says, 'If Mathurin Roze de Chantoiseau's scheme to reduce the French national debt had been as successful as his bouillon-selling establishments, he might have prevented the French Revolution.'

During the last part of the 18th century the *Hôtel d'Aligre* also housed the Central Office of Chimney Sweeps, where large numbers of small boys were employed to clean chimneys for 8 *sols*. If your chimney was more than four floors up it was half-price - and we can only imagine what percentage of this the poor chimney sweeps got for their labour. Another occupant of the *hôtel* during the same period was a goldsmith called Maillart, who numbered among his customers none other than Louis XVI himself. In 1782 the king wished to honour Tsar Paul the First with a gift, and Maillart, who was chosen for this privilege, made an exquisite snuff-box for the Russian potentate.

Directly opposite, at numbers 106 and 108, was a dispensary belonging to an apothecary named Charles-Louis Cadet de Gassincourt. Cadet, who was 20 when the Revolution broke out, belonged to a family of pharmacists, but his real origins were the subject of popular gossip at the time, for he was generally said to be one of the many illegitimate sons of Louis XV. Number 130, further down the road at the intersection with rue du Louvre, also has an association with Louis XV. During the 18th century there was a fashion boutique here, owned by a Monsieur Dulac, and here you would have spied Louis's favourite mistress, the lovely Madame du Barry, going into the shop to buy her *mouches* (false beauty spots), a must at the extravagant and theatrical court of Versailles.

➥Cross the road, and at number 145 you will see an imposing baroque façade standing rather dramatically at an oblique angle to the street. This is the Temple de l'Oratoire, a Protestant church that was built in the 1620s by Pierre de Bérulle, founder of an association of parish priests known as the *Congrégation des Pères de l'Oratoire* - an evidently well-endowed institution, for a few years earlier it had bought the original building on this site for 90,000 *livres*. At that time, Louis XIII wanted the new church to be incorporated into the projected new wing of the Louvre, hence its peculiar angle, for it was never intended to form part of rue Saint-Honoré. There were two houses in front of it then, separating it from the street, with a small covered alley behind them giving access to the church. After the demolition of these two houses in 1745, the church's present façade was constructed by an architect named Caquet. Behind the church spread several large convent buildings belonging to the *Congrégation des Pères*, as well as an enormous library that by the end of the 18th century contained 37,750 rare and valuable volumes. On December 14th 1792 the Convention issued a decree abolishing the Oratorians and taking over their buildings for the storage of military material brought down from Saint-Denis. The church was then used successively for meetings of the local district Assembly, as a military store, a revolutionary club and a meeting place for the various societies that were constantly springing up at the time.

By 1793 the Oratoire had a red cap of Liberty over its doorway, and housed a large number of strange and idealistic organizations, such as *The Static Society*, *The Galvanic Society* and *The Society of Observers of Man*. During the Directory period the rather more pragmatic *Office of Mortgages and Debts* took up residence in one of the convent buildings, and stayed there until rue de Rivoli was opened in 1854. In 1797 the secretary of this office was the writer Choderlos de Laclos, who fifteen years earlier had provoked a scandal and become an overnight celebrity with the publication of his novel *Les Liaisons Dangereuses*. This sudden fame brought him into contact with all the well-known figures of the time, notably the Duc d'Orléans, who employed Laclos as a speech-writer, put him in charge of his political campaigns, and even extended his professional duties to include accompanying the duke when he fled to England after the royal flight to Varennes. Laclos was a member of the Jacobin Club and wrote, with Brissot, the petition which led to the massacre on the Champ-de-Mars, but his relations with Philippe d'Orléans eventually brought him under suspicion, and he was arrested and imprisoned along with other supporters of the renegade duke. He escaped being guillotined with the Orleanists, but was kept in prison until December 1794, probably because of his suspected affinity with Robespierre. On being liberated Laclos was given his post of secretary in the Mortgage Office, but when Napoléon came to power, he joined the Rhine Army and died of dysentery in Italy. Laclos was nothing like the Vicomte de Valmont, the morally corrupt protagonist of his novel; he was by all accounts a happily married man who enjoyed throughout his life a reputation as a devoted father and a faithful husband. But he was clearly familiar with the social behaviour of the *ancien régime*, and some say he wrote the book to expose the decadence of the era.

It was in 1811, under Napoléon Bonaparte, that the Temple de l'Oratoire became a Protestant church, and has remained so ever since. Unfortunately it's now closed to the public, following vandalism and theft of church property, so you are unable to go in and look at this splendid monument. It does open for services, however, on Sunday mornings and religious feast days, so you could see it then, and ➥if you want to make a group visit you should telephone 01 42 60 21 64. On the corner of rue de l'Oratoire, which runs alongside the church, there used to be a little bookshop that like many other businesses in the city did not hesitate to profit from the popularity of the Revolution to make a sale. In November 1790 you could buy here a pair of engraved sheets of images of revolutionary events, each one coming with a free gift of twenty medallions which '*could also serve beautifully as decorative buttons.*' I'm sure sewing these on to your coat would have helped keep you off the list of suspects.

At number 149, on the corner of rue Marengo, was a barrier in the street known as the *Barrière des Sergents,* guarded by 25 policemen. It had been there since 1551 and remained until 1804, being only once dismantled in 1747 to honour the triumphant return of Louis XV from his campaign in Holland. Between number 149 and the corner of the Place du Palais-Royal you now find a large new building containing the Louvre boutique and a branch of the Club Med Gym. But in the 18th century it was where several small streets went off from the main road, and on this side of rue Saint-Honoré was a pastry shop owned by a man named Ragueneau. The shop also had a café, a favourite haunt for the literary bohemians of the day, who, like bohemians of any period, were usually broke, but so favoured by Ragueneau that he habitually let them pay with poems or short stories. Nor did he shrink from lending them money, which they usually spent drinking somewhere else, so it's not surprising then that Ragueneau soon went bankrupt, and was obliged to take up the rather eccentric post of Molière's candle-snuffer.

Later, in 1772, a milliner by the name of Rose Bertin opened up her boutique, *Au Grand Mogul*, on this block of rue Saint-Honoré where it meets Place du Palais-Royal. It was Rose's second shop in Paris, and she had already established herself as the most fashionable *modiste* in the capital, counting among her most important customers Marie-Antoinette, who used to visit the shop twice a week. Rose was blamed at the time for the extravagance of the queen, whose annual expenditure here for many years was about l00,000 *livres*, but thanks to her wealthy royal patron, Rose was able to close the shop in April 1789 and open a new one in rue de Richelieu, which she bought for 180,000 *livres*. Another of Rose's valued customers was the Comtesse Jeanne du Barry, another big spender, who in the decade leading up to the Revolution spent nearly 80,000 *livres* in Madame Bertin's fashion paradise. Jeanne's final view of her favourite shop, however, was more akin to hell than heaven. It was from a tumbril on her way to execution, and her last moments are famous for the spectacle of unleashed terror that she gave as she passed along rue Saint-Honoré. She was 50, and despite being a little overweight, was still beautiful, and so loved life that she couldn't believe she would really be killed. She sobbed and screamed desperately, her hands outstretched, imploring the spectators to save her, but to no avail. When the tumbril arrived here at the *Barrière des Sergents*, Jeanne not only saw Rose Bertin's former shop, she also caught sight of the staff of *A la Toilette*, the nearby fashion boutique where she had worked as a young girl. There they were, those who were once her friends, all lined up on the iron balconies overlooking the street, shouting insults at her. On recognizing some of the older employees, she lifted her head up and let out a hysterical laugh so loud and piercing that it could be heard above the noise of the jeering crowd.

➡ Cross over rue Marengo and continue along rue Saint-Honoré, where in a house on the site of the present number 194 lived the republican 'King of the Directory', Jean-Nicolas-Paul-François Barras. This was his home at the beginning of the Revolution, when he was merely an anonymous onlooker during the storming of the Bastille. Born into one of the oldest noble families in Provence, Paul Barras was blonde and sensual with exceptionally pale blue eyes that, despite their emptiness, never failed to seduce. His only thoughts were for women and adventure, and, unimpressed by the options open to him in France, he decided to satisfy his desire to see the world by becoming a gentleman soldier. After enrolling in the regiment of Langudoc, he took part in the campaign in the Indies, where he distinguished himself by intrepid actions in the face of danger. But military life did not leave Barras enough time to indulge his taste for pleasure and dissipated living, so he resigned and went to Paris, where he very quickly squandered his family fortune. Returning to Provence, he married a wealthy woman who was conveniently indifferent to his philandering, and then came back to Paris in 1792 as a deputy in the National Convention. Although an ardent republican who voted for the death of the king, Barras was always careful to avoid compromising himself politically, so was rarely heard speaking from the rostrum.

In April 1793 he was sent on a mission to Marseille with Stanislas Fréron, with whom he conducted some very dubious business deals that made him quite rich, and it was during this period in the south of France that the cruel streak in Barras's nature became very evident when he ordered the summary execution of huge numbers of suspects. This, and his personal and financial immorality, brought Barras the contempt of Robespierre, who almost had him arrested on several occasions. Having contributed to the persecution of both the Hébertists and the Dantonists, he then began to feel personally threatened by Robespierre's increasing hostility. Along with many other deputies, Barras saw the writing on the wall, and on the evening of 9 *Thermidor* they sprang into action.

As Commander-in-Chief of the Paris Army, Barras took a leading role in this overnight coup d'etat, and by the following morning Robespierre had been deposed. Then Barras's career really took off. He already had considerable power in the Convention, and he used it to fight the monarchist backlash that began gathering momentum during 1795. On October 5th (*13 Vendémiaire*) of that year he once again commanded the Paris Army, this time against royalist insurgents who tried to topple the Convention. With his young protégé, Napoléon Bonaparte, Barras successfully led the coup that left several holes in the wall of Saint-Roch Church, and the 'whiff of grapeshot' along rue Saint-Honoré. By the end of the month the Convention had been replaced by the Directory, and Barras was named one of the five Directors who would run the country. But it was a group divided by political differences, and Barras, with Reubell and La Révellière, formed the republican 'triumvirate' that gradually consolidated their power by suppressing a succession of attempted royalist coups.

Barras developed a friendship with Bonaparte over the years , but it was a rather volatile one, for they were both continually suspicious of each other. It was through Barras that Bonaparte met Joséphine, who had formerly been Barras's lover, and some say that Barras manoeuvred Napoléon into the marriage to get Joséphine off his hands. By 1798 the 'sly little Corsican' began to pose too much of a threat to Barras, who got him out of the way by sending him to Egypt, but when Bonaparte came back triumphant Barras no longer had the power to resist the coup d'etat that, on November 9th 1799 (*18 Brumaire*), overthrew the Directory and established Napoléon as ruler of France. Barras knew when he was beaten. He sent a letter of resignation saluting *'the return of the illustrious warrior to whom I have had the good fortune of opening up the path to glory',* and indicated his intention of *'returning with joy to the ranks of ordinary citizen.'* But such submissive rhetoric from the likes of Barras would have been viewed with suspicion by anyone, especially Bonaparte, who gradually ordered him further and further from the capital, until in 1810 he sent him into exile in Rome. Barras was able to return to France only after the defeat of Napoléon, when he re-settled in Paris and spent his remaining years in relative luxury, writing his memoirs, and entertaining a circle of friends composed exclusively of royalists.

On the site of number 202 there used to be a small street called *cul-de-sac de l'Opéra*. On the left-hand corner of this *cul-de-sac*, forming part of the Palais-Royal, was a theatre built by Richelieu in 1639 that later became the Royal Opera. On the right-hand corner was another theatre, begun in 1763 when the Royal Opera burned down. This theatre, designed by Moreau, took seven years to build, and was also destroyed in 1781 by a fire that claimed 21 victims. There were however some dramatic rescues, like that of the celebrated dancer Marie-Madeleine Guimard, saved by a stage-hand who dragged her from a flaming box and carried her out of the theatre rolled in a wet sheet. Thanks to this courageous act, Mlle Guimard lived to dance for another eight years, retire at 45, marry a fellow dancer and live to the age of 71. The house that now stands at number 202, which is a listed historic building, was built after 1784, when rue de Valois was opened, absorbing the *cul-de-sac de l'Opéra*. It houses a bakery and patisserie called Ragueneau, no doubt in deference to its more famous predecessor at number 149.

➡ You are now in front of the Palais-royal, home of the Duc d'Orléans, who at a convenient moment in the Revolution became Philippe-Egalité. This was one of the most bustling squares in the city then, alive with the coming and going of local residents and tradesmen, the hurried figures of the numerous deputies who lived in or around rue Saint-Honoré, and the more leisurely movement of promenading Parisians who came regularly to see the palace and gardens of the revolutionary duke. Throughout the Revolution the Place du Palais-Royal was the scene of many events and processions, some joyous, but many bloody. A week after the storming of the Bastille, Paris was in the grip of a frightened and uncontrollable populace who on July 22nd accused the new Controller of Finances, Foulon, of being responsible for food shortages, and savagely assassinated him. They also killed his son-in-law Berthier, whose mutilated body was dragged through the muddy streets, while his heart was brandished on the end of a cutlass. The horrific procession stopped at a café on this part of rue Saint-Honoré, near rue de Richelieu, where some of the customers are reported to have seized Berthier's still throbbing entrails and dipped them into their drinks.

Later on, in the summer of 1792, the air here was alive with patriotic fervour and the beating of drums, as an enrolment centre was set up to recruit young soldiers for the defence of the nation. Not long after, on September 2nd, the square saw another hideous trophy paraded in triumph, the head of the Princesse de Lamballe, who had just been slaughtered at the *Petite Force* prison. The frenzied mob held it high on the end of a pike in front of the windows of the Palais-Royal, where the Duc d'Orléans, was dining with his mistress, the blonde and beautiful Agnès Buffon. Hearing so much shouting in the square below, they went to the window, where they saw the long blonde hair of the duke's unfortunate sister-in-law flying around the pike as it was jolted about by the crowd. *'My God!'* said a white-faced Agnès, *'it'll soon be my head that they're carrying in the street!'* Nearly two years later, Parisians taking an evening stroll under those same windows were stunned by the news of the fall of Robespierre, brought to the square by deputies on horseback. By then the Duc d'Orléans had lost his head, but Agnès, despite her fears and her outspoken criticism of the Revolution, had kept hers firmly on her shoulders.

The following day, Robespierre was seen sitting silently in a tumbril as it rolled past the Palais-Royal, now re-named *Maison Égalité*. He was among the last of those who took this route of the condemned, and you will meet up with him again in Walk Eight, when he passes by his own house on his final journey.

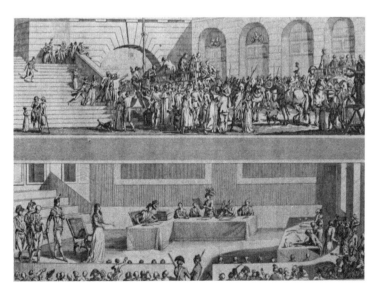

The Girondins leaving the Conciergerie in a tumbril, on their way to execution. (Courtesy of Musée Carnavalet, Cabinet des Arts Graphiques, Paris)

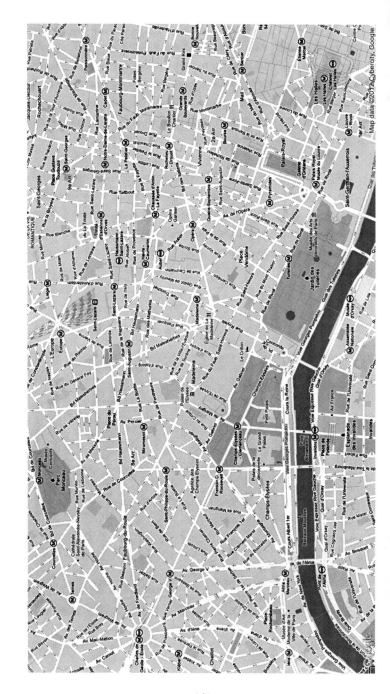

Walk Number Eight

THE ROUTE OF THE CONDEMNED
II. THE GUILLOTINE - AND AFTER

Rue Saint-Honoré - Place Vendôme - Place de la Concorde - Chapelle-Expiatoire - Parc Monceau

From the Conciergerie prison sad processions of tumbrils set off each afternoon, transporting the daily batches of victims destined for the guillotine in the Place de la Concorde, known then as *Place de la Révolution*. In walks number seven and eight you will follow in their footsteps, from prison cell to scaffold to grave, at the same time getting to know some of the residents of the area and the events that took place there. Walk eight takes you through Robespierre's neighbourhood to the site of the famous Jacobin Club, where he reigned supreme during the Terror, and if you want to get better acquainted with this redoubtable revolutionary, you can have lunch or dinner in the same place where he ate every evening with his adopted family. After witnessing the last moments of the most famous patriots in the *Place de la Révolution*, and then following them to their burial place, you will end your walk at a highly subversive dinner party.

The Route of the Condemned
II. The Guillotine - and After

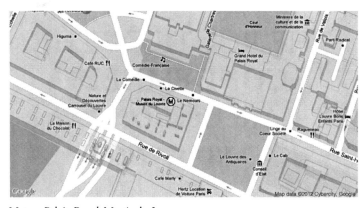

Metro: Palais-Royal-Musée du Louvre

➡You come out of the metro into the Place du Palais-Royal, where you will join up again with the procession of tumbrils carrying condemned prisoners on their final journey to the scaffold in the *Place de la Révolution* (Concorde). ➡Walk to the north side of the square, go left on rue Saint-Honoré and walk up to number 155 (Gallimard bookshop). Between here and rue de Rohan was the site of the old *Quinze-Vingts* hospice for the blind, founded in 1254 and demolished in 1781 when the gardens and arcades of the Palais-Royal were being planned. At number 157 is La Civette, a tobacco shop that takes its name from the small cat-like animal shown on its beautiful sign. It was first established as a tobacconist in 1754 in a prime location next door to the Palais-Royal, but in 1829 the Duc d'Orléans decided to enlarge his property, and the shop had to move to new premises a few houses down near rue de Richelieu. Five years later it moved again, to its present position, which is the site of the church that had belonged to the *Quinze-Vingts* Hospice. During the 18th century the shop owed its reputation to the generosity of the Duchesse de Chartres, Louise de Bourbon-Conti, who founded it for a young couple whom she wished to help, and who, together with her husband the Duc de Chartres, attracted its illustrious clientele. Voltaire, Diderot and Benjamin Franklin were all regular customers, as well as Louise's father-in-law, the Duc d'Orléans, and other residents of the Palais-Royal like Chamfort, who would often stop here to buy tobacco before going to drink at the nearby *Café de la Régence*. According to reports of the time, it was not unusual for more than 100 *écus* worth of tobacco to be sold in a day at La Civette. It is the oldest cigar shop in Paris, and was of course regularly visited by that most famous of cigar-smokers, Winston Churchill.

Rue Richelieu.

I	Former Quinze-Vingts Hospice for the Blind (demolished 1781)
II	La Civette
III	Café Mirabeau
IV	Hôtel d'Angleterre
V	Librairie Lagrange
VI	Saint-Honoré Gate/Café de la Régence from 1854 until its closure
VII	Comédie-Française
-----	Former position of rue Richelieu and rue Saint-Honoré

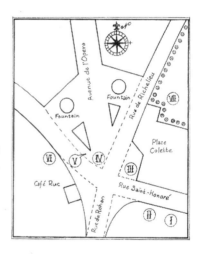

➥Cross rue Saint-Honoré to Place Colette (the side that is nearest rue de Richelieu). Before Place André Malraux and Avenue de l'Opéra were opened, rue de Richelieu came all the way down to form a corner with rue Saint-Honoré - about where you are standing - the actual corner is now part of the road (see plan) so don't stand there or you might get run over! On one corner (probably this side nearest the Palais-Royal) was a café named *Café Mirabeau*, and on the opposite corner (in Place André-Malraux) stood a large building known as the *Hôtel*

d'Angleterre, where a Monsieur Hubault rented out furnished apartments. He also ran a rather disreputable gambling room there, which still existed during the Directory period, and when the *Hôtel d'Angleterre* refused to pay its taxes, Monsieur Hubault received unswerving support from the customers in his little casino, who staged a rebellion against the official collectors when they came to the house. Hubault probably used the unpaid taxes to decorate his establishment in the sumptuous style of the *ancien régime*, provoking the newspaper, *Le Patriote Français*, to comment with astonishment on the absence of any action against '*this house, which, as God knows, is so beautifully furnished.*' Hubault also ran a restaurant in the *Hôtel d'Angleterre*, where many hard-up deputies could get a buffet supper at a fixed price of 42 *sous*.

There were three deputies living in Hubault's furnished apartments who no doubt took advantage of being able to eat so cheaply, and without having to leave the building. One of them was Maximin Isnard, a deputy from the Var who allied himself with the Girondins, but often voted with the Montagnards, and was in fact the major cause of the hostility between the two factions. He succeeded in keeping his name off the Girondin arrest warrant in June 1793 by voluntarily suspending himself of his duties, but not for long, for three months later, as he walked out of his apartment on to rue Saint-Honoré, he was met by a juror from the Tribunal who tried to arrest him. Thanks to his legendary physical strength, Isnard overcame his aggressor, escaped to the safety of a friend's house and proceeded to spread rumours of his own death. He remained in hiding until after Robespierre's death, when he returned to the Convention and became one of the most violent Thermidoreans. On a mission in the south, Isnard was responsible for the hunting out and execution of scores of 'terrorist' republicans, and did nothing to stop the massacre of all the prisoners in the Saint-Jean fort in Marseille. After being made a baron during the

Empire, Isnard survived the restoration of the monarchy by becoming a fervent royalist, racked with remorse for having voted for the death of the king.

Next to the *Hôtel d'Angleterre* was a bookshop and publishing house called *Librairie Lagrange*, which in January 1790 brought out 'The almanac of Patriots.' This most important publication, which praised the National Assembly at enormous length, was soon to be found in the eager hands of every dedicated revolutionary, and possessing it became a guaranteed proof of good citizenship. It was just one in the never-ending succession of emblems and tokens that flooded the capital in the early months of the Revolution. The most earnest would display these insignia with pride and conviction, while those more sceptical of the new era were wise enough not to dismiss them too disdainfully.

Rue Saint-Honoré.
➡You now need to cross back over to the other side of rue Saint-Honoré, either by crossing to Place André-Malraux and then crossing over to the Café Ruc, or by crossing back to La Civette, and crossing rue de Rohan over to the Café Ruc. Then continue along rue Saint-Honoré and stop at number 161 and 163, site of the *Saint-Honoré Gate* where in 1429 Joan of Arc tried to enter Paris and liberate it from the English. Number 161 is also the site of the *Café de la Régence*, where all the great chess masters played for more than 150 years, and where the artist David was sitting when he made his famous sketches of Danton and Marie-Antoinette as they made their final journey along rue Saint-Honoré in a tumbril. You'll learn more about this celebrated café when you go on the walk that takes you around the Palais-Royal. The lion and lioness languishing above the entrance of number 165 were put there by a fur merchant who used to ply his trade there. As you go along rue Saint-Honoré I'll be pointing out houses on both sides of the street, so I won't keep telling you to cross over - I will leave it up to you

- but I warn you to be really careful when you do cross, for this is a very busy street and Parisian drivers, as you probably know by now, are not too keen on stopping for pedestrians.

The French Revolution pioneered many changes in social attitudes and behaviour, and an ex-naval doctor named Retz at the *Bureau of the Annals of the Art of Healing* was part of this trend. His office was over the road at number 238 rue Saint-Honoré, which was either part of 248 or was where you now see the west side of Place André-Malraux. There Retz could be found hard at work protecting the moral welfare of future generations of revolutionaries, and to this worthy end he published in 1790 a 'Guide to young people of both sexes on their entry into the world.' His purpose in writing this was to *'warn of the deplorable effects that can result from youthful misdemeanours'*, an aim that might still be dear to the heart of many a modern social worker. Stay on this side (the south side) of rue Saint-Honoré and walk along to the corner of rue de l'Echelle, where during the Revolution you found one local tradesman who was evidently not at all interested in pioneering any social changes. He traded here as a *tabletier*, which seems best translated as someone who works with wood, but specifically on small items like trinket boxes, chess boards, dominoes, and small toys. Heavily suspected of royalism, he came under the eye of a government spy called Rousseville, who on September 25th 1793 reported that *'the tabletier at the sign of the Green Monkey is selling little boxes containing locks of Capet's* [Louis XVI's] *hair.'* Rousseville also noted with alarm that several jewellers in the vicinity were making *'rather large silver rings that opened with a secret lock and concealed in their top part a little piece of the clothing of Mr Veto* [Louis XVI]*, who has become a saint for having murdered his subjects.'* We don't know what happened to these reckless tradesmen, but it was the beginning of the Terror, so it didn't bode well!

Also on the corner of rue de l'Echelle, at number 252, a manufacturer named Launoy who was busy producing vegetable-based red dyes. In an age where red caps abounded and everything from sashes to sofas was coloured red, white and blue, business must have been booming for Monsieur Launoy. 254 was the home of deputy Pierre–Toussaint Durand–Maillane, a lawyer who wrote extensively on canon law, was one of the authors of the Civil Constitution of the Clergy, and survived the Terror to become a deputy in the Thermidorean government. In his memoirs he talks about how difficult it had been to be a deputy on the Right during the period when the Montagnard faction dominated, when he and his colleagues could not openly oppose the Mountain out of fear for their lives, and so maintained silent non-alliance. He also refers to yet another group in the Assembly, known as 'the Stomach', that was sandwiched between the Right and the Mountain and considered itself wiser than the Right. Durand-Maillane did not agree, preferring to view them with contempt for not taking any stand at all, silent or otherwise.

Between numbers 256 and 274 is a row of old houses, one of which, number 270, was the home of the revolutionary feminist Marie Olympe Grouze, known as Olympe de Gouges. Born into a modest family in 1748, she married at age 17 to a man she didn't love, who died a year later, leaving her alone with her baby son Pierre. Olympe moved immediately to Paris, where she began writing, having financially useful love affairs and getting in with the aristocracy. After producing several plays, essays and anti-slavery tracts, and championing the cause of women of all ages, including single mothers, in 1791 Olympe wrote her 'Declaration of the Rights of Women and the Female Citizen'. In this she challenges the inherent sexism of the revolutionary ideal of equality, exhorts women to demand their own national assembly, and cites *perpetual male tyranny* as the only obstacle to women being able to exercise their natural rights. Her thinking was decidedly ahead of its time, and Olympe's Declaration is inspiring reading to any woman who has lived through the feminist revolution of the 20th century. In 1793 she paid with her life for her challenge to the male dominated world in which she lived when the Tribunal condemned her to death for royalist writings. Olympe's militant genes were hopefully passed down through many descendants in both Britain and the United States, for her son Pierre had two daughters, one of whom married an English officer while the other married an American politician/planter from Virginia.

Number 272 was the home of the Montagnard deputy Marc-Guillaume Alexis Vadier, born into a wealthy family and acquiring vast amounts of land in his home town of Pamiers, before going on to become the President of the Committee of General Security. In this role he evolved into one of the most pitiless proponents of the Terror, responsible for the arrest of numerous patriots, including Danton, Desmoulins and also Robespierre, with whom he came to blows over the condemnation of the Sainte-Amaranthe family. Vadier was without mercy towards those he hated. He considered the king a '*bandit with a crown*', called Danton '*a stuffed turbot*', and it was Vadier's denunciation at the heart of the so-called 'prison conspiracy' that resulted in the arrest and execution of several innocent people, including Desmoulins's young wife Lucile. You might be hoping that Vadier got his comeuppance eventually, but he didn't really, because he succeeded in denouncing Robespierre and surviving 9 *Thermidor*. However, he was later condemned to deportation along with his colleague Billaud-Varenne, but managed to escape and go into hiding until he was liberated by a general amnesty. During the Directory Vadier spent several years in prison, and at the age of 80 was exiled as a regicide, but he escaped the guillotine to which he had condemned so many of his compatriots. Vadier's fondness for denouncing blameless people seemed to run in the family. In June 1794 a man called

Jean Paul Cazes was guillotined for being a counter-revolutionary, but Sanson assures us in his memoirs that *'everyone knows that Cazes was accused on the denunciation of Vadier's son, to whom this poor man had refused to give his daughter's hand in marriage.'*

Number 272 was also the office of a merchant called Béraud who was so inspired by the achievements of the revolutionary era that he determined to record them for posterity. In May 1790 he published a directory called 'The Instructive Annals', consisting of an alphabetical table of discoveries made in medicine, physics, mechanics, painting and agriculture. It was renewable each year, and subscribers received at the same time Béraud's 'Universal and methodical code of the laws which have governed France since 1789.'

At number 278 you will find a quaint little shop, nestling in the shadow of a large art-deco building. In 1761 this was a fashion boutique called *Aux Traits Galants* run by a silk merchant named Buffault and his wife, and in the same year a ravishing 18-year-old blonde began working at another *boutique de mode* nearby, run by Monsieur and Madame Labille. Professional contacts often brought Buffault to the Labille's establishment, where he spied the pretty salesgirl named Jeanne Bécu, and singled her out for a romantic adventure. Buffault was not alone, however, in his passion for Jeanne, who was more than generous with her favours, despite Monsieur Labille's earnest attempts to protect his sales-girls. But Jeanne would later give up all these frivolous episodes, for the likes of Buffault could not compete with the more promising future offered to Jeanne by a viscount named Jean du Barry. The romantically engraved flowers and violins above the doorway, the tiny staircase behind the counter and the pretty sculpted face on the inside wall just to the left of the door, are all evocative reminders of the elegant little shop that once belonged to Madame du Barry's paramour.

The tradition is now faithfully maintained by Véronique, aka Lady Sandwich, the charming manager of this little snack bar. She is a worthy successor to Mr and Mme Buffault, having succeeded in creating here an atmosphere of the romantic past in a context of modern commerce.

➥Continue along to Passage Saint-Roch, where directly opposite was a restaurant called *Chez Philpin*, where you could have a copious dinner for 3 *livres*, including wine. Philpin was one of many Parisian *traiteurs* who opened restaurants in the abandoned shops that had belonged to the wealthy traders of the old regime. Next to *Chez Philpin*, opposite the church, was a music shop run by Monsieur Bonin, who sold musical scores and stringed instruments. He too was swept up in the tide of revolutionary commerce, and in May 1792 you could spot for sale amongst the cellos and violins a commemorative poster of the new Declaration of the Rights of Man. It cost 12 *sols*, but for 4½ *livres* you could have one that was engraved on glass with a gold border.

At number 286 is the Eglise de Saint-Roch, founded in 1521 when a little chapel was built on the site of the transept of the present church. It was Louis XIV who laid the foundation stone of Saint-Roch in March 1653, but due to lack of funds, construction was slow and the church was not consecrated until July 1740. At 126 metres in length, it is almost as big as Notre Dame and one of the most spacious churches in Paris. Saint-Roch is unusual in possessing three chapels, one of which has been dedicated to the memory of wartime deportees. The first chapel you see as you enter, and the most beautiful, was built in 1709 with the proceeds of a lottery. It has a lovely painted dome showing a scene from the Assumption, and over the altar is a work by Falconet called 'Divine Glory', a dramatic explosion of golden sun rays interlaced with floating clouds and celestial cherubs. Saint-Roch contains many fine paintings and sculptures, an organ case dating from 1755 which is one of the most beautiful in France, and the wonderful gilded pulpit by Challe is supported by four wooden sculptures representing the cardinal virtues of Temperance, Strength, Prudence and Justice. They were carved in 1940 from some old wooden beams taken from the roof of the Louvre.

During the 18th century Saint-Roch was the most fashionable church in Paris, patronized by many of the most notable figures of the *ancien régime*. The great designer of French gardens, André Le Nôtre, was buried at Saint-Roch, as well as Diderot in 1784, and Molière had his baby baptized here. You can also see the tomb of another Frenchman to get involved in the American Revolution, the Comte de Grasse, who beat the English at Chesapeake Bay on September 5th 1781, and later became captain of the Cincinnati Society of Yorktown.

In the early days of the Revolution, a Parisian speculator tried to buy Saint-Roch Church, with the idea of building a road through part of it, and converting the rest into shops. Fortunately he didn't succeed, and being in the centre of Jacobin territory, the church was able to remain as a silent witness to the succession of revolutionary events that took place on its doorstep. The first, on January 6th 1789, was the festival of Epiphany, when Paris was freezing under a blanket of thick snow. It was so deep that the local aristocracy coming to attend Mass at Saint-Roch arrived in sleighs that were parked alongside the sedan chairs under the porch of the church. The pews usually occupied by the poorer residents of the area were empty, so the neighbourhood gentry were alone, listening from their privileged seats at the front to the sermon being given by the despairing curate. He implored them, with tears in his eyes, to pray and to donate money for those absent parishioners who were too exhausted by poverty and hunger to attend church.

The fur-clad nobles listened indifferently, but it was an indifference they would not be able to maintain for long.

A few months later, in the hysteria of the storming of the Bastille, the populace directed its rage against Jacques de Flesselles, Provost of Merchants. The entry of food into the capital was being blocked by the presence of foreign troops around the city gates, and Parisians blamed Flesselles for this, accusing him of feeding the Court at the expense of the people. Late in the afternoon of July 14th the Abbot of Saint-Roch, Claude Fauchet, who had just returned from the front line of the attack on the Bastille, rushed into the church gasping for breath, his long robe in shreds from the day's fighting. He found himself confronted by a huge crowd of parishioners, all violently opposed to Flesselles, all eager for action. He pleaded with them not to destroy the purity of that historic day by staining with blood the very cradle of Liberty. But Fauchet's dramatic metaphors were in vain, for Flesselles' head was soon to be seen paraded outside the Palais-Royal on the end of a pike

The curate of Saint-Roch, whose name was Marduel, continued working for the welfare of his flock, and on September 9th 1789, with food shortages still rife in the city, he put up a notice outside the church entitled *'Recipe for economic rice.'* Perhaps because many people could not afford the utensils necessary for efficient cooking, Marduel must have intended his 'economic rice' to be prepared and served in a communal soup-kitchen, for the recipe required twenty pounds of rice, two pounds of salt, two pounds of butter and six pounds of potato flour. This was all to be cooked in six buckets of water, and Marduel concluded his instructions by proudly declaring that this would produce 400 servings of very healthy and agreeable food.

During the Easter week of 1790, Marie-Antoinette was seen several times praying at Saint-Roch, in the company of Lafayette. This was an imprudent act at a time when the clergy had become allied with the royalist faction, and were in increasing conflict with the Assembly over the future of church property. It was precisely because of clerical sympathy for the monarchy that the queen decided to come to Saint-Roch, but her Easter prayers that year brought her under a great deal of suspicion. By the autumn of 1793 Marie-Antoinette had perished on the scaffold and the country was in the grip of dechristianisation. In November the triumph of atheism was celebrated everywhere by the pillaging of churches. Every object that represented the old faith was systematically broken or burned, and Saint-Roch was no exception. What was not destroyed by the band of looters who invaded the church on November 20th was carried by a group of patriots to the National Convention, where the deputies could not wait to get their hands on the sacred vases, reliquaries, crucifixes and other priceless treasures from Saint-Roch. After the Terror the Republican Arts Society outlined a proposal to turn the church into a sculpture studio, declaring that it received favourable light from every angle, making it ideally suited to this purpose. However, the plan was abandoned after a protest from the *sans-culottes* of a local section who had already taken up residence in the church and held their meetings there.

Saint-Roch Church was not spared from the violence of the Revolution, and carries even to this day the visible marks. By the autumn of 1795 sympathy was escalating for the royalist faction, particularly in Paris, where they felt their power in the new Directory government greatly diminished, so supported by the bourgeoisie, the royalists staged a rebellion with the aim of laying siege to the Tuileries and attacking the Convention. To counter this revolt, Paul Barras was given command of the army, and had the excellent idea of adding to his list of generals his friend Bonaparte, who was fast becoming renowned for his military talent. At 4 p.m. on October 5th (*13 Vendémiaire*) royalist rebels poured into rue Saint-Honoré and opened fire, but Barras's cannons immediately returned the attack, leaving the road strewn with *émigrés* and nobles. But those who survived this onslaught didn't give up. Instead they beat a retreat into Saint-Roch and opened fire again on the Convention's troops, who, after several rounds, succeeded in blowing off the porch of the church. The defeated rebels barricaded themselves in the church tower for several hours, before surrendering to the victorious Convention at 8 o'clock that evening.

➡ When you leave the church, look at the façade and you will see several rectangular marks on the stone - traces of repair work to the holes made by republican cannons on that day when Napoléon Bonaparte's future glory was assured. The following March the Directory government decided to try and win popular support by glorifying France's military successes with a *Festival of Youth* in honour of war veterans and the young who were destined to take up armed service. The Saint-Honoré neighbourhood celebrated this event at Saint-Roch, by then renamed *Temple of the Spirit* and draped with tricolour hangings for the occasion. An altar was built in the middle of the church, surrounded by a circle of little vases filled with perfumed oil that burned in honour of the nation. This colourful occasion, attended by all the local dignitaries, opened with a concert of patriotic hymns and songs performed by a group of artistes from nearby theatres. After several speeches, the veterans distributed arms to all the young recruits, along with a voting card for those among them who were over 21.

The new cult of *Théophilanthropie* was introduced at Saint-Roch in 1797, by which time anti-Catholic feeling had gathered so much momentum that a local administrator named Leclerc was dismissed for insulting the new religion. Leclerc was described by his opponents as a superstitious fanatic *'who liked only the religion that gave people blood to drink and flesh to eat.'* But after the triumph of Napoléon the Catholic religion began to filter its way back into French society, and in 1800 Easter Mass was celebrated at Saint-Roch. On this occasion the collection was taken by Madame Juliette Récamier, who wafted around the church in one of her legendary white muslin dresses that were to become the hallmark of fashion during the Empire period. Juliette's grace and beauty created such a sensation that many members of the congregation stood on chairs or climbed up pillars just to get a glimpse of her - and 20,000 *francs* were collected that day! This was the first of many masses and religious ceremonies to take place at Saint-Roch up until the end of the Empire, including the funeral of Dazincourt, a professor at the Conservatory of Music who had once taught drama to Marie-Antoinette. Once the monarchy was restored, Saint-Roch returned to Catholicism, and a Mass was held in remembrance of Louis XVI and his queen. On this occasion the church was filled with aristocrats and clergy offering prayers for the souls of the departed monarchs, and the ceremony was followed by distribution of bread to the poor.

Next to Saint-Roch Church was a bookshop called *Librairie J. J. Rousseau*, owned by a royalist named Dufart. In December 1792, when Louis XVI was about to be tried for treason and the royalist party decided to make a discreet demonstration in support of the 'martyr king', Dufart bravely, and at great risk, played his part. On sale in his shop over that Christmas season was an allegorical engraving reverently entitled 'The Rosebush of the Temple', showing a little rose tree with five roses, each representing a member of the imprisoned royal family. But survival was the name of the game in those days, so by 1794 Dufart had become Citizen Dufart, and received a diploma from the National Convention for his books of war hymns to the glory of the nation's victorious armies, for his anthology entitled 'The Little Songbook of the Republic', and for his patriotic verses sung to great applause on the stage of every major theatre in the country. Perhaps Dufart developed all this revolutionary zeal on hearing of the fate of two of his colleagues, a 60-year-old printer named Jacques François Froullé and another bookseller, Thomas Levigneur, both decapitated for having written and published an account of Louis XVI's *'last twenty-four hours of anguish'*. Froullé had been a long-standing friend of Thomas Jefferson, who always considered this kindly gentleman to be his favourite Parisian bookseller.

➡ On coming out of the church, turn right briefly on rue Saint-Roch, which runs alongside the west wall of the church, where you can see the old name of the street engraved on the church wall. It was given this name - *rue de la Montagne* - during the Revolution, in honour of the left-wing faction of the Assembly. At number 18, which leans against the foundation stone of the church, is an interesting old shop which became a hairdressing establishment in 1630, but now sells a wonderful array of antiques and trinkets, and has a stone staircase that looks ancient but is in fact a very artistic replica, and the pride and joy of the owner. This shop might have already been there when they started building the church in 1653, and is so small it's impossible to go in without getting into conversation with the owners, who are delightful. Further along on the right, to the left of the church steps, if you look carefully at the base wall of the steps, you can see some 18th-century graffiti - fragments of dates from the revolutionary period - and right next to this you will notice a little wooden shed or lock-up, painted dark green, that seems to have been long abandoned. This used to be a *cordonnier* (shoe maker and repairer), who was still there until quite recently, and next door at number 20 is a restaurant called La Cordonnerie, to remind us of this unique *petit-commerçant*, one of the last of many now disappeared from the streets of Paris. La Cordonnerie serves traditional cuisine that is sometimes prepared before your very eyes by the chef Hugo, who took over the restaurant from his parents, and now runs it with his wife Valerie. This lovely one-story 17th-century house is also quite likely to be older than the church, and at number 24 is another beautiful building dating from the early 1700s, where the priests of Saint-Roch used to live. At the outbreak of the Revolution there were more than 60 of them living in this house.

➡Now go back to rue Saint-Honoré and cross over to the south end of rue Saint-Roch, which runs between rue Saint-Honoré and rue de Rivoli and was originally called *cul-de-sac du Dauphin*. It was in this street that Bonaparte assembled his troops for the attack on the royalist rebels in Saint-Roch Church, and in honour of this victory the cul-de-sac was temporarily re-named *rue du Treize-Vendémiaire*. But for most of the Revolution it was known as *rue de la Convention*, for it led to the main entrance of the *Salle de Manège* where the National Convention sat. When the Assembly decided to follow the king to Paris in October 1789, it was Doctor Guillotin who chose the *Manège*, considering it the most hygienic place available in a city that, in Guillotin's view, was extremely unhealthy. Redecoration began immediately and continued day and night, despite terrible weather, attracting swarms of curious visitors to this part of rue Saint-Honoré. The grandeur of such an operation inspired the onlookers, who tried in vain to light up the work area with torches that were immediately extinguished by the wind and the pouring rain.

Being the principal means of access to the Assembly, rue Saint-Roch was always alive with the continual coming and going of deputies. One of the most dramatic moments for this little street was the morning of January 16th 1793, when it was invaded from the early hours by a huge crowd of people, for this was the day when the fate of the king would be decided, and they were waiting eagerly for the arrival of the deputies. Danton, Desmoulins, Marat and Robespierre all entered the *Manège* to the sound of applause and shouts of acclaim, while Brissot and the Girondins, out of favour for their moderate attitude regarding Louis XVI's guilt, hurried past quickly to avoid the threats, raised fists and sabres that were brandished at them. Some members of the crowd were lucky enough to have a ticket for the *Manège* public gallery, where places had been reserved in the first row for certain high-class prostitutes who had clients among the deputies. There were also places kept for Philippe-Egalité's mistresses, who arrived in carriages in *rue de la Convention*, decked out with tricolour ribbons and feathers, eager to see the rebel duke vote for his cousin's death. Once the deputies were all installed and the trial under way, a calm fell among those waiting outside for news. Every so often a snippet of information would filter through. They heard how Danton had voted, then Marat, Desmoulins, Philippe-Egalité, each time followed by a murmur of speculation about the final outcome. Then the word they had been waiting for was heard up and down the entire length of the street. '*Death*'. It was over. The tyrant-king would pay for his crimes on the scaffold. The crowd straight away expressed their approval, but as they made their way home that day along rue Saint-Honoré, there was a strange and surreal silence in the air, and an unexplainable sadness in many hearts.

➥Continue along rue Saint-Honoré to number 209, which dates from the 17th century, and is where Doctor Guillotin had his surgery after the Revolution was over. Having narrowly escaped being decapitated himself during the Terror, Guillotin lived in this house until 1814, when he died at the age of 76 from anthrax of the shoulder, possibly contracted through his work in the field of vaccination. The house has an interesting and rather lovely sign, decorated with painted circles and bearing the name *E. Millien* in gold and black letters.

Over the road at number 320 was the home of Bertrand Barère de Vieuzac, notorious member of the Constituent Assembly and described by the historian Michelet as *'the licenced liar of the Committee of Public Safety.'* You will meet up with him again further down the road at number 350, where he lived in someone else's house for much of the revolutionary period.

At number 211 you find what is left of the *Hôtel de Noailles*, once one of the great noble residences of Paris, and from 1711 the home of the family of Marie-Adrienne-Françoise de Noailles, better known as Madame Lafayette. The original façade on rue Saint-Honoré has been replaced, but the interior façade is still visible. You will be seeing this in a little while, but first ➡you're going to visit the site of one of the most famous of the revolutionary political clubs. Walk a little bit further along from the *Hôtel de Noailles*, cross the the road and turn right on rue Marché Saint-Honoré, opened in 1807 on the site of the *Couvent des Jacobins*. It was in 1218 that the Dominicans first established their order in Paris, in a hospice on rue Saint-Jacques (in Latin, *Sanctus Jacobus*, from which they took the name Jacobin). Four centuries later when the order was reformed, they bought 10 acres of land along rue Saint-Honoré and built a chapel surrounded by a vast complex of convent buildings. The main entrance, which was situated approximately where rue Marché Saint-Honoré meets rue Saint-Honoré, had a central arch for carriages and a smaller one on each side for pedestrians. As you turn into rue Marché Saint-Honoré you will be walking through that entrance, accompanied no doubt by many famous ghosts, for this was where Robespierre and his fellow Jacobins walked every time they went into their famous club. Directly in front of you as you entered the large interior courtyard was the chapel, a simple building with a spacious attic lit by a row of dormer windows. The attic housed the convent's impressive library, which by the time of the Revolution contained over 20,000 volumes, many of them precious rarities. Behind the church were the convent buildings, and behind these an enormous garden extended all the way to rue Gomboust, where there was another smaller entrance.

After 175 years of peaceful existence, the Jacobin Convent was destined to become one of the major focal points of revolutionary turbulence. When the Assembly moved from Versailles to Paris in autumn 1789, the *Club Breton* came with them and rented the convent refectory for 200 *francs* a year. The following year they moved into the library above the church, where the annual rent was 400 *francs* but gave much more space to the rapidly growing club. The convent was suppressed very early in the Revolution, however, and its 80 Jacobin friars soon found themselves expelled and their premises firmly taken over by the Breton Club, which was re-named *Société des Amis de la Constitution*. In March 1790 Maximilien Robespierre became its President, and a set of rules was formulated excluding passive citizens and women from membership. On April 1st 1791 the club moved down into the church itself, changing its name to the Jacobin Club, and in the course of that year began to exercise more and more influence on political events.

By the end of the year Robespierre's dominance was beginning to be apparent. On December 16th 1791, when Brissot tried to justify the war to his fellow members, he got little sympathy from the Incorruptible, who two days later replied with a powerful speech against the war. Evoking all the horrors of military conflict, he decried the idea of political 'missionaries' intent on spreading the Revolution abroad. '*War makes the bed of despotism*' he shouted, then declared with chilling foresight that the French might end up with a Caesar, or a Cromwell. But in saying this Robespierre was not thinking of his own future reign as a revolutionary despot, but was actually alluding to Lafayette, whom he viewed as a potential military dictator - not realizing of course that a certain Bonaparte was waiting in the wings for his moment to come. The reference to Cromwell must have been duly noted by the English deputation visiting the Jacobin Club that day - who were probably much more frightened of Robespierre than of Lafayette.

December 18th 1791 was a turbulent session at the Jacobin Club, and very daunting for the visiting English deputation seen here. Club members advocated deposing the king, and Robespierre railed against supporters of the war, warning that they risked ending up with a ruler like Cromwell. (Author's private collection)

They might well have heard a lot of anti-monarchist rhetoric that day - enough to make an 18th-century Englishman tremble - for the Jacobin Club was now beginning to advocate the overthrow of the king. This eventually led to a split in its members, many of whom, including Lafayette, left to form the Feuillant Club on the other side of the road. This left the way clear for Robespierre to take precedence in the Jacobin club, which became all powerful after the fall of the monarchy, dominating both the Commune and the Convention.

The Jacobin Club was like a magnet in rue Saint-Honoré, drawing an assortment of converted nobles and monks, deputies and journalists, to its great arched doorway where the tricolour standard was proudly crowned with a red revolutionary bonnet. Smaller clubs occasionally sprang up on the same premises, like the *Fraternal Society of the Two Sexes*, whose membership increased considerably in 1790 when it grafted itself on to the Jacobin Club. It was at the Fraternal Society that journalist Jacques-René Hébert, founder of the newspaper *Le Père Duchesne*, met Marie-Françoise Goupil, a former nun - a fateful meeting for Françoise, for her subsequent marriage to Hébert led her to the scaffold. After the death of Robespierre the Jacobin Club lost most of its members, who feared the consequences of any continued association with the former idol now dubbed a treacherous dictator.

There were some, however, who surely must be admired for their courage if not for their ideas, who stayed on and persisted in demanding a return to the Terror. But they did not stay long. On the night of November 11th 1794, while these intrepid Jacobins, some still sporting red bonnets, were busy declaiming one of their incendiary motions against the National Convention, a long column of eccentrically dressed, monocled young men was making its way down rue Saint-Honoré. They were known as *Muscadins*, the new 'gilded youth' who were openly nostalgic for the monarchy and roamed around Paris in gangs provoking fights with anyone who showed sympathy for the Revolution. They wore wigs and musk perfume, hence their name, and affected a disdainful manner of speaking without pronouncing the 'r.' They were often to be seen with their female counterparts who were even more noticeable in very tight-fitting dresses made out of transparent gauze. The *Muscadins* were 'fops' in every respect, except that they carried lead bludgeons, and that night they were going to finish off the Jacobins. The club was soon under siege, and the *Muscadins* went to work with their weapons on the terrified members, who scattered in every direction trying to save themselves. Stones were thrown, women were whipped, some raped, and the interior of the church was vandalised, while hundreds of people crowded outside on the street hurling abuse at the escaping club members. The fighting spread across rue Saint-Honoré all the way down to the Tuileries Gardens, where the fugitive Jacobins continued to be assailed by their *muscadin* opponents. There were rumours that the attack had been organized by the Committee of General Security, who certainly did nothing to stop it, and the next day the Jacobin Club was closed and its entrance sealed.

Jacobins and Muscadins fight it out in the Tuileries Gardens. After the death of Robespierre a few stalwart Jacobins tried to keep the Jacobin Club going, but attacks by these gangs of monarchist fops eventually put an end to their efforts, and the club was closed. (Author's private collection)

The following year the entire convent was demolished, but not before a final rather bizarre ceremony on January 21st 1795 that truly put an end to the Jacobin Club. An evening paper called 'The Messenger' reported that 3,000 citizens marched from the Palais-Royal to the main courtyard of the former club carrying a dummy representing a Jacobin. This grotesque figure, draped in a long red cloak and wearing a black wig and a crown, held a dagger in one hand and in the other a wallet and a goblet of blood. By flickering torchlight the crowd stood in silence while a young citizen solemnly condemned the symbolic Jacobin to be burned and its ashes thrown into the sewers. The sentence was carried out immediately to cries of '*Vive la Justice!*' and the ashes were then transported in a chamber pot to the sewers of Montmartre.

➡ On your way up rue du Marché-Saint-Honoré you will see a street to your right called rue Saint-Hyacinthe, used by the Jacobins to gain access to their club. This road was originally a *cul-de-sac*, ending at number 8 with the boundary wall of the convent, and at number 8*bis* you can see the club's secondary entrance, which is now all that remains of the original Jacobin Convent. The redoubtable figure of Robespierre, in his powdered wig and favourite cornflower-blue frock-coat, passed many times through this huge arched doorway, as did the inscrutable Saint-Just, and Georges Couthon in his wheelchair. Earlier on in the Revolution, before they formed their own club, you would have also seen the provocatively dishevelled Danton and his petulant companion, Desmoulins, who both must have revelled in the attention they got from the regular gathering of curious onlookers. After the Massacre on the Champ-de-Mars the club was attacked by a band of soldiers who held the Jacobins responsible for the killings, and it was into this little street that the terrified club members ran in a desperate attempt to save themselves. No-one was killed in fact, and those brave enough to leave by the main entrance suffered nothing more than the boos of the crowd who were waiting in rue Saint-Honoré.

➡ Now go back to rue du Marché-Saint-Honoré, turn right and continue towards the market. The houses to your left stand on the site of the church where the Jacobin Club met, and the main entrance was directly opposite rue Saint-Hyacinthe. ➡ If you would like to eat dinner with the ghosts of Robespierre and his fellow Jacobins, there is a restaurant at number 15 Place du Marché-Saint-Honoré called Brasserie Saint-Honoré, situated where the end of the church would have been. You'll find a plaque on the wall there, and the owners of the restaurant have also put up an old street map showing the Jacobin Convent during the 17th century. On May 17th 1795 the National Convention ordered the entire convent to be demolished and replaced by a public market called *Marché du 9 Thermidor*. In the official proposal the Jacobin monks were described as *'monsters whose name recalls the disastrous Inquisition they established,'* and the Jacobin Club as an *'infernal abyss which vomited like a devouring lava all the scourges that have afflicted France.'* Official memories seem to be short, however, for when the market was opened in 1810 it was under the name *Marché des Jacobins*. It got its present name sixteen years later.

When you have finished looking round the market, ➥go back to rue Saint-Honoré. As you emerge from rue du Marché Saint-Honoré back into rue Saint-Honoré you are walking through the original entrance of the Jacobin Club, and if you had been coming out of the club on March 14th 1794 you would have seen a procession of tumbrils carrying the Hébertists

The Hébertists pass by the entrance of the Jacobin Club on their way to the guillotine on March 14th 1794. This print gives a good impression of what the rue Saint-Honoré looked like during the Revolution. (Courtesy of Musée Carnavalet, Cabinet des Arts Graphiques, Paris)

towards the scaffold. It was a sobering sight, for Hébert himself, the legendary *Père Duchesne* and leader of this faction, who had made so many people tremble with fear by his bloodthirsty rhetoric, was now trembling with fear himself. Hébert, who sobbed in terror all the way to the guillotine, was one of the few victims of the Revolution to show such fear when faced with execution.

You are now going to have a look at what remains of the lovely *Hôtel de Noailles*, childhood home of Madame Lafayette. ➡The best way to do this is to go into the St. James and Albany Hotel, which has been built around it - its main entrance is on rue de Rivoli, but you should go in via the Bar Saint James at number 6 rue du 29 Juillet. This street is almost directly opposite, on the other side of rue Saint-Honoré, as you come back out of rue du Marché Saint-Honoré. Go into the bar and walk through the arcades that link the hotel's two entrances, and you will see on the left the courtyard and façade of the only building remaining from the original *Hôtel de Noailles*. You could also take the opportunity to sit down for a while and have a drink in the bar while reading about this historic residence - and don't forget to visit the toilets so you can see the lovely vaulted stone walls of the basement. The de Noailles family must have had a wonderful wine cellar there. If the weather is good, you can sit out in the courtyard itself, and get an even better view of this truly beautiful house, which was built in 1687 and at the time covered a huge area stretching right down to the Tuileries gardens. It consisted of several buildings and gardens, and it was from one of these gardens (perhaps the one you're in now) that a horrified 9-year-old Adrienne de Noailles saw through a bedroom window the disfigured face of her mother, the Duchesse d'Ayen, who was recovering from smallpox. The duchess survived her illness, only to suffer a much worse fate later on.

After acquiring the house in 1711, Adrien-Maurice de

Noailles, comte et duc d'Ayen, and later the second Maréchal de France, installed his ever-growing family here. By filling his new home with fine furniture, oriental vases, Renaissance paintings and the best art treasures of the time, he turned it into a veritable museum that was soon worth a fortune. The Maréchal was an intelligent and highly respected man, whose ardour would later be seen in his great-granddaughter, Adrienne, future wife of General Lafayette. She kept many fond memories of her childhood in this house, where she and her sisters were cared for by a governess who, instead of reading them fairy tales, preferred to tell them stories from the Old Testament. This was heaven for Adrienne, who thought fairy tales were absurd, and carried piousness to such a degree that she has been rather unjustly described in retrospect as frigid.

Perhaps piety was the only refuge for this intense and anxious adolescent, for at 14 she was led into a marriage that had been arranged by her parents when she was just 12 years old. Marie Paul Yves Roch Gilbert du Mottier, marquis de Lafayette was only two years older than Adrienne, and at first the match was opposed by his future mother-in-law partly on account of his extreme youth. He was also an orphan - his father died two months before his birth and his mother when he was 12 - and what's more he was an orphan with an immense, ready-made fortune, all of which spelled moral danger to the very correct duchess. Adrienne later recalled the terrible and lengthy dispute that resulted between her parents, who fumed at each other for days before a glorious reconciliation on September 21st 1772. Adrienne was so relieved that she noted the date, which *'will never fade from my memory or from my heart!'* The wedding, one of the most celebrated aristocratic marriages of the century, took place on April 11th 1774 in the private chapel of the *Hôtel de Noailles*, where many of the guests who attended the reception must have marvelled at the splendour of the magnificent residence.

Adrienne had an older sister, whose name, Anne Jeanne Baptiste Pauline Adrienne Louise Cathérine Dominique de Noailles, is surely one of the longest in French history. It sometimes led to confusion, and when tragedy struck later and the executioner Sanson had to put her on his list of victims, he wrote her name as Angélique Jeanne Louise Delphine, while on another list of victims of the Terror she appears as Noailles, A. J. B. A. P. L. C. D. In accounts of her life she is sometimes referred to as Anne-Dominique, and sometimes as Louise, which to simplify things is what I will call her. A short time before her sister Adrienne's wedding, Louise had married her cousin, Louis-Marie, vicomte de Noailles, who would later be one of the first nobles to renounce his privileges at the start of the Revolution. Louise went with her husband to live in Versailles, but Adrienne remained at the *Hôtel de Noailles* after her marriage while Lafayette left to serve with his regiment. During the winter of 1774 the Duchesse d'Ayen decided to hold a series of intimate dinners here for the friends of her two new sons-in-law, a decision that according to her daughter was taken solely to avoid *'mortally displeasing'* her husband. But the evenings proved to be so successful that the duchess had a delighted stream of noble teenagers at her door, coming back for more.

The *Hôtel de Noailles* was the Lafayettes' home for the first ten years of their marriage, and Adrienne was living here when her husband went to to America to fight against the English. She was still only 17 and expecting her second child when he left in April 1777, and she wrote in her memoirs, *'I was pregnant, and I loved him dearly. My father and the rest of the family were all in a violent rage against him.'* Their anger was soon forgotten, however, when he came back in February 1779, and three days later was honoured by a visit from Marie-Antoinette (see the plaque in the garden). After this Lafayette went once more to America, and returned to Paris after his final victory on January 21st 1782. He hurried immediately to the *Hôtel de*

Noailles, where to his surprise he found everyone out, for his return had coincided with the celebrations at the Hôtel-de-Ville for the birth of the dauphin. But this didn't prevent him from getting a hero's welcome, for as the news spread of his return, a huge crowd of admirers was soon milling around in the street outside the *Hôtel de Noailles*, waiting for a glimpse of the red-haired young hero. Then Marie-Antoinette's carriage arrived, followed by a small procession of other noble vehicles, one of which contained Adrienne Lafayette and several members of her family. Finally came the moment the spectators had been waiting for as Lafayette, resplendent in his American uniform, emerged from the house and proudly received the acknowledgement of his queen.

The Lafayettes left the *Hôtel de Noailles* in 1784 and moved to rue de Lille, leaving the Duchesse d'Ayen with her younger daughters. Lafayette's part in the Revolution was very closely linked with the fate of the royal family, and after the monarchy fell he surrendered to the Austrians and spent the rest of the Revolution in prison. Although Adrienne was later arrested, and also spent time in prison, she managed to survive the Terror, despite her aristocratic roots. This was a time of emigration, and many of Adrienne's family left France, notably her brother-in-law, the Vicomte de Noailles, who fled to England. But for those who remained, the situation got rapidly worse.

After Louis XVI was deposed in 1792, Adrienne's parents decided to leave the *Hôtel de Noailles* for a while, for they could no longer stand all the disturbances that continually took place around the neighbouring Tuileries Palace. A few days later they were both summoned to the Hôtel-de-Ville, questioned about their reasons for leaving their usual domicile, and ordered to return home. The following year the Duc d'Ayen began to have increasing problems with the authorities regarding residence certificates, and was obliged to flee to Switzerland, leaving the Duchesse d'Ayen in Paris with her eldest daughter Louise, who had decided not to join her husband in England, but to stay and take care of her mother – a decision that would cost her her life. They were joined at the *Hôtel de Noailles* in September by the duchess's mother-in-law, the Maréchale de Noailles, who had just become a widow, and just one month later all three women were put under house arrest. During this time a very courageous priest named Carrichon used to come to the house regularly to attend to their religious needs, a dangerous activity for all concerned at a time when every day the Terror escalated in the capital, when every day the three women learned of some new catastrophe, relatives and friends arrested, guillotined. They received visits from officials, who questioned them on their thoughts and actions, while an inventory was made of all their possessions, prompting the duchess to try and save her diamonds by selling them to a jeweller - who consequently perished on the scaffold a few days later.

Then, in May 1794, they were taken from the *Hôtel de Noailles* and put into the Luxembourg Prison. Two months later, five days before the fall of Robespierre, the Maréchale de Noailles, the Duchesse d'Ayen and her daughter Louise were taken to the *Place du Trône-Renversé* and guillotined along with 42 other victims. Louise's parents-in-law had also been executed shortly before this. This multiple tragedy is the reason why you find the tomb of Lafayette and his wife in the graveyard at Picpus, for this cemetery is reserved exclusively for the families and descendants of those victims of the Terror who were buried there in the communal graves, and it was Madame Lafayette who created this descendants' cemetery.

As for the *Hôtel de Noailles*, it was re-named *Maison de Noailles* and suffered the usual revolutionary transformations, first being occupied by several committees, then by a printer named Cussac, and later the *Commission of Seventeen*. This was a committee that had been created, in the inquisitorial spirit of the time, to examine the conduct of government employees during the period of the Convention. After 9 *Thermidor* the *Hôtel de Noailles* was occupied by the *Café de Vénus*, a working-class paradise where citizens could dance under a trellis of vines by the smoky light of Chinese lanterns. Its owner, an entrepreneur called Vénua, had emptied the *hôtel* of all its art treasures, put up modern wallpaper and gingham curtains, and sat his customers at rough wooden tables where they ate ice-cream with pewter spoons. Later on, deciding to go a bit more upmarket, Vénua changed the name of his establishment to *l'Odéon de l'Hôtel de Noailles*, put up his prices, and soon replaced his working-class clientele with Parisian high society.

At the turn of the 19th century the *Hôtel de Noailles* became the residence of the Consul, before being given back to the de Noailles family when the monarchy was restored. But perhaps the house had too many unhappy memories, for the new duke sold it soon afterwards to an Englishman called Lord Henry Egerton, whose father had constructed the canal linking Manchester and Edinburgh. He remained there to the end of his life, restoring the house to much of its former glory with his collection of precious and rare objects and his magnificent library. But Sir Henry's eccentric behaviour made him the talk of the neighbourhood. On one occasion he caused great amusement by bringing a law suit against a stray pig that had eaten a baby (this did happen occasionally in the streets of 18th-century Paris). On another occasion the entire community was woken up in the middle of the night by a fanfare of trumpets and hunting horns coming from Egerton's garden, where the semi-paralysed lord, carried by costumed lackeys behind a pack of hounds, was honouring the feast of Saint Hubert by chasing an exhausted fox around his estate. His two favourite dogs, called *Bijou* and *Riche*, would often take their place amongst the invited guests at his lordship's famous and excellent table, where, with a serviette placed lovingly around their necks, they would be solemnly served each of the elegant dishes coming out of Lord Egerton's kitchen.

One day Egerton decided he was tired of his residence and resolved to leave. The whole household was thrown into six months of furious activity in preparation for the grand departure, and finally he was on his way. As his carriage moved away along rue Saint-Honoré, it was escorted by thirty members of his domestic staff and followed by fifteen carriages filled with luggage. But a few hours later astonished local residents saw the entire convoy returning to the *hôtel*, where Sir Henry explained that he had stopped in Saint-Germain to have dinner, a meal so revolting that it boded ill for the rest of the journey. So he came back to Paris, and never left again. In 1830 the major part of the *Hôtel de Noailles* disappeared with the opening of rue Algers and rue Mont-Thabor.

➡Leave the hotel by the Bar Saint James, turning right into rue du 29 Juillet, left on rue Saint-Honoré and continuing along to number 334. This lovely old house was built in 1660 and at the beginning of the 18th century it belonged to the extremely wealthy Adrien-Maurice de Noailles whom you already met back at the *Hôtel de Noailles*. His family had acquired number 334 as a dowry in 1671, but after he bought the much bigger *Hôtel de Noailles*, he rented out 334, which subsequently became known as the *Petit Hôtel de Noailles*. In the 1780s it was the residence of Louis-Marie-Athanase de Loménie, comte de Brienne, Minister of State for War, and one of the many nobles and financiers who just before the Revolution occupied most of the property between the Jacobin Convent and rue Royale. Louis-Marie-Athanase was the brother of the more well-known member of the Loménie family, the cardinal and statesman, Etienne-Charles de Loménie de Brienne, who in November 1793 ended up in prison after a life alternating between politics and religious office. As a wealthy, aristocratic, high-ranking cleric, to say nothing of his dissolute lifestyle, Cardinal Loménie was bound to end up in a revolutionary prison, but he was later sent back home and put under house arrest, where he died, some say by his own hand, but more probably from apoplexy. When Louis-Marie-Athanase heard his older brother was dying, he rushed to his deathbed, and was immediately arrested, along with his two sons Alexis-François aged 36, and Martial aged 30, a bishop who had renounced his beliefs. Imprisoned with them were Louis-Marie-Athanase's 29-year-old niece, Anne-Marie-Charlotte, the divorced wife of an emigrated count, and another relative called Charles de Loménie, who was 33 and a Knight of Saint-Louis and the Order of Cincinnatus. All five were guillotined on May 10th 1794, on the same day as Louis XVI's sister, Madame Elisabeth, who travelled in the same tumbril as Martial de Lomènie and his father, and whose prayers and exhortations during the fatal journey persuaded Martial to retract his religious renunciation and die repentant. The unfortunate Loménie family had been rounded up as 'co-conspirators' in the trial of Madame Elisabeth, and their former home is now occupied by a shop called B. Biberon et fils. If you want to take home a high-class handbag from Paris, this is the place to get it.

Number 219 directly opposite is also 17th-century. It was here that in 1793 the Farmer-General Jean-Baptiste de Boulogne set up his office to liquidate the French East India Company, a colonial trade monopoly whose unofficial objective was to attract money from unwary investors. The National Convention eventually decided to put an end to its fraudulent activities and appointed as liquidators the deputies Chabot and Basire, two residents of rue Saint-Honoré, who did not hesitate at this chance to profit from the situation. Another deputy, Joseph Delaunay, had already prepared the ground by launching a bitter attack on financial companies in general, and the East India Company in particular, thus provoking a panic that lowered the price of its stock. After buying up the devalued stock, they then proceeded to accord clemency to the company, which sent the price up again and enabled Chabot, Basire, Delauney and probably several other deputies to make a lot of money. Danton was more than likely implicated in this fraudulent affair which contributed to the condemnation of all those involved. De Boulogne was probably innocent in the East India swindle, but was nonetheless guilty of being a Farmer-General, and consequently guillotined in May 1794.

Number 350 rue Saint-Honoré is early 18th-century and used to be part of a much larger house whose former grandeur can be easily imagined from the beautiful ceiling and rich gold panelling that are visible, if the light is right, through the first floor windows. From 1774 it belonged to Charles-Pierre de Savalette de Langes, an extremely rich official at the Royal Treasury and holder of several important public offices. He was at the forefront of cultural life in the capital, and in 1791, when the revolutionary government launched an idealistic initiative to elevate the position of the arts, he lent them his house for a cultural brainstorming between representatives of the Assembly and a carefully chosen assortment of authors and composers. De Savalette also counted a good number of politicians among his circle of friends, one of whom was Bertrand Barère de Vieuzac, a brilliant lawyer from Tarbes near the Spanish border, who lived as a guest in de Savalette's house during most of the Revolution.

Barère's political career, beginning as a monarchist and then becoming a Robespierrist, is a remarkable study in survival. He began his legal studies at the age of 15, showing an extraordinary intelligence that throughout his life enabled him to adapt to all situations. When first elected as a deputy, he observed more than he spoke, and founded a newspaper called *Le Point du Jour*, in which he reported in detail the proceedings of the Assembly. Barère was described by his contemporaries as *'sweet, reserved and noble'*, and his charm, good looks and silken voice opened doors everywhere. When he later presided over the trial of Louis XVI, and still later sat on the Committee of Public Safety, his deceptively gentle manner and poetic rhetoric enabled him to administer pitilessly harsh judgments with personal impunity - and very flowery language, which earned him the nickname 'the Anacreon of the guillotine', after a poet in ancient Greece who wrote lyrically about love, lust and wine. Despite a promise made to his wife to always defend the king, Barère was equally merciless towards the fallen monarch, refusing an appeal to the people or any form of suspended sentence. However, he often used his persuasive talents to help his friends, sometimes even to save them from death, as in the case of his generous host, de Savalette, who was arrested in 1793 in this house. Barère describes the incident in his memoirs.

'One day, to my astonishment, I was woken up with a start by M. de Savalette, accompanied by guards and members of the Committee of the local section…it was 4 o'clock in the morning: "I am being arrested," he told me, "in accordance with a warrant issued by the committee of the local section."' Barère was given no reason for the arrest, and he warned the officers that he intended to take action that very morning. But he was worried. *'I could not get a wink of sleep for the rest of the night, after M. de Savalette left for prison. At 9 o'clock I ran to see Pache, the Mayor and leader of the Commune; I demanded the reasons for the arrest.'* Barère threatened to make a complaint to the Committee of Public Safety, which meant Robespierre, and extracted a promise from the mayor to free his friend that day, a promise that was honoured. Savalette returned home, relieved and thankful, at 2 o'clock that afternoon. The reason for his arrest was a loan of 7 million *livres*, made two years earlier to Louis XVI's brothers, the Comte d'Artois and the Comte de Provence, to enable them to emigrate. Under revolutionary law he was guilty of treason, and was therefore very fortunate to have the friendship of Barère.

Much less fortunate, however - and much less guilty - was the poet André Chénier, whose father came here on June 25th 1794 asking Barère for a reprieve for his condemned son. The old man wept despairingly, and implored Barère, who in the end could no longer stand his pathetic pleas and placated him with a most ambiguous reply. *'Don't worry, your son will come out in three days.'* Three days later André Chénier did indeed come out of prison, along with 44 other victims, all destined for the guillotine. It was Chénier who, ironically, was reputed to have translated at the age of 14 the poems of Anacreon, the Greek poet for whom Barère was nicknamed.

Because of his competence and *sang-froid* as an administrator, Barère always maintained the friendship of Robespierre, despite accusations of moderation, and he managed to choose just the right moment to switch his loyalties when Robespierre fell. But the Thermidoreans were not taken in, and would not forgive him for his lack of conviction. Barère was still living in this house, and describes himself what happened on March 2nd 1795. *'I was peacefully sitting in my bedroom...at 10 o'clock in the evening, three men, two of them armed, a justice of the peace and two national guards, burst in. The first of these henchmen informed me that he had come to put the seals on my papers and possessions, and that a decree from the Convention had condemned me to deportation to Cayenne. I passed the night in the calm of innocence. The next day, at 8 o'clock, several armed men were posted at the entrance to Savalette's house, on the main staircase, and right up to my bedroom door. M. de Savalette, who had learned that morning of my condemnation, came to embrace me and support me in my misfortune. Real friends such as this are rare in Paris.'* (Hénard, 1908-09)

A carriage arrived and took Barère away amidst an immense hue and cry along rue Saint-Honoré, where a large crowd of spectators, mostly women, had gathered to send off the disgraced revolutionary. Barère was a survivor, though, and while awaiting deportation in a prison in Saintes, he escaped, and lived in hiding until he could continue his political career under Napoléon. With the return of the monarchy, he was exiled as a regicide and went to Belgium, returning in 1830 to be elected deputy yet again in his home department. But when this election was declared void due to a legal flaw, Barère returned to his home town disappointed and sick, and died there in 1841 at the age of 86.

Before leaving number 350, have a look at the inner courtyard and the rather lovely 18th-century staircase to the left as you go in through the covered arch. There is a curious postscript to the story of de Savalette's house. At the restoration of the monarchy, a woman called Jenny Savalette de Langes came to Paris, claiming to be the illegitimate daughter of the former owner of number 350. She bitterly lamented her unfortunate family heritage, complaining that she was penniless because her father had neglected her, preferring to loan his fortune to the king's two brothers. Her plight evoked so much sympathy that she was awarded a lifetime pension by Louis XVIII, Charles X and Louis-Philippe, she was given a job managing the post-office at Villejuif, and an apartment at Versailles was also put at her disposition. Here she received an endless stream of highborn royalist visitors, who would spend hours listening to her stories of hardship and compensate her with gifts and offers of financial help, so that by the time she died in 1858 Mlle Savalette de Langes had accumulated a small fortune. But when the neighbours began to lay out her body in preparation for burial, they found to their astonishment that the charming *Mademoiselle* de Langes was in fact a *monsieur*! For all those years the high society of Paris had been handing over their fortunes to a very clever con-man, who had even persuaded one of his visitors to give him, among other treasures, a bed-cover of silken lace that had belonged to Louis XIV.

Opposite 250, numbers 229, 231, 233 and 235 were originally a single building belonging to the *Couvent des Feuillants* where Lafayette and other royalist moderates established their club in July 1791. These houses were not part of the actual convent, but were built with convent funds in 1782 and rented out by the monks to generate extra income. If you look at the entire group of buildings from the other side of the road, you will see more clearly the symmetry of the original construction and, on the roof of 231, a pretty baroque pediment with circular windows and a coat of arms surrounded by palms and laurel leaves. The main entrance to the convent was directly opposite Place Vendôme, where the south part of rue de Castiglione meets rue Saint-Honoré, and the church where the Feuillant Club met was situated directly behind numbers 229-235. In the interior courtyard of number 229 can be seen to the right the only part of the actual convent that still remains - an enormous round stone wall which was the chevet of the church - yet another of Paris's historical secrets that is now unfortunately hidden behind an entrance code. There should, nonetheless, be a plaque here to commemorate this historic political club.

The entire convent was closed in 1790 by the revolutionary government, who a few months later lent the church to the artist David so he could paint his famous 'Tennis Court Oath.' David was not able to create his masterpiece undisturbed, though, for it was also within the massive stone wall of this church that the members of the Feuillant Club held their meetings. But Dr. Guillotin, one of the instigators of the famous oath, came to David's rescue with a scheme to separate off the part of the church being used by the artist. So while David was immortalizing on canvas the Revolution's first defiant step towards the demise of King Louis, on the other side of a paper screen the members of the Feuillant Club were planning his comeback. The club was founded in May 1791 by the Marquis de Lafayette, under the name *Club de 89*, with the aim of establishing a more democratic form of monarchy. Most of its members also belonged to the Jacobin Club, but after the royal family's attempted escape, the question of the monarchy caused a division of opinion among the Jacobins. As a result the *Club de 89* faction defected, moved across the road to the Feuillant Convent and re-named itself the *Club des Feuillants*. They were joined by several Jacobins favouring a constitutional monarchy, including the 'triumvirate' of Pierre Barnave, Adrien Duport and Alexandre de Lameth.

Lafayette left no doubts about the aim of his club. Just days after its formation he gave orders to fire at the people on the Champ-de-Mars, people who had gathered to sign a Jacobin petition demanding the dethronement of Louis XVI. For just over a year the Feuillant Club remained in opposition to both the Cordeliers and Jacobin clubs, enjoying a small moment of glory in June 1792 when, after the fall of the Girondin government, all but two of the new ministers were Feuillants, and unknown ones to boot. But the cause they were championing was fast becoming a lost one. Barnarve's efforts to persuade Marie-Antoinette to act more favourably towards the Constitution all ended in failure, and on August 10th 1792 the Tuileries Palace was attacked and the royal family forced to take refuge in the *Manège* under the protection of the National Assembly. Louis and his family spent the next three nights in the Feuillant Club before being imprisoned in the Temple. Without its *raison d'être* the club rapidly went out of existence, and the church later became a cafeteria serving the *Manège*.

Before being demolished in 1804, the Feuillant Convent witnessed one of the many humiliations that marked the last weeks of Louis XVI's life, when on December 11th 1792 he appeared before the Convention to hear the long list of charges to be brought against him. Louis entered the *Manège* by way of the huge arched doorway of the Feuillant Convent, where a crowd of about a hundred local market workers had gathered, waiting for his arrival. Escorted by the mayor of Paris, the king emerged from his carriage dressed in a sombre brown outfit and protected from the cold by a light brown frock-coat. His face was pale and unshaven, and his formerly plump cheeks had become so thin that they almost hung on his collar, but despite his pitiful appearance, the onlookers were without mercy. As the king walked slowly through the convent entrance, they sang a loud chorus of the *Marseillaise*, purposely raising the volume on the words 'impure blood'. Louis didn't seem to register much reaction to this torment as he passed through the vaulted entrance into the inner courtyard, for he was besieged by painful memories. It was in this courtyard, which now forms the first few metres of rue de Castiglione, that he had furtively handed to his valet, Thierry de Ville d'Avray, the key to the famous *armoir de fer*, which had contained so much incriminating evidence against him. It was also from this same courtyard, on August 13th 1792, that he and his family had been ushered into carriages and taken away to their final captivity in the Temple prison.

The house at number 352, with its splendid doorway and balcony, dates from 1710. I was very sorry to see that the old semi-circular windows of the *entresol* have been replaced by modern shop windows, for behind them was the home, after the Terror, of the widow of the Marquis de Condorcet, one of the most refined and humane of the revolutionaries and described by Michelet as *'the last of the philosophers'*. In 1786 he married Sophie de Grouchy, who was twenty years younger than him and whom he loved passionately. She was intelligent and very pretty, and during the early years of their marriage her *salon* was one of the most brilliant in Paris, attracting all the most prominent philosophers and scientists of the age. Sophie was a loyal wife, supporting Condorcet both politically and personally, and when he was denounced in 1793 and forced to go into hiding, she risked her own life every evening by making a clandestine visit to his hideout in rue Servandoni.

During this fraught period Madame Condorcet took refuge herself at her sister's home in Auteuil, but every morning she would set off for Paris by foot, and come here to number 352, where a friend of her husband's kept a lingerie shop. Here, in a small, badly-lit room with an oppressively low ceiling, she would spend the day drawing portraits. Portraiture had become a popular means of earning a living during the Terror, when the constant threat of death provoked many to rush to have a last souvenir made of a loved-one about to be denounced. By May 1794 Sophie believed her husband to be safely over the Swiss border, so she carried out a promise she had made to him, and obtained a divorce. This was to protect the inheritance of their daughter in the event of her husband's possessions being taken by the State, but Sophie did not realise that it was already too late, for Condorcet had committed suicide two months earlier in his prison cell. After the Revolution was over Madame Condorcet made this her residence, continued drawing portraits and miniatures and bought the lingerie boutique, turning it into a haberdashery shop that enabled her to supplement her meagre income. The shop is now a women's clothing store on one side and a luggage shop on the other.

PLACE VENDÔME.
➡ You are now going to cross over to the north side of rue de Castiglione and take a short detour to look at this elegant square begun at the instigation of Louis XIV in 1685 with the purchase of a large *hôtel* and lands belonging to Capuchin nuns. The entire convent, which stood on the site now occupied by numbers 360 to 364 rue Saint-Honoré, was immediately demolished to make way for the new square. On either side of rue de Castiglione leading to the Place Vendôme are two elegant *hôtels* of identical style, with balconies decorated with

gilded images of the Sun King. These were both built at the same time as the Place Vendôme, on the site of the original *Hôtel Vendôme* belonging to the convent. Number 2 Place Vendôme (and 356 rue Saint-Honoré) was built in 1707, and in 1788 was owned by a notary-public named Jean Raguideau de La Fosse, who in 1796 wrote the marriage contract between Joséphine and Napoléon.

You're now going to take a brief walk around Place Vendôme, which, with its arcades and columns and wonderful mansard roofs, must be one of the most splendid examples of 18th-century French architecture. Construction of these beautiful houses was begun in 1702, and still not finished when the square was inaugurated in 1715 as a homage to Louis XIV. By 1720 the work was completed, achieving admirably its objective of enhancing the beauty of the city and facilitating traffic in the streets adjoining rue Saint-Honoré. It was called *Place Louis-le-Grand* until 1792, when its name was changed to *Place des Piques*, presumably on account of the decapitated heads that were displayed there on pikes. During the Revolution the square was a constant scene of popular demonstrations that continued even up to 1796 when the plates that had been used to print the infamous *assignats* were ceremoniously burned here.

The centrepiece of the square during the 18th century was an equestrian statue of Louis XIV, splendidly be-wigged and decked out in Roman robes. On the evening of August 13th 1792, when the newly de-throned Louis XVI left the Feuillant Club with his family on his way to the Temple prison, the first sight that met his eyes as he crossed the square was the desecrated statue of his glorious ancestor. It had been torn down the previous day by an angry crowd, causing the accidental death of a luckless woman called Rose Violet, who was selling copies of Marat's newspaper, *L'Ami du Peuple*, in the centre of the square. The base of the statue remained in place but empty until

1810, when Napoléon added a bronze column, at the very top of which stood a triumphant statue of the conqueror, also wearing Roman apparel and a laurel crown. The column survived numerous changes, but after being in the centre of *communard* gunfire in 1871, the column and statue were both taken down and re-built.

Soon after its inauguration the Place Vendôme became a favourite residence for the rich, who built a succession of illustrious *hôtels* that you can still see today. Most of these houses were owned by financiers and Farmers-General, as well as bankers, treasury officials and entrepreneurial nobles, making of the area a sort of residential stock exchange. The Place Vendôme was, in a way, a microcosm of the epoch, for the experience of many of its residents ran the entire gamut of trends and events that characterized the progress of the Revolution - nobility, wealth, financial speculation and the good life, harshly transformed by the enlightened ideas of their own era into enforced social change, disgrace, denunciation and death. Their homes became government offices, revolutionary ministers sat in their living rooms, and many who had previously held court here ended up on the scaffold. Some, such as the writer Brillat-Savarin, who lived at number 4 and was a deputy in the Constituent Assembly, decided to emigrate, sensing the danger he was putting himself in by opposing the Terror.

Others were less fortunate, like Jacques Paulze at number 6, a Farmer-General who in 1771 married his 13-year-old daughter, Marie-Anne-Pierrette, to the young chemist, Antoine Lavoisier. Paulze was a successful financier, a director of the East India Company, and his daughter's marriage added the world of science and letters to his already impressive social circle. His considerable influence opened many doors for the aspiring young Lavoisier, but in 1794 they both found themselves behind one door he could not open - that of the Conciergerie.

When they came through it on May 8th of that year, it was on their way to the guillotine, along with 26 other Farmers-General.

The night of January 20th 1793 saw high drama in the Place Vendôme, when Louis-Michel Lepeletier de Saint-Fargeau was brought back, blood-stained and mutilated, to his parents' house at number 8. Lepeletier, a deputy from the nobility, had been stabbed that evening by a royalist in a café at the Palais-Royal, following his vote for the death penalty at Louis XVI's trial. Lepeletier's subsequent death at about 1 o'clock in the morning here on the first floor of his family home, was turned into a veritable cult by his fellow patriots, who decided to display his body in the middle of the Place Vendôme. They lifted on to the pedestal, which had previously served as a base for the statue of Louis XIV, the bed where the martyr had taken his last breath, and where he now lay, naked to the waist, exposing to all who passed the terrible gaping wound which had killed him. The murderer's sabre lay on the bloody sheets beside him, a wreath of flowers and oak leaves crowned his ashen face, and his blood-soaked clothes were attached to the end of a pike and decorated with cypress leaves. The pedestal, draped in white, was similarly adorned with oak and cypress, and the long stream of mourners went in single file up two stairways lit by torches and candles. The *coup de grace* of this macabre spectacle was the ceremonial placing, at the foot of the bed, of a large stone from the Bastille, on which was engraved the letter of condolence that the Assembly had written to Lepeletier's mother. This rather exaggerated funereal pomp, conceived for the most part by the artist, David, continued with a procession through the streets of Paris, led by soldiers carrying naked sabres. Then came deputies and friends, followed by groups of mothers leading their children and holding in their reverent hands copies of Lepeletier's 'Plan for Public Education.' It ended with the burial of the martyred deputy in the Panthéon, the highest honour that could be afforded any patriot, and as the convoy set off from the Place Vendôme, one small, sad figure, covered with black veils, walked alone behind the corpse. It was Lepeletier's daughter, an orphan at 11 years old, who would be adopted by the French nation and declared a 'daughter of the Republic.'

Some of the square's residents were more astute than others, not only surviving, but actively profiting from the new regime. Number 10 was owned by a marquis named de Malateste who in addition to escaping the guillotine, also had the audacity to rent his house to the office of the revolutionary Finance Committee. Two years later in 1792 he had tenants from the office of departmental administration, who stayed there until 1799, and by the time Napoléon became emperor, the marquis was still living happily in his house, which stayed in the family until his son finally sold it in 1842. Number 12 was originally the home of a prince, but by 1777 it was occupied by a mere baron, Baudard de Saint-James, royal treasurer and financier. He accumulated a small fortune, part of which he lent to the jewellers Boehmer and Bassanges to enable them to make the famous diamond necklace that brought scandal to the court of Marie-Antoinette. He clearly had bad judgement in his choice of business ventures, leading to bankruptcy in 1787, when his house was bought by another financier, Claude Denis Dodun, an administrator in the East India Company. In 1792 Madame Dodun offered the hospitality of their home to the Girondin deputy and orator, Pierre Victurnien Vergniaud, who was likened to Danton for his belief in the inviolability of political leaders and his contempt for his enemies. Madame Roland, who was well acquainted with most of the Girondin deputies, considered Vergniaud the most eloquent orator of the Assembly, whose speeches were *'strong in logic, burning with ardour and sparkling with beauty. However,'* she added, *'I don't like him one bit.'* She found him egocentric, disdainful and lazy, as did many people, but his talent for speaking was undeniable, and the political dinners that he held here at number 12 were legendary for their brilliance and importance. It was at one of them that the decision was taken to offer the Ministry of Justice to Danton following the overthrow of the monarchy. Vergniaud was later guillotined with his fellow Girondins, and Claude Denis Dodun suffered the same fate for his involvement in the East India Company.

After the Revolution, number 12 was home to Marie-Joseph Chénier, the younger brother of the guillotined poet André Chénier. Marie-Joseph was also a writer, but more political than his brother, becoming a deputy in the Convention in 1792 and voting for the king's death. But with the imprisonment and execution of his brother, the Revolution became a nightmare for Marie-Joseph, and he welcomed the fall of Robespierre with great enthusiasm. He was a very active Thermidorean, and at the time he lived in this house, he was Inspector-General for public instruction, a post that he lost in 1806 for making references to tyrants when writing about the Napoleonic regime. His works continued to displease the emperor, to the point of being banned from all the theatres in France, so Marie-Joseph was forced to earn his living teaching literature in a boarding school. He died in Paris, poor and bedridden, at the age of 49.

There were some strange goings-on at number 16 for a number of years, starting in 1778, when the house was taken over by a mysterious German doctor named Franz Anton Mesmer, who claimed that he had discovered 'animal magnetism', a celestial fluid that exerted a direct influence on our bodies. He also claimed that he was able to control this magnetic fluid, presenting his new phenomenon as a means of curing nervous illnesses, and after a few initial successes, people began to flock to 16 Place Vendôme in large numbers. His 'cures' became so popular that he would seat groups of twelve to fifteen patients at a time around his famous tub containing water, iron filings and ground glass. This magical solution was covered by a huge lid pierced with holes containing iron rods protruding on each side. One end of the rods plunged into the water and the other was held by the patient, who applied it to the afflicted part of their body, while a long cord linking all the patients ensured that the precious fluid was not lost. Mesmer would then stroll around the circle behind the patients, laying on his hands, whispering therapeutic phrases and being generally mystical, as a result of which hundreds of happy Parisians were cured of their neuroses.

Dr Franz Anton Mesmer made hundreds of ailing Parisians happy with his magical tub of iron filings, water and ground glass. His mesmerising career was eventually halted by a sceptical committee of Enlightenment figures like Benjamin Franklin, who decided it was all in the mind of the patient. (Author's private collection)

Mesmer's success was so great that he decided to install different types of tubs, some for the rich, on whom he took care to lay his own hands, and others for the poor, who had to content themselves with the less expensive hands of his assistant. Throughout the entire procedure could be heard the sound of a glass armonica being played in a corner of the room, no doubt further mesmerizing the already transfixed patients. The effects of all this were reported as ranging from none at all, through a spectrum of reactions including laughter, yawning, trembling, sweating, crying and convulsions. Faces became cadaverous, and when people appeared to be on the point of dying of suffocation, they would suddenly revive, laugh, throw themselves on the floor and leap up and down like a spring. Those patients who were in extreme distress would be escorted by Dr Mesmer to another room known as the Crisis Room, where under his expert care they gradually sank into a langorous reverie before joyously declaring themselves cured.

Dr. Mesmer's spectacular success enabled him to eventually leave this house for larger, more luxurious premises, and indeed he seemed to become mesmerized by his own popularity. On the corner of rue René-Boulanger he fashioned a tree into a communal tub, where thousands of people, many poor and homeless, would come and cling on to Mesmer's famous iron rods in the hope of a magic cure. When he demanded a *château* and a large tract of land from the government, a commission was appointed to investigate his work. Guillotin, Bailly and Franklin were all part of this group, which came to the conclusion that Mesmer's success was due to the imagination of his patients. In 1784 the discredited but rather wealthy doctor left for England, where he died in obscurity in 1815, although he has left us the word, 'mesmerize', to remember him by.

The house at number 20 follows a pattern typical of the era. After decades of being inhabited by the noble and wealthy, it was occupied at the outbreak of the Revolution by a family of bankers called Pache, and the following year by several committees of the Constituent Assembly. In 1791 it was the headquarters of the East India Company before being bought the year after by Madame Aubeterre, a lady from the *bourgeoisie*. In 1815 the house returned to its aristocratic tradition when it became the home of the Duc de Lévis and his family. Tragedy struck at number 22, acquired in 1780 by a wealthy but ill-fated financier, Magon de La Balue, who was decapitated in 1794 at the age of 81. Guillotined along with him were his brother, aged 80, his daughter, his son-in-law, his grandson, his nephew, and his tenant, the Marquis de Saint-Pern. In 1795, one year after this multiple tragedy, the house was returned to Magon's rightful heirs.

➡Cross over rue de la Paix to the other side of Place Vendôme, where number 21 was also owned by a Farmer-General called Darnay, who seemed to have escaped the guillotine, for his name does not figure on the list of his fellow Farmers-General executed on 19 *Floréal*. Darnay sold this house in 1789 to Lheritier de Brutelle, a botanist and former royal advisor, who just before the Revolution created the *Société Linnéenne de Paris*, based on the Linnean Society in London. Lheritier embraced the Revolution to the point of leading a National Guard battalion and being a judge on the Tribunal, but probably because of his earlier Court connections, he was kept under house arrest here during the Terror. In a rare gesture of regard for the activities of their prisoners, however, the revolutionary authorities permitted him to continue his study of the grasses growing in the square, provided he was always accompanied by two guards. The results of his work were to be put into a book called 'The Flora of the Place Vendôme', which he was still working on in 1800 when he was found with his throat cut in front of his country house. There was no known reason for Lheritier's assassination, which remains to this day an unsolved mystery.

In 1707 number 19 witnessed the wedding of one of the youngest brides in Paris, when 12-year-old Marie-Anne Crozat was married to the Comte d'Evreux. Her father, Antoine Crozat, had started out as a lowly cashier, but through clever speculation and commerce became the richest financier in France. Much later, in 1787, the *hôtel* was bought by a banker by the name of Louis Pourrat, whose financial speculations were rewarded less agreeably in 1794 by the guillotine. Antoine

Crozat had also previously owned number 17, which in 1787 was occupied by the 59-year-old Italian composer Niccolo Piccinni. Piccinni's famous rivalry with Gluck had reached civil war proportions in the earlier part of the decade, when Parisians seemed to no longer care about the philosophical leanings of their contemporaries. 'Piccinnist or Gluckist?' was the all-important question, and each new work presented by either one provided the field for a new battle. Piccinni got involved in this situation unwillingly, for he was of a modest nature and hated fighting of any kind, and although the war was ultimately won by Gluck, the two composers were not unfriendly, and always maintained a high professional regard for each other. When the Revolution broke out, Piccinni was obliged to leave France, but he returned in 1798 to become an inspector at the Conservatoire. Piccinni did not own number 17, and while he was living there his landlady, the Marquise de Béthune, sold it to Nicolas Deville, another of the ill-fated Farmers-General to be guillotined in 1794.

The Hôtel de la Grande-Chancellerie at number 13 is the Ministry of Justice, where on August 11th 1792 Georges-Jacques Danton took up residence as Minister of Justice following the overthrow of the monarchy. Camille Desmoulins was appointed Secretary of Seals, so Lucile Desmoulins and Gabrielle Danton moved with their husbands to the ministerial apartments here, where Lucile says *'we passed three fairly merry months.'* They were also joined by Pierre and Louise Robert, and Fabre d'Eglantine, who was Secretary-General. Danton was thrilled with his new power, which rather went to his head, and he immediately began to dominate the others, permitting Fabre to lodge at the Ministry, but flatly refusing to let him bring his actress girlfriend, Caroline Rémy. The victorious little group could hardly believe that they were to eat off the same tables, work at the same desks and sleep in the same beds as the former Chancellors of France. Gabrielle in particular, the modest daughter of a café owner, was particularly overwhelmed. For a brief period they all lived in unprecedented luxury in the enormous rooms of this beautiful *hôtel*, where they delighted in the panelled walls, the ceilings decorated exotically with sensual gods and celestial angels, and the exquisite Gobelins tapestries that hung everywhere. In the ministerial offices Danton and his friends gaily ordered entire meals to be brought to them from the best restaurants in rue Saint-Honoré, to sustain themselves as they worked through the day's business. But their moment was short-lived. On November 9th Danton was replaced by Dominique Joseph Garat, who as Minister of Justice would have the unenviable task of telling Louis XVI that he had been sentenced to death. Meanwhile Danton and his friends had to leave their temporary paradise and go back to the relative modesty of their own homes - and we will return to the relative modesty of the houses of rue Saint-Honoré, where you are now very near the home of the street's most famous resident, Maximilien Robespierre.

Before leaving this lovely square take a look at number 1, which was once the emblem of another little revolution, another republic fighting for its freedom. In 1842 this house was occupied by the Embassy of the Republic of Texas, whose independent status was acknowledged and supported by France until it became an American state three years later. You can see an inscription on the building, telling how *'by the Franco-Texan Treaty of 29 September 1839 France was the first nation to recognize the Republic of Texas, independent state between 1836 and 1845.'*

➡Turn right back on to rue Saint-Honoré and continue along to number 368, built in 1705 and the home of Louis-Adrien Prévost d'Arlincourt, another Farmer-General executed during the Terror. Louis-Adrien had a son called Charles-Victor, who was only 5 when his father was guillotined, but grew up to be a successful novelist. At the height of his popularity he was dubbed 'The Prince of the Romantics' and considered a serious rival to Victor Hugo. A little way along at number 263 on the other side of the road there used to be an Augustinian convent called *The Daughters of the Assumption*, which before the Revolution was a retreat for widows, deserted wives and ladies wishing to do penance. The convent was closed in 1793, and transformed first into barracks, then a warehouse, before being demolished in 1898, leaving only the chapel, which still stands here and since 1850 has been the Polish Church of Paris.

On the night of May 10th 1796 a disturbance broke out here on the street outside the convent when the police came to arrest François-Nöel Babeuf. More generally known by his Roman name of Gracchus, Babeuf was the leader of a group of former *Montagnards* intent on reviving Robespierrism, and was accused of plotting against the Directory. Having already escaped once from the police that day, Babeuf now found himself surrounded, and he hid behind some large carts full of grain that were being deposited in the warehouse. He owed his escape that night to the help of local residents, first taking refuge until nightfall with the wife of a cart-owner living in one of the former convent houses, and then being spirited to safety by a local locksmith called Didiée. But his luck didn't last, and he was arrested a few days later with 36 others in what was known as the 'Conspiracy of Equals', a plot to overthrow the Directory government and establish a pure democracy based on egalitarian communism. The word 'communism' didn't exist then, of course, but it has often been used to describe Babeuf's ideas, which centred around the need for armed proletarian revolt against a bourgeois Directory government. After a very long trial that acquitted most of those accused, Babeuf and his principle accomplice, Augustin Darthé, were condemned to death. On hearing the sentence, Babeuf's son handed a dagger to his father, who stabbed himself, but not fatally, and he was still wavering between life and death as he was lifted on to the guillotine.

➥Across the road at number 2 rue Duphot is a tiny and very pretty 18th-century house, built at an angle to the street, with a lovely old clock and scrolled emblem over the door. Rue Duphot was opened on the site of the former *Couvent des Filles de la Conception*, and if you had been walking in this part of rue Saint-Honoré at the beginning of the Revolution, you may have caught a glimpse of a young nun called Marie-Marguérite-Françoise Goupil going through the convent's huge entrance doorway that stood where you now find number 386 rue Saint-Honoré. Later in the walk you will meet up again with this young woman, who renounced her religious vows and became the wife of one of the Revolution's most colourful journalists.

Continue now on the same side of the street to 398 rue Saint-Honoré. On a hot July morning in 1791 an unknown carpenter named Maurice Duplay woke up in this house, not knowing that an action he would take that day would enter his name in the annals of revolutionary history. The temperature in Paris was soaring, and by afternoon the sun burned down relentlessly on the heads of a crowd of citizens who had gone to the Champ-de-Mars to sign a petition against the king. When this gathering turned into a massacre, the authors of the petition, notably absent from the bloody scene, took the prudent step of leaving the capital immediately, knowing they would be arrested if they went home. There was one exception to this unheroic behaviour, spotted amongst the terrified crowd fleeing from Lafayette's bullets. He walked slowly home, his green eyes meditating behind the thick glass of his spectacles, and as he passed along rue Saint-Honoré, a group of people, recognizing the familiar olive-green outfit, shouted *'Vive Robespierre!'* One man added, *'If we must have a king, why not him!'* Maximilien Robespierre found himself surrounded, and recognizing the danger of such an ovation, began struggling to get away.

As his eyes darted frantically from one house to another, searching in vain for the home of a friend where he could take refuge, the resident of a nearby house came to his rescue. It was Duplay, who approached the besieged deputy and offered him shelter in the house that he rented from the nuns of the neighbouring *Couvent des Filles de la Conception*. Robespierre accepted gratefully and never returned to his former lodgings in rue de Saintonge, remaining in the home of Maurice Duplay until the morning of 9 *Thermidor*, the day of his demise. I am sure Robespierre derived great satisfaction from living in an atmosphere of good honest work amongst Duplay's carpenters and woodworkers. Danton of course used to always contemptuously refer to the Duplay household as a *'temple of planers and prattlers'* where he considered his rival to be surrounded by fools and gossips. But it was an ideal situation for Robespierre, who seemed to re-discover there the security and comfort of the family life that he had lost at such an early age.

➡ Go through the covered alleyway leading into the inner courtyard of 398 - there is an entry code, but it's not on during the day. This was Maurice Duplay's timber yard, where you would have seen Robespierre's dog, Brount, running around amongst the planks of wood that were piled up everywhere. On the right of the courtyard there was a garden and a small shed, and on the left is the building where Robespierre lived, which at the time only had a ground and first floor, but has since had several more storeys built on to it. The French do not have the Anglo-American habit of turning the homes of their famous ancestors into mini-museums, so you can only content yourself with looking and leave the rest to your imagination, since the former apartment of the Incorruptible is now somebody's office. Look up to the left at Robespierre's lodgings, where on the first floor you will see four windows, and directly underneath them was a large shed, used by Duplay's workmen for cutting and storing the wood. The first window on the far right was an antechamber, serving as Robespierre's *cabinet de toilette*, and the second on the right was his bedroom, which also doubled as a study, and contained a wooden bed, a table and four cane chairs. The bed cover of blue and white floral damask was made by Madame Duplay out of one of her dresses, and on the pine shelves the very orderly deputy had arranged in neat piles all his speeches, reports and other writings, next to his precious volumes of philosophy. Racine and Rousseau, however, were never on the shelves, for they remained permanently open on the table where Robespierre sat each evening by the light of a single candle, forcing his exhausted eyes to read one more chapter or write yet another manuscript.

Robespierre at the window of his lodging in Maurice Duplay's house. On the desk is a piece of paper, a quill pen, and an open book propped up against the wall - perhaps his beloved Rousseau. Through the window the sky is visible, for the house only had two storeys then, and the wood used by Duplay's workmen is stacked up against the wall outside. Robespierre is wearing his favourite blue coat. (Courtesy of Société des Amis de Robespierre, Paris)

Robespierre was assisted in his work from time to time by Duplay's nephew, Simon Duplay, who occupied the room to the far left and was known as 'Peg-Leg Duplay' after losing his left leg at the battle of Valmy. The room between Simon's and Robespierre's was occupied by the Duplays' young son, whom Robespierre affectionately nick-named 'our little patriot.' At first Robespierre used the main staircase immediately to the left on entering the courtyard, but the more important and well-known he became, the more his host felt the need to protect him, so Duplay had the rather over-accessible main entrance closed off and at the far end of the building a door leading to another small staircase was installed leading directly to Robespierre's lodging. To get to it you first had to pass through either the dining room or the workers' shed, which further protected Robespierre from unwanted visitors. There is still a very old wooden staircase behind this door, but it is not Robespierre's original staircase, which was removed to accommodate a baker's oven in 1811, when it was taken away intact and installed in a country house just outside Paris.

At the far end of the courtyard is the part of the house where Maurice Duplay lived with his family. This used to be a wonderful restaurant called *Le Robespierre*, run by Madame Christianne Rollet and her son Jean-Marc, who re-created the atmosphere of Robespierre's time in this house with such excellence that coming here was like stepping into history. Sadly they have gone, and it is now occupied by another restaurant called Aux Delices de Manon, with its entrance next door at number 400. If by chance you are here on a day when the entry code prevents you from going in to look at the courtyard, you should go into the restaurant, walk all the way to the back then round to the right, and you can see the courtyard through the French windows. Look up and you will see to the right the four windows, where the wood sheds stood underneath, and the door to the right where Robespierre's private staircase was built.

If you decide to eat here you can sit and read about Robespierre and his adopted family while having lunch or dinner in the company of their ghosts, and if you sit in the very end section, by the French windows, they may be eating with you, for this was the Duplay's dining-room. Eat in the part just before getting to the French windows and you will be in their living-room, where every evening after dinner Robespierre would pronounce his thoughts on philosophy and revolution before an admiring audience of Duplays. On Thursday evenings you might have seen any one of an illustrious group of friends who attended the Duplay's weekly *salon* - Desmoulins, Couthon, Saint-Just, or the artist David - all sitting in earnest conversation on the mahogany chairs that were scattered around the room, and when the air was not echoing with words of revolution and liberty, it resounded to the music of Philippe Buonarroti on the harpsichord. Buonarroti was a Florentine noble whose excessive enthusiasm for the French Revolution had obliged him to flee his native Italy, and he was one of the few foreigners to be awarded honorary French citizenship. Philippe Le Bas, the young deputy who married the Duplays' youngest daughter, Elisabeth, also contributed to the music at these *soirées révolutionnaires* by playing the violin and singing love-songs.

Duplay, already a successful bourgeois businessman, was more than pleased at the improvement that Robespierre's presence brought to the quality of his life. He was a family man who, in addition to his young son, had four adult daughters all educated at the convent next door. Three of them, what's more, were still at home and unmarried, and no doubt lingered a little longer than usual over their *toilette* that first morning, before going down to have breakfast with the interesting new lodger. Madame Duplay also regarded the enigmatic deputy with interest, her hopes suddenly high for a prestigious alliance for one of her daughters - maybe more than one, for after all, he must know all the most important men in the Assembly! She began to see glimpses of a bright future for herself and her husband, whose talent as a cabinet-maker had resulted in a thriving business that had become one of the most familiar landmarks of rue Saint-Honoré. Always intensely interested in politics, Duplay followed the progress of the Revolution avidly, and as a member of the Jacobin Club he had already spent many hours listening to Robespierre's speeches. Duplay was, in his own way, ambitious to make his mark on society, and by coming to Robespierre's aid in this way, he was perhaps satisfying his desire to become 'someone.' His generous gesture paid off, for later on he was given the post of juror on the Revolutionary Tribunal, where he sat in judgement of those accused of crimes against the nation.

For Robespierre it was a good move in all respects. His new home was in the heart of revolutionary territory, being only a few steps away from both the Convention and the Jacobin Club, where he spent most of the day. What's more his new quarters were far more agreeable that his rather squalid room in rue de Saintonge, and the generous Duplay ordered one of his apprentices to build the shelves for Robespierre's book collection and the large table where he could work on his interminable speeches and decrees. As well as these material luxuries - for luxuries they were to the spartan deputy - Robespierre also knew for the first time since the death of his mother the pleasure of being in a family environment. He was held in reverence by the entire household, who would sit and listen admiringly while he read out key passages from his beloved Rousseau.

For Eléonore Duplay, the eldest daughter, it was more than reverence that kept her transfixed whenever the Incorruptible took up his habitual stance against the mantelpiece and lectured to the Duplays. She loved Rousseau, to be sure, but not as much as she loved Robespierre, and to the end of her days she nurtured in her heart a jealously guarded obsession with her beloved Maximilien. Mr Duplay would have liked nothing better than to marry his daughter to the increasingly important deputy, but alas, Eléonore's love seemed to be unrequited. Although she described herself as Robespierre's '*fiancée*' (gossips said his mistress), and although after his death she was known as the 'widow Robespierre', there is not much evidence to suggest that her love was ever returned. There was one person, though, who would have disagreed with this, and that was the Duplay's physician, Dr Souberbielle, who claimed there was great affection between Eléonore and Maximilien, and that they considered themselves 'engaged'. Eléonore was, according to most descriptions, no beauty, with dark, heavy features, an unfashionably large mouth, and a perpetually sad expression. But even had she been vivacious and pretty - like her younger sister Elisabeth who fulfilled Madame Duplay's dream by marrying Robespierre's handsome colleague, Philippe Le Bas - it would probably have made no difference. Maximilien was married to the Revolution, and was not that much of a ladies' man, preferring the discreet adoration he had always enjoyed, at a safe distance, from many of the women who met him.

And as Robespierre's fame grew, he began to receive this adoration on a daily basis, in the form of bundles of fan-mail delivered to the door of the Duplay house. One letter, from a very rich young English woman called Miss Shepen, begged him not to be contemptuous of the English and offered him an enormous sum of money for his cause. Some wrote asking him to visit their homes, while others, like this letter from a young widow, bore dramatic witness to the amorous effect of political power. *'Since the beginning of the Revolution I have been in love with you, but I was bound in marriage and I had to overcome my passion. Today, since I am free, having lost my husband in the Vendée war, in the presence of the Supreme Being I make my declaration to you.'* She then made a proposal of marriage, offering as her dowry *'the true virtues of a good republican woman and an income of 40,000 francs.'* She ended by imploring him to *'think of this unfortunate who lives only for you.'* These letters were clearly very important to Robespierre, for he kept all of them, and after his death the inventory of his possessions included several boxes of them, found on the dusty shelves that Duplay's workmen had put up for him.

In the security and adulation of his new *ménage*, Robespierre's simple puritanism began to give way to slight stylishness. Although he would never give up the powdered wig of the old regime, he did abandon his much loved olive green attire for a more up-to-the-minute striped outfit and highly fashionable seamless hose. But at the same time the inscrutable self-assurance, paranoia and peculiar vanity that characterized the last period of his life became more apparent, at times reaching psychotic proportions. Those who recall visiting Robespierre in rue Saint-Honoré tell some strange stories. Barbaroux was struck by the way his room was decorated almost exclusively with his own image, repeated in every possible art form. '*He was painted on the right hand wall, engraved on the left, his bust was in one corner, his bas-relief in the opposite corner. On the tables were half a dozen little engraved Robespierres.*' When Barras and Fréron became the objects of unjust accusations, they came to see the redoubtable deputy, to get assurance of his friendship and support. In his memoirs Barras leaves us an astonishing image of Robespierre, as he describes how, after managing to get past the formidable Eléonore, they entered his room.

'*Robespierre stood there, wrapped in a sort of bathrobe. He was freshly out of the hands of his hairdresser, and was covered in white powder. He was not wearing his spectacles, and through the powder which made his already white face even whiter, we saw two strained eyes unable to recognize us. He put on his glasses and stared at us, and we greeted him in the simple manner of the times. He did not return the greeting, but turned towards his mirror...he took a knife and scraped off the powder which was hiding his face, carefully respecting the angles of his hair-do. He then took off his bathrobe, and placed it on the chair next to us in such a way as to cover our clothes with powder…He washed himself in a bowl which he held in one hand, cleaned his teeth and spat out the water several times on our feet, without speaking a word.'* (Hénard, 1908-09). This ceremony over, they dared to speak and explain the purpose of their visit, but Robespierre maintained his silence, and they wondered if he had been offended by their use of *tu*, according to revolutionary custom. So they continued, but this time addressing him with the more respectful *vous* of the old regime. Robespierre was indifferent. He remained silent, and they eventually left having heard not one word from the lips of the Incorruptible, lips on which, Barras adds, *'I perceived a sort of yellowish foam, which was not at all reassuring.'*

Robespierre's capacity for maintaining silence was one of his strengths when dealing with problems or adversaries. The other was spying, and he regularly received detailed reports on the movements of anyone he suspected or felt threatened by. Gradually number 398 rue Saint-Honoré became a focal point of the Revolution, and one of the busiest doorways in Paris. Past the piles of wood stacked up in the alley and the courtyard came a continual stream of carpenters, labourers, deputies, spies, admirers and, occasionally, enemies. For although Robespierre was protected in his new home by Duplay's timber yard and workshop, which formed a buffer between the house and the street outside, unwanted visitors sometimes still got in.

On May 22nd 1794 a young girl knocked on the door and asked to speak to *'the Incorruptible.'* It was 20-year-old Cécile Renault, whom you met at the start of Walk Seven on the Boulevard du Palais. Her request was refused, and Cécile replied, rather insolently, that as a public figure he should always be ready to speak with anyone who came to see him. Her attitude aroused the suspicions of Eléonore and the two other people with her, who immediately arrested Cécile as 'suspect' and took her directly to the Committee of General Security. She protested, saying that under the old regime, if you wanted to have an audience with the king, you were treated with more respect. *'Would you prefer to have a king, then?'* she was asked. Cécile replied from the heart to this dangerous question, saying *'I would spill every drop of my blood to have one. That is my opinion, and you are all tyrants.'* Her interrogator asked her why she would rather have a king, and she told him, *'I would prefer one king to fifty thousand tyrants, and I went to Robespierre's house just to see what a tyrant is like.'*

After her interrogation, however, Cécile was searched, and two knives were found hidden in her dress. It remains a mystery whether she actually intended to kill Robespierre, but several people observed that she seemed somewhat disturbed in her ideas and behaviour. Another curious fact is that before leaving for rue St. Honoré she had been to see a café owner by the name of Payen, and had asked him to look after a parcel containing a complete outfit of clothes. When asked later why she had done this, she replied, *'In the place where I am bound to be taken, I will be glad to have some clean clothes to wear.'* *'What place are you talking about?'* asked her interrogator. *'Prison,'* replied Cécile, *'and then to the guillotine.'* Which is exactly where she did go, on 29 *Prairial* (June 17th), a day known thereafter as the *Great Red Mass*. Cécile went to her death with 53 other victims, which included her father, brother and aunt, all condemned at the same time as co-conspirators, and all wearing the red robe of murderers and poisoners.

Sanson, the executioner, had his own view of young Cécile. On the day of her arrest he wrote, *'The enormous daggers of citizeness Cécile Renault seem to have been no more than two little folding knives...similar to those that children use to eat with, and could only hurt the hand of the person who uses them...it is difficult to understand how she could have entertained the idea of such a difficult crime when she was so poorly armed...the simplest, and perhaps the most likely explanation is that her mind is deranged.'* (Sanson, 1998). But unfortunately for Cécile, on the day before her visit to Robespierre, an attempt was made on the life of another deputy, Collot d'Herbois. In this case there was no doubt that murder was intended, for the assailant, an unemployed neighbour called Henri Admiral, fired two shots, both of which missed. There was no question about Admiral's fate in such circumstances, and Sanson saw immediately that this also sealed the fate of Cécile Renault.

'Robespierre will never leave to Collot all the glory of dying for one's country; he knows only too well the advantages of it, especially when you can add to that glory the good fortune of still being alive - the trial will take its course.' A few hours after Cécile's visit the Duplay house was filled with local Jacobins, who had come to reassure Robespierre and rejoice in his good fortune to be still alive. He received them in silence, seated before his dinner, which he calmly continued to eat in front of the unwanted visitors. Undeterred, they persisted in their reassurances and shouts of indignation, while the object of their outbursts sat eating an orange, his favourite fruit, which he always took obsessive pride in being able to peel with one hand.

The covered entrance you came in by is not the one Robespierre used. In his day it was directly in front of you (if you're standing in the courtyard looking towards rue Saint-Honoré) but it has since been moved over to the right, creating a much more closed courtyard. Robespierre's original entrance alley was filled in and has become the ground floor, but on the first floor you can still see the rooms that were above that entrance. Anyone coming to the Duplay house would have walked straight in under those rooms directly from the street, rather than turning right and then left into the courtyard as you do nowadays. The rooms above the entrance were occupied by

Charlotte Robespierre, Maximilien's sister, and their younger brother Augustin Robespierre. The intimacy of the Duplay family with Robespierre provoked bitter jealousy in Charlotte, who in their home town of Arras had been used to being the mistress of her brother's household. So in 1794 she successfully persuaded him to leave rue Saint Honoré for another lodging in nearby rue Saint-Florentin. But not for long, for when Maximilien became ill, the shrewd Madame Duplay seized the moment and visited him. She easily convinced him that he was not sick but was merely missing his 'family', telling him he was like her own son, and thus touching the grief that was still buried deep in Robespierre's heart for his own mother. He could not resist such an earnest show of concern, and was soon persuaded to return to the fold, much to the chagrin of his sister, who never forgave Madame Duplay as long as she lived. And Charlotte lived a long time, her celebrated name bringing her a pension from successive governments right up to the time of her death in 1834. The only member of the Duplay family she remained in contact with was Elisabeth, whose husband Philippe Le Bas remained faithful to Robespierre to the end and shot himself at the Hôtel-de-Ville on the night of 9 *Thermidor*. Charlotte continued to make frequent and welcome visits to Elisabeth and her son, also called Philippe, both of whom treated the aging *demoiselle* with an almost royal deference.

Charlotte's attempt to remove her brother from the influence of the Duplays came shortly before the Festival of the Supreme Being, an event intended to be the glorification of everything that Robespierre had struggled for and believed in. On that day, June 8th 1794, the whole of rue Saint-Honoré was festooned with garlands of flowers and patriotic banners, and in the courtyard of the Jacobin Club a Tree of Liberty was covered with a tricolour blaze of marguerites, cornflowers and poppies. The pavement outside the Duplay house was strewn with rose petals, where young girls holding bouquets and young men waving palms cheered wildly as the Incorruptible appeared in the doorway. He was magnificently dressed in a cornflower blue coat and yellow nankin breeches, a wide silk tricolour belt encircled his exquisite lace shirt, his hat was adorned with a tricolour rosette, and white silk hose and silver shoe buckles completed the splendour of his outfit. It was to be his finest hour. The entire Duplay family followed him out, bursting with pride, while Eléonore held against her heart the bouquet of wheat and wild flowers that Maximilien would hold during the ceremony.

The enthusiasm of the crowd momentarily gave all Robespierre's dreams an aura of reality, but as the day progressed and he heard voices describing him as the 'revolutionary pope' and threatening him with 'Brutus's dagger', he became suddenly aware of the hatred he had brought upon himself. He saw a mortally dark cloud gathering over his life, and he returned home that evening deeply troubled. To the excited questions and self-contented chatter of the Duplay family he could only utter sadly and prophetically, '*You will not see me around for very long.*' With that he retired to his room, and just seven weeks later his words became reality. On the morning of July 27th he left the Duplay house for the last time and set off for the Assembly. As he passed by the Jacobin Club, bathed in morning sunshine, he could not have realised that it would be his last look at this place, so dear to his heart, where only the night before he had been acclaimed by his fellow members. But on the benches of the Convention a storm was brewing. As he walked in Robespierre was met by a wall of hostility, and after being denounced by almost all his former supporters, he was outlawed and put under arrest. Aided by the Paris Commune, he took refuge with his remaining friends in the Hôtel-de-Ville, where, on the famous night of 9 *Thermidor*, the Incorruptible was finally overcome.

From then on Robespierre's home was the scene of drama and tragedy. At six in the evening of 10 *Thermidor*, as three tumbrils rolled along rue Saint-Honoré, the shutters of the Duplay house were, as usual, firmly closed. But today Robespierre was not behind them, cloistered in his room, poring over his books in an attempt to block out the horrible scene from his mind. He was sitting impassively in the first tumbril, his fractured jaw enveloped in a blood-stained handkerchief, his glassy green eyes staring out at the sea of hostile faces who were rejoicing at his fate. His comrades accompanied him, some mutilated and half-dead, but bound, nonetheless, by ropes from shoulder to ankle, presumably to prevent any attempts at escape or rescue. It was hardly necessary. Hanriot, drunk and terrified, ranted incoherently, the ashen-faced Couthon sat in the back of the cart, his forehead bandaged and his paralysed legs dangling over the side, while Augustin Robespierre, who had courageously chosen to share the fate of his older brother, groaned in agony every time the tumbril jolted his broken leg. Saint-Just remained dignified and stoic, his god-like beauty lending itself admirably to the role of revolutionary martyr.

As the tumbrils passed *rue de Luxembourg* (now rue Cambon) they began to slow down, and came to a halt outside the Duplay house. There followed a grotesque ceremony, conceived no doubt as a final torment for the Incorruptible before dying. As a band of *sans-culotte* women, known as 'the furies of the guillotine', danced around the tumbrils singing the revolutionary song *Ça ira*, another *sans-culotte* arrived with a bucket of ox-blood and a broom. Plunging the broom into the bucket, he then proceeded to splash the house with the blood, which ran down the walls, on to the street and into the gutters. This gory spectacle was applauded wildly by the crowd of delighted spectators who had been lining this part of the street since early morning. Deprived of his glasses, Robespierre was perhaps mercifully spared too clear a view of this macabre pantomime, but he was nonetheless observed to close his eyes - and think of Rousseau? Who knows.

The tumbrils continued on their way, and the crowd followed them, leaving the house in silence. Behind the bloodstained walls, in the back room on the first floor, two sisters lay prostrate on the bed that stood by the far window. Indifferent to the evening sun that shone softly on the convent garden below, they both wept desperately, Eléonore for her lost '*fiancée*' Maximilien, and Elisabeth for her husband, Philippe. The very next day they were both arrested, but did not remain in prison long. Elisabeth, still fearing for her safety, changed her name, dressed herself as a woman of the people, and worked down by the Seine as a laundress to support herself and her baby son. In later life she took up residence in rue de Tournon, where she lived surrounded by portraits of her family, including those of Robespierre in all his most elegant outfits. Eléonore lived for another 40 years, but could never really shed the terror of those dreadful days of *Thermidor* 1794. Nor could she shed the passion she had for Robespierre, whom she continued to adore even more in death than she ever had while he was alive, for in her own mind she was Maximilien's widow, and she lived in that belief for the rest of her life. But to the rest of the world she maintained an almost fearful silence on the subject of her obsessive love for the man who became, after his death, the scapegoat of the Revolution.

What then was the fate of the Duplays, the couple who for three years had centred their entire existence around the care and protection of the most feared and powerful man in France? As soon as Robespierre was denounced, the inevitable soldiers came here to rue Saint-Honoré and arrested them. Madame Duplay was imprisoned in *Sainte-Pélagie*, where on the morning of 11 *Thermidor* she was found hanging from a hook over the window of her cell. Her death remains somewhat of a mystery. Some say that a group of enraged prisoners strangled her on discovering her to be the traitor who had given hospitality to the dethroned tyrant. Others say that, faced with a hostile prison and the possibility of imminent execution, she chose to commit suicide. As for Monsieur Duplay, he was taken to the *Prison du Plessis* in the old college of Louis-le-Grand, where his ill-chosen house-guest had been educated. He later appeared before the Tribunal, where he had formerly sat as a juror, in a trial that was one of the last to take place in the infamous court before it was abolished. He was tried in company with Fouquier-Tinville and his fellow jurors, but had the good fortune to be judged after the repeal of the notorious Law of 22 *Prairial*, thus escaping the blade of the guillotine to which he had condemned so many of his countryman. Unlike them, Duplay had the privilege of a real interrogation, where he had the chance to defend himself, as a result of which he was acquitted, and returned to his house on rue Saint-Honoré.

But Duplay had developed a real taste for 'being someone', and resumed playing host to those of his former friends who did not feel threatened by continued association with Robespierre. Among those who were often seen here during this period were the former Marquis d'Antonelle, the Italian Utopian revolutionary Philippe Buonarotti, and two people who eventually led Duplay into a second brush with the law. One was his neighbour, a locksmith named Didiée, and the other was Augustin-Alexandre Darthé, former Public Prosecutor of the notoriously pitiless tribunals in Arras and Cambrai. They were both accused in the 'Conspiracy of Equals' with Babeuf, whom you met a little while ago being rescued by Didiée when he was hiding behind some carts full of grain near the *Daughters of the Assumption Convent*. Babeuf had been arrested earlier that day when he was spotted coming out of a house on rue Saint-Honoré, and although no-one can be sure, it is thought he was coming out of number 398, casting deep suspicion on Duplay and leading to his arrest a few days later, along with his son Jacques-Michel, Darthé, Didiée, Antonelle and Buonarotti. Once again fortune smiled on Duplay, who was acquitted for lack of evidence, as were all his friends except Darthé, who, seen as Babeuf's principle collaborator, was guillotined. Duplay's innocence in this affair is highly questionable, but not only did he come through it unscathed, he then went on to become a municipal officer in the Paris Commune, and his son, who was just 19, was given the post of Finance Minister. After this Duplay retreated into a quieter life in his now rather famous house, which he was able to buy in 1796 for 38,000 *francs*. If you go to the Père-Lachaise cemetery, you will see against the wall in an obscure corner an old worn gravestone with the name 'Duplay' engraved on it several times. Here are buried Maurice Duplay, who died aged 79 in Paris on June 30th 1820, Eléonore Duplay, who died aged 64 on July 26th 1832, and Jacques-Michel Duplay, administrator of hospices, who died aged 69 in 1847.

➡ As you come out of the restaurant in the Duplay house, almost opposite, just before you get to rue Saint-Florentin, was where Robespierre was walking when Duplay rescued him and took him to the safety of his home. On the corner of rue Saint-Florentin is number 273, site of a house which was the home of Abbé Sieyès, author of the pamphlet entitled 'What is the Third Estate?' He lived here during the Revolution, and in April 1797 he narrowly escaped being murdered in his own home by a man named Poule, who was a fanatical priest but fortunately for Sieyès a rather inadequate assassin. After three unsuccessful attempts, Poule finally got into the apartment and fired two shots that caused minor injuries to Sieyès' arm and stomach. When he was arrested Poule declared that he intended to assassinate the entire National Convention - a slightly overambitious goal for such a bad shot - and Sieyès, who recovered very rapidly, was less than pleased to learn that his assailant had not been condemned to death, but merely to twenty years in jail. Convinced that prisoners generally found a way of escaping, Sieyès gave the concierge at number 273 strict instructions. *'When Citizen Poule asks for me, tell him I'm out.'*

On the site of the modern building at number 275 there used to be a house dating from the 17th century. In an apartment on the third floor lived a deputy named Louis Héron whose talents as a police agent for the Committee of General Security eventually secured him the unofficial post of spy for Robespierre. He started in the footsteps of his father as a furrier to the aristocracy, but after being refused the favours he felt he deserved, Héron became violently anti-royal for the rest of his life. He played his part with ferocious enthusiasm in the overthrow of Louis XVI, and was the major force behind the orgy of arrests that characterized the revolutionary period. Héron favoured the company of extremists like Marat, who was often pursued by the law for his violent opinions, and in 1790 used Héron's apartment here as one of his many hiding places. Héron himself managed to avoid the ultimate judgement that befell so many revolutionaries, but was arrested after 9 *Thermidor*, then released following a general amnesty in 1795. Héron would no doubt have thoroughly enjoyed the café on the ground-floor of his house. It was called *Au Saint-Esprit*, and later in the Revolution became the most popular meeting-place for people wanting to watch the tumbrils of condemned victims as they passed by on the last leg of their fateful journey. By now they were almost at the end of rue Saint-Honoré, and knew that on turning the next corner they would be faced with the silhouette of the guillotine, dark against the sky, its great steel triangular blade suspended above the scaffold, waiting.

RUE ROYALE.

If you still have the courage, ➡ make the fateful left turn into rue Royale, nowadays a wide, elegant street that originally started as a muddy path leading down to the Seine. The transformation into its present splendour began in 1758, as part of the opening of the *Place Louis XV* (now Place de la Concorde), when the architect Ange-Jacques Gabriel designed two matching façades to be built on either side of the street. Gabriel was obviously very pleased with his work, for after their completion he moved into number 8, where some of the original wood panelling still exists. It is these two façades, comprising numbers 1 to 15 and 2 to 14, that you see as you turn left into rue Royale, magnificent examples of 18th-century architecture that now number among the protected historic buildings of Paris. Their beauty was no doubt lost on those who had the misfortune to view them from a tumbril, for at this point they knew that what remained of their lives could now only be counted in minutes.

As you follow them down to the scaffold, you will see on your right at number 3 the most famous of all Parisian restaurants, Maxim's, founded in 1893 by Maxime Gaillard, an employee in a bar at number 23, who bought it when it was an ice-cream parlour with a bankrupt owner. A century earlier, at the time when the tumbrils were passing by, Maxim's was the abandoned residence of Armand-Emmanuel du Plessis, duc de Richelieu, who had the foresight to emigrate back in 1790 when he was still just 24 years old. Had he not taken this wise decision, the duke would have probably found himself waving goodbye to his house as he headed towards his fate in the Place de la Concorde. As it turned out he waved goodbye to it anyway when he emigrated, for he went to Russia and became first mayor of Odessa, then governor-general of what is now Ukraine. He remained there until the restoration of the monarchy under Louis XVIII, and is considered to be the founder of the port and town of Odessa.

Place de la Concorde.

Place de la Concorde. This lovely square has had many names over history, beginning as *Place Louis XV*, then becoming *Place de la Révolution*. In 1826 it was re-named *Place Louis XVI* in honour of the king who was executed there in 1793. (Courtesy of Musée Carnavalet, Cabinet des Arts Graphiques, Paris)

Gabriel's plans for the construction of this enormous square were first begun in 1757, when it was just a vast expanse of undeveloped land, completely empty except for the royal marble depot in the north part. It was bordered by the muddy path to the north that is now rue Royale, by the river to the south, and on its east side was the Tuileries Palace. To the west the Champs-Elysées was no more than a tree-lined clearing leading to the woodcutters' cottages in the village of Chaillot. Gabriel transformed this space into a grand octagonal concourse surrounded by a 20-metre wide ditch that was landscaped with flowers and bushes to form a sunken garden all around the new square. There were six stone bridges across the ditch giving access to the square, and at each of the eight angles was a small pavilion containing steps leading down to the gardens below, which, predictably, became a favourite haunt for prostitutes, and remained so until the ditch was filled in in 1852. The square itself was divided into four large lawns, each surrounded by green-painted barriers, and in the centre was an equestrian statue of Louis XV, dressed in a Roman toga and crowned with laurels. The corners of the statue's pedestal were decorated with bronze representations of the four virtues exemplified by the benevolent monarch - strength, justice, prudence and peace. Not all Louis's subjects were convinced, however, as evidenced by an irreverent placard hung around the horse's neck just a few days after the statue was inaugurated in 1763. *'Oh beautiful statue - Virtue at its feet, Oh beautiful statue - and Vice in its seat.'* But this little hint of the tempest to come did not concern the majority of Parisians, who came in their hundreds to promenade in the extravagant new *Place Louis XV*.

Work also began on a new bridge, the Pont de la Concorde, that was finally completed in 1790, and in 1794 David organized the addition of the statue 'The Horses of Marly' at the entrance to the Champs-Elyséees. The idea of adorning the eight corner pavilions with statues symbolizing the principle cities of France was born in 1795, but not actually realised until the reign of Louis-Philippe, when the statues were installed along with the elegant lamps and fountains. The famous Egyptian obelisk was put there in 1836, and is the oldest monument in Paris, dating from the time of Ramses II, thirteen centuries before Christ. This 220,000-kilo column was sent from Luxor as a gift to Louis-Philippe, and its installation attracted thousands of people. The name of the square was changed several times with each political regime, becoming *Place de la Révolution* in 1792, *Place de la Concorde* in 1795, then reverting to *Place Louis XV* in 1814. In 1826 it was re-named *Place Louis XVI*, and if you look on the corner of rue Boissy d'Anglas you will see that name engraved on the wall. But this homage to the decapitated monarch was short-lived, and in 1828 Louis XV yet again took pride of place on the name plate until 1830, when it became permanently Place de la Concorde.

Before the Revolution the square was often the scene of grandiose spectacles. On May 30th 1770, to honour the marriage of the future Louis XVI and Marie-Antoinette, there was a fireworks display here, part of a great celebration that attracted all the city's nobles. They arrived in their carriages along rue Royale, followed by a multitude of Parisians, most of whom were in varying states of intoxication, having drunk all along the way at the public fountains that were running with wine to honour the occasion. But panic broke out during the display when a rocket went in the wrong direction, setting alight the *Temple to Hymen* in the middle of the square. People rushed in all directions, and several of the spectators' stands collapsed, resulting in the death of 133 people, many of whom fell into the sunken gardens and were suffocated by those who fell on top of them. Every year during August and September was the *Saint Ovid Fair*, when for a month the square bustled with commercial activity as Parisians wandered up and down the aisles of boutiques and stalls, amusing themselves at fairground games. This event was also struck by disaster in 1777, when a fire broke out and destroyed all the stalls.

On the north side of the new square Gabriel designed the two twin palaces that still stand today. With their Corinthian columns, their four elegant triangular frontons and allegorical decoration, they form the familiar façade that has appeared over the years in so many photos and engravings of the Place de la Concorde. Built between 1760 and 1775, they were originally intended to lodge the city's most important ambassadors, but were never used for this purpose. Number 2, to your left as you enter the square, was designated immediately as the royal furniture depository (*Garde-Meuble*), where Louis XVI's first valet set himself up in a sumptuous apartment. Marie-Antoinette also had a small *pied-à-terre* here that she used when visiting the capital, and it was from the windows of this little apartment that she watched in 1788 the hunting of a deer around the *Place Louis XV*. The horrible finale of this entertainment, laid on for her by her brother-in-law, the Comte d'Artois, took place by torchlight, when the unfortunate animal was caught by the pursuing hounds at the entrance to the Tuileries gardens. Another violent spectacle was later witnessed through these same windows, but this time Marie-Antoinette wasn't watching it, she was the principle actor in the scene taking place below. At the windows were a group of revolutionary officials, appointed to be present at the queen's execution on October 16th 1793. A year earlier, during the night of September 11th 1792, a band of thieves broke into the royal depository and made off with the Crown's precious diamond collection. The captured thieves were guillotined here in Place de la Concorde, but only a small percentage of the jewels were recovered, and the theft provoked a scathing attack by Interior Minister Roland on the Paris Commune, who were responsible for the surveillance of the royal treasure. Much earlier, in July 1789 when the people of Paris were looking for weapons, before storming the Bastille they came here to pillage the cannons and other weapons that were stored in the *Garde-Meuble*. Number 2 Place de la Concorde is now the Ministry of the Navy.

July 13th 1789. Before storming the Bastille people went to other places to arm themselves, including the royal furniture depository in Place de la Concorde, where they found cannons and other weapons. (Author's private collection)

The second of the palaces built by Gabriel, to your right on entering the square, was divided up after its construction and sold as four separate houses. It is now number 4 and known as the Hôtel de Coislin after it first owner, the formidable Marquise de Coislin, who bought it in 1776, survived the Revolution and died here in 1817 at the age of almost 100. The story goes that she was visited here one evening by the King of Sweden, who, wishing to honour her with an incognito visit, had himself announced as 'Count Wasa.' The marquess did not recognize the name, and refused to see him. When it was explained who he really was, she replied, *'I don't know how they do it in Sweden, but in Paris I receive only those who have demanded audience, or those to whom I have accorded it.' Noblesse* clearly didn't *oblige* this particular marquess. A more famous - and hopefully more polite - resident of number 4 was the celebrated writer François René Chateaubriand, whose older brother, Jean-Baptiste, had sealed his fate by marrying the grand-daughter of Malesherbes, defence lawyer at Louis XVI's trial. Jean-Baptiste's marriage opened social avenues that enabled him to help his younger brother by acquainting him with the best literary salons and eventually presenting him at Court. He paid for this privilege with his life, however, for Jean-Baptiste and his wife were among the numerous members of the Malesherbes family guillotined during the Terror. François-René, more fortunate than his older brother, survived the Revolution, and came to live in this house with his wife for two years at the beginning of the Empire. But his hostility to Napoléon, sparked off by the execution of the Duc d'Enghien in 1804, led to his departure from France in 1806, when he began his travels in the middle-east. François-René is immortalized in the name of a cut of tenderloin steak known as the Chateaubriand Steak, created by his chef, who served it with a white wine and shallot sauce flavoured with lemon, butter and tarragon. Chateaubriand's lovely Hôtel de Coislin is now the property of the Emir of Qatar.

The king's Secretary was the very first resident of number 6, which in 1889 was owned briefly by the Pope, until it was sold to the Automobile Club in 1901 along with number 8. Ange-Jacques Gabriel, the royal architect who designed the building, was the first owner of number 8, where under the Republic and the Empire a café flourished on the first floor under the management of Corazza, who already had another successful café at the Palais-Royal. If you want luxury during your visit to Paris, you can stay at number 10, which now forms part of the beautiful Hôtel Crillon. It takes its name from the second owner, the Duc de Crillon, who bought it in 1788, lost it during the Revolution through emigration, but whose family re-gained it in 1820. They remained there until 1907, when it was bought, along with the first two buildings in rue Boissy d'Anglas, by the *Societé des grands magasins et hôtels du Louvre*, who turned all three buildings into the Hôtel Crillon.

When you look at these two lovely columned façades, standing now in such peaceful contrast to the endless movement of the Place de la Concorde, it is hard to believe that they witnessed the last violent moments of almost half the people guillotined in Paris during the Revolution. In the space of thirteen months 1,119 people were beheaded in this square by Dr Guillotin's machine, which was installed here permanently between May 11th 1793 and June 9th 1794. It had made its first appearance in the square, re-named *Place de la Révolution*, in October 1792, for the execution of the royal diamond thieves that you just read about, and then it came back three months later, on January 21st, when Louis XVI was guillotined before a vast crowd of his former subjects. On this occasion the scaffold was placed between the middle of the square and the pavilion holding the statue dedicated to the town of Brest - about twelve metres in from the pavilion. When you look at the two plans showing the square then and now you can see that the Place de la Concorde is still pretty similar to what it was during the

Place de la Concorde.

A Statue of Ville de Brest

B Position of guillotine for Louis XVI's execution

C Position of guillotine from 11th May 1793 to 8th June 1794

D Obelisk

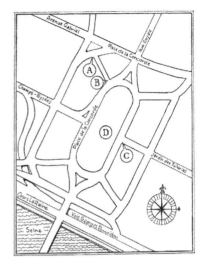

Revolution. At the time of Louis's execution the centre of the square was occupied by an enormous stone and plaster figure representing Liberty, replacing the statue of Louis XV that had been toppled by an angry mob the day after the dethronement of the king. 'Liberty' - by all accounts not the most beautiful of statues - was a bronze-coloured Amazonian figure holding a lance and wearing a red revolutionary bonnet. She dominated the square from her throne, set on the very pedestal that had accommodated 'Louis the Beloved', whose unfortunate heir was that day about to become 'Louis the Shortened.' The guillotine did not return to Place de la Concorde until 11th May 1793, when the Convention moved from the *Manège* to the Tuileries Palace and did not want the instrument of death on their doorstep (it had been right outside one of the Palace courtyards). This time it would stay for thirteen months, and stood half-way between the statue of Liberty and the entrance to the Tuileries Gardens (see plan).

    The irreverence of the nickname 'the Shortened' given to Louis XVI after his execution bears no relation to the sober atmosphere that reigned throughout Paris on the day that he was guillotined, when he arrived at the foot of the scaffold in a closed carriage, accompanied by his confessor, the Irish priest Abbé Edgeworth. The king had spent most of the journey reciting psalms, and those close to him on that day were all astonished at the piety and dignity that he displayed to the last. He insisted on removing his own jacket and opening his shirt without assistance from the executioners, and at first resisted having his hands bound. Edgeworth, however, with tears in his eyes, persuaded Louis that *'in this new outrage I see one last resemblance between Your Majesty and the God who is about to be your reward.'* As soon as he mounted the scaffold, Louis broke free from Edgeworth and his guards, ran to the edge of the platform and began addressing the crowd. *'I die innocent of the crimes with which I am charged, I pardon my enemies, and I pray to God that the blood you are about to shed will not be visited on France.'* The rest of his speech was lost in a sudden roll of drums, as the monarch was seized by Sanson's assistants and attached to the plank. The drums stopped, the blade fell, and France no longer had a king. When Sanson displayed Louis's head to the people, they replied with a unanimous cry of *'Long Live the Nation!'* followed by a heavy silence. Then came the ritual dipping of handkerchiefs in blood, the rush for fragments of the victim's

'The stupor was universal' wrote Restif de la Bretonne after seeing Louis XVI decapitated. The king's confessor, Abbé Edgworth, continues to pray, turning away as Sanson shows Louis's head to the people. (Author's private collection)

clothing and hair sold off by Sanson's assistants at exorbitant prices, while cakes and pies were peddled around the scaffold. Then gradually a surreal silence set in, and the crowd dispersed without saying a word. A vast range of emotions began to grip the hearts of every citizen that evening when, according to Restif de la Bretonne, *'the stupor was universal.'*

The same soul-searching did not follow the execution nine months later of Marie-Antoinette, who arrived at the scaffold in a tumbril, protected from the chill of autumn by no more than a white linen dress. Her shoulders were covered by a muslin *fichu*, a plain white bonnet concealed her cropped grey hair, and her hands were tied behind her back like a common criminal. Throughout the journey from the Conciergerie she had suffered with resolute indifference the jeers and insults of a contemptuous populace, maintaining a fixed, absent stare right up to the moment when she descended from the tumbril. She made her way firmly and bravely towards the guillotine, her feet clad in a pair of dainty slate-blue satin shoes that she had kept carefully in a box throughout her imprisonment, and as she went up the steps of the scaffold she seemed in such a hurry that she tripped and lost one of them. She also trod on Sanson's foot, provoking her famous apology, *'I beg your forgiveness, Sir, I did not do it on purpose.'* It is my belief that this apology was a genuinely spontaneous act of noble courtesy on the queen's part, but if you want to look more deeply, you might choose to see it as an unconscious apology to the French nation for her crimes, so many of which stemmed from coming to France as an insouciant teenager and being thrown into a dangerous world of political turmoil and intrigue. To the astonishment - and irritation - of those who loathed her, Marie-Antoinette died with a courage and dignity that was never attributed to her during her lifetime, but this did not prevent the day of her execution from becoming an orgy of rejoicing at the demise of the hated *Madame Veto*.

Apart from these royal victims, there were many other well-known names from the Revolution who met their end in the Place de la Concorde. It was here that Maximilien Robespierre and his bedraggled band of supporters paid the price of tyranny, going to their death in sober silence, most of them wounded and bandaged, some unable to walk. Robespierre was executed last, and his turn brought a moment of horrific drama when Sanson ripped off the bloodstained bandage that was holding together his broken jaw, causing Robespierre to break his silence with a piercing cry of agony. Some victims tried to add an element of theatrical drama to their final moments. The 21 Girondin deputies, led by Jacques-Pierre Brissot, sang the *Marseillaise* throughout the entire length of their journey from the Conciergerie, and continued singing as each one of them kissed the others goodbye and mounted the scaffold. Their inspiration and ally, Manon Roland, died here ten days later, on November 10th 1793, with characteristic courage and dignity, and without sparing the crowd a last expression of her contempt for the hypocrisy of the Revolution. Stopping for a few moments to contemplate the colossal figure of Liberty in front of her, she exclaimed, *'Oh Liberty, what crimes are committed in your name!'*

After Manon's execution the number of these 'crimes' would escalate dramatically, entire families sometimes being exterminated all at once. Such was the case of the family of Lamoignon de Malesherbes, former minister to Louis XVI and a staunch advocate of freedom of the press, the rights of Jews and Protestants, and the humane treatment of prisoners. It was probably this very compassion for the oppressed that led him to return from emigration to defend Louis XVI in his hour of need, but he could not save the king, and nor in the end could he save himself. On April 22nd 1793 (3 *Floréal*), at the age of 73, Malesherbes stood at the foot of the guillotine, watching in tragic despair as his 48-year-old daughter, Marguérite, his grand-daughter Aline-Thérèse, aged just 28 and her young husband, Jean-Baptiste Chateaubriand, were all decapitated before him. Marguérite's husband, Lepeletier de Rosanbo, former president of the Paris parliament, had already been guillotined two days before, and revolutionary thirst for the blood of the Malesherbes would not be quenched until the old man's 76-year-old sister and his two private secretaries had also suffered the same fate. Another victim of his past to die here on the same day as Malesherbes was Isaac René Guy le Chapelier, author of the notorious Le Chapelier Law that prohibited strikes and workers' associations, thus preventing the creation of trade unions in France until 1864.

A famously innocent victim whose death was accompanied by a certain theatrical touch was Madame Elisabeth, Louis XVI's sister. She was the last to be executed of 24 prisoners, all of whom bowed their heads in deference as they passed the princess, and then kissed her before mounting the steps to the scaffold. This display of defiance was not lost on one *sans-culotte*, who shouted, *'Grovel all you like - she's done-for, like the Austrian whore!'* Then it was the turn of the princess herself. As she was being attached to the fatal plank, her muslin *fichu* slipped off, exposing her shoulders and provoking a reaction in keeping with her very modest nature. *'In the name of decency, cover me up!'* she implored. Her piety and obvious innocence of any real crime touched everyone, even the furies of the *Place de la Révolution*, who, instead of their usual grotesque display of joy, remained relatively silent when Madame Elisabeth's head rolled into the leather bag at the foot of the guillotine.

The courage that people consistently showed in the face of a violent and public death is quite remarkable. There were, however, two notable exceptions to this. One was Jacques-René Hébert, who as the legendary *Père Duchesne* had mocked so many of the victims of the Revolution and expressed unmitigated joy at the daily slaughter of the nation's enemies. He invented scores of macabre expressions for being guillotined, but when it was finally his turn to *'sneeze into the bag'*, or *'play the hot hand'*, he could not take his own medicine, and went to his death white with terror and weeping. The other exception to the rule of bravery was Madame du Barry, whose petrified screams froze the assembled crowd as they saw the former royal mistress dragged to the scaffold. It took several men to hold her down while she was being attached to the plank, her arms and legs flailing in all directions as she struggled to free herself. Her shrieks as Sanson released the lever were so blood-curdling they reduced the spectators to stunned silence.

In contrast, one of the most conspicuously fearless victims of the guillotine was Charlotte Corday, executed for the murder of Marat. Her final moments are described by Sanson, who remained fascinated by her stoic calmness, which he had hardly ever seen in any of his many victims. During the first part of the journey from the Conciergerie there was a clap of thunder, then a storm broke out and rain poured down, soaking Charlotte's long red traitor's robe, which clung to her body and provoked a series of lewd comments from the bystanders. But Charlotte remained impassive, and Sanson remained fascinated. *'At every possible moment, I turned to look at her, and the more I looked the more I wanted to see her. It wasn't, however, because of her beauty, great as it was; but it seemed impossible to me that she could remain to the end as gentle and as courageous as I saw her then; I needed reassurance that she had her weakness like the others; but, I don't know why, every time I turned my eyes towards her, I trembled in fear that she would falter. However, what I considered to be impossible did happen. For the two hours that she was next to me her eyelids did not tremble, and her face did not betray one moment of anger or indignation...As we arrived in the Place de la Révolution, I got up and placed myself in front of her to protect her from the sight of the guillotine. But she leaned forward to look, saying: I have the right to be curious, I've never seen one before! I believe, nonetheless, that her curiosity made her pale; but that only lasted an instant, and almost immediately she regained her colour.'* (Sanson, 1988)

Charlotte's final moments on the scaffold are described accurately but with great romanticism by Klaus, a German historian, who was an eye-witness to the execution. *'She looked on the surging multitude with ineffable sweetness, and when the people greeted her with strident shouts, one glance from her beautiful eyes was often enough to silence them. Her smile was the only outward sign of her emotions. As she approached the scaffold, she looked as if she was reaching the end of a tiring journey. She was alone. Without assistance, she climbed the steps of the bloodstained apparatus, and did not even change colour. Only when her neck was bared before the crowd did a more intense tint come to her virginal cheeks. Her noble head, her bare shoulders, the tranquil look which she cast round her, produced the most profound impression. Already half transfigured, she seemed an angel of light.'* To Sanson's continued amazement, Charlotte hastened to the guillotine and placed herself in position on the plank of her own accord, and Klaus's quixotic account ends as *'the fatal blade fell, and cut off the most beautiful of heads...Thus ended Charlotte Corday, the sublime maiden of Caen.'* (Tannahill, 1966)

But when the executioner's assistant picked up her head and displayed it to the crowd, the mystique of Charlotte Corday continued to affect Sanson, who admitted that *'although familiar with this kind of spectacle, nonetheless I was frightened. I had the impression that it was on me that those half-open eyes were fixed, and that I saw in them yet again that penetrating and irresistible sweetness that had so astonished me.'* Sanson was so transfixed by his young victim that he forgets to relate how one of his assistants, enraged by the murder of his hero, Marat, took the severed head and slapped it. This provoked the legendary story of how Charlotte's disembodied face blushed at the outrage, thus proving that death by decapitation is not instantaneous. This is probably pure fantasy, and more rational observers contend that her face became red from the blood that was on the hands of the assistant who slapped it.

'Famous last words' is the name of the game when you take on the role of heroic revolutionary martyr, and Georges Danton must surely take the prize for this. He had already begun throwing out a few while still at the Conciergerie, the most notable - and typical - of which concerned his regret at leaving the Republic in such disarray. *'If I left my balls to Robespierre and my legs to Couthon the Committee might last a bit longer.'* Danton was the last to be executed of his group of compatriots, all of whom died with courage. When the handsome and cultivated Hérault de Séchelles, who was the first to go, wanted to kiss Danton farewell, the executioner, anxious to get on with the day's work, tried to separate them. *'Imbecile!'* shouted Danton, *'You won't stop our heads from kissing each other in the same basket!'* When Hérault mounted the scaffold, as if in a dream he turned his eyes upwards towards a window, where a mysterious female hand, elegantly clad in a white glove, waved him a last farewell. Camille Desmoulins slipped a bunch of his beloved Lucile's hair into Sanson's hands, charging him with the unenviable task of delivering it to her parents. Once attached to the plank, Camille found the strength to face the supreme moment by shouting 'Lucile!' at the top of his voice as the blade fell. At last it was Danton's turn. There had been fourteen executions in quick succession, and he had to take care not to slip over as he waded across the wooden boards that were swimming with his friends' blood. Looking up at the dripping blade he tried to reassure himself by repeating quietly but audibly the words that Desmoulins had once used to describe the new beheading machine, *'It's only a sabre cut.'* Then in an instant of vulnerability he thought of his young wife, and whispered, *'So my beloved, I'll never see you again!'* then quickly regained his strength, muttering to himself, *'Come on, Danton, no time for weakness!'* In a second all his characteristic arrogance and bravado returned, and, ensuring that he controlled the spectacle to the very last, he turned to the executioner and demanded, *'You show my head to the people, Sanson. It's well worth the trouble.'*

—ooOoo—

There is one last part to this walk, taking you to the two places where all the victims of the *Place de la Révolution* were buried after their executions. However, having just done a very long and tiring walk, you might prefer to defer this for another day - the walk ends in a lovely park so you could combine it with a picnic. Whenever you do it, however, bear in mind that the Chapelle Expiatoire, which is an important visit in this part of the walk, is only open on Thursday, Friday and Saturday between 1 p.m. and 5 p.m., so make sure you choose one of those afternoons. ➡You begin right here in Place de la Concorde, leaving it from the north-east corner of the square via rue Saint-Florentin at the end of rue de Rivoli. This street was opened in 1640 and used to be called *cul de sac de l'Orangerie*, since it ended at the Orangery of the Tuileries Gardens. Number 2 is the Hôtel de Saint-Florentin, which was the residence of the Venetian ambassador until 1793, when he was thrown out and his embassy turned into a saltpetre warehouse. The Italian gentleman should not have had too many regrets, however, for had he stayed, during the year that followed he would have had to put up with the occasional but nonetheless disturbing sight of tumbrils full of doomed prisoners passing by his house as they took a short-cut through rue Saint-Florentin into the *Place de la Révolution*.

The Hôtel de Saint-Florentin was built in 1767 and its first owner was Louis Phélypeaux, duc de la Vrillière et comte de

Saint-Florentin, one of Louis XV's ministers, who was well-known for his generosity in handing out *lettres de cachet*. When Louis XV was on his deathbed it was La Vrillière who had the unenviable task of getting Madame du Barry out of Versailles. He did this in a letter, in which he wrote - with some embarrassment, for he had formerly been on obsequiously good terms with the king's mistress - *'I hope, Madame, that you will be in no doubt as to the pain I feel in being obliged to inform you that you are prohibited to appear at Court, but I must execute the orders of the king.'* La Vrillière was not one to inspire respect, it seems, for his epitaph reads, *'Here lies, despite his rank, a rather common man.'*

This description would not fit the second owner of the Hôtel de Saint-Florentin, who was Jacques Charles, duc de Fitz-James, great-grandson - albeit illegitimate - of James II of England. He sold it in 1784 to the Princesse de Salm-Salm, and in 1792 the Venetian ambassador moved in, until he was obliged to leave the following year so his embassy could be filled up with saltpetre. After the Revolution it was the home of Charles Maurice de Talleyrand, who was a minister under the Empire. It was while living here that Talleyrand turned against Napoléon's foreign policy, secretly supporting Czar Alexander I, and in 1814 he proclaimed the overthrow of Napoléon and the return of the Bourbons. Following this the Czar lived here as Talleyrand's guest for a short while, before moving to the Elysée palace, and it was in the Hôtel de Saint-Florentin that the charter was drawn up establishing a constitutional monarchy in France under Louis XVIII. This house was the last of Talleyrand's many Parisian residences, and he died here in 1838 at the age of 84.

Number 7 rue Saint-Florentin dates from 1761 and was built by an architect named Louis Le Tellier. The house was later owned by his son, Louis-Pierre Le Tellier, who was at the Tuileries Palace, performing his duties as first *valet de chambre* to

Louis XVI, on the fateful night of August 10th 1792 when the Parisian mob broke in and invaded the palace. The royal family were saved by fleeing across the Tuileries Gardens, but the staff remained in the palace, and many of them found themselves at the mercy of the mob, who were so enraged not to find the king and queen that they proceeded to murder their employees instead. Louis-Pierre was among the unlucky ones who were killed that night. This house is now occupied by *Le Médiateur de la République*, whose logo is a woman wearing a red revolutionary bonnet, and the house next door at number 9 was built at the same time and by the same architect as number 7. During the years just before the Revolution number 9 was the office of Louis XVI's War Minister, the Marquis de Ségur, who was imprisoned in *La Force* prison during the Terror, escaped with his life, but then found himself in poverty. Napoléon awarded him a pension in 1800 but he only lived to enjoy it for one year.

Number 11 was built in 1767 and was the property of Caroline Louise Amélie, marquise de Crussol d'Amboise, who with such a name should have been more prudent than to still be living here in 1793, when privilege and aristocracy were being hunted down throughout the city. She was put under house arrest and held prisoner here in her own home for eleven months, until April 1794, when she was taken to the Conciergerie. There her fate became entwined with that of Louis XVI's sister, Madame Elisabeth, who appeared before the Tribunal accused of conspiracy against the nation. But a conspiracy needs accomplices, so sitting with the princess on the benches of the accused were 23 other prisoners, one of whom was the Marquise de Crussol, along with a diverse group that combined the greatest names in France with the most humble. It included a pharmacist, a tailor and a domestic servant, together with no less than five members of the Loménie de Brienne family, whom you met a little while ago on rue Saint-Honoré, and even though they didn't know each other, all 23 prisoners were found guilty of the same conspiracy and condemned to death. The next day, before leaving for the guillotine, Madame Elisabeth was brought into the room where Madame de Crussol and the other 'co-conspirators' were waiting, and on seeing the king's sister the men bowed and the women stopped crying. The princess called to her side one of the Loménie brothers, Martial, the former Archbishop of Sens, and Sanson described how *'after a few minutes of conversation she bowed her head, and we saw Loménie's lips whispering a prayer, without doubt an absolution...that would have been a great consolation for the poor woman.'*

After receiving her absolution she stayed with her fellow prisoners, comforting them, praying with them, and helping them to face their ordeal with courage, including one woman who was sobbing and distraught because her 20-year-old son had to die with her. The next day Martial de Loménie accompanied Madame Elisabeth in the tumbril, and *'talked to her of God who would compensate for her martyrdom,'* to which she replied, *'It's enough that you take care of my safety; charity must not make you forget the care of your own soul.'* The piety and unselfishness of this totally innocent princess was astonishing to all around her, including Madame de Crussol, whose final act at the scene of execution was clearly inspired by it. Her name was the first to be called out when they arrived at the scaffold, and as she made her way to the steps, she stopped before the princess, knelt in respect and asked if she could kiss her before dying. '*With all my heart,*' replied the king's sister, giving Madame de Crussol a reassuring smile. It was the Marquise de Crussol's example that prompted all the remaining prisoners, noble or otherwise, to do the same, each kneeling before the princess and kissing her, and each receiving a smile of solidarity from the royal prisoner as they went to face their final moment.

➡Cross over rue Saint-Honoré, continue straight ahead along rue du Chevalier de Saint-Georges and then left into rue

Duphot, where you will be walking through the former *Couvent des Filles de la Conception*, which stood where rue Duphot was built. One of the nuns, Marie-Françoise Goupil, was 35 years old in June 1790 when city officials visited the convent to interrogate its 24 residents about their future intentions. The nuns were obliged to state whether or not they intended to stay in the convent and continue their devotions, a difficult and dangerous decision, for the new laws were becoming increasingly punitive towards religious orders. 23 resolute voices nonetheless declared their determination to live, and, if needs be, die faithful to their vows. Only one voice remained silent, and that was Françoise, who when pressed for an answer told the officials that she could not make up her mind. The following year, after much reflection, and probably sensing the mounting danger of remaining in any religious institution, she bade farewell to her colleagues and began the task of re-integrating herself into the radically changed society that she found outside the convent walls.

Her life went well at first. For renouncing her vows Françoise was rewarded by the state with a pension of 700 *livres*, and she decided to liven up her social life by joining the 'Fraternal Society of the Two Sexes.' Here she met her Prince Charming in the person of Jacques René Hébert, more well-known as the controversial journalist, *Père Duchesne*. Physically they made an odd couple, for Hébert was small and dapper, while Françoise has been described as resembling an enormous spider! But they seemed to suit each other admirably, and their joy was completed in February 1793 with the birth of a daughter, whom they gave the fashionably Roman name of Scipion-Virginie. Françoise's happiness was short-lived, however, for little more than a year later Hébert was arrested and taken to prison, and at 6 o'clock the same evening, the soldiers returned for Françoise, leaving her baby in the care of a friend. Hébert was executed on March 24th 1794, and his completely innocent wife was tried along with the equally innocent Lucile Desmoulins and guillotined on April 14th.

➡ As you go along the north part of rue Duphot you are walking in the garden of Françoise Hébert's former convent, where she might well have retreated for reflection when making her decision to leave the convent. ➡ At the end of the street turn right on to Boulevard de la Madeleine, cross over immediately and take the fourth road to the left, which is rue de Caumartin. On the corner at numbers 1 and 3 (and 2 Boulevard de la Madeleine) you will see the circular façade, with statues and floral insignia, of the Hôtel Marin-Delahaye. This beautiful residence was built in 1779 for a Farmer-General called Charles-Marin Delahaye, whose son Etienne-Marie Delahaye, also a Farmer-General, was guillotined in May 1794. His other son, Philippe-Antoine, sold the house in 1792 to the Marquis de Giac, an aristocrat who dared to remain in Paris during the Terror, and as a result also ended up under the fatal blade.

During the last few months of his life de Giac rented part of his house to someone who may well have been responsible for sending him to the guillotine, for it was none other than the 'Angel of Death', Antoine Saint-Just. He was the youngest of the revolutionaries and one of the most pitiless in his administration of justice, famously declaring that *'Liberty is a bitch who must be bedded on a mattress of corpses.'* In the spring of 1794 - as the Great Terror was beginning - Saint-Just moved here into an apartment on the second floor, just above the *entresol*, where he had three rooms, an antechamber and a small bathroom. After his previous modest lodgings in rue Gaillon this was luxury for the young deputy, who perhaps took on this new apartment with a view to a change in his personal life, although it remains a mystery who the lady in question would have been. He had finished the affair with his childhood sweetheart, Thérèse-Louise Thorin, and the woman who was most interested in him, Henriette Le Bas, sister of deputy Philippe Le Bas, held little allure for Saint-Just, who found it difficult to adjust to a girl who took snuff. For much of the time that he rented this apartment, Saint-Just was out of Paris on missions at the northern frontier, where he was present at the Battle of Fleurus on June 26th. When on his return to Paris he found the Committee of Public Safety in a state of chaos, he rallied to the support of Robespierre, who was now politically alone but for a small group of faithful supporters. Robespierre was arrested, and Saint-Just went with him, following him the next day to the guillotine. After his execution, when the town officials came here to do an inventory and put the seals on Saint-Just's apartment, they discovered that the young patriot had been living beyond his means, had not paid any rent for some time, and had left his landlord nothing but *'an old blue suit and a wicker basket full of papers.'*

Several years earlier during the last part of 1789 this *hôtel* was home briefly to Saint-Just's political opposite, the Comte de Mirabeau, who, with the rest of the government, had followed the Court to Paris in October. His moment of glory as hero of the Assembly had by now passed its summit, and he soon found himself on the extreme right of the Assembly, nursing his frustrated hopes for a constitutional monarchy. Shortly after coming to Paris the Assembly passed a decree that deprived Mirabeau of the possibility of becoming a Minister, signalling for the great orator a period of relative isolation, both sentimentally and politically, during which time his health began to deteriorate. The Assembly's new headquarters in the Manège were damp and airless, and Mirabeau would often attend sessions wearing a bandage over his eyes to alleviate his persistent and increasingly severe conjunctivitis. In 1790 he began secret negotiations with the king, which would be revealed - after Mirabeau was dead - by the contents of the 'iron wardrobe' discovered in the Tuileries Palace. Mirabeau later moved to rue Chaussée d'Antin, where he died on April 2nd 1791 at the age of 42, disillusioned by political failure and exhausted by a life of debauchery and excess.

➡ Go back to Boulevard de la Madeleine, turn right and immediately right again into rue de Sèze, which was not created until 30 years after the Revolution, but is named after one of Louis XVI's three defence lawyers, Romain de Sèze. ➡ Go all the way to the end of this street, keep straight on past the back of the Madeleine Church on your left (which was an abandoned building-site during the Revolution) and rue Tronchet to your right, named after another of the lawyers who defended Louis XVI. Continue straight ahead into rue Chauveau-Lagarde, also built 30 years after the Revolution and whose name commemorates one of Marie-Antoinette's defence lawyers. ➡ Walk along until you get to the intersection with rue de l'Arcade and stop. A little further down, at the other end of rue Chauveau-Lagarde, is Boulevard Malesherbes, reminding us of the courageous 71-year-old lawyer who came out of retirement to be Louis XVI's third advocate.

Louis XVI, on trial for his life, sits with his lawyers, all of whom suffered as a result of defending the king. One of them went to prison, another had to go into hiding, and the third ended up on the scaffold along with several members of his family. (Courtesy of Musée Carnavalet, Cabinet des Arts Graphiques, Paris)

Why, you may be wondering, has this area become such a memorial to royal defenders? The reason is simple. Two or three blocks away is the site of the *Cimetière de la Madeleine* where the king and queen were buried following their executions, and you are now standing on the route taken by the rickety, bloodstained carts as they rolled away from the Place de la Concorde, carrying the mutilated remains first of Louis XVI, and nine months later of Marie-Antoinette. They left the Place de la Concorde via rue Boissy d'Anglas and came up from the left on rue de l'Arcade, so ➡if you now turn right on rue de l'Arcade you will be joining them on their path towards the royal couple's final resting place. Rue de l'Arcade was home to the young Robespierriest deputy Philippe Le Bas during 1793 when he was courting Elisabeth Duplay, youngest daughter of Robespierre's host on rue Saint-Honore. Their subsequent marriage was truly one made in heaven, which unfortunately was where Philippe went after only one year of domestic bliss.

➡Turn left towards the end of this street on Passage Puteaux and continue straight on into rue Tronson du Coudray. If you are here on a weekend the Passage Puteaux will be closed, and you will have to continue on rue de l'Arcade, turn left on rue des Mathurins, left on rue Pasquier and right into rue Tronson du Coudray, which was created during the Revolution as a short-cut through an old priory. It remained a nameless path until 1820, but later in the century was given its present name commemorating Guillaume Tronson du Coudray, the second of Marie-Antoinette's defence lawyers. ➡At the end of this street you turn right on rue d'Anjou, which leads you directly into Square Louis XVI, but first turn briefly to the left and look at 52 rue d'Anjou. It is now the Compagnie Générale des Eaux, but was formerly known as *Hôtel de Bouville*, where in 1834 there lived a marquis by the name of Alexandre Destutt de Tracy. On May 20th of that year he went to the local town hall to register the death of his father's old friend, Lafayette. The 77-year-old general had died that day a short way down the road, and ➡if you are interested in going later on to see the house where this famous French patriot and American citizen breathed his last, it's at the other end of rue d'Anjou at number 8, very near rue Faubourg Saint-Honoré. Now walk a bit further along to number 48 rue d'Anjou, where there used to be a house bought in 1816 by Louis XVIII from the previous owner, Pierre-Louis Ollivier Desclozeaux, who had been *chef de cuisine* for a marquis. He then became churchwarden for the area as well as being a lawyer for the Paris Parliament, and during the Revolution Desclozeaux was one of the most important residents of the neighbourhood. After the Revolution he bought the *Cimetière de la Madeleine*, which bordered on to his house, and which you will be coming to soon.

➡Go back now, past rue Tronson du Coudray and rue des Mathurins, and continue along rue d'Anjou, stopping when you get to rue Lavoisier on your left. This street was built over the garden of a grand residence called *Hôtel de Chazelles* which used to stand where you now see 59 rue d'Anjou (directly opposite rue Tronson du Coudray). It was the home of a Farmer-General named Jacques Paultz, comte de Chazelles, whose daughter Marie-Anne spent her childhood here before marrying in 1771 at the age of 13. Her bridegroom was a 28-year-old chemist by the name of Antoine Lavoisier, and surprisingly it was a marriage based not on financial interests but on mutual love between the happy couple, who soon became the two most fashionable young people in Paris. Like his father-in-law, Lavoisier was also a Farmer-General, which would prove the downfall of both of them during the Terror, and on May 8th 1794 poor Marie-Anne had the misfortune to lose both her father and her husband to the guillotine. Although generally known as Lavoisier's devoted wife, Marie-Anne was a very intelligent woman who contributed enormously to her husband's work with her translations into French of numerous scientific works, notably one on phlogiston, an element of combustion. Her translation enabled Lavoisier to fully understand the research in this field and eventually disprove it, thus paving the way for his own work on combustion and subsequent discovery of oxygen. Marie-Anne was also an accomplished artist, having studied with Jacques-Louis David, and she put this talent to use by making wonderful drawings of Lavoisier's laboratory, his experiments and scientific instruments.

After ten years as a widow Marie-Anne re-married, this time to an Anglo/American scientist called Sir Benjamin Thompson, Count Rumford, who had fought with the British during the American Revolution, and is credited with a variety of inventions including the Rumford fireplace, the coffee percolator, wax candles and thermal underwear. His title of Count Rumford must have been viewed with a certain degree of suspicion by his fellow citizens in the United States, where titles had been abolished. The French didn't mind, though, and even immortalized the American aristocrat by naming a nearby street after him. Marie-Anne didn't like him quite as much as that, so she divorced him after four unhappy years of marriage, and *rue de Rumford* has since been absorbed by Boulevard Malesherbes. But despite this lapse into European obscurity, Count Rumford has been well-honoured by his fellow Americans, who have transformed his house in Woburn, Massachusetts into a museum. Another well-known figure of the revolutionary period, archeologist Alexandre Lenoir, died in a house on rue Lavoisier in 1839 at the age of 77, after a life heroically spent saving works of art that were threatened with destruction by the Revolution.

Cimetière de la Madeleine.

➡At rue Lavoisier you are standing in the Square Louis XVI, and you can see the back of the Chapelle Expiatoire, which was built in 1826 in memory of Louis XVI and Marie-Antoinette. ➡Go back and turn left on rue des Mathurins then left again on rue Pasquier, which will bring you to the Chapel entrance, and then go into the gardens and sit down amongst the trees to read about this memorial to the king and queen who were brought down by a revolution. Square Louis XVI was built on the site of the former *Cimetière de la Madeleine*, created in 1721, when it was the cemetery serving the parish of *La Madeleine*, and was the burial place of the Swiss Guards who were killed defending the Tuileries Palace on the night the monarchy was overthrown. They were not the first victims of a violent death to be buried here. In May 1770 a huge trench was dug to receive the remains of 133 people who had been suffocated or crushed to death when a massive crowd of Parisians tried to leave *Place Louis XV* (Concorde) and rue Royale after a fireworks display to honour the marriage of Louis XVI and Marie-Antoinette. The cemetery, which received on average 160 bodies each year, stood alone in the middle of an area of marshland, and was surrounded by a wall 2½ metres high.

On January 21st 1793 the headless body of Louis XVI was brought along rue d'Anjou to about this point. The dead monarch was dressed in a white shirt, grey breeches, grey silk hose, and a white piqué coat, and was lying in an open coffin with his severed head placed between his legs. His remains were lowered into a grave 3½ metres deep, dug about three metres from the wall that separated the cemetery from rue d'Anjou. Louis was laid to rest on a bed of quicklime, then another layer was thrown on top of his body, which was then covered with earth while an assortment of vicars, abbots and priests prayed around the grave. Louis's coffin cost 6 *livres* and he'd had to pay 25 *livres* to the gravediggers. A similar ritual was repeated nine months later after the execution of Marie-Antoinette, who also had to pay 25 *livres* to have her own plot and avoid being thrown into a communal grave. What's more, it is said that Sanson had not arranged for a grave to be dug, nor provided for any kind of tomb, and that Joly, the gravedigger, left the queen's remains lying out on the open grass while a hole in the ground was hurriedly prepared for her. Given the hatred towards Marie-Antoinette at the time of her execution, this sad anecdote could well be true, and also lends credence to the story that Marie Grosholtz (Madame Tussaud) took the opportunity to rapidly make a death mask of the dead queen that can still be seen in her London museum.

As well as the king and queen, the *Cimetière de la Madeleine* also contains the remains of numerous other victims of the Revolution, including Charlotte Corday, who murdered Marat and was guillotined on July 17th 1793. Also buried here were the 21 Girondin deputies, executed October 31st of the same year, the revolutionary feminist Olympe de Gouges, the former Duc d'Orléans, Philippe-Egalité, Madame Roland and Louis XV's former mistress the Comtesse du Barry.

Chapelle Expiatoire.

➡ You should now go in and see the interior of the Chapelle Expiatoire, which was designed by architects Hippolyte Lebas and Pierre Fontaine, with a crypt that stands on the exact spot where the two royal victims were buried in 1793. The origins of the chapel go back to the time of the Terror, to March 1794 to be exact, when local residents began lodging complaints about the odours coming from the cemetery, resulting in its closure. Two years later a carpenter named Isaac Jacot bought the entire plot, which was then re-sold by Jacot's creditors in 1802 to Pierre-Louis Desclozeaux, who had been living next door at 48 rue d'Anjou since 1789. In acquiring this land, Desclozeaux, who was a royalist sympathizer, wished to protect the graves of the king and queen from any possible looting or profanation. To this end he restored and heightened the walls of the cemetery, which he then turned into his private garden, creating an arbour of cypresses and weeping willows around the royal graves.

At the Restoration of the monarchy Louis XVIII immediately began a search for the bodies of Louis XVI and Marie-Antoinette, a search that eventually brought him to Desclozeaux's door. Since his house looked out on the cemetery, he had been a witness to the burial of the royal victims, and was able to tell Louis XVIII exactly where they were. This information was confirmed by Pierre Seveste, the grandson of one of the gravediggers, and following their instructions the bodies of the two former monarchs were soon found and exhumed. In gratitude for this invaluable service to the monarchy, Louis XVIII awarded Desclozeaux the *Cordon de Saint-Michel* and a lifetime pension that transferred to his two daughters after his death. Seveste must have been an actor of some kind, for to him and his descendants Louis awarded the privilege of opening a theatre in the suburbs where he could produce plays performed in Parisian theatres. The bodies of the king and queen were exhumed on January 18th and 19th 1815, put in coffins on the 20th, and taken to join their fellow deceased monarchs in the Basilica of Saint-Denis on the 21st - twenty-two years to the day that Louis XVI had been executed. The following January Desclozeaux sold the cemetery and his house to Louis XVIII for the sum of 160,000 *francs*.

Once Louis had possession of the terrain he authorized work to begin immediately on the construction of a monument that would be a permanent symbol of monarchy and a place of expiation, where people could go and pray for the soul of the martyred king. This project was paid for out of the king's personal funds and those of Louis XVI's daughter, the Duchesse d'Angoulême, formerly Madame Royale. The chapel, which was inaugurated in 1826, is built in the style of a classical Greco-Roman temple, and the entrance, with its dark doorway standing behind four Doric columns, gives the impression of a burial vault. It is flanked on each side by a row of nine low arcades resembling a cloister and containing memorials to the Swiss

Guards who were murdered while defending the royal family at the Tuileries Palace on the night of August 10th. Inside the chapel to your right you see a statue by the Monegasque sculptor, François Bosio, showing Louis XVI ascending to heaven, supported by an angel symbolizing Louis's confessor, the Irish priest, Abbé Edgeworth. Marie-Antoinette is also on the left, sculpted by Cortot, who shows her kneeling at the feet of the figure of Religion in the form of the king's sister, Madame Elisabeth. To the right of the statue of Louis XVI is a picture of him, hand on heart, writing his will in the Temple prison. To the left of the statue of Marie-Antoinette, by the stairs, is a picture made of her in 1793 at the Conciergerie, showing her wearing widow's weeds. There are two staircases leading down to the vaulted crypt, where an altar stands on the very spot where for 22 years lay buried the remains of the last king of the *ancien régime*.

You may wonder how they were so sure that the right remains were exhumed and taken to Saint-Denis so long after the king and queen had died. A report at the time describes the digging work, which revealed *'five feet underground...on a bed of lime 10 to 12 inches thick, in a coffin 5½ feet long, containing a large number of bones, including an intact skull: the position that they were placed in indicating that it had been detached from the trunk.'* The fact of a deep grave filled with quicklime left little doubt that it was the king's grave, and in the case of Marie-Antoinette, her identity was confirmed by the fact that her grave contained fragments of the stockings she wore in prison, and *'two rather well-preserved elastic garters.'* The writer Chateaubriand made the rather ridiculous claim to have recognized the queen's smile on the skull that was found in the *Cimetière de la Madeleine*, and although this was no doubt apocryphal and over-dramatic, his account of it in his memoirs makes for rather macabre reading. During the queen's last days at Versailles, Chateaubriand had once seen her walk by with her children on her way to Mass, and as she went past she smiled graciously at him. *'I will never forget that look,'* he writes passionately, *'which would so soon be extinguished. When Marie-Antoinette smiled, the shape of her mouth was so well-delineated that the memory of that smile (a horrifying thing) made me recognize the jaw of the daughter of kings when they discovered the unfortunate woman's head during the exhumations of 1815.'*

➡ On leaving the chapel turn left on rue Pasquier, immediately left again along the side of the chapel on Boulevard Haussmann, then cross over the road and turn right into rue d'Anjou. After complaints from local residents resulted in the closure of the *Cimetière de la Madeleine* in March 1794, the remains of the victims of the guillotine had to be buried somewhere else, and the Paris Commune chose a piece of land running alongside the Farmers-General Wall near the *Barrière de Monceau* to the northwest of Paris. The tumbrils transporting the remains left the *Cimetière de la Madeleine* and continued past it along rue d'Anjou, where you are now joining up with them. Follow them as they cross rue de la Pépinière, continue straight along rue Joseph-Sansboeuf and bear left into rue du Rocher, which leads directly to the new cemetery. This street used to be part of the old route from Paris to Argenteuil, and was scattered with windmills along the section north of rue de Vienne. This northern part of the street was called *rue des Errancis*, meaning 'crippled or maimed people', which rather takes on the air of a sick joke when you learn that the same name was given to the cemetery opened at its north end in 1794, to receive the mutilated victims of the guillotine.

➡ Before crossing rue de Vienne have a look at number 26 rue du Rocher (on the right hand side). The Duc de Chartres - future Philippe-Egalité - had a little house here before moving into his 'folly' in the Parc Monceau, which you will come to later. This street was also home to the painter Pierre Prud'hon, who after the Revolution lived at number 32, where you now see the EDF complex - which I'm sure he would not have approved of. Born in 1758, he was the thirteenth child of a stone-cutter, studied in Paris and Dijon and spent three years in Rome just before the outbreak of the Revolution, which he ardently supported. While in Italy he came into contact with a number of visiting German artists whose influence pushed his style towards romanticism, an influence that is very visible in many of the portraits he did between 1794 and 1796. During this time he had fled Paris, fearing persecution for his Jacobin ideas by Thermidorean reactionaries, and he lived in hiding in Franche-Comté, making his living by painting portraits of important people. Prud'hon returned to Paris during the Directory, where for a while he lived in near poverty, reduced to designing manufacturers' labels and commercial letterheads. When the city architect presented his project for a column on the Pont-Neuf to honour the victories of the Republic, several artists also drew their conception of the proposed obelisk, which in the end was never built. Prud'hon's design was far prettier that the rather heavy official version, and is a good example of the sensuality of his work, even for a military monument. After the turn of the century things got better for Prud'hon, and in 1805 he painted a portrait of Joséphine in her house at Malmaison. He remained in Paris, and died in his house here in 1832 at the age of 65.

Cimetière des Errancis.

➥At the end of rue du Rocher is the Place Prosper-Goubaux, where during the 18th century you found the *Barrière de Monceaux*, one of the customs points in the Farmers-General Wall. The area to the south of this square, more precisely the space formed by the Boulevards Malesherbes and Courcelles and rues Monceaux and Rocher, was the site chosen by the Commune for disposing of the victims of revolutionary justice (see plan). After having all the trees cut down, they opened up several large communal graves where 943 people were buried in

Plan showing position of Cimetière des Errancis over present day streets.

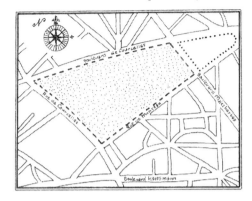

Boundary of Duc d'Orléan Folie de Chartres

Boundary of the Cimetière des Errancis

the 78 days between March 24th and June 9th 1794. In addition to these, another 176 victims were brought here after the coup of 9 *Thermidor*, some during July and August 1794, and the rest in May of the following year.

The list of these victims is long and impressive, for it contains the majority of the most well-known figures of the Revolution. The first were the Hébertists on March 24th, followed on April 5th by Danton and his friends, who included Desmoulins, Fabre d'Eglantine, Hérault de Séchelles and the former Capuchin monk Chabot. A week later Hébert's widow, Françoise Goupil, and Lucile Desmoulins, both executed on April 13, were re-united here with their husbands, and next came the Farmers-General, including scientist Antoine Lavoisier and his father-in-law. Then it was the turn of the Nicolaï family, the Malesherbes family, and the king's sister Madame Elisabeth along with her 'co-conspirators', which included five members of the Loménie family. After 9 *Thermidor* it was Robespierre's turn, along with his younger brother Augustin and his colleagues Saint-Just, Couthon, Hanriot, and the shoemaker Simon who had been in charge of young Louis XVII in the Temple prison. Also among the Robespierrists was the deputy Philippe Le Bas, who was already dead, having shot himself at the Hôtel-de-Ville during the siege the previous night. But they guillotined his corpse anyway. In May 1795 the body of Antoine Fouquier-Tinville, the Public Prosecutor and mainstay of the Revolutionary Tribunal, was brought to the *Cimetière des Errancis* along with fifteen of his colleagues.

After the Revolution the cemetery continued to be used for burials by the first four *arrondissements* of the Right Bank, but by the spring of 1797 the residents were making the usual protests that were always being made in those days by people unfortunate enough to live next to a cemetery. As a result it was closed, the land sold off in small lots, and a public dance hall known as *La Chaumière* flourished on part of the former burial-ground until 1860. When Louis XVIII came to the throne and organized a search for the place where his sister, Madame Elisabeth, had been buried, he contacted the gravedigger, Joly, who told him that he had buried 18 people on the day of her execution, only one of which was a woman. He then went on to say that the bodies, which had all been buried naked, could be found in a certain grave, and that Madame Elisabeth's would be in a certain row. But Joly's credibility - or memory - was put into serious doubt when it was discovered that there had actually been 25 victims that day, and ten of them were women, so Louis called off all plans for exhumation. In the middle of the 19th century the remains of all the victims buried in the *Cimetière des Errancis* were dug up and taken to the Catacombs, where you can still see them today. A few years later apartment buildings went up on the site of the former cemetery, and I sometimes wonder how many of the residents of this fashionable area of Paris realise that they are living on the spot where for half a century lay the remains of the founding fathers of modern France.

La Folie de Chartres.

➥Leave Place Prosper-Goubaux by Boulevard de Courcelles, which corresponds to the covered path that ran alongside both the exterior and interior of the Farmers-General Wall. Between numbers 1-5, which are in Place Prosper-Goubaux, and Boulevard Malesherbes, you are walking along what used to be the northern edge of the *Cimetière des Errancis*. ➥Continue along the boulevard until you get to number 35, where there was another customs house in the Farmers-General Wall known as the *Barrière de Chartres*. It stood between the little village of Monceaux and the present-day rue de Monceau, in the middle of an area of land that was deserted but for a few windmills and hunting sheds. In 1778 the future Philippe-Egalité, then still Duc de Chartres, bought a large piece of this land and turned it into a wonderful park. It became known as the *Folie de Chartres*, a fantasy world created by the landscape architect, Carmontelle, who combined Greek temples, Chinese pagodas and a Tartar marquee with pyramids, pavilions, windmills and obelisks, all hidden away amongst woods, vineyards, rivers, ponds and islands, where marble nymphs danced on fashionable 'antique' ruins. The *Folie de Chartres* was the origin of the present-day Parc Monceau, which is now, however, less than half the size of the duke's original wonderland (see plan).

In 1787 the Farmers-General Wall ran along the northern limit of the *Folie de Chartres*, and in order not to spoil the view from the park of the open countryside on the other side, that section of the wall was replaced by a wide moat. However, as a precaution against goods being smuggled into Paris duty-free by way of this moat, a colonnaded rotunda toll-house was built where customs officers maintained continual observation of the area. This construction is the Rotonde de Chartres that you still see today at the entrance to the park, and which is now a listed national monument. In the upper part of this observation post the Duc de Chartres created a large *salon* with a panoramic view of the Plain of Monceaux - a view that was enjoyed by the many patriots who were invited to the rebel duke's dinner table. The *Folie de Chartres* was later confiscated by the revolutionary government, and after going through various royal owners, at one point being returned to the Orléans family, it was decreed property of the city of Paris in 1852 and has since become the Parc Monceau that we know today. As well as the observation rotunda, there still exists from the Duc de Chartres' original *Folie* a river, a small wood, a hill of rocks with a grotto and a bridge, and a large oval pond surrounded by an arcade of Corinthian columns ➡that you can see as you approach the park along Boulevard de Courcelles. There are also some very old trees, including an elm tree that dates back almost to the Revolution.

The Duke who would be King.

Before losing yourself in the pleasant greenery of the Park Monceau, here is a short but intriguing story about the man who created it. When Paris was in a state of political panic just before the overthrow of the monarchy, a large group of people, including Danton and Robespierre, were invited for a stay at the *Folie de Chartres*. One evening they were all at dinner in the *salon* of the former Duc de Chartres - who was now Duc d'Orléans but had changed his name to the more revolutionary Philippe-Egalité, and whose ambitions regarding the throne were general knowledge in certain circles. By the end of the evening, any doubts that Danton and Robespierre may have had about deposing Louis XVI had disappeared. One of the guests at the dinner table that night was Pierre Louis Roederer, a public prosecutor in Paris, who tells this interesting tale of intrigue and conspiracy.

'I remember that, during a stay at Mousseaux (Monceau) *from the 15th to the 20th of July 1792, one evening we were shown a list written by the hand of the ex-Minister of the Marine,*

Bertrand-Molville, and annotated by that of the queen...There were three-hundred names and five categories: 1. execution; 2. galley-slave; 3. imprisonment for life; 4. exile for life; 5. banishment or a term of imprisonment; and, for all, total confiscation of property. The Dukes of Orléans, Biron and d'Aiguillon, plus sixty members of the Constituent Assembly were in the first category, along with Robespierre, Pétion, and Marat. The second category was scarcely less numerous, and I had the honour to figure among them...The Duc d'Orléans was filled with consternation...Barbaroux, who already saw himself in the galleys for life, asked us what we intended to do. "As for me" he added, "my decision is made: I'm waiting for the Marseillais: once they arrive, I shall put myself at their head, I'll go to the Palace and I'll kill the king and the queen, or I'll die on the steps of the palace staircase."' (Christophe, 1964)

The guests were all terrified, including Robespierre, who rarely accepted invitations to social occasions, and had only done so because of the seriousness of the situation. Curiously, Danton's name did not appear anywhere on the list, giving credence to the generally accepted gossip that he was paid off by the Court. However, he reacted as violently as Barbaroux, especially when the Duc d'Orléans proposed fleeing to England. Roederer describes Danton's response to this. *'I'll slit the throat of any bastard who thinks of clearing off! Dammit, the wine is poured, we have to drink it. Let's not talk rubbish, let's follow Barbaroux and attack the Tuileries: such an act will disarm the royalists: they'll tremble, they'll flee, and our success will be total.'*

Pétion and Danton, both suspecting the National Guard at the Tuileries of being less than patriots, then dreamed up a treacherous scheme for disposing of Mandat, the commander who had replaced Lafayette. They weren't just going to put him out of office; they planned to kill him. *'Dead men don't come back!'* declared Danton. *'This manner of getting rid of poor Mandat astonished several of us who were there,'* continued

Roederer. *'Danton replied: "Better to eat the beast than to be eaten by it." We could have argued that there was no sense in the idea, but we kept quiet. It was therefore resolved that we would attack the Palace as soon as there were enough Marseillais to encourage the people of Paris…One person, to whom we did not cease to promise the crown, furnished what money he had left to pay the men of the 10th of August.'* (Christophe, 1964)

The tale becomes even more treacherous when we learn that the list was in fact a forgery made by the hand of a certain Dupart, commissioned by a henchman of the Duc d'Orléans, and paid for with the favours of the actress Théroigne de Méricourt, who had long been the object of Dupart's fantasies. The *person* referred to was of course the Duc d'Orléans, who, despite embracing the revolutionary cause and changing his name, was widely suspected of wanting to become king. Memories of past events are often distorted in the mind of those relating them, but if Roederer's are correct, the monumental decision to overturn the French monarchy was precipitated by a non-existent situation.

Hopefully by now it is the beginning of a lovely sunny evening, a perfect time to enjoy the Parc Monceau and re-live some of the history of Philippe-Égalité's former folly. ➡When you have finished exploring, you can get the métro (Monceau, line 2) to Etoile (3 stops). There you can get line 1, which goes directly into the city centre.

Robespierre at the Jacobin Club demanding Lafayette's dismissal from his post.
(Authors private collection)

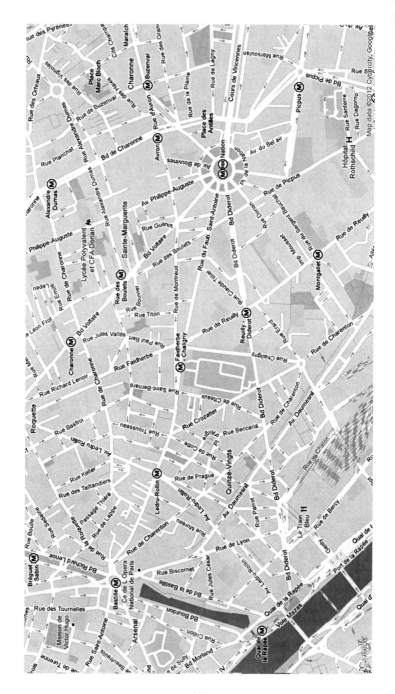

Walk Number Nine

Sans-Culottes, the Terror, and a Path of False Hope

Rue Saint-Antoine - Place de Vosges - Bastille - Faubourg Saint-Antoine - Doctor Belhomme's Clinic - Place de la Nation - The Picpus Cemetery

For four centuries the inhabitants of the Faubourg Saint-Antoine lived in the shadow of the grim mediaeval fortress known as the Bastille. For them it was an ever-present symbol of royal despotism, so it isn't surprising they chose it as a target on July 14th 1789, a day in French history that has never been forgotten. As you visit the Faubourg Saint-Antoine - which unfortunately has been forgotten by many of today's visitors to Paris - you will be walking with the ghosts of hundreds of unsung popular heroes, for this was the cradle of the *sans-culotte* revolution. The sans-culottes of Paris played a vital part in pushing the Revolution towards many of its most radical reforms. But it was a violent process, culminating in a Reign of Terror that saw hundreds of hard-working citizens denounced, often by neighbours or even their own family. People lived in fear of the guillotine, and would do anything - and pay anything - to avoid being sent to the Tribunal, which meant almost certain death. Some did this by becoming 'patients' at Doctor Belhomme's clinic, where money bought safety. But for how long?

Sans-Culottes, the Terror and a Path of False Hope

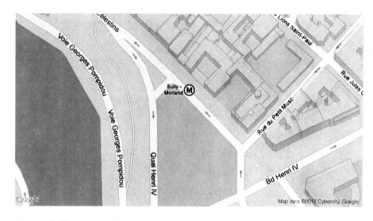

Metro: Sully-Morland

By starting at this point you are able to approach the Bastille by rue Saint-Antoine, and then follow the original path that led to the prison. ➡Take Exit 3 (Bd Henri IV) from the metro, and turn right into rue du Petit-Musc, where on your left at number 1 is the *Hôtel Fieubet* (you will find more information about this lovely house in Walk Number 5). During the Revolution you would have seen the *Couvent des Célestins* at numbers 2 to 8 (look up high to see the numbers), without doubt one of the city's most beautiful convents which was unfortunately demolished at the beginning of the 20th century. Its luxurious gardens and magnificent cloister built around 50 Corinthian columns were constant objects of praise, although the same could not be said for its community of *Célestin* monks, who were so corrupt they were evicted from their convent ten years before the Revolution had even started. The confiscated buildings were meant to be occupied by the Hôtel-Dieu hospital, but remained abandoned until 1791, when they became the new home of *l'Institut National des Sourds-Muets*, created in

1760 by Abbé l'Epée. At that time it was located on rue des Moulins near the Louvre, and was the first free public school for the deaf in the world,

Before moving here, the school had been raised to the status of 'National Institution' in 1789 on the death of Abbé l'Epée, who was replaced by another priest from Bordeaux. His name was Abbé Sicard, a former pupil of l'Epée, who owed his new post to the excellent progress of one of his star students, Jean Massieu. But Sicard's humanitarian activities could not spare him from the dangers of the time. On August 26th 1792 he was accused of sheltering nonjuring priests, arrested and put in the *Abbaye* prison, but the very next day Massieu, who had followed Sicard to Paris, presented a petition to the National Assembly. *'Citizen president, return Sicard to his children: it is he who has taught us what we know; without him we would be like animals. Since he was taken from us, we are sad and full of sorrow.'* This plea must have moved the deputies, for Sicard was released on September 2nd - and not a moment too soon, for that very day the terrible massacres began in the prisons of Paris, some of the worst being at the *Abbaye*. Sicard returned triumphant to his school, which in 1960 changed its name to Institut National de Jeunes Sourds and is now located at 254 rue St Jacques in the 5th arrondissement. For more information you can call them on 01 53 73 14 00 or visit their website: http://www.injs-paris.fr.

➡ Turn left on rue des Lions Saint-Paul, a street full of beautiful houses, many from the 17th century - look out for people going in and coming out, so you can get a glimpse of some of the old cobbled courtyards. At number 3 is an 18th-century house with a fountain in the courtyard dating from the reign of Louis XV, while number 8 echoes the street name with its old lion's head that is a bit broken but still lovely, and an old lantern that also has a lion on it. Go down to number 12, a classic Louis XIII *hôtel* that has the date 1675 engraved on the right-hand façade of the courtyard, although the house is actually older than that. During the height of the Terror this elegant residence was transformed into a prison for people accused of forging *assignats*. They would not have stayed long, however, for theirs was a crime that was shown little mercy by the Tribunal - perhaps because so many of the false notes were produced in England - and the perpetrators hardly ever escaped the guillotine.

➡Go back and turn left on rue Beautreillis, a name from 1556 recalling the trellises of the *Hôtel Saint-Pol* which was built on the site of this street for the young Charles V when he returned from exile in 1358 after the death of Etienne Marcel. Still traumatized by the murder of two counsellors at his palace, he preferred to live in this new *hôtel* that held no unpleasant memories and where he could sleep in security. It was more a village than a house, occupying the entire space between present-day rue du Petit-Musc, rue Saint-Paul, rue Saint-Antoine and the Seine, and it comprised several buildings, gardens, orchards, fishponds and even a menagerie with lions - which is probably how rue des Lions Saint-Paul got its name. But by the time it was demolished by François I in 1543 it had become very dilapidated, having been unoccupied for nearly a century.

At number 6 of this street is a rather wonderful doorway, standing all alone looking severely in need of a house - and a clean. Until 1961 a wonderful 17th-century *hôtel* stood behind this entrance, and was home to an impressive succession of counsellors, magistrates and other high-level dignitaries. The last of these was Anne-Louis Pinon, Marquis de Saint-George, who during the Revolution was invited to 'share with the Nation' his numerous properties, including this one - no doubt as a punishment for the emigration of his son, who had fought with the royalists. The Marquis was lucky, for people were guillotined for less at the time, and he even survived to get his property back when Napoléon came to power. But the name on the doorway does not belong to any of these illustrious men of the *ancien régime*. Jean-Louis Raoul was a file manufacturer from the Aveyron region, who bought the house in 1810 from the Pinon de Saint-George family and set up his file factory in the gardens. The house cost him 28,000 *livres*, but he had to pay another 4,000 for the house's magnificent collection of Venetian mirrors. This was a lot of money, but I am sure Jean-Louis felt it was worth it, for the mirrors were specially manufactured with mercury and considered precious even at the time. It is very sad to know that these wonderful mirrors were still intact in the house when it was demolished, along with some wood panels containing paintings attributed to the French rococo artist, Jean-Antoine Watteau. The only two things that survived are an ancient clock, known as the *horloge des dauphins*, which is now on the wall of the new apartment building - and this lovely old doorway. A local resident named Michel Cribier has written a wonderful history of this lost mansion, so if you read French you should check it out at www.cribier.net/Hotel-Raoul. It contains some marvellous photos of the interior of the house just before its demolition, and Mr Cribier really brings to life the *hôtel* that stood behind this solitary relic of a bygone age.

There are some houses on this street that would have been considered old even at the time of the Revolution, like the one at number 7, hidden unfortunately behind high walls, which was built in 1596 and is a perfect example of a 16th-century Parisian bourgeois residence. Its original wells are still in the courtyard, and it even has a trellis covered with vines that you can see growing over the top of the wall to the right. Number 9, which is badly in need of repair on the first floor, and has had some of its upstairs windows filled in, was also built in 1596 and used to belong to a magistrate. The house opposite at number 10, dating from 1640, was owned during the 17th century by the family of the Prince de Monaco, and later belonged to Valton, Louis XVI's wine steward.

A sense of the past permeates much of rue Beautreillis because of the age of its houses, like number 11, built in 1635, and 16 and 20, both of which are 17th-century. The tiny little house at number 16 was built on the site of a Renaissance indoor tennis court, and during the latter part of the 18th century was owned by Jean-Baptiste Machault d'Arnouville, Controller-General of Finances under Louis XV. His attempts to reform direct taxation by the reduction of fiscal privileges brought the rage of the aristocracy upon him, but it was falling out of favour with the king's favourite mistress, Madame de Pompadour, that led to his disgrace and exile from Court in 1757. When Louis XVI succeeded to the throne, his first choice for chief minister was Machault, who had by then acquired the nickname *acier poli* which means either 'polished steel' or - a more subtle possibility - 'polite steel' - it translates either way, but was probably the latter, for Machault was known for being cold but courteous. Despite his 73 years, he was still open to new ideas, professed to be a Jansenist, and had far too much character for Louis XVI's aunt Adélaïde, who successfully pushed her wavering nephew into giving the post to Maurepas, a less provocative and more compliant candidate. Machault's personality also attracted the suspicion of certain revolutionary judges, who had him arrested during the Terror, and left him to die in prison at the age of 93.

The *Hôtel de Charny* at number 22 is a good example of how the times changed over the 18th century. It was built in 1676 as the home of a marquis, but little more than a hundred years later it belonged to a clerk, who sold it just before the Revolution to a man named Lombard, a building contractor who was in the business of paving the city streets. Lombard was probably able to afford this house by economising on the quality of his work, for Parisian cobblestones were notorious at the time for their dangerously irregular shape and the pools of muddy water that formed in their concave surface. When he died in 1792 Lombard left the house to his daughter, whose lawyer husband was Joseph Coffinhal, the brother of Jean-Baptiste Coffinhal, infamous vice-president of the Revolutionary Tribunal. This lesser-known Coffinhal was also a Tribunal judge, and during the Directory was among those who sent the Robespierrist conspirator Babeuf to the guillotine. But he moved with the times, avoiding the fate of his brother, who was executed after 9 *Thermidor*, and by the time of the Empire Joseph Coffinhal had become Baron Dunoyer.

➥When you get to rue Saint-Antoine you will be opposite rue de Birague, leading to the Place de Vosges, and you are now going to take a look at this elegant and historic square built for Henri IV in 1605 and so much admired by all visitors to Paris. ➥Cross over rue Saint-Antoine and walk straight down rue de Birague and into Place de Vosges. For almost a century this square was the heart of the aristocratic quarter of Paris, and thus a centre of gallantry and intrigue where duelling was a regular occurrence, despite being officially forbidden by Richelieu. It was also the scene of sumptuous feasts and grandiose theatrical presentations, beginning with the square's inauguration in April 1612, when the celebrated Queen Margot had a special moveable platform constructed that could roll her as close as possible to the ballet that was performed in the gardens . Directly in front of you as you walk down rue de Birague you can see, above the entrance to the square, the King's Pavilion, which was sold in 1799 as national property. The Place de Vosges was called *Place Royale* until the Revolution, when it was re-named successively *Place des Fédérés and Place de l'Indivisibilité.* During this time the square was levelled off so the National Guard could do manoeuvres, and in July 1792 a military recruitment centre was set up, then replaced the following year by an arms production workshop. It was the presence of a military installation in the middle of the square that saved the decorative wrought-iron railings from being pillaged and used as pikes during the *journées révolutionnaires*. This was a temporary grace, however, for Louis-Philippe later succeeded in getting them all removed, for reasons unknown to anyone but him, resulting in the rather more ordinary ones you see now. The square retained the name *Place de l'Indivisibilité* until 1799, when it was promised that the first regional department to pay all its taxes could give its name to a square in the capital. It thus became Place de Vosges.

This square had no celebrated revolutionary residents, although there were two families of notable victims, one of whom lived at number 9 (to your left as you enter the square). The doors are usually open and you can go into the courtyard and look at the art galleries that now occupy the ground floor of these lovely buildings. At the same time you can see the beauty and splendour in which this family lived. Their name was de Nicolay, and three of them were guillotined during the Terror for a range of 'crimes', not least of which was belonging to a family that had produced one of the most eminent magistrates of the *ancien régime*. He was Jean-Aymard de Nicolay, who died here in 1785, unaware that he was leaving his descendants to pay with their lives for the privileges he had enjoyed. His son, Aymard-Marie-Charles Nicolay, who like his father was President of the *Chambre des Comptes*, was guillotined at the age of 47 on July 7th 1794, and two days later his 24-year old son Aymard-Marie-Léon suffered the same fate. Another family member, 57-year old Aymard-Charles-François de Nicolay, also perished on the scaffold, for the double crime of emigrating, then coming back and offering to defend Marie-Antoinette. At the same time their house was confiscated as national property, but returned in 1795 to one of the surviving family members, Aymard Théodore de Nicolay, who despite the fate of his relatives still had the courage to use his title of marquis.

In this pretty courtyard of the Nicolay house you can see a delightful statue of a rather mischievous looking boy being fed grapes by an even more mischievous looking cherub. There is a restaurant on the ground floor called L'Ambroisie, opened in 1985 by Bernard Pacaud, who is considered one of the greatest chefs in Paris, maybe in all of France. The decor is sober but refined, and the cuisine, as the restaurant's name suggests, is worthy of the gods, and includes such specialities as *marjolaine de foie gras* (goose liver, truffles, and celery), and *marinière* of sea bass with rosemary and artichokes. The dishes change with the seasons, so there might be Breton lobster or turbot, and truffles abound. It is strictly *à la carte* and is costly, but not only will you be enjoying the best of French gastronomy and a magnificent selection of wines, you might well be dining with the ghost of France's greatest magistrate and his less fortunate descendants. (Reservations: 01 42 78 51 45).

Between 1776 and 1790 the house at number 4 (to your right as you enter the square) had a tenant who is worthy of mention, for he was accused in 1789 of plotting to kidnap Louis XVI and kill Bailly and Lafayette. His name was Thomas de Mahy, known as the Marquis de Favras, an invented title that he took from his native town of Favras near Blois. In 1789, after several years of adventure that included a marriage with the daughter of a prince, he arrived in Versailles, where he immediately made attempts to ingratiate himself with the king's ministers. But they were otherwise engaged in the turbulent spring of 1789, and Favras could find no-one ready to pay any heed to his opportunistic offers of advice. So after the storming of the Bastille he decided to make his fortune by spiriting the king away from the revolutionary tempest that was brewing. Louis's brother, the Comte de Provence, known as Monsieur, was a good listener, and provided an interested ear for Favras's extravagant scheme, as a result of which Monsieur negotiated a loan of 2 million *francs* from bankers Schaumel and Sartorius, to finance the raising of the necessary troops. Favras was so pleased with the success of his plan so far that he couldn't help talking about it just a little too much, and word got to Lafayette that he and Bailly were both to be murdered as part of this daring coup. Favras was arrested on Christmas eve of 1789, having been denounced by some officers to whom he had confided his secret, although some say it was the banker Schaumel who betrayed Favras, perhaps hoping to exonerate himself from the affair.

Overnight a glut of posters appeared all over Paris accusing Monsieur of stirring up a plot for the escape of the royal family and the assassination of Lafayette and Bailly, all with the aim of installing himself as regent. When questioned Favras made no mention of the king's brother, believing that Monsieur would feel the weight of *noblesse oblige*, and protect him. But Monsieur did no such thing. He went in person to defend himself before the Commune, wearing his most sombre outfit, and declaring with his winning smile and a manner most sincere that he had never set eyes on the Marquis de Favras. As for the 2 million borrowed from Schaumel, he had naturally taken the loan to cover his personal expenses, a lie that was given credibility by his reputation as one of the biggest spenders in the royal family. Favras never knew who his betrayer was, for the judge refused to disclose it, and throughout the trial Favras continued to believe that Monsieur would intervene to save him. But help never came, and he was executed in the *Place de Grève* on the evening of February 19th 1790 - on the gallows rather than the more noble death by decapitation. As the crowd pressed around the scaffold, which was lit up by several flaming torches, one of the onlookers shouted to the unfortunate Favras, '*Jump, Marquis!*' Favras may have been a bogus aristocrat, but it was he who behaved like a gentleman at the end, taking the identity of his accomplices to his commoner's grave, while Monsieur, the Comte de Provence - second highest of French nobility - turned out to to be rather less than noble.

At number 2 was the second family of notable victims living in the Place de Vosges. In 1786 this house became the property of the widowed Marquise de La Vieuville, who rented it to Louis Bruno, Comte de Boisgelin, a royal musketeer and member of the strongly monarchist Breton nobility. He was married to Marie-Cathérine Stanislas de Boufflers, a lady-in-waiting to Louis XVI's aunt, Madame Victoire, and the de Boisgelins were still living here in 1789, when the count represented the nobility at the Estates-General. Despite his antipathy towards the Revolution, Louis Bruno remained in Paris but did his best to keep out of the limelight. He should have followed the example of his older brother, Jean-de-Dieu Raymond, Archbishop of Aix, who was unwilling to take the constitutional oath imposed on the clergy and emigrated to England in 1792. The count's younger brother, Pierre Marie Louis, was an officer in the king's army, and after commanding a counter-revolutionary regiment, he too emigrated with his troops to Corsica. But Louis Bruno heedlessly remained until 1794, when he and his wife were arrested and taken to the Luxembourg prison. They were both guillotined on July 7th 1794 as part of the first 'batch' of 68 victims from this prison, which also included their neighbour from number 9, Aymar-Charles-Marie Nicolaï. The count's two cousins were also victims of the Revolution. One was a soldier, Gilles-Dominique, guillotined at the age of 40 four days before the count and countess, and the other was an abbot who was murdered during the massacres of September 1792. You can go in and look at part of the home of the unfortunate de Boisgelin family, for there is an art gallery on the ground floor as well as a restaurant at number 2*bis* called La Place Royale. Here you can sit either in the old-world ambiance of the interior or on the lovely terrace under the arcades, and enjoy traditional cuisine and very friendly service.

➡Go back along rue de Birague and turn left on rue Saint-Antoine, which is built on top of the solidly paved surface of the original Roman road that led from Paris to Melun. It was always an important street, being the main thoroughfare of the Marais linking the centre of the city with the Saint-Antoine gate and the adjoining faubourg. By the mid-18th century rue Saint-Antoine was a bustling hive of activity, with eight schools, two fire stations, two coach hiring points, and one of the capital's 36 mail boxes, where three times a day you could drop off your letters and packages. There were also five *caffés* where you could sample the fashionable new black brew from Italy, play a game of chess, catch up on the latest news or find a sympathetic ear for your problems - unless of course you happened to be a soldier or a domestic servant, or simply a loud, flashy type, in which case you weren't allowed in. During the Revolution rue Saint-Antoine was part of the second 'route of the condemned' between the Conciergerie and the scaffold, and during June and July 1794 it witnessed the passage of endless processions of tumbrils. The first 73 victims of this frightening period, known as the Great Terror, stopped at the Place de la Bastille, where the guillotine stood for three days, while the remaining 1,306 continued along to Place de la Nation.

➡Stay on the north side of the street for the moment and walk along to Impasse Guéménée. Go into the courtyard of number 4, apparently once referred to as *Cul-de-Sac de Ha Ha*, on account of its merry atmosphere, and it certainly lived up to this nickname when I was there. I had a delightful time chatting and joking with one of the residents and M. Delranc, locksmith and specialist in metal joinery who has a wonderful workshop at the far end of the courtyard. If you speak French you should go and say hello and I'm sure he will be happy to talk to you about the house, the street and the area in general. In the courtyard of number 4 is an 18th-century building which is all that remains of the *Couvent des Filles-de-la-Croix*. To the left as you enter you can still see the beautiful stone staircase of this residence, and to the right is one of the original convent walls. Also on the right you would have found the entrance to the convent, where the novices slept in two rooms on the second floor, and their initiated sisters prayed in solitude in cells under the mansard roof. On the first floor were two apartments for paying *pensionnaires*, while the ground floor was occupied by the convent library, which at the outbreak of the Revolution contained over 1,300 religious volumes. The sisters here belonged to a teaching order, and in 1789 had 25 pupils paying up to 400 *livres* to live in the residential buildings. In addition to the boarders, the sisters also received day students, who were divided into two groups and educated free of charge, under conditions of work that would never be accepted by today's teachers. One class consisted of no less than 80 pupils who were taught to read, write and count, while the other was a nursery class containing 40 very small children. When the convent was closed by the revolutionary government, the nuns left voluntarily after the women of the Faubourg Saint-Antoine threatened to publicly whip them, as they had already done to their fellow sisters across the road at the the *Couvent de la Visitation Saint-Marie* (you'll come to this later). The *Couvent des Filles-de-la-Croix* was declared national property and sold in 1797 to a hosier from rue Saint-Honoré for 165,900 *livres*. There is not a lot left of this once lovely convent, but another of the buildings can still be seen in the courtyard of 8*ter* if there is no entry code stopping you. But even if you can't see that, look at the wall of number 8, where you can still see the outline of a doorway that was one of the original convent gates.

➡Cross back to the other side of rue Saint-Antoine where, at number 21 on the corner of rue du Petit-Musc, you can see the lovely old *Hôtel d'Ormesson*. It dates from 1617 and got its name in 1759 from the owner, Marie-François de Paule Le Fèvre d'Ormesson. In 1775 it was inherited by his son, Henri-François, a Controller-General of Finances who refused a job as mayor of Paris when it was offered to him in 1792.

Perhaps he lacked ambition, but more probably he was scared - and with good reason - of the consequences of power at such a turbulent time. But despite trying to keep a low profile he was still imprisoned during the Terror, then released after 9 *Thermidor*, eventually regaining possession of his house, which was sold in 1812 to a bookseller called Favart. After destroying the beauty of the façade by various additions to the building, Favart turned the *hôtel* into a school from which has grown the present Ecole des Francs-Bourgeois. The right and left hand wings of the building on either side of the entrance have been cleaned and restored, giving you an idea of how beautiful the house must have been, with its gilded balconies and pretty red brick façade. Unfortunately the central building of the *hôtel* is very neglected and almost black with dirt, apparently due to the criteria for restoration, which require a building to be original. The central building has had additions made to it, including those made by Favart, which disqualifies it, but if these are removed, then finances can be authorized to complete the restoration. Let's hope it happens! In the meantime, you can go and look at the interior courtyard of this old *hôtel*, where to your right as you enter is a wonderful old turret. Before going in, however, you should first go to the *Acceuil* (to your left as you go through the entrance arcade) and let them know you are there to look at something in this book.

At number 17 is a Protestant church, L'Eglise Réformé de Sainte-Marie, all that is left of the *Couvent des Filles de la Visitation Sainte-Marie*. This convent was built in 1632, and its first chaplain was Saint Vincent de Paul, who stayed here until 1660, by which time he was almost 80. The convent owned many of the buildings between here and the Bastille, including several of the shops at the end of the road in front of the prison, and much of this property was damaged during the storming of the Bastille. When the Civil Constitution of the Clergy was introduced, the convent became national property and was sold, and the Mother Superior, Anne-Madeleine Chalmette, was expelled along with her 53 nuns, who were publicly whipped in front of the church by a group of women from *Les Halles*. The same humiliating punishment was later meted out to the revolutionary feminist actress, Théroigne de Méricourt, who opened a republican club in this church after its closure. Giving it the provocative name of *Popular Club of Armed Women*, she hoped to use it to mobilize the women of the Faubourg Saint-Antoine. But she hadn't reckoned on the reaction of their husbands, who, while being good patriots and believing in liberty and equality, preferred their wives to stay at home. Théroigne had to be rescued from an angry crowd of these disgruntled husbands by local police agents and a dozen national guards, who escorted her to a carriage and made her promise never to bring her disruptive ideas to the neighbourhood again.

After this the church was turned into a warehouse for confiscated books. Some of them were piled up in front of the coat of arms of a family named Coulanges, hiding it from view and thus enabling it to escape the subsequent pillages - and it's still there today. These pillages were started in March 1793 by an opportunistic builder named Scellier, and lasted for four months, during which time the church was emptied of all its paintings, copper and marble, including the altar and the marble floor. After the Revolution the nuns tried, unsuccessfully, to get their convent back, and in 1796 the entire complex was sold for 168,000 *francs*, then demolished to make way for the opening of rue Castex. The only part of the convent that escaped this destruction was the Chapel, which in 1803 became the Protestant church that you see here today. There is a guided tour every other Sunday at 4 p.m., when you can visit the interior of the church and see the revolutionary phrygian bonnet that is sculpted on the lintel of one of the side doors - one of the church's only two remaining souvenirs of the Revolution. The other is outside on the façade in rue Saint-Antoine - an inscription saying *'laws and acts of the public authority.'* This church has recently been restored, revealing it in all its former beauty.

➡Approaching Place de la Bastille you pass rue Lesdiguières, a narrow street that bordered the prison entrance. As the enormous crowd poured toward the Bastille on July 14th 1789 some of the attackers came into this street and tried to enter the fortress by climbing over the wall. There was already a *boulangerie* on the corner even then - in fact there has been a bakery at number 11 rue Saint-Antoine since 1776, so this must be one of the oldest in the country and probably experienced all the revolutionary turmoil associated with the price of bread. Here you would have seen angry queues, rioting and even looting, for bread shortages were at the heart of much of the violence that marked the beginning of the Revolution, and it was lack of bread, in fact, that caused the eventual defeat of the Faubourg Saint-Antoine as a revolutionary force. Poor harvests had caused the price of the standard 4lb loaf to soar from 9 to 12 *sous* at the end of 1788, and rumours of speculation and corruption spread like wildfire in the long queues that became a daily sight outside the city's bakeries. People frequently spent the whole day waiting at the baker's door without receiving anything, and violence became more and more common. Even the royalist press sympathized. *'Food was snatched from the hand...workshops were deserted; workmen and craftsmen wasted their time in quarrelling...and, by losing working time in queuing, found themselves unable to pay for the next day's supply. This bread, moreover, seized with such effort, was far from being of good quality: it was generally blackish, earthy and sour. Swallowing it scratched the throat, and digesting it caused stomach pains.'* (Cobb, 1988). The writer of this article then went on to describe the *'beautiful bread'* that he had seen served *'in great abundance'* to the ministers and deputies at Versailles, *'delivered by the bakers themselves'*. It's not surprising that the women from the Faubourg

Saint-Antoine who went to bring the king and queen back to Paris in October 1789 set off shouting *'Let's get the baker and the baker's wife!'*

When the king was brought back to the capital, with him came 60 wagons of grain and flour, and everyone thought this would mean cheaper bread. But despite the establishment of a price maximum, the queues and pillaging persisted, while repeated issue of paper money led to serious inflation. The municipal authorities in Paris tried to keep prices as low as possible by paying the difference between the real price and the imposed price, provoking harsh comments in the Convention from provincial deputies who were furious to see Parisians paying less for bread than their rural constituents. Apparently indifferent to the hungry people waiting at their doors, many bakers would keep back part of their grain, bake it in secret and sell the loaves at inflated prices to the rich. As a result, hoarding became a crime, and the fate of a farmer called Thibaut served as a warning to those considering speculation. When his farm was searched, it was discovered that he had not only been hoarding grain, he had even been feeding it to his horses. After his arrest Thibaut tried to bribe the judges, who were unmoved by his offer of money, calling him a coward who was *'more vile than the gold you lay before us.'* He was guillotined on January 21st 1794.

After the fall of Robespierre bread shortages produced more bloodshed. Another bad harvest caused bread to become more and more scarce and expensive, culminating the following May in the revolt known as the *journées de Prairial* when the Convention was invaded by hundreds of women demanding bread. Violence broke out, a deputy was murdered, and troops were sent to suppress the Faubourg Saint-Antoine, which quickly surrendered for lack of real leadership. When the *sans-culottes* began their revolution it was because they were hungry for bread, and when it ended they were still hungry. Nowadays there is no violence or looting at number 11 rue Saint-Antoine, and their bread is delicious - but you may still have to queue for it!

Before the demolition of the Bastille there was a row of quaint two-storey houses lining rue Saint-Antoine between the *Couvent des Filles de la Visitation Sainte-Marie* (now the Protestant church you just saw) and the entrance to the prison. Of these little houses, which originally belonged to the convent, only one remains at number 7, and is now occupied by a restaurant. Throughout the 18th century this house belonged to the governor of the Bastille, who rented it out, but by the outbreak of the Revolution the Bastille guards were using it as a place to change into their uniforms on their way to work. It was conveniently situated just next to the *Magasin des Armes* (see plan of *La Prise de la Bastille*), where they probably also stopped off, once in uniform, to pick up their weapons. If you look at the plan you'll see that this arms depot stood behind the house, so after getting in uniform, maybe they were able to leave the house from a rear entrance and go straight into the depot to get their weapons. After Governor de Launay surrendered, several Bastille guards were taken prisoner, but some of them never got to the Hôtel-de-Ville for they were massacred along the way. The first one to die was Joseph Miray, who was killed with a pike under these very windows, right outside the house at number 7, where he had changed into his uniform a few hours earlier.

Later on this house was known for a long time as *A la Friture* (referring to the crackling sound of fish frying), so it's appropriate it should still be a restaurant, and until very recently it was a very atmospheric place called La Bastoche, a slang word for *Bastille*. I was very sad to find that it had closed, since the two women who ran it, Lise and Sylvie, had really managed to maintain the historical feeling of the house and its association with the Bastille. But things change quickly in Paris, and it has now become Le Comptoir de Maître Kanter, a name evoking the famous Berlin brewer who brought German beer to Paris, Alsace-Lorraine, Belgium and even North Africa and America. Here you can enjoy the cuisine of Alsace, and their particular speciality, *Flammekueche*, a delicious *tarte flambée,* covered with cream, onions and bits of bacon. It comes with several different toppings, including tuna, goat cheese and smoked salmon, and looks rather like a pizza. They also serve sauerkraut (*choucroute*) and a variety of other meat, fish and pasta dishes, as well as offering a fixed-price menu at 14.90 euros and a children's menu at 5.50 euros. If you have a sweet tooth, try one of their *Flammekueches sucrés*, with banana and chocolate, or apple and cinnamon. Apart from the excellent food, it's also worth eating here to see the interior of the house. With its low ceilings and lovely old beams, you'll be transported back to the 18th century, and if you have a table by the window on the first floor, you'll have a good view of the opposite side of the street as it widens into rue des Tournelles. This was where you had to turn off if you were leaving the city by the Saint-Antoine gate, and you can still see there the simple but attractive façade of 8*bis* rue Saint-Antoine on the far corner. This house was built at the same time as the Bastille, and between the second floor windows and the roof are circular mouldings that were added in the 17th century. As well as the nice view, the upstairs rooms of Le Comptoir de Maître Kanter also have old beamed ceilings and give the feeling of not having changed since the Bastille was stormed. So don't let your visit to Paris pass without eating here, for as well as the *Flammekueche* experience, it gives you the chance to see inside the only house that now remains of those little houses that formed part of the Bastille neighbourhood.

The Bastille.

➧Standing on the corner of rue Jacques-Coeur outside the bank at number 5 you are on the site of the Bastille entrance where the invading mob of Parisians entered the prison from rue Saint-Antoine on July 14th 1789 (see the plaque - look up, it's very high on the wall). Looking from here into the Place de la Bastille, directly in front of you at the end of rue Saint-Antoine was the outside wall of the prison, and beyond that the walls of the *Tour de la Liberté*, one of the prison's eight towers, part of which you can still see in Square Henri-Galli. When you walk up towards the end of the street you can see the position of these walls traced on the road. Despite the presence of the Bastille, this end of rue Saint-Antoine was a lively place, partly due to its proximity to the city gate, which saw an endless stream of traders and travellers. It was invariably blocked with various forms of public transport on offer to the new arrivals in the city, who could hire a horse-drawn cab here at any time of day or night for 20 *sols* an hour. If they were not in a hurry there were sedan-chairs pulled along by a man - one called a *brouette*, which was rather like a wheelbarrow, and another more elegant version known as a *vinaigrette*. At the end of the street, against the prison wall, was a row of two-storey houses, built in 1643 for the *Couvent des Filles de la Visitation Sainte-Marie*, but by 1789 they were the property of the Bastille and rented out by the governor to a variety of tradesman. Here you could find without any problem a café, a cobbler, a grocer or a potter, you could buy sweets for your children, buttons for your overcoat, and you could even get a shave and a haircut. The prison wall turned this end of rue Saint-Antoine into a *cul-de-sac*, so it must have been very congested, for as well as the shops, pedestrians, travellers and various forms of transport, there were always several vehicles filled with water standing in the street, at the ready for the city fireman who were stationed in the first courtyard of the Bastille.

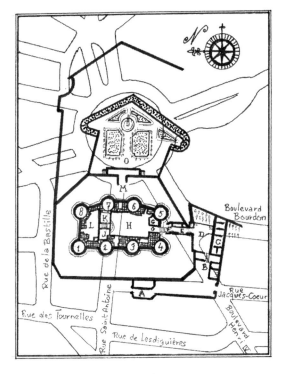

Plan showing position of the Bastille over present day streets.

A Cour du Passage
B Premiers pont-levis
C Hôtel du gouverneur
D Cour du Gouverement
E Avenue conduisant au fort
F Ponts-levis du fort
G Corps de garde
H Grande cour intérieure
I Bâtiment de Pétat-major
J Anciennes cuisines
K Salle du Conseil
L Cour du Puits
M Ancien chemin du bastion
N Escalier du jardin
O Jardin du Bastion

1 Tour du Puit
2 Tour de la Liberte
3 Tour de la Bertaudiere
4 Tour de la Baziniere
5 Tour de la Comté
6 Tour du Trésor
7 Tour de la Chapelle
8 Tour du Coin

➥You are now going to take the path of the 'Conquerors of the Bastille.' As you go around you can follow the route on the plan, which shows the exact position of the fortress superimposed on the present-day streets. To gain access to the prison you had to ➥turn right off rue Saint-Antoine through a huge doorway leading into a courtyard called *Cour du Passage* which roughly corresponds with the present-day rue Jacques-Coeur, although, as you can see on the plan, the first part of it went directly through the bank! To your right was the arms depot, barracks housing the prison guards, and lodgings for wounded soldiers, while along the left-hand side you saw the brightly coloured awnings of several little shops that provided prisoners with some of the 'extras' to which most of them were accustomed - for contrary to its mythical reputation, the Bastille was the most luxurious of prisons. ➥Just before you get to the end of rue Jacques-Coeur, stop and look at the engraving in this book showing the storming of the Bastille (you will find this picture on the next page). You are now standing almost exactly where the cannon is standing in the picture, and between the

Storming of the Bastille. This is in the *Cour du Passage*, the first courtyard the crowd entered from rue Saint-Antoine. A shop has been knocked down, giving a view of the moat, and beyond the moat is the path leading to the main drawbridge, where crowds of people are trying to get into the prison. (Author's private collection)

crowd and the actual prison you can see the little shops that sold 'extras' to the Bastille prisoners.

Towards the end of this passage it widened into a large courtyard known as the *Cour de l'Avancée*, which stretched across Boulevard Henri IV at its junction with rue Jacques-Coeur. ➡Here the crowd of invaders turned left and saw directly in front of them the first drawbridge, called *l'Avancée*, which stood where you now see the shoe shop Emeric on the opposite corner at 46 Boulevard Henri IV. As they surged forward, armed with with an assortment of pikes, scythes and razors, one of their leaders, Louis Tournay, cried out in fury, '*I want the Bastille!*', and proceeded to shatter the chain of the drawbridge with an axe. ➡The crowd followed Tournay across the bridge into the *Cour du Gouverneur*, which was where Boulevard Bourdon meets Place de la Bastille. To their right was the Governor's residence, and directly ahead, on the opposite (eastern) pavement of the Boulevard Bourdon, was a terrace planted with trees. ➡As you go across the first part of the crossing that leads towards the middle of the road, you will be walking through the *Cour du Gouverneur*, and the island in the middle is roughly at the entrance to a narrow path about ten yards long leading to a second drawbridge. This path corresponds to the second crossing that leads you into the Place de la Bastille. As you arrive at the pavement on the other side of this crossing you will be on the site of the second drawbridge that gave access to the *Grande Cour*, principal courtyard of the prison. Nowadays the crossing leads much more invitingly to two cafés There is the Lounge Bar, which has a good selection of beer, and looks out directly on to the site of the second drawbridge, part of the moat, and beyond the moat to the governor's courtyard where most of the combat took place. ➡Alternatively, a few steps round the corner is the Café Français, which has a large terrace situated in the southern half of the *Grande Cour* of the prison. Choose the view you want, then sit down and have a drink or lunch while reading about the legendary Bastille and the dramatic events that took place here over two centuries ago.

THE MYTH OF THE BASTILLE.

'Who knows what has gone on in the Bastille, who it imprisons, who it has imprisoned? But how can we write the history of Louis XIII, of Louis XIV and of Louis XV, if we do not know the history of the Bastille? That which is most interesting, most curious, most remarkable took place within its walls. The most interesting part of our history is thus hidden from us for all time: nothing more is revealed by this abyss than by the silent void of the tomb. Henri IV kept the royal treasure in the Bastille. The Encyclopaedia, locked up there by Louis XV, is still rotting away in the Bastille. Oh solid walls of the Bastille, that have known during the past three reigns the sighs and moans of so many victims, if you could speak, how your own true and terrible tales would belie the timorous flattery of history!... We have a history of the Bastille in five volumes, which offers several unusual and bizarre anecdotes; but nothing of which we would so much like to learn, nothing, in a word, which could throw any light on certain State secrets that are covered with an impenetrable veil.' (Mercier, 1947)

Thus wrote Louis Sebastien Mercier in his *Tableau de Paris,* published between 1781 and 1788, perpetuating in his own way the endless romanticising of a Bastille full of sighing and moaning and political intrigue. But the inhabitants of the Faubourg Saint-Antoine viewed it rather differently. Every day for nearly 400 years they had seen the sun set behind its forbidding silhouette. It was always there, solid and impenetrable, a constant reminder of the power of princes. Over the centuries it came to be seen by these poor and hard-working people as a symbol of cruelty, oppression and despotism, not only towards the prisoners inside it, but towards themselves as well. So it isn't surprising that they seized upon it as a focus of violence on that hot July day two centuries ago, but by 1789 the reality that lay behind its 2-metre thick walls was light years away from the legends about the famous fortress that had been passed down over the centuries. The conquerors of the Bastille were the first to realize this when they released the prisoners at the end of their day of siege. Having been raised on tales of hundreds of starving wretches languishing in chains for decades in damp, vermin-ridden dungeons, they were astonished to find only seven people, all clean and well-fed, only one of whom had been there more than five years.

The Construction of the Bastille.

The origin of this famous building dates back to the Hundred Years' War and, ironically, to the first Frenchman in history to organize a *journée révolutionnaire* against the monarchy. His name was Etienne Marcel, Provost of Merchants, who in 1356, wishing to isolate Parisians from the victorious English, extended the limits of the northern half of the capital by constructing a new city wall. One of its many gates was situated at the eastern extremity of the city, at the far end of rue Saint-Antoine on the route to Vincennes. This gate, known as the *Porte Saint-Antoine*, looked like a little castle, complete with portcullis and drawbridge, and was flanked by two round towers that were later named *Tour de la Chapelle* and *Tour du Trésor*. They were the first of the eight towers that would become the famous prison, and the entire construction was named *Bastille Saint-Antoine*, since a *bastide* or *bastille* meant 'little bastion'.

By 1357 Etienne Marcel had become one of the most powerful leaders of the *bourgeoisie*, and succeeded that same year in imposing on the dauphin (future Charles V) a reform that gave fiscal control to the Estates-General. Confronted with royal opposition, Marcel and his supporters staged a rebellion. On February 22nd 1358 they invaded the palace and brutally murdered two royal counsellors in front of the horrified dauphin, who, after being forced to endorse the new ordinance, fled the city. For a short time Etienne Marcel controlled Paris. In an attempt to save its citizens from the tyranny of the house of Valois, he planned to deliver the capital into the hands of Charles II of Navarre (known as Charles the Bad) and his English allies, who were busy capturing as much French territory as possible. This subversive operation was to take place at the *Port Saint-Antoine* in the afternoon of July 31st 1358, and might well have been successful if the guardians at the gate had not refused to give Etienne Marcel the keys to the city. Instead they butchered him and his accomplices with an axe in front of the gate, and their mutilated bodies were later stripped naked and thrown into the Seine.

With Etienne Marcel out of the way Charles V returned triumphantly to Paris, and wasted no time in improving the defences of the capital. The new Provost, Hugues Aubriot, who is generally given credit as constructor of the Bastille, added two more towers to the *Porte Saint-Antoine*, those of *de la Liberté* and *de la Bertaudière*. A gate was built between them, with a moat and a drawbridge opening out on to the end of rue Saint-Antoine, which went right through the middle of the little fortress. In order to leave Paris by this gate you now had to cross two drawbridges and two moats, go through two portcullises and walk across 18 metres of courtyard between the two gates. To spare traders and travellers this lengthy and rather intimidating process, Aubriot decided to move the *Porte Saint-Antoine* a bit further northeast, to a spot which is approximately where today's rue de la Bastille meets Boulevard Beaumarchais. Adequate defence was needed for this new gate, as well as for the neighbouring royal residence, the *Hôtel Saint-Pol*, so Aubriot almost trebled the size of the *Bastille Saint-Antoine* by adding four more towers to the north and south of the existing ones. The towers were 24 metres high with a diameter of 11 metres, and the whole thing was surrounded by a wide moat filled with water from the Seine. Around the moat was the exterior wall of the fortress, which cut right across the end of rue Saint-Antoine, turning it into a *cul-de-sac*. So in order to leave the city you now had to turn left at the end of rue Saint-Antoine where it met the prison, and then right on to a new road that ran alongside the north wall. It was called *petite-rue-Saint-Antoine*, corresponding almost exactly to the present-day rue de la Bastille, and running parallel to the two north towers, *du Coin* and *du Puits* (wells). These two towers, along with the Council Chamber and the kitchens, formed a new courtyard known as the *Cour du Puits*, containing several wells and surrounded by the 18-metre high walls of buildings reserved for domestic staff and the servants of certain prisoners. In reality the *Cour du Puits* was a garbage dump for the kitchens, and the putrid smells produced by accumulated potato peelings, greasy water and horse manure, wafted over the wall and across the path of people entering or leaving Paris by the new *petite-rue-Saint-Antoine*.

The eastern facade of the Bastille at the time of Charles V. All eight towers are built, and on the right is the new Porte Saint-Antoine, with its bridge and port-cullis. The Arsenal, which stood where we now see the column in the Place de la Bastille, was built two centuries later in the rural space on the left of the picture. (Author's private collection)

As you can see from the plan, the prison was not on the site of the famous column which now stands in the middle of Place de la Bastille. The eastern point of the city wall cut across this area until 1557, when Henri II decided to fortify the wall with several bastions, one of which was put next to the east wall of the Bastille. It was in the form of a large triangle with a moat and a small lookout tower at the eastern point, and the entire construction was connected to the prison by a raised walkway supported by two stone arches, remains of which can still be seen today. Since the bastion was on unconsecrated ground, it was later used as a burying place for Jewish and Protestant prisoners and for those who committed suicide. Later still the Marquis de Launay, last governor of the Bastille, turned it into his private garden where he permitted certain prisoners to take the air, and by this time access to the bastion was by way of a gate out of the governor's courtyard leading to a covered walkway around the exterior wall. With the completion of this bastion in 1559, the construction of the Bastille complex was fully realized.

THE PRISON.

The Bastille was equipped from the start with cells, and its first prisoner was, ironically, the man who built it, Hugues Aubriot, charged with heresy and sentenced to a regime of bread and water. It was Cardinal Richelieu who transformed the Bastille from military citadel into a state prison for enemies of the Crown, but in reality there were never very many people locked up there, and as prisons go it was the least redoubtable. It could only hold a maximum of 50 prisoners, and by the reign of Louis XVI it took in an average of nineteen per year. Up to the beginning of the 18th century, however, some prisoners were kept in the kind of cells associated with the popular legend of the Bastille. They were situated at the bottom of the towers, beneath ground level, so were often swimming with water and contained all the usual elements of a good dungeon - rotting straw, rats, spiders, mildew and unbearable smells. In 1709 Constantin de Renneville spent eleven months in one of these, at the end of which *'my eyes were almost out of my head, my nose was like a medium-sized cucumber; more than half my teeth, once healthy, had fallen out from scurvy; my mouth was swollen and scabby and my bones protruded through my skin in more than ten places.'* By the reign of Louis XV these cells were assigned only for punishment, and Louis XVI refused their use for anything or anyone.

For the most part the Bastille was reserved for aristocrats, for whom a stay within its walls had no dishonour attached to it, because they were ordered into 'enforced residence' there by means of a *lettre de cachet* from the king himself. These celebrated documents, issued under the royal seal and authorizing arrest and imprisonment without trial, did, however, disrupt the lives of many a noble delinquent during the *ancien régime*. During his younger years Mirabeau was constantly pursued by *lettres de cachet* issued against him on the request of his own father, resulting in several years of imprisonment in different jails. A typical *lettre de cachet* would read, *'Monsieur the Governor, in sending to my castle of the Bastille Mr. X——, this letter is to inform you of my intention that you receive and keep him there in top security, until my further instruction.'* Nearly all prisoners in the Bastille came there by way of one of these notorious pieces of paper, and the process of admission was carried out in the best possible taste. The prisoner would be called for at his home by a representative of the prison governor, who accompanied him to the Bastille in a carriage, although some people, on receipt of their letter, turned up voluntarily to present themselves to the governor. When a new prisoner arrived, as he came into the *Cour de l'Avancée*, the shopkeepers and guards would respectfully turn the other way to preserve the anonymity of the new arrival. At the first drawbridge he was received by the king's Lieutenant and taken to see the governor, who would interrogate him about his situation and what kind of treatment should be given to him. When this was established, his sword, jewels and money were taken from him, along with other high-risk items like knives and scissors. A room would then be assigned to him, and from that moment on, to further respect his anonymity, he would never be identified by name, but by his location in the prison. So if, for example, he was on the 3rd floor of the *Tour de la Bertaudière*, he would be known as '*3rd Bertaudière.*'

Most prisoners were of noble origin and included heretics, conspirators, and writers deemed subversive or salacious, like the Bastille's most famous literary prisoner, the Marquis de Sade. The lawyer and journalist Simon-Nicolas Henri Linguet spent two years here as a result of his unrestrained mockery of almost all the other writers of his time. Another famous literary figure to find himself behind these walls in 1717 was Voltaire, for allegedly putting into verse a rumour that the Regent was having incestuous relations with his own daughters. Since the poem in question made all sorts of biblical references to Ammonites and Moabites, Voltaire, who was educated by the Jesuits, denied the charge with another poem, advocating that *'a poet from the Jesuits only knows the Sodomites.'* This irreverent defence did not help his cause, and he spent a year locked up on the first floor of the *Tour du Coin*, where he wrote 'Oedipus'. Later recognized as unjustly imprisoned, Voltaire was awarded 2,000 *livres* and a gold medal by the Regent, whom he thanked for paying for his food, but added *'I beg your Royal Highness not to take further charge of my lodging.'* Cardinal Louis de Rohan, and all the others implicated in the affair of the queen's diamond necklace, came to the Bastille for varying periods of time, including the young Nicole Leguy, who had posed as Marie-Antoinette, and who for one fleeting moment became a heroine for the entire nation when she gave birth in the Bastille on May 12th 1786.

One of the most legendary prisoners was the famous 'Man in the Iron Mask', who was brought to the Bastille from the island of Sainte-Marguerite on September 18th 1698. The identity remains unknown of this mysterious man who always wore a mask, not of iron, but of black velvet, and who spent five years and two months in a room in the *Tour de la Bertaudière*. On November 19th 1703 the medical officer, Dujonca, noted in his diary that the unknown prisoner *'felt slightly unwell yesterday as he was leaving Mass. He died today, at 10 o'clock in the evening, without having suffered great illness.'* After the funeral Dujonca added, *'I have learned since that they wrote in the register "Mr. de Marchiali, whose burial cost 40 livres."'* The identity of this enigmatic character has been variously given as Louis XIV's twin brother, his illegitimate son, the son of Mazarin and Anne of Austria, or even Voltaire, but a more realistic probability is that he was Count Mattioli, minister to the Duke of Mantua. Speculation about this fascinating historical phenomenon has been endless, and if you want to read more about it here is a website that gives a well-researched account of all the various theories.

http://www.straightdope.com/columns/read/2047/who-was-the-man-in-the-iron-mask

Escape attempts were relatively rare at the Bastille, but the most spectacular figure in this regard was Jean-Henri Latude, who was compromised in an intrigue surrounding Madame de Pompadour. He spent a total of 35 years in different prisons, including the Bastille, where in 1756 he made one of his numerous and usually unsuccessful attempts to get free. This time, however, he and an accomplice named d'Alègre managed to get over the walls by way of a rope-ladder that can still be seen today in the Carnavalet Museum. But their freedom was short-lived, and three months later Latude was arrested again and sent back to the Bastille - this time to one of the underground dungeons! A few prisoners were unlucky enough to leave the Bastille for the scaffold. The last person to do this was Thomas Arthur de Lally-Tollendal, a French general of Irish Jacobite descent, who went to Scotland with Bonny Prince Charlie in 1745 and later fought against the English during the Seven Years' War. Following his defeat at Madras and his surrender at Pondicherry after a heroic struggle, he became a scapegoat for France's military failure in India and was imprisoned in the Bastille. His trial for treason must be one of the longest in history - it lasted three years - and at the end of it he was condemned to death and decapitated in the *Place de Grève* (Hôtel-de-Ville) in 1766. With the help of Voltaire, Lally-Tollendal's son, Trophime Gérard, was able to get his father's name rehabilitated by royal decree in 1778. Escape or execution were uncommon, however, and most people just waited for the arrival of the second *lettre de cachet* authorizing their release. The letter also required the departing prisoner to swear a signed oath that he would never reveal anything of what he had seen during his imprisonment, and the majority of prisoners remained faithful to their oath. This helps to explain how the mystery of the Bastille was perpetuated, along with its accompanying legends of atrocious treatment in rat-infested dungeons, possibly the product of the imagination of a public deprived of the truth.

Some, however, were unable to remain silent about their imprisonment, notably Constantin de Renneville, Latude and Linguet, whose writings were all that was known about the Bastille at the outbreak of the Revolution. Their memoirs were widely read at that time, and have left us some vivid images of what life was like in the Bastille during the 18th century. Despite his initial nightmare in the dungeon, de Renneville gives generally praiseworthy accounts, particularly about the food, which at times seems to have rivalled the best restaurants in Paris. The governor received money from the king to feed and maintain his prisoners, sums that differed considerably according to their status - for example, he got 50 *livres* for a prince of the blood, while a lawyer only merited 5. But there was always enough to eat, and sometimes the meals were veritable feasts, so much so that some prisoners asked if they could have less food and keep the money that was saved. It was with great fondness that de Renneville remembered mealtimes at the Bastille, when there were *'always several main dishes, soup, entrée, spicy sauces, desserts and two bottles of wine, burgundy or champagne. On Fridays and Lenten days I had six dishes and a wonderful crayfish soup. My fish dish contained a large sole and a perch - all paid for by the king.'* In 1759 another prisoner, writer and historian Jean-François Marmontel, had *'an excellent soup, a succulent slice of beef, a leg of capon oozing with grease* [they appreciated cholesterol in those days], *a small plate of fried artichokes, another of spinach, a beautiful Crésane pear, fresh grapes and the best Moka coffee.'* Latude was obviously used to a high standard of food at the Bastille, for on one occasion he complained that the chickens were not sufficiently well-larded.

In addition to these sumptuous meals, many prisoners also received regular supplements. Tavernier, one of the seven to be released when the Bastille was stormed, was furnished with 1½lbs of tobacco, 4 bottles of *eau-de-vie*, 62 bottles of wine, 3 bottles of beer, 30lbs of bread, 3lbs of candles, a turkey, pigeons, 2lbs of coffee, 3lbs of sugar, oysters, chestnuts, apples and pears - just for the month of May 1787. During March of the same year Tavernier is noted as receiving supplements of tobacco, 4 bottles of *eau-de-vie,* 4 of wine, 6 of beer, coffee, sugar, chicken, cheese, etc., all of which were in addition to the regular copious regime offered by the kitchens of the Bastille. Perhaps several bottles of *eau-de-vie* every month explains why two other prisoners, Marguérite de Launay, Baronne de Staal and Louis-Isaac Lemaistre de Sacy, both counted their two-year stay in the Bastille amongst the best years of their lives. In Marguérite's case it might have also had something to do with the love affairs she had there, not only with a fellow prisoner, but also with her gaoler.

As well as being fed by the king, many prisoners were also dressed by him if they couldn't afford to supply enough of their own clothing. They got used to being able to order at will according to their needs any personal items they lacked, and some even complained if the quality was not up to standard. Latude was able to make his escape from the Bastille by ordering a large number of handkerchiefs, towels and hose, plus thirteen dozen shirts, all of which he used to make his famous ladder. Most prisoners not only ate and dressed luxuriously, they could also live in surroundings that were as close to home as possible, because before the 18th century the rooms assigned were empty, so moving into the Bastille was like moving house. Local residents always knew when a new prisoner arrived, for a procession of servants, sweating under the weight of elegant furniture and heavy boxes, would be seen filing through the prison entrance on rue Saint-Antoine. Some prisoners rented furniture from the Bastille, and if they had no money to do this the governor could always manage to secure a grant for them - a practice that was abused by many prisoners, who rented a minimum of the cheapest items and saved the rest of the grant money for when they were released.

By the reign of Louis XVI, all rooms were furnished, but prisoners were permitted to bring along their personal possessions, including family paintings, tapestries, cushions and curtains, bookshelves, mirrors, screens and candlesticks. Many prisoners brought so much that it's hard to imagine where they put it. The Marquis de Sade had his own writing desk and chair, a library of over 130 books, as well as a huge wardrobe to accommodate the vast quantity of silk shirts, frock-coats, tailcoats, dressing gowns and assorted foot ware that came with him to the Bastille. He also brought in his own bedding, and imported almost the entire contents of his *cabinet de toilette*, including a range of perfumes that no doubt helped to fuel his exotic imagination. Because they were privileged prisoners, most of the residents of the Bastille were treated with respect, continuing to maintain their normal level of self-esteem, and few of them ever displayed any of the humility that comes with loss of freedom. On Linguet's second day of imprisonment, he was visited by the Bastille's official barber, who offered his services with a courteous bow. Linguet replied with irritation, *'Who are you and why are you disturbing me?' 'Monsieur, I am the Bastille barber,'* came the reply, to which Linguet snapped, *'Then shave me and leave me in peace!'* Most prisoners, however, were grateful for this welcome daily visit from the prison barber, who would arrive with a basin, perfumed soap, a dainty chin towel edged with lace and a big silver kettle to heat up the water. Of course some prisoners brought their own domestic help with them, so life went on exactly as if they were at home, and many of them quickly formed social circles among the other prisoners. Cardinal de Rohan brought two of his servants to the Bastille with him, and on one occasion gave a dinner party for twenty people.

Another privilege accorded to prisoners in the Bastille was permission to bring domestic pets such as dogs, cats and even birds. In addition to being company for the prisoners, they also performed the vital job of eliminating the uninvited rodents that infested even these relatively luxurious prison cells. The only person who didn't mind the vermin was Latude, one of the Bastille's most colourful characters, who, when put into an underground dungeon after his attempted escape, made pets of the 26 rats that inhabited his cell. He gave them all names and trained them to beg or do tricks in exchange for pieces of his food, which they then politely ate off his plate. After this communal meal, Latude would serenade his companions with an improvised flute, watching affectionately, like a fond parent, as the rats played and fought their way endlessly around his cell. When he was finally let out of the dungeon he transferred his affections to a colony of pigeons that flew into his room. Unlike Linguet, who wrote of his time in the Bastille as a living death, incarceration seemed to bring out in Latude his most reflective and inventive qualities, as well as provoking in him an immense desire for freedom that he translated into his numerous attempts at escape. He finally gained his release in 1784, and Louis XVI awarded him a pension of 400 *livres* in recognition of his wrongful imprisonment.

In the summer of 1788 the Bastille had only one more year left before it was destroyed by the Revolution. By this time the prison regime was at its most humane - the few prisoners that it contained even had a billiard table at their disposal - so it isn't surprising that some people were not in a hurry to gain their liberty. One prisoner asked if he could delay his release in order to finish a poem he was writing, and another preferred to stay on at the Bastille until he had found an apartment. But prisons, whatever their level of comfort, have a curious and often tragic effect on their occupants. Sebastien Mercier tells the story of a very old man who was freed from the Bastille by an amnesty at the beginning of Louis XVI's reign. For 47 years he had known only the four cold stone walls of one of the prison's more unpleasant cells, his body was frail and wasted, and what hair he had left had turned white and metallic. When he was told he could leave, he stood staring in a dream-like state, his eyes blinded by the light of day, as a prison guard ushered him into a carriage and accompanied him to his former home. When they arrived, the old man found his home replaced by a public building, and he could not recognize a single face or find one neighbouring house that looked familiar. People came to stare at him out of curiosity, including one of his former domestic servants, whom he did not recognize. But the servant recognized the old man, and informed him with thoughtless indifference that his wife had died 30 years earlier of sadness and misery, and his children had all left for distant places. Distraught with grief, the old man went to the government minister who had released him, bowed courteously and asked to return to the Bastille. He tried to explain how he felt. *'Separated from society, I have lived with myself. Here I can live neither with myself nor with these new men for whom my despair is but a dream. The worst is not to die, but to be the last to die.'*

THE STORMING OF THE BASTILLE.

This most famous event of the French Revolution, universally portrayed as a heroic siege in which a crowd of courageous citizens took the place by force, has been painted with the same apocryphal brush as the entire history of the Bastille. Some say the fortress itself was never 'taken', for the governor had already surrendered and handed over the keys before any of the attackers entered the prison. However, the crowd had nonetheless already entered two courtyards and shattered the chain of the drawbridge between them, which could be construed as 'taking' the fortress. But however you see it, the importance of this event is indisputable, because it was seen as an act of popular triumph over royal despotism, and thus became the principal ideological symbol of the Revolution.

So who were 'the men of July 1789'? The storming of the Bastille was very much a local event, for 70 percent of the crowd came from the adjacent Faubourg Saint-Antoine, so it was largely an army of joiners, carpenters, cabinet-makers, mirror-polishers and factory workers that pressed through the *Cour de l'Avancée* that afternoon. It contained three principal elements - ordinary working people from the city's faubourgs, a bourgeois militia created to keep order, plus out-and-out brigands, armed with clubs and pikes, who had spent the preceding 36 hours attacking prisons, intimidating pedestrians, breaking into wine shops, armouries and bakeries, and looting the toll-booths of the Farmers-General Wall. The major quest, however, was for arms, and this began at 9 o'clock in the morning of the 14th at Les Invalides. The next stop was the Bastille, where the initial aim was not to take the fortress itself but to seize the vast quantities of gunpowder, cannons and other weapons that were rumoured to be stocked within its towers - false rumours as it turned out, for all they found when they finally got in was 35,000 lbs of powder, 3 cannons in the courtyard, 6 rampart guns, and on top of the towers 15 rather rusty cannons that were used for celebrations.

When they arrived, the crowd from Les Invalides quickly joined up with a growing group of artisans from the Faubourg Saint-Antoine that had been gathering outside the walls of the Bastille since the previous evening. Inside, the Marquis Bernard-René de Launay, the last governor of the Bastille, was feeling distinctly apprehensive. Having been born in the Bastille, where his father had also been governor, de Launay had hardly any experience of combat, and possessed little flair for military strategy. The troops at his disposal were not only insufficient for the task at hand, the loyalty of some of them, notably the *Invalides*, could not be counted on, and he was not sure how he could effectively deploy the 250 barrels of powder their commander had sent along with them. The air bristled with rumours that de Launay had sent for massive reinforcements, and public fear mounted at the sight of several cannons pointing from the towers in the direction of the Faubourg. The assembly of electors, alerted to this fact, immediately sent a delegation to force the governor to remove the cannons. At 10 a.m. de Launay received these delegates with excessive courtesy, inviting them in for *déjeuner*, and then informed them that he could not remove the guns without the king's permission. He could, however, move them back. Meanwhile the crowd waiting below were becoming more and more agitated, and when they saw the cannons being moved back, they assumed that it was in order to re-charge them. Panic broke out, and at about 11.30 a.m. another delegation was brought, headed by a lawyer named Jacques Thuriot de la Rosière. Within one hour Thuriot emerged from his meeting with de Launay and conveyed to a sceptical crowd the governor's assurances that the cannons were not loaded and would not be fired if no attack was made on the Bastille.

At this point the crowd could possibly have got what they had initially wanted from the Bastille - its stock of arms - without any blood being shed. It was a crucial and decisive moment, especially for the governor, whose life hung dangerously in the balance. Unfortunately for de Launay a few members of the crowd chose to greet his promise with a chorus of boos, which in an instant transformed the general insecurity into mass delirium. '*I want the Bastille!*' came the cry from Louis Tournay, who leaped up on to the roof of a perfume shop that was built onto the gate of the governor's courtyard, and jumped down to the other side, landing right in front of the governor's house. He was quickly joined by several others, and within minutes the chain was broken and the drawbridge opened, causing the first fatality of the siege as it came crashing down on one of the attackers. Hundreds of people surged into the courtyard and began to draw near the prison entrance, firing a few shots at the soldiers who were standing guard on the observation platform.

The crowd was agitated and defensive, for most of them didn't realise that the bridge had been opened by their own side, and they presumed that the governor had let them into the courtyard in order to massacre them. Suddenly cannon shots rang out as several attackers fell to the ground, provoking a general retreat and giving credibility to their suspicions, although it is unlikely that the order for this onslaught was given by de Launay - it was more probably issued by the commander of the *gardes-suisses*. It was now 1.30 in the afternoon and relative calm reigned for about half an hour until a third delegation turned up from the Hôtel-de-Ville waving white handkerchiefs, demanding that the governor stop firing, hand over his armoury to the people and install a detachment of bourgeois militia in the fortress. This had no effect, and not long afterwards an elector named Ethis de Corny was sent to make another demand for surrender. As he calmed the crowd and evacuated them to the rear of the governor's courtyard, a white flag appeared on top of the fortress. But as Ethis and his fellow delegates approached the entrance, firing broke out, one of the attackers fell to the ground, and the delegation withdrew to threatening shouts from the defenders of the Bastille.

By mid-afternoon the crowd were beginning to get exhausted from fighting and discouraged by de Launay's apparent betrayal of trust. They tried setting fire to the drawbridge by launching three cartloads of burning straw at it, an unsuccessful manoeuvre that merely resulted in seriously burning the governor's house and the adjacent kitchen, which had been their only places of retreat from the cannon fire. A young girl, Mlle Monsigny, daughter of an *Invalides* captain, unwisely appeared at the entrance to the courtyard, and was immediately grabbed by a group of attackers who thought she was Mlle de Launay. When they threw her onto a cartload of hay and threatened to set light to it if the governor refused to surrender, her father, who witnessed the scene from the top of one of the towers, cried out in horror and was immediately felled by gunshots. Fortunately Mlle Monsigny was saved from becoming a human firebomb by a valiant citizen named Aubin Bonnemère, who managed to drag her to safety. This dramatic incident was followed by the sudden arrival at 3.30 p.m. of a detachment of about 60 *gardes-françaises*, several hundred armed citizens dragging five cannons behind them, and all led by Pierre-Augustin Hulin, a defector from the *gardes-suisses* who had recently been appointed as director of the royal laundry. Close on their heels came another huge column of armed citizens, led by Lieutenant Jacob Elie of the Aquitaine infantry, bringing with them cannons that had been taken from Les Invalides. It was Hulin and Elie who brought some kind of military order to the rampaging crowd, and succeeded in getting the cannons into the governor's courtyard and placing them at the prison entrance, directly in front of the second drawbridge. The crowd then began shouting *'Down with the bridge! Down with the bridge!'*

While all this drama was taking place below in the courtyard, what, you might be wondering, was going on inside the Bastille? The story was told later by one of de Launay's soldiers in a magazine called *La Bastille Devoilée* (The Bastille Unveiled). *'About 4 o'clock in the evening, the governor, urged by his non-commissioned officers to surrender the Bastille, realising himself that he could not sustain the siege for long without provisions, seized the fuse from one of the cannons in the inner courtyard with the intention of setting light to the powder in the Tour de la Liberté, which without doubt would have blown up part of the faubourg Saint-Antoine and all the houses next to the Bastille, if two officers had not kept him from carrying out this intention. They forced him to withdraw at the point of a bayonet...It was at that moment that Monsieur de Launay asked the garrison what he should do, for he saw no other course of action but to blow himself up rather than expose himself to being slaughtered by the mob, whose rage could no longer be escaped...the soldiers replied that it would not be possible to fight much longer, that they would submit to any fate rather than cause so many citizens to perish, and that it would be more advisable to send the drum up on to the towers, beat the retreat, hoist a white flag and capitulate. The governor, having no flag, offered them a white handkerchief.'* (Charpentier, 1790)

Just as the crowd were about to open fire with their strategically placed cannons, they saw the white banner waving above the fortress, and at the same moment a piece of paper appeared through a slit in the wall of the second drawbridge. But how were they to reach it if the bridge remained closed? Being a neighbourhood of carpenters, planks of wood were readily available, and the longest one they could find was placed precariously over the moat, while several men stood on the end of it to hold it in place. Venturing on to this dangerously unstable improvised bridge was rather like 'walking the plank', and the entire crowd held its breath as the first heroic attempt to cross it was made by one of their number, a shoemaker, who lost his balance just before the end and fell into the moat. One eye-witness maintained that he was killed by a shot from the parapet. Another man then tried his luck, and although the identity of this person who succeeded in seizing the paper has never been established with certainty, some say it was Stanislas-Marie Maillard, a bailiff who afterwards adopted the title 'Captain of the Volunteers of the Bastille' and would later gain notoriety for presiding over the so-called tribunals during the September massacres. He reached across the moat and took the piece of paper, walked carefully back along the plank to safety, and handed the note to Hulin, who read it to the assembled crowd. It was capitulation! Through the opening in the wall came the voice of an officer, asking them to retire with the honours of war, which they refused to do. The officer then said that they would like to yield and lay down their arms if it was promised that the soldiers would not be massacred, to which the crowd replied *'Lower the bridge, nothing will happen to you.'* The defender of the Bastille concludes his story. *'It was on this promise that the governor gave the little drawbridge key that he had in his pocket to corporal Gaiard and officer Pereau, who opened the gate and lowered the bridge...It is plain to see that the Bastille was not taken by assault. No breach was made. We defy anyone to prove that there was; entry was made after we had lowered the bridge.'*

Governor de Launay ordered the bridge to be lowered because he believed this promise, and perhaps the attackers also believed it at the moment they made it, but once the way was clear a frenzy broke out. They poured across the bridge, only to find that the gate on the other side was still closed. One of the *Invalides* came to open it, a man named Béquard, who had

Maillard walks over the moat on a plank of wood, successfuly reaching the piece of paper on which was written the capitulation of the governor of the Bastille. After this the drawbridge was lowered and the attackers poured into the main prison courtyard. (Author's private collection)

earlier been one of those responsible for holding a bayonet at de Launay and stopping him from exploding the *Tour de la Liberté*. Seconds after letting them in Béquard was attacked by one of the crowd who mistook him for a turnkey, cut off his hand and seized it as a trophy. Poor Béquard had no luck that day, despite having saved the Faubourg Saint-Antoine from being blown up, for later on, after being mistaken yet again for an enemy of the people, he was horribly mutilated and then hanged in the *Place de Grève*, while his severed hand, still clutching the key to the Bastille, was paraded around the capital. Once inside the *Grande Cour*, despite the efforts of Elie and Hulin to keep the fighting under control, the crowd began to kill the *Invalides* and Swiss guards who had laid down their arms on the orders of de Launay. For a short while chaos reigned as the crowd proceeded to destroy everything in its path, loot the administrative buildings and throw sheaves of documents out of the window. The disorder was so great they even shot some of their own people, before disappearing in the direction of the cells to release the remaining prisoners.

It all happened very quickly, and about fifteen minutes later governor de Launay, his face white and drawn, appeared in the courtyard escorted by Hulin and Elie. He had fought with courage, but now knew it was all over, and resigned himself to his fate. He was taken out of the Bastille into rue Saint-Antoine, followed by an enormous crowd that accompanied him and his escorts all the way to the Hôtel-de-Ville, shouting insults, spitting and threatening to cut his head off or hang him on the spot. It was all that Hulin and Elie could do to prevent this from happening, and during the journey three staff-officers of the Bastille and three *Invalides* were slaughtered. They finally came to a halt in front of the Hôtel-de-Ville, where a cook by the name of Denot said they should take the prisoner into the building. At this suggestion de Launay protested. *'Let them kill me!'* he pleaded, unable to tolerate his ordeal any longer, and he kicked Denot so hard that the young man fell to the ground in agony. As he fell, a bayonet was hurled from the crowd into de Launay's stomach, giving the signal for the massacre to begin. Within seconds he was covered with wounds from knives, bayonets and swords, and as he fell into the gutter someone finished him off with a pistol. By then Denot had sufficiently recovered from his blow to rise to his feet and become a momentary hero by providing the crowd with a much needed trophy. Taking his pocket-knife, he proceeded to saw off de Launay's head, declaring confidently that being a cook he knew *'how to work with meat.'* It was 6 o'clock in the evening, and for the rest of that day and night the head of the ill-fated governor was paraded on a pike throughout the streets of the city, to screams of joy and victory from celebrating Parisians.

When the hysteria had died down, it was possible to assess the final toll of this historic day. In terms of human life the figures were relatively low, considering the hundreds of people involved in the attack - 83 were killed on the spot, another 15 died later from their wounds, there were 60 cases of serious in

The Bastille governor resigns himself to his fate as he is brought into rue Saint-Antoine and sets off towards the Hôtel-de-Ville followed by a threatening crowd. They are seen here passing the *Couvent des Filles de la Visitation Sainte-Marie*, nowadays the Protestant Église Réformé de Sainte-Marie. (Author's private collection)

jury and 13 people were permanently maimed. The Bastille itself was badly damaged. Doors and windows were broken, offices were looted, and many of its historic archives, including prison registers, were destroyed - those that survived are now housed at the library of the Arsenal. It was not until rather late in the day that the attackers of the Bastille remembered the prisoners. They included four forgers, who had all arrived within the previous two years, and a lunatic brought from Vincennes in 1784 who, on leaving the Bastille, was transferred immediately to the mental hospital at Charenton. There was one classic Bastille prisoner, the Comte de Solage, incarcerated by a *lettre de cachet* at the request of his family, and the seventh prisoner was Tavernier, accused in 1757 of being an accomplice of the regicide Damiens. He had been fortunate to escape the terrible traitor's death suffered by Damiens, but instead had lived for 32 years in the Bastille, where he was found, thin and demented and unable to understand what was going on, when the conquerors of the Bastille entered his cell. He was sent to end his days at the Charenton hospital.

Restif de la Bretonne, always on the scene at every event of the Revolution, was a witness to this dramatic day, which he describes with his usual perceptive vision of how the future will unfold. He also expresses a worthy concern for his country's documentary heritage that he sees flying in the air all around him. *'I went to see the siege of the Bastille begin and already it was all over: the entire place had been taken. Fanatics were throwing papers, precious historical documents, from the top of the towers, into the ditches...A destructive spirit hovered over the city...I see it now, this dreaded Bastille, on which I had never dared to cast my eyes...I see it fall with its last governor!...I see a cloud of evil rising above the unfortunate French capital.'* (Restif de la Bretonne, 1986)

THE CONQUERORS OF THE BASTILLE.

After it was all over, the 'conquerors of the Bastille', in the words of Saint-Just, went from fear to audacity. At first many of them went into hiding, frightened of the reaction of the city in general and the municipal authorities in particular, but they were quickly enticed out of their hideouts by a story - completely apocryphal - that was rapidly making its way around town. It concerned a certain *Comte de Lorges*, a mythical prisoner from the Bastille, who had supposedly been found, skeletal and white haired, lying chained up and nearly naked in a cell that was swimming with water. Engravings were already on sale depicting his liberation, showing him being supported out of prison like a corpse from the grave, his long white beard flowing down to his knees. It was the title, 'Victim for Years and Years of Tyranny and Despotism', that persuaded people to come out of hiding, eager to take on their new role of revolutionary hero. No time was wasted in drawing up a list of 'conquerors', which eventually contained 863 names, only 200 of whom were Parisians, the rest coming either from the provinces or abroad. Honours were awarded in all directions, medals glinted on the chest of hundreds of proud patriots, and certificates of merit decorated the modest walls of almost the entire

Faubourg Saint-Antoine. The following June 954 combatants received the honours of the nation, which consisted of a uniform and a complete set of weapons. On the barrel of each gun and on the blade of each sabre was engraved *'Given by the Nation to—-, Conqueror of the Bastille'*, and as an expression of the nation's gratitude, the Assembly presented a certificate to each one of them and a pension to those who were wounded during the siege. Some of these pensions were still being paid by the time of the Second Empire!

The Demolition of the Bastille.

On July 15th the Bastille was evacuated by order of General Lafayette, who installed one of the electors from the Hôtel-de-Ville as temporary governor. His name was Soulès, a bourgeois from the Faubourg Saint-Antoine, who was understandably unnerved as night began to fall over the sinister towers of the old prison. Unable to sleep, he roamed about the abandoned fortress into the small hours of the next morning, inspecting the entire length of the outside wall. At about 3 a.m. he was crossing the drawbridge leading out into the *Cour de l'Avancée* when he suddenly found himself surrounded by a contingent of bourgeois militia. Their leader, an unknown volunteer, was a giant of a man with a scarred face and a booming voice. *'Who are you?'* Soulès demanded angrily, incensed by the intrusion. *'I am Captain Danton of the Cordeliers battalion,'* came the reply, *'and we have come to visit the Bastille. And, may I ask, who are you?'* When Soulès replied that he was the new governor, Danton looked stupefied, retorting that the Bastille no longer had a governor, at which Soulès took out of his pocket a piece of paper signed by Lafayette and waved it under Danton's nose. But it was too dark to decipher the document, so Danton brushed it aside contemptuously and ordered his men to arrest the so-called governor. There was not a guard in sight or within earshot to heed Soulès' pleas for help as Danton and his battalion marched him out of the Bastille and along rue Saint-

Antoine. It was a dangerous journey for Soulès, for the population was still agitated from the previous day's events, and Danton's soldiers had to use their bayonets at every corner to fend off potential lynch-mobs. They took Soulès to the Cordeliers headquarters, where the local residents wanted to shoot him, but Soulès managed to persuade them to take him to the Hôtel-de-Ville, where Lafayette, who had to be got out of bed and brought from his home in rue Saint-Honoré, was able to verify that he had indeed appointed Soulès as governor.

After this attempt by Danton to take control of the Bastille, other local patrol groups were eager to do the same, so in order to avoid any more violence, the electors decreed that the entire fortress be demolished. This mammoth operation, which cost 850,000 *livres*, was put in the hands of Pierre-François Palloy, an architect and self-styled 'conqueror of the Bastille', although his claim to the title is questionable, for the first time he arrived at the fortress was on the 15th. The building trade was booming in Paris, where Palloy had constructed many of the bourgeois residences of the Left Bank, so he was already extremely wealthy. What's more he had grown very fond of money and success, so this golden opportunity to exploit the rapidly escalating revolutionary fever was seized upon by Palloy, who dropped his image of property speculator and became *Patriote Palloy*. From the ruins of the legendary dungeon Palloy built another legend, a veritable cult that turned the Bastille into the most powerful icon of the Revolution. His building site employed 800 workers at 45 *sous* a day, and soon became a popular 'promenade', where both Mirabeau and Beaumarchais were to be seen taking the air amidst the ruins, while patriotic parents, including the Duc and Duchesse d'Orléans, came to walk their children around the spot where liberty had triumphed. The former prisoner, Latude, who was now something of a folk hero, took groups of visitors on guided tours, pointing out with pride the exact location of his cell, and explaining how he made his daring escape with the famous improvised rope-ladder. Latude's tours were especially popular with female visitors, many of whom opted to spend a night in one of the cells, which gave them the dubious privilege of being able to boast first-hand acquaintance of the rats and insects that had been Latude's 'friends'!

It was Mirabeau who ceremoniously felled the first stone, and what pleasure he must have derived from swinging a pickaxe at the walls that had formerly held him captive. As the hated fortress came tumbling down, each stone was chipped and carved into a miniature Bastille, and *'to perpetuate the horrors of despotism,'* one was sent to each of the 83 newly-formed departments of France. You can see examples of these models in the Carnavalet Museum. Some of the stones were used to build the *Pont Louis XVI* (now Pont de la Concorde), so that the vanquished fortress could be trodden under the feet of the populace, and various other parts of the Bastille were transformed into a range of toys, medals and swords, all sold at enormous profit. Palloy managed to find some commercial use for every relic of the old prison, even distributing as prizes to certain 'apostles of liberty' small boxes containing fragments of a crust that had formed from the prisoners' breath on the ceilings of their cells! From the marble mantelpieces a game of dominoes was made and presented to the dauphin, while the pages of the prison registers became sets of playing cards. The general party atmosphere that prevailed throughout the demolition of the Bastille was interrupted for a while, however, on the grim discovery underneath the Bastion of the bones of hundreds of Jews, Protestants and prisoners who had committed suicide. Some of them had been there for 200 years, and Mirabeau remarked, with his customary caustic humour and well-known hatred of the old regime, *'The Ministers lacked foresight, they forgot to eat the bones.'*

By October 1789 all that was left of the Bastille was a wall 50 centimetres high, giving a spectacular new perspective to the sunset in the Faubourg Saint-Antoine. Most of the building had been sold off piecemeal as souvenirs or offered as patriotic prizes, but Palloy had not yet exhausted the Bastille business, and early the following year he further demonstrated his talent, this time as an impresario, when he organized a ceremony on the site of the demolished fortress. A huge quantity of iron balls, chains and prison bars were all assembled to form a revolutionary shrine in the middle of the ruins, and as several hundred labourers all swore an oath to the Constitution, the metallic mountain miraculously fell down to reveal a gigantic altar of flowers. It took a year for the demolition to be completed, and on July 14th 1790 the *Fête de la Fédération* was held to mark the first anniversary of the storming of the Bastille. Poplar trees were planted along the site of the fortress walls, forming the outline of the eight towers, and each tree bore the name of one of

'Ici l'on danse'. Parisians dance at a party held on the illuminated ruins of the Bastille. By July 14th 1790 the famous prison had been demolished, but Parisians continue to dance in the streets on this day every year. (Courtesy of Musée Carnavalet, Cabinet des Arts Graphiques, Paris)

the departments of France. In the centre was an obelisk covered with patriotic inscriptions, and the whole thing was illuminated at night to the delight of the hundreds of Parisians who came to marvel at this notorious site transformed into a wonderland. Over the entrance was a sign saying *Ici l'on danse* (We dance here), so that is exactly what they did, for three days and three nights, and Parisians have continued to dance in the streets on Bastille Day ever since.

Palloy's last public appearance in Place de la Bastille was on July 10th 1791, when Voltaire's remains were transferred to the Panthéon. His coffin was placed in the middle of the square on an allegorical rock made from prison stones, bearing the inscription *'Receive in this place, where despotism enchained you, Voltaire, the homage that the Nation renders you.'* A huge crowd gathered the following morning at 8 o'clock, waiting to accompany Voltaire to his final place of honour, but heavy rain delayed their departure until 2.30 p.m. Then Palloy walked proudly at the head of the procession of 'conquerors', who were followed by contingents from revolutionary clubs and colleges, market porters and citizens from the Faubourg Saint-Antoine armed with pikes. Some carried stones from the Bastille that had been sculpted into busts of Benjamin Franklin, Mirabeau and Rousseau, and a theatre group heralded the *pièce de résistance*, a statue of Voltaire sitting in a chair, carried by scholars dressed in old-fashioned clothes. Last of all came the horse-drawn float carrying the coffin. On top of this was an antique bed containing a wax effigy of Voltaire sleeping, an enormous ensemble that was almost as high as the second storey of the houses on rue Saint-Antoine. Palloy must have been proud of this gargantuan finale to his Bastille saga, but many Parisians, historians and visitors to the city have often expressed regret that this classically sinister mediaeval fortress, with its darkly shrouded past and mysterious legends, was not kept to become the 'Tower of London' of the French capital.

Palloy continued to make a business out of the Revolution, and in August 1792 he was responsible for building a reinforcing wall around the Temple dungeon in preparation for the arrival of the royal prisoners. But his opportunistic past caught up with him during the Terror, when he was arrested for embezzlement of national property and put in *La Force* prison just before 9 *Thermidor*. He escaped the guillotine and managed to get himself acquitted, at which point he left Paris and moved to Sceaux, where he continued to sell anything he could to anyone who was willing to pay. Palloy was just as adaptable in politics as he was in business, going from *sans-culotte* in 1793 to royalist during the Restoration, and he even tried to profit from his 'patriotic' past to find a suitable husband for his daughter. In 1796 he wrote to the Republican Army, offering her in marriage to *'an honest and virtuous warrior who has constantly fought for his fatherland on foreign soil since the Revolution.'* When Charles X came to the throne Palloy sang his praises in a poem that earned him the *Ordre du Lys* (Order of the Lily), but in 1830 he was obliged to dust off his revolutionary cap and resume the identity of 'conqueror of the Bastille' for a short time, until the advent of Louis-Philippe, when he was inspired yet again to more royalist poetry. The new king was so touched by the verses, entitled *Le Souverain Chéri*, that he offered Palloy a pension, which he accepted and enjoyed until his death in 1835 at the age of 80.

Three years after Palloy's last public appearance here, the huge space left by the demolished Bastille saw one last period of drama before the Revolution ended. Every day for two months the long procession of tumbrils passed across it on their way to the guillotine in the *Place du Trône-Renversé* (Nation). The site was still unpaved, and the uneven ground was often very muddy on rainy days, obliging the cortege to slow down or even stop as it went across. It was just such a day on July 22nd 1794 when Father Carrichon, a priest from the Oratory, followed the tumbrils containing the three de Noailles women, one of whom was Lafayette's mother-in-law. Carrichon was their personal confessor, and had promised to give them final absolution as they went to their death, and it was the knowledge of this that maintained the women's spirits during their final hours, as their eyes darted desperately from one side of the street to the other in an attempt to spot the courageous priest. He had to disguise himself as an ordinary citizen, for Catholic worship was forbidden and he was risking his life in performing this service. Carrichon has left his own account of this most terrible day of his life.

> *'The storm was at its worst, and the wind was raging, tormenting the women in the first tumbril, especially the maréchale de Noailles. Her large bonnet blew away, revealing her grey hair. She wobbled unsteadily on her miserable bench, her hands tied behind her back. A group of spectators, who stood by the road in spite of the storm, recognized her and augmented her torment by their insults, which she bore with patience. There she is, that marshall's wife who used to ride in a beautiful carriage, in a tumbril like the rest of them! The cries continued; the sky was blacker, the rain heavier. We arrived at the crossroads at the entrance to the faubourg Saint-Antoine. I walked ahead, examined the spot, and thought: this is the best place to accord them what they so desire. The tumbrils slowed down. I turned towards them. I made to Mme de Noailles a sign that she understood perfectly. Mother, M. Carrichon is going to give us absolution. They immediately lowered their heads with an air of repentance, contrition, tenderness, hope and piety. I raised my hand and with my head covered I pronounced the formula of absolution. I shall never forget this beautiful scene. From that moment, the storm subsided, the rain diminished. I praised the Lord, and so did they. Their expression conveyed contentment, security, elation.'* (Lasteyrie, 1868)

Place de la Bastille.

During the Revolution the government acquired an enormous amount of property and land by confiscation, but not much was done to develop these acquisitions, and revolutionary Paris gave very little evidence of real urban planning. In May 1794, however, in the midst of the Terror, a group of architects commissioned by Antoine-Léon-Anne Amelot de Chaillou, administrator of the public domain, began to plan the best utilisation of the state's new property. This committee worked for the next few years on a variety of projects to beautify the capital, before being abolished by the Directory government in 1799. One of the reforms they put forward was the restriction on the height of houses in proportion to the width of the street, a project that was calculated with admirable mathematical precision. They also had a proposal for the site of the demolished Bastille, where they planned to construct a huge esplanade in the form of a star, rather like the one you see nowadays in Place Charles de Gaulle at the end of the Champs-Elysées. But the project was never realised, and the site of the Bastille remained empty for many years, during which time it was periodically occupied by a strange assortment of monuments.

The Fountain.

Once demolished the Bastille gave its name to the huge empty space that had been created at the entrance to the Faubourg Saint-Antoine. On August 10th 1793 the first anniversary of the fall of the monarchy was celebrated all over Paris, with various events in all the major squares of the city. In Place de la Bastille it was called *Fête de la Régénération*, where the centre of attention was an enormous plaster of Paris statue of a rather Egyptian looking goddess sitting on an elevated throne. Surveying the population from above with a sober expression, she crossed her arms in a corpse-like position, while from her breasts, which she appeared to be squeezing, spurted fountains of 'water of regeneration.' Hérault de Séchelles, the President of the Convention, collected some of this sacred liquid in a goblet, which he reverently put to his lips before passing it round a huge circle of elderly men each carrying the banner of his department. Then it was the turn of the deputies to file past and regenerate themselves, and once this official consecration of the fountain was over, a swarm of spectators rushed over to the gushing goddess to quench their ideological thirst. Afterwards they gathered round the enormous statue and sang, to the tune of the *Marseillaise*, a song honouring the goddess and exhorting people to *'tear away the mask and blood-stained daggers of imperious papism, and smother the cruel serpents that are the offspring of fanaticism.'*

Fête de la Régénération, August 10th 1793. This Egyptian style goddess dispensed 'water of regeneration' which was collected in a goblet and passed around first to a succession of dignitaries and deputies, and then to an eager crowd of patriotic citizens. (Author's private collection)

The Guillotine.

Most of those singing were blissfully unaware that revolutionary fanaticism was creeping up on them at that very minute. The Assembly had already decreed, a fortnight earlier, that tradesmen hoarding bread and other essential foodstuffs would be guillotined. There had been a Revolutionary Tribunal for six months, and just one month later the infamous Law of Suspects would put an end to freedom of expression, and provide judges with an endless supply of prisoners. Palloy himself was one of them, and if he had not had the good fortune to catch the Tribunal on one of its very few good days, he might have met his death much earlier on the very spot where he had made his fortune, for on June 9th 1794 the guillotine was installed in Place de la Bastille. The previous day had been the *Fête de l'Être-Suprême*, and the grim-looking death machine had been moved from the *Place de la Révolution* (Concorde) out of sight of the procession. Sanson's carpenters worked all night by torchlight to dismantle the guillotine, transport it and put it up again in Place de la Bastille, where it only stayed for three days, but long enough to provoke loud protests from the local residents. In his memoirs Sanson describes the first of these three days - and at the same time gives away a few of his own feelings about revolutionary justice.

'We counted on the citizens of the patriotic faubourg, poor but hard-working, to be a more enthusiastic audience than that of the Tuileries area; we were most mistaken. We arrived by rue Antoine with 18 prisoners in three tumbrils. When we emerged into the square, we were greeted by cries, boos and even hissing. These people are not as reserved as those in the Place de la Révolution, and perceiving that the unfortunate prisoners showed not the least sign of being aristocratic, they did not hesitate to pity them and to express their sentiments loudly. The nearer we got, the worse the situation became. I saw men in their shirtsleeves, wearing work-aprons, searching for their wives in the crowd and taking them away by force. By the time the last victims mounted the scaffold the square was almost deserted. The Committee spies, whom we know so well, were most disconcerted; they had assumed that the people would unhitch the tumbrils and lead these so-called enemies to the guillotine themselves, but these very people have given a good lesson to those who profess to know them.' (Sanson, 1988)

These very people also informed the authorities of the potential health hazards of having the guillotine on their doorstep. These hazards were considerable, for the ground in the square was not sufficiently absorbent, and the area around the scaffold quickly became a pool of infection that cast an unbearable odour over the entire neighbourhood. So on June 12th Sanson's carpenters had another sleepless night when the guillotine was dismantled and transported yet again to the *Place du Trône-Renversé* (Nation). In the three days that it stood in Place de la Bastille 73 people were decapitated, and their bodies buried in the Sainte-Marguerite Cemetery, which you will come to later.

THE ELEPHANT.

Under Napoléon another fountain was planned for Place de la Bastille, to be placed there in honour of the arrival in Paris of a new water supply from the river Ourcq, which crossed the square by way of an underground canal. The fountain was to take the form of a vast elephant, cast in bronze from expropriated Spanish cannons, with water coming out of its trunk. The first stone was laid in the middle of the square on December 2nd 1808, the fourth anniversary of Napoléon's coronation, and on this the foundations of the statue were built. The elephant itself was never realised, but the architect, Jean-Antoine Alavoine, made a 24-metre high model in lathe and plaster, which was put on show on the south side of the square at the entrance to rue de Charenton. The project was eventually abandoned, but the model remained for many years as an object of curiosity for visitors and Parisians alike. In 1847 this once majestic elephant, which was by then a dilapidated ruin and a nest for hundreds of rats, was sold by the city of Paris for 3,833 *francs*. I can't tell you who bought it, but as far as I can see, the city got the better deal.

THE COLUMN.

The elephant was still there at the end of 1830, when a law was passed authorizing the construction of a new monument in Place de la Bastille. This time it was to be a column in honour of the men killed earlier that year during the 'Glorious Three' - July 27th, 28th and 29th, three days of fighting that deposed Charles X. The architect in charge was once again Alavoine, who at that moment was working on the seventh blueprint for his now ageing elephant, and must have been relieved to at last have something to build on the foundations that still stood embarrassingly empty in the middle of the square. The bronze column was constructed in three parts, each representing one day of combat, and at the top is the spirit of Liberty *flying away, breaking her chains and spreading light.*' The entire construction is 52 metres high, and stands on top of an underground funeral grotto holding the bones of the victims of those three glorious days. On July 24th 1848, after the transfer into the grotto of yet more bones from victims of the *journées révolutionnaires* the previous February, Louis-Philippe's throne was ceremoniously burned at the foot of the column. In 1871 the column itself was a victim of revolutionary violence, when soldiers from the Commune set fire to a barge full of petrol and sent it along the canal underneath the column. Enormous flames belched from both entrances of the canal, burning the vaulted ceiling of the grotto and turning it into a red-hot inferno, while outside the monument was pelted with 50 firebombs. But miraculously Alavoine's column stood firm, and still stands today on the site of the bastion of the Bastille, which in the last years of the fortress had become governor de Launay's private garden, where he used to let his favourite prisoners take their daily walk.

➡If you would like to see some remains of the Bastille you should go down into the metro station. Walk around the north part of the square and you will find an entrance where

Boulevard Beaumarchais meets Boulevard Richard-Lenoir. Go down on to the platform of Line 5, direction Place d'Italie, where there is a vestige of the rampart that joined the bastion to the main part of the prison. ➡On the opposite platform (direction Bobigny) you can see part of the counterscarp wall which ran along the eastern side of the moat. These are the only parts of the ancient fortress that are still in their original position.

THE FAUBOURG SAINT-ANTOINE.

➡Leaving the Place de la Bastille, walk eastwards and take rue du Faubourg Saint-Antoine. In the late 18th century this road was the principal thoroughfare between the Bastille and the *Barrière du Trône*, and took you through the Faubourg Saint-Antoine, a veritable breeding ground of revolutionary activity. It is slightly off the beaten track and seldom explored by visitors, for it contains none of the renowned tourist 'sights' that have made Paris so famous. But as you visit the area you will be walking with the ghosts of hundreds - perhaps thousands - of unsung popular heroes, for the Faubourg Saint-Antoine was the cradle of the *sans-culotte* revolution. Over the years it earned a reputation as *'the crater from which revolutionary lava regularly erupted',* for it was in the forefront of all popular revolts during the Revolution and for a century afterwards, and still retains some of its image as a bastion of the Left.

In addition to its political significance, the Faubourg Saint-Antoine has always played an important role in the economic life of the city, for it was a major producer of furniture as well as a centre of wallpaper production, pottery, glass polishing, mirror-making and the manufacture of saltpetre. Most of the artisans who inhabited the area were carpenters and cabinet makers, and it remains to this day a centre of furniture production, where numerous small workshops continue to occupy

'The crater from which revolutionary lava regularly erupted.' The rue du faubourg Saint Antoine was in the forefront of all popular revolts during the Revolution and for a century afterwards. Scenes like this were all too familiar to the residents of this militant neighbourhood. (Author's private collection)

many of the rear courtyards of the buildings. These modern-day carpenters use age-old methods handed down by their predecessors to produce a variety of furniture which is then displayed and sold in the local shops. In the 18th century the production of wooden furniture was a domain in which the different types of work were strictly delineated. Carpenters (*charpentiers*) were divided into two groups, according to the size of cutting axe used, since this decided the size of the pieces of wood you worked with. If you worked on the smallest parts of a building you were a joiner (*menuisier*), and if you made doors, windows, chests or sideboards, or if you worked with ebony, you were a cabinet-maker (*ébéniste*). Since the 15th century a royal ordinance had granted the furniture makers of the Faubourg Saint-Antoine exemption from the restrictive authority of the guilds, which enabled them to give free rein to their creativity. They experimented with wood from a variety of origins, developed decorative specialities like tortoise-shell inlay, nut and cedar veneers, and produced imitations of Chinese furniture. They were pioneers in the use of marquetry and decorative bronze, as well as being official suppliers to the royal family and the Court, a privilege that simultaneously generated enormous jealousy and thus contributed to the development of anger and revolt. What's more, it is questionable whether or not these favourable conditions enabled them to earn a good living. At the beginning of the Revolution a cabinet-maker named François-Joseph Dehm, working at 270 rue du Faubourg Saint-Antoine in one room and with no shop or showroom, could hardly earn enough to support his wife and five children. Another cabinet-maker, Antoine-Charles Balin, who was also a Justice of the Peace in the *Quinze-Vingt* Section of the faubourg, was arrested after 9 *Thermidor*. He told his judges, *'I was poverty-stricken before the Revolution, and I'm still poverty-stricken.'*

A good many of the houses on rue du Faubourg Saint-Antoine date at least from the 18th century, like number 18, known at that time by its sign, *L'Agneau-Pascal* (the Pascal Lamb), which used to still be there, but now seems to have disappeared from its niche. As you walk in this area you should look in all the doorways and entrances, for you never know what old cobbled courtyard or beamed arches you might catch a glimpse of. A lot of these doors have entrance codes nowadays, but sometimes they don't function during the day, so if you press the button just underneath the numbers, the door might open and you can go in and look - but always discreetly because people live in these places. There are beams on the ceiling of the entrance to number 33, and along the side you see old boundary stones, with grooves around the top for rope, where people tied up their horses. The courtyard is paved with big cobblestones, and as you go in, there is an old well to your right that's now used as a plant pot. If the door is open ➥ take a look at the Cour Nom-de-Jésus at number 47, and then cross over and go into Passage de la Boule-Blanche at number 50. This little street was opened in 1700 to connect the Faubourg Saint-Antoine with the *Caserne des Mousquetaires* (Musketeers' Barracks) at the other end of the passage. It was at number 9 of this passage that the famous murderer, Pierre François Lacenaire, killed one of his victims, most of whom were bank messenger-boys. Lacenaire is also known as a poet, a very intelligent individual who purposely got himself arrested for a minor crime so he could learn to become a crook in prison, which he called his 'criminal university'. He was guillotined in 1836 at the age of 33, and is portrayed in Marcel Carné's film *Les Enfants du Paradis*, a more recent film with Daniel Auteuil, and Lacenaire's crimes also inspired Dostoevsky to write 'Crime and Punishment'. If you can, go in and have a look at the courtyard of number 9, for it is very lovely, despite its grim past, and also gives a good idea of the kind of places where the *sans-culottes* lived and worked.

➡Go to the end of the Passage de la Boule-Blanche where directly in front of you, at 28 rue de Charenton, is an eye hospital that dates back to 1254. It stands on the site of the *Caserne des Mousquetaires-Noirs*, built in 1699 for the 2nd company of royal musketeers whose horses were always draped in black. They accompanied the king on all his military campaigns, and even if the king himself was not commanding, it was always the Black Musketeers who served his chief general, the *Maréchal de France* (Marshall of France). A celebrated *Mousquetaire Noir* was the marquis de Lafayette, who came here in 1760 at the age of 13 to begin his military education. A few years later Cardinal de Rohan - more famous for his part in the affair of the queen's diamond necklace - became administrator of the *Hospice des Quinze-Vingts*, an institution for the blind on rue Saint-Honoré, founded in 1260 by Louis IX (Saint-Louis). The name *quinze-vingts* refers to the number of beds - 15 times 20 beds - that Louis requested for 300 blind patients. These patients that the king was so concerned for were 300 knights, seized in the Holy Land by Saracen soldiers, who put out their eyes, and when they finally returned to France Louis ordered the building of this hospital specifically to care for them, ordaining that there should never be more than three 300 patients. The hospital was still there on rue Saint-Honoré 500 years later, when Cardinal de Rohan sold it in 1780 for a mammoth 6.3 million *livres*, and transferred it here to the *Caserne des Mousquetaires-Noirs*, which had been closed since 1775. These much larger premises enabled him to increase the number of patients to 800, all of whom received 4 *francs* a day, and every child born there was given 10 *centimes* a day until the age of 16. (The term *franc* was used at the time in accounting as a synonym for the *livre tournois*, a unit of currency created by Jean, King of the Franks, in 1360.)

During the Revolution the hospital would have witnessed a great deal of violence all around it, for this area was the scene of frequent *sans-culotte* revolts that continued into the next century. In 1848, during another revolution, when the Archbishop of Paris, Mgr Denys Affre, tried to mediate between soldiers and rebels battling on the barricades, he paid for his efforts with his life. After being shot down at the entrance to rue du Faubourg Saint-Antoine, he was sheltered at the house of the hospital's curate, where he died, and his blood-stained shirt is still kept in the Eglise de Saint-Antoine-des-Quinze-Vingts (66 Avenue Ledru-Rollin). After the Revolution the hospital remained here under the direction of the government, and it's still here - now called Centre Hospitalier National d'Ophtalmologie des Quinze-Vingts. Unfortunately most of the buildings of the Black Musketeers' *Caserne* were demolished during the 1960s and rebuilt, but the main entrance at number 28 and the buildings next to it are originals from 1699. ➡Go through the main entrance, follow the *piétons* signs and walk across to the right, where you can go and look at the hospital chapel, the only other original building remaining. (If you can't find it ask at the *Acceuil* at the entrance.) In 1791 the parish of *Saint-Antoine-des-Quinze-Vingts* was created, and this little chapel became its seat until the construction of the new church on Avenue Ledru-Rollin in 1903. The chapel did not entirely escape the impact of the Revolution. It was rented to a coal merchant in 1793, but was restored by Abbé Dubois in 1799 and received a renewed benediction in May of the following year.

➥Now go back along Passage de la Boule-Blanche, right on rue du Faubourg Saint-Antoine, and then right again at number 56 into Cour du Bel-Air. This interesting old passage has now been beautifully restored, and according to legend the house directly in front of you when you enter was frequented by the most famous of the musketeers, D'Artagnon and his companions, and has a magnificent staircase known as the *escalier des Mousquetaires-Noirs*. Incidentally, if you are a fan of Dumas's swashbuckling heroes, it seems they were real people, and you can read all about them at this website: http://www.awesomestories.com/flicks/the-musketeer/the-real-dartagnan.

Walking into the Passage du Chantier at number 66 will give you a real feeling of where the *sans-culottes* lived and worked. It is still full of furniture makers, and the tradition of producing the furniture in the back and selling it in the shops on the street is going on to this day. Look through the windows of some of the shops, like Atelier Paul about half way down on the left, and you will see old stone walls and open beams that must certainly have been witness to much revolutionary ranting, plotting and action.

➥Coming back into rue du Faubourg Saint-Antoine, at number 61 on the other side of the road is the Trogneux Fountain, one of four that were built in the city during the 18th century, and until its installation in 1720 the faubourg had no local water supply. This one was named after a neighbourhood brewer, and is still working, although the water that comes out of the two lions' heads is not drinkable, so don't try it!

➥Another passage worth looking at is the Cour de l'Etoile d'Or at number 75, which is enormous and really evokes old Paris. As you enter the first courtyard you will see a sundial bearing the date 1757 on the facade of the house directly in front of you. This was the principal house (*maison de maître*) of the passage, separating the two courtyards and dating from 1640 - much older than the sundial, which has been somewhat changed from its original aspect by substantial restoration. Find the staircase to the right marked *escalier* F and press the white square button that lights up the staircase - then try to imagine places like this without the benefit of electric lighting, and you can see how the *sans-culottes* were able to organize a revolt without ever being observed. ➡Now have a look into the Cour des Trois Frères with its vaulted, beamed entrance, where to your right as you enter is a lovely old staircase, and on the left an old door with lace curtains at the window, all of which bring to mind images from old French films. The look of many of these little alleys in the Faubourg Saint-Antoine has not changed a great deal for decades, and some of them still seem to have retained the atmosphere of revolutionary times. When you look behind some of the entrances, you will often see a maze of passages that can easily be imagined peopled with *sans-culottes*, going about their work by day, and at night gathering together to plan the next *journée revolutionnaire*. The artisans and workers of the faubourg had no official political voice, but maintained a high level of involvement in the political life of the city through regular meetings and discussions both in their workshops and in the local cafés and taverns, and of course through insurrection. They were the most violent supporters of the Revolution, which is why Hanriot rushed to the faubourg on the night of 9 *Thermidor* to raise support for the outlawed Robespierre amongst the *sans-culotte* community. But by then most of their leaders, who could have moved the faubourg into action, had already been eliminated by Robespierre's own regime of terror, and those left were either against him or too frightened to take action.

The Sans-Culottes.

'The sans-culotte is a true man of nature...a patriot who is robust in mind and body...who used to be called a man of the people, frank, cordial, sometimes rough, but always humane, even in those revolutionary instants when a veil is thrown over the image of humanity. The true sans-culotte desired the death of the tyrant and of all conspirators; you will see him where traitors are passing on their way to execution, you will even see him crowding around their scaffold, for humanity in no way excludes justice. The two Brutuses were true sans-culottes; the older one kissed his son as he condemned him to death; the other wept in his father's arms before stabbing him.' (Challamel, 1843)

Despite its idealism, this description of a *sans-culotte*, which appeared in the newspaper *Révolutions de Paris* in 1793, is also rather alarming in its extremism. So who were they, these 'robust men of nature', these latter-day Brutuses? And why the name *sans-culotte* - meaning 'without breeches'? Believe it or not it was the aristocrats who started it. At the beginning of the Revolution the expression was coined contemptuously by certain members of the nobility to ridicule the working man's habit of wearing ordinary trousers rather than aristocratic knee-breeches and hose. But the popular press cleverly turned this insult to their advantage by seizing on the name and adopting it with glory, so that soon many middle-class Jacobins were abandoning their silk stockings and elegant perfumes, and affecting the style of the faubourgs. The true friend of the Revolution wore trousers held up by braces, and a short, narrow-fitting jacket, known as a *carmagnole*, which had very short lapels and was decorated with lots of buttons. He wore a scarf around his neck, carried a pike in his hand, and on his head, of course, was the all-important *bonnet-rouge* decorated with a tricolour cockade. *Sans-culottes* dropped the use of *vous* in favour of the more informal *tu*, and never addressed anyone as *monsieur* or *madame*, but simply as *citoyen* or *citoyenne*. These 'working-class heroes' were revered in the popular press, especially by the pipe-smoking *Père Duchesne* in Hébert's radical newspaper, where in issue number 313 he describes a typical day in the life of a *sans-culotte*.

> *'From early morning he is merry as the day is long, and at the crack of dawn he picks up his tools and sings the Carmagnole; when he has worked hard all day he goes to relax at the section, and when he appears amongst his brothers, one shakes his hand, another pats him on the shoulder...he has no fear of being denounced, he is never threatened with domiciliary visits...when he returns in the evening to his garret, his wife greets him with a kiss, his little kids run to embrace him, his dog jumps around licking him...he tells them that a general, a traitor, a Brissotin has been guillotined...he then eats with the appetite of a true worker...after that he goes to bed, sleeps peacefully and snores all night long.'*

(Hardman, 1973)

By the time the monarchy was toppled in the summer of 1792 the term *sans-culotte* had become synonymous with the political views and objectives of the working people of Paris, the small shop-keepers and craftsmen of popular quarters like the Faubourg Saint-Antoine. Their political arena was to be found in the 48 sections created in 1790 for the Paris Commune, and in the summer of 1792, by forcing the hand of the Assembly, they got permission for these popular sections to operate in permanent session. That moment marked the beginning of the *sans-culotte* revolution.

Although there were not very many of them - a maximum of 5,000 in Paris - their power was now indisputable, and until spring 1794 no individual or group could take control in Paris without first winning their support. They had their own newspaper that was originally called *L'Ami des Citoyens*, but was later changed to *L'Ami des Sans-Culottes*, a change that the editor explained to his readers on the front page. '*The word citizen includes both good and bad citizens, and I am not, nor do I wish to be, a friend of bad citizens.*' There was, apparently, no such thing as a bad *sans-culotte*. They also had their own song, the celebrated *Ca Ira!*, which became the anthem of the *sans-culotte* movement. Literally meaning 'that will go', this French expression has been variously translated at 'That'll be ok', 'That'll do', 'That'll work', 'Everything will turn out fine', or even 'There is hope', but in the context of the revolutionary *Ca Ira!* it could well be seen as a mixture of all of them. The song's lyrics began benignly in 1789 with '*When the aristocrat protests, the good citizen will laugh in his face*', but by 1793 it had become the anthem of a lynch-mob - '*Aristocrats to the gallows! We'll string up the aristocrats!*' The power of the *sans-culottes* was not confined to Paris - they were feared throughout the country. On one occasion a group of actors in Chartres were performing a play containing some decidedly anti-revolutionary dialogue, and unbeknownst to them, in the audience that day were Gonchon and Forcade, two *sans-culotte* orators from the Faubourg Saint-Antoine. When the most unpatriotic part of the play was wildly applauded by the audience, Gonchon stood up and said, '*I see you don't realise that the sans-culottes from the faubourg Saint-Antoine are here.*' The applause stopped instantly, as Gonchon climbed up on the stage and declared to the intimidated spectators, '*We have overthrown the kings, and we will easily overthrow the kings of the theatre.*'

➡Continue along rue du Faubourg Saint-Antoine to numbers 106-118. On this site, now Square Trousseau, stood the *Hospice des Enfants-Trouvés* (Foundling Hospital), known in the 18th century as the *Hospice des Enfants-Exposés*. The hospital and its chapel had existed since the 17th century, and it was in the cemetery of the chapel that the mutilated body of the Princesse de Lamballe was buried, after having been paraded in the streets of the Marais, while her head was on a pike on its way to the Temple prison. In 1748 another branch of the Foundling Hospital was built next to Notre Dame Cathedral, so that mothers, who usually abandoned their babies at night in order to hide their shame, did not have to risk the dangers of the faubourg after dark.

➡ Keep going along rue Saint-Antoine, looking in on the Cour du Saint-Esprit at number 127, and as you walk don't forget that during the Great Terror this was another 'route of the condemned', where daily processions of tumbrils took condemned prisoners to the guillotine in what is now Place de la Nation. The street was always lined with crowds of local residents, as well as people from other parts of the city who came to cheer and jeer at the unfortunate victims being jolted along to their doom. On one occasion a military deserter named Victor Notter was in one of the tumbrils because of his much-loved dog, who had been responsible for his arrest by recognizing him at the wrong moment. The dog followed his master all the way from prison to the scaffold, barking and leaping around the wheels of the tumbril as it rolled along rue du Faubourg Saint-Antoine. You will meet up with this soldier and his best friend again later on when they reach the scaffold. The executioner Sanson recalled another day, when there were 23 women in one tumbril, *'of various ages and backgrounds, all equal in their despair, by the terror, by the horror of their fate.'* Sanson describes the terrible journey, *'where each turn of the wheel is marked by a teardrop, by a cry of anguish, by a supplication; those ashen, stony faces, those wild eyes, the pleas of those unhappy souls going some to Heaven, some to Hell, would dishearten the most determined of us.'*

It was during this time of Terror when the tumbrils came along here that Sanson began to become increasingly disturbed by his job. *'My strength is at its limit, and at times my heart fails me,'* he wrote on 29 *Prairial*, when the guillotine took 54 victims. It was a terrible day for Sanson. *'It is like a dream from which I want to tear myself without being able to. I make the preparations for these executions without realizing what is going to happen, carrying out my duties with the mechanical regularity of an automaton...then comes the sound of the blade which brings me back to reality. I never hear it now without flinching, without my entire body breaking out in a cold sweat. Then a kind of rage takes hold of me; without realizing that I should be cursing myself first, I silently utter a thousand curses on these policemen who, sabre in hand, brought these unfortunates here with their hands tied; to those stupid people who watch them die without venturing a single movement or gesture to save them; and to the sunshine that illuminates it all. At the end, I leave, crushed, broken by the anguish in my soul, wanting to cry but unable to find one tear.'* (Sanson, 1988)

➼Keep following Sanson along rue du Faubourg Saint-Antoine, but stop and look in on the Passage Saint-Bernard at number 159, which has a restaurant, Le Brespail, where you can sit on a lovely little terrace right in the passage. It is by all accounts a very good restaurant, with cuisine from the Ariège region in Gascony, where the word *brespail* means a sort of improvised meal. But with *foie-gras*, *cassoulet* and lots of Armagnac on the menu, this charming little restaurant doesn't sound very improvised to me. The tiny passage at number 179 has some pretty windows, and in the tradition of the faubourg is also home to several furniture makers. ➼Continue walking until you get to where the road widens at metro Faidherbe-Chaligny. There used to be a covered market in the middle of the road here called *La Petite-Halle*, built in 1643 and which functioned right up to 1940. The mother-superior of the neighbouring *Abbaye royale de Saint-Antoine-des-Champs* (you'll come to this next) had ten butcher's stalls here, giving her a monopoly on the sale of meat in the entire faubourg. In 1719 a fountain was built next to the market - companion to the Trogneux fountain that you saw earlier - called Fontaine de Montreuil, which served the whole faubourg, including the butchers of *La Petite-*

Halle. The foundation stone was laid on September 20th 1719 in a ceremony presided over by the Provost of Merchants, accompanied by drums, trumpets and the distribution of alms to local workers. It is also on this same spot that a riot broke out on April 27th 1789 leading to the pillaging and burning of the Réveillon wallpaper factory, which you'll come to shortly.

➡ Across the road at number 184 is the Hôpital Saint-Antoine, which stands on the site of the former *Abbaye Royale de Saint-Antoine-des-Champs,* founded at the end of the 12th century. This was for a long time one of the richest and most important abbeys in Paris - which is not surprising if all their abbesses were as good at business as the butcher of *La Petite-Halle* - and in addition to business, the mother-superior administered justice throughout the faubourg. The abbey served as a refuge for delinquent women led astray by life, who would come here to save their souls through devotion to God, but it also received women who believed that prevention was better than cure, and came here to flee the temptations of the world before succumbing to them. At the outbreak of the Revolution the abbey was closed and confiscated by the government, who turned part of it into a military storehouse, and rented out the rest to local residents. Market gardeners grew fruit and vegetables, including melons and lentils, and some of them developed little vineyards, orchards and flower gardens that all flourished here. Then in 1793, with the definitive closure of all religious institutions, the *Quinze-Vingts Section* set up a saltpetre factory in the abbey buildings. These were dangerous times for religion, but the nuns here were much luckier than many others, for none of them was executed during the Terror. Ten of them continued to live together in a rented house in Paris, until they were eventually arrested and imprisoned, but then saved by the fall of Robespierre on 9 *Thermidor*. The youngest of them, Sister Augustin de Vergèses de Chabannes, went to England, where she founded a Cistercian-Trappist abbey that still exists today.

After the Revolution, the post-*Thermidor* government deemed care of the body to be more important than care of the soul, and turned the abbey into a hospital, naming it *Hospice de l'Est*, by way of a thank you to the *sans-culottes* of this eastern end of the city for their contribution to the Revolution. Starting with 230 beds, it has evolved over two centuries into the huge hospital you see now, where not much is left of the original abbey, but if you go in through the entrance you will see some of the buildings re-constructed in 1770 by the architect Goupil. Directly facing the entrance is the Clock Pavilion, which was renovated in 1764 and is all that remains of the abbey's cloistered courtyard. ➡You should now go back out through the hospital entrance, turn left and walk down to number 170*bis* rue du Faubourg Saint-Antoine, where you will see a door with pillars that belonged to the abbey's original gatehouse.

At this point the tumbrils continued straight on along rue du Faubourg Saint-Antoine heading for Place de la Nation, but you are going to take a different route. ➡After passing the Hôpital Saint-Antoine, cross over rue de Chaligny and rue de Reuilly, and have a look at the houses at numbers 202 and 206 rue du Faubourg Saint-Antoine, both of which were built during the Revolution and give a good example of the architecture of the period. 206 has some nice carvings on each side of the central window, and along the top of it you can see a typical revolutionary rod design. ➡Now go back and turn left into rue de Reuilly, which began as a dirt road leading to the village of Charenton, and in 1781 counted among its residents the youngest brother of Louis XVI, Charles-Philippe, Comte d'Artois, later to become Charles X. Having so many older brothers, Artois never expected to become king, and consequently opted from an early age for the life of a libertine. He had a little house at this end of the street where he could escape from the bustle and intrigue of Versailles, and it was here that his mistress, Louise de Polastron, used to visit him regularly. She was the sister-in-law of the queen's favourite, Yolande de Polignac, who in 1782 brought this angelic 17-year old to Versailles as a new 'toy' for Marie-Antoinette. Artois had known her since she was 15, had been constantly at her bedside when she was stricken with measles in 1781, and it wasn't long before the ravishing teenager became his mistress. Their union turned out to be a long-lasting and happy one, and when Artois emigrated in 1789 she accompanied him into exile. Louise's death from consumption in 1804 provoked a dramatic transformation in the Comte d'Artois, converting him overnight from frivolity to religious devotion.

➥Continue down rue de Reuilly to number 11, where in 1772 a wealthy bourgeois by the name of Antoine Joseph Santerre bought a house and opened a *brasserie* called *L'Hortensia*. A *brasserie* nowadays is a place where beer and other alcohols are drunk, but the word actually means brewery, and originally it was a place where beer was produced. There were twelve breweries in the Faubourg Saint-Antoine during the time of the Revolution, producing all sorts of beer at all seasons, but the beer brewed in March was always considered the best. Santerre bought his brewery with a family inheritance, and had the necessary capital - and space - for the business of brewing. During the time he lived here there was a round tower built on to the top of the first floor where barley was stored, while the entrance to the courtyard, where the brewing took place, was at number 13. Despite his wealthy bourgeois background, his nickname 'King of the Faubourgs', and a rather aristocratic obsession with horse-racing, Santerre was a dedicated patriot who in times of hardship always generously shared his wealth with the local residents. The popularity this brought him later enabled him to drum up local support for the overthrow of Louis XVI, and when it happened, it was Santerre who replaced Mandat as commander and persuaded the National Guard to join the invasion of the Tuileries.

Santerre was a rather contradictory character, and had no reputation for cruelty or wickedness. When the Tuileries palace was attacked, Santerre showed extreme concern for the safety of the royal family, escorting them to a safe refuge in the Feuillants Club, and as chief of the Temple guard during their imprisonment, he also displayed a moderate and courteous attitude that contrasts strangely with his behaviour a few months later when Louis XVI was executed. Having accompanied the deposed king to the Convention for his trial and then to the scaffold, he then ordered the drums to be rolled as Louis tried to address the crowd, thus preventing the king's last words from being heard by the people. Santerre seemed to be making it clear that in his most public moments he wanted no shadow of royalism to be cast over his identity as *sans-culotte* leader. His house was always a focal point for subversive activity, and during the period leading up to the overthrow of the monarchy he had a stream of visitors, including the Duc d'Orléans. On the morning of June 20th 1792 the neighbourhood bristled with tension as Louis Legendre, a butcher from the Cordeliers district, and several other militants from the Faubourg Saint-Antoine all assembled at Santerre's house to organize one of the most legendary popular revolts of the Revolution. Later that day a huge crowd invaded the Tuileries Palace and forced Louis XVI to put on a red republican bonnet and drink the wine of the people from a common gourd.

Santerre's experience as commander of the National Guard convinced him that he was well suited to military service, so he requested a posting in the Vendée. But he turned out to be totally incapable, and after a succession of failed campaigns he was recalled to Paris, arrested on suspicion of *Orléanism* and put in the *Carmes* prison. By the time he was released after 9 *Thermidor* Santerre's political career was over, and he returned to rue de Reuilly to find that his wife had not only left him but had also brought the brewery to financial ruin. Undeterred, he sold his house and re-made his fortune by speculating in state property, only to lose it all again in an ill-managed business deal. Although Santerre retired from political activity after the Revolution, his past glory - and immense power - as a popular leader and revolutionary general was never quite forgotten. When unrest broke out in the Faubourg Saint-Antoine on the eve of Napoléon Bonaparte's coup d'etat in 1799, the future emperor immediately issued a warning. *'Tell Santerre that at the first sign of trouble, I'll have him shot.'* As a soldier, however, he was not remembered with quite so much awe. When reports circulated that he had died at the battle of Saumur, a humorous epitaph was circulated, making fun of his profession as a brewer: *Ci-Gît le général Santerre, qui n'eût de Mars que la bière* (Here lies General Santerre, Who knew of war only the bier/beer.) The reports of Santerre's death turned out to be greatly exaggerated, and the 'King of the Faubourgs' lived on for several more years until he died in poverty in Paris on February 6th 1809.

It is really very sad that this historic brewery, so irrevocably linked with the *sans-culotte* movement, has been totally demolished. But it is, at least, gratifying to see that the residents of today's Faubourg Saint-Antoine have recognized the significance of this famous brewer, by having a plaque put up on the wall in his honour. It reads, *'To the brewer Santerre, General-in-Chief of the National Guard of Paris. The residents of the faubourg Saint-Antoine. 1752-1809.'*

We'll now leave Santerre and his friends to their revolts and conspiracies and ➡continue down rue de Reuilly to number 20, where nowadays you see a complex of military barracks called the Caserne de Reuilly. (The number 20 is not marked but the building is opposite a new college called J. Fr. Oeben.) These barracks were built in 1830 on the site of the former *Manufacture Royale des Glaces*, where mirrors were produced of a quality and beauty rivalled only by those of their great

Venetian competitors. It began in the 17th century when a group of glass-blowers from Venice set up business in a row of houses on rue de Reuilly, where their work was protected by royal favour. The mirrors were made in factories near Cherbourg, and then brought here to be softened, polished and silvered. Under Colbert's ministry the industry flourished and a new building was constructed, with several huge galleries on two different levels, all equipped with benches for polishing and silvering. It took about twelve days to polish a 2-metre mirror, but before that it had to be 'softened', a process of equalizing the surface by rubbing one mirror against the other. When working with a very big mirror, the polisher had to be lowered towards it on a large wooden arc that was suspended like a spring from the ceiling. There were about 1,000 workers here during the *ancien régime*, and if there was an excess of polishing to be done, the workforce was supplemented with inmates of the *Bicêtre* prison. During the Revolution the number of workers fell to 500, and by 1791 there was such a shortage of polishers that 70 prisoners were employed in the workshop at *Bicêtre*.

On March 28th 1790 you would have seen the unusual sight of a cortege of royal carriages going right past Santerre's brewery and stopping here where you are standing. For on that day the *Manufacture Royale des Glaces* was honoured by a visit from the king and queen, an event which, despite the revolutionary climate, evoked in the district a surge of royalist sentimentality worthy of the age of Louis XV. The following day the District Secretary addressed the local assembly and recalled *'the intense joy manifested at the sight of Their Majesties, who came to honour us yesterday with their presence...in one of the workshops the president of the district made a speech in which, after describing with eloquent simplicity the needs of the inhabitants of the faubourg, who lived in large part by the aid administered by Their Majesties, he requested the continuation of this, reassuring their sacred persons of the intense and sincere gratitude of all the workers of the faubourg, and the ardour of their wishes for the prosperity of all the royal family. The king replied that he neither knew nor desired any other happiness than that which he shared with his people...the queen, casting a look full of tenderness and sensitivity on the workers who surrounded her on all sides, and shedding tears of emotion, added that the relief of the people was the constant object of their concerns, and often even of their anxieties. Their Majesties then visited the different workshops, addressing their remarks to both bosses and workers, posing questions to each relative to their rank and position and all full of kindness.'* This eulogy went on and on, describing Louis XVI as *'the dearest and most worthy of beings'* and *'father of the people'*, claiming that *'no king had ever done so much for the happiness of his subjects'*, and even suggesting that *'however glorious the title of "Conquerors of the Bastille" might be for the inhabitants of the faubourg Saint-Antoine, it is not so close to their hearts as that of being faithful to the law and to the king.'* (BHVP 10065, No. 210)

After that dose of royalism - unexpected in this neighbourhood - ➡you should now go back to rue du Faubourg Saint-Antoine, cross over the road, continue on rue Faidherbe and turn immediately right into rue de Montreuil, which was originally a dirt track leading to the village of Montreuil and became an official road in 1750. At number 31, now a 20th-century building, stood a country house known as the *Folie-Titon*, named after its original 17th-century owner, Maximilien Titon, a royal arms manufacturer. In 1765 part of this property became the Manufacture Royale de Papiers Peints (Royal Wallpaper Factory) owned by a paternalistic but very successful capitalist named Jean-Baptiste Réveillon, who employed nearly 400 workers in his magnificent factory. Beginning first as a haberdasher, he started importing flock wallpaper from England and gained popularity when one of his imports, a particularly lovely blue English design, was chosen by Marie-Antoinette for the walls of her private *cabinets* at Versailles. After opening his factory here, Réveillon began producing wallpaper himself, becoming such a talented specialist in both colour and texture that it was not long before he had permisson to add *Royale* to his factory name. Behind the building was a beautiful garden, and both the factory and its grounds were open to the public. In 1783 Réveillon permitted two aeronauts, Pilâtre de Rozier and the Marquis d'Arlandes, to use his garden, where, aided by Réveillon's unique paper-joining techniques, they constructed a hot air balloon in which they made the first free flight in history. These historic balloons were covered with colourful and highly-decorative paper produced by Réveillon's workforce.

Six years later the factory became the centre of a riot on April 27th 1789, a week before the opening of the Estates-General, where Réveillon was running as a candidate. A few days before the riot, rumours had been spread by the Duc d'Orléans that Réveillon intended to reduce the daily wage of his workers to 15 *sous*. The reality was that Réveillon, who was well-known for his benevolence towards his employees and to the hard-working poor in general, had made a speech urging that the price of bread be brought down to 15 *sous*, so people could afford it. The rumours were denied by Réveillon, whose workers were actually paid rather better than many, receiving between 35 and 50 *sous* for a day's work. But all this was eclipsed by Réveillon's enormous personal wealth and his magnificent home standing provocatively in the middle of the modest Faubourg Saint-Antoine, making him a symbol of all that was hated by the local residents. The public anger fuelled by all the rumours was soon directed at Réveillon and his family, who, terrified for their lives, took refuge in the Bastille, while a violent crowd of 300 people poured down rue du Faubourg Saint-Antoine and gathered around the hated fortress, where they burned an effigy of Réveillon. People came from all around to join them, and it was a crowd of nearly 3,000 who then set off from the Bastille and back to rue de Montreuil to invade both the factory and

In the run-up to the Estates-General rumours spread that wallpaper manufacturer, Jean-Baptiste Réveillon, was going to lower his workers' wages. As a result his house on rue Montreuil was pillaged, looted and burned and Réveillon and his family had to take refuge in the Bastille. (Author's private collection)

Réveillon's personal residence. It was an extremely violent attack. The enraged crowd started several fires, burned all the books and accounts, threw furniture out of the windows into the street, and looted or destroyed everything in sight, turning this end of rue de Montreuil into a veritable battle ground. Casualties were taken to number 23, the home of a surgeon named Emtal, who did a noble job of cleaning and bandaging wounds and giving general first aid, while 25 dead bodies were piled up in the house of a gardener living at number 8.

Réveillon was not the only victim. A similar attack was made on the premises of a neighbouring saltpetre merchant named Henriot, also suspected of intending to reduce his workers' wages. Henriot himself took refuge in the dungeon at Vincennes, but leaves a vivid account of the terrifying experience of his wife, who was hiding in the room of one of their lodgers. *'Concealed between two mattresses, her children next to her, she expected to be killed at any moment. A shower of stones, thrown from the street, fell by her side and on top of the very mattress that covered her...suddenly the rioters knocked on the door and forced the lodger to open it. They wanted to come in; they said they knew I was hidden there...these furies then ran amok in my workshops and my home; they threw my furniture, clothes and papers into the flames...what they could not take, they destroyed...and since my entire fortune consists of my workshops, my furniture and the money or securities I had in my home, it is literally true to say that I am entirely ruined.'* (BHVP 957368 8379). Henriot calculated his loss at 71,734 *livres*, declaring that of this sum he could only hope to recover around 6,000 *livres* of debts *'owed by honest people.'*

It took two days to quell the revolt, which counted nearly 100 dead and several hundred injured, and resulted in the total destruction of both Henriot's and Réveillon's property. Henriot described himself as a victim of sedition, and wrote that *'my wife, my children and I are without bread and without a home.'* The Réveillon riot was one of the first manifestations of the Revolution to come, and, according to an anonymous open letter to the king, written two days after the revolt by a *'zealous citizen of the faubourg Saint-Antoine'*, it would not be the last. This anonymous pamphleteer does not mince his words in his prophetic warning to Louis XVI. *'Sire, I dare to announce to you that things have come to a head; the groaning of your people will transform itself into fury.'*

➡ Walk back now along rue de Montreuil and stop at number 23, where the surgeon named Emtal gave emergency treatment to the wounded during the two days of the Réveillon riots. When you cross over rue Faidherbe you are walking on the site of the former number 8 rue de Montreuil, where a gardener lived, and during those two days of rioting his property was used to pile up almost 80 bodies, all victims of the violence.

➡Continue down and along rue du Faubourg Saint-Antoine, then turn right on rue Saint-Bernard, a street dating from 1620. There are some lovely stone carvings over the door of number 18, which has a very nice courtyard and in the 18th century was a popular tavern called *Cabaret du Petit-Saint-Bernard*, no doubt a favourite meeting place for local *sans-culottes*. At number 17 on the left is Dos San Carlos, an interesting mirror shop, whose owner continues the real tradition of this area, still producing glass and mirrors in the same way as the original Venetian mirror-makers of the Faubourg Saint-Antoine, and you'll see shops selling wood too, all in the spirit of the neighbourhood's history. ➡Keep following the road, which makes a zig-zag at the corner of rue Chanzy, until you get to number 36, the Eglise Sainte-Marguerite. (You will see the church at the end, and you go left and right to get to the entrance.) This church was built in 1627 to serve the growing population of the Faubourg Saint-Antoine, which reached nearly 40,000 by the beginning of the 18th century. It was one of the few churches not to be closed during the Revolution, since its clergy had sworn the Constitutional Oath, and it thus witnessed many of the social changes of the period. The vicar of Sainte-Marguerite's was one of the first priests to take advantage of a new law permitting members of the clergy to marry, and for a short while the church was renamed *Temple de la Liberté et de l'Egalité.*

The Cimetière Sainte-Marguerite opened in 1637, and by the middle of the 18th century contained 34 communal graves. The escalating number of deaths in the community necessitated the building of two charnel houses that were used after the outbreak of the Revolution as a depot for military equipment, and in 1792 as a meeting place for officials of the Montreuil section. Between June 9th and 12th 1794, when the guillotine was briefly moved to the Place de la Bastille, this cemetery was used to bury the 73 people who were decapitated there. It was also the final destination for the first few victims executed in the *Place du Trône Renversé* (Nation) before the Picpus Cemetery was opened. The brevity of the guillotine's stay in Place de la Bastille (three days) was due to pressure from local residents, who, having given so much of their energy and blood for the patriotic cause, were outraged to see their neighbourhood becoming the killing field of the Revolution.

On June 8th 1795 a child died in the dungeon of the Temple prison. Two days later he was buried in a communal grave in the Sainte-Marguerite Cemetery, after being carried without ceremony through the streets of Paris in the company of about 40 assorted officials. The child's name was given as Louis XVII, the young dauphin who had been imprisoned with his royal parents in 1792. Once night had fallen the grave-digger retrieved the coffin under cover of darkness, opened it up and saw to his astonishment that the boy's skull had been sawn open during an autopsy. He closed the coffin and put it in a lead container, hastily drew a *fleur-de-lys*, symbol of royalty, on the top, and buried it again in a different place. The body of this enigmatic boy was exhumed half a century later in 1846, and again in 1894, when examination of the remains revealed them to be those of a boy of about 15 to 18, whereas the dauphin was just 10 when he died. The mystery of the Child of the Temple has never been solved, and the inevitable stories of substitutes provoked a wave of pretenders. Some rumours suggested that he had been poisoned. What we do know is that the dauphin was taken from his mother, Marie-Antoinette, in July 1793, and moved to the most secure part of the Temple prison, where he was given a 'good patriotic education' by the *sans-culotte* cobbler, Simon. However, confined to his room and left in filthy conditions, his physical and psychological health suffered irrevocably, and he died having spent the whole of his brief reign in captivity. The mysterious boy is now commemorated by a small gravestone over the spot where he was re-buried after the last exhumation in 1894. It carries the simple inscription 'L... XVII

1785-1795.' If the results of the 1894 examination were correct, then the boy in this grave is not Louis XVII at all, but exactly who he is we will never know. In order to look at this sad little monument you need to ask a church official to unlock the gate to the cemetery, which nowadays is reduced to a small courtyard. The church *Acceuil* is open from 9a.m.-12 noon and 2-5 p.m. on weekdays, and 10a.m.-12 noon on Saturdays.

➡Continue along rue Saint-Bernard, turn left on rue de Charonne, and walk down to numbers 51 and 53, where you will see the Hôtel de Mortagne, built in 1661. And you will see it, don't worry, despite the new building which appears to stand in its place. You just have to walk through the arch of the new building, and in front of you will be the beautiful Hôtel de Mortagne. If the entrance code is functioning, push the button under the numbers to get in - with the usual reminder that this is a private residence. In the middle of the 18th century, Jacques de Vaucanson, a collector of moving models and industrial machines, was looking for a bigger place to house his collection. He bought this house, which at the time was in the middle of fields and hedgerows, and installed his eccentric assortment of mechanical flute-players, tambourinists, and chess-players, as well as his famous duck that could flap its wings and swallow grain. This collection was one of the first acquisitions of the Conservertoire des Arts et Métiers created by the National Convention on October 10th 1794. There is an inscription on the house about de Vaucanson, who died here in 1782 at the age of 73. He invented methods of weaving that revolutionized the manufacture of tapestries at Les Gobelins, but he was equally well-known for his morally unconventional life-style, having lived intimately not only with his niece and his sister-in-law, but also with a nun from Longchamp Abbey.

After Vaucanson's death the *hôtel* was bought by Louis XVI for The King's Clockwork Exhibition, which was open to the public under the direction of a noble *savant* called De Vandermonde. In September 1793 the great French mathematician, Gaspard Monge, inventor of descriptive geometry, took a vacation from maths for a while to carry out experiments in metallurgy in this house. France was at war, and Monge, along with Vandermonde and a chemist called Berthollet, had been ordered by the Committee of Public Safety to do this work as a contribution to the country's steel industry, essential for arms production. So for a while this elegant house became a scientific laboratory. When Vandermonde died in 1796, his successor transferred the entire clockwork collection to the Conservatoire des Arts et Métiers, and turned the Hôtel de Mortagne into a free lodging-house for inventors, one of whom was an Englishman named Milne who invented a machine for spinning cotton. The entrance hall is all you can see of this beautiful house, but it is worth looking at for the lovely carvings and terracotta cameos that adorn the walls.

➡ Now go back eastwards along rue de Charonne, passing the rather spectacular Salvation Army building on the right, until you get to number 99, which was the site of a Benedictine convent called Couvent de Notre-Dame de bon-Secours. It has now sadly been replaced by a 1960s apartment block, but you can see some of the original interior façade if you go into the little street to the right of the building, called Cité du Couvent. Go to the end of this street and look to your left, where you can see what is left of the convent buildings. This would have been part of the inner courtyard, and despite the modern block in front of it, you can sense the monastic tranquillity that still pervades its lovely arches. But it was not only monks who led a life of seclusion in this peaceful cloister during the years leading up to the Revolution. Married women were locked up here on the orders of their husbands, who paid the kindly Benedictines handsomely for their hospitality. The convent was closed at the outbreak of the Revolution, thus liberating these unfortunate women who, in a new era of liberty and equality, hopefully found the means to take revenge on their husbands. The buildings were taken over in 1802 by the first cotton mill in France, visited in 1804 by Napoléon, who told the mill owner, *'Between us we have waged a tough war on English industry, but so far the manufacturer has been much happier than the Emperor.'*

➥ Another former convent with an eye to business was the Priory of La Madeleine-de-Traisnel at number 100 opposite. There is not much left of it now, but the entrance and the arcades on the street are original, and if you go into the courtyard, on your left you will see the façade of the former chapel with its original door. In 1911 three coffins from the 18th century were found in an underground vault of this priory, containing remains of three members of the Lafayette family. Up until the Revolution, the sisters of this establishment ran a very profitable business marketing a cosmetic product called *eau-de-vie de lavande*. With such a name, one wonders if perhaps they drank it as well, and with all this walking, a drink might not be such a bad idea. ➥If you continue in the same direction, the metro Charonne is just a few steps down the road, where you should find a nice café to relax and read about your next stop, the infamous clinic that a certain Doctor Belhomme ran during the Terror.

➥After leaving your café, continue walking eastward along rue de Charonne. This street began as a path leading from Paris to the village of Charonne, but became a proper road at the beginning of the 17th century, and is dotted with old shops and picturesque alleys going off on either side. These have mostly appeared since the 19th century, and at the time of the Revolution this end of rue de Charonne was quite rural, with fields stretching out behind the few houses that stood along the street. ➥Keep walking until you get to number 161.

Doctor Belhomme's Clinic.

As you look at the vast complex of modern apartment buildings at number 157-161 rue de Charonne, you might be wondering why I've brought you here. But don't be fooled by its exterior appearance, for behind it you will find what remains of one of the more sinister establishments of the revolutionary period. Jacques Belhomme has gone down in history as the bogus doctor who 'saved' rich aristocrats from the guillotine by lodging them here at vast expense, and then throwing them to the mercy of the Tribunal once their money had run out. Hard truth or pure legend? This is now being debated, but in the meantime ➡ you can see what is left of this celebrated establishment by going through the entrance of number 159 into the public park that has been built on Dr Belhomme's garden. Most of the biggest trees here are very old, some dating back to the 18th century, for when the present-day estate was built, they were dug up and later re-planted, in order to retain some of the appearance and atmosphere of Belhomme's original garden. The housing estate was opened in 1974 on the site of the clinic buildings, which had stood here, run-down and abandoned, until the beginning of the 1970s, when they were all tragically demolished. All, that is, but one very elegant and pretty 18th-century house that was miraculously saved from the bulldozers by the petitions and protests of the residents of the new apartments - to whom we owe an enormous debt of gratitude. You will understand why when you see the house they saved, which is now a listed building and owned by the City of Paris.

➡ To find it, as you enter the park follow the path with the playground immediately to the right, then take the path that goes off to the right (with the playground still on your right) and then veers around to the left. In front of you you will see the *Pavillon Colbert*, a baroque jewel amidst the modern architecture, and all that remains of Dr Belhomme's clinic. Built by the grandson of Jean-Baptiste Colbert, Minister to Louis XIV, it served as a lodge for Colbert when he went hunting in the woods and meadows around the village of Charonne. It is now a club for senior citizens, whom you might see through the windows, playing cards in the rooms where Belhomme's patients lived. The house has been restored, but the re-decoration has remained faithful to the original style, and one of the rooms has an interesting vaulted ceiling. If you look discreetly through the last window to the right of the main entrance you might be able to see this room, which is now used for playing billiards.

But what of the house's most well-known owner? Jacques Belhomme never strayed far from his roots, for he was born in the village of Charonne in 1737, and when he first rented his property in 1769 this part of rue de Charonne was within the outer limits of his village. Some say he was a carpenter by trade, others say a dealer in mirrors, but he called himself 'Doctor', a title for which he was by all accounts totally unqualified. Despite his lack of credentials, however, the clinic that he opened in his rented premises was such a success that he was able to buy the entire property in 1787 for 18,000 *livres*. His patients consisted of backward children and lunatics, who were all very well-looked after, for Belhomme compensated for his own lack of professional knowledge by engaging several competent and respected specialists. One of these specialists was Philippe Pinel, one of the founders - some say the father - of modern psychiatry, who was advisory physician to Belhomme during the 1780s. It was during this time that Pinel began to develop his system of observing patients and writing up case studies, so in this way Belhomme's patients probably made an important contribution to the evolution of today's psychiatry. But Pinel apparently failed to convince Belhomme himself to adopt his ground-breaking approach to the treatment of the mentally ill.

There were about 35 lunatics lodging in Belhomme's clinic by the time the Revolution broke out, a revolution that was to bring him a small fortune. The first victims of this turbulent era were the noble rich, and Belhomme gave them the opportunity of using what was left of their riches to buy their freedom. He offered the hospitality of his clinic to the growing number of imprisoned aristocrats, who, on the pretext of illness, were able to leave prison for the security of Dr Belhomme's clinic. Although their lodgings here were fairly mediocre, they naturally compared favourably with any of the prisons they had been in, and since the area was quite rural, they also benefited from fresh air and tranquillity. Another advantage was the permission of visits, and many residents were able to re-discover here some of the social pleasures and elegance of their former existence.

The privilege of being locked up in Dr Belhomme's clinic cost 250 *livres* a month, but this was a small price to pay when the alternative was the Tribunal and almost certain death. For Belhomme it meant a guaranteed income, a percentage of which he no doubt paid to the authorities. There is no evidence to prove it, but some believe that he had made a deal with Fouquier-Tinville, who must have delighted in this opportunity to fleece the aristocrats of their last remaining wealth. For the residents it was a tenuous arrangement, for according to the traditionally accepted theories about Dr Belhomme, once their money ran out and they could no longer pay for their lodgings, they found themselves out on the street without further discussion. From there it was only a short route, via the Conciergerie, to the guillotine. One of the many unfortunate inmates who suffered this fate, after having handed over his last resources to Dr Belhomme, was the lawyer and journalist Simon Linguet, whom you met at the Bastille. Linguet was an intelligent misfit who throughout his career attracted a great deal of attention for his angry and violent attacks on powerful aristocrats as well as on most of his fellow writers. This activity earned him his two-year stay in the Bastille in the early 1780s, memories of which must have made Dr Belhomme's hospitality seem all the more sweet, and his forced departure all the more bitter. Also among those thrown out were Delphine de Rochechouart, Duchesse de Châtelet, whose husband had already been executed, and Béatrix de Choiseul, Duchesse de Grammont. Both these unlucky ladies were guillotined on April 22nd 1794, at the same time as the equally unlucky Malesherbes family. A more fortunate duchess was Marie-Amélie Penthièvre, widow of the former Duc d'Orléans, Philippe-Egalité. Not only did she manage to keep up her payments at Belhomme's clinic until the overthrow of Robespierre, she also found consolation there in the arms of another resident, a deputy from Toulouse named Jean-Marie Rouzet, whose passion for Marie-Amélie later led him to abandon his entire family and follow her into exile.

As the Terror mounted, so did the number of Dr Belhomme's clients, and by 1793 his premises needed enlarging, so he rented the house next door at number 163, an attractive early 18th-century mansion called *Hôtel de Chabanais*. It was not very large, just two floors and a mansard roof, but enough to accommodate the overflow from Belhomme's rapidly expanding clientele, and it had the added advantage of a ground floor building linking it to the main clinic. Once the dividing wall was taken down between the two properties, Belhomme found himself with an enormous garden, an impressive complex of buildings and a rapidly expanding business. But there was trouble ahead.

In January 1794 two of his residents, municipal soldiers from Belhomme's own former regiment, who were genuinely ill, denounced him to their section commander, complaining that they hadn't been given any food during their stay at the clinic. An arrest warrant was put out for Belhomme, who took refuge first in the *Collège des Ecossais* before becoming a resident himself at another 'clinic', lesser-known than his own, run by Citizen Coignard in rue de Picpus. You'll be visiting this later, during the last part of the walk. Belhomme didn't stay at the Picpus clinic very long, for at the end of March he was transferred to the Conciergerie, and his wife took over the running of the clinic until 9 *Thermidor*, when all the residents left to enjoy their new-found liberty. In the meantime Belhomme had been accused of misuse of public funds and inhumanity to the poor, and sentenced to six years hard labour in the penal colony of Guyana. But a week after the fall of Robespierre he appealed successfully against his judgment, was acquitted, and came back to the clinic. With the money he had made during the Revolution he bought the *Hôtel de Chabanais* at number 163, and continued in business until his death in 1824 at the age of 87. Belhomme's son, who was a genuine doctor, transformed it into an asylum for 'renowned lunatics', and remained here until 1852.

This then is the macabre picture that, until recently, history has painted of Jacques Belhomme - the ruthless opportunist who fleeced the rich and threw them out to face their destiny when they had no more money. He is portrayed as a dealer in liberty - an increasingly scarce commodity in 1794 - who exploited the laws of supply and demand by continually putting up his prices until some people were paying 1,000 *livres* a month to escape from the hands of the executioner. Stories like this are probably apocryphal, and there are now some who believe that Belhomme has been misjudged, and that his aim in lodging these wealthy fugitives from the guillotine was to enable him to offer his establishment without charge to the poor. There is even some doubt now as to whether exhaustion of funds was ever the reason for turning people out. If Belhomme had made a deal with Fouquier-Tinville, it might well have been because he was harassed, or even threatened with arrest himself, if he didn't co-operate with the authorities - people were guillotined for less than that at the time. The jury is still out on Dr Belhomme, so you will have to decide for yourself whether this enigmatic character was a pitiless moneymaker or a subversive do-gooder.

Apart from this lovely house, the only other thing that remains from Belhomme's clinic is the front door. It was moved during the demolition to form part of the boundary of the new park, and the best way of looking at it is to ➡ return to rue de Charonne, turn right, then right again on rue Léon Frot, and take the fifth turning on the right, which is Passage Courtois. At the end of this alley you will see the great stone arched doorway that was the original entrance to the clinic, and which used to stand where you now find the entrance to number 161 rue de Charonne. There are two numbers on it - 161*bis*, which is the more recent number, and 32, which is engraved in the stone and was the number during the Revolution. It was through this doorway that Belhomme welcomed his residents when they first arrived, their pockets full - and - if legend has its way - through the same doorway that he threw them out when their pockets were empty.

➡ Return to rue de Charonne and turn left, continuing eastwards to number 177 on your left, where you see the Eglise du Bon-Pasteur. It stands on the site of the original neo-Gothic church, built in 1873 by Arthur Verhaegen for the large local community of furniture makers and wood-workers who spoke only Flemish. They had been brought from Belgium the previous year to replace the numerous French workers who had died or been imprisoned during the 1871 Commune. It remained a Flemish church until 1904, when it was given back to Paris, but 1972 saw its demolition and replacement by the modern building you see now. Along with the new church was built a complex of low-income housing, health facilities and a cultural centre.

Place de la Nation.

➥Your next stop is Place de la Nation, and you can reach it either by metro (continue in the same direction to metro Alexandre-Dumas, go two stops to Nation, and take the exit for Avenue du Trône), or on foot. In this case you you should walk back and turn left down Avenue Philippe-Auguste, a walk of about 10-15 minutes that will lead you directly into the north side of Place de la Nation. Bear left around the square, crossing Avenue de Bouvines and Avenue de Taillebourg until you get to Avenue du Trône.

Development of this enormous square, which was situated on the main route between Paris and Vincennes, began in the 17th century. Progress was slow, however, and at the time of the Revolution it still resembled a vast field that was given a circular form by the surrounding trees. The ground was grassy and uneven, and on the south side, beyond the encircling trees, a large expanse of vines and vegetable gardens stretched all the way to the convent at Picpus. It was given the name *Place du Trône* in 1660, the year of Louis XIV's coronation, in honour of the throne that was built here to receive the newly crowned monarch and his queen, Marie-Thérèse. Returning from the coronation ceremony in Rheims, the procession stopped here while the whole of Paris paid homage to the royal couple, seated gloriously on their throne in the middle of the square.

1787 saw the completion of the notorious Farmers-General Wall that was built around Paris for the collection of customs duty. One of its 60 barriers, the *Barrière du Trône*, was placed at the eastern edge of the *Place du Trône*, where architect Claude Nicolas Ledoux constructed the two enormous Doric columns that you see on either side of the Avenue du Trône. The base of these columns had been built much earlier to accommodate a triumphal arch to the glory of Louis XIV, a project that was never realised. But when the Farmers-General Wall was built, the foundations served as sentry-boxes, where all traffic coming in and out of Paris was stopped and inspected for taxable merchandise. Payment of duty was settled in one of the adjacent toll-houses, the two square stone buildings where customs personnel lived at that time, and which you still see today.

The Farmers-General Wall was an object of intense hatred throughout the city, described at the time as '*le mur murant Paris qui rend Paris murmurant*' (the wall enclosing Paris that leaves Paris grumbling). Two days before the storming of the Bastille it became the target of an attack by angry crowds, who forcibly broke through the wall in several places very near the *Barrière du Trône*. They looted and set fire to many of the toll-booths around Paris, in the hope of ridding the city of these crippling taxes and the resulting high food prices, but they had to wait almost two years, until May 1st 1791, for the barriers to be officially closed. On this occasion the *Place du Trône* was the scene of great merriment, as people danced all night to the sound of music and cannon fire, and over 300 cartloads of wine were brought through the barrier free of tax. Surprisingly, and fortunately for us, their festivities did not degenerate into the destruction of the two toll-houses, and these charming old buildings, which are now national monuments, have been restored as apartments by the Public Housing Office. The statues at the top of the two columns, portraying Saint-Louis and Philippe-Auguste, were added in 1845.

In 1793, after the overthrow and execution of the king, the square was re-named *Place du Trône Renversé* (the overturned throne), and for six weeks of the following year it became the setting for the most sombre spectacle of the Revolution. Up until June 1794 the guillotine had been permanently installed in *Place de la Révolution* (now Concorde), but on the 8th of that month Robespierre proposed a festival to honour the Supreme

Being and the Goddess of Reason. This was to be on the Champ-de-Mars, followed by a procession ending at the Tuileries Gardens - a route that went directly through *Place de la Révolution* - and the prospect of passing by the guillotine did not seem at all festive to the organizers of the event. As well as the sight of the dreadful machine, the ground around the scaffold was permanently soaked in blood, for according to official calculations, every time they guillotined someone blood spattered approximately four metres in all directions. So it was decided that the guillotine be moved further out of the city, and for three days it operated in the Place de la Bastille, until the residents complained and it was moved yet again. This time they took it to the city limits and installed it here, on June 13th 1794. To see the exact place, walk over to Place de l'Ile de la Réunion, which is behind the toll-house on the south side of the square (see plan), where you will see a plaque on the wall. This was the most deserted part of the *Place du Trône Renversé*, with not a house in sight, and the fields of vines and vegetables that stretched beyond it to the south have since been replaced by the buildings of Boulevard de Picpus, giving it the form of a square. It is hard nowadays to imagine the scenes of slaughter that took place here in such a peaceful little spot where in summer you can take welcome refuge from the glaring sun of the Place de la Nation, and relax on a bench in the shade of the linden trees.

It was already a shady spot two centuries ago, probably the only agreeable aspect for the victims of the sweltering summer of 1794, lined up under the trees waiting their turn to climb the steps of the scaffold. The processions of tumbrils generally arrived here in the late afternoon, filled with prisoners condemned by the Tribunal that morning. The sun poured relentlessly down on them during their journey from the Conciergerie, which was long and exhausting, taking about 45 minutes to get to the Place de la Bastille and then another 45

Plan of Place du Trône Renversé during the Revolution.

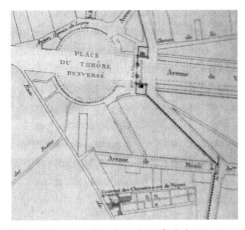

- Side of the guillotine in the Place de L'Ife de la Réunion
- ---- Route taken by tip-carts from the guillotine to the Jardin de Picpus

along rue du Faubourg Saint-Antoine. Once out of the tumbrils, the prisoners were placed in several rows with their backs to the guillotine, while the accompanying guards formed a semicircle between them and the crowd. At the call of their name, each prisoner turned around and walked towards the scaffold, accompanied to the top of the steps by two assistants, who immediately pushed them towards the guillotine. As soon as they were attached to the plank, it was flipped over into a horizontal position and the wooden collar slammed down around their neck with a thud. The last two sounds the victims heard were the click as Sanson released the lever, and the whirring of the blade as it flew down on to the back of their neck. It was all over in a matter of seconds, and the severed head and body were thrown on top of an ever-mounting pile of mutilated remains in a large red-painted wagon that stood at the foot of the wooden steps. When their turn came, the prisoners would have to walk past this cart and its grisly contents as they began the ascent to the scaffold, knowing that within less than 60 seconds they would be in it themselves.

During that terrible summer this little square became a veritable theatre of horror. To receive the copious amounts of blood that poured from the bodies of the victims a large hole had been dug underneath the scaffold, which was covered each evening by planks of wood. But the ground was too hard to absorb it efficiently, and after a few days unbearable sulphurous fumes began to envelop the square. So the hole was filled in, and after that the blood was collected in a lead-lined wheelbarrow that presumably was emptied somewhere more isolated than a public square. There were fewer spectators at the gruesome spectacles here than there had been at the *Place de la Révolution*, partly because of the distance from the city centre. But also because people had begun to tire of the continual bloodshed, and fear gripped the population of Paris, for it was during this time of the Great Terror that the guillotine began to claim the majority of its victims from among the common people. When you study the lists of those executed during this period, you see an alarming assortment of shoemakers, greengrocers, café owners, haberdashers, clockmakers, domestic servants and labourers. Cheering an undeserving aristocrat into the next world was one thing, but when it was your next-door neighbour it was another matter, and at this point in the Revolution many of the 'furies' who continued to animate these mass executions were die-hards who had been paid by the authorities for their performance. This could be a profitable activity, for in addition to being paid for providing a regular stream of shouting and insults, they also persuaded the waiting prisoners to hand over shoes, items of clothing and other objects that were of no further use to them.

Apart from the revulsion of cheering fellow workers to an unjust death, local residents also became increasingly disgusted by the more tangible consequences of all this butchery on their doorstep. Disposal of bodies was a constant problem for the authorities, and at first the victims of the *Place du Trône* were sent for burial in the Montreuil section, but the people living there complained bitterly, as did the residents around the Eglise Sainte-Marguerite, where bodies were also taken. Sanson recounts the protests of those working in this church, who *'declared that the foul odours are becoming unbearable and if they keep piling up bodies in the narrow cemetery that surrounds the workshop an epidemic will very soon break out among the employees.'* Sanson wrote this on 4 *Messidor*, and two days later he executed the deserter, Victor Notter, whom you met as he was followed on the final journey by his faithful dog. Sanson was clearly moved by this pathetic scene, describing what happened when Notter arrived at the scaffold.

'When he got out of the tumbril, the soldier caressed the poor animal, who showered his master with affection; he begged several people to take it and adopt it, but not one either wanted or dared to. When the final moment of separation came, the dog did not want to leave its master; despite the cries, the threats and the blows, it followed him on to the platform. One of my men threw it down; it tried once again to climb the steps, as though it had realised that the soldier needed help. When the body was thrown in the basket, the animal began howling in sorrow; a policeman stabbed it with the point of a knife. This crowd, almost without emotion when it is merely Christians being killed, became outraged over a dog. It was clear they were going to attack the policeman; stones were thrown at the guillotine; a worker picked up the dog and took it away in his apron.' (Sanson 1988)

The first executions to take place in this square were on June 14th 1794 (26 *Prairial* Year II), a day that saw 38 heads roll into the leather sack, including those of Jean-Baptiste Lerebours and his colleague Fréteau, counsellors of the Paris Parliament, and 26 counsellors from the Toulouse Parliament. Guillotined with these disgraced politicians were a baker, a wig-maker, a fruiterer, a printer and a farmer. There was also an unfortunate man named Jean Paule Cazes who was officially condemned as a counsellor of the Toulouse parliament, but according to Sanson, *'everyone knows that Cazes was charged on the denunciation of Vadier's son to whom this poor man had refused to give his daughter's hand in marriage.'* As the number of daily victims mounted, the executions were carried out with increasing efficiency, presided over by the impeccably-dressed Sanson, who would always be seen, just before the gruesome spectacle was about to commence, putting on his blood-stained protective over-garment. At the foot of the platform stood the sober figures of the two bailiffs from the Tribunal, dressed all in black with a chain around their neck, ready to make their official report of the proceedings.

Victims were condemned in *fournées* (batches), and on that first day it was a batch of counsellors. Two days later there was a batch of 42 prisoners from the *Bicêtre* prison, first in a series of 'prison conspiracies', and on June 25th Sanson and his assistants sent to their fate 23 people from the Vendée. On the 27th it was the turn of the 71-year old Maréchale de Biron and the 79-year old Maréchal de Mouchy, a relative of Madame Lafayette. This old gentleman's major crime had been trying to protect the king from invading rioters when the Tuileries was attacked on June 20th 1792. He was put in prison with his wife, who opted to share his fate and accompany him to the scaffold. With them in the same tumbril was the journalist Simon Linguet, one of the more colourful prisoners in the Bastille, who, having experienced first-hand the justice of the old regime, now found himself a victim of the new one. On July 6th 22 more members of the Toulouse Parliament were executed, followed by three batches from the Luxembourg prison, the first on July 7th, when a record 68 people were guillotined, including the architect Richard Mique, who created Marie-Antoinette's idyllic hamlet in the Trianon at Versailles. He had been arrested with his son on charges of conspiring to save the queen, and they both perished together. Also among the victims of July 7th was an 80-year old priest named Abbé de Salignac Fénelon, who had devoted himself to helping orphaned chimney sweeps, several of whom came that day to ask for his release. As they followed his tumbril along the entire route, Fénelon consoled them, saying, '*Don't cry, it is the will of God.*' Standing on the scaffold in his last moments, he asked Sanson to untie his hands, so he could give a last blessing to the children, a request that was granted, and many of the spectators could be seen furtively bending their knee to receive the abbot's benediction.

The second batch from Luxembourg was three days later, when 46 more prisoners met their fate, and the third on July 22nd, when the three de Noailles women were guillotined along with 42 others. The old Maréchale de Noailles was the first of the three women to die. Wearing a dress of black taffeta, she sat, motionless and exhausted, on a block of stone next to the scaffold, waiting to be seized by Sanson's assistants. She did not have to wait long, for she was third on the list that day. The scissors flashed as they cut away the neck of her black dress, and within seconds she was gone. The Maréchale's daughter-in-law, the Duchesse d'Ayen, was number ten, and she was followed by her own daughter, the Viscomtesse de Noailles, sister to Madame Lafayette. Their last moments were watched by the priest, Père Carrichon, who had followed in disguise behind the tumbril and given a clandestine blessing to the three women during the journey. In his account of this terrible day, he relates *'how happy Madame d'Ayen was to die before her daughter, and her daughter for not having to go before her mother!'* The next day was a group of 46 prisoners from the Carmes prison, including the Prince de Salm Kyrburg, accused of spying for the Austrians, and General Alexandre de Beauharnais, estranged husband of the future Empress Joséphine. Two days later it was the turn of the young poet, André Chénier, who died in the company of Léonard Autié, the queen's hairdresser, and 33 other fellow prisoners from Saint-Lazare.

Perhaps the most memorable execution to take place here was that of the Carmelites of Compiègne, whose martyrdom on July 17th 1794 has inspired a book, a film and an opera. All along the route leading to the scaffold the voices of the sixteen nuns, raised in song to the praise of the Lord, reduced the crowds by the roadside to an awe-struck silence. They remained standing throughout the entire journey, despite the fact that two of them were almost 80 years old, and the tumbril jolted them harshly to and fro as they made their way along the bumpy road. On arriving in the square, they were lined up next to the scaffold, where, draped in their white habits, they began singing the *Veni Creator Spiritus* in unison, with such enormous force that the crowd still remained silent even as Sanson's assistant came to take the first victim. She was Marie-Jeanne Meunier, a novice, and at 28 the youngest of the group. Before allowing herself to be taken by the executioner, she walked over to the Mother Superior, Sister Lidoine, knelt down and asked permission to die. As she mounted the scaffold, she continued to sing with the others until the instant when the blade of the guillotine severed her head from her body. One by one, each of them did the same, each one kneeling and asking permission to die, each one singing up to their final breath, until only the Mother Superior was left, standing alone under the trees, singing. As she climbed the wooden steps, she continued to sing the *Veni Creator* until her lone voice was silenced by the falling knife.

Only three days after the guillotine was installed here, Sanson and his assistants excelled themselves by executing 61 people in the space of 24 minutes, an achievement that won Sanson official congratulations in the Convention from the deputy Barère. This was the day known as 'The Red Mass', when all the victims were grouped together as regicides, due no doubt to the presence among them of Cécile Renault, a 20-year old girl who had visited Robespierre with two little knives in the folds of her bodice. With her in the tumbril were her father, her brother and her aunt, who was a nun, as well as several others who had been tried at the same time and thrown in for good measure to give the impression of a conspiracy. Among them was Madame de Sainte-Amaranthe, who ran a gambling house in the Palais-Royal, and who apparently looked so beautiful draped in red that she started a new fashion in Paris known as 'the Sainte-Amaranthe shawl'. She was guillotined with her daughter, Charlotte-Rose, aged 19, and her 17-year old son Louis, who numbers among the Revolution's youngest victims. Rumours had flown around the Conciergerie, and continued to be related around the scaffold, about the two Sainte-Amaranthe women, one of whom was said to have been Robespierre's lover, the other to have refused the advances of Saint-Just. The Law of Suspects, passed the previous September, required the arrest of not only the entire family of a suspect, but of as many others connected directly or indirectly to that person. Consequently this batch of 29 *Prairial* also included Charlotte-Rose's husband, Charles Sartine, his mistress, the actress Maria Grandmaison, and her maid, Marie-Nicole Bouchard.

Despite the official praise from Barère, this was a traumatic day for Charles-Henri Sanson, who at 55 was feeling his age and beginning to suffer emotionally from the strain of his position. *'My strength is exhausted,'* he wrote afterwards, *'and this afternoon my courage failed me, when someone showed me a cartoon which is going around town, in which I am seen guillotining myself, amidst a sea of severed heads and bodies.'* His courage had also failed him on the scaffold that terrible day of 29 *Prairial* on seeing Marie-Nicole Bouchard, the 18-year old maid who only looked about 14 and evoked universal sympathy. '*She was so frail and thin, so delicate that even a tiger would have pity,*' he wrote, and one of his assistants refused to tie her hands, protesting that it was not his job to execute children. Even the crowd of spectators was outraged, shouting '*No children!*', and by the time Nicole arrived on the scaffold, Sanson was at his wits' end. He was seized with an impulse to save her, '*an inspiration that told me: destroy the guillotine rather than let it take this child.*' But when he heard the shrill voice of the pathetic young girl asking, while being attached to the plank, '*Citizen, am I in the right position?*' it was too much for him. '*I turned round in haste, my eyes clouding and my knees trembling. Marin took over the execution, and told me: You're ill - go home and I'll continue here alone. I hurried down from the scaffold without replying, and left without looking behind me. For the rest of that day I had hallucinations, so badly that on the corner of rue Saintonge, when a beggar approached me for money, I thought it was her, and I nearly fell backwards. That evening at dinner, I saw bloodstains on the tablecloth.*' (Sanson, 1988)

•

Sanson's panic reaction at having to carry out this execution stands out in peculiar contrast to the calm resignation of the victim who was about to suffer the ordeal. The presence of the guillotine had a powerful and complex effect on the population of Paris, sometimes giving a *raison d'être* to people whose lives were otherwise destined for insignificance and anonymity. Writing later about what motivated Cécile Renault, Sanson's grandson leaves us a chilling comment on the psychological effect that the Terror had on ordinary people. '*Everything in her revealed a vague desire to end her life...considering the pathetic means with which she intended to achieve her objective, one wonders if Cécile Renault was not of a weak spirit, distraught, who had in her turn caught this contagious fever of death that pushes so many, their emotions carried away by the times we live in, to brave the guillotine.*' (Sanson, 1988)

The last executions to take place in this little square were on July 27th 1794, the famous 9 *Thermidor*, when all Paris was buzzing with rumours of the impending fall of Robespierre.

At the Palais de Justice the tumbrils stood in the Cour de Mai, their 45 occupants waiting anxiously for the moment of departure towards the guillotine. The authorities, fearing riots in the Faubourg Saint-Antoine, advised Fouquier-Tinville to postpone the executions until another time, but Fouquier was unmoved, and ordered the tumbrils to set off. The crowds along the route, however, had had enough of these horrific processions. They tried to stop the tumbrils, and instead of taunting the victims with insults, urged them to escape and save themselves. But the prisoners hesitated, for many of them were exhausted by months of imprisonment, had long given up any hope of survival, and perhaps preferred execution to the possibility of being massacred on the streets. They did not have the chance to get out of the tumbrils, however, for at that moment Hanriot arrived with several guards, the crowd dispersed and the procession resumed its journey to the scaffold. Among those guillotined that day was 25-year old Thérèse-Françoise de Stainville, Princesse de Grimaldi-Monaco. An opponent of the Revolution, she had returned from Rome in 1793 when Monaco was annexed by France, in order to avoid being listed as an *emigré* and losing her property to the State. She died along with an array of carpenters and chemists, ironmongers and astronomers, hat makers, farmers, students and notaries, as well as a couple named Loison, owners of a puppet theatre, who were accused of putting counter-revolutionary propaganda into the mouths of their marionettes.

Every evening, once the executions were over and the crowds had dispersed, a large tip cart, lined with lead, would set off from the little square. It contained the heads and bodies of the day's victims, and was painted red to camouflage the bloodstains that covered it. ➡You are now going to follow the path taken by this cart as it transported its doleful cargo to the Picpus Cemetery, final resting place of the victims of the Great Terror. ➡Leave Place de l'Ile de la Réunion by Boulevard de Picpus, which was formed in 1864 from the various circular roads and boulevards that followed the Farmers-General Wall. In 1794 it was called *Chemin de Ronde de Saint-Mandé*, and was situated on the side of Boulevard de Picpus with uneven numbers. ➥Stop when you get to Villa de Saint-Mandé on the right. This little street corresponds approximately to the point where the convoy turned right and cut across the fields, so you should turn right here as well and follow the cart as it continues on its bleak journey. ➥At the end of Villa de Saint-Mandé you get to Avenue de Saint-Mandé, which opened in 1697 and used to lead to the village of Saint-Mandé. It already had its present name in 1794, and if you had been walking along it then you would have seen fields on either side all along the road. At this point the convoy crossed over the Avenue and went into the fields on the other side, continuing through them in a straight line until they arrived at the wall of the former Picpus Convent. Here they entered the garden through a temporary entrance that had been hastily constructed by the authorities to shorten the journey from the scaffold and, no doubt, to divert public attention from their sinister operations. You are unable to follow this last part of their journey, for the path is now covered with buildings, and the temporary entrance closed up. To reach the main entrance of the Picpus Cemetery, turn right along Avenue de Saint-Mandé, turn sharp left on rue de Picpus and walk down to number 35.

THE PICPUS CEMETERY.

It is open every day except Mondays and Public Holidays, October to Easter from 14h-16h, and Easter to September from 14h-18h, guided visits Tuesday-Sunday at 14h30 and 16h by the curator, Mr Jean-Jaques Faugeron. The admission fee is 2.50 Euros, and the guided tour is in French, but you can also go around the garden and cemetery on your own. If you decide to do this, what you read here will tell you the same story as that told by Mr Faugeron during his guided visit, and you can follow the plan as you walk around the garden. But before you do, ➥you should find a place to sit, and read the sad and dramatic story of what happened in this lovely garden.

The first religious community here was the convent of the Dames-Chanoinesses de Saint-Augustin, founded in 1640, when ten Augustinian nuns were brought here from Rheims by the Archbishop of Paris. Their Superior was Mother Suzanne Tubeuf, whose brother was Intendant of Finances and owner of the *Hôtel Tubeuf* that now houses the Bibliothèque Nationale. He bought a house and seven acres of land for his sister in the village of Picpus, where she established her religious community and gradually added more buildings to enlarge the convent. There was a hostel for young girls that remained open until the 1960s, and the convent also took in retired ladies, some of whom were ladies of the Court who came here to end their lives in a religious environment. One of the most famous of these residents was Marguerite-Louise d'Orléans, grand-daughter of Henri IV and wife of Cosme III of Medici, the Grand Duke of Tuscany. When she died here in 1721 she merited a commemorative inscription in the chapel describing her as the 'Very High and Very Virtuous Princess.' On the eve of the Revolution there were 40 nuns here who not only ran the hostel and looked after the *pensionnaires*, they also cultivated the land.

In 1789 all religious institutions were ravaged by revolutionary torment, and the convent of the *Dames-Chanoinesses* was no exception. The girls' hostel was ransacked by an invading mob, who forced out all the residents and then attacked the rest of the convent, demolishing the chapel dating from the reign of Louis XIII, and selling off all the valuable stone and stained glass. Despite this turmoil and destruction, the nuns refused to be driven out, and a survey of the clergy made in 1790 revealed that there were still 40 nuns practising their religion here. But their determination was thwarted in May 1792 when they were forcibly thrown out and the entire convent confiscated as national property. Instead of immediately selling it, as they usually did, the revolutionary government decided to hold on to this particular property, which they rented to a citizen named Riedain, a rather well-off market gardener, who lodged in the house at the entrance and cultivated the garden. He did not, however, occupy any of the other convent buildings, which had been badly damaged when they were ransacked in 1789 and needed more repair work than Riedain's budget permitted.

These convent buildings remained empty for two years, until the beginning of 1794, when Riedain decided to sub-let some of them to a man named Eugène Coignard, who was in the same business as our friend Dr Belhomme and already had a little clinic next to the convent, so he welcomed the opportunity to enlarge his establishment. There were several similar clinics at the time in different parts of Paris, where those who could afford it were able to escape the rigours of revolutionary prisons and the guillotine. It was an expensive form of salvation, however, starting with the payment of several bribes - to Fouquier-Tinville, the bailiffs at the Tribunal, the Director of Prisons and other police officials. These formalities could sometimes amount to as much as 15,000 *livres*, before you even entered the clinic. Then came the rent, which covered nothing but an empty room, so furniture, bedding, food and water, even firewood, had to be paid for separately, at inflated prices. For Coignard it was an excellent way to pay his own rent to Riedain while restoring his new buildings to a habitable state, and one of his first clients, ironically, was Dr Belhomme himself, who for a very short time sought refuge here from Fouquier-Tinville. Other residents worthy of mention were Raymond Romain de Sèze, the youngest of Louis XVI's defence lawyers, who stayed here for 18 months, the Comte de Buffon and the Marquis de Sade.

By the middle of 1795 the residents in Coignard's clinic had all left. Some were released by the Directory government, but of those that remained here in custody, many demanded their liberty or a change of prison, because they could no longer tolerate the smells coming from the far end of the garden. To explain this strange phenomenon we must go back to the summer of 1794. The guillotine had been moved for the third time and installed at the *Barrière du Trône-Renversé*, where the mass executions of the Great Terror commenced on June 14th. When they began this terrible slaughter, the authorities had not thought about where to bury the bodies, for since the area was all countryside they probably assumed they could empty the corpses into one of the public pits. But remembering the protests made by people living in previous locations of the guillotine, they decided to look for a more discreet place to dispose of the victims. It was then that they remembered the domain of the *Chanoinesses* that they had confiscated two years earlier, and which was conveniently close to the new site of the scaffold.

On the morning of June 14th inspectors from the Commune came to see Riedain and asked to visit his garden. Riedain was not worried about this, for he still had six years to go on his lease, and he invited them to make a full inspection, assuring them that their land was well-maintained. After going all round the property, including the lower end of the garden, the inspectors left without saying a word, so Riedain contentedly assumed that he had successfully passed the annual inspection of state property and promptly forgot about the matter. You can imagine his surprise, therefore, when the following morning one of his employees came running to him in a panic and informed him that during the night a large opening had been made in the north wall of his property. Riedain went to investigate, and not only did he find the enormous hole in the wall, he also saw 35 labourers busily engaged in digging a ditch and constructing a fence to close off the end of the garden. When he questioned the workmen they were very evasive and simply muttered some vague references to 'the work of the Nation.' So Riedain asked to see their superior, and along came citizen Coffinet, a Commune inspector, who explained that the Nation needed Riedain's garden to bury the bodies of the enemies of the Republic. When Riedain continued to protest Coffinet simply replied, *'Sir, if you are not satisfied, you'll be the first one in there.'*

The stupefied Riedain persisted in his complaints, but the work continued, and he soon saw a wooden doorway, complete with formidable locks and bolts, being built into the opening in the wall. They cut down trees, ripped out bushes and vines and trampled on the flowers that Riedain had cultivated with such care. When the fence was completed it shortened his garden by several metres, and was high enough that no-one could see the sinister operations taking place on the other side. It hid nothing, however, from the second-floor of the clinic, where white-faced residents stared from the windows in silent horror at the sight of the two enormous holes being dug in the garden below. One was 20ft deep and measured 25ft by 15ft, while the other larger one measured 30ft by 20ft and was 24ft deep. A third grave was also prepared, for it was the height of the Terror and they intended to guillotine a lot of people, but this one was never used, thanks to the arrest and execution of Robespierre on 9 *Thermidor*. Otherwise, instead of the 1,306 bodies buried there, we would find 7,000, which was the number of executions planned, and we would never have heard of Empress Joséphine, for she was scheduled to appear before the Tribunal on 12 *Thermidor*, and would now most certainly be lying in one of these communal graves.

As soon as the holes were dug, the bodies started coming. Every evening the blood-soaked red carts rattled their way into Riedain's garden and unloaded their cargo next to a chapel that stood near the new entrance. It was built in the form of a little grotto, and had been given the name 'Garden of Desolation' by the nuns who used it for solitary prayer. It was now occupied by officials of the Republic responsible for making an inventory of the victims' clothing, and they protested bitterly about their conditions of work. There was no glass in the windows of the chapel, so the candles that lit their 'office' were continually being blown out by the wind, and to illustrate their complaint these excellent bureaucrats calculated that without proper light certain items could easily be overlooked, causing a loss to the State of 100 *livres* per outfit. At first the clothing was given as payment to the grave-diggers, who had the gruesome job of undressing the mutilated bodies before throwing them into the graves. But as the number of executions rose, it was decided that the clothing should be donated to the city's poorhouses, reserving only shoes, stockings and scarves for the cemetery workers, although as business got still better, even this concession was withdrawn. Once all clothes had been removed and noted, the bodies were buried. They didn't throw them into the graves indiscriminately, however, but arranged them carefully in rows, filling the spaces with the severed heads, and to do this the workers had to go down into the graves and step over the corpses that had been put there the previous day. They couldn't use quicklime, which would have prevented them from walking around on the bodies in this way, so when each day's operation was completed, a thin layer of earth was all that separated the decomposing bodies from the air of the garden and surrounding neighbourhood. There was, after all, no point in closing it up when it was going to be used again the next day, and to make matters worse the summer of 1794 was torridly hot, so it was not long before complaints came pouring in from the local residents.

On July 9th a petition - representing schools, clinics, farmers and retired citizens who had been attracted to Picpus by the purity of the air - warned of the dangers they were being exposed to, and demanded immediate action. *'Citizens, do not suffer that men who, during their lives, were declared enemies of the people and the Republic, should assassinate you after their death.'* Inspector Coffinet made another visit to the graves, and an official decision was pronounced by the Commune. *'What Inspector Coffinet proposes consists of establishing in these graves a wooden floor with trap-doors for access. This is the only means we can employ at present.'* This of course had little effect, and in addition made the burial workers' job even more horrific, for the graves were now covered and they had to climb down under the wooden floor and carry out their gruesome task in the dark. Many of them, even the most hardened, threatened to quit, no longer able to stand the terrible odours and the putrefied liquid that floated in the graves. But nothing more was done until July 17th, when the Commune finally ordered the graves to be covered with quicklime, and herbs to be burned in the garden during the burials. By this time the effect of all this trauma on the people living within the former convent was disastrous. Healthy people lodging in the clinic demanded to leave, and Riedain's wife, increasingly disturbed by the daily scenes of horror, had a nervous breakdown and had to be taken to a hospital on the other side of the city.

After 9 *Thermidor* the burials ceased, but the graves stayed open for a year, and it was not until June 1795 that they were officially closed up and the opening in the wall filled in. At the same time Riedain decided to write to the Convention asking for compensation for his terrible ordeal. Surprisingly he was successful, and also managed to get his lease extended, so was able to resume cultivation of the garden for a few months until the Convention changed their mind and put the property up for sale. In 1796 two citizens named Le Jemptel and Cordival, both well-aware of what had gone on here, bought the entire property with a view to speculation. In November they re-sold the part of the land containing the communal graves to the Princess of Hohenzollern-Sigmaringen, sister of the Prince of Salm-Kyrbourg, guillotined on July 23rd 1794. Knowing what was going to happen to him, the prince had written to his sister from prison, asking her to try and find his burial site and take his body back to Germany. This had been her intention in coming to Paris, and she only decided to buy the entire parcel of land when she realized how impossible it would be to find her brother's remains. The princess immediately had a wall built to separate her land from the rest of the garden and protect it from vandalism. Her family remained the owner until 1926, and during the 19th century several members of the family were buried in the little garden amongst the common graves. So for some time this little plot was German territory, and during the Second World War, when Paris was occupied, these graves were always respected and protected, because it was known that there was a German prince buried here, along with several members of his family.

Once the princess had bought the communal graves, nothing changed until 1802. Then the garden had a new visitor, Anne-Pauline-Dominique de Noailles, Marquise de Montagu, who came here with her sister, Madame de Lafayette. Five members of their family had been guillotined, and for two years they'd been searching for the site of their graves, always without success, until 1802, when they had the good fortune to meet Mademoiselle Pâris, a lace maker whose father and brother had also been executed during the Great Terror. This young girl had had the courage not only to witness the execution of her two dearest relatives, but also to take the considerable risk of following at a distance behind the cart that transported their bodies to Picpus. She was thus able to show Madame de Montagu exactly where the five members of the de Noailles family were buried. But the visit ended in disappointment when the two sisters discovered that the plot of land had already been acquired by the German princess, who was not willing to sell it. However, they determined to buy the remaining land adjacent to the graves, but had to do so clandestinely, since all activity connected with the site was closely surveyed.

Buying the property collectively seemed to be the best option for Mme de Montagu and Mme de Lafayette, so with the help of a notary named Maître Lherbette, they formed a company to raise subscriptions from the relatives of victims buried at Picpus. In August 1803 they had enough to buy the convent and the remaining part of the garden, and had a stone cross built at the entrance to the communal graves. The majority of those who subscribed were from the nobility, who not only had the money to do so, but also knew more about where their various relatives had been executed. Many commoners could not read or write, and had no idea where a relative might have been taken after leaving their first prison in the local *château* or gaol, so they often never knew what happened to them. What's more they were scared, for even up to 1805 the domain of Picpus was watched by the police, and in that year the police chief, Fouché, received an anonymous denunciation, revealing the existence of *'an establishment designed to perpetuate the memory of misfortunes that the Government would prefer to forget.'* Fouché might well have succeeded in foiling Madame de Montagu's plan, had his investigations not identified one of the subscribers as Eugène de Beauharnais, son of the Empress Joséphine, and step-son of the Emperor Napoléon himself. At that point Fouché decided to abandon the affair, leaving Madame de Montagu free to continue her activities.

The first thing she did was to re-establish a religious community in the convent, the Congregation of the Sacred-Heart and the Perpetual Adoration, who came here in 1805 and have remained to this day. Their Superior was Henriette Aymer de la Chevalerie, a former socialite whose grim experience in a revolutionary prison had led to a desire to take religious vows and retreat from the world. At first the nuns rented the convent, but thanks to various donations and purchases, they now own one half of the property, and in 1805 Madame de Montagu made a deal with the Princess de Hohenzollern, who agreed to unite her little plot with the rest of the garden. A gate was installed and a new cemetery established in the adjoining part of the garden, reserved for descendants of those people buried in the communal graves. The first funeral in the new cemetery was that of Marie Joséphine Freteau, whose husband had been in the first batch of executions on June 14th 1794, and two years later she was joined by Madame de Lafayette, who died at midnight on Christmas Eve 1807 after a very painful illness. In 1830 the clandestine association set up by Madame Montagu in 1802 was re-named Societé Civile de l'Oratoire et du Cimetière de Picpus and now owns the other half of the property not owned by the religious community. The families of the original subscribers are still co-owners, and their share is passed on by inheritance, but can never be sold. They have perpetual concessions in the cemetery, where approximately every two years the burial takes place of a descendant of one of the victims guillotined at the *Place du Trône*.

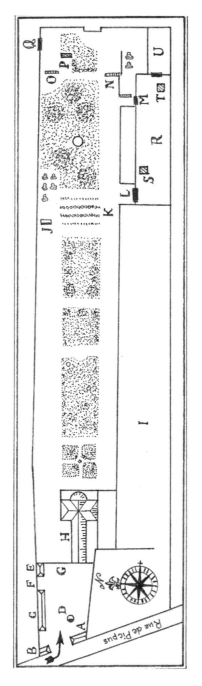

Plan of the Picpus Garden and Cemetery.

➡ You should now use the plan to tour the garden and cemetery, following the letters indicating the different things to look at as you go round.

A. This is one of the three original houses that citizen Riedain occupied.

B. Another of the houses occupied by Riedain.

C. These little lodgings - known as *chambrettes* - were the stables, and horses were kept here right up until 1930. They are now used as a *pension* by girls from the lycée Saint-Michel (on the other side of the wall at the far end of the garden) who are preparing for entrance exams into higher education.

D. This statue of the Virgin is a reminder of another later revolution. There used to be a well here, and in 1870 during the revolt of the Commune, a group of *Communards* invaded the convent and threatened to throw the sisters into the well. The Mother Superior was luckily able to persuade one of their number, who had more compassion - and authority - than his comrades, to spare them this terrible fate. The *Communards* eventually left the convent without harming anyone. But realising that the incident could repeat itself with much worse consequences, the Mother Superior decided to fill in the well, and put the Virgin in its place, as a symbol of their gratitude to God for saving them from death.

E. This house, which is the oldest in the 12th arrondissement, dates from the reign of Louis XIII, and as you go through the gate into the garden you can see the other side of it. It is the third of Riedain's houses, built in 1640 with just one floor, and the second storey has been added since Riedain lived here.

F. This wall, which stretches along the north side of the garden on both sides of the Louis XIII house, was much lower at first. Originally the land went right up to the round modern building you see in the distance on the other side of the wall, and belonged to the Picpus Fathers, but this land was confiscated in 1905 on the separation of church and state, and a wall built to separate it from the convent. It was built on to the already existing lower part of the wall - you can see it below the line of cement - which is much older and was the original wall around the religious community established here by Mme de Montagu in 1805.

G. On either side of the door to the garden are two plaques. The one on the left refers to the official visit by the American General Pershing in July 1917, when he greeted his famous military ancestor with the words *'Lafayette, here we are!'* In fact the words were first uttered discreetly by Pershing's aide-de-camp Colonel Stenton, but Pershing made them famous by repeating them next to Lafayette's grave. On the right hand side is another plaque about Lafayette himself, giving the date of his birth in 1757 and his death in 1834. He asked specifically to be buried here in the Picpus Cemetery, next to his wife, who was from the de Noailles family and had lost five relatives to the guillotine during the Terror.

H. This church was built in 1841 on the site of the original chapel demolished in 1789. It is built on simple lines, in the style of Louis-Philippe, and inside, in the two transepts, are two enormous plaques giving the names of all the people who were guillotined on the *Place du Trône-Renversé* from 26 *Prairial* to 9 *Thermidor*. There were 1,306 victims, and when you examine the names and professions, you can see that a large number were from the ordinary ranks of the people - 60 percent in fact. On the plaque to the right look for the name of 21-year old Amélie Saint-Pern, *femme* Cornuillier, listed as being guillotined on 1 *Thermidor* (19th July). In fact she was never executed, for she was in an advanced state of pregnancy and was granted a suspension of her sentence until the birth. But 9 *Thermidor* intervened, and Amélie lived to testify the following year at Fouquier-Tinville's trial.

I. This area behind the trees, bushes and dividing wall is where the present religious community lives, and where the original convent stood prior to the Revolution. It was here that Coignard established his clinic, in several buildings that unfortunately no longer exist. From the windows of this clinic groups of anxious residents watched, as workmen dug the enormous graves - in which several of those residents ended up being buried.

J. Statue of the Madonna.

K. There were still cows at Picpus up until the 1950s, and the two stone walls on either side of this mossy path both date from 1640, and were kept in place simply because this was where the cows were brought past.

L. The main gate to the Descendants' Cemetery.

M. A secondary entrance to the Descendants' Cemetery.

N. A small fragment of the original fence dividing up Riedain's garden.

O. This is the principal fragment of the same fence, the one that Riedain saw being put up on the morning of June 15th 1794, and which deprived him of several metres of garden. It is made of heart of oak, which was transported by river and left to dry for a long time, accounting for its solidity, and any potentially damaging humidity has been absorbed by the ivy behind it. The fence ran the entire width of the garden between the two principal boundary walls.

P. This monument commemorates the position of the chapel known as the 'Garden of Desolation' to the nuns who used it, and which was used during the Terror as an inventory office. Here the victims' clothes and possessions were sorted through and itemized, and then distributed first to the gravediggers and later to the poor.

Q. This is where the enormous wooden doorway, furnished with heavy locks and bolts, was installed on June 15th 1794, enabling the daily cartloads of decapitated bodies to be brought into the garden, stripped of their clothing and buried in the communal pits. The gate you see now has been built recently, but above it you can still see the original wooden lintel that supported the wall above the opening made in June 1794. It was through this entrance that 1,306 victims came to their final resting place.

R. This is the Descendants' Cemetery, founded in 1805 by Mme de Montagu and her sister Mme de Lafayette. Here you will find graves belonging to some of the most prominent noble families of France, including the Malesherbes family, who lost numerous relatives during the Terror, and names like de Noailles, de Nicolay, and de Beauharnais, as well as Récamier and Tascher de la Pagerie (Josephine's descendants).

S. Only two people are buried here who have no connection with the guillotine. One of them is the famous writer G. Lenotre, whose tombstone can be found in this part of the cemetery. He wrote a wonderful series of books on the Revolution, and was given the honour of a grave in the Picpus Cemetery in recognition of all his research and writing about this turbulent period. One of his books, *Le Jardin de Picpus*, is about the history of this cemetery, and if your French is good enough it is well worth reading - you can buy a copy from Mr Faugeron on your way out.

T. The tomb of the Lafayette family. This is where General Lafayette was buried in 1834 next to his wife, Adrienne, who had died 27 years earlier in 1807, and at the time of her death made her husband promise to be buried by her side. When Lafayette was laid to rest the American flag was placed here in honour of all he had done for the USA, and in recognition of his dual nationality that some of his descendants still possess today. The flag is changed every year on July 4th, when there is a ceremony here in the presence of the American ambassador, and during World War II, throughout the entire German occupation, the Picpus Cemetery was the only place in France that continued to fly the American flag.

U. Behind the iron gate you will see the little garden containing the communal graves of those guillotined during the Great Terror. There are two graves in this garden, situated under the two large rectangular areas of gravel. The smaller one is in the back and contains 1,002 people, and the one nearest you is larger, but contains only 304 bodies, for it was never filled, thanks to the downfall of Robespierre. Amongst the victims buried in this garden is the poet André Chénier, who was guillotined two days before the end of the Terror at the age of 31. Just before his execution he is said to have declared, *'I leave nothing for posterity; and yet,'* he added, tapping his forehead, *'I had something here!'* Chénier was being modest, for he left a great deal to posterity, and I will leave you with some lines from one of his poems. It is a part of his sixth elegy, *Aux frères de Pange*, where prophetically, he describes the anguish of dying too young. In the imagines himself after death, in a place where his visiting friends can still feel the bonds of friendship. It is a touching image, that remind us with tragic poignancy of how the Revolution snuffed out the lives of so many young people who had not yet had the chance to live.

> *Je meurs. Avant le soir j'ai fini ma journée.*

Scarce open to day's light, my rose is faded.

> *A peine ouverte au jour, ma rose s'est fanée.*

Life has held for me such fickle sweetness;

> *La vie eut bien pour moi de volages douceurs;*

And, hardly tasting it, behold, I die.

> *Je les goûtais à peine, et voilà que je meurs.*

But, oh! how soft would rest my ashes,

> *Mais, oh! que mollement reposera ma cendre,*

If, when e'er a strong and tender impulse

> *Si parfois un penchant impérieux et tendre*

Guides you to the tomb where I am sleeping,

> *Vous guidant vers la tombe où je suis endormi,*

Your eyes approaching think to see their friend!

> *Vos yeux en approchant pensent voir leur ami!*

(Chénier, 1920)

WALK NUMBER NINE

Barrière du Trône, showing the site of the scaffold during the Great Terror.
(Authors private collection)

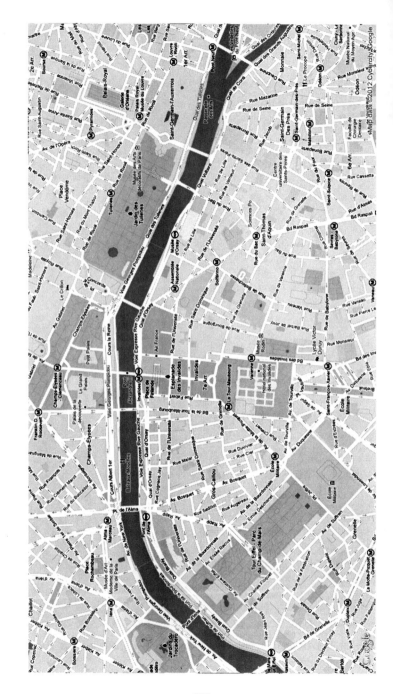

Walk Number Ten

Power and Glory

Faubourg Saint-Germain - Invalides - Ecole-Militaire - Champ-de-Mars

This walk begins in the Faubourg Saint-Germain, seat of the rich and powerful for nearly three centuries, and home to the Empress Joséphine when she was still known as Rose. By 1792 most of its residents had emigrated, and the Revolution moved in, taking over great houses like the Hôtel de Salm, occupied by a political club, and the Palais Bourbon, which became the seat of the Directory government. Here were the roots of today's 7th arrondissement, still a bastion of the republican establishment and home to numerous government ministries. The walk ends on the Champ-de-Mars, where you'll re-live the best and worst of the revolutionary era. It was the scene of the euphoric Festival of Federation - the Revolution's greatest moment of optimism - and the execution of Paris's first mayor, astronomer Sylvain Bailly, which must rank among the Revolution's more regrettable acts.

Power and Glory

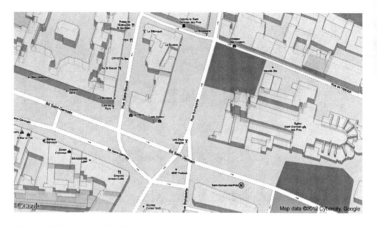

Metro: Saint-Germain-des-Prés

Faubourg Saint-Germain.

➡Turn right on leaving the metro along Boulevard Saint-Germain, and keep going until you reach rue des Saints-Pères. You are about to meet up with the doomed aristocracy of the *ancien régime*, for it was in the Faubourg Saint-Germain that for nearly 300 years the rich and powerful lived and ruled. Nowadays embassies and government ministries occupy many of its grand *hôtels*, which in the days of Talleyrand and Madame Récamier witnessed some of the most sumptuous parties in town. At that time the centre of Paris was the Cité area, and the Faubourg Saint-Germain was a suburb encompassing the rising middle-classes of Saint-Germain-des-Près, and the aristocratic mansions of Les Invalides. It is into this elegant faubourg that you are now going to venture, the Paris of the *ancien régime*, where the nobility enjoyed their greatest moments of glory. The Revolution made an urban desert of this privileged quarter, which rather shocked a young British member of parliament who came here in 1790. '*The aristocrats are melancholy and miserable to the last degree. This makes the society at Paris very gloomy; the number of deserted houses is immense, and if it were not for the deputies, ambassadors, and some refugees from Brussels, there would be scarcely a gentleman's coach to be seen in the streets.*' Many of the residents, seeing the writing on the wall, had emigrated during the early years, while others with less foresight ended their days on the scaffold.

RUE DES SAINTS-PÈRES.

This street already existed in mediaeval times, and during the 16th century was still a small path cutting at its northern end right through a garden belonging to Queen Margot, who owned all the land between rue Jacob, rue de l'Université and the Seine. ➡Cross over Boulevard Saint-Germain and take a look at the house at 53 rue des Saints-Pères. It dates from the 18th century and during the Revolution was the home of an actress from the Comédie-Française named Louise Contat, the most idolized actress in town. This 'Queen of Paris', as she was known, was famed for her interpretation of Beaumarchais's plays, and especially for her legendary portrayal of Suzanne in 'The Marriage of Figaro'. Hers was a life of *galanterie*, involving a succession of amorous adventures with assorted aristocrats, each of whom fathered one of her five children. She was a passionate monarchist, although her royalism didn't stop her from socializing with more republican colleagues. One of them, fellow actor François Joseph Talma met his future wife, a dancer named Julie Carreau, at a *soirée* that Louise gave here during the first year of the Revolution. It was also while she was living in this house that she was arrested in 1793, and imprisoned with several other actresses in the prison of *Sainte-Pélagie*. The Queen of Paris's house is now a branch of Sonia Rykiel, who was named 'Queen of Knits' by the Americans, so she's in the right place.

➦ Return across the boulevard and continue north on rue des Saints-Pères. It might surprise you to know that the little Square Taras Chevchenko to the right on the corner of Boulevard Saint-Germain used to be a burying-ground for plague victims during the Middle Ages. The square stands on the site of the *Cimetière Saint-Père*, which originally belonged to the Protestants, and was returned to them in 1576 by the Edict of Nantes. For the next 28 years Protestant burials took place here '*in the accustomed manner*', meaning '*by night, without noise, scandal or ceremony*', but they were still often the object of vandalism. When 29-year-old Claude Arnault died in 1603, after a short but illustrious life as king's secretary, treasurer, counsellor and notary, because of his Protestant beliefs his body had to be carried to the cemetery at 10 o'clock at night by four local 'picklocks'. Two weeks later his black marble tombstone, inscribed with gold lettering, was vandalized by a group of Catholic extremists, who objected to the attention attracted by such a beautiful tombstone. As a result Arnault's family were obliged to cover the stone with plaster. The Protestants lost their cemetery yet again in 1604, when it was returned to the parish of Saint-Sulpice, who resumed their former activity of burying plague victims here.

Five years later the cemetery was given to the *Hôpital de la Charité*, which had just taken over the *Chapelle Saint-Père* that stood next to the square at numbers 49 and 51 rue des Saints-Pères. This chapel was replaced in 1732 by the church you see now, and this was closed at the beginning of the Revolution. A year or so later, when the Convention decided that Paris needed more teaching hospitals, Jean Corvisart, official doctor to the revolutionary government, and the architect Clavareau, suggested putting one in the abandoned church. Work began in 1795 with a false ceiling dividing the nave into two floors, the lower one serving as a walkway for students, while upstairs there was an amphitheatre with dissection tables, a pathology room, and a mortuary for the study of anatomy. The grand opening of the new *Ecole de Médicine Clinique* took place in May 1799, and it was at this same school, nearly a century later, that Louis Pasteur presented his paper on a rabies vaccine. Since 1942 the Ukrainian Catholic Church of Paris has occupied the lower part of the *Chapelle Saint-Père*, where you can still admire the sixteen ionic columns built by Clavareau. Other revolutionary features that he added to this church can also be seen above the main entrance, where there is a sculpture of Aesculapius, the Roman god of healing, and between the columns on either side of the doors are two carved bundles of rods, ancient emblem of the power of Roman magistrates that was incorporated into the symbolism of the Revolution.

The more modern building that you see beyond the church between numbers 39 and 45 rue des Saints-Pères belongs to the faculty of medicine of the University of Paris. I will leave you to form your own opinion about this bit of wartime architecture, which has been described as a disgrace to the Saint-Germain-des-Prés quarter and the Paris skyline. It stands on the site of the former *Hôpital de la Charité* that took over the *Chapelle Saint-Père* in 1609. This hospital had existed here since 1606, and was run by a group of Augustinian monks whose order required them to become surgeons and pharmacists and take care of the sick. By 1789 it was considered the best-kept hospital in Paris, known for its airy rooms and scrupulous cleanliness - a rare commodity at the time! The 208 beds were arranged with a suitable space between them, and had only one patient in each, an innovation that was studiously ignored in other Parisian hospitals such as the Hôtel-Dieu. During the Revolution the hospital was re-named *Unité* and from 1791 women were admitted in a small gesture for sexual equality - another rare commodity, even during this era when equality was trumpeted from every rooftop. The *Hôpital de la Charité* remained here until its demolition in 1937, and counted among its patients the Italian artist, Modigliani, who died there in 1920 at the age of 36.

Opposite the faculty of medicine, at numbers 26 and 28, is a beautiful old *hôtel* now occupied by the Ecole des Ponts et Chaussées (School of Civil Engineering). It was originally composed of three houses dating from the 1640s, two (numbers 24 and 28) built directly on the street, and a third one (number 26) set further back. The houses didn't seem to bring much luck to their occupants, but on the contrary seemed to predispose them to being decapitated. In 1689 the owner of number 26 was Claude Tiquet, a counsellor in the Paris Parliament, almost dispatched to eternity on two occasions by his wife, who was reserving her more generous side for a captain of the guard. In those days a mere attempt at murder was sufficient grounds for a death penalty, and the unfortunate Madame Tiquet met a horrible death in the *Place de Grève* (Hôtel-de-Ville) at the hands of a very incompetent executioner who had to hack at her six times with his axe before her head came off. The *hôtel* was reconstructed in 1768 by the architect Antoine, for another counsellor called Jacques de Frécaut-Lanty, who sold it in 1772 for 120,000 *livres*. But the malediction caught up with him later on, and poor Jacques found himself in a tumbril on his way to the guillotine one hot summer day in 1794, 8 *Thermidor* to be exact, just one day before the end of the Terror. He was 81 years old. Charles Brochet de Saint-Prest, the man who bought Jacques's property, was no more fortunate. He didn't even live here, but rented the houses to a Public Prosecutor called Armand Joly de Fleury, whose wife, Elisa de Fleury, was guillotined on 6 *Thermidor*. I don't know what happened to her husband, but Brochet de Saint-Prest, their landlord, had already been decapitated two weeks before Madame de Fleury. This was decidedly not a promising address. Things got a bit better later on, when a German doctor called Samuel Hahnemann, the founder of homeopathic medicine, came to Paris in

1835 and set up a practice of his new and unknown medical treatment in this house, now known as the *Hôtel de Fleury*. Since its occupation in 1845 by the Ecole des Ponts et Chaussées, this lovely old *hôtel* has enjoyed a more peaceful existence.

Rue de l'Université.

➡ Turn left on rue de l'Université, where numbers 1 to 6 all date from the 17th century. Number 10 is from the same period and was the birthplace of one of the most celebrated financiers of the Faubourg Saint-Germain, Samuel Bernard. He was born in this house on November 28th 1651, spent his childhood here, and still owned it in 1710, when he rented it to a marquis. If property prices went up as fast as they do these days, Samuel must have ended up very rich. And he did. He was, in fact, a good example of just how rich some of the residents of this area were. It is said that he accumulated during his lifetime a fortune of 60 million *livres*, which explains why he was able to lend considerable sums of money to both Louis XIV and Louis XV.

Many old Parisian houses were demolished when new streets were created in the 19th century, taking with them all the history that had taken place within their walls. A good example is at numbers 7 and 9, where there used to be a house that disappeared when rue du Pré aux Clercs was opened in 1845. It had been built in 1639, was known as *Hôtel Villeroy* and in 1793 was the home of the engineer Claude Chappe, who invented aerial telegraph based on a semaphore relay system. He developed this system with his brothers, one of whom, Ignace Chappe, was a deputy, and persuaded the Legislative Assembly to support the building of a relay system between Paris and Lille for the transmission of military information. By 1792 the system was up and running, and consequently during the Terror Parisians could get news of military victories and defeats via Claude Chappe's semaphore relay stations. In 1793 he installed the system here in his house, which became the Telegraph Administration centre with Chappe as its Director. Chappe tried to market the system, but was eventually besieged by competition from others seeking to profit from his invention. Some claimed to have already invented the same system much earlier, others claimed to have a better system, and some even accused him of stealing the idea from the military. Overwhelmed by all these challenges, Chappe fell into a deep and dangerous melancholy. *'On 9 Thermidor the Robespierrists said I corresponded with the Austrians. In Prairial people said I was an aristocrat, in Vendémiaire I was a terrorist. Thus I would be hung by some, guillotined by others, and perhaps burnt as a sorcerer by the Vendéens.'* Chappe was unable to shake off his depression, and when he later fell ill, he started suspecting his enemies of poisoning him. It all ended here in 1805, when Chappe committed suicide by throwing himself down a well in the yard of the *hôtel*, and was found several hours later when some Telegraph employees saw his hat lying by the well. The *Hôtel Villeroy* continued to be the Telegraph Administration until 1834, and was demolished eleven years later.

Number 14, currently under renovation, was built in 1663 for Jean Petitot, an artist specializing in portraits on enamel, which were very fashionable at the time, and customarily offered by Louis XIV as a reward for services rendered. Petitot had plied his trade at the English Court up until 1649, when his patron, King Charles I, was executed, and he had to leave England. Number 14 remained in Petitot's family until 1757, when it was sold to the Marquis de Saint-Priest, then passed on to his heir, Antoine de Sartine, who in 1759 had become chief of the Paris police. In this position of power, Sartine made enormous improvements to the quality of life in the capital, including better street cleaning, street lighting, public water fountains and the introduction of the city's first public toilets. He had a reputation for being humane but incredibly efficient, and his methods soon became the benchmark for municipal administration throughout Europe. Equally renowned was Sartine's network of spies, which he used to root out criminals and expose social scandals, all of which were communicated to the king. As a result, the number of *lettres de cachets* issued during Sartine's fifteen years as police chief was higher than at any other time, and was one of the things that eventually sullied his reputation and brought public anger upon him when the Revolution broke out. Sartine had the good sense to heed this writing on the wall, and emigrated, but his son Charles-Antoine was not quite so prudent. He remained in Paris, where he had the misfortune to marry a young girl by the name of Charlotte-Rose Sainte-Amaranthe, who was executed during the Terror with her mother and her younger brother. Because of the pitiless Law of Suspects, poor Charles-Antoine was scooped up with various others connected to the Sainte-Amaranthe family, and guillotined with the 'batch' of 29 *Prairial*. A month later another member of the Saint-Priest family became a victim of the Terror. This time it was Julie-Agathe de Saint-Priest, aged 42, guillotined for conspiracy against the Republic and for reading letters from her *émigré* husband.

The house at number 18 was already at least 100 years old when the writer François René de Chateaubriand moved into it in January 1792 after his return from America. During the few short months that he lived here he got married, decided he would be safer out of the country, and emigrated the following July. His older brother, Jean-Baptiste, did not have the same foresight, and perished two years later when the Tribunal condemned him along with his wife and most of her family, the luckless Malesherbes. Like Charles Antoine de Sartine, whom you just met at number 14, Jean-Baptiste de Chateaubriand was a victim of marrying into the wrong family. In 1808 number 18 was home to Claude Chauveau-Lagarde, one of the lawyers who, with Malesherbes, had courageously defended Louis XVI at his trial. He also took on other risky cases, defending Charlotte Corday, the Girondin leader Brissot, the king's sister Madame Elisabeth, and Marie-Antoinette. Unlike Malesherbes, Chauveau-Lagarde survived the Revolution, despite being condemned to death in his absence, then later defending himself so brilliantly that he was acquitted. He was 53 when he came to live here, and was still practising law, still defending royalists, which he continued to do until the end of his career.

At number 24 you find the *Hôtel de Senneterre*, built in 1670 and named after the last family to live in it before the Revolution. Comte Henri-Charles de Senneterre bought the house in 1772 for 160,000 *livres*, and it remained in the family until 1794. The count had a daughter, Marie-Charlotte, who had considerably enhanced the family's status by marrying the Marshal of France, Louis de Conflans, Marquis d'Armentières. She was now Marquise d'Armentières, and although barely 25 years old, possessed a considerable fortune with which she set about enlarging the family home by buying two neighbouring houses. On the death of her father, the entire property was inherited by her son, who by then was about 14 years old. Four years later the Revolution broke out and this very young man quickly saw that being a rich aristocrat was going dangerously out of vogue, so he married before he turned 20 and took his bride out of the country, leaving his mother in the family residence. She was now a widow, and made the unwise decision to remain in her home, perhaps not believing things would get so bad. When the Terror began, it was too late to leave, and it would not be long before soldiers came here to arrest her. She was sent before the Tribunal, and on 8 *Thermidor*, one day before the fall of Robespierre, the 44-year-old marquise was guillotined.

Meanwhile, her son's wife had given birth to a son, Charles-Louis-Gabriel de Conflans, born during their emigration. He was still a teenager when he returned to Paris, thirteen years after his grandmother's execution, to claim his property, which had been seized in the interim by the revolutionary government and put up as a prize in a lottery. It was won with a 50 *livre* ticket by an entrepreneur who immediately sold it for a huge profit, and by the time Charles de Conflans made his claim the *hôtel* was on its seventh owner, a Monsieur Guénoux de Boissy, who flatly refused to part with it. It took five years of legal action before de Boissy agreed to sell his house back to Charles, who immediately re-sold it, presumably for a profit, otherwise all his efforts seem rather a waste of time. A century later it was bought by the city of Paris with a view to demolition, but fortunately they changed their mind at the last minute and handed it over to the government. Judging by the present state of the building, though, no-one seems to have made up their mind what to do with this potentially lovely *hôtel*.

The charming early 18th-century house opposite at number 13 became an artillery depot during the Revolution, and now belongs to Sciences Po, the French School of Political Science. At the beginning of the 19th century number 15, dating from 1681, belonged to one of Joséphine's grandsons. The elegant *Hôtel Bochart de Saron* at number 17 was built in 1639, and six years later had its youngest 'mistress of the house' ever when 13-year-old Elisabeth de Rambouillet married the owner, her first cousin Tallemant des Réaux. The house gets its name from the family of magistrates who took up residence here at the end of the 17th century, the last one of whom, Gaspard Bochart de Saron, was guillotined at the age of 64 as part of a 'batch' from the Paris Parliament. In addition to his parliamentary role, Bochart de Saron was also a scientist who owned a sizable collection of astronomical instruments, and whose work contributed to the classification of the distant 'comet' Uranus as a planet.

Earlier in the Revolution, in 1790, Charles-Maurice de Talleyrand lived in this house, when he was a deputy in the Constituent Assembly. Talleyrand was born in 1754 into a very distinguished family, and would certainly have become a soldier but for a club-foot, which proved too much of a handicap for the rigours of military life. Talleyrand cited a fall as the cause of this physical condition, but it was actually due to a genetic disorder known as Marfan's Syndrome, and it had an enormous effect on Talleyrand's future. Not only did it prevent him from becoming a soldier, it also deprived him of his right, as the oldest son, of inheritance by *primogéniture* when an official family decision judged that Talleyrand's physical condition made him unfit for the military service that this involved. Consequently all the titles, estates and offices that went with this inheritance were given to his younger brother, Archambaud Joseph, evoking considerable resentment in the young Talleyrand and probably contributing to his life-long cynicism. Following all this early disappointment, he decided to opt for a career in the church, was ordained in 1774, and thanks to the influence of his uncle, the archbishop of Rheims, Talleyrand rose rapidly to the position of bishop by 1788. The following year he was elected by the clergy to the Estates-General, and soon became embroiled in revolutionary politics. He supported the nationalization of church property, and was one of the few bishops to go along with the Civil Constitution of the Clergy, but in 1791 he decided to break his church connections, and resigned from his bishopric.

When the Constituent Assembly was dissolved, Talleyrand left his house and went on a diplomatic mission to London to try and extract a promise of neutrality from the English. On hearing the news of Louis XVI's overthrow he rushed back to Paris, only to be sent immediately on another London mission by the new Minister of Justice, Georges Danton. It was while Talleyrand was there that rumours began to spread about his complicity with the Duc d'Orléans, and when the National Convention formally accused him, he came back to Paris to try and clear his name. This proved to be impossible, and when he left yet again for England his name was put on the list of *émigrés*, and he was declared under arrest. During the few brief periods that Talleyrand spent in Paris during this turbulent time, he lodged over the road at number 30, maybe to remain unseen during an era of constant denunciation. At the end of 1793 he was thrown out of England, and left for America, where he remained until 1796 - a sensible decision, given his status in France. On his return to Paris Talleyrand's life took a turn for the better, and he was soon one of the key figures not only on the political scene, but also in the extravagant social life of the Faubourg Saint-Germain. You will meet up with him again very shortly.

The rather dirty façade of the *Hôtel Cambacérès* at number 21 masks the former glory of this once elegant but asymmetrical mansion, built in 1639 for a king's counsellor. If you look in the far right window of the first floor, however, you can catch a glimpse of the magnificent gilded mirrors, symbols of opulence, which have reflected three centuries of smiling nobility. They are now more likely to reflect the smiling faces of French civil servants, for this house has been occupied for 85 years by the Ministry of Finance. The State has recently authorized its transfer into the private sector, and it is now going to be restored, so you'll be able to see it in all its original splendour. ➡ To get an idea of the size of these old *hôtels*, go round the corner into rue Sebastien-Bottin and look at the back of the *Hôtel Cambacérès*, where you can see the garden, the carved wooden shutters on the interior of the windows, and the lovely arched doorway at the very back.

➡ Now go back to rue de l'Université and turn left, cross rue du Bac, continue down rue de l'Université and look at the beautiful carved doorway of number 33. This was one of the many houses owned by various members of the Nicolaï family, two of whom were guillotined during the Terror. Despite their Italian roots, they were one of the *grandes familles* of France, and since 1506 had held the post of *Premier Président* in the Paris *Chambre des Comptes* (Chamber of Accounts). The house at number 43 with the pointed roofs, iron gate and jigsaw carving around the entrance, stands on the site of an earlier *hôtel* that belonged to Lafayette's brother-in-law, Louis Marie, vicomte de Noailles. He fought with Lafayette against the British in America, and when the Revolution began he represented the nobility at the Estates-General. Despite his dismay at the attack on the Bastille, de Noailles soon got swept up in the tide of revolutionary fervour, and was one of the first nobles to renounce his privileges on the night of August 4th 1789. He returned to military service, but being fundamentally a product of the *ancien régime*, he was unable to accept the appalling lack of discipline amongst the troops, and he resigned. With a passport issued by the Commune and official permission from the Ministry of War, he left France without the stigma of *émigré*, going first to England and then to the United States. Louis-Marie left behind his wife, Anne-Dominique (Madame Lafayette's sister), who remained with her mother and grandmother in the de Noailles family home on rue Saint-Honoré. Rather than abandoning them to their fate, Anne-Dominique chose to share it with them, and all three women were guillotined on the same day in July 1794. Louis-Marie resumed his military service in 1802 in Santa Domingo, and his career ended as it had begun - fighting the British. He died in 1804 of wounds received in a battle with an English ship near Havana, Cuba.

Number 47-49 (formerly number 371) was where Napoléon's future wife, Joséphine de Beauharnais, came to live in September 1794 after her release from prison, where she had narrowly escaped the guillotine. She rented her lodgings from a kindly lady called Madame de Kreny, who did everything she could to help the rather destitute Joséphine, and eventually became her closest confidante. Joséphine was still known at this time by her real name of Rose, and lived here with her two children, Eugène aged 13, and 11-year-old Hortense, the future Queen of Holland. Since her release Rose had been living off her lover, Louis Hoche, whom she'd met in prison and who was so crazy about Rose that he would have given her anything he owned, and did, quite regularly. This was a time in her life when the future Empress was the most successful hustler in town, for she borrowed from anyone and everyone, including her two servants, who rarely saw any wages. Famine was rife in the capital during that winter, and it became the custom for people to bring their own bread to dinner parties, but Rose's friends told her not to worry. She successfully inflicted her Creole charm on everyone, was universally liked for her warmth and easy-going nature, and despite the modesty of her living situation, was out and about constantly, at parties, dinners, and the public dance halls that were all the rage after 9 *Thermidor*. It is quite likely that Rose and her closest friend, Thérésia Tallien, danced from time to time in their former prison at the Carmes Convent, which had been turned into a *bal public*. Thérésia was now the wife of Jean Lambert Tallien, whom some said she married out of gratitude for provoking 9 *Thermidor* and getting her out of prison. Rose was the godmother of their daughter, Thermidor-Rose-Thérésia - a suitably flamboyant name for a baby who was born in a theatre foyer.

It was at the Tallien's home that Rose met up again with Paul de Barras, the ambitious 'King of the Republic', who was at this time without doubt the most powerful member of the Convention. Always on the lookout for wealthy saviours, Rose immediately set her sights on him, but he rather took his time, which didn't fit in with Rose's scheme at all, and she let him know it. *'It's a long time since I've had the pleasure of seeing you,'* she wrote to him. *'It's most unkind of you to abandon an old friend. I hope you will be sensitive to this reproach. I now live at number 371 rue de l'Université.'* She got no response, and had to write a second note informing him that she had a cold, and telling him off yet again for not visiting her, before the hard-nosed deputy deigned to appear in rue de l'Université. Meanwhile Rose continued her 'business deals' which brought her a varied assortment of financial loans and gifts, enabling her to move from her modest lodgings here in August 1795 to a little house near the Faubourg Montmartre. It was way beyond her means, but Rose would very soon not have to worry about that.

At number 51 is the Hôtel de Soyécourt, with columns and little stone benches built into the wall on either side of its grand entrance. It was the home of three Spanish ambassadors in the last years of the *ancien régime*, firstly the Count of Fuentès, who was succeeded by Abarca de Boleo, Count of Aranda. When writer Caron de Beaumarchais was involved in arms trafficking, he was frequently to be seen among de Boleo's dinner guests. The third ambassador was Fernand Nunez, who replaced de Boleo in 1786, and was on close terms with Marie-Antoinette. It was to Nunez that the queen disclosed, in January 1791, her intention to escape from France. The *hôtel* takes its name from the Comtesse de Soyécourt, who inherited it in 1715 and started much of the enlargement and restoration that has made the *hôtel* what it is today. At her death her son, Joachim-Charles, Comte de Soyécourt, inherited the property and completed the work his mother had begun, then rented it to the Austrian ambassador, who was later replaced by the Spanish. Joachim-Charles had a daughter, Camille de Soyécourt, who was born in 1757, maybe in this house. She was to suffer considerable tragedy during the first half of her life, which she bravely turned into good works during the second. By the time the Revolution broke out Camille had become a Carmelite nun, and suffered all the hatred and persecution that was dealt out to the religious community at the time, but miraculously survived the massacres and executions.

Other members of her family were not so fortunate however. Her father, Joachim-Charles, ended up in the *Couvent des Carmes*, which had been transformed like many other convents into a revolutionary prison. He was imprisoned there at the same time as Joséphine, and on 5 *Thermidor* he was condemned along with 46 others, including Alexandre de Beauharnais, Joséphine's ex-husband, whom he had befriended in prison. That afternoon they both found themselves in the same tumbril, which took them to the guillotine in the *Place du Trône* (Nation). The 25 victims who made the same journey the following day included Camille's younger sister, Catherine-Louise-Silvain de Soyécourt, who was also born in this house. The heartbroken Camille was determined to restore the *Prison des Carmes*, where her father had spent his last months, and return it to its rightful occupants. Three years later, now aged 40 and known in the church as Mère Camille, she began the systematic purchase of the entire convent, and brought back the Carmelite community that had been expelled during the Revolution. The Hôtel de Soyécourt was confiscated in 1794 and occupied by a government ministry before being returned to the de Soyécourt family in 1815.

Rue de Poitiers.

➡ Cross the road, walk back to rue de Poitiers, and look at the house on the corner at number 11 (and 60-64 rue de l'Université), another one that was seized by the government in 1794 and put up for lottery. The lucky winner this time was a man named Hartmann, who sold it three years later for 40,000 *livres*. You can't see much of this house, since it is masked on rue de l'Université by a high wall and thick foliage, but you need have no doubt that its grandeur and dimensions were a bargain at 50 *livres*, which was the price of Hartmann's lottery ticket.

Turn into rue de Poitiers, and on your left at number 12 you will see a very lovely house called *Hôtel de Poulpry*, built in 1700. Its owner in the 1780s, the Marquise de Poulpry, emigrated at the beginning of the Revolution, and her house became the offices of the local municipal authority. When she came back in 1800, she got permission to sell the property while the municipality was still in it, then half a century later the *hôtel* was once more the scene of political activity, this time involving a group of monarchists, who moved in under the name of *Comité de la rue de Poitiers*. Further down the street you can see the rear façade of number 65 rue de Lille (and 10 rue de Poitiers), an elegant mansion with fabulous windows all the way round. This house has long been home to dukes and marquises, and has graced this corner since 1706.

RUE DE LILLE.

➡Continue on rue de Poitiers until it meets rue de Lille. This street used to be called *rue de Bourbon* before the Revolution, and was given its present name in 1792 to commemorate the victory of the city of Lille over the Austrians. As you arrive at rue de Lille, directly in front of you is the rear façade of the Musée d'Orsay, formerly a railway station, *Gare d'Orsay*. At the outbreak of the Revolution this was a huge lumber yard known as *La Tour d'Argent*, which was owned by the Marquis de La Vrillière and extended right down to the river's edge. Also on the site of the museum was a quadrangle of buildings occupied by a company called *Coaches for the Court*, which organized transport for the king and his entourage when they came to Paris from Versailles or the other royal residences around the capital. During the Revolution it became a barracks, first for the police, and then for the Consular Guards in 1800. At that time the area was known as the *Quartier Eugène* after Joséphine's son, Eugène de Beauharnais, who commanded the Consular Guards and who lived at number 78 of this street (see below). During the 19th century a government administrative building, the *Palais d'Orsay*, was put up on the site of the *Quartier Eugène*, and was occupied by various ministries before being burned down by the Commune in 1871. Strangely enough, the charred remains of the *Palais d'Orsay* became one of the most romantic sites of Paris, bringing inspiration to poets, and joy to botanists, who discovered all kinds of interesting new flowers springing up constantly amidst the ruins. Thus it remained for 27 years, until the *Gare d'Orsay* was built in its place in 1898, later being turned into the present Museum.

➥Turn left into rue de Lille and go past the main façade of number 65, now annexed to number 67, which was built at the same time as 65 and is known as the *Hôtel du président Duret*. In 1792 number 67 became the property of a marquis called Antoine Jean Gailliot de Mandat, who was a captain in the *Gardes Françaises* at the outbreak of the Revolution. He quickly switched to the winning side, became president of a municipal military committee, and was named as a commander in the National Guard. When Lafayette resigned as commander-in-chief in October 1791, no successor was named, so it was decided that each commander would take his turn at the post for a period of two weeks. Unfortunately for Mandat his turn coincided with the grand coup against the monarchy the following year, making of him a pawn in the game of deposing the king. He took charge of defending the Tuileries on August 9th, but at 5 a.m. the next morning he was summoned by the newly-formed Commune, who suspected him of being on the wrong side, perhaps because of his aristocratic roots. Mandat was discharged of his duties and put under arrest, but he never got to prison, for a pistol shot ended his life as he was walking down the steps from the Hôtel-de-Ville, and his body was thrown unceremoniously into the Seine. Surprisingly, throughout his entire revolutionary career, Mandat managed to hold on to this noble residence, which after his death was passed to his son, who remained here all through the Terror until 1797. Some people, it seems, got away with it.

During the Revolution number 71 belonged to a more famous marquis, Jean Antoine de Condorcet, who was born in the Aisne district in 1743, and became the most brilliant mathematician of his day. He entered the Academy of Sciences at just 26, became its permanent secretary eight years later, and entered the Academie-Française by the time he was 40. He was friends with all the great philosophers of the time, and wrote prolifically in defence of the rights of black people, and of human rights in general. Because of his passionate belief in the perfectibility of the human race, teaching people became a life-time preoccupation for Condorcet, and one that he pursued when he worked for a while in Turgot's ministry. He was a great enthusiast for the Revolution, and used it as a vehicle for the promotion of his ideas about education, which he considered one of the most fundamental human rights. His marriage rather late in life to Marie-Louise-Sophie de Grouchy was for both of them a match made in heaven, and brought Condorcet much happiness in the last six years of his life.

In 1791, at about the same time as he bought this house, Condorcet openly declared himself a republican, which earned him many enemies at the time, with the exception of the Girondin leader Brissot, who was always his ally. When Condorcet was attacked in the Assembly, Brissot jumped to his defence with the most eloquent words in praise of his friend's admirable evolution *'from philosopher to politician, from academician to journalist, from aristocrat to Jacobin.'* The reason for the attack had been Condorcet's project for public instruction, which proposed a non-religious curriculum and equal education for boys and girls. This was too progressive, even for revolutionaries, and the project was rejected, but Brissot's declaration left the Assembly silenced for a few brief moments. Condorcet almost always voted with the Girondins, and when it came time to judge the king he refused the death penalty and voted for permanent imprisonment. He rejected all involvement in factional warfare, and tried in vain to persuade Brissot and his friends to reconcile their differences with the Montagnards. For this reason perhaps Condorcet was not arrested with the Girondins, but he was denounced a few months later and declared under arrest. He immediately fled to a friend's house in rue Servandoni and remained there in hiding for eight months. When he was eventually caught in March 1794, he poisoned himself in his prison cell.

➡Continue along rue de Lille to number 79. This is the 18th-century *Hôtel de Lannion*, which you can't see very well from here, since it is masked by another building, but ➡if you go round the corner to 5*bis* rue de Bellechasse you can see it through the railings - and if you are there when the gates open you will get a glimpse of its elegant entrance. In 1836 an English woman was living here called Charlotte Walpole Atkins who in her youth had been an actress at Drury Lane Theatre in London. Like her more famous predecessor, Nell Gwyn, Charlotte was rather fond of royalty, but not in quite the same way. A staunch monarchist, she was horrified by the execution of Louis XVI and took up the cause of his imprisoned widow with admirable courage, arriving in Paris at the beginning of April 1793 with the intention of using part of her inheritance to liberate Marie-Antoinette. She succeeded in getting an audience at the Temple prison, where she arrived in disguise and talked to the queen about her escape plan, an incredibly dangerous act that put her own life in jeopardy. But despite her pleas, Charlotte was unable to persuade Marie-Antoinette to leave without her children. She begged her, she implored her. Her heroism knew no limits, even to the point of proposing that the queen put on Charlotte's own disguise and leave the prison in her place, but to no avail. Her failure was compensated, however, by being able to contribute to future escape attempts, for during her visit to Paris Charlotte made the acquaintance of the Baron de Batz. He was busy collecting money for a new plan to get the royal family out of the Temple, so Charlotte handed part of her fortune over to him, bringing his capital up to 20 million *livres*. None of it, unfortunately, could save the queen in the end. Charlotte Atkins died here in 1836, and I wonder if she chose to live here because she knew that her brave plan for the queen's salvation had not been the first to be hatched in this house. Legend has it that the Princesse de Lamballe and Axel de Fersen, Marie-Antoinette's two most dedicated friends, met here in 1791 to organize the royal escape that took place in June of that year.

➠Go back and turn left into rue de Lille. During the final years of the *ancien régime*, before the Revolution shattered for ever the *vie-en-rose* of the country's rich and privileged, many wealthy foreigners were drawn, as they still are, to the delights of the French capital, and would create palaces here that often surpassed the grandeur of those built by the Parisian aristocracy. A good example of this is the magnificent Hôtel de Salm immediately to your right at number 64 rue de Lille, one of the most admired of all Parisian residences that even inspired one architect to produce a replica of it in San Francisco. It was completed in 1784 for Frederick III, Prince de Salm-Kyrburg, a long-time resident of Paris who lived here with his sister, Amélie de Saxe, Princesse de Hohenzollern-Sigmaringen. The gardens extended all the way to the Seine, and could be seen from the wall of the Tuileries Gardens, where Thomas Jefferson used to regularly sit and admire the splendour of his favourite Parisian mansion. The opulence of the prince's house rather masked the fact that he was in debt up to his eyebrows, and continually besieged by angry creditors. But this did not stop him and his sister from holding the most sumptuous *soirées* that were attended enthusiastically by all the high society of the capital, most of whom did not care much for the prince but thoroughly enjoyed his parties. A frequent guest was Joséphine, who lived at the time in rue Saint-Dominique and became instant friends with Princesse Amélie. When the Revolution disturbed the tranquillity of the neighbourhood, Prince Frederick initially sided with the royalists, but it was not long before he became an 'Orléanist' and began sympathizing with the new regime. By 1792 he was so impressed with political developments in France that he transferred some of them to his own principality, where he abolished what remained of feudalism and introduced the French constitution. Frederick was obviously sincere in his enthusiasm for the Revolution, for he accepted Lafayette's offer of a post as commander in the National Guard, requiring him to give up a royal pension of 20,000 *livres* a year - no small sacrifice for someone whose financial situation was so dire that his furniture and possessions were seized by the authorities. He even tried, without success, to raise money by putting his *hôtel* up for lottery.

The Hôtel de Salm, now the headquarters of the Legion of Honour. Thomas Jefferson confessed to being *'violently smitten'* by this magnificent house, which he admired regularly from the Tuileries Gardens. It belonged to a German prince, who went to the guillotine during the Terror. (Authors private collection)

In the course of 1793 things got increasingly dangerous for people like Frederick, who decided to leave for England with his son and his sister. Before leaving Amélie proposed taking along Eugène and Hortense de Beauharnais, the two young children of Joséphine, who readily accepted the offer, glad of the chance to get them away from the dangers of the capital. The little group of fugitives had already got as far as Saint-Pol in the region of Artois when the children's father, Alexandre de Beauharnais, found out about the plan and intercepted them. The entire party was stopped in Saint-Pol and the two children were taken back to Paris, but the interruption proved fatal for Frederick, who was questioned and arrested. His house was searched by agents of the Committee for General Security, who then realized that they'd confused him with his cousin, the Prince de Salm-Salm, whose *Hôtel de Saint-Florentin* was on the other side of the river. But the committee members weren't concerned, and Frederick remained under house arrest until the end of March 1794, when he was put in the *Prison des Carmes* on the orders of Fouquier-Tinville, who accused him of being a '*secret agent of the German coalition.*' Frederick must have felt at home in prison, for his whole neighbourhood seemed to be there. On the first day he ran into Alexandre de Beauharnais, whose intervention had led to Frederick's unpleasant predicament, and he also met up with the Comte de Soyécourt from rue de l'Université. Then came the arrival of Joséphine, who was the only one of the four to survive. Frederick and his two neighbours all appeared before the Tribunal on 5 *Thermidor* and departed together for the guillotine, leaving Joséphine behind, shocked and terrified.

Amélie continued to live in the Hôtel de Salm during her brother's imprisonment, and two years after his death she bought the plot of land in the garden of the Picpus Convent where he had been buried with all the other victims of the Terror. The Hôtel de Salm was confiscated briefly after Frederick's execution, and at the end of August 1794 it was badly damaged by the explosion of a powder magazine at Grenelle. The following year Frederick's family re-gained possession of the house, but it remained under the control of their creditors, who auctioned off all the furniture and rented the house to a thoroughly unscrupulous arms dealer by the name of Claude Lenthereau. Under the assumed name of Comte de Beauregard, he bought a *château* and kept several mistresses, including Mademoiselle Lange, a well-known actress from the Comédie-Française, who received 10,000 *livres* a day from her ostentatious lover. He also gave the most extravagant parties here that were the talk of the entire neighbourhood. This went on for four years until Beauregard had a visit from the police, was arrested on charges of fraud and publicly branded with a hot iron before going to prison for four years.

At the same time that Beauregard was leading his high-life here, the Hôtel de Salm was also being used as a public dance hall called *Le Bal Lambert*. This was held in one of the *hôtel's* grandiose ballrooms and the manager was obviously trying to attract a high-class clientele, for dancing in boots was prohibited. There was also a political club here, founded in 1797 under the name *Cercle Constitutionnel* or *Club de Salm*, which counted among its members Talleyrand and Madame de Staël, daughter of Louis XVI's former minister, Jacques Necker. Its members were all moderate republicans, and their aim was to fight the royalist revival that was gaining ground at the time. In 1804 the *hôtel* was sold to the Legion of Honour, which has remained here ever since, and it now houses the Legion's museum. Despite being burned in 1871 by the Commune, who installed one of their generals here, the façade of this magnificent house suffered hardly any damage, so you can still see the Hôtel de Salm in all the same glory that was once the pride and joy of the ill-starred Frederick de Salm-Kyrburg.

➡ Now walk down to number 93 rue de Lille, with its beautiful statues above the entrance and very elegant entresol windows. When Louis XVI and his family were brought to Paris in October 1789, they were followed by the government, who brought with them all their paperwork, past and present, and number 93 is one of the houses where the Comte de Montmorin, Minister of Foreign Affairs, hastily arranged the archives of his department. At that time he was the most influential person in the new government and worked in close cooperation with Mirabeau to establish a constitutional monarchy. After the failed royal escape to Varenne, de Montmorin resigned from his post, and with two of his colleagues continued trying to influence the king. However, the nickname 'Austrian Committee' given to them by their critics rather overestimated their power, for Louis refused to listen to anything they said. When the monarchy was overthrown, de Montmorin went into hiding, but was rapidly found, arrested and imprisoned in the *Abbaye*, where he was killed during the September massacres. At the time when de Montmorin brought his archives here the house was occupied by an aristocrat called Archambaud Joseph de Talleyrand-Perigord, Comte de Talleyrand, whose wife, Madeleine-Henriette-Sabine, was guillotined on 8 *Thermidor* at the age of 31. Their landlord, a counsellor called Joseph Duruey, was also executed during the Terror. It was Archambaud Joseph who was given all the rights of *primogéniture* that should have belonged to his older brother, the more famous Charles-Maurice de Talleyrand, one of the most colourful residents of this area whom you met in rue de l'Université. Archambaud Joseph, who was eight years younger that his brother and by all accounts very handsome, survived the Revolution by emigrating, and was eventually made Duc de Talleyrand in 1817.

The *Hôtel de Beauharnais* at number 78 is named after Joséphine's son, Eugène de Beauharnais, who bought it in 1803 and lived here with his sister Hortense until his departure for Italy two years later. Eugène spent 1.5 million *francs* on structural modifications and elaborate decoration, including the eagles - symbols of power - over the gate, all of which turned it into a residence worthy of his new title of 'Prince of the

Empire'. All this work has remained intact, and much of Eugène's furniture is still in place in the bedrooms, bathrooms, the fabulous Pompeian-style *salon* and the Turkish *boudoir*. If you are lucky enough to pass by when the main entrance doors are open, you will see the wonderful Egyptian façade that Eugène had built on to his *hôtel*. He left in 1805 to become Viceroy of Italy and married Augusta, the daughter of Maximilian I of Bavaria.

Next door at number 80 is the *Hôtel de Seignelay*, built in 1714 and owned at the end of the 18th century by Armand-Joseph de Béthune, duc de Charost, who was imprisoned during the Terror, but saved from death by 9 *Thermidor*. His only son, Armand-Louis-François de Béthune, was not so lucky, and went to the scaffold in April 1794 at the age of 23. Eleven years earlier Armand-Joseph had married for a second time with Henriette-Adélaïde de Tourzel, oldest daughter of Louise Elisabeth, duchesse de Tourzel, governess to the royal children and more often referred to as Madame de Tourzel. During the king and queen's attempted escape to Varennes it was Madame de Tourzel who assumed the role of 'Baronne de Korf', and when the royal family was imprisoned in the Temple she accompanied them briefly, but was taken out just before the September massacres and put into *La Force*. However she and her daughter Pauline both miraculously escaped the massacre thanks to the intervention of a member of the Commune called Hardy, who hid them in Vincennes for six months. After 9 *Thermidor* she lived here in this house, in an apartment on the first floor, and twice a week she would set off for the Temple to visit Madame Royale, daughter of Louis XVI and Marie-Antoinette. Before her execution the queen gave her dog, Coco, to Madame de Tourzel, who looked after it in this *hôtel*, and the little grave where Coco was buried can still be seen in the garden.

➥ When you get to Boulevard Saint-Germain turn right and take the pedestrian crossing to the other side. As you cross, take a look to your right at the Pont de la Concorde, begun in 1788 and completed three years later, and which contains most of the stones from the demolished Bastille. ➥ On the other side of the crossing turn obliquely right into the end part of rue de Lille. Number 123 was home briefly to Lafayette in 1799, when he returned to France after the coup d'etat of 18 *Brumaire* (11 November) that brought Napoléon Bonaparte to power. Although he refused to have any official post in the new government, Lafayette did not actively oppose Bonaparte, and had even predicted his future glory. *'Who will give the country the government it desires?'* he wrote to a friend three weeks before the coup. In his eyes Bonaparte was the only choice. *'He can become master of France...because he is the man who did so much at the siege of Toulon, at the events of Vendémiaire, who was linked with Barras, Tallien, Fréron, and because in the end he is not unpleasant to look at.'* Lafayette knew from experience what it took to make a national hero - a few good victories, good contacts and good looks. Two weeks later he wrote, with rather less perception, to his wife, assuring her that Bonaparte would never want to be an autocrat. But after his first meeting with the new head of state he was immediately disillusioned. Bonaparte was furious to find out that Lafayette had returned to Paris without his permission, and sent Talleyrand to his house with orders to leave, which Lafayette flatly refused to do. Surprisingly Bonaparte gave in, mostly thanks to a visit from Madame Lafayette, who so charmed him that he agreed to let her husband stay, on condition that he didn't cause any trouble. Napoléon got the last word, though, when a ceremony was held two months later to commemorate the death of George Washington, and he forbade Lafayette's name to be mentioned in any of the speeches.

When Lafayette came to live at number 123 in 1799 he was no stranger to the neighbourhood. He had spent nearly ten years here with his family before and during the Revolution. If you walk back a few metres along rue de Lille in the direction of the boulevard, you will pass number 119, site of the house that Lafayette bought in 1784 when he moved out of his wife's family home (*Hôtel de Noailles*). This was the first time his young wife Adrienne had been separated from her mother, and every day she would go back to rue Saint-Honoré to spend several hours with her. The corner where you are standing was very busy in those days, for Adrienne's husband was now a national figure of considerable importance, and their home on rue de Lille received a continual stream of visitors associated with Lafayette's various political projects. In 1787 he was busy defending civil rights for Protestants, so Adrienne had a succession of Protestant ministers passing through her *salon*. When he got involved in the campaign to end the slave trade, her house was filled with abolitionists, and of course there were frequent visits from all Lafayette's American friends. It was here that Adrienne and her husband received all the most eminent citizens of the United States, including Benjamin Franklin, John Adams, and Thomas Jefferson.

The Revolution played havoc with Adrienne's orderly world, as her life became linked with every turbulent event that took place. Although she shared her husband's opinions with some sincerity, she was nonetheless horrified by some of the things that happened. Her daughter, Virginie de Lafayette, who was only 7 at the beginning of the Revolution, remembered her at this time as accepting all the demands that were made by the municipal authorities *'to bless the flag, or carry out other various patriotic rituals'* while at the same time *'imploring ceaselessly the mercy of God'*. Virginie described how Lafayette's involvement in the Revolution affected her mother's state of mind. *'My father kept permanent open house. My mother did the honours and showed his numerous friends around the house with great charm, but what she suffered can only be judged by those who heard her talk about it. She saw my father at the head of a revolution of unknown duration...she tolerated with unbelievable strength the continual dangers to which he was exposed. Never, she told us, did she see him leave the house during that time without thinking that she was saying goodbye for the last time.'* Adrienne was a pious Catholic, and actively opposed the oath that the clergy were required to take, resulting in her *salon* being filled with non-juring priests and nuns seeking protection. When Lafayette invited to dinner members of the clergy who had taken the oath, Adrienne entertained them politely but did not hide her views, for religion was one subject on which she could not compromise herself. Sometimes she had whole armies at her door. When Lafayette got it into his head to resign as commander of the National Guard, Virginie saw her mother do the honours once more. *'My father...to avoid all entreaties, left the house. My mother stayed there, overjoyed at his resolution, and was charged by him to receive in his place the municipality and the sixty battalions who came to beseech him to resume his command.'* (Lasteyrie, 1868)

Unfortunately for Adrienne her husband did return to his post, and on the day that he led the troops during the massacre on the Champ-de-Mars she and her children sat petrified inside their house while a furious crowd amassed outside shouting their intention to murder Madame Lafayette and present her head to her husband. The street where you are standing became a battleground, and the whole family came dangerously close to being massacred that day. *'We had doubled the guard, who were fighting them off in front of the house; but the brigands were on the point of entering the house, having scaled the wall of the garden which borders the Place du Palais-Bourbon, when a group of cavalry, who were passing by, dispersed them.'*

In 1791 the Lafayette family all left Paris for Chavaniac (just south of Clermand-Ferrand), where they stayed with a relative, remaining together until Lafayette was called again for active duty. It was while she was still in Chavaniac that Adrienne got news of the overthrow of Louis XVI, of the mass hatred towards Lafayette that had broken out in the capital, and eventually the good news that he had got out of the country safely. Later on she was arrested, and brought to Paris, where she was imprisoned for two weeks in *La Force*, and then transferred to *Le Plessis*, the former *Collège Louis-le-Grand* where her husband had been educated. These were terrible days for Madame Lafayette. She was now separated from her husband and children, and on leaving Paris for Chavaniac in 1791 she had also said goodbye to her mother and sister, not realizing she would never see either of them again. She did not find out about their execution or that of her grandmother until after 9 *Thermidor*, when she sent a letter to the *Luxembourg* prison, where she thought they were still alive and about to be liberated. The reply from the gaoler at *Luxembourg* told her everything.

Rue de Courty.

➡Continue in the same direction past number 119 and turn right on rue de Courty, which is also associated with the name Lafayette. In 1801, six years after her release from prison, Madame Lafayette came back to Paris with her sister, Pauline, Marquise de Montagu, and rented rooms in this little street in a modest lodging-house run by one of their former domestic servants. Their objective in coming to the capital was to find the communal graves where their mother, sister and grandmother had been buried after being guillotined during the Terror. They spent nearly two years looking for the exact site of the graves before meeting Mademoiselle Pâris, a courageous lace maker who had followed the decapitated bodies of her own father and brother from the scaffold to the garden of Picpus, where all the victims were thrown. Mademoiselle Pâris was able to tell the two sisters the location of the graves, and once they knew this they set about raising money to buy the site. While all this was going on the two women lived here under false names, for their mission was not without danger. All activity connected with the Picpus graveyard was closely observed by the police, and the negotiations of the two sisters came very close to being exposed by police-chief Fouché, until he discovered that one of those contributing money to the scheme was none other than the Emperor's step-son, Eugène de Beauharnais.

RUE DE L'UNIVERSITÉ.

➥From rue de Courty turn right and you're back on rue de l'Université, where at number 108 is a house dating from the beginning of the 18th century. Unfortunately you can't see it since it's covered by a wall crowned with ivy and bearing a rather old notice relating to the law of July 1881 forbidding bill-stickers. The house number is also very small, but you will see it on the wall to the right, under the commemorative plaque. It was in this house that Anne-Robert Jacques Turgot, Louis XVI's disgraced finance minister, died of gout on March 18th 1781, after much physical suffering and personal bitterness over his political downfall five years earlier He had tried in vain to influence the 22-year-old king and steer him on to the path of reason, but when he saw that his days as minister were numbered, Turgot wrote an emotional letter to Louis, berating him for offering '*neither help nor consolation*'. He did not mince his words concerning the king's incompetence in running the affairs of state. '*You lack experience, Sire!...Consider, Sire, that following the course of nature, you will have fifty years to reign, and imagine the progress that could be made by this present chaos which, in just twenty years, has come to the point we see now. Oh! Sire, do not wait for such a fatal experience to befall you, and learn to profit from the experience of others...Never forget, Sire, that it was weakness that put Charles I's head on the block.*' (Manceron, 1972). Turgot's prophetic pleas did not impress the young Louis, who dismissed him twelve days later and sent him into exile.

By 1779 Turgot had returned from banishment, but was so afflicted by the gout that he was scarcely able to walk. He sold off some of his family heirlooms and with the profits he bought this house, known at the time as the *Hôtel de Viarmes*, where he spent his last two years of life - years that were hardly characterized by peace of mind. He spent most of his time lashing out critically at all his former political rivals, particularly Jacques Necker, whom he described as '*obnoxious*' and '*bloated*' with glory. Turgot's most generous words were reserved for the Americans, who in his view '*could become the model for all others, as long as they never seek to resemble our old Europe, a mass of divided powers, fighting with each other over territory or commercial profit.*' He wrote this to his English friend, Richard Price, a liberal Unitarian pastor in Newington Green, with whom he shared a belief in the unlimited perfectibility of man. Turgot and Price exchanged their ideas in a correspondence that was intercepted so often by the French authorities that Turgot eventually advised Price not to reply, for '*they open my letters and consider me too much a friend of liberty for a minister - even a disgraced minister.*' Turgot wrote a lot of letters in this house, for letter-writing was all that was left to him now he was no longer able to get out and visit people. His correspondents included Condorcet and Adam Smith, the Scottish economist who had befriended Turgot during his stay in France during the 1770s. Despite his bitterness, in his last letter to Condorcet Turgot affirmed his belief that there was more good in the world than evil, but he must have been hard put to believe it on his death-bed, which was noticeably bereft of any member of his family. He was not one to complain, however, and managed to repress his choking and death-rattle enough to give the impression of sleeping peacefully. It was such a convincing impression, what's more, that the few friends who were there left the room for a while, and when they came back Turgot had already died, alone. An autopsy revealed over 40 small stones in his liver. '*If he had had them in his heart,*' they said, '*he would have been more suited to being a Minister.*'

After Turgot's death, his absent relatives suddenly appeared to claim their inheritance, which contained rather more than they bargained for. Among his effects was a collection of papers and letters that contained so many potentially explosive state secrets that the frightened heirs decided to burn them, although fortunately for history Turgot had sent copies of some of them to other people. They then sold his house to a marquis, who emigrated at the beginning of the Revolution, leaving the property to fall into the hands of the government. It was put up for lottery in 1795, and won by a Belgian merchant, who sold it for a huge profit the following year. Turgot would not have been too pleased to know that in 1803 Madame Germaine de Staël, the daughter of the 'obnoxious' Necker, lived here for a few months, before being exiled by Napoléon. Since her return to Paris at the end of the Revolution she had increasingly irritated the authorities by her writings and liberal politics which attracted to her *salon* all the educated rebels of the day. Her activities were closely surveyed by Napoléon Bonaparte, well-known for his loathing of political women, and when Necker brought out a book on the economic policies of the *ancien régime*, Napoléon seized the occasion to get rid of this female thorn in his side. He accused her of collaborating with her father on the book, resulting in her exile to Italy and Germany, where she got a much warmer welcome from the powers that be.

➡ Go across the square in front of Turgot's house (Place du Président Edouard Herriot), cross rue Aristide-Briand, continue westwards along rue de l'Université and stop outside number 126, The Palais-Bourbon, now the seat of the National Assembly. The façade most familiar to visitors is the one on the other side, facing the Seine, where 25 steps lead up to a monumental 75-metre Corinthian colonnade. This was added by Napoléon in 1806 at the same time as he ordered the completion of the Eglise de la Madeleine on the opposite side of the river. The façade you see on this side is the original entrance of the palace built in 1722 for Louise-Françoise, Duchesse de Bourbon, the legitimized daughter of Louis XIV and his mistress, the Marquise de Montespan. The original architect was an Italian named Ghirardini, who died before completing his work, and the Italianate design, based on Le Grand Trianon at Versailles, is hardly visible now underneath the considerable changes made later on by the duchess's grand-son, Louis-Joseph de Bourbon, Prince de Condé. A true prince of the blood, skilled in the art of war and Grand-Master of the King's House at the age of 15, the Prince de Condé nonetheless did not get on very well with Marie-Antoinette. He therefore avoided the Court at Versailles, and spent most of his time at his magnificent palace at Chantilly, which was as much admired by foreign visitors then as it is now. The minute the Revolution broke out Louis-Joseph emigrated and raised an army in defence of the royalist cause, leaving his Parisian palace to be confiscated by the government and turned into *La Maison de la Révolution*. At first it was used as a prison, then in 1798, during the Directory, it was occupied by the Council of Five Hundred, who held their meetings in the Prince de Condé's former living rooms. If you visit the interior of the Palais-Bourbon, you will see in the entrance hall a magnificent bronze sculpture made in 1891 by Jules Dalou. It shows the dramatic session of the National Assembly in Versailles on June 23rd 1789, when the deputies refused to leave the hall and Mirabeau hurled his celebrated threat to the Marquis de Dreux-Brézé.

➡Walk further down rue de l'Université keeping the Palais-Bourbon on your right and you'll see number 128, another smaller palace, the Hôtel du Petit-Bourbon, former home to Armand de Lesparre, Marquis de Lassay, 17th-century adventurer and a close friend of the Duchesse de Bourbon next door. It was built at the same time and by the same architects as the Palais-Bourbon, and was later acquired by the Prince de Condé, who incorporated it into his palace, thus completing his monopoly on property in the immediate vicinity. During the Revolution it was occupied by the *Ecole Centrale des Travaux Publics*, one of the many schools created by the new government and which in 1795 became the celebrated and prestigious Ecole-Polytechnique. Courses began here in December 1794 and took place in the Prince de Condé's former administrative offices, which, if the doors are open, you can see on either side of the long driveway leading up to the house. The Hôtel du Petit-Bourbon has had a floor added since the days of the Prince de Condé, but its original 18th-century lines and graceful elegance can still be seen and appreciated. It is nowadays the official residence of the president of the National Assembly, and is linked by a gallery to the Palais-Bourbon.

Place du Palais-Bourbon.

➡Go back to the Place du Palais-Bourbon, and walk across the road to the left hand side of the square (with odd numbers). It was opened in 1778 when the Prince de Condé got permission to change the direction of part of rue de Bourgogne and create this lovely square in front of his palace. It started out with its present name, but was given a new one with each political change that took place, before returning to the original one in 1815. Thus it has successively been *Place de la Maison-de-la-Révolution, du Conseil-des-Cinq-Cents, du Palais-du-Corps-Legislatif,* and *de la Chambre-des-Deputés.* The creation of this square, and the construction of the surrounding houses, was a speculative operation for the Prince de Condé in much the same way as the Palais-Royal was for the Duc d'Orléans. When Napoléon's younger brother, Lucien Bonaparte, lived in the Hôtel de Brienne around the corner, he installed his mistress, a widow named Alexandrine de Bleschamp, in the house at number 7 Place du Palais-Bourbon, where you now see the entrance to a garage. It is said that the love-struck Lucien ordered the construction of a tunnel, known as 'the conjugal underground', which led him discreetly - and frequently - out of the Hôtel de

Brienne and directly *chez* Alexandrine. His visits became so frequent, in fact, that in 1803 he decided to dispense with his subterranean wanderings, and married the object of his desire in a ceremony that took place on the same day as the baptism of their child - the first of ten.

RUE SAINT-DOMINIQUE.
➡ Leave Place du Palais-Bourbon by rue de Bourgogne, where on your right is a florist called Moulié. Above it on the corner wall you can still see, albeit very faintly, the letters *St* scratched out by vandals during the Revolution. ➡ Continue along rue de Bourgogne and turn left (eastward) on rue Saint-Dominique, where the first house on the right is number 35, the *Hôtel de Broglie*, a lovely house with beautiful shell carvings under the windows on the left-hand side of the façade. It got its name from a family of aristocrats who owned it from 1724 until 1810, and at the time of the Revolution the two most prominent members of this noble dynasty were Victor-François, Duc de Broglie, and his son Prince Claude-Victor, whom you will meet later on in this walk. This house belonged to another branch of the de Broglie family, and they sold it in 1810 to Baron Jean Corvisart, who as official physician to the emperor was at the height of his glory. He originally began studying as a lawyer, a career that would very probably have led him into revolutionary politics, a passport in those times to an early death by decapitation, so the day he decided quite by chance to attend a hospital lecture was for him a lucky one. Immediately drawn to the mysteries of medicine, he switched his field of study, qualified in 1782 and went on to found the *Hôpital de la Charité*. He was good friends with Joséphine, and it was thanks to her introduction that Corvisart became Napoléon's personal doctor, and remained so even after the imperial divorce. Napoléon's second wife, Marie-Louise de Lorraine, was a guest in this house when she was pregnant with her son, who was known as the 'King of Rome'. Corvisart's home became famous not only for

its illustrious resident, but also for the sumptuous parties he held in it, which in the end contributed to his financial ruin.

Opposite the Hôtel de Broglie is number 16, built in 1724 and home in 1788 to Louis Pierre de Chastenet, Comte de Puységur when he was Minister of War in Necker's government. Puységur was loyal to the king, and raised a small contingent of gentlemen to defend the Tuileries on the night the monarchy was overthrown, but after this he very sensibly emigrated, not returning until Napoléon came to power. Number 14, the Hôtel de Brienne, dates from 1714 and takes its name from the Comte de Brienne, who bought it in 1776. He was the older brother of the celebrated cardinal, Loménie de Brienne, who became Louis XVI's controller-general of finances in 1787, and whose conservatism in the face of reform eventually led to the convocation of the Estates-General. While at Court Loménie de Brienne used his influence to put the Comte de Briennne at the head of the of Ministry of War, a post that he only kept until 1788, when he was replaced by his next-door neighbour at number 16, the Comte de Puységur. The Comte de Brienne should have followed his neighbour's example and emigrated, but he chose to remain, buying up adjoining gardens to enlarge his house, and sharing it with his younger brother, whose own home was nearly burned down by an agitated crowd in 1787. This act of vandalism against the cardinal's property was just one of many signalling the torment to come, warning signs that were not heeded by either of the two brothers, who both remained in France throughout the Revolution. Despite swearing the patriotic oath and becoming a constitutional bishop in Sens, Loménie de Brienne was arrested in November 1793, but being ill he was kept prisoner in his home. There he died of apoplexy the following February, in the arms of the Comte de Brienne, who had rushed to Sens on hearing of his brother's grave condition. Shortly afterwards he too was arrested and guillotined, a victim of his aristocratic past.

After the Revolution the Hôtel de Brienne became the property of Lucien Bonaparte, who restored it and filled it with wonderful pieces of art - and constructed the underground tunnel to the home of his lover, Alexandrine de Bleschamp. Lucien had been a widower since 1800, and lived in this house with his two daughters, Christine and Charlotte, and his sister Elisa, but shortly after moving here he met Alexandrine and it was love at first sight. Thanks to the amorous tunnel, there was no limit to their romantic trysts either here or at Alexandrine's home in the Place du Palais-Bourbon. But when Lucien decided to dispense with the 'conjugal underground' and get married, it evoked such disapproval from his brother, Napoléon, that Lucien and his family left Paris and went to live in Italy. Napoléon gave the empty house to his mother, Madame Letizia, who was respectfully known as *Madame Mère*. She was one of the few women of the era who resisted, with no trouble at all, the temptation to spend a fortune on interior decoration and furniture in order to impress her friends. Although Napoléon gave her a million a year for this purpose, she scrupulously saved as much of it as she could, provoking reproach from her son for living *'like a bourgeoise from rue Saint-Denis.'* He impressed on her that for the sake of protocol she should be seen to spend a million a year, to which she replied, *'Then give me two.'* For several years *Madame Mère* lived out a peaceful existence in this house, saving money and playing cards with her entourage of geriatric statesman, before selling it to the government in 1817, since when it has been occupied by the Ministry of Defence.

Numbers 10 and 12 are also offices of the Ministry of Defence. Number 10 was built in 1784 for the *Couvent des Filles de Saint-Joseph*, which since 1641 had been taking in poor orphan girls, educating them in the Christian faith and training them in a useful job such as embroiderer. At the age of 20 they went out into the world with three possibilities before them - work, marriage or the Church. As well as taking in orphans the convent also continued the time-honoured tradition of receiving retired ladies of the Court and discarded royal mistresses. The most notable of this latter group was Madame de Montespan, who came here when she was supplanted in Louis XIV's affections by Madame de Maintenon. Celebrated for her beauty, Madame de Montespan had become the king's mistress at the age of 27 and bore him eight children, six of whom survived and were legitimized by Louis XIV. Another aristocratic lady to retire here was Marie-Anne de Vichy-Chamrond, Marquise de Deffand, who was 50 and almost blind when she arrived in 1747. This didn't stop her from opening a famous *salon* here, romantically decorated in *moiré* silk wallpaper covered in buttercups, where she received some of the most illustrious figures of the day, including Turgot, Voltaire and Horace Walpole. Despite such a stimulating entourage, she suffered constantly from that most tedious of afflictions, *ennui* (world-weariness), which she put down to *'deprivation of emotion coupled with the pain of not being able to do without it.'*

If you like 19th-century churches you have probably noticed the Notre Dame look-alike set back in a square opposite numbers 10 and 12. This is the Basilique Sainte-Clotilde, and it's worth going in to have a look at the interior. This lovely mini-cathedral, which was the first neo-Gothic church to be built in Paris, has a beautiful carved wooden pulpit, and the painted chapels and stained glass windows are quite wonderful.

➡Continue along rue Saint-Dominique, where just before the end of the street you will see Place Jacques Bainville and rue Solférino. Here you should sit on one of the benches in Place Jacques Bainville and read about Madame Félicité de Genlis, who for a short time was the mistress of the Duc d'Orléans. Félicité was married to Charles-Alexis Brûlart, Marquis de Sillery, Comte de Genlis, and she lived here where you now see 11*bis* rue Saint-Dominique, which stands on the site of a *hôtel* known as the *Pavillon d'Orléans*. It was originally part of the *Couvent des Dames de Bellechasse*, which was closed by the revolutionary government in 1790, and its demolition in 1905 was a great loss, for it had been the home of one of the most interesting women of the 18th century. Félicité de Genlis seemed to be the woman who had everything. She was beautiful, charming, intelligent and knowledgeable, she had no trouble seducing men, spoke several languages, cultivated wonderful gardens and played sublimely on the harp. She was also very socially ambitious, and was able to indulge this with the blessing of her husband, who didn't seem bothered by Félicité's continual efforts to be admitted into other people's households. When she was presented to Philippe, Duc de Chartres (future Philippe-Egalité) with a view to becoming a lady-in-waiting to the Duchesse de Chartres, Félicité immediately started a liaison with Philippe. It would turn into an intense affair that did not last long, but led to an enduring friendship between Félicité and not only the duke, but also the duchess, who never knew about her 'companion's' passionate interlude with her husband.

In the mid 1750s the Duc d'Orléans put her in charge of the education of several of his children, including the future Louis-Philippe, and she thus became, in practice if not in name, the first woman *gouverneur* of royal princes. The children spent much of their time with Félicité here in the *Pavillon d'Orléans*, where she gave them not a moment of repose, continually subjecting them to educational experiments based on the ideas of Rousseau. She covered the walls of the children's bedrooms with maps of the world, Roman history, French history, mythology, in fact anything likely to arouse curiosity in their young minds. She took them on visits to factories, where they learned how things were made - one of these visits was to the Maille mustard factory - and they also visited cabinet makers, locksmiths, mirror polishers, potters and metal workers. Félicité was tireless, and expected her charges to be the same. *'We rose at 6 o'clock, winter or summer, were fed on milk, roast meat and bread; never any treats, never any sweets,'* was how Louis-Philippe later described her educational methods to the writer Victor Hugo, *'forced labour, little pleasure...it is she who got me used to sleeping on bare boards.'* But despite her severity and the rigorous regime she inflicted on them, the children all seemed to adore their teacher, particularly the teenage Louis-Philippe, who confessed to Hugo that *'I have never been in love except for once in my life, and that was with Madame de Genlis...she was 36 and I was 17.'* When he was 15 he offered her a ring as a new year's present, with the touching dedication engraved on it, *'What would I have been without you?'* His two brothers, the dukes of Montpensier and Beaujolais, also gave her engraved rings saying, *'To love you is my duty'* and *'I am your work and I offer you mine'.*

In 1781 the royal children were joined in their classes by a young 'orphan' named Pamela. She had been brought over from England in rather mysterious circumstances, officially so she could help the young princes in their study of English, but in reality she was the result of the amorous liaison that Félicité

Madame de Genlis gives a harp lesson to her pupil, Adélaïde d'Orléans, while on the left of the picture Pamela holds the music book in place. Pamela was the daughter of Philippe-Egalité and Madame de Genlis, conceived during their brief affair. (Author's private collection)

had had with the Duc d'Orléans. Baby Pamela had been sent to England shortly after her birth, then later brought back to take her place among the Orléans children - to whom she apparently bore a striking resemblance. By the time she was a teenager, and the Revolution was under way, Pamela was admired by many of the duke's political friends, and even Camille Desmoulins courted her for a while.

Despite being her mother, Félicité didn't get on that well with Pamela, but she loved her job, finding the whole realm of education and the development of the young so consuming that she wrote several books on the subject. She was one of the few women of her time to devour knowledge as widely and profoundly as her male contemporaries, and she wrote several books aimed at women, whom she firmly believed to be every bit as intelligent as men - not a common belief at the time. When the Revolution broke out she shared the enthusiasm of the Duc d'Orléans for the new regime, believing, like him, that it would give the Orléans branch of the royal family the chance to ascend the throne. During this time she continued to live here in the *Pavillon d'Orléans*, until her emigration in October 1791, at the insistence of the Duchesse d'Orléans, who was horrified by every aspect of the Revolution. It was while she was in England that she learned two years later of the execution of both her husband, Charles-Alexis, and her former lover, the Duc d'Orléans, who had become Philippe-Egalité. During this time Pamela met and married Lord Edward Fitzgerald, an Irish aristocrat and revolutionary. They had two children, but in 1798 Edward died in Newgate Prison in Dublin of wounds sustained while trying to escape arrest.

Madame de Genlis remained in exile until 1800, when Napoléon permitted her to return to France, gave her lodgings with the librarian of the Arsenal, and a pension of 6,000 *livres* paid out of his own account, in exchange for which she had to write him a weekly report containing all her vast knowledge about life at Court during the *ancien régime*. Napoléon for once suppressed his animosity towards worldly, accomplished women in the interests of obtaining this coveted information. As well as her 'tell-all' documents for Napoléon, Félicité continued to write prolifically - *'everything that came into my head'* she said - producing a total of 80 works, including some popular historical biographies, and her brilliant and informative *Mémoires sur le XVIII siècle et sur la Révolution*. Her writings turned out to be an enormous asset to Félicité when the Bourbons returned to the throne and she lost the privileges she had under Napoléon, for she then found herself having to live off her royalties. But Felicité's wish to see an Orléans on the throne was granted just months before her death in 1830, when her former pupil, Louis-Philippe, became king. This original and complex woman died at the age of 84, having lived a rich and interesting life, despite much criticism from her contemporaries as someone too fond of intrigue, too prone to dishonesty and hypocrisy, and too sure of herself.

The last three houses on the right, numbers 1, 3 and 5 at the end of rue Saint-Dominique are all 17th-century. When repairs were carried out at number 3, a hideout used at the time of the Terror was revealed between the ceiling of the second storey and the floor of the third. Before the Revolution this house was the property of the Comte de Guerchy, who later became ambassador to England. He also owned number 1, the *Hôtel de Tingry*, which dates from 1695 and was named after a prince who bought it in 1734, the Prince de Tingry, also the first owner of the magnificent Hôtel de Matignon which you will see in rue de Varenne. The *Hôtel de Tingry* was later the home of Charles-Daniel de Talleyrand-Périgord and his wife, Alexandrine de Damas d'Antigny, parents of the more famous Charles-Maurice de Talleyrand. Throughout his entire life Talleyrand hated these parents who, despite descending from the most noble families in France, had very little fortune. For Talleyrand they were a constant reminder of his childhood, always a source of bitterness, when according to him he was dropped by his nurse, resulting in a deformed foot and a permanent limp. The cause of Talleyrand's club foot was actually a genetic disorder known as Marfan's Syndrome, but he probably genuinely believed it was the result of an accident. Whatever the cause, as a consequence he lost any hope of a military career, was despatched to a seminary, and later saw his inheritance, which as the eldest son was rightfully his, passed on to his younger brother. *'That accident affected my entire life,'* he lamented. *'It was that which persuaded my parents that I could not be a soldier...that made them push me into another profession. This seemed to them to be more favourable to the advancement of the family. For, in the great houses, it is the family that one loves, much more than the individuals, especially young individuals whom one does not really know yet. I don't like this idea one bit...I shall stop thinking about it.'* (Manceron, 1972-87).

Boulevard Saint-Germain.

➡ At the end of rue Saint-Dominique bear right into Boulevard Saint-Germain and stop opposite number 246, which has flags on either side of the entrance. ➡ It is not advisable to try and cross the road at this point, so just look at the house from where you are now. Before Haussmann's grand boulevards, rue Saint-Dominique extended up to here, and this house, built in 1722, was number 62 of that street. It was probably the end house of a *cul-de-sac*, and was known as *Hôtel de Roquelaure* after the duke who first bought it. At his death his daughters sold it for 460,000 *livres* to a magistrate named Mathieu-François Molé de Champlâtreux, the son-in-law of multi-millionaire financier Samuel Bernard whom you met on rue de l'Université. Molé was born in 1705, enjoyed all the delights and privileges of the *ancien régime*, and died in 1793, just before the harsh hand of revolutionary justice could catch up with him. It was only just in time, though, and Molé's son, Edouard François Mathieu Molé, also a magistrate and counsellor in the Paris Parliament, was not so lucky. After emigrating to Brussels, he came back to Paris to comply with the law relating to *émigrés*, believing, no doubt, that revolutionary law would reward honesty. He was arrested and released twice, then arrested for a third time in January 1794, and went to the guillotine on April 20th along with numerous magistrates and other members of the Paris Parliament.

After his execution the house was confiscated by the government, who used it as a refuge for people afflicted with ringworm and scabies, before returning it after the Revolution to Molé's son, Louis Mathieu Molé, who had been just 13 years old when his father was guillotined. He sold the house in 1808 to former deputy, Jean-Jacques Cambacérès, who at that time was at the height of his glory as Napoléon's favourite. In addition to being president of the Senate, the emperor had named him arch-chancellor and made him Prince and Duke of Parma. You would have seen a lot of carriages in the street here, for Cambacérès gave the most luxurious parties and gourmet dinners at this house, and his extravagance and eccentricity were often the object of gossip and malicious comments. '*The poor man rather resembled an ancient sexual perversion,*' wrote Madame Cavaignac, referring to Cambacérès' homosexuality, '*a perversion ravaged by boredom.*' At the Restoration of the monarchy Louis XVIII bought the house and gave it to Philippe-Egalité's widow, the Duchesse d'Orléans, but at her death it returned to the Crown. It is now a government ministry, along with number 248, which used to be the home of Cardinal Cambacérès, brother of the arch-chancellor.

RUE DE GRENELLE.
➡Turn right off Boulevard Saint-Germain into rue Saint-Simon, and at the end take a left into rue de Grenelle. Until the 18th century this was a lane known by various names,

including *chemin aux vaches* (cow path) and *chemin de la Justice*, for it led to the gallows of the Saint-Germain Abbey. At number 73 is the *Hôtel de Gallifet*, built for a magistrate named Talon in 1739 on the site of a former parish cemetery. You can't see much of this house, for it's concealed by a very large gate, but an awful lot of partying went on behind that gate. When Talon died his widow, Madeleine Chauvelin, sold the garden to Louis, Marquis de Gallifet, who built another house in it. Louis was a dashing young man, 27 years old and with all the attributes of an 18th-century beau - impeccably well-mannered, an exquisite dancer, and imbued with an insatiable passion for entertainment. Having been declared unfit for military service, he was awarded a pension that relieved him of the necessity to earn a living, leaving him free to lead a life of *galanterie.* Not long after building his house in the garden, he struck up a liaison with Emilie, estranged wife of the Comte de Mirabeau, who was languishing at the time in the dungeon of Vincennes following yet another *lettre de cachet* against him. But revolutionary France was no place for Louis de Gallifet, who speedily emigrated after his country property in Salerne was invaded by farm workers and the intendant of his manor held for ransom. After Louis's departure the government seized the *Hôtel de Gallifet* and installed the Ministry of External Relations, predecessor of the present-day Ministry of Foreign Affairs. In 1797 the Minister was the former bishop Talleyrand, the local doyen of party-givers, and when you go past the other side of this house on rue de Varenne you will hear more about the memorable *soirées* and receptions he held here. You will also be able to see the splendour of the *hôtel*'s magnificent colonnaded façade. In 1821 the Marquis de Gallifet's heirs came back to claim their family home, and the ministry had to vacate the *hôtel*, which by the end of the 19th century was rented to the Italian ambassador. Eventually the embassy bought the property and enlarged it in 1938 with the purchase of the *Hôtel de Boisgelin* which stands behind it on rue de Varenne.

Rue du Bac.

➡Turn right on to rue du Bac, named after the ferry (*bac*) that crossed the Seine where you now see the Pont Royal. The ferry service first began in 1550 and was used to transport the stones for the construction of the Tuileries Palace. This narrow and lively part of rue du Bac used to be entirely taken up by a religious community, and you can see to your left at number 85 some of the remaining convent buildings. To get a better look at them, go through the passageway into the lovely stone courtyard of number 83, where to your right you will see some of the walls and beams of the former convent, which was called *Couvent des Récollettes*, and stretched all along this block. Like many other Paris convents, it was closed in 1790 and three years after the Revolution its church was occupied by a succession of unlikely enterprises. During the Directory it opened as the *Théâtre des Victoires Nationales*, then every Thursday and Sunday for 22 years it became a ballroom called the *Salon de Mars,* and between 1830 and 1860 it was a concert hall, *Pré-aux-Clercs*, whose audiences were so politically radical that the church became one of the breeding-grounds of the 1870 Commune.

The beautiful bas-reliefs depicting two angels that surround the window over the door on the corner of rue de Varenne are now listed pieces of Parisian architecture. ➡To get a better view of them, cross over rue de Varenne and look at them from the opposite side of rue du Bac. These delightful seraphs are part of number 98 rue du Bac (now the gift shop Pylones), an attractive *hôtel* that seems an unlikely location for a tavern, but that is what it was in 1804, when Georges Cadoudal, leader of the royalist conspirators known as *Chouans*, lived here in hiding in a room on the first floor. It was Cadoudal's accomplices who four years earlier had organized an explosion outside the Tuileries with the intention of killing Napoléon Bonaparte, and at this corner tavern, called *Cabaret de la Cloche d'Or* (Golden Bell Tavern) and also known as

Cabaret des Deux-Anges (Two Angels Tavern), Cadoudal and his fellow conspirators met in secret to plan another attempt on Napoléon's life. The owner of the tavern was Denoud, a dedicated royalist and in total sympathy with Cadoudal and his friends, who arrived here for their meetings in diverse disguises, some coming as peasants, others as horse-dealers or other kinds of tradesmen. But time was running out for this intrepid band of rebels, and after a dramatic chase through Paris, Cadoudal and eleven of his colleagues were arrested, tried and guillotined on June 25th 1804.

➡ Before turning into rue de Varenne, walk down to number 102 rue du Bac, an 18th-century *hôtel* generally thought to be the one occupied before the Revolution by the Swedish ambassador, Baron Erik de Staël-Holstein, and where Germaine Necker lived after she married him in 1786. Erik became ambassador, in fact, thanks to his father-in-law, the Swiss banker Jacques Necker, who only consented to the marriage on the condition that Erik be given the post - a very necessary condition, for although he came from fine old Swedish nobility, Baron de Staël-Holstein had no money. Germaine, who was just 20 when she married, remained very attached to her father, loving him to a degree that bordered on religious worship, and supporting him fervently during his political crises as Louis XVI's Finance Minister. In contrast to her passion for her father, she found her husband cold and distant, and at times perhaps regretted not having married William Pitt the Younger, a match that had been proposed at one point. Despite living with an ambassador, Germaine's lack of diplomacy in posing questions and airing her views frequently resulted in political or social blunders that raised the eyebrows of many a Swedish diplomat.

Over the years Germaine acquired a little more discretion, and by the outbreak of the Revolution her *Salon* on rue du Bac was one of the most celebrated in Paris. It probably took place behind the elegant first-floor windows above the entresol, where every political development was discussed with as much rigour and detail as in the National Assembly. Most of those who attended were sympathetic to the introduction in France of a constitutional monarchy along the lines of that in England, and discussions were dominated by Germaine's brilliant intellect. She was a formidable woman. Despite her luxuriant black hair and ebony eyes, she was not considered a beauty in her time, but every time she took the floor at meetings of her *salon*, the entire gathering was dazzled by the magic of her speech. Jacques Necker was exiled in 1790, but Germaine did not join her father immediately. Her decision to leave came two years later, when the September massacres put her in fear for her own life and that of her friends. On the morning of September 3rd, while the killing was still going on, she packed her belongings and left immediately, declaring, *'For me there is no more France.'*

RUE DE VARENNE.

➡ Now go back to the intersection and turn left into rue de Varenne, which has a magnificent collection of elegant mansions. Number 50 is the other side of the *Hôtel Gallifet* (see rue de Grenelle above), headquarters of the Italian Cultural Institute. It's closed on the weekend, but open Monday to Friday, 10h-13h and 15h-18h, and if you are an Italianophile and speak French you might like to go to some of the activities organized here (Tel: 01 44 39 49 39, website: www.iicparigi.esteri.it). It is from here on rue de Varenne that you can see, by going through the covered arch into the courtyard beyond, the colonnaded main façade of this lovely neo-classical building. It was amongst the elegant columns and luxurious décor of these salons that Foreign Minister Talleyrand organized his magnificent receptions, attended by all the top dignitaries of the day. One of the most glittering of these events took place on January 3rd 1798, *'in honour of Madame Bonaparte'*. The guest of honour, however, was out of town, in the arms of her lover, Hippolyte Charles, so

Talleyrand had to keep putting off his party, much to the exasperation of the gardener, Muller, who was three times obliged to bring out 930 decorative shrubs, only to have to put them all away again each time. Joséphine finally returned to Paris, and Talleyrand sent out a fourth round of decidedly politically-correct invitation cards that reminded his guests to support the commercial war being waged between France and Britain, and to refrain from wearing any garments manufactured by the English. The salons had all been perfumed with amber, and the star of the evening was resplendent in a yellow gown embroidered in black. To complete her outfit, Joséphine wore a gold skullcap that provoked a certain amount of stifled laughter amongst some of the other women, who formed a triumphal arch for her to pass under - as if she were a queen. Despite having arrived at the party in a bad mood, Joséphine ignored this veiled mockery and carried out her role graciously, while simultaneously trying to forget all her other woes - the chilly welcome she'd had from her husband on her return to Paris, her embarrassingly unsuccessful attempts to explain her lateness, and her misery at not being with her beloved Hippolyte.

For one of the invitees, Jacques Necker's daughter, Germaine de Staël, this fête was the occasion of her first meeting with Napoléon Bonaparte. The encounter turned out to be decidedly icy, which is not surprising, for Germaine's dazzling intellect and love of politics were just what the chauvinistic Corsican hated in a woman. Germaine offered the victorious General a laurel branch, which he refused, thus setting the tone for the conversation that followed. *'General, what kind of woman do you like most? —Mine. —I see. But what kind do you respect most? —The kind who is best at looking after her house. —I see yet again. But, in the end, who would be the best woman for you? —The one who bears the most children, madame.'* Napoléon then turned his back on her, and from that moment she numbered among his enemies.

The house opposite at number 47, *Hôtel de Boisgelin*, has been an annexe of the *Hôtel de Gallifet* since 1938, when it was bought by the Italian embassy. It was built in 1732, but the first floor was added half a century later by the archbishop of Aix-en-Provence, Boisgelin de Cucé, a more fortunate member of the Boisgelin family, three of whom were guillotined during the Terror. After becoming president of the Constituent Assembly, he was completely opposed to the Civil Constitution of the Clergy and joined the rapidly swelling ranks of *émigrés* who crossed the Channel to England. At number 56 you find the former home of Henriette, Marquise de Gouffier de Thoix, who gave her name to this house, which dates from 1719 and has a beautifully carved wooden door. Despite her French name, Henriette had English roots, for her older sister was the Duchess of Portsmouth, one of Charles II's favourites. This lovely *hôtel*, with its decorated bas-reliefs and the magnificent sculpted shell over the entrance, was one of the many houses won in a lottery during the Revolution, this time by a jeweller named Gillot, who was later obliged to return it to the former owners.

➡ Now walk along to the Hôtel de Matignon at number 57, which was covered up for restoration work when I was last there, so I could not see it. I hope it's uncovered by the time you go to see it, for it is without doubt the grandest and most beautiful of all the mansions of the Faubourg Saint-Germain, and contains the biggest private garden in Paris. It was built in 1721 for Christian-Louis de Montmorency, whose titles were almost as numerous as his military victories - he was Duc de Luxembourg, Prince de Tingry, and later became Maréchal de France under Louis XV. Construction of the *hôtel* was not even finished when he went to live in another house on rue Saint-Dominique, having sold this one to his niece's husband, another heavily titled individual called Goyon de Matignon, also Comte de Thorigny and Governor of Normandy. During the mid-18th century this mansion became the property of Honoré-Camille,

Prince de Monaco, who had spent much of his life in France - quite a bit of it breeding horses on his Normandy estate of Thorigny. He died here in the Hôtel de Matignon in 1795, having come back to it after being released from prison in 1794. Honoré had been arrested the previous year when France annexed Monaco, but he was saved from the guillotine by 9 *Thermidor*. After his death the Hôtel de Matignon was confiscated, but returned in 1804 to his children, who ceded it to that ubiquitous Saint-Germain resident, Talleyrand. You would have been ill-advised to be his neighbour during the three years that followed, for on the orders of Napoléon, Talleyrand gave four extravagant and very noisy receptions every week at the Hôtel de Matignon, before selling it to the State. Later Louis XVIII continued the game of musical mansions by swapping Matignon with the Elysée Palace, which had just been reclaimed by the Duchesse de Bourbon on her return from emigration. After numerous changes of ownership, the Hôtel de Matignon was confiscated once again during World War I and occupied by the courts of arbitration set up under the Treaty of Versailles. Nowadays it is the official residence of the French Prime Minister.

Number 72 is the *Hôtel de Castries*, birthplace of Armand Charles de la Croix, duc de Castries, who later fought against the English in America, particularly distinguishing himself at the battle of Yorktown. His childhood had been privileged and harmonious, and not without originality. His father, the Maréchale de Castries, had always shown a strong interest in the education and development of Jean-Nicolas Pache, the young son of his Swiss concierge, and when the boy was old enough he put him in charge of the education of his own children. Jean-Nicolas, who was also born in this house, evidently carried out the job successfully, for the young Armand Charles went on to study mathematics and physics under Gaspard Monge, and it was maybe this *avant-garde* aspect of his upbringing that led him to sympathize with the Revolution at first. But as soon as he realized that the aristocracy would be wiped out along with the monarchy, Armand Charles changed his mind and joined the royalists, breaking with his long-time friend Lafayette.

As a result of this change of loyalties, the Duc de Castries found himself challenged to a duel on November 11th 1790 by his political rival Charles Lameth, who was badly wounded in the fight, and rumours instantly spread that the duke had dipped his sword in poison. Fearing for the life of Lameth, who was a patriotic defender of the National Assembly, an enormous crowd gathered in rue de Varenne the next day and descended on the *Hôtel de Castries*, shouting *'Everyone to the duke's house! Vengeance for Lameth!'* The duke had taken the wise precaution of getting out of his house and taking refuge with a friend, having been warned by the hastily printed brochures that were circulating giving a vivid description of the duel and a violent denunciation of the victor. After climbing

The Hôtel de Castries at 72 rue de Varennes, home of the Duc de Castries. In November 1790 rumours of foul play during a duel led to a pillage of the duke's house, where everything was destroyed or thrown out of the windows, while La Fayette stood by with his soldiers and did nothing to stop it. (Courtesy of Musée Carnavalet, Cabinet des Arts Graphiques, Paris)

over the iron gates and breaking the windows with iron bars, the crowd poured into the house and destroyed everything in sight, ripping bedding and tapestries to shreds, breaking mirrors and throwing furniture out of the windows. A short distance away, within sight of the house, Lafayette stood with his troops, his sabre at the ready, but presumably to defend himself, it seems, for he gave no order to intervene and save the *Hôtel de Castries*. By the time the crowd left 30 minutes later, the house was on fire and the interior in ruins. The Duc de Castries emigrated as soon as possible after this, and joined his father in Switzerland.

In the meantime the duke's former teacher, Jean-Nicolas Pache, had been launched into a political career by his benefactor, the Maréchal de Castries, who got him first into the Ministry of the Navy, and then, with the help of Necker, he progressed to the position of Controller of the King's House. But Pache, who was an independent soul, ultimately chafed at all this aristocratic sponsorship, resigned from his post and left for his native soil in Switzerland. By this time Pache was 32 and happily married, a fact that astonished Madame Roland when she met him just before his departure. *'I saw, at M. Gibert's, a most interesting sight: a happy couple. It is the first one I have seen. I saw a married philosopher, an enlightened spouse, a tender and wise father…with a virtuous companion…of simple tastes, sound judgement, a peaceful exterior and the greatest veneration for her dear husband.'* From the standpoint of her less than passionate marriage, Madame Roland simply couldn't get over it. She had nothing but praise for this *'strong and noble soul'* who seemed to her to be the epitome of all that was virtuous, and it was perhaps through her influence that Pache later got a job in Roland's ministry.

Madame Roland was eventually to be disappointed with Pache, however, when he broke with her husband's party in favour of the more radical Montagnards, and joined the campaign to bring down Roland and his colleagues. *'The baseness, the atrocity of this behaviour filled me with indignation and contempt,'* she wrote in her memoirs, and then went on to decry Pache's fraudulent misuse of government money as Minister of War. From his virtuous and quasi-privileged beginnings, Pache seemed to end up an object of derision, and Sebastien Mercier described him as the leader of *'a monstrous group formed from amongst the principal actors of the September massacres.'* And that was not all. *'He was Swiss,'* said the chauvinistic Mercier, *'more fatal to France than an enemy army.'* Despite all this bad press, Pache went on to become Mayor of Paris in 1794, but good fortune was often short-lived in those days. He was arrested soon afterwards and imprisoned as an ally of the Hébertists, but was one of the lucky ones who survived. Pache retired from politics at the start of the 19th century and died in the Ardennes in 1823.

The Castries family also owned number 76 rue de Varenne, built in 1760 and known as the *Petit Hôtel de Castries*. The entire block between numbers 72 and 80 is nowadays occupied by the Ministry of Agriculture and Fisheries, where modern bureaucrats share their offices with the ghosts of this privileged quarter, most of whom are noble, but not all. The *Hôtel-de-Villeroi* at number 78, for example, is probably haunted by a few Thespian spectres, since it was not built for an aristocrat, but for an actress named Charlotte Desmares, who made her début at the Comédie-Française in 1690 at the tender age of 8. She had a preference for playing the role of queens, and followed closely in the footsteps of her English counterpart, Nell Gwyn, in her tendency to choose high-born lovers, who included the dauphin and the future Regent, father of her daughter. Later on she became the mistress of Antoine Hogguer, Baron de Presle, who built this house for her in 1724 in the garden of his own *Hôtel de Rothelin* at 101 rue de Grenelle, but since it was a very long garden, the house ended up being on rue de Varenne. The amorous pair used to meet regularly in one house or another, using the garden for access, until Antoine went bankrupt a year later and they had to abandon their multi-residence urban life-style for the relative modesty of the suburbs. Charlotte died, still in the suburbs, at the age of 71.

After the departure of the two lovers, number 78 was occupied first by the ambassador of Holland, then by Horace Walpole, the English ambassador, before being sold by Hogguer's liquidators to François-Louis, duc de Villeroi, who gave it his name. He was succeeded at his death in 1766 by his nephew, Gabriel-Louis, who became the new Duc de Villeroi and invited an impressive succession of princes and princesses to his table - it was even graced on one occasion by the King of Denmark, Christian VII. But despite his glittering social life, the new Duc de Villeroi's domestic life was far from blissful, so two years after inheriting the *Hôtel-de-Villeroi* he sold it and moved to rue de Lille, while his wife moved to rue de l'Université. Later on Gabriel-Louis would become a victim of the Revolution, being judged *'guilty of plotting against the safety and sovereignty of the people'*. For this he was guillotined on April 28th 1794 at the age of 63, having already been judged by his fellow prisoners, one of whom described him as *'the most worthless of men'*.

But however worthless he might have been, the duke certainly knew how to lay on entertainment, and while he lived here in rue de Varenne he excelled himself. To delight his guests he had a small theatre built in the house, with 110 seats and featuring a well-known actress of the *ancien régime*, Claire de la Tude, more generally known as La Clairon. She was in her mid-40s when she took the stage at the *Hôtel-de-Villeroi*, and not long after, in 1770, she was the star performer at the Opera House in Versailles during the festivities to honour Marie-

Antoinette's arrival in France. La Clairon was still enjoying a reputation as a grand lady of theatre just before the Revolution, when the young Hérault de Séchelles, future Dantonist, sought her out for elocution lessons with a view to improving his public speaking. She was considered one of the greatest actresses of her time, but was also very vain, once saying of Mme de Pompadour that *'she owes her royalty to chance; I owe mine to my genius.'* La Clairon was getting on for 50 when she melted the heart of Charles-Frédéric d'Anspach-Bayreuth, a German nobleman thirteen years her junior, who whisked her off to his principality. She stayed there for seventeen years, until she was replaced in his affections by Lady Elizabeth Craven, an English writer who married him and whisked him off to England. When La Clairon returned, somewhat heartbroken, to Paris, she found a radically changed city, and a revolution in the making. She went to live in the Marais at the home of her adopted daughter, where she stayed, surrounded by admirers, until her death in 1803.

Across the road at number 69 is the *Hôtel de Clermont*, built in 1708 and sold to the Comte Durfort d'Orsay in 1768 by a desperate duchess trying to pay off her husband's debts. Durfort d'Orsay, who was married to a princess and had no such financial problems, was a great patron of the arts and spent his time collecting paintings and sculptures from all over the world, many of which are now in the Louvre. During the count's ownership, the *Hôtel de Clermont* rather resembled a museum itself, with room after room filled with art treasures, while guests in his dining room sat amongst marble columns that came from Nero's palace in Rome. When Durfort d'Orsay said goodbye to all that and emigrated at the beginning of the Revolution, his house was confiscated and then sold in 1798 to a gentleman named Le Breton. He in turn rented it to the Marquis d'Avèze, an aristocrat who was decidedly ahead of his time. He had a huge annexe built on to the garden façade and turned it into a public gym and sports club - 18th-century style - called

Jeux Gymniques (gymnastic games). Here exercise-conscious Parisians came to do dancing, fencing, wrestling, horse-riding, real tennis, archery, discus throwing, horse-racing, athletics and a variety of other popular sports of the time. Many of these activities were held in the gardens, while cafés and restaurants were installed in the out-buildings, and the house itself became an auction room. It was a highly ambitious enterprise, perhaps too ambitious, for - not unlike many a modern fitness club - it went bankrupt after a very short time and the property was bought out by a restaurant owner. The *Hôtel de Clermont* now houses the offices of the Minister of State responsible for relations with Parliament.

At 73 you have the *Grand Hôtel de Broglie*, although it doesn't look very grand at the moment - it needs a bit of paint. It was sold in 1752 for 130,000 *livres* to Victor François, duc de Broglie, who lived here with his son Claude-Victor, Prince de Broglie. The duke had been made Marshall of France by Louis XV, and was still in active service on July 11th 1789, when at the age of 70 he commanded the troops that encircled Versailles to protect the king. A week later he emigrated, not because he felt too old to cope with a revolution, but in order to raise an army of *émigrés* that joined forces with the Prussians and invaded the region of Champagne. Later on he was in the pay of the English and the Russians, and was at the point of returning to France when he died in Munster at the age of 86. His son, Claude-Victor, was not so fortunate, for he opted for politics, initially choosing to represent the nobility at the Estates-General. Later on he joined the Constituent Assembly, and even became its president for a while, before going back to the family tradition of soldiering. Unable to accept the fall of the monarchy, Claude-Victor resigned from his post and left for the provinces, which immediately branded him as 'suspect', and he was arrested, tried by the Tribunal and guillotined on June 27th 1794. The house was seized, put up for lottery and won by a merchant from Hamburg, who sold it for 90,000 *livres* - less the cost of his lottery ticket.

Another historic *hôtel* stands at number 77, the *Hôtel de Biron*, which dates from 1731 and before the Revolution was the property of the Maréchal (Marshal) and Peer of France, Louis-Antoine, duc de Biron. He was as much a *bon-vivant* as Talleyrand, and his house was famous for the expensive parties he held and the lavish beauty of its gardens that were open to the public. He died in 1788 as old as the century and in happy ignorance of the horror that was to befall those who came after him. His *Hôtel de Biron* was left in equal shares to his widow, the Maréchale Françoise-Pauline, Duchesse de Biron, and his brother, Charles-Antoine de Gontaut, but the Revolution was to take its toll on the Biron family. The first victim was Charles-Antoine's son, Louis-Armand de Lauzan, who had become Duc de Biron on the death of the Maréchal. He represented the nobility at the Estates-General, and took part in the delirious renunciation of privilege during the night of August 4th, after which he was heard to say, on leaving the hall, '*Gentlemen, what have we done?*' He later returned to military service, commanding the Rhine army, but after several disputes with a Jacobin general, was recalled to Paris and asked to explain himself, which he did, but with his peculiar brand of cynical humour. This did not go down very well with the committee, who immediately branded him suspect and threw him in prison. He retained his amused air of *sang-froid* to the end. When the Tribunal asked him his name, he told them, '*Cabbage, Turnip, whatever you like.*' He smiled as his death sentence was read out, declaring as he left the room, '*Well, my friends, that's over, I'm going.*' When he returned to his cell to pass his final night in prison, one of his fellow prisoners, Beaulieu, was astounded at his attitude. '*He maintained his serene, laughing air, full of grace, which he had always had, and for which he was considered the most likeable and courteous of French noblemen...he requested a chicken and a bottle of Bordeaux wine, completely emptied the bottle and ate almost all the chicken...he read for the rest of the day and then lay down to sleep on a wretched mattress, furnished by the concierge, as peacefully as if he were in his own house. One of the gendarmes assured me that he snored all night.'* (Dauban, 1977). When Sanson came to fetch Louis-Armand the next morning, he found him eating oysters. *'Would you permit me to finish my last dozen oysters?'* he asked the executioner, who replied, *'I am at your command.'* The duke found this highly amusing, laughed loudly and answered, *'No, zounds! Unfortunately I am at yours.'*

There were to be three more victims in the Biron family. After Louis-Armand it was the turn of Armand-Louis-François de Béthune-Charost, son of another of the Maréchal's nephews, Armand Joseph de Béthune, duc de Charost. Father and son were both in prison together at *La Force*, and Armand-Joseph had the good fortune to be saved by 9 *Thermidor*, but not before seeing his son taken away to the Tribunal and condemned to death. Armand-Louis-François was guillotined in April 1794 with 34 other victims, most of whom were magistrates or ex-nobles, and the Great Terror of the summer of 1794 would take two more Birons. One of them was the widowed Maréchale herself, aged 71, who shared a tumbril with Louis-Armand's widow, 48-year-old Amélie de Boufflers. They were guillotined on June 27th, leaving the imprisoned Armand-Joseph de Béthune and the late Maréchal's brother, Charles de Gontaut, as the only surviving heirs to the *Hôtel de Biron*. Charles already owned half of it by inheritance, and when Armand-Joseph got out of prison he made a deal with Charles, who ceded the entire property to him in exchange for 4,200,000 *livres*, paid in *assignats*. Armand-Joseph remained here until he died in 1802 from smallpox, which he had contracted during an official visit to a hospital in his capacity of mayor of the locality. This magnificent *hôtel* and its English-style gardens have since become the Rodin Museum (entrance at number 79), so when you go in to enjoy the beauty of Rodin's sculptures, you can have a glimpse at the same time of the splendour in which the Biron family lived.

RUE DE GRENELLE.

➥At the end of rue de Varennes turn right on Boulevard des Invalides, which from 1760 formed the eastern limit of this noble and wealthy suburb. ➥Walk up one block and turn right into rue de Grenelle to have a look at a few more opulent mansions, starting with number 127 on the left, the magnificent neo-classical *Hôtel de Châtelet*, built twenty years before the Revolution for the Duc de Châtelet, son of Voltaire's friend, Madame Châtelet. The duke and his wife, Diane Adelaïde de Rochechouart, duchesse de Châtelet, came from two of the most illustrious noble families of France, and unfortunately were destined to suffer the fate that the Revolution dealt out to the country's most privileged. The Duc de Châtelet was a colonel of the *Gardes Françaises*, commanding them during the Réveillon riot in the Faubourg Saint-Antoine, and in this role he became increasingly unpopular with the population of Paris. He made many attempts to escape from the capital, but despite all efforts by his friends and colleagues to protect him, he was eventually arrested at the beginning of the Terror and guillotined. The house was confiscated and the Duchesse de Châtelet took shelter in Doctor Belhomme's clinic for a while, but she too ended up on the scaffold.

Opposite at number 142 is the *Hôtel de Chanac de Pompadour*, now the Swiss Embassy, built in 1750 for an upper-class abbot and later occupied by the bishop of Rennes. In 1785 it became the property of Baron Pierre-Victor de Besenval, a handsome and charming Swiss aristocrat who was part of Marie-Antoinette's intimate circle of friends and advisers. As colonel in the Swiss Guards he was put in command of troops surrounding Paris in July 1789, and it was Besenval who ordered the Prince de Lambesc to charge on the people in the Tuileries

Gardens. At the same time he realised the way things were going, and decided to protect himself, so during the siege of the Bastille he issued orders that were designed to avoid mass slaughter. As a result, he was arrested and judged by the court at Châtelet for his attitude and his actions, but was acquitted thanks to the protection of Jacques Necker. After that Besenval withdrew from public life, but remained in Paris and lived a surprisingly peaceful existence throughout the entire revolutionary period, including the Terror. At his death he became a rare phenomenon - an aristocrat who died peacefully in his bed of natural causes, in Paris, in the summer of 1794.

Numbers 136-140 used to be all one mansion, the *Hôtel de Sens*, built in 1722 and the home of royalty and nobility until the Revolution. In 1797 the author Louvet de Couvray moved his bookshop here from the arcades of the Palais-Royal, where it had been attacked and looted by gangs of *muscadin* thugs. He didn't have long to appreciate his sumptuous new surroundings though, for he died here of tuberculosis a few months later, exhausted and saddened by life. His wife, Lodoïska, who had been the love of his life, took opium in an unsuccessful attempt to kill herself, with apparent lack of concern for their 3-year-old son Félix, sleeping in another room. She kept Louvet's coffin in the house for eight months, then moved to a château in the Loiret department, where her husband was finally buried in the garden. Lodoïska died 30 years later when her bedroom caught fire, and Félix inherited the château, keeping it until his death in 1845.

➥When you have finished looking at Louvet de Couvray's house, turn around and walk back to Boulevard des Invalides, cross over it (rue de Talleyrand will be on your right) and continue straight ahead into Place des Invalides - where you have cannons pointing at you! If you like walking and have the energy, ➥you can get a marvellous view of the magnificent Hôtel des Invalides by turning right on to Avenue du Maréchal

Gallieni and walking straight ahead towards the Seine. Stop at the Pont Alexandre III, which was built at the turn of the 20th century and is the widest and one of the loveliest of the Parisian bridges. If you are of a romantic spirit, don't miss seeing it at night, when its picturesque lanterns casting magical shadows and silhouettes will fill you with nostalgia for the *Belle-Epoque*. Turn round at the bridge and look back, for from here you have the best view of the Invalides, whose dome, modelled on Saint-Peter's in Rome, has been re-gilded, making this building one of the most splendid architectural sights in Paris.

➡ If you don't want to walk to the bridge, you should at least cross over, veer to the right and have a look at the magnificent mansion on the corner of rue de Talleyrand and rue de Constantine. If you've been up to the bridge you should walk back via rue Constantine and stop at rue de Talleyrand to look at this lovely house (you'll have to crane your neck a bit to see over the very high wall). It is number 1 rue de Talleyrand, known as the *Hôtel de Monaco-Sagan*, now the Polish Embassy, but once the home of a princess. In 1772 Marie-Cathérine de Brignole, Princesse de Monaco, had just separated from her first husband, Prince Honoré III, and decided to have a house built for her in Paris. She chose this spot very near the Palais Bourbon so she could be close to her lover and future husband, the Prince de Condé, who lived there. Marie-Cathérine probably spend most of *her* time there too - she certainly didn't spent much time here in her new house, preferring to rent it out to the British Embassy, but in 1790 things started to look decidedly dangerous for anyone royal. So the princess left for England with her paramour, and the *Hôtel de Monaco-Sagan* was seized by the revolutionary government. When Monaco was annexed to France in 1793, her ex-husband, Honoré III, was imprisoned, as was their daughter-in-law, Françoise-Thérèse de Choiseul Stainville, also known as Princesse de Monaco. Honoré survived the Terror, and died in Paris in 1795, but Françoise-Thérèse was not so lucky. After spending time in several revolutionary prisons, she was finally condemned to death in July 1794, becoming one of the very last victims of the Terror, guillotined in the late afternoon of 9 *Thermidor* when Robespierre was already under arrest. For French film buffs, you might like to know that Edouard Molinaro's wonderful film *Le Souper*, about a dinner between Talleyrand and Fouché, was filmed in this house.

Hôtel Royal des Invalides/Musée de l'Armée.

➥You should now cross back to Place des Invalides and go into the main entrance of the *hôtel*. Before giving you the history of the Invalides, here are some practical points about seeing the Hôtel des Invalides.

It is open every day from 10h to 17h, and from 10h to 18h during the summer. For more information you can telephone 01 44 42 38 77. If you don't wish to visit the Invalides, or even wander through it (and you can just wander through it without buying a ticket), you should follow these alternative instructions for getting to the Ecole Militaire, which is the next stop. ➥Continue in the same direction on Place des Invalides (cannons to your left, the Seine to your right) and walk around the Hôtel des Invalides with the gardens on your left. If you want to read about the Invalides this would be a good place to find a bench and sit down amongst the trees. When you come to the junction with rue Fabert, turn left and keep walking, pass rue de Grenelle on your right, cross Boulevard de la Tour Maubourg and continue straight ahead on Avenue de la Motte-Picquet. Walk along this avenue to Place Joffre, where you will be standing in front of the main façade of the Ecole-Militaire. (You should now go to the end of the description of Hôtel des Invalides and join the walk again.)

If you want to visit the Hôtel des Invalides, you have two options. You can get a ticket and see the whole thing, including Napoléon's tomb, the Army museum and the two churches. If you just want to get a feel of the place and what it might have been like during the Revolution, you can wander around the courtyard, arcades and corridors without buying a ticket.

➡ If you decide to buy a ticket and see the whole thing, you need to go all the way through to the south entrance, for the ticket office is there - unless you want to pay by credit card, and don't mind grappling with machines, in which case you can buy your ticket here by the north entrance, on your right as you enter.

➡ If you just want to wander without a ticket, you enter by the north entrance that faces the Seine, (where you are now), and you will see ahead of you the main courtyard, called the Cour d'Honneur, with an arcade on either side of it. The best view of the Cour d'Honneur is to go up the wonderful staircase leading to the Army Museum and walk around the upper gallery (*Galerie Supérieure*). There are cannons all around the gallery, and from here you get an excellent view of the courtyard and the 60 dormer windows in the roof, all decorated with sculpted coats of arms and heraldic symbols. This gallery gives a real feeling of being in a fort, with the simple wooden doors all along the sides - perhaps the soldiers quarters - and from here you also get a good view of the three sundials over the pediments of the north, west and east facades of the Cour d'Honneur. ➡ When you go back down, look underneath the galleries to see the old, rather primitive looking beams that are holding them up - in stark contrast to the grandiose exterior of the building, with its gilded dome. Cannons are everywhere, including the carts used to drag them along - probably the same kind of thing that was used by the conquerors of the Bastille, and the crowd of women who marched on Versailles. You can ➡ wander past the Soldiers'

Church (*Eglise Saint-Louis-des-Invalides*), which seemed closed up when I was there, and then by the side of the Dome Church (*Eglise du Dôme*) and out by the south entrance.

SOME HISTORY.

In 1604 a hospital for wounded soldiers (*invalides*) was founded by Henri IV, but it was not until the reign of Louis XIV that construction of this *hôtel* was begun on the *Plaine de Grenelle*. At that time it was outside the city limits, on the other side of the *Boulevard du Midi*, nowadays called Boulevard des Invalides. The foundation stone was laid on November 30th 1671, and five years later 6,000 *invalides* were admitted. Supervised by the architects Libéral-Bruant and Jules Hardouin-Mansart, the construction of this huge complex, built around a series of courtyards, took 35 years, and by the time it was completed in 1706 it housed one of the most exalted institutions of the *ancien régime*.

The Hôtel des Invalides contains two churches. The first, which you enter through the main courtyard, is the Eglise Saint-Louis-des-Invalides, designed by Libéral-Bruant for use by the soldiers. In 1794 the crypt was invaded by vandals, who showed surprising respect in sparing the tombs of the 420 former governors of the Invalides buried there. The crypt contains the tomb of Rouget de l'Isle, composer of the *Marseillaise*, and you can also see the casket containing the heart of the legendary Mlle de Sombreuil, who saved the life of her father, the last pre-revolutionary governor of the Invalides, by supposedly drinking a glass of blood. The second church, designed by Jules Hardouin-Mansart, is the Eglise du Dôme, or 'Royal Chapel' intended for use by the king. This was begun in 1677 to the glory of the Sun-King, and is one of the most beautiful landmarks in Paris, with its golden dome that, at 105 metres high, can be seen from numerous points in the city. It was gilded for the first time in 1815, and the four arcades above the dome used to contain gilded lead statues of the Four Virtues, but these were brought down and melted during the Revolution, probably for the manufacture of cannons. At the same time the dome was decorated with an enormous red revolutionary bonnet that turned out to be a dangerous symbol of patriotism, for it was so heavy it fell off, bringing with it the ball and cross from the top of the building.

At the end of the crypt of the Eglise du Dôme you can see the tomb of Napoléon Bonaparte, which has been described as the most ostentatious tomb in the world outside of the Egyptian pyramids. The body of the defeated emperor was brought back in December 1840 from the island of Saint Helena, where he had died in exile. In a solemn ceremony ordered by Louis-Philippe, the former emperor's remains were carried through Paris in a snowstorm and left on display underneath the dome for two months, before being laid to rest in the Chapelle Saint-Jérôme of the Eglise du Dôme. Twenty years later the imperial tomb was completed and Napoléon's body re-buried on April 2nd 1861. His remains lie in six coffins, each one inside the other, and the great man was apparently finally laid to rest in boots that were coming unstitched. Another remarkable but rather unappetizing detail about the imperial corpse was discovered in 1840, when his body was exhumed and it was observed that Napoléon's toe-nails had grown since his death, making holes in his socks. Scientific research was a little less advanced in 1840, and although those exhuming the body might have seen toe-nails that measured more than they had at death, we know that this is an illusion, caused by the retraction of skin and tissue after death, making the toenails appear longer. I have no explanation for the holes in the imperial socks, except perhaps that the great Bonaparte was only concerned with outward appearances, even in his coffin.

The day before the storming of the Bastille a delegation

from the Hôtel-de-Ville arrived at the Invalides demanding weapons for the newly-formed militia. The governor, Charles François Virot, Marquis de Sombreuil, politely refused to act without authorization from Versailles. The following day a crowd of about 30,000 gathered here at the gates of de Sombreuil's *hôtel*, where there were 5,000 *invalides* quite capable of fighting off any invasion. But de Sombreuil knew only too well that they would refuse to fire on their fellow citizens, and there was nothing he could do to prevent the insurgents from invading the Invalides armouries. Nearby on the Champ-de-Mars Colonel de Besenval (whom you just met on rue de Grenelle) issued no orders to his troops to stop the invasion, having been warned by his officers that the soldiers would refuse to march against the people. The crowd left the Hôtel des Invalides with 32,000 guns and a dozen cannons, but no gunpowder, which is what they had expected to find here. Governor de Sombreuil escaped unharmed, and the insurgents set off with their loot to attack the Bastille, where governor de Launay did not have as much luck as de Sombreuil.

During the Revolution the Hôtel Royal des Invalides did not change as much as many other Parisian institutions. In

On the morning of July 14th 1789 a huge crowd of insurgents descended on the Hôtel des Invalides and raided the armouries. They took 32,000 guns and a dozen cannons, and then set off with their loot to attack the Bastille. (Author's private collection)

1792 it became the *Hôtel National des Invalides*, and in August of that year it was invaded again, this time for pikes and sabres that were used during the overthrow of the monarchy, and at the same time many of the symbols of royalty were destroyed, including a bas-relief over the main entrance showing Louis XIV in Roman costume. In 1793 the Eglise du Dôme was re-named *Temple de Mars*, and the *Invalides* became known as *Pensionnaires de la République* and had to swear an oath to the Constitution. In December of that year a national festival was held on the Champ-de-Mars to celebrate the liberation of Toulon from the English, and on the way the procession stopped here to collect the *Invalides*, who joined the triumphal march to the Champ-de-Mars. Napoléon had a great affection for these veterans of the nation, and was often to be seen in the Cour d'Honneur presiding over the official review of the *Invalides*. He seemed to feel at home at the Hôtel des Invalides, in fact, which is why he chose to celebrate the anniversary of the storming of the Bastille here on July 14th 1800, his first Bastille Day as head of state.

Before leaving the Invalides you should take a look at the Army Museum, where you will find the richest collection of military memorabilia and art in the world. You can follow here the development of arms, from the cross-bow of the dark ages to the more sophisticated weapons of modern warfare. There is an interesting presentation of the Occupation in France during World War II, complete with a model of the allied landing on the Normandy beaches. On the second floor of the east building you will find the section devoted to relics of the revolutionary period, including the uniforms of the Swiss Guards, the National Guard, and other soldiers of that era. You can also see the arms and uniforms of the *ancien régime*, the swords belonging to Lafayette, Louis XVI and Louis XVIII, and a tiny one belonging to Charles-Louis, the dauphin who died in the Temple prison. There are a good number of objects relating to the

Napoleonic period, such as the cannon-ball that killed Turenne, one of his military chiefs, trophies seized from the Mamelukes during the campaign in Egypt, and a reconstruction of the emperor's bedroom on the island of Saint Helena where he lived in exile.

➥ Leave the Invalides museum by the south exit leading on to Avenue de Tourville, opened in 1780, except for the first part (directly alongside the Hôtel des Invalides) which dates from 1680 when the *hôtel* was being built. It was called *Avenue des Invalides* until 1805, when it was re-named in honour of the Comte de Tourville, a 17th-century Vice-Admiral and Marshall of France. ➥ Turn right on to Avenue de Tourville as you leave the museum, go to the end and bear left at Place de l'Ecole Militaire into Avenue de La Motte-Picquet and walk down to Place Joffre, where you will be standing in front of the main façade of the Ecole-Militaire.

Ecole Militaire.

The origins of this prestigious military academy go back to 1750, when a financier by the name of Pâris-Duverney came to Louis XV with a proposal for the construction of a college for 500 poor gentlemen, preferably the sons of officers who had been killed or severely wounded in the service of their country. The ultimate success of this proposal was largely thanks to the king's mistress, Madame de Pompadour, who is credited with uttering those rather prophetic words, '*Après nous, le déluge.*' She had enormous influence over Louis XV, and was so strongly in favour of the academy project that Louis agreed to build it, writing in response to her entreaties, '*Approved, the project, approved, little beloved, because you want it so much.*' In the new school, which would become as prestigious as the neighbouring Hôtel des Invalides, the disadvantaged young men were to be educated in the military arts and trained to become officers. The building is a beautiful example of French classical architecture, designed by Jacques-Ange Gabriel and built on lands that had formerly belonged to the abbeys of Saint-Germain and Sainte-Geneviève. Progress was slow, partly due to lack of funds, and Madame de Pompadour spent considerable sums of her own money on the construction of this academy. In 1755 she wrote to Pâris-Duverney promising to pass him her entire revenue for that year to pay the fifteen journeymen who were working on the building, while Louis XV pleased his 'little beloved' even further by contributing more funding from the proceeds of a lottery and a tax on playing cards. Classes began from 1760 on, but of the school's three benefactors, Louis was the only one who lived to see the final completion of all the buildings in 1770. Madame de Pompadour died in 1764 of lung congestion, and Pâris-Duverney died at the age of 84 just a few days before the last stone of the chapel was put in place.

When they stipulated that the school was for 'gentlemen' they really meant it, for all applicants, who were between 8 and 11 years old, were asked to present proof of four generations of nobility on their paternal side, and had to be able to read and write. Once accepted they studied all the sciences necessary to the art of warfare, and left at the age of 20 with a troop to command and an allowance of 200 *livres*. In 1776 the minister of war was the Comte de Saint-Germain, who thought the Ecole-Militaire was run too extravagantly, and closed it down. For eighteen months it was used as barracks for several battalions of bodyguards, and then the minister thought better of his decision and re-opened the school, but with a few reforms. The name was changed to *Ecole des Cadets-Gentilshommes*, and top students from provincial military academies were now able to come here for special training programmes. It was thanks to one of these programmes that a rather withdrawn 15-year-old Corsican from the military college at Brienne made his debut in the capital, along with four of his fellow students and their teacher, Father Berton. His arrival at the Ecole-Militaire was duly noted in the register of admissions: *'22 October 1784, de Buonaparte (Napoleone), born the 15th of August 1769 (Student of the King)'*. After spending one year here, Napoléon Bonaparte left for Valence with the rank of sub-lieutenant in the artillery, and an optimistic report card predicting that he could *'go a long way given the right circumstances'*.

In 1787 the Ecole-Militaire was closed down again and handed over to the municipal authorities. Their plan was to take patients out of the Hôtel-Dieu hospital, where the putrid air of central Paris often made them even sicker than they were to begin with, and bring them to live here, where the purity of the air would hopefully aid their recovery. This laudable project never got off the ground, however, and instead the abandoned academy was occupied by a tailor in charge of making and repairing National Guard uniforms. Two years later the revolutionary government took over the school, transforming it first into a wheat and flour warehouse, then into headquarters for the cavalry, and the building did not escape the violence of the later years of the Revolution. On the night when the monarchy was overthrown, the crowd went first to the Hôtel des Invalides looking for weapons, and then they descended on the Ecole-Militaire, where they found nothing but 26 ceremonial swords. A week later the chapel was vandalized, the statues on the main staircase were hurled to the bottom of the steps, and later on all symbols of royalty were attacked. A marble statue of Louis XV was destroyed, the *fleur-de-lys* decorations on the facade were scratched out, and the entire contents of the library taken away. After the Revolution the building became headquarters for the Consular Guard, the Imperial Guard, and on the restoration of the monarchy, the Royal Guard, and it is now occupied by all the high-level military academies of France.

The Ecole-Militaire is closed to the public, so you are unable to see its two chapels, one of which is called the Pupils' Chapel and nowadays serves as the Officers' Mess. The principal chapel is a beautiful example of Louis XVI architecture, luxuriously decorated with Corinthian columns and a series of paintings about the life of King Louis IX, more usually known as Saint-Louis. It was here, in May 1785, that the young Napoléon Bonaparte received his confirmation from Monseigneur de Juigny, Archbishop of Paris. Napoléon came back to his old school much later, when he was Emperor, to celebrate his birthday in a lavish party held in the chapel, which at the time was being used as a dance hall.

The Champ-de-Mars.

➡ Go across the road and and stand in the Place Joffre, where you can see the Champ-de-Mars stretching out before you. This massive expanse began as a vineyard in the 16th century, and was later occupied by market gardeners who grew vegetables for the citizens of Paris. When construction began on the Ecole-Militaire, the Champ-de-Mars was first used to stockpile building materials, and then turned into a terrain for manoeuvres for the students, and for reviewing the king's troops. To prepare this training ground enormous quantities of earth had to be brought in, dug over and levelled, resulting in a space large enough to hold 10,000 soldiers lined up on parade. It was surrounded by wide, deep ditches that made it impossible to get into the field except by one of five small stone drawbridges that were all equipped with iron grilles and guarded day and night. Eight rows of elm trees were planted along the two long sides, and next to these an immense hedge formed the final barrier separating the field from the land outside.

Before the Champ-de-Mars became a theatre of Revolution, it was used on several occasions for non-military events, including a couple of 'firsts'. In 1780 two Parisian gentlemen settled a bet here by competing against each other on horseback, thus turning the field into the capital's first race-course and causing excited gossip throughout the city and at Versailles. The Champ-de-Mars was also the scene of the first experimental flights in the hot-air balloon invented by the Montgolfier brothers. Their attempts were followed by others, including a physician named Jacques Charles, and then by the Robert brothers, who on August 27th 1783 launched a balloon with no basket or passengers, the first of its kind to be designed on scientific principles. The design was not very well calculated, however, for the balloon fell to earth 45 minutes later just north-east of Saint-Denis, into the little hamlet of Gonesse, where the dramatic descent of this mysterious UFO sent the inhabitants into a petrified panic. On March 2nd of the following year another intrepid aeronaut, Jean-Pierre Blanchard, declared that he had resolved the problems of steering these capricious vessels in the right direction, and to prove his point set out from the Champ-de-Mars in another state-of-the-art aircraft. His intention was to land at La Villette, in the north-east corner of Paris, but he too clearly had some homework to do, for he ended up in Billancourt in the south-west corner. Whether he subsequently did his homework is also debatable, for in 1819 his wife Sophie was somewhere above Paris setting off fireworks from one of her husband's balloons, when a massive explosion sent her flying to an untimely death. This rhyme about Blanchard that was circulating at the time suggests that some people were already cynical about space travel, even in the 18th century!

He flies away from the Field of Mars
And lands his craft in the neighbouring grass
A mountain of money is now in his grasp
It is thus, messieurs, that we head for the stars.
(Hillairet, 1963)

Mme Sophie Blanchard clearly had too much confidence in the expertise of her husband, Jean-Pierre, who built the hot air balloon in which she fell to her death in 1819. Jean-Pierre had been flying balloons since the 1780s, when he was one of several aeronauts to take off from the Champ-de-Mars. (Author's private collection)

Fête de la Fédération.

The Revolution brought the Champ-de-Mars into the forefront as a stage for a succession of events, both joyous and tragic. There was almost a riot here the day after the storming of the Bastille when a crowd of suspicious Parisians, discovering a convoy of wheat on its way to the Champ-de-Mars, tried to follow it into the field, only to be prevented by the ditches, the drawbridges and iron railings. Fortunately violence was avoided, and by the spring of 1790 the atmosphere in Paris was decidedly patriotic when both Lafayette and Louis XVI came here to review the National Guard. The most memorable celebration to be seen on the Champ-de-Mars was the *Fête de la Fédération* -

the very first 'Bastille Day' - that took place on July 14th of that same year. The purpose of the event, which was attended by 300,000 people from all over France, was to bring together representatives of the National Guard from around the entire nation, and to swear a communal oath of fidelity to the king, the nation and the law. It was attended by the royal family and a huge contingent of courtiers, who sat on a raised gallery built on to the façade of the Ecole Militaire, where Louis XVI sat on a throne in the centre, with the president of the National Assembly to his right. The gallery was covered, which turned out to be a wise precaution, for the festival was drenched throughout the day by a violent deluge of rain.

➡ If you have not already done so, cross over the Place Joffre on to the lawns of the Champ-de-Mars, where the first thing you will see is the 'Wall for Peace'. It was created in the year 2000 by Parisian artist Clara Halter and architect Jean-Michel Wilmotte, and you can leave your own message for peace in the cracks in the wall. Peace was certainly in the air during the four weeks leading up to the *Fête de la Fédération*, when hundreds of people came here with spades and shovels to help prepare the ground and put up the *Autel de la Patrie* (Altar of the Fatherland). They had to level off the earth on 100 hectares of land, build up more than 3,000 metres of embankment, and distribute several tons of sand in order to stop the esplanade from becoming a sea of mud. The newspaper *Chronique de Paris* reported this moving and unprecedented sight, when people's emotions reached dizzy heights of patriotic bliss as they worked together and sang in unison the new revolutionary song, *Ca ira!* ('Everything will be fine!'). It was thanks to this spontaneous effort by the citizens of Paris that the Champ-de-Mars was ready in time for the festival, and in the darker times that followed, their collective memory of this euphoric experience soon became a symbol for them of the Revolution's most glorious moment.

'It is impossible to give a description of the works in the Champ-de-Mars, which are beyond reality. Foreigners who arrive by the Versailles road cannot get enough of the spectacle: "What a people, these Parisians!" they say to each other, their eyes swimming with tears that are impossible to hold back at the sight of such general devotion. It has to be seen, this ant-hill of citizens, this activity, this gaiety in the face of the hardest work; it has to be seen, this long chain they form to pull the overloaded carts; enormous stones move under their force; they could drag mountains. There is absolutely no-one who does not want to contribute to the raising of the altar of the fatherland: a military band precedes them; everyone walks in threes, carrying a spade or a pickaxe on their shoulder; their rallying cry is this refrain, so well-known now, from the new song called "The National Chimes". Everyone sings at once: ça ira, ça ira, ça ira: Yes, ça ira, repeats everyone who hears them. Nobody feels exempt from work on account of age, sex or condition...the inhabitants of distant villages come running, with their mayor at their head, wearing his sash, a spade on his shoulder. They all have their flags or ensigns. On that of the charcoal burners is written "the last sigh of the aristocrats"...some only come at night, having spent the entire day in back-breaking work. The labourers on the Pont Louis XVI [Concorde] come with their tools, their tip carts, their wheelbarrows, after finishing their day... We saw a woman, already well advanced in age, and obviously not used to fatigue, make more than twenty trips carrying earth in her apron...many deputies came there to work; Wagons were pulled by priests wearing cassocks, others by monks; pulling one cart we saw messieurs Sieyès and Beauharnais; we noticed that they pulled more to the left than to the right, apparently out of habit. You who still think of returning to the old administration, come to the Champ-de-Mars; observe, and yield with good grace to necessity, if reason cannot convince you.' (Rossel, 1982)

➥Walk towards the Eiffel Tower, either on the lawn or on one of the paths, until you get to the pond, with a road going around it, that is situated right in the middle of the Champ-de-Mars. It was on the site of this pond, on a 25-foot platform, that the altar of the fatherland was built. An awful lot took place here, so ➡ find somewhere to sit and take a good look at this circle surrounded by traffic, which two centuries ago was the sacred altar that saw some of the most colourful and spectacular events of the Revolution. The day of the *Fête de la Féderation* had finally arrived. The people of Paris began assembling here at dawn, armed with brightly coloured umbrellas against the rain that, however torrential, could never have dampened their spirits. All morning and into the afternoon they awaited the arrival of the procession that had started out at 7 o'clock in the morning from the *Boulevard Saint-Antoine* (now Boulevard Beaumarchais). By early afternoon it could be seen moving slowly along the other side of the Seine towards the floating bridge that had been specially constructed for the occasion, at the point where you now see the Pont d'Iéna. When the procession arrived at the improvised bridge, it turned left and crossed over it, entering the Champ-de-Mars through a massive 25-metre high triple arch that had also been put up specially for the festival. The top of this arch had been turned into an observation point by those spectators with the courage and agility to get to the top, where they had the most spectacular view of the procession as it came over the bridge, passing underneath them on to the Champ-de-Mars.

The procession was led by the Paris cavalry and grenadiers, who arrived to thunderous applause, followed by the Paris electors, representatives, and the presidents of the municipal districts. The deputies from the Constituent Assembly, accompanied by one battalion of old men and another of children, were also welcomed with an enthusiasm bordering on hysteria as they took their place on the royal platform, where Marie-Antoinette sported - perhaps with some embarrassment - a hat with tri-colour feathers. After the deputies came the *fédérés*, the

National Guardsman from every province in France whose presence in the capital, despite the general feeling of national unity, nonetheless provoked slight apprehension amongst monarchists and patriots alike. But their fears were unfounded. The behaviour of these provincial militia was exemplary, for many of them had been moved, some to almost royalist sentiments, when they met the king and queen two days earlier at the royal inspection. Two hundred priests, all wearing tricolour sashes around their white robes, assembled around the altar, where Talleyrand, Bishop of Autun, stood at the top waiting to officiate at the Mass. Talleyrand might well have been the only cynic in the entire gathering. Maintaining his patriotic reverence and solemn expression, he turned to his colleague, Abbé Louis, who was assisting him, and whispered, '*Whatever you do, don't make me laugh.*'

The ceremony was reported in detail in a newspaper called *Courier de l'Europe*, which was printed in London. '*When everyone was in place the historic scarlet flag and the departmental banners were carried to the top of the steps of the esplanade at the base of the altar to be blessed. Once the blessing was done, the cannons were fired, and Monsieur, the bishop of Autun, pontifically celebrated the Mass, after which the major-general of the federation* [Lafayette] *came to the altar and swore the oath, which was repeated by all the fédérés, naked sword in hand to the sound of a volley of gunfire from the artillery. The president of the National Assembly swore it next, and this oath was repeated by all the members, among whom M. d'Orléans took his place. The municipality and all the civil officers swore it at the same time, as well as all the spectators, to the sound of a second round of gunfire from the artillery. The King was placed on a raised throne in the middle of a covered gallery, enriched with blue and gold hangings...His Majesty had on his right the president of the National Assembly, and he was surrounded by all the deputies. This monarch, wearing the royal mantle, then swore the noble oath "to employ the power which is delegated to him by the constitutional law of the State only for the maintenance of the Constitution, and for the execution of laws." A third general volley was fired after His Majesty's oath... The Queen attended the federation with the Royal Family in a superbly-decorated box that had been built immediately behind the King's throne. The ambassadors and distinguished foreigners were also present in a box which had been prepared for them at a short distance from that of the Queen... The Te Deum was sung after the oath, three hundred drums and as many wind instruments were heard between each verse, and no-one seemed to notice that from 8 o'clock in the morning until 4 o'clock, it had been pouring with rain accompanied by a very cold north wind.'* (Rossel, 1982)

At the *Fête de la Féderation* Lafayette takes wine from a stranger, showing no suspicion that someone might want to poison him. This makes him a hero in the eyes of the public, who instantly see him as a true friend of the people.
(Authors private collection)

This account did not mention an unexpected gesture made by the Queen after Louis XVI had sworn his oath. As the king finished speaking, she took the dauphin in her arms, lifted him up and presented him to the people, a spontaneous act of solidarity that got a standing ovation from the delighted crowd. But the indisputable champion of the day was Lafayette, who provoked a minor delirium of hero-worship when a complete stranger approached him and offered him some wine. Accepting it without hesitation, Lafayette took a huge draught, seemingly oblivious of any possibility that someone might want to poison him. This transformed him in the eyes of everyone, at least for that day, into a true friend of the people. When it was all over the *fédérés* all fell out of their ranks and began embracing each other, and cries of joy were to be heard all over the Champ-de-Mars as the public began leaving and making their way back home. Later that evening many of them went to the public dance that was held on the ruins of the Bastille, beginning a tradition for July 14th that continues to this day.

Not everyone was so deliriously happy about the *Fête de la Fédération*, however. Mirabeau complained about the hero-worship shown to Lafayette, making contemptuous mockery of the *fédérés* that he had seen *'falling at the knees of the dictator, kissing his clothes, his hands, his boots, the saddle of his horse!'* A newspaper in Provence attacked *'the brilliant throne'* that had been provided for the king, which *'seemed to paralyse everybody and transform patriotic spirits into royalist ones.'* But for the most part the whole nation experienced a true feeling of unity and hope, as well as a desire to show their love for their king, and the sincerity of all those present, with the notable exception of Talleyrand, cannot be doubted.

But revolutions progress within their own parameters, and this one was no exception. A notice posted in the newspaper, *Le Moniteur*, three weeks before the Festival, demonstrates that even in such a euphoric atmosphere there were still strict limits on Equality and Fraternity. *'Given that the moment is approaching when the family pact must be sworn by ALL the French people on the altar of the fatherland, that this important and sacred ceremony cannot fail to attract to Paris a huge number of French people and foreigners, eager to take part in the festival of Liberty and to be present at this sublime spectacle, that order and decency must accompany the day of oath, the police department has ordered that the decree authorizing the arrest of beggars, able-bodied or disabled, healthy or sick, women and children, will be put into rigorous operation. SIGNED, Bailly, mayor.'* (Rossel, 1982)

MASSACRE ON THE CHAMP-DE-MARS.

The repeat performance of the Festival of Federation the following year bore no comparison to the euphoria of 1790. Lafayette was given a chilly reception, and a general air of tension and discontent hung over the event. The next day there was general chaos, as thousands of people from the city's political and popular clubs came back to the Champ-de-Mars to protest against the National Assembly's attitude towards the king, an attitude they found far too sympathetic. Louis was no longer very popular with more radical patriots. A petition drafted by the Cordeliers Club demanding the end of the monarchy and the establishment of a republic had already been circulated around the capital, and within 24 hours it had more than 6,000 signatures. The 'problem of the king' was coming to a head, with its first explosion on July 17th, when Parisians were called to the Champ-de-Mars by the leaders of the Cordeliers Club, to collect more signatures on the altar of the fatherland.

The occasion got off to a bad start with a prank that turned violent, and ultimately triggered off the massacre. Two men, a wig-maker and a disabled soldier, seeking to amuse themselves, hid underneath the sacred altar, where they carved a hole in the wooden floor with the intention of looking up the skirts of the *citoyennes* as they passed across the platform to sign the petition. They were so excited by their plan, however, that they forgot to lower their voices, and were discovered before they'd had time to enjoy their improvised observatory. The agitated crowd dragged them out from underneath the altar, assuming, without bothering to question them, that the two *voyeurs* were planning to blow up the good people of Paris. At first they took them to the local police commissioner, who seemed convinced of their harmlessness and let them go. But their liberty was short-lived, for the now angry crowd took the law into their own hands and lynched the two unfortunate pranksters. When mayor Bailly got news of it, he declared martial law and sent more troops to the Champ-de-Mars, where Lafayette was already installed with the National Guard.

Lafayette had his soldiers positioned on the edge of the esplanade, intending to keep his distance, keep his calm, and not give orders to fire, even though shots from the crowd had come dangerously close to them. But when Bailly's reinforcements poured in from all sides, carrying the red flag signifying martial law, the situation became explosive. All of a sudden the sound of gunfire broke out again and the soldiers charged into the crowd, shooting every which way at the terrified citizens who tried in vain to protect themselves from the volley of bullets. Among them was Robespierre, the only one of the Jacobin leaders who'd had the courage to be present. It was after he fled from here that the carpenter Maurice Duplay gave Robespierre shelter in his home on rue Saint-Honoré, where he stayed until the end of his life. But for the protection of the National Guard, Lafayette may well have been massacred that day by the now hysterical Parisians, some of whom took off immediately towards his house with the intention of murdering his family. When it was all over there was enormous disagreement between the patriots and the municipal authorities as to the number of victims, which was in reality about 50.

After this unfortunate incident the festivals around the altar of the fatherland did not have quite the same feeling of national unity, and the pyramid build on it in 1792, to the glory

When citizens gathered on the Champ-de-Mars to sign a petition calling for the overthrow of the king, it ended in disaster. Mayor Bailly declared martial law and sent troops, who opened fire, killing about fifty innocent people. (Author's private collection)

of citizens who had died fighting for their country, was a great disappointment to many present. As the king arrived symbols of the *ancien régime* were attached to a nearby tree and burnt, and the crowd cheered, not for Louis but for Jérôme Pétion, the new mayor of Paris. The next time Louis appeared in public would be the following January, when he mounted the scaffold. In 1793 the Festival of Federation was cancelled at the last moment, depriving Charlotte Corday of the chance to carry out her initial plan, which was to murder Marat on the Champ-de-Mars, in full view of the assembled nation. In this way she hoped not only to rid France of a monstrous tyrant, but also to add to the symbolism of the *Fête de la Fédération* in future years.

A fortnight earlier there had been a celebration here of the Constitution of Year I, drafted by Hérault de Séchelles. It was adopted by all the members of the Assembly, who came to the Champ-de-Mars to swear, in the presence of the people, to maintain liberty, equality, the safety of persons and property, the unity of the Republic and the Rights of Man. Hérault de Séchelles found himself the star of another festival on August 10th of the same year, when he addressed the crowd from a temple raised in memory of those who had died during the overthrow of the monarchy one year earlier. This event was the work of artist Jacques-Louis David, who, in addition to the *Fountain of Regeneration* at the Bastille, had also built a colossal figure of Hercules standing on a mountain on the Esplanade des Invalides. This allegorical figure, shown fighting a dragon, was supposed to represent the French people battling against the evils of federalism, which had been rearing its head all over the country. Dozens of cities and departments were now in open revolt over the growing supremacy of Paris, in particular in Caen, Lyon, Bordeaux and Marseille. Charlotte Corday was from Caen, and her action had been part of this rebellion, so the political symbolism of David's Hercules was no accident. It was a silent warning to those fomenting the so-called 'Federalist Revolt', and a harbinger of the despotic terror that the capital would soon wield over the entire nation.

The Festival of the Supreme Being.

Throughout the Revolution religion had been a continual source of contention and division, and during the Terror the persecution of Catholic priests, monks and nuns reached tragic extremes. But despite this Robespierre firmly believed that a religion was necessary for the stability and unity of the country, provided it was one of tolerance, one that was not hampered by old dogmas but which gave people principles to live by. With his inflexible sense of morality and his lyrical and devouring passion for virtue, Robespierre actually had all the makings of a good Protestant fundamentalist. But he had rejected Christianity, so in its place he introduced the Cult of the Supreme Being, which is best described as a secular religion, centred around a brand new deity, the Goddess of Reason. Robespierre was completely dedicated to this new belief, and June 8th 1794 was to be his finest hour, when all that he had worked towards, ideologically and politically, would be celebrated by the entire nation. David was commissioned to organize the event, which started in the Tuileries Gardens and culminated in a glorious ceremony here on the altar of the fatherland.

By this time the Champ-de-Mars had been re-named *Champ de la Réunion*, and on the site of the altar an enormous symbolic mountain rose dramatically to the sky. It was decorated with allegorical columns and statues, and growing out of a hillock at the top was a 'Tree of Liberty'. The procession was led by Robespierre carrying a bunch of wheat, followed by two columns, one of men, another of women, and behind them a battalion of adolescents. Someone carrying violets symbolized 'Childhood', another crowned with myrtle represented 'Adolescence', a third wearing a sash of oak leaves was 'Virility', and last came 'Old Age' with hair decorated by vine branches and olive leaves. As the deputies made their way to the top of the mountain, more than a few of them suppressed the urge to laugh at the exaggerated solemnity of the occasion, and many more burned inside with resentment at the absolute power that Robespierre and his entourage now wielded over the rest of the Assembly. But the ceremony continued. Robespierre made a long speech. Hymns were chanted to 'Virtue'. Everyone sang the *Marseillaise* to new words by Marie-Joseph Chénier, whose brother André languished in prison and would be guillotined a few weeks later, two days before Robespierre met the same fate. Today, however, Robespierre was drunk with joy. But even though, from the top of his mountain, the 'Incorruptible Defender of the People' could not see the yawns of his audience, all the incense and rose-petals that fell in his path did not blind his eyes to reality. When he got home that night he announced to the assembled Duplay family, '*You will not see me around for very long.*'

The Festival of the Supreme Being, in honour of the Goddess of Reason, symbolized everything that Robespierre had worked towards. It was his finest hour. But less than two months later, he was dead. (Courtesy of Musée Carnavalet, Cabinet des Arts Graphiques, Paris)

The Execution of Mayor Bailly.

A few months before Robespierre's finest hour the Champ-de-Mars, at that time re-named *Champ de la Fédération*, became yet again the scene of bloodshed. But this time it was the judicial kind, when on November 12th 1793 Jean-Sylvain Bailly, the 57-year-old former mayor of Paris, paid for his role in the massacre that had taken place here two years earlier. The people could never forgive him for this, and their final revenge was to have him guillotined here at the scene of his crime against the nation. At 9 o'clock that morning the executioner, Charles-Henri Sanson, received orders to dismantle the guillotine and transport it across the river to the *Champ de la Fédération*. The plan for revenge was orchestrated in macabre detail, and Sanson's memoirs show that the odious treatment of Bailly began in prison well before his execution. *'The wardens at the Conciergerie...treated Bailly with a violence that left no doubt that they had received orders to do so. One, mimicking the accent of a valet who announces the arrival of guests, shouted as Bailly came in, "Monsieur Bailly, ex-butcher of the former tyrant!" Another, as Bailly was leaning over to secure his garters, pushed him so harshly that he fell backwards...the cruelty of his gaolers had not dampened the courage of this illustrious scholar...when my assistants took him away from his persecutors, he adjusted his shirt with a smile and said, "It's just that I'm a bit old for these games."'* (Sanson, 1988). Bailly continued in this spirit of good-natured humour, and when Sanson had finished the *toilette*, he began helping Bailly on with his overcoat, provoking the prisoner to quip, *'Are you worried that I'll catch a cold?'*

The tumbril set off with a red flag attached to the back of it, the symbol of martial law that had been flourished by Bailly's troops during the massacre, and Sanson had been given orders to burn it in front of the prisoner before the execution. As the cortège was moving along the Champs-Elysées, it was discovered that the carpenters had forgotten some essential beams for the construction of the scaffold, so they had to go back and get them, and put them on the tumbril with the condemned prisoner. Twice during this interruption the crowd of spectators tried to jump on to the cart and seize Bailly, who had to be protected by the gendarmes that followed the procession. When the tumbril set off again, the jolting to and fro of the pieces of wood bothered Bailly so much that he accepted Sanson's suggestion to get out and walk, leaving him open to attack. Almost immediately a teenage boy ran up and grabbed the coat that he had around his shoulders, leaving the astonished Bailly lying on his back in the mud, watching in horror as his coat was ripped to shreds. Sanson quickly got his prisoner back in the tumbril, which was then pelted with stones and other objects, and when Sanson rebuked the crowd, Bailly told him, *'It would be regrettable to have learned to live with honour for 57 years, and to not know how to die with courage for a quarter of an hour.'*

Champ-de-Mars.

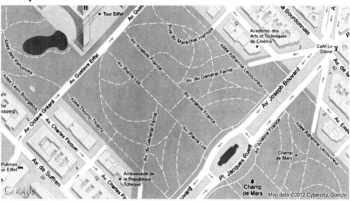

After an hour and a half they reached the Champ-de-Mars. Fouquier-Tinville's instructions required Sanson to place the scaffold half-way between the altar of the fatherland and the present-day Place du General Gouraud (see plan), exactly the same position, in fact, that the troops had occupied when they fired on the people. ➡If you stand facing the Eiffel Tower, you should take the path to the right of the pond (Avenue Joseph Bouvard) and stop about half-way along it, where it crosses Allée Adrienne Lecouvreur. The name of this *allée* is not marked, but the spot where Bailly's tumbril arrived on that cold November afternoon was where you now see a pedestrian crossing, and the rather lyrical sign *'Reservé aux Cavaliers allure moderée'*. It was here, where nowadays a steady succession of joggers pass by, that the authorities wanted to kill Bailly. Sanson was anxious to get his prisoner's agony over as soon as possible, and immediately ordered his assistants to put the beams in place on the scaffold. But as they were beginning their work, a general murmur of discontent began to spread among the spectators, who declared that *'the ground that had drunk the blood of martyrs could not be soiled by the blood of a scoundrel, that Bailly would not be executed in the Field of Federation.'* Sanson protested and called on the help of the gendarmes, who conveniently disappeared, as a voice in the crowd shouted, *'You can proclaim*

martial law, you've got Bailly and the red flag in your hands; as for us, we're going to put the guillotine in its proper place, we'll do the work ourselves, if you're too lazy!' As the crowd began to dismantle the guillotine, Sanson found himself separated from Bailly, who was being dragged along by a sea of people, his shirt and face covered in mud, and blood running from a graze on his forehead. He tried to keep calm, but his face was very pale, and he showed visible relief when he found Sanson, his executioner, who seemed at that moment to be his only friend.

Sanson was instructed to execute Mayor Bailly on the Champ-de-Mars, scene of the massacre he was blamed for. Sanson's assistants begin to put up the scaffold, but the people protest, and force them to dismantle it and take it outside the boundaries of the Champ-de-Mars. (Courtesy of Musée Carnavalet, Cabinet des Arts Graphiques, Paris)

After the crowd had been calmed a little by the intervention of a local official, it was decided to move the guillotine to the north corner of the Champ-de-Mars, where nowadays the Avenue de la Bourdonnais meets the Quai Branly (see plan). While his assistants put the dismantled machine on to the tumbrils, Sanson took charge of his exhausted prisoner, and they set off through the field towards the Seine. You are going to go with them, so ➡turn into Allée Adrienne Lecouvreur in the direction of the river (same direction as the Eiffel Tower), and take it as far as Avenue Sylvestre de Sacy. Turn around at this point and look behind you. Try to imagine the scene on this peaceful path, with no buildings next to it, no Eiffel Tower, just the crowd, surging forward, dragging the dismantled guillotine as it was thrown to and fro on the tumbril - and a bedraggled, despairing Bailly, supported on his final walk by the executioner.

➡ Turn right on Avenue Silvestre de Sacy (you will see the Eiffel Tower to your left), pass Avenue Elisée Reclus, then turn left on Avenue de la Bourdonnais. Here the crowd came to a halt, unable to decide where to set up the guillotine. They discussed at great length, no doubt all part of their programme of revenge against Bailly, who stood in the icy rain, protected from the cold by nothing more than his shirt, torn to shreds and revealing several lacerations on his chest and back. He was shivering, and his teeth chattered so loudly that one of his tormentors asked him, *'Are you trembling, Bailly?'* to which he replied, *'No, I'm cold.'* At that moment he seemed to lose his strength, threw his head back, closed his eyes and fell into the arms of a gendarme and the executioner, murmuring, '*A drink! A drink!*' One of the spectators responded to this by throwing some liquid mud in Bailly's face, a gesture so low that the rest of the crowd cried out their indignation, and someone came running with a bottle of wine to pour into Bailly's half-open mouth.

Finally it was decided to put the guillotine at the bottom of one of the outer ditches surrounding the Champ-de-Mars, ➡ in a spot which more or less corresponds to where a tree now stands in front of numbers 6-8 Avenue de la Bourdonnais. I wonder what the residents of this rather chic Parisian street would think to know that such a harrowing scene took place right outside their elegant apartments. By now the crowd was quieter, tired perhaps by the energy they had expended in their fury, and sobered without doubt by Bailly's amazing courage in the face of such an ordeal. He had to be supported up the steps of the scaffold, and when he got to the top he heaved a sigh of relief and smiled. *'Quickly, quickly, let's get it over with, please.'* But he was not to have his wish, for Sanson still had to carry out the final ritual of burning the red flag before he could put poor Bailly out of his misery. This was no easy task either, for the stove that had been brought along for the purpose was so inefficient they eventually had to break some of the planks from the scaffold and create an improvised brazier. This all took time, and Bailly was showing signs of fainting again by the time Sanson took his arm and led him to the guillotine. Realizing that this time his agony really was almost over, he seemed to revive. As he tied the poor man to the plank, Sanson whispered, *'Courage! Courage! monsieur Bailly.'* Bailly turned his head to the right and replied, in a firm and audible voice, *'Ah! Now I'm within sight of home, and...'* Bailly never finished his sentence, and we can only hope that he reached home safely.

To get home safely yourself, the best way is to ➡ keep walking towards the Seine to the end of Avenue de la Bourdonnais, turn right along Quai Branly and walk to the Pont de l'Alma RER station. Here you can get the RER C line, which takes you directly into the centre of town (Saint-Michel).

Louis XVI-era lantern at the entrance of a Parisian mansion. (Authors private collection)

Glossary of French Terms

(Certain words in this glossary have more than one meaning in French, but I have restricted my translations to the meanings relevant to this book)

A

abbaye	abbey
allée	path
ami	friend
ancien régime	old regime
armoire	wardrobe
arrondissement	postal/administrative district of Paris
assignat	paper money issued during the Revolution, initially as government bonds 'assigned' from church property that had been confiscated and nationalized
auberge	inn
autel	altar

B

bague	ring
bal public	public dance hall
Belle Epoque	Paris's heyday at the end of the 19th/beginning of the 20th century
bière	means either beer or bier (as in coffin)
bonnet Phrygian	red cap worn by *sans-culottes* and radical revolutionaries, inspired by the hat worn in ancient times by Phrygian galley slaves
bonnet rouge	same as *bonnet Phrygian*
bon vivant	person who enjoys luxury, especially food and drink
borne	low stone posts along the side of Paris streets

bosquet	grove
boucher/boucherie	butcher/butchery or butcher's shop
boue	mud
boulangerie	bakery
bouquiniste	bookseller, nowadays refers to bookstall owners along the quays of the River Seine (comes from *bouquin*, slang for book)
bourg	village or small market town
bourgeois	middle-class, in 18th century meant any non-noble person of high social standing
bourgeoisie	the middle-classes
bourreau	executioner, headsman
brasserie	brewery, nowadays means café/bar
Brissotin	supporter of the politician Brissot, more usually referred to as a *Girondin*

C

cabaret	tavern
cabinet	small room for receiving people or working
cabinet de toilette	toilet
cahiers de doléances	books of grievances presented by the people to the king at the Estates-General
Ca Ira!	revolutionary song and slogan, literally means 'it will go' but can best be translated as 'everything will be fine' or, in more modern language, 'it'll be OK'.
carmagnole	1. costume worn by workers in the Piedmontese town of Carmagnola, adopted by soldiers of Marseille and then by *sans-culottes*
	2. a round sung and danced by revolutionaries
carré	square
carrière	quarry or pit
caserne	barracks

chambre	1. bedroom
	2. chamber or court of law
Chambre des Comptes	financial court, created in 1320, which controlled the accounts of foreign agents
champ	field
chanoine/chanoinesse	canon (clergyman)/canoness
chaussée	highway, roadway, carriageway
chouannerie	royalist counter-revolutionary movement created in 1793 by the Cotereau brothers, whose habit of rallying their men with a cry like that of a *chat-huant* (screech owl) resulted in the name *chouan* being given to its members
ci-devant	formerly, of former days
un ci-devant	an aristocrat who lost his/her title during the Revolution
cimetière	cemetery
cité	city
citoyen/citoyenne	citizen/citizeness
cloître	cloister
cocarde	rosette or cockade
coiffure	hairstyle/hairdo
collier	necklace
comité	committee
communard	member of the Paris Commune, a revolutionary government that was formed in Paris and took control in March 1871
comte/comtesse	count/countess
condamné	a condemned person
contre-révolution	counter-revolution
coup-de-grâce	final or decisive stroke, finishing touch
cour	courtyard
couvent	convent
couvert	cutlery, place setting for a dining table, or a cover charge in a restaurant (used in this

	book as *Grand Couvert*, the room where the king and queen ate at Versailles)
cuisine	kitchen or cuisine
culotte	breeches (historical meaning) - nowadays means trousers

D

dauphin	title of the eldest son and heir of the king of France
dauphine	title of the *dauphin*'s wife
déjeuner	morning meal in the 18th century, eaten at 10.30 or 11.00 a.m., nowadays means lunch
de rigeur	required by fashion or etiquette
droit	right
duc/duchesse	duke/duchess

E

eau-de-vie	literally 'water of life', a strong alcoholic brandy or liqueur
école	school
écu	means 'shield', so given in 14th century as name of unit of money bearing the shield of France. Originally made of gold, first silver *écu* (1641) was worth 3 *livres*, last silver *écu* was issued during Year II of the Republic (1794)
égalité	equality
église	church
émigré	emigrant, referred to people who left France to escape the Revolution
enceinte	surrounding wall or rampart around a city or fortress
les Enragés	radical revolutionaries (1792-3) led by Jacques Roux, forerunners of socialism

entremet	a dish served between the roast and the dessert, could be sweet or savoury
entresol	low-ceilinged floor between ground and first floor of a house, often with oval or half-circular windows
estaminet	old word meaning small café

F

faubourg	inner suburb, refers to village-like communities around the centre of Paris
fédéralisme	federalism, or Federalist Revolt, movement beginning in summer 1792, opposing the Jacobins and the domination of Paris over the rest of the country
fédéré	name given to the national guardsmen of the *Fédération Nationale* of 1789, a movement dedicated to national unity, which was celebrated at the *Fête de la Fédération* in July 1790 on the Champs-de-Mars the *fédérés* were sent to Paris from the provinces for this festival, and later played a major role in the overthrow of the monarchy in August 1792
Ferme-Générale	General Farm - private company whose members paid a fee to the king in exchange for the right to impose taxes
Fermier-Général	Farmer-General - member of the *Ferme-Générale* - there were forty of them, and in 1780 they had a wall built round Paris, the notorious *Mur des Fermiers-Généraux*, with several customs houses for the collection of duty
fête	festival
fichu	scarf, usually of muslin, worn around the shoulders and crossed over at the front

	preserved modesty by covering the bodice and shoulders, or an overplunging neckline
fille-de-joie	loose woman or prostitute, literally means 'girl of joy'
fleur-de-lys	lily motif, traditional symbol of royalty
La Fronde	series of civil rebellions against absolute monarchy during Louis XIV's childhood andthe regency of Anne of Austria - got its name from a streeturchins' game of the time

G

galant	1. gallant, courtly, gentlemanly, courteous 2. amorous - *la vie galante* or a life of *galanterie* = a life of amorous adventures, the life of a courtesan
garde-française	royal household regiment, defected to the revolutionary cause just prior and during the storming of the Bastille
garde-nationale	citizen's militia, created just before the storming of the Bastille to protect the people and assure the continuation of the Revolution - called the *garde-bourgeoise* up until August 7th 1789
garde-Suisse	royal regiment, composed of Swiss soldiers, that defended the king and his household
gare	station
gendarme	policeman - originally meant 'men-at-arms' (*gens d'armes*)
Gironde	department in the southwest of France, in the region of Aquitaine
Girondins	political group consisting of several deputies from the *Gironde*, hence their name - their leader was Brissot, and their inspiration was

	Madame Roland
grande noblesse	high aristocracy
greffe	clerk's office - in prisons it referred to the administrative room where prisoners were received when entering or leaving the prison
greffier	clerk (of the court) who worked in the *greffe*
guichet	1. in 18th century prisons it referred to administrative windows or checkpoints between different parts of the prison - nowadays it is the word used for bank and post-office windows and ticket booths in train stations, cinemas etc.

2. the *guichets* of the Louvre and Tuileries were narrow, covered passages connecting the exterior of those palaces with the interior courtyards |
| *guingette* | open-air café or dance hall |

H

hôtel	private mansion - often referred to as a *hôtel particulier*

I

île	island/isle, e.g. *île Saint-Louis*
l'Incorruptible	The Incorruptible - nickname given to Robespierre, who never accepted a bribe
les Incroyables	literally means 'the Incredibles', a group of royalist dandies during the Directory
les Indulgents	people who in 1793/4 called for an end to the Terror, notably Danton and Desmoulins
Invalides	disabled ex-soldiers who reside at the *Hôtel des Invalides*

J

jardin — garden

jeu de paume — indoor tennis court where real (royal) tennis was played

jeunesse dorée — literally means 'gilded youth', another name for the *Incroyables*

journée — day - i.e. *les journées d'Octobre* = the October days

journée révolutionnaire — day of revolutionary action

L

lanterne — streetlamp, used for lynching - *les aristocrats à la lanterne!* = string up the aristocrats!

lettre de cachet — 'letter with a seal', issued by a monarch to authorize imprisonment without trial

limonadier — café owner or manufacturer of softdrinks (feminine = *limonadière*)

livre — old unit of French money, replaced by the franc during the Revolution

M

mairie — town hall

maison — house

maison de santé — clinic - used by the wealthy during the Revolution to avoid imprisonment - most famous was the one run by Dr. Belhomme

manège — riding-school - the *Manège* of the Tuileries became seat of the National Assembly

marais — a marsh or swamp

Le Marais — 1. area of Paris in the 4th arrondissement
2. name given to lower benches in National Assembly occupied by moderate and right-wing deputies

marquis/marquise — marquis/marquess

Marseillais	soldiers (*fédérés*) from Marseille, played major role in the overthrow of the monarchy
La Marseillaise	French national anthem, originally called War Hymn of the Rhine Army, written by Rouget de Lisle in 1792
mercerie, mercier	haberdashery, haberdasher
les Merveilleuses	'Marvellous women' - female companions of the *Incroyables*
moiré	having a watered or wavelike pattern
Monsieur	title of the king's oldest brother
montagnard	deputy belonging to the political group known as *La Montagne* (see below)
La Montagne	The Mountain, left-wing faction led by Danton and Robespierre - they occupied the highest benches in the National Convention, hence their name
mousquetaire	musketeer
mur	wall
muscadins	another name for the *Incroyables* - name comes from the musk perfume they wore
musée	museum

N
noblesse	nobility

O
officier de bouche	literally means 'officer of the mouth' - an official in charge of the kitchens of an aristocratic household - many of those who had held this prestigious position sub-sequently opened restaurants when their masters emigrated or were arrested during the Revolution - thus began French gastronomy

P

pailleux	a prisoner who slept on straw (*paille*)
palais	palace
parlement	parliament
parloir	visiting room where people can talk - used in 18th century prisons (origin of 'parlour')
parterre	flower beds, borders
patisserie	cake or pastry/ shop where they are sold
patois	provincial dialect
patrie	fatherland
pavillon	pavilion or wing of a building
paysan	peasant/rural (adjective); country man or woman; farm worker; peasant (pejorative)
peintre	painter, artist
pension	boarding house
pensionnaire	boarder, guest
petite-noblesse	gentry, minor nobility
petit-peuple	lower classes
pique	pike - weapon of the *sans-culottes*
chambre à la pistole	prison cell containing beds
place	square - i.e. *Place de la Concorde*
La Plaine	'The Plain', another name for Le Marais, where moderate and right-wing deputies sat
pont	bridge
porte	door, gate
préfecture	police headquarters
prévôt	provost

Q

quai	quay
quartier	quarter, area or neighbourhood

R

raison	reason
raison d'être	reason for being/living/existing
reine	queen
roi	king
rue	street

S

salle	room, hall
salon	1. living-room, often used for meetings of literary or political groups
	2. exhibition hall
salon de thé	tea room
(garder son) sang-froid	(keep one's) cool, calm - also means cold-bloodedness
sans-culottes	radical revolutionaries, mostly small property-owners, artisans or working-class name comes from habit of wearing long trousers instead of the traditional knee-breeches (*culotte*) of the old regime
savant	scholar, scientist
seigneur	overlord, lord of the manor, master
seigneurial	relating to the *seigneur*, i.e. *seigneurial* courts, rights, etc.
septembriseurs	nickname given to the men who carried out the massacres of September 1792 - the word comes from *briser* meaning 'to break'
serment	oath
soirée	party or social evening
sol	another word for *sou*, the smallest unit of currency
sortie	exit
soupirant	suitor, beau, or admirer (from *soupirer* meaning to sigh)

sous-sol	basement or cellar
Suisses	see *garde-Suisse*

T

tableau	picture
La Terreur	The Terror
9 Thermidor	27th July 1794, key date in the Revolution, marking the overthrow of Robespierre and the end of the Terror
Tiers	means 'third', refers to the Third Estate at the Estates-General
tocsin	alarm bell that was rung throughout a city in the event of an emergency
une tour	a tower
traiteur	caterer (nowadays also means delicatessen)
tricoteuse	literally means 'knitter', name given to women who cheered and counted the heads around the foot of the guillotine, some of whom used to knit during the executions. They were sometimes known as 'furies' and would also animate sessions of the Assembly, trials of suspects and processions of tumbrils heading for the scaffold.
trompe l'oeil	a style of painting giving an illusion of reality- literally means 'deceives the eye'
tu, vous	two forms of 'you', the second one was virtually abolished during the Revolution as an undesirable symbol of the formal protocol of the *ancien régime*

V

vainqueur	conqueror
13 Vendémiaire	5th October 1795, when Barras crushed a royalist rebellion against the National

Convention - he was aided by Napoléon Bonaparte, who was thus brought into the forefront of the political scene and nicknamed *'General Vendémiaire'*

vertu virtue - Robespierre's major preoccupation

BIBLIOGRAPHY

DIARIES WRITTEN DURING THE REVOLUTION

Desbassayns, Henry Paulin Panon, *Voyage à Paris pendant la Révolution*, ed. M.H. Bourquin-Simonin (Perrin, Paris 1985).

Desmoulins, Lucile, *Journal, 1788-1793*, ed. P. Lejeune (Editions des Cendres, Paris 1995).

Floriban, Célestin Guittard de, *Journal de Célestin Guittard de Floriban, bourgeois de Paris sous la Révolution 1791-1796*, ed. R. Aubert (France-Empire, Paris 1974).

Gouverneur Morris, *A Diary of the French Revolution by Gouverneur Morris, 1752-1816, minister to France during the Terror*, ed. B.C. Davenport (Harrap, London 1939).

EYE-WITNESS ACCOUNTS AND PERSONAL MEMOIRS FROM THE PERIOD

Adams, John, *The Works of John Adams, Second President of the United States* I, *Life of the Author*, ed. C.P. Adams (Little and Brown, Boston 1856).

Blagdon, Francis W., *Paris as it was, and as it is; or a sketch of the French Capital, illustrative of the effects of the revolution, in a series of letters, written by an English traveller during the years 1801-1802* (Gutenberg EBook No. 8998, Salt Lake City 2005).

Bourrienne, Louis Antoine Fauvelet de, *Mémoires de M. de Bourrienne, ministre d'état; sur Napoléon, le directoire, le consulat, l'empire et la restauration*, 10 vols. (Ladvocat, Paris 1829).

Charpentier and Louis Pierre Manuel, *La Bastille Dévoilée* (chez Desenne, Paris 1790).

Elliot, Grace Dalrymple, *Journal of My Life During the French Revolution* (R. Bentley, London 1859).

Lasteyrie, Virginie de, *Vie de Madame de Lafayette* (Techener fils, Paris 1868).

Mercier, Louis-Sébastien, *Tableau de Paris* (Horizons de France, Paris 1947).

Paine, Thomas, *Writings of Thomas Paine* III, *French Revolution*, ed. M.D. Conway (G.P. Putnam's Sons, New York 1894).

Paine, Thomas, *Writings of Thomas Paine* IV, *the Age of Reason*, ed. M.D. Conway (G.P. Putnam's Sons, New York 1894).

Restif de la Bretonne, Nicolas Anne Edmé, *Les Nuits de Paris ou le Spectateur Nocturne*, ed. M. Delon (Gallimard, Paris 1986).

Roland de la Platière, Marie-Jeanne, *Mémoires particuliers de Mme Roland*, ed. Fs. Barrière (Firmin Didot, Paris 1847).

Sanson, Charles-Henri, *La Révolution Française vue par son Bourreau*, ed. M. Lebailly (L'Instant, Paris 1988).

Tannahill, Reay, *Paris in the Revolution* (The Folio Society, London 1966).

Tourzel, Louise-Élisabeth de, and François Des Cars, *Mémoires de Madame la duchesse de Tourzel, gouvernante des enfants de France pendant les années 1789, 1790, 1791, 1792, 1793, 1795*, 2 vols. (Plon, Paris 1884).

Twiss, Richard, *A Trip to Paris in July and August 1792* (Minerva Prefs, London 1793).

Vigée Lebrun, Elisabeth, *Memoirs of Madame Vigée Lebrun (1755-1842)*, ed. L. Strachey (Doubleday, Page & Company, New York 1903).

Villefosse, René Héron de, *Voyage au Temps de la Douceur de Vivre* (Les Publications Techniques et Artistiques, Paris 1947).

Wairy, Louis Constant, *Mémoires de Constant, premier valet de chambre de l'empereur, sur la vie privée de Napoléon, sa famille et sa cour* (Gutenberg EBook No.28176, Salt Lake City 2009).

Contemporary Documents from the Bibliothèque Historique de la Ville de Paris

Desmoulins, Camille, *Le Vieux Cordelier*, No. VII, BHVP 986, Res. 25, Folio 44, 85.

Desmoulins, Camille, *Letters*, BHVP 985, Res. 24, Folio 5, 12, 105, 156, 158, 160, 165.

Desmoulins, Horace, *Letters*, BHVP 986, Res. 25, Folio 206.

Desmoulins, Lucile, *Letters and Notes*, BHVP 986, Res. 25, Folio 144, 175, 180, 185, 186, 187.

Duplessis, Annette, *Letters*, BHVP 987, Res. 26, Folio 51.

Duplessis, Claude, *Letters*, BHVP 987, Res. 26, Folio 4.

Fréron, Stanislas, *Letters*, BHVP 986, Res. 25, Folio 144.

Exposé Justificatif Pour le Sieur Henriot, Salpétrier du Roi, Fauxbourg Saint-Antoine, BHVP 957368 8379.

Extrait des procès-verbaux des registres de l'Assemblée générale du District de Sainte Marguérite, par M. l'abbé de Ladeveze, Secrétaire du district et aumônier du bataillon, BHVP 10065, No. 210.

Inventory taken at the Desmoulins' apartment after their execution, BHVP 985, Res. 24, Folio, 83.

Lettre au Roi par un Citoyen zélé, Habitant du Fauxbourg Saint-Antoine, relativement aux désastres arrivés au Fauxbourg Saint-Antoine, à Paris, le Lundi 27, la nuit suivante, et le lendemain 28 Avril 1789, BHVP 961209 1296, AB-611.

THE CONTEMPORARY PRESS

Desmoulins, Camille, *Le Vieux Cordelier*, ed. P. Pachet (Belin, Paris 1987).

'Letters on the subject of the Concert of Princes, and the Dismemberment of Poland and France', *Morning Chronicle* 20 July 1792 - 25 June 1793, ed. by a Calm Observer (G.G.J.&J. Robinson, London 1793).

Rossel, André, *Histoire de France à travers les Journaux du Temps Passé* (A l'Enseigne de L'Arbre Verdoyant, Paris 1982).

The French Revolution, General

Bertaud, Jean-Paul, *Les causes de la Révolution Française* (Colin, Paris 1992).

Carlyle, Thomas, *History of the French Revolution* (Ward, Lock, Bowden & Co., London 1891).

Cobb, Richard and Colin Jones, *The French Revolution* (Salem House Publishers, Topsfield 1988).

Doyle, William, *The Oxford History of the French Revolution* (Oxford University Press, Oxford 1990).

Manceron, Claude, *Les Hommes de la Liberté* I-V, *Les Racines 1744-1789* (Laffont, Paris 1972-87).

Michelet, Jules, *Histoire de la Révolution Française* (Rouff, Paris 1869).

Pernoud, Georges and Sabine Flaissier, *The French Revolution* (Secker & Warburg, London 1962).

Roberts, John Morris, *The French Revolution* (Oxford University Press, Oxford 1997).

Schama, Simon, *Citizens* (Vintage Books, New York 1989).

The History of Paris, General

Davis, Richard Harding, *About Paris* (Harper & Brothers, New York 1895).

Cetekk, Claude, *Nous avons bâti Paris* (Inter-Livres, Paris 1987).

Gourdon de Genouillac, Nicolas-Jules-Henri, *Paris Moderne, suite de Paris à Travers les Siècles, Histoire Nationale de Paris et des Parisiens* (F. Roy, Paris 1892).

Hillairet, Jacques, *Connaissance du Vieux Paris*, 3 vols. (Gonthier, Paris 1963).

Hillairet, Jacques, *Dictionnaire Historique des Rues de Paris*, 2 vols. (Les Editions de Minuit, Paris 1963).

Hillairet, Jacques, *Evocation du Vieux Paris*, 3 vols. (Les Editions de Minuit, Paris 1952).

Pitte, Jean-Robert, *Paris, Histoire d'une Ville* (Hachette Livre, Paris 1993).

The French Revolution, Specific

Arasse, Daniel, *The Guillotine and the Terror* (Penguin, London 1991).

Badinter, Robert, *Libres et Egaux, l'Emancipation des Juifs sous la Révolution Française 1789-1791* (Fayard, Paris 1989).

Challamel, Augustin and Wilhelm Ténint, *Les Français sous la Révolution* (Challamel, Paris 1843).

Chaussinand-Nogaret, Guy, *1789, Collection Cabinet des Estampes de la Bibliothèque Nationale* (Banque Nationale de Paris/Hervas, Paris 1988).

CNAM, *Les Arts et Métiers en Révolution* (Musée National des Techniques, Paris 1988).

Decaux, Alain, *Histoire des Françaises*, 2 vols. (Librairie Académique Perrin, Paris 1972).

Deloche, Bernard and Jean-Michel Leniaud, *La Culture des Sans-Culottes* (Les Editions de Paris/Les Presses de Languedoc, Paris/Montpellier 1989).

Favier, Jean, *Chronique de la Révolution 1788-1799* (Larousse, Paris 1988).

Fournet, Louis-Henri, *Le Journal de la Révolution* (Sides, Paris 1988).

Guedj, Denis, *La Révolution des Savants* (Gallimard, Paris 1989).

Guillot, Renée-Paule, 'Marie Tussaud: Une Femme de "têtes"', *Historia* 494 (1988).

Gupta, Abhijit, 'Child from Chittagong', *The Telegraph*, March 11th 2008.

Hardman, John, *French Revolution Documents, Volume II, 1792-95*, (Barnes & Noble, New York 1973).

Hastier, Louis, *La Vérité sur l'Affaire du Collier* (Cercle du Bibliophile, Genève 1970).

Izard, Georges, *Les Coulisses de la Convention* (Hachette, Paris 1938).

Lamartine, Alphonse de, *Histoire des Girondins*, 2 vols. (Christiaens, Brussels 1847).

Lenotre, G., *Les Grands Jours du Tribunal Révolutionnaire* (Flammarion, Paris 1933).

Levy, Barbara and Paul Lagriffoul, *Les Sanson, une dynastie de bourreaux* (Mercure de France, Paris 1976).

MacDonogh, Giles, *A Palate in Revolution, Grimod de La Reynière and the Almanach des Gourmands* (Robin Clark, London 1987).

Manceron, Claude and Anne Manceron, *La Révolution Française, Dictionnaire Biographique* (Renaudot, Paris 1989).

Mercier, Alain, *1794, L'Abbé Grégoire et la création du Conservatoire National des Arts et Métiers* (Musée National des Techniques, Paris 1989).

Roberts, J.M. and R.C. Cobb (eds.), *French Revolution Documents*, 2 vols. (Blackwell, Oxford 1966-1973).

Rousseau, J. J., *Du contrat social ou Principes du droit politique* (Marc Michel Rey, Amsterdam 1762).

Various Authors, 'Thomas Paine in England and in France', *Atlantic Monthly* Vol. 04, No. 26 (1859).

Walter, Gérard, *Le Procès de Marie-Antoinette* (Complexe, Bruxelles 1993).

The History of Paris, Specific

Arnold, Wendy, *The Historic Hotels of Paris* (Thames and Hudson, London 1990).

Association du Souvenir de Picpus, *Les Victimes de Picpus 1794-1994* (Société de l'Oratoire et du Cimetière de Picpus, Paris 1993).

Babeau, Albert Arsène, *Paris en 1789* (Librairie de Firmin-Didot, Paris 1892).

Boulant, Antoine, *Les Tuileries, palais de la Révolution (1789-1799)* (published by the author, Nimes 1989).

Brazier, Nicolas, *Histoire des petits théâtres de Paris depuis leur origine*, 2 vols. (Allardin, Paris 1838).

Cain, Georges, *Nouvelles Promenades dans Paris* (Flammarion, Paris 1908).

Caron, Pierre, *Paris pendant la Terreur: Rapports des agents secrets du ministre de l'Intérieur*, 7 vols. (Picard, Paris 1910-1978).

Christ, Yvan, Jean-Marc Léri and Alfred Fierro, *Vie et Histoire - 1er arrondissement* (Hervas, Paris 1999).

Dauban, Charles Aimé, *Les Prisons de Paris sous La Révolution, d'après les relations des contemporains* (Slatkine-Megariotis Reprints, Genève 1977).

Espezel, Pierre d', *Le Palais-Royal* (Calmann-Lévy, Paris 1936).

Fierro, Alfred, Jean-Marc Léri and Andrée Jacob, *Vie et Histoire - 4ème arrondissement* (Hervas, Paris 1998).

Groetschel, Yves, *Village XVII, Saint-Victor, Sorbonne* (Village Communication, Paris 1996).

Groetschel, Yves, *Village XVIII, Jardin des Plantes, Val-de-Grâce* (Village Communication, Paris 1996).

Hénard, Robert, *La Rue Saint-Honoré* II, *De la Révolution à nos Jours* (Emile-Paul, Paris 1908-1909).

Hervier, Dominique and Marie-Agnès Férault, *Le faubourg Saint-Antoine, Un double visage* (APPIF, Paris 1998).

Jacob, Andrée and Jean-Marc Léri, *Vie et Histoire - 6ème arrondissement* (Hervas, Paris 1988).

Jarry, Paul, *Vieilles Demeures Parisiennes* (Plon, Paris 1945).

Laveau, Noël, *Paris Révolution* (Loysel, Paris 1989).

Le Moël, Michel and Jean Colson, *Vie et Histoire - 5ème arrondissement* (Hervas, Paris 1990).

Lenotre, G., *Le jardin de Picpus* (Perrin, Paris 1928).

Lenotre, G., *Paris Révolutionnaire* (Perrin, Paris 1906).

Lenotre, G., *Vieilles maisons, vieux papiers*, 6 vols. (Perrin, Paris 1929-1930).

Poisson, Georges, *Paris au temps de la Révolution* (Bonechi, Florence 1989).

Poisson, Michel, V. Mesny and J. de Wismes, *1792: Les Massacres de Septembre* (Mairie du 6e Arrondissement, Paris 1992).

Rice, Howard C., *Thomas Jefferson's Paris* (Princeton University Press, Princeton 1976).

Tulard, Jean, *Nouvelle Histoire de Paris: La Révolution* (Hachette, Paris 1989).

Versailles

Caffin-Carcy, Odile and Jacques Villard, *Versailles et la Révolution* (Editions d'Art Lys, Versailles 1988).

Caffin-Carcy, Odile, Jacques Villard and Jean-Pierre Babelon, *Versailles, le Château, la Ville, ses Monuments* (Picard, Paris 1991).

Gruyer, Paul, *Huit Jours à Versailles* (Hachette, Paris 1920).

Kemp, Gerald van der, *Versailles, a guide to the Palace* (Editions d'Art Lys, Versailles 1973).

Meyer, Daniel, *Versailles* (Editions d'Art Lys, Versailles 1991).

Biographies

Aulneau, Joseph, *La Comtesse du Barry et la fin de l'ancien Régime* (Denoël, Paris 1937).

Becker, Marianne, *Maximilien, Histoire de Robespierre*, 3 vols. (M. Becker, 1989-1999).

Bourson, Pierre-Alexandre, *Robespierre ou le délire décapité* (Buchet Chastel, Paris 1993).

Cabanès, Augustin, *La Princess de Lamballe, Intime, D'après les Confidences de son Médecin* (Albin Michel, Paris 1922).

Campan, Jeanne Louise Henriette, *Mémoires de Madame Campan*, ed. Mme Carette née Bouvet (Albin Michel, Paris 1920).

Castelot, André, *Joséphine* (Perrin, Paris 1965).

Castelot, André, *Madame du Barry* (Perrin, Paris 1989).

Castelot, André, *Marie-Antoinette* (Perrin, Paris 1993).

Castelot, André, *Philippe-Egalité, le Prince Rouge* (Sfelt, Paris 1950).

Chamfort, Sébastien Roch Nicholas, *Maximes et Pensées* (Mille et Une Nuits, Paris 1997).

Christophe, Robert, *Danton* (Perrin, Paris 1964).

Christophe, Robert, *Mademoiselle de Sombreuil, héroine de la Révolution Française* (Plon, Paris 1965).

Huertas, Monique de, *Madame Royale, L'énigmatique destinée de la fille de Louis XVI* (Pygmalion, Paris 1999).

Korngold, Ralph, *Robespierre, Le Premier des Dictateurs Modernes* (Payot, Paris 1936).

Labracherie, Pierre, *Camille Desmoulins* (Hachette, Paris 1948).

Lafue, Pierre, *La Tragédie de Marie-Antoinette, Les Complots pour Délivrer la Reine* (Mondiales, Paris 1965).

Lardaàs, Henri, *La Vie Privée de Mirabeau* (Hachette, Paris 1949).

Lecomte, Georges, *La Vie Amoureuse de Danton* (Flammarion, Paris 1927).

Le Corbeiller, Armand, *Le Calvaire de Madame Roland* (Calmann-Lévy, Paris 1942).

Lenéru, Marie, *Saint-Just* (Grasset, Paris 1922).

Morton, Brian N. and Donald C. Spinelli, *Beaumarchais and the American Revolution* (Lexington Books, Lanham 2003).

Roujon, Jacques, *Ce bon monsieur Danton* (Plon, Paris 1929).

Scurr, Ruth, *Fatal Purity, Robespierre and the French Revolution* (Chatto & Windus, London 2006).

Sédouy, Jacques-Alain de, *Le comte Molé ou la Séduction du Pouvoir* (Perrin, Paris 1994).

Sipriot, Pierre, *Louis XVII et les mystères du Temple* (L'Archipel, Paris 1994).

Thompson, J.M., *Robespierre and the French Revolution* (English Universities Press, London 1952).

Vendôme, duchesse de, *Madame Elisabeth de France* (Flammarion, Paris 1942).

Vinot, Bernard, *Saint-Just* (Fayard, Paris 1985).

POETRY AND SONGS

Chénier, André Marie, *Poésies* (Mignot, Paris 1920).

Marty, Ginette and Georges Marty, *Dictionnaire des chansons de la Révolution, 1787-1799* (Tallandier, Paris 1988).

Restaurants

Gaudry, François Régis, *Mémoires du restaurant* (Aubanel, Paris 2006).

Spang, Rebecca L., *The Invention of the Restaurant: Paris and Modern Gastronomic Culture* (Harvard University Press, Cambridge 2001).

Lightning Source UK Ltd.
Milton Keynes UK
UKOW04f0629060514

231161UK00006B/39/P